Numerical Algorithms

Numerical Algorithms

Methods for Computer Vision,
Machine Learning, and Graphics

Justin Solomon

 **CRC Press**
Taylor & Francis Group
Boca Raton London New York

CRC Press is an imprint of the
Taylor & Francis Group, an **informa** business

AN A K PETERS BOOK

CRC Press
Taylor & Francis Group
6000 Broken Sound Parkway NW, Suite 300
Boca Raton, FL 33487-2742

Printed on acid-free paper
Version Date: 20150105

International Standard Book Number-13: 978-1-4822-5188-3 (Pack - Book and Ebook)

Library of Congress Cataloging-in-Publication Data

Solomon, Justin.
   Numerical algorithms : methods for computer vision, machine learning, and graphics / Justin Solomon.
      pages cm
  "An A K Peters Book."
  Includes bibliographical references and index.
  ISBN 978-1-4822-5188-3 (alk. paper)
  1. Computer algorithms. 2. Computer vision. 3. Image processing. 4. Machine learning. I. Title.

QA76.9.A43S65 2015
005.1--dc23
                                                   2014048905

Visit the Taylor & Francis Web site at
http://www.taylorandfrancis.com

and the CRC Press Web site at
http://www.crcpress.com

In memory of Clifford Nass
(1958–2013)

Contents

PREFACE   xv

ACKNOWLEDGMENTS   xix

SECTION I **Preliminaries**

CHAPTER   1 ▪ Mathematics Review   3

1.1   PRELIMINARIES: NUMBERS AND SETS   3
1.2   VECTOR SPACES   4
      1.2.1   Defining Vector Spaces   4
      1.2.2   Span, Linear Independence, and Bases   5
      1.2.3   Our Focus: $\mathbb{R}^n$ 7
1.3   LINEARITY   9
      1.3.1   Matrices   10
      1.3.2   Scalars, Vectors, and Matrices   12
      1.3.3   Matrix Storage and Multiplication Methods   13
      1.3.4   Model Problem: $A\vec{x} = \vec{b}$ 14
1.4   NON-LINEARITY: DIFFERENTIAL CALCULUS   15
      1.4.1   Differentiation in One Variable   16
      1.4.2   Differentiation in Multiple Variables   17
      1.4.3   Optimization   20
1.5   EXERCISES   23

CHAPTER   2 ▪ Numerics and Error Analysis   27

2.1   STORING NUMBERS WITH FRACTIONAL PARTS   27
      2.1.1   Fixed-Point Representations   28
      2.1.2   Floating-Point Representations   29
      2.1.3   More Exotic Options   31
2.2   UNDERSTANDING ERROR   32
      2.2.1   Classifying Error   33
      2.2.2   Conditioning, Stability, and Accuracy   35
2.3   PRACTICAL ASPECTS   36
      2.3.1   Computing Vector Norms   37

2.3.2	Larger-Scale Example: Summation	38
2.4	EXERCISES	39

SECTION II **Linear Algebra**

CHAPTER 3 ▪ Linear Systems and the LU Decomposition 47

3.1	SOLVABILITY OF LINEAR SYSTEMS	47
3.2	AD-HOC SOLUTION STRATEGIES	49
3.3	ENCODING ROW OPERATIONS	51
3.3.1	Permutation	51
3.3.2	Row Scaling	52
3.3.3	Elimination	52
3.4	GAUSSIAN ELIMINATION	54
3.4.1	Forward-Substitution	55
3.4.2	Back-Substitution	56
3.4.3	Analysis of Gaussian Elimination	56
3.5	LU FACTORIZATION	58
3.5.1	Constructing the Factorization	59
3.5.2	Using the Factorization	60
3.5.3	Implementing LU	61
3.6	EXERCISES	61

CHAPTER 4 ▪ Designing and Analyzing Linear Systems 65

4.1	SOLUTION OF SQUARE SYSTEMS	65
4.1.1	Regression	66
4.1.2	Least-Squares	68
4.1.3	Tikhonov Regularization	70
4.1.4	Image Alignment	71
4.1.5	Deconvolution	73
4.1.6	Harmonic Parameterization	74
4.2	SPECIAL PROPERTIES OF LINEAR SYSTEMS	75
4.2.1	Positive Definite Matrices and the Cholesky Factorization	75
4.2.2	Sparsity	79
4.2.3	Additional Special Structures	80
4.3	SENSITIVITY ANALYSIS	81
4.3.1	Matrix and Vector Norms	81
4.3.2	Condition Numbers	84
4.4	EXERCISES	86

CHAPTER   5 ▪ Column Spaces and QR   91

5.1   THE STRUCTURE OF THE NORMAL EQUATIONS   91
5.2   ORTHOGONALITY   92
5.3   STRATEGY FOR NON-ORTHOGONAL MATRICES   93
5.4   GRAM-SCHMIDT ORTHOGONALIZATION   94
       5.4.1   Projections   94
       5.4.2   Gram-Schmidt Algorithm   96
5.5   HOUSEHOLDER TRANSFORMATIONS   99
5.6   REDUCED QR FACTORIZATION   103
5.7   EXERCISES   103

CHAPTER   6 ▪ Eigenvectors   107

6.1   MOTIVATION   107
       6.1.1   Statistics   108
       6.1.2   Differential Equations   109
       6.1.3   Spectral Embedding   110
6.2   PROPERTIES OF EIGENVECTORS   112
       6.2.1   Symmetric and Positive Definite Matrices   114
       6.2.2   Specialized Properties   116
                6.2.2.1   Characteristic Polynomial   116
                6.2.2.2   Jordan Normal Form   116
6.3   COMPUTING A SINGLE EIGENVALUE   117
       6.3.1   Power Iteration   117
       6.3.2   Inverse Iteration   118
       6.3.3   Shifting   119
6.4   FINDING MULTIPLE EIGENVALUES   120
       6.4.1   Deflation   120
       6.4.2   QR Iteration   121
       6.4.3   Krylov Subspace Methods   126
6.5   SENSITIVITY AND CONDITIONING   126
6.6   EXERCISES   127

CHAPTER   7 ▪ Singular Value Decomposition   131

7.1   DERIVING THE SVD   131
       7.1.1   Computing the SVD   133
7.2   APPLICATIONS OF THE SVD   134
       7.2.1   Solving Linear Systems and the Pseudoinverse   134

	7.2.2	Decomposition into Outer Products and Low-Rank Approximations	135
	7.2.3	Matrix Norms	136
	7.2.4	The Procrustes Problem and Point Cloud Alignment	137
	7.2.5	Principal Component Analysis (PCA)	139
	7.2.6	Eigenfaces	140
7.3	EXERCISES		141

SECTION III Nonlinear Techniques

CHAPTER 8 ■ Nonlinear Systems   147

8.1	ROOT-FINDING IN A SINGLE VARIABLE		147
	8.1.1	Characterizing Problems	147
	8.1.2	Continuity and Bisection	148
	8.1.3	Fixed Point Iteration	149
	8.1.4	Newton's Method	151
	8.1.5	Secant Method	153
	8.1.6	Hybrid Techniques	155
	8.1.7	Single-Variable Case: Summary	155
8.2	MULTIVARIABLE PROBLEMS		156
	8.2.1	Newton's Method	156
	8.2.2	Making Newton Faster: Quasi-Newton and Broyden	156
8.3	CONDITIONING		158
8.4	EXERCISES		158

CHAPTER 9 ■ Unconstrained Optimization   163

9.1	UNCONSTRAINED OPTIMIZATION: MOTIVATION		163
9.2	OPTIMALITY		165
	9.2.1	Differential Optimality	166
	9.2.2	Alternative Conditions for Optimality	168
9.3	ONE-DIMENSIONAL STRATEGIES		169
	9.3.1	Newton's Method	170
	9.3.2	Golden Section Search	170
9.4	MULTIVARIABLE STRATEGIES		173
	9.4.1	Gradient Descent	173
	9.4.2	Newton's Method in Multiple Variables	174
	9.4.3	Optimization without Hessians: BFGS	175
9.5	EXERCISES		178
9.6	APPENDIX: DERIVATION OF BFGS UPDATE		182

CHAPTER 10 ▪ Constrained Optimization   185

10.1	MOTIVATION	186
10.2	THEORY OF CONSTRAINED OPTIMIZATION	189
	10.2.1 Optimality	189
	10.2.2 KKT Conditions	189
10.3	OPTIMIZATION ALGORITHMS	192
	10.3.1 Sequential Quadratic Programming (SQP)	193
	10.3.1.1 Equality Constraints	193
	10.3.1.2 Inequality Constraints	193
	10.3.2 Barrier Methods	194
10.4	CONVEX PROGRAMMING	194
	10.4.1 Linear Programming	196
	10.4.2 Second-Order Cone Programming	197
	10.4.3 Semidefinite Programming	199
	10.4.4 Integer Programs and Relaxations	200
10.5	EXERCISES	201

CHAPTER 11 ▪ Iterative Linear Solvers   207

11.1	GRADIENT DESCENT	208
	11.1.1 Gradient Descent for Linear Systems	208
	11.1.2 Convergence	209
11.2	CONJUGATE GRADIENTS	211
	11.2.1 Motivation	212
	11.2.2 Suboptimality of Gradient Descent	214
	11.2.3 Generating A-Conjugate Directions	215
	11.2.4 Formulating the Conjugate Gradients Algorithm	217
	11.2.5 Convergence and Stopping Conditions	219
11.3	PRECONDITIONING	219
	11.3.1 CG with Preconditioning	220
	11.3.2 Common Preconditioners	221
11.4	OTHER ITERATIVE ALGORITHMS	222
11.5	EXERCISES	223

CHAPTER 12 ▪ Specialized Optimization Methods   227

12.1	NONLINEAR LEAST-SQUARES	227
	12.1.1 Gauss-Newton	228
	12.1.2 Levenberg-Marquardt	229
12.2	ITERATIVELY REWEIGHTED LEAST-SQUARES	230

12.3	COORDINATE DESCENT AND ALTERNATION	231
	12.3.1 Identifying Candidates for Alternation	231
	12.3.2 Augmented Lagrangians and ADMM	235
12.4	GLOBAL OPTIMIZATION	240
	12.4.1 Graduated Optimization	241
	12.4.2 Randomized Global Optimization	243
12.5	ONLINE OPTIMIZATION	244
12.6	EXERCISES	248

SECTION IV Functions, Derivatives, and Integrals

CHAPTER 13 ▪ Interpolation   257

13.1	INTERPOLATION IN A SINGLE VARIABLE	258
	13.1.1 Polynomial Interpolation	258
	13.1.2 Alternative Bases	262
	13.1.3 Piecewise Interpolation	263
13.2	MULTIVARIABLE INTERPOLATION	265
	13.2.1 Nearest-Neighbor Interpolation	265
	13.2.2 Barycentric Interpolation	266
	13.2.3 Grid-Based Interpolation	268
13.3	THEORY OF INTERPOLATION	269
	13.3.1 Linear Algebra of Functions	269
	13.3.2 Approximation via Piecewise Polynomials	272
13.4	EXERCISES	272

CHAPTER 14 ▪ Integration and Differentiation   277

14.1	MOTIVATION	278
14.2	QUADRATURE	279
	14.2.1 Interpolatory Quadrature	280
	14.2.2 Quadrature Rules	281
	14.2.3 Newton-Cotes Quadrature	282
	14.2.4 Gaussian Quadrature	286
	14.2.5 Adaptive Quadrature	287
	14.2.6 Multiple Variables	289
	14.2.7 Conditioning	290
14.3	DIFFERENTIATION	290
	14.3.1 Differentiating Basis Functions	291
	14.3.2 Finite Differences	291
	14.3.3 Richardson Extrapolation	293

14.3.4   Choosing the Step Size   294

14.3.5   Automatic Differentiation   295

14.3.6   Integrated Quantities and Structure Preservation   296

14.4   EXERCISES   298

CHAPTER 15 ■ Ordinary Differential Equations   303

15.1   MOTIVATION   304

15.2   THEORY OF ODES   305

15.2.1   Basic Notions   305

15.2.2   Existence and Uniqueness   307

15.2.3   Model Equations   309

15.3   TIME-STEPPING SCHEMES   311

15.3.1   Forward Euler   311

15.3.2   Backward Euler   313

15.3.3   Trapezoidal Method   314

15.3.4   Runge-Kutta Methods   315

15.3.5   Exponential Integrators   316

15.4   MULTIVALUE METHODS   318

15.4.1   Newmark Integrators   318

15.4.2   Staggered Grid and Leapfrog   321

15.5   COMPARISON OF INTEGRATORS   322

15.6   EXERCISES   324

CHAPTER 16 ■ Partial Differential Equations   329

16.1   MOTIVATION   330

16.2   STATEMENT AND STRUCTURE OF PDES   335

16.2.1   Properties of PDEs   335

16.2.2   Boundary Conditions   336

16.3   MODEL EQUATIONS   338

16.3.1   Elliptic PDEs   338

16.3.2   Parabolic PDEs   339

16.3.3   Hyperbolic PDEs   340

16.4   REPRESENTING DERIVATIVE OPERATORS   341

16.4.1   Finite Differences   342

16.4.2   Collocation   346

16.4.3   Finite Elements   347

16.4.4   Finite Volumes   350

16.4.5   Other Methods   351

16.5   SOLVING PARABOLIC AND HYPERBOLIC EQUATIONS   352

16.5.1	Semidiscrete Methods	352
16.5.2	Fully Discrete Methods	353
16.6	NUMERICAL CONSIDERATIONS	354
16.6.1	Consistency, Convergence, and Stability	354
16.6.2	Linear Solvers for PDE	354
16.7	EXERCISES	355

Bibliography   361

Index   369

Preface

COMPUTER science is experiencing a fundamental shift in its approach to modeling and problem solving. Early computer scientists primarily studied *discrete* mathematics, focusing on structures like graphs, trees, and arrays composed of a finite number of distinct pieces. With the introduction of fast floating-point processing alongside "big data," three-dimensional scanning, and other sources of noisy input, modern practitioners of computer science must design robust methods for processing and understanding real-valued data. Now, alongside discrete mathematics computer scientists must be equally fluent in the languages of multivariable calculus and linear algebra.

Numerical Algorithms introduces the skills necessary to be both *clients* and *designers* of numerical methods for computer science applications. This text is designed for advanced undergraduate and early graduate students who are comfortable with mathematical notation and formality but need to review continuous concepts alongside the algorithms under consideration. It covers a broad base of topics, from numerical linear algebra to optimization and differential equations, with the goal of deriving standard approaches while developing the intuition and comfort needed to understand more extensive literature in each subtopic. Thus, each chapter gently but rigorously introduces numerical methods alongside mathematical background and motivating examples from modern computer science.

Nearly every section considers real-world use cases for a given class of numerical algorithms. For example, the singular value decomposition is introduced alongside statistical methods, point cloud alignment, and low-rank approximation, and the discussion of least-squares includes concepts from machine learning like kernelization and regularization. The goal of this presentation of theory and application in parallel is to improve intuition for the design of numerical methods and the application of each method to practical situations.

Special care has been taken to provide unifying threads from chapter to chapter. This strategy helps relate discussions of seemingly independent problems, reinforcing skills while presenting increasingly complex algorithms. In particular, starting with a chapter on mathematical preliminaries, methods are introduced with *variational* principles in mind, e.g., solving the linear system $A\vec{x} = \vec{b}$ by minimizing the energy $\|A\vec{x} - \vec{b}\|_2^2$ or finding eigenvectors as critical points of the Rayleigh quotient.

The book is organized into sections covering a few large-scale topics:

I. Preliminaries covers themes that appear in all branches of numerical algorithms. We start with a review of relevant notions from continuous mathematics, designed as a refresher for students who have not made extensive use of calculus or linear algebra since their introductory math classes. This chapter can be skipped if students are confident in their mathematical abilities, but even advanced readers may consider taking a look to understand notation and basic constructions that will be used repeatedly later on. Then, we proceed with a chapter on numerics and error analysis, the basic tools of numerical analysis for representing real numbers and understanding the quality of numerical algorithms. In many ways, this chapter explicitly covers the high-level themes that make numerical algorithms different from discrete algorithms: In this domain, we rarely expect to recover *exact* solutions to computational problems but rather approximate them.

II. Linear Algebra covers the algorithms needed to solve and analyze linear systems of equations. This section is designed not only to cover the algorithms found in any treatment of numerical linear algebra—including Gaussian elimination, matrix factorization, and eigenvalue computation—but also to *motivate* why these tools are useful for computer scientists. To this end, we will explore wide-ranging applications in data analysis, image processing, and even face recognition, showing how each can be reduced to an appropriate matrix problem. This discussion will reveal that numerical linear algebra is far from an exercise in abstract algorithmics; rather, it is a tool that can be applied to countless computational models.

III. Nonlinear Techniques explores the structure of problems that do not reduce to linear systems of equations. Two key tasks arise in this section, root-finding and optimization, which are related by Lagrange multipliers and other optimality conditions. Nearly any modern algorithm for machine learning involves optimization of some objective, so we will find no shortage of examples from recent research and engineering. After developing basic iterative methods for constrained and unconstrained optimization, we will return to the linear system $A\vec{x} = \vec{b}$, developing the conjugate gradients algorithm for approximating $\vec{x}$ using optimization tools. We conclude this section with a discussion of "specialized" optimization algorithms, which are gaining popularity in recent research. This chapter, whose content does not appear in classical texts, covers strategies for developing algorithms specifically to minimize a single energy functional. This approach contrasts with our earlier treatment of generic approaches for minimization that work for broad classes of objectives, presenting computational challenges on paper with the reward of increased optimization efficiency.

IV. Functions, Derivatives, and Integrals concludes our consideration of numerical algorithms by examining problems in which an entire *function* rather than a single value or point is the unknown. Example tasks in this class include interpolation, approximation of derivatives and integrals of a function from samples, and solution of differential equations. In addition to classical applications in computational physics, we will show how these tools are relevant to a wide range of problems including rendering of three-dimensional shapes, x-ray scanning, and geometry processing.

Individual chapters are designed to be fairly independent, but of course it is impossible to orthogonalize the content completely. For example, iterative methods for optimization and root-finding must solve linear systems of equations in each iteration, and some interpolation methods can be posed as optimization problems. In general, Parts III (Nonlinear Techniques) and IV (Functions, Derivatives, and Integrals) are largely independent of one another but both depend on matrix algorithms developed in Part II (Linear Algebra). In each part, the chapters are presented in order of importance. Initial chapters introduce key themes in the subfield of numerical algorithms under consideration, while later chapters focus on advanced algorithms adjacent to new research; sections within each chapter are organized in a similar fashion.

Numerical algorithms are very different from algorithms approached in most other branches of computer science, and students should expect to be challenged the first time they study this material. With practice, however, it can be easy to build up intuition for this unique and widely applicable field. To support this goal, each chapter concludes with a set of problems designed to encourage critical thinking about the material at hand.

Simple computational problems in large part are *omitted* from the text, under the expectation that active readers approach the book with pen and paper in hand. Some suggestions of exercises that can help readers as they peruse the material, but are not explicitly included in the end-of-chapter problems, include the following:

1. Try each algorithm by hand. For instance, after reading the discussion of algorithms for solving the linear system $A\vec{x} = \vec{b}$, write down a small matrix A and corresponding vector $\vec{b}$, and make sure you can recover $\vec{x}$ by following the steps the algorithm. After reading the treatment of optimization, write down a specific function $f(\vec{x})$ and a few iterates $\vec{x}_1, \vec{x}_2, \vec{x}_3, \ldots$ of an optimization method to make sure $f(\vec{x}_1) \geq f(\vec{x}_2) \geq f(\vec{x}_3) > \cdots$.

2. Implement the algorithms in software and experiment with their behavior. Many numerical algorithms take on beautifully succinct—and completely abstruse—forms that must be unraveled when they are implemented in code. Plus, nothing is more rewarding than the moment when a piece of numerical code begins functioning properly, transitioning from an abstract sequence of mathematical statements to a piece of machinery systematically solving equations or decreasing optimization objectives.

3. Attempt to derive algorithms by hand without referring to the discussion in the book. The best way to become an expert in numerical analysis is to be able to reconstruct the basic algorithms by hand, an exercise that supports intuition for the existing methods and will help suggest extensions to other problems you may encounter.

Any large-scale treatment of a field as diverse and classical as numerical algorithms is bound to omit certain topics, and inevitably decisions of this nature may be controversial to readers with different backgrounds. This book is designed for a one- to two-semester course in numerical algorithms, for computer scientists rather than mathematicians or engineers in scientific computing. This target audience has led to a focus on modeling and applications rather than on general proofs of convergence, error bounds, and the like; the discussion includes references to more specialized or advanced literature when possible. Some topics, including the fast Fourier transform, algorithms for sparse linear systems, Monte Carlo methods, adaptivity in solving differential equations, and multigrid methods, are mentioned only in passing or in exercises in favor of explaining modern developments in optimization and other algorithms that have gained recent popularity. Future editions of this textbook may incorporate these or other topics depending on feedback from instructors and readers.

The refinement of course notes and other materials leading to this textbook benefited from the generous input of my students and colleagues. In the interests of maintaining these materials and responding to the needs of students and instructors, please do not hesitate to contact me with questions, comments, concerns, or ideas for potential changes.

JUSTIN SOLOMON

Acknowledgments

PREPARATION of this textbook would not have been possible without the support of countless individuals and organizations. I have attempted to acknowledge some of the many contributors and supporters below. I cannot thank these colleagues and friends enough for their patience and attention throughout this undertaking.

The book is dedicated to the memory of Professor Clifford Nass, whose guidance fundamentally shaped my early academic career. His wisdom, teaching, encouragement, enthusiasm, and unique sense of style all will be missed on the Stanford campus and in the larger community.

My mother, Nancy Griesemer, was the first to suggest expanding my teaching materials into a text. I would not have been able to find the time or energy to prepare this work without her support or that from my father Rod Solomon; my sister Julia Solomon Ensor, her husband Jeff Ensor, and their daughter Caroline Ensor; and my grandmothers Juddy Solomon and Dolores Griesemer. My uncle Peter Silberman and aunt Dena Silberman have supported my academic career from its inception. Many other family members also should be thanked including Archa and Joseph Emerson; Jerry, Jinny, Kate, Bonnie, and Jeremiah Griesemer; Jim, Marge, Paul, Laura, Jarrett, Liza, Jiana, Lana, Jahson, Jaime, Gabriel, and Jesse Solomon; Chuck and Louise Silverberg; and Barbara, Kerry, Greg, and Amy Schaner.

My career at Stanford has been guided primarily by my advisor Leonidas Guibas and co-advisor Adrian Butscher. The approaches I take to many of the problems in the book undoubtedly imitate the problem-solving strategies they have taught me. Ron Fedkiw suggested I teach the course leading to this text and provided advice on preparing the material. My collaborators in the Geometric Computing Group and elsewhere on campus—including Panagiotis Achlioptas, Roland Angst, Mirela Ben-Chen, Daniel Chen, Takuya Funatomi, Tanya Glozman, Jonathan Huang, Qixing Huang, Michael Kerber, Vladimir Kim, Young Min Kim, Yang Li, Yangyan Li, Andy Nguyen, Maks Ovsjanikov, Franco Pestilli, Chris Piech, Raif Rustamov, Hao Su, Minhyuk Sung, Fan Wang, and Eric Yi—kindly have allowed me to use some research time to complete this text and have helped refine the discussion at many points. Staff in the Stanford computer science department, including Meredith Hutchin, Claire Stager, and Steven Magness, made it possible to organize my numerical algorithms course and many others.

I owe many thanks to the students of Stanford's CS 205A course (fall 2013) for catching numerous typos and mistakes in an early draft of this book; students in CS 205A (spring 2015) also identified some subtle typos and mathematical issues. The following is a no-doubt incomplete list of students and course assistants who contributed to this effort: Abraham Botros, Paulo Camasmie, Scott Chung, James Cranston, Deepyaman Datta, Tao Du, Lennart Jansson, Miles Johnson, David Hyde, Luke Knepper, Warner Krause, Ilya Kudryavtsev, Minjae Lee, Nisha Masharani, David McLaren, Sid Mittal, J. Eduardo Mucino, Catherine Mullings, John Reyna, Blue Sheffer, William Song, Ben-Han Sung, Martina Troesch, Ozhan Turgut, Blanca Isabel Villanueva, Jon Walker, Patrick Ward, Joongyeub Yeo, and Yang Zhao.

David Hyde and Scott Chung continued to provide detailed feedback in winter and spring 2014. In addition, they helped prepare figures and end-of-chapter problems. Problems that they drafted are marked DH and SC, respectively.

I leaned upon several colleagues and friends to help edit the text. In addition to those mentioned above, additional contributors include: Nick Alger, George Anderson, Rahil Baber, Nicolas Bonneel, Chen Chen, Matthew Cong, Roy Frostig, Jessica Hwang, Howon Lee, Julian Kates-Harbeck, Jonathan Lee, Niru Maheswaranathan, Mark Pauly, Dan Robinson, and Hao Zhuang.

Special thanks to Jan Heiland and Tao Du for helping clarify the derivation of the BFGS algorithm.

Charlotte Byrnes, Sarah Chow, Rebecca Condit, Randi Cohen, Kate Gallo, and Hayley Ruggieri at Taylor & Francis guided me through the publication process and answered countless questions as I prepared this work for print.

The Hertz Foundation provided a valuable network of experienced and knowledgeable members of the academic community. In particular, Louis Lerman provided career advice throughout my PhD that shaped my approach to research and navigating academia. Other members of the Hertz community who provided guidance include Diann Callaghan, Wendy Cieslak, Jay Davis, Philip Eckhoff, Linda Kubiak, Amanda O'Connor, Linda Souza, Thomas Weaver, and Katherine Young. I should also acknowledge the NSF GRFP and NDSEG fellowships for their support.

A multitude of friends supported this work in assorted stages of its development. Additional collaborators and mentors in the research community who have discussed and encouraged this work include Keenan Crane, Fernando de Goes, Michael Eichmair, Hao Li, Niloy Mitra, Helmut Pottmann, Fei Sha, Olga Sorkine-Hornung, Amir Vaxman, Etienne Vouga, Brian Wandell, and Chris Wojtan. The first several chapters of this book were drafted on tour with the Stanford Symphony Orchestra on their European tour "In Beethoven's Footsteps" (summer 2013). Beyond this tour, Geri Actor, Susan Bratman, Debra Fong, Stephen Harrison, Patrick Kim, Mindy Perkins, Thomas Shoebotham, and Lowry Yankwich all supported musical breaks during the drafting of this book. Prometheus Athletics provided an unexpected outlet, and I should thank Archie de Torres, Amy Giver, Lori Giver, Troy Obrero, and Ben Priestley for allowing me to be an enthusiastic if clumsy participant.

Additional friends who have lent advice, assistance, and time to this effort include: Chris Aakre, Katy Ashe, Katya Avagian, Kyle Barrett, Noelle Beegle, Gilbert Bernstein, Elizabeth Blaber, Lia Bonamassa, Eric Boromisa, Katherine Breeden, Karen Budd, Lindsay Burdette, Avery Bustamante, Rose Casey, Arun Chaganty, Phil Chen, Andrew Chou, Bernie Chu, Cindy Chu, Victor Cruz, Elan Dagenais, Abe Davis, Matthew Decker, Bailin Deng, Martin Duncan, Eric Ellenoff, James Estrella, Alyson Falwell, Anna French, Adair Gerke, Christina Goeders, Gabrielle Gulo, Nathan Hall-Snyder, Logan Hehn, Jo Jaffe, Dustin Janatpour, Brandon Johnson, Victoria Johnson, Jeff Gilbert, Stephanie Go, Alex Godofsky, Alan Guo, Randy Hernando, Petr Johanes, Maria Judnick, Ken Kao, Jonathan Kass, Gavin Kho, Hyungbin Kim, Sarah Kongpachith, Jim Lalonde, Lauren Lax, Atticus Lee, Eric Lee, Jonathan Lee, Menyoung Lee, Letitia Lew, Siyang Li, Adrian Lim, Yongwhan Lim, Alex Louie, Lily Louie, Kate Lowry, Cleo Messinger, Courtney Meyer, Daniel Meyer, Lisa Newman, Logan Obrero, Pualani Obrero, Thomas Obrero, Molly Pam, David Parker, Madeline Paymer, Cuauhtemoc Peranda, Fabianna Perez, Bharath Ramsundar, Arty Rivera, Daniel Rosenfeld, Te Rutherford, Ravi Sankar, Aaron Sarnoff, Amanda Schloss, Keith Schwarz, Steve Sellers, Phaedon Sinis, Charlton Soesanto, Mark Smitt, Jacob Steinhardt, Charlie Syms, Andrea Tagliasacchi, Michael Tamkin, Sumil Thapa, David Tobin, Herb Tyson, Katie Tyson, Madeleine Udell, Greg Valdespino, Walter Vulej, Thomas Waggoner, Frank Wang, Sydney Wang, Susanna Wen, Genevieve Williams, Molby Wong, Eddy Wu, Kelima Yakupova, Winston Yan, and Evan Young.

I

Preliminaries

CHAPTER 1

Mathematics Review

CONTENTS

1.1   Preliminaries: Numbers and Sets 3
1.2   Vector Spaces 4
     1.2.1   Defining Vector Spaces 4
     1.2.2   Span, Linear Independence, and Bases 5
     1.2.3   Our Focus: $\mathbb{R}^n$ 7
1.3   Linearity 9
     1.3.1   Matrices 10
     1.3.2   Scalars, Vectors, and Matrices 12
     1.3.3   Matrix Storage and Multiplication Methods 13
     1.3.4   Model Problem: $A\vec{x} = \vec{b}$ 14
1.4   Non-Linearity: Differential Calculus 15
     1.4.1   Differentiation in One Variable 16
     1.4.2   Differentiation in Multiple Variables 17
     1.4.3   Optimization 20

I N this chapter, we will outline notions from linear algebra and multivariable calculus that will be relevant to our discussion of computational techniques. It is intended as a review of background material with a bias toward ideas and interpretations commonly encountered in practice; the chapter can be safely skipped or used as reference by students with stronger background in mathematics.

1.1   PRELIMINARIES: NUMBERS AND SETS

Rather than considering algebraic (and at times philosophical) discussions like "What is a number?," we will rely on intuition and mathematical common sense to define a few sets:

- The *natural numbers* $\mathbb{N} = \{1, 2, 3, \ldots\}$

- The *integers* $\mathbb{Z} = \{\ldots, -2, -1, 0, 1, 2, \ldots\}$

- The *rational numbers* $\mathbb{Q} = \{a/b : a, b \in \mathbb{Z}, b \neq 0\}$

- The *real numbers* $\mathbb{R}$ encompassing $\mathbb{Q}$ as well as *irrational* numbers like π and $\sqrt{2}$

- The *complex numbers* $\mathbb{C} = \{a + bi : a, b \in \mathbb{R}\}$, where $i \equiv \sqrt{-1}$.

The definition of $\mathbb{Q}$ is the first of many times that we will use the notation $\{A : B\}$; the braces denote a set and the colon can be read as "such that." For instance, the definition of $\mathbb{Q}$ can be read as "the set of fractions a/b *such that* a and b are integers." As a second example, we could write $\mathbb{N} = \{n \in \mathbb{Z} : n > 0\}$. It is worth acknowledging that our definition of $\mathbb{R}$ is far from rigorous. The construction of the real numbers can be an important topic for practitioners of cryptography techniques that make use of alternative number systems, but these intricacies are irrelevant for the discussion at hand.

$\mathbb{N}$, $\mathbb{Z}$, $\mathbb{Q}$, $\mathbb{R}$, and $\mathbb{C}$ can be manipulated using generic operations to generate new sets of numbers. In particular, we define the "Euclidean product" of two sets A and B as

$$A \times B = \{(a, b) : a \in A \text{ and } b \in B\}.$$

We can take *powers* of sets by writing

$$A^n = \underbrace{A \times A \times \cdots \times A}_{n \text{ times}}.$$

This construction yields what will become our favorite set of numbers in chapters to come:

$$\mathbb{R}^n = \{(a_1, a_2, \ldots, a_n) : a_i \in \mathbb{R} \text{ for all } i\}.$$

1.2 VECTOR SPACES

Introductory linear algebra courses easily could be titled "Introduction to Finite-Dimensional Vector Spaces." Although the definition of a vector space might appear abstract, we will find many concrete applications expressible in vector space language that can benefit from the machinery we will develop.

1.2.1 Defining Vector Spaces

We begin by defining a vector space and providing a number of examples:

Definition 1.1 (Vector space over $\mathbb{R}$). A *vector space* over $\mathbb{R}$ is a set $\mathcal{V}$ closed under addition and scalar multiplication satisfying the following axioms:

- *Additive commutativity and associativity:* For all $\vec{u}, \vec{v}, \vec{w} \in \mathcal{V}$, $\vec{v} + \vec{w} = \vec{w} + \vec{v}$ and $(\vec{u} + \vec{v}) + \vec{w} = \vec{u} + (\vec{v} + \vec{w})$.

- *Distributivity:* For all $\vec{v}, \vec{w} \in \mathcal{V}$ and $a, b \in \mathbb{R}$, $a(\vec{v}+\vec{w}) = a\vec{v}+a\vec{w}$ and $(a+b)\vec{v} = a\vec{v}+b\vec{v}$.

- *Additive identity:* There exists $\vec{0} \in \mathcal{V}$ with $\vec{0} + \vec{v} = \vec{v}$ for all $\vec{v} \in \mathcal{V}$.

- *Additive inverse:* For all $\vec{v} \in \mathcal{V}$, there exists $\vec{w} \in \mathcal{V}$ with $\vec{v} + \vec{w} = \vec{0}$.

- *Multiplicative identity:* For all $\vec{v} \in \mathcal{V}$, $1 \cdot \vec{v} = \vec{v}$.

- *Multiplicative compatibility:* For all $\vec{v} \in \mathcal{V}$ and $a, b \in \mathbb{R}$, $(ab)\vec{v} = a(b\vec{v})$.

A member $\vec{v} \in \mathcal{V}$ is known as a *vector*; arrows will be used to indicate vector variables.

For our purposes, a scalar is a number in $\mathbb{R}$; a *complex* vector space satisfies the same definition with $\mathbb{R}$ replaced by $\mathbb{C}$. It is usually straightforward to spot vector spaces in the wild, including the following examples:

Example 1.1 ($\mathbb{R}^n$ as a vector space). The most common example of a vector space is $\mathbb{R}^n$. Here, addition and scalar multiplication happen component-by-component:

$$(1, 2) + (-3, 4) = (1 - 3, 2 + 4) = (-2, 6)$$
$$10 \cdot (-1, 1) = (10 \cdot -1, 10 \cdot 1) = (-10, 10).$$

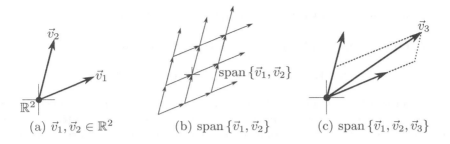

(a) $\vec{v}_1, \vec{v}_2 \in \mathbb{R}^2$ (b) span $\{\vec{v}_1, \vec{v}_2\}$ (c) span $\{\vec{v}_1, \vec{v}_2, \vec{v}_3\}$

Figure 1.1 (a) Vectors $\vec{v}_1, \vec{v}_2 \in \mathbb{R}^2$; (b) their span is the plane $\mathbb{R}^2$; (c) span $\{\vec{v}_1, \vec{v}_2, \vec{v}_3\}$ = span $\{\vec{v}_1, \vec{v}_2\}$ because $\vec{v}_3$ is a linear combination of $\vec{v}_1$ and $\vec{v}_2$.

Example 1.2 (Polynomials). A second example of a vector space is the ring of polynomials with real-valued coefficients, denoted $\mathbb{R}[x]$. A polynomial $p \in \mathbb{R}[x]$ is a function $p : \mathbb{R} \to \mathbb{R}$ taking the form*

$$p(x) = \sum_k a_k x^k.$$

Addition and scalar multiplication are carried out in the usual way, e.g., if $p(x) = x^2 + 2x - 1$ and $q(x) = x^3$, then $3p(x) + 5q(x) = 5x^3 + 3x^2 + 6x - 3$, which is another polynomial. As an aside, for future examples note that functions like $p(x) = (x-1)(x+1) + x^2(x^3 - 5)$ are still polynomials even though they are not explicitly written in the form above.

A weighted sum $\sum_i a_i \vec{v}_i$, where $a_i \in \mathbb{R}$ and $\vec{v}_i \in \mathcal{V}$, is known as a *linear combination* of the $\vec{v}_i$'s. In the second example, the "vectors" are polynomials, although we do not normally use this language to discuss $\mathbb{R}[x]$; unless otherwise noted, we will assume variables notated with arrows $\vec{v}$ are members of $\mathbb{R}^n$ for some n. One way to link these two viewpoints would be to identify the polynomial $\sum_k a_k x^k$ with the sequence $(a_0, a_1, a_2, \ldots)$; polynomials have finite numbers of terms, so this sequence eventually will end in a string of zeros.

1.2.2 Span, Linear Independence, and Bases

Suppose we start with vectors $\vec{v}_1, \ldots, \vec{v}_k \in \mathcal{V}$ in vector space $\mathcal{V}$. By Definition 1.1, we have two ways to start with these vectors and construct new elements of $\mathcal{V}$: addition and scalar multiplication. *Span* describes all of the vectors you can reach via these two operations:

Definition 1.2 (Span). The *span* of a set $S \subseteq \mathcal{V}$ of vectors is the set

$$\text{span}\, S \equiv \{a_1 \vec{v}_1 + \cdots + a_k \vec{v}_k : \vec{v}_i \in S \text{ and } a_i \in \mathbb{R} \text{ for all } i\}.$$

Figure 1.1(a-b) illustrates the span of two vectors. By definition, span S is a *subspace* of $\mathcal{V}$, that is, a subset of $\mathcal{V}$ that is itself a vector space. We provide a few examples:

Example 1.3 (Mixology). The typical well at a cocktail bar contains at least four ingredients at the bartender's disposal: vodka, tequila, orange juice, and grenadine. Assuming we have this well, we can represent drinks as points in $\mathbb{R}^4$, with one element for each ingredient. For instance, a tequila sunrise can be represented using the point $(0, 1.5, 6, 0.75)$,

---

*The notation $f : A \to B$ means f is a function that takes as input an element of set A and outputs an element of set B. For instance, $f : \mathbb{R} \to \mathbb{Z}$ takes as input a real number in $\mathbb{R}$ and outputs an integer $\mathbb{Z}$, as might be the case for $f(x) = \lfloor x \rfloor$, the "round down" function.

representing amounts of vodka, tequila, orange juice, and grenadine (in ounces), respectively.

The set of drinks that can be made with our well is contained in

$$\text{span} \{(1,0,0,0), (0,1,0,0), (0,0,1,0), (0,0,0,1)\},$$

that is, all combinations of the four basic ingredients. A bartender looking to save time, however, might notice that many drinks have the same orange juice-to-grenadine ratio and mix the bottles. The new simplified well may be easier for pouring but can make fundamentally fewer drinks:

$$\text{span} \{(1,0,0,0), (0,1,0,0), (0,0,6,0.75)\}.$$

For example, this reduced well cannot fulfill orders for a screwdriver, which contains orange juice but not grenadine.

Example 1.4 (Cubic polynomials). Define $p_k(x) \equiv x^k$. With this notation, the set of cubic polynomials can be written in two equivalent ways

$$\{ax^3 + bx^2 + cx + d \in \mathbb{R}[x] : a, b, c, d \in \mathbb{R}\} = \text{span} \{p_0, p_1, p_2, p_3\}.$$

Adding another item to a set of vectors does not always increase the size of its span, as illustrated in Figure 1.1(c). For instance, in $\mathbb{R}^2$,

$$\text{span} \{(1,0), (0,1)\} = \text{span} \{(1,0), (0,1), (1,1)\}.$$

In this case, we say that the set $\{(1,0), (0,1), (1,1)\}$ is *linearly dependent*:

Definition 1.3 (Linear dependence). We provide three equivalent definitions. A set $S \subseteq \mathcal{V}$ of vectors is *linearly dependent* if:

1. One of the elements of S can be written as a linear combination of the other elements, or S contains zero.

2. There exists a non-empty linear combination of elements $\vec{v}_k \in S$ yielding $\sum_{k=1}^{m} c_k \vec{v}_k = 0$ where $c_k \neq 0$ for all k.

3. There exists $\vec{v} \in S$ such that span $S = \text{span}\, S \backslash \{\vec{v}\}$. That is, we can remove a vector from S without affecting its span.

If S is not linearly dependent, then we say it is *linearly independent*.

Providing proof or informal evidence that each definition is equivalent to its counterparts (in an "if and only if" fashion) is a worthwhile exercise for students less comfortable with notation and abstract mathematics.

The concept of linear dependence provides an idea of "redundancy" in a set of vectors. In this sense, it is natural to ask how large a set we can construct before adding another vector cannot possibly increase the span. More specifically, suppose we have a linearly independent set $S \subseteq \mathcal{V}$, and now we choose an additional vector $\vec{v} \in \mathcal{V}$. Adding $\vec{v}$ to S has one of two possible outcomes:

1. The span of $S \cup \{\vec{v}\}$ is *larger* than the span of S.

2. Adding $\vec{v}$ to S has no effect on its span.

The *dimension* of $\mathcal{V}$ counts the number of times we can get the first outcome while building up a set of vectors:

Definition 1.4 (Dimension and basis). The *dimension* of $\mathcal{V}$ is the maximal size $|S|$ of a linearly independent set $S \subset \mathcal{V}$ such that span $S = \mathcal{V}$. Any set S satisfying this property is called a *basis* for $\mathcal{V}$.

Example 1.5 ($\mathbb{R}^n$). The *standard basis* for $\mathbb{R}^n$ is the set of vectors of the form

$$\vec{e}_k \equiv (\ \underbrace{0,\ldots,0}_{k-1\ \text{elements}},\ 1,\ \underbrace{0,\ldots,0}_{n-k\ \text{elements}}\ ).$$

That is, $\vec{e}_k$ has all zeros except for a single one in the k-th position. These vectors are linearly independent and form a basis for $\mathbb{R}^n$; for example in $\mathbb{R}^3$ any vector (a,b,c) can be written as $a\vec{e}_1 + b\vec{e}_2 + c\vec{e}_3$. Thus, the dimension of $\mathbb{R}^n$ is n, as expected.

Example 1.6 (Polynomials). The set of monomials $\{1, x, x^2, x^3, \ldots\}$ is a linearly independent subset of $\mathbb{R}[x]$. It is infinitely large, and thus the dimension of $\mathbb{R}[x]$ is ∞.

1.2.3 Our Focus: $\mathbb{R}^n$

Of particular importance for our purposes is the vector space $\mathbb{R}^n$, the so-called *n-dimensional Euclidean space*. This is nothing more than the set of coordinate axes encountered in high school math classes:

- $\mathbb{R}^1 \equiv \mathbb{R}$ is the number line.

- $\mathbb{R}^2$ is the two-dimensional plane with coordinates (x, y).

- $\mathbb{R}^3$ represents three-dimensional space with coordinates (x, y, z).

Nearly all methods in this book will deal with transformations of and functions on $\mathbb{R}^n$.

For convenience, we usually write vectors in $\mathbb{R}^n$ in "column form," as follows:

$$(a_1, \ldots, a_n) \equiv \begin{pmatrix} a_1 \\ a_2 \\ \vdots \\ a_n \end{pmatrix}.$$

This notation will include vectors as special cases of *matrices* discussed below.

Unlike some vector spaces, $\mathbb{R}^n$ has not only a vector space structure, but also one additional construction that makes all the difference: the *dot product*.

Definition 1.5 (Dot product). The dot product of two vectors $\vec{a} = (a_1, \ldots, a_n)$ and $\vec{b} = (b_1, \ldots, b_n)$ in $\mathbb{R}^n$ is given by

$$\vec{a} \cdot \vec{b} \equiv \sum_{k=1}^{n} a_k b_k.$$

Example 1.7 ($\mathbb{R}^2$). The dot product of $(1, 2)$ and $(-2, 6)$ is $1 \cdot -2 + 2 \cdot 6 = -2 + 12 = 10$.

The dot product is an example of a *metric*, and its existence gives a notion of geometry to $\mathbb{R}^n$. For instance, we can use the Pythagorean theorem to define the *norm* or *length* of a vector $\vec{a}$ as the square root

$$\|\vec{a}\|_2 \equiv \sqrt{a_1^2 + \cdots + a_n^2} = \sqrt{\vec{a} \cdot \vec{a}}.$$

Then, the distance between two points $\vec{a}, \vec{b} \in \mathbb{R}^n$ is $\|\vec{b} - \vec{a}\|_2$.

Dot products provide not only lengths and distances but also angles. The following trigonometric identity holds for $\vec{a}, \vec{b} \in \mathbb{R}^3$:

$$\vec{a} \cdot \vec{b} = \|\vec{a}\|_2 \|\vec{b}\|_2 \cos \theta,$$

where θ is the angle between $\vec{a}$ and $\vec{b}$. When $n \geq 4$, however, the notion of "angle" is much harder to visualize in $\mathbb{R}^n$. We might *define* the angle θ between $\vec{a}$ and $\vec{b}$ to be

$$\theta \equiv \arccos \frac{\vec{a} \cdot \vec{b}}{\|\vec{a}\|_2 \|\vec{b}\|_2}.$$

We must do our homework before making such a definition! In particular, cosine outputs values in the interval $[-1, 1]$, so we must check that the input to arc cosine (also notated $\cos^{-1}$) is in this interval; thankfully, the well-known Cauchy-Schwarz inequality $|\vec{a} \cdot \vec{b}| \leq \|\vec{a}\|_2 \|\vec{b}\|_2$ guarantees exactly this property.

When $\vec{a} = c\vec{b}$ for some $c \in \mathbb{R}$, we have $\theta = \arccos 1 = 0$, as we would expect: The angle between parallel vectors is zero. What does it mean for (nonzero) vectors to be perpendicular? Let's substitute $\theta = 90°$. Then, we have

$$0 = \cos 90° = \frac{\vec{a} \cdot \vec{b}}{\|\vec{a}\|_2 \|\vec{b}\|_2}.$$

Multiplying both sides by $\|\vec{a}\|_2 \|\vec{b}\|_2$ motivates the definition:

Definition 1.6 (Orthogonality). Two vectors $\vec{a}, \vec{b} \in \mathbb{R}^n$ are perpendicular, or *orthogonal*, when $\vec{a} \cdot \vec{b} = 0$.

This definition is somewhat surprising from a geometric standpoint. We have managed to define what it means to be perpendicular without any explicit use of angles.

Aside 1.1. There are many theoretical questions to ponder here, some of which we will address in future chapters:

- Do all vector spaces admit dot products or similar structures?

- Do all finite-dimensional vector spaces admit dot products?

- What might be a reasonable dot product between elements of $\mathbb{R}[x]$?

Intrigued students can consult texts on real and functional analysis.

1.3 LINEARITY

A function from one vector space to another that preserves linear structure is known as a *linear* function:

Definition 1.7 (Linearity). Suppose $\mathcal{V}$ and $\mathcal{V}'$ are vector spaces. Then, $\mathcal{L} : \mathcal{V} \to \mathcal{V}'$ is *linear* if it satisfies the following two criteria for all $\vec{v}, \vec{v}_1, \vec{v}_2 \in \mathcal{V}$ and $c \in \mathbb{R}$:

- $\mathcal{L}$ *preserves sums:* $\mathcal{L}[\vec{v}_1 + \vec{v}_2] = \mathcal{L}[\vec{v}_1] + \mathcal{L}[\vec{v}_2]$

- $\mathcal{L}$ *preserves scalar products:* $\mathcal{L}[c\vec{v}] = c\mathcal{L}[\vec{v}]$

It is easy to express linear maps between vector spaces, as we can see in the following examples:

Example 1.8 (Linearity in $\mathbb{R}^n$). The following map $f : \mathbb{R}^2 \to \mathbb{R}^3$ is linear:

$$f(x, y) = (3x, 2x + y, -y).$$

We can check linearity as follows:

- *Sum preservation:*

$$\begin{aligned}
f(x_1 + x_2, y_1 + y_2) &= (3(x_1 + x_2), 2(x_1 + x_2) + (y_1 + y_2), -(y_1 + y_2)) \\
&= (3x_1, 2x_1 + y_1, -y_1) + (3x_2, 2x_2 + y_2, -y_2) \\
&= f(x_1, y_1) + f(x_2, y_2) \ \checkmark
\end{aligned}$$

- *Scalar product preservation:*

$$\begin{aligned}
f(cx, cy) &= (3cx, 2cx + cy, -cy) \\
&= c(3x, 2x + y, -y) \\
&= cf(x, y) \ \checkmark
\end{aligned}$$

Contrastingly, $g(x, y) \equiv xy^2$ is not linear. For instance, $g(1, 1) = 1$, but $g(2, 2) = 8 \neq 2 \cdot g(1, 1)$, so g does not preserve scalar products.

Example 1.9 (Integration). The following "functional" $\mathcal{L}$ from $\mathbb{R}[x]$ to $\mathbb{R}$ is linear:

$$\mathcal{L}[p(x)] \equiv \int_0^1 p(x)\, dx.$$

This more abstract example maps polynomials $p(x) \in \mathbb{R}[x]$ to real numbers $\mathcal{L}[p(x)] \in \mathbb{R}$. For example, we can write

$$\mathcal{L}[3x^2 + x - 1] = \int_0^1 (3x^2 + x - 1)\, dx = \frac{1}{2}.$$

Linearity of $\mathcal{L}$ is a result of the following well-known identities from calculus:

$$\int_0^1 c \cdot f(x)\, dx = c \int_0^1 f(x)\, dx$$

$$\int_0^1 [f(x) + g(x)]\, dx = \int_0^1 f(x)\, dx + \int_0^1 g(x)\, dx.$$

We can write a particularly nice form for linear maps on $\mathbb{R}^n$. The vector $\vec{a} = (a_1, \ldots, a_n)$ is equal to the sum $\sum_k a_k \vec{e}_k$, where $\vec{e}_k$ is the k-th standard basis vector from Example 1.5. Then, if $\mathcal{L}$ is linear we can expand:

$$\mathcal{L}[\vec{a}] = \mathcal{L}\left[\sum_k a_k \vec{e}_k\right] \text{ for the standard basis } \vec{e}_k$$

$$= \sum_k \mathcal{L}[a_k \vec{e}_k] \text{ by sum preservation}$$

$$= \sum_k a_k \mathcal{L}[\vec{e}_k] \text{ by scalar product preservation.}$$

This derivation shows:

> **A linear operator $\mathcal{L}$ on $\mathbb{R}^n$ is completely determined by its action on the standard basis vectors $\vec{e}_k$.**

That is, for any vector $\vec{a} \in \mathbb{R}^n$, we can use the sum above to determine $\mathcal{L}[\vec{a}]$ by linearly combining $\mathcal{L}[\vec{e}_1], \ldots, \mathcal{L}[\vec{e}_n]$.

Example 1.10 (Expanding a linear map). Recall the map in Example 1.8 given by $f(x, y) = (3x, 2x + y, -y)$. We have $f(\vec{e}_1) = f(1, 0) = (3, 2, 0)$ and $f(\vec{e}_2) = f(0, 1) = (0, 1, -1)$. Thus, the formula above shows:

$$f(x, y) = x f(\vec{e}_1) + y f(\vec{e}_2) = x \begin{pmatrix} 3 \\ 2 \\ 0 \end{pmatrix} + y \begin{pmatrix} 0 \\ 1 \\ -1 \end{pmatrix}.$$

1.3.1 Matrices

The expansion of linear maps above suggests a context in which it is useful to store multiple vectors in the same structure. More generally, say we have n vectors $\vec{v}_1, \ldots, \vec{v}_n \in \mathbb{R}^m$. We can write each as a column vector:

$$\vec{v}_1 = \begin{pmatrix} v_{11} \\ v_{21} \\ \vdots \\ v_{m1} \end{pmatrix}, \vec{v}_2 = \begin{pmatrix} v_{12} \\ v_{22} \\ \vdots \\ v_{m2} \end{pmatrix}, \cdots, \vec{v}_n = \begin{pmatrix} v_{1n} \\ v_{2n} \\ \vdots \\ v_{mn} \end{pmatrix}.$$

Carrying these vectors around separately can be cumbersome notationally, so to simplify matters we combine them into a single $m \times n$ matrix:

$$\begin{pmatrix} | & | & & | \\ \vec{v}_1 & \vec{v}_2 & \cdots & \vec{v}_n \\ | & | & & | \end{pmatrix} = \begin{pmatrix} v_{11} & v_{12} & \cdots & v_{1n} \\ v_{21} & v_{22} & \cdots & v_{2n} \\ \vdots & \vdots & \vdots & \vdots \\ v_{m1} & v_{m2} & \cdots & v_{mn} \end{pmatrix}.$$

We will call the space of such matrices $\mathbb{R}^{m \times n}$.

Example 1.11 (Identity matrix). We can store the standard basis for $\mathbb{R}^n$ in the $n \times n$ "identity matrix" $I_{n \times n}$ given by:

$$
I_{n \times n} \equiv \left(\begin{array}{cccc} \vert & \vert & & \vert \\ \vec{e}_1 & \vec{e}_2 & \cdots & \vec{e}_n \\ \vert & \vert & & \vert \end{array} \right) = \left(\begin{array}{ccccc} 1 & 0 & \cdots & 0 & 0 \\ 0 & 1 & \cdots & 0 & 0 \\ \vdots & \vdots & \vdots & \vdots & \vdots \\ 0 & 0 & \cdots & 1 & 0 \\ 0 & 0 & \cdots & 0 & 1 \end{array} \right).
$$

Since we constructed matrices as convenient ways to store sets of vectors, we can use multiplication to express how they can be combined linearly. In particular, a matrix in $\mathbb{R}^{m \times n}$ can be multiplied by a column vector in $\mathbb{R}^n$ as follows:

$$
\left(\begin{array}{cccc} \vert & \vert & & \vert \\ \vec{v}_1 & \vec{v}_2 & \cdots & \vec{v}_n \\ \vert & \vert & & \vert \end{array} \right) \left(\begin{array}{c} c_1 \\ c_2 \\ \vdots \\ c_n \end{array} \right) \equiv c_1 \vec{v}_1 + c_2 \vec{v}_2 + \cdots + c_n \vec{v}_n.
$$

Expanding this sum yields the following explicit formula for matrix-vector products:

$$
\left(\begin{array}{cccc} v_{11} & v_{12} & \cdots & v_{1n} \\ v_{21} & v_{22} & \cdots & v_{2n} \\ \vdots & \vdots & \vdots & \vdots \\ v_{m1} & v_{m2} & \cdots & v_{mn} \end{array} \right) \left(\begin{array}{c} c_1 \\ c_2 \\ \vdots \\ c_n \end{array} \right) = \left(\begin{array}{c} c_1 v_{11} + c_2 v_{12} + \cdots + c_n v_{1n} \\ c_1 v_{21} + c_2 v_{22} + \cdots + c_n v_{2n} \\ \vdots \\ c_1 v_{m1} + c_2 v_{m2} + \cdots + c_n v_{mn} \end{array} \right).
$$

Example 1.12 (Identity matrix multiplication). For any $\vec{x} \in \mathbb{R}^n$, we can write $\vec{x} = I_{n \times n} \vec{x}$, where $I_{n \times n}$ is the identity matrix from Example 1.11.

Example 1.13 (Linear map). We return once again to the function $f(x, y)$ from Example 1.8 to show one more alternative form:

$$
f(x, y) = \left(\begin{array}{cc} 3 & 0 \\ 2 & 1 \\ 0 & -1 \end{array} \right) \left(\begin{array}{c} x \\ y \end{array} \right).
$$

We similarly define a product between a matrix $M \in \mathbb{R}^{m \times n}$ and another matrix in $\mathbb{R}^{n \times p}$ with columns $\vec{c}_i$ by concatenating individual matrix-vector products:

$$
M \left(\begin{array}{cccc} \vert & \vert & & \vert \\ \vec{c}_1 & \vec{c}_2 & \cdots & \vec{c}_p \\ \vert & \vert & & \vert \end{array} \right) \equiv \left(\begin{array}{cccc} \vert & \vert & & \vert \\ M\vec{c}_1 & M\vec{c}_2 & \cdots & M\vec{c}_p \\ \vert & \vert & & \vert \end{array} \right).
$$

Example 1.14 (Mixology). Continuing Example 1.3, suppose we make a tequila sunrise and second concoction with equal parts of the two liquors in our simplified well. To find out how much of the basic ingredients are contained in each order, we could combine the recipes for each column-wise and use matrix multiplication:

	Well 1	Well 2	Well 3		Drink 1	Drink 2		Drink 1	Drink 2	
Vodka	1	0	0		0	0.75		0	0.75	Vodka
Tequila	0	1	0		1.5	0.75	=	1.5	0.75	Tequila
OJ	0	0	6		1	2		6	12	OJ
Grenadine	0	0	0.75					0.75	1.5	Grenadine

We will use capital letters to represent matrices, like $A \in \mathbb{R}^{m \times n}$. We will use the notation $A_{ij} \in \mathbb{R}$ to denote the element of A at row i and column j.

1.3.2 Scalars, Vectors, and Matrices

If we wish to unify notation completely, we can write a scalar as a 1×1 vector $c \in \mathbb{R}^{1 \times 1}$. Similarly, as suggested in §1.2.3, if we write vectors in $\mathbb{R}^n$ in column form, they can be considered $n \times 1$ matrices $\vec{v} \in \mathbb{R}^{n \times 1}$. Matrix-vector products also can be interpreted in this context. For example, if $A \in \mathbb{R}^{m \times n}$, $\vec{x} \in \mathbb{R}^n$, and $\vec{b} \in \mathbb{R}^m$, then we can write expressions like

$$\underbrace{A}_{m \times n} \cdot \underbrace{\vec{x}}_{n \times 1} = \underbrace{\vec{b}}_{m \times 1}.$$

We will introduce one additional operator on matrices that is useful in this context:

Definition 1.8 (Transpose). The *transpose* of a matrix $A \in \mathbb{R}^{m \times n}$ is a matrix $A^\top \in \mathbb{R}^{n \times m}$ with elements $(A^\top)_{ij} = A_{ji}$.

Example 1.15 (Transposition). The transpose of the matrix

$$A = \begin{pmatrix} 1 & 2 \\ 3 & 4 \\ 5 & 6 \end{pmatrix}$$

is given by

$$A^\top = \begin{pmatrix} 1 & 3 & 5 \\ 2 & 4 & 6 \end{pmatrix}.$$

Geometrically, we can think of transposition as flipping a matrix over its diagonal.

This unified notation combined with operations like transposition and multiplication yields slick expressions and derivations of well-known identities. For instance, we can compute the dot products of vectors $\vec{a}, \vec{b} \in \mathbb{R}^n$ via the following sequence of equalities:

$$\vec{a} \cdot \vec{b} = \sum_{k=1}^{n} a_k b_k = \begin{pmatrix} a_1 & a_2 & \cdots & a_n \end{pmatrix} \begin{pmatrix} b_1 \\ b_2 \\ \vdots \\ b_n \end{pmatrix} = \vec{a}^\top \vec{b}.$$

Identities from linear algebra can be derived by chaining together these operations with a few rules:

$$(A^\top)^\top = A, \qquad (A + B)^\top = A^\top + B^\top, \qquad \text{and} \qquad (AB)^\top = B^\top A^\top.$$

Example 1.16 (Residual norm). Suppose we have a matrix A and two vectors $\vec{x}$ and $\vec{b}$. If we wish to know how well $A\vec{x}$ approximates $\vec{b}$, we might define a *residual* $\vec{r} \equiv \vec{b} - A\vec{x}$; this residual is zero exactly when $A\vec{x} = \vec{b}$. Otherwise, we can use the norm $\|\vec{r}\|_2$ as a proxy for the similarity of $A\vec{x}$ and $\vec{b}$. We can use the identities above to simplify:

$$\|\vec{r}\|_2^2 = \|\vec{b} - A\vec{x}\|_2^2$$
$$= (\vec{b} - A\vec{x}) \cdot (\vec{b} - A\vec{x}) \text{ as explained in §1.2.3}$$

```
function MULTIPLY(A, x⃗)
    ▷ Returns b⃗ = Ax⃗, where
    ▷ A ∈ ℝᵐˣⁿ and x⃗ ∈ ℝⁿ
    b⃗ ← 0⃗
    for i ← 1, 2, ..., m
        for j ← 1, 2, ..., n
            bᵢ ← bᵢ + aᵢⱼxⱼ
    return b⃗
```

(a)

```
function MULTIPLY(A, x⃗)
    ▷ Returns b⃗ = Ax⃗, where
    ▷ A ∈ ℝᵐˣⁿ and x⃗ ∈ ℝⁿ
    b⃗ ← 0⃗
    for j ← 1, 2, ..., n
        for i ← 1, 2, ..., m
            bᵢ ← bᵢ + aᵢⱼxⱼ
    return b⃗
```

(b)

Figure 1.2 Two implementations of matrix-vector multiplication with different loop ordering.

$$= (\vec{b} - A\vec{x})^\top (\vec{b} - A\vec{x}) \text{ by our expression for the dot product above}$$
$$= (\vec{b}^\top - \vec{x}^\top A^\top)(\vec{b} - A\vec{x}) \text{ by properties of transposition}$$
$$= \vec{b}^\top \vec{b} - \vec{b}^\top A\vec{x} - \vec{x}^\top A^\top \vec{b} + \vec{x}^\top A^\top A\vec{x} \text{ after multiplication}$$

All four terms on the right-hand side are scalars, or equivalently 1×1 matrices. Scalars thought of as matrices enjoy one additional nice property $c^\top = c$, since there is nothing to transpose! Thus,

$$\vec{x}^\top A^\top \vec{b} = (\vec{x}^\top A^\top \vec{b})^\top = \vec{b}^\top A\vec{x}.$$

This allows us to simplify even more:

$$\|\vec{r}\|_2^2 = \vec{b}^\top \vec{b} - 2\vec{b}^\top A\vec{x} + \vec{x}^\top A^\top A\vec{x}$$
$$= \|A\vec{x}\|_2^2 - 2\vec{b}^\top A\vec{x} + \|\vec{b}\|_2^2.$$

We could have derived this expression using dot product identities, but the intermediate steps above will prove useful in later discussion.

1.3.3 Matrix Storage and Multiplication Methods

In this section, we take a brief detour from mathematical theory to consider practical aspects of implementing linear algebra operations in computer software. Our discussion considers not only faithfulness to the theory we have constructed but also the *speed* with which we can carry out each operation. This is one of relatively few points at which we will consider computer architecture and other engineering aspects of how computers are designed. This consideration is necessary given the sheer number of times typical numerical algorithms call down to linear algebra routines; a seemingly small improvement in implementing matrix-vector or matrix-matrix multiplication has the potential to increase the efficiency of numerical routines by a large factor.

Figure 1.2 shows two possible implementations of matrix-vector multiplication. The difference between these two algorithms is subtle and seemingly unimportant: The order of the two loops has been switched. Rounding error aside, these two methods generate the same output and do the same number of arithmetic operations; classical "big-O" analysis from computer science would find these two methods indistinguishable. Surprisingly, however,

$$A = \begin{pmatrix} 1 & 2 \\ 3 & 4 \\ 5 & 6 \end{pmatrix}$$

(a)

1	2	3	4	5	6

(b) Row-major

1	3	5	2	4	6

(c) Column-major

Figure 1.3 Two possible ways to store (a) a matrix in memory: (b) row-major ordering and (c) column-major ordering.

considerations related to computer architecture can make one of these options much faster than the other!

A reasonable model for the memory or RAM in a computer is as a long line of data. For this reason, we must find ways to "unroll" data from matrix form to something that could be written completely horizontally. Two common patterns are illustrated in Figure 1.3:

- A *row-major* ordering stores the data row-by-row; that is, the first row appears in a contiguous block of memory, then the second, and so on.

- A *column-major* ordering stores the data column-by-column, moving vertically first rather than horizontally.

Consider the matrix multiplication method in Figure 1.2(a). This algorithm computes all of b_1 before moving to b_2, b_3, and so on. In doing so, the code moves along the elements of A row-by-row. If A is stored in row-major order, then the algorithm in Figure 1.2(a) proceeds linearly across its representation in memory (Figure 1.3(b)), whereas if A is stored in column-major order (Figure 1.3(c)), the algorithm effectively jumps around between elements in A. The opposite is true for the algorithm in Figure 1.2(b), which moves linearly through the column-major ordering.

In many hardware implementations, loading data from memory will retrieve not just the single requested value but instead a block of data near the request. The philosophy here is that common algorithms move linearly though data, processing it one element at a time, and anticipating future requests can reduce the communication load between the main processor and the RAM. By pairing, e.g., the algorithm in Figure 1.2(a) with the row-major ordering in Figure 1.3(b), we can take advantage of this optimization by moving linearly through the storage of the matrix A; the extra loaded data anticipates what will be needed in the next iteration. If we take a nonlinear traversal through A in memory, this situation is less likely, leading to a significant loss in speed.

1.3.4 Model Problem: $A\vec{x} = \vec{b}$

In introductory algebra class, students spend considerable time solving linear systems such as the following for triplets (x, y, z):

$$3x + 2y + 5z = 0$$
$$-4x + 9y - 3z = -7$$
$$2x - 3y - 3z = 1.$$

Our constructions in §1.3.1 allows us to encode such systems in a cleaner fashion:

$$\begin{pmatrix} 3 & 2 & 5 \\ -4 & 9 & -3 \\ 2 & -3 & -3 \end{pmatrix} \begin{pmatrix} x \\ y \\ z \end{pmatrix} = \begin{pmatrix} 0 \\ -7 \\ 1 \end{pmatrix}.$$

More generally, we can write any linear system of equations in the form $A\vec{x} = \vec{b}$ by following the same pattern above; here, the vector $\vec{x}$ is unknown while A and $\vec{b}$ are known. Such a system of equations is *not* always guaranteed to have a solution. For instance, if A contains only zeros, then no $\vec{x}$ will satisfy $A\vec{x} = \vec{b}$ whenever $\vec{b} \neq \vec{0}$. We will defer a general consideration of when a solution exists to our discussion of linear solvers in future chapters.

A key interpretation of the system $A\vec{x} = \vec{b}$ is that it addresses the task:

Write $\vec{b}$ as a linear combination of the columns of A.

Why? Recall from §1.3.1 that the product $A\vec{x}$ encodes a linear combination of the columns of A with weights contained in elements of $\vec{x}$. So, the equation $A\vec{x} = \vec{b}$ sets the linear combination $A\vec{x}$ equal to the given vector $\vec{b}$. Given this interpretation, we define the *column space* of A to be the space of right-hand sides $\vec{b}$ for which the system $A\vec{x} = \vec{b}$ has a solution:

Definition 1.9 (Column space and rank). The *column space* of a matrix $A \in \mathbb{R}^{m \times n}$ is the span of the columns of A. It can be written as

$$\text{col } A \equiv \{A\vec{x} : \vec{x} \in \mathbb{R}^n\}.$$

The *rank* of A is the dimension of col A.

$A\vec{x} = \vec{b}$ is solvable exactly when $\vec{b} \in \text{col } A$.

One case will dominate our discussion in future chapters. Suppose A is square, so we can write $A \in \mathbb{R}^{n \times n}$. Furthermore, suppose that the system $A\vec{x} = \vec{b}$ has a solution *for all* choices of $\vec{b}$, so by our interpretation above the columns of A must span $\mathbb{R}^n$. In this case, we can substitute the standard basis $\vec{e}_1, \ldots, \vec{e}_n$ to solve equations of the form $A\vec{x}_i = \vec{e}_i$, yielding vectors $\vec{x}_1, \ldots, \vec{x}_n$. Combining these $\vec{x}_i$'s horizontally into a matrix shows:

$$A \begin{pmatrix} | & | & & | \\ \vec{x}_1 & \vec{x}_2 & \cdots & \vec{x}_n \\ | & | & & | \end{pmatrix} = \begin{pmatrix} | & | & & | \\ A\vec{x}_1 & A\vec{x}_2 & \cdots & A\vec{x}_n \\ | & | & & | \end{pmatrix}$$

$$= \begin{pmatrix} | & | & & | \\ \vec{e}_1 & \vec{e}_2 & \cdots & \vec{e}_n \\ | & | & & | \end{pmatrix} = I_{n \times n},$$

where $I_{n \times n}$ is the identity matrix from Example 1.11. We will call the matrix with columns $\vec{x}_k$ the *inverse* A^{-1}, which satisfies

$$AA^{-1} = A^{-1}A = I_{n \times n}.$$

By construction, $(A^{-1})^{-1} = A$. If we can find such an inverse, solving any linear system $A\vec{x} = \vec{b}$ reduces to matrix multiplication, since:

$$\vec{x} = I_{n \times n}\vec{x} = (A^{-1}A)\vec{x} = A^{-1}(A\vec{x}) = A^{-1}\vec{b}.$$

1.4 NON-LINEARITY: DIFFERENTIAL CALCULUS

While the beauty and applicability of linear algebra makes it a key target for study, non-linearities abound in nature, and we must design machinery that can deal with this reality.

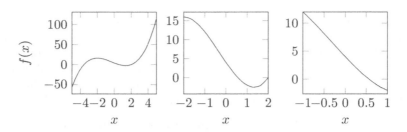

Figure 1.4 The closer we zoom into $f(x) = x^3 + x^2 - 8x + 4$, the more it looks like a line.

1.4.1 Differentiation in One Variable

While many functions are *globally* nonlinear, *locally* they exhibit linear behavior. This idea of "local linearity" is one of the main motivators behind differential calculus. Figure 1.4 shows that if you zoom in close enough to a smooth function, eventually it looks like a line. The derivative $f'(x)$ of a function $f(x) : \mathbb{R} \to \mathbb{R}$ is the slope of the approximating line, computed by finding the slope of lines through closer and closer points to x:

$$f'(x) = \lim_{y \to x} \frac{f(y) - f(x)}{y - x}.$$

In reality, taking limits as $y \to x$ may not be possible on a computer, so a reasonable question to ask is how well a function $f(x)$ is approximated by a line through points that are a finite distance apart. We can answer these types of questions using infinitesimal analysis. Take $x, y \in \mathbb{R}$. Then, we can expand:

$$f(y) - f(x) = \int_x^y f'(t)\,dt \text{ by the Fundamental Theorem of Calculus}$$

$$= yf'(y) - xf'(x) - \int_x^y tf''(t)\,dt, \text{ after integrating by parts}$$

$$= (y - x)f'(x) + y(f'(y) - f'(x)) - \int_x^y tf''(t)\,dt$$

$$= (y - x)f'(x) + y\int_x^y f''(t)\,dt - \int_x^y tf''(t)\,dt$$

$$\text{again by the Fundamental Theorem of Calculus}$$

$$= (y - x)f'(x) + \int_x^y (y - t)f''(t)\,dt.$$

Rearranging terms and defining $\Delta x \equiv y - x$ shows:

$$|f'(x)\Delta x - [f(y) - f(x)]| = \left| \int_x^y (y - t)f''(t)\,dt \right| \text{ from the relationship above}$$

$$\leq |\Delta x| \int_x^y |f''(t)|\,dt, \text{ by the Cauchy-Schwarz inequality}$$

$$\leq D|\Delta x|^2, \text{ assuming } |f''(t)| < D \text{ for some } D > 0.$$

We can introduce some notation to help express the relationship we have written:

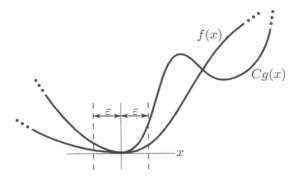

Figure 1.5 Big-O notation; in the ε neighborhood of the origin, $f(x)$ is dominated by $Cg(x)$; outside this neighborhood, $Cg(x)$ can dip back down.

Definition 1.10 (Infinitesimal big-O). We will say $f(x) = O(g(x))$ if there exists a constant $C > 0$ and some $\varepsilon > 0$ such that $|f(x)| \leq C|g(x)|$ for all x with $|x| < \varepsilon$.

This definition is illustrated in Figure 1.5. Computer scientists may be surprised to see that we are defining "big-O notation" by taking limits as $x \to 0$ rather than $x \to \infty$, but since we are concerned with infinitesimal approximation quality, this definition will be more relevant to the discussion at hand.

Our derivation above shows the following relationship for smooth functions $f : \mathbb{R} \to \mathbb{R}$:

$$f(x + \Delta x) = f(x) + f'(x)\Delta x + O(\Delta x^2).$$

This is an instance of Taylor's theorem, which we will apply copiously when developing strategies for integrating ordinary differential equations. More generally, this theorem shows how to approximate differentiable functions with polynomials:

$$f(x + \Delta x) = f(x) + f'(x)\Delta x + f''(x)\frac{\Delta x^2}{2!} + \cdots + f^{(k)}(x)\frac{\Delta x^k}{k!} + O(\Delta x^{k+1}).$$

1.4.2 Differentiation in Multiple Variables

If a function f takes multiple inputs, then it can be written $f(\vec{x}) : \mathbb{R}^n \to \mathbb{R}$ for $\vec{x} \in \mathbb{R}^n$. In other words, to each point $\vec{x} = (x_1, \ldots, x_n)$ in n-dimensional space, f assigns a single number $f(x_1, \ldots, x_n)$.

The idea of local linearity must be repaired in this case, because lines are one- rather than n-dimensional objects. Fixing all but one variable, however, brings a return to single-variable calculus. For instance, we could isolate x_1 by studying $g(t) \equiv f(t, x_2, \ldots, x_n)$, where we think of $x_2, \ldots, x_n$ as constants. Then, $g(t)$ is a differentiable function of a single variable that we can characterize using the machinery in §1.4.1. We can do the same for any of the x_k's, so in general we make the following definition of the *partial derivative* of f:

Definition 1.11 (Partial derivative). The k-th *partial derivative* of f, notated $\frac{\partial f}{\partial x_k}$, is given by differentiating f in its k-th input variable:

$$\frac{\partial f}{\partial x_k}(x_1, \ldots, x_n) \equiv \frac{d}{dt}f(x_1, \ldots, x_{k-1}, t, x_{k+1}, \ldots, x_n)|_{t=x_k}.$$

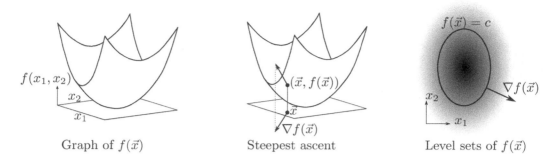

Graph of $f(\vec{x})$ Steepest ascent   Level sets of $f(\vec{x})$

Figure 1.6 We can visualize a function $f(x_1, x_2)$ as a three-dimensional graph; then $\nabla f(\vec{x})$ is the direction on the (x_1, x_2) plane corresponding to the steepest ascent of f. Alternatively, we can think of $f(x_1, x_2)$ as the *brightness* at (x_1, x_2) (dark indicates a low value of f), in which case ∇f points perpendicular to level sets $f(\vec{x}) = c$ in the direction where f is increasing and the image gets lighter.

The notation used in this definition and elsewhere in our discussion "$|_{t=x_k}$" should be read as "evaluated at $t = x_k$."

Example 1.17 (Relativity). The relationship $E = mc^2$ can be thought of as a function mapping pairs (m, c) to a scalar E. Thus, we could write $E(m, c) = mc^2$, yielding the partial derivatives

$$\frac{\partial E}{\partial m} = c^2 \qquad\qquad \frac{\partial E}{\partial c} = 2mc.$$

Using single-variable calculus, for a function $f : \mathbb{R}^n \to \mathbb{R}$,

$$f(\vec{x} + \Delta\vec{x}) = f(x_1 + \Delta x_1, x_2 + \Delta x_2, \ldots, x_n + \Delta x_n)$$

$$= f(x_1, x_2 + \Delta x_2, \ldots, x_n + \Delta x_n) + \frac{\partial f}{\partial x_1}\Delta x_1 + O(\Delta x_1^2)$$

by single-variable calculus in x_1

$$= f(x_1, \ldots, x_n) + \sum_{k=1}^{n}\left[\frac{\partial f}{\partial x_k}\Delta x_k + O(\Delta x_k^2)\right]$$

by repeating this $n - 1$ times in $x_2, \ldots, x_n$

$$= f(\vec{x}) + \nabla f(\vec{x}) \cdot \Delta\vec{x} + O(\|\Delta\vec{x}\|_2^2),$$

where we define the *gradient* of f as

$$\nabla f(\vec{x}) \equiv \left(\frac{\partial f}{\partial x_1}(\vec{x}), \frac{\partial f}{\partial x_2}(\vec{x}), \cdots, \frac{\partial f}{\partial x_n}(\vec{x})\right) \in \mathbb{R}^n.$$

Figure 1.6 illustrates interpretations of the gradient of a function, which we will reconsider in our discussion of optimization in future chapters.

We can differentiate f in any direction $\vec{v}$ via the *directional derivative* $D_{\vec{v}}f$:

$$D_{\vec{v}}f(\vec{x}) \equiv \frac{d}{dt}f(\vec{x} + t\vec{v})|_{t=0} = \nabla f(\vec{x}) \cdot \vec{v}.$$

We allow $\vec{v}$ to have any length, with the property $D_{c\vec{v}}f(\vec{x}) = cD_{\vec{v}}f(\vec{x})$.

Example 1.18 ($\mathbb{R}^2$). Take $f(x, y) = x^2 y^3$. Then,

$$\frac{\partial f}{\partial x} = 2xy^3 \qquad\qquad \frac{\partial f}{\partial y} = 3x^2 y^2.$$

Equivalently, $\nabla f(x, y) = (2xy^3, 3x^2 y^2)$. So, the derivative of f at $(x, y) = (1, 2)$ in the direction $(-1, 4)$ is given by $(-1, 4) \cdot \nabla f(1, 2) = (-1, 4) \cdot (16, 12) = 32$.

There are a few derivatives that we will use many times. These formulae will appear repeatedly in future chapters and are worth studying independently:

Example 1.19 (Linear functions). It is obvious but worth noting that the gradient of $f(\vec{x}) \equiv \vec{a} \cdot \vec{x} + \vec{c} = (a_1 x_1 + c_1, \ldots, a_n x_n + c_n)$ is $\vec{a}$.

Example 1.20 (Quadratic forms). Take any matrix $A \in \mathbb{R}^{n \times n}$, and define $f(\vec{x}) \equiv \vec{x}^\top A \vec{x}$. Writing this function element-by-element shows

$$f(\vec{x}) = \sum_{ij} A_{ij} x_i x_j.$$

Expanding f and checking this relationship explicitly is worthwhile. Take some $k \in \{1, \ldots, n\}$. Then, we can separate out all terms containing x_k:

$$f(\vec{x}) = A_{kk} x_k^2 + x_k \left(\sum_{i \neq k} A_{ik} x_i + \sum_{j \neq k} A_{kj} x_j \right) + \sum_{i, j \neq k} A_{ij} x_i x_j.$$

With this factorization,

$$\frac{\partial f}{\partial x_k} = 2 A_{kk} x_k + \left(\sum_{i \neq k} A_{ik} x_i + \sum_{j \neq k} A_{kj} x_j \right) = \sum_{i=1}^{n} (A_{ik} + A_{ki}) x_i.$$

This sum looks a lot like the definition of matrix-vector multiplication! Combining these partial derivatives into a single vector shows $\nabla f(\vec{x}) = (A + A^\top) \vec{x}$. In the special case when A is symmetric, that is, when $A^\top = A$, we have the well-known formula $\nabla f(\vec{x}) = 2 A \vec{x}$.

We generalized differentiation from $f : \mathbb{R} \to \mathbb{R}$ to $f : \mathbb{R}^n \to \mathbb{R}$. To reach full generality, we should consider $f : \mathbb{R}^n \to \mathbb{R}^m$. That is, f inputs n numbers and outputs m numbers. This extension is straightforward, because we can think of f as a collection of single-valued functions $f_1, \ldots, f_m : \mathbb{R}^n \to \mathbb{R}$ smashed into a single vector. Symbolically,

$$f(\vec{x}) = \begin{pmatrix} f_1(\vec{x}) \\ f_2(\vec{x}) \\ \vdots \\ f_m(\vec{x}) \end{pmatrix}.$$

Each f_k can be differentiated as before, so in the end we get a matrix of partial derivatives called the *Jacobian* of f:

Definition 1.12 (Jacobian). The *Jacobian* of $f : \mathbb{R}^n \to \mathbb{R}^m$ is the matrix $Df(\vec{x}) \in \mathbb{R}^{m \times n}$ with entries

$$(Df)_{ij} \equiv \frac{\partial f_i}{\partial x_j}.$$

Example 1.21 (Jacobian computation). Suppose $f(x, y) = (3x, -xy^2, x + y)$. Then,

$$Df(x, y) = \begin{pmatrix} 3 & 0 \\ -y^2 & -2xy \\ 1 & 1 \end{pmatrix}.$$

Example 1.22 (Matrix multiplication). Unsurprisingly, the Jacobian of $f(\vec{x}) = A\vec{x}$ for matrix A is given by $Df(\vec{x}) = A$.

Here, we encounter a common point of confusion. Suppose a function has vector input and scalar output, that is, $f : \mathbb{R}^n \to \mathbb{R}$. We defined the gradient of f as a column vector, so to align this definition with that of the Jacobian we must write $Df = \nabla f^\top$.

1.4.3 Optimization

A key problem in the study of numerical algorithms is optimization, which involves finding points at which a function $f(\vec{x})$ is maximized or minimized. A wide variety of computational challenges can be posed as optimization problems, also known as variational problems, and hence this language will permeate our derivation of numerical algorithms. Generally speaking, optimization problems involve finding extrema of a function $f(\vec{x})$, possibly subject to constraints specifying which points $\vec{x} \in \mathbb{R}^n$ are *feasible*. Recalling physical systems that naturally seek low- or high-energy configurations, $f(\vec{x})$ is sometimes referred to as an *energy* or *objective*.

From single-variable calculus, the minima and maxima of $f : \mathbb{R} \to \mathbb{R}$ must occur at points x satisfying $f'(x) = 0$. This condition is *necessary* rather than *sufficient*: there may exist saddle points x with $f'(x) = 0$ that are not maxima or minima. That said, finding such critical points of f can be part of a function minimization algorithm, so long as a subsequent step ensures that the resulting x is actually a minimum/maximum.

If $f : \mathbb{R}^n \to \mathbb{R}$ is minimized or maximized at $\vec{x}$, we have to ensure that there does not exist a single direction Δx from $\vec{x}$ in which f decreases or increases, respectively. By the discussion in §1.4.1, this means we must find points for which $\nabla f = 0$.

Example 1.23 (Critical points). Suppose $f(x, y) = x^2 + 2xy + 4y^2$. Then, $\frac{\partial f}{\partial x} = 2x + 2y$ and $\frac{\partial f}{\partial y} = 2x + 8y$. Thus, critical points of f satisfy:

$$2x + 2y = 0 \qquad \text{and} \qquad 2x + 8y = 0.$$

This system is solved by taking $(x, y) = (0, 0)$. Indeed, this is the minimum of f, as can be seen by writing $f(x, y) = (x + y)^2 + 3y^2 \geq 0 = f(0, 0)$.

Example 1.24 (Quadratic functions). Suppose $f(\vec{x}) = \vec{x}^\top A\vec{x} + \vec{b}^\top \vec{x} + c$. Then, from Examples 1.19 and 1.20 we can write $\nabla f(\vec{x}) = (A^\top + A)\vec{x} + \vec{b}$. Thus, critical points $\vec{x}$ of f satisfy $(A^\top + A)\vec{x} + \vec{b} = 0$.

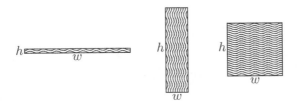

Figure 1.7 Three rectangles with the same perimeter $2w + 2h$ but unequal areas wh; the square on the right with $w = h$ maximizes wh over all possible choices with prescribed $2w + 2h = 1$.

Unlike single-variable calculus, on $\mathbb{R}^n$ we can add nontrivial *constraints* to our optimization. For now, we will consider the *equality-constrained* case, given by

$$\text{minimize } f(\vec{x})$$
$$\text{subject to } g(\vec{x}) = \vec{0}.$$

When we add the constraint $g(\vec{x}) = 0$, we no longer expect that minimizers $\vec{x}$ satisfy $\nabla f(\vec{x}) = 0$, since these points might not satisfy $g(\vec{x}) = \vec{0}$.

Example 1.25 (Rectangle areas). Suppose a rectangle has width w and height h. A classic geometry problem is to maximize area with a fixed perimeter 1:

$$\text{maximize } wh$$
$$\text{subject to } 2w + 2h - 1 = 0.$$

This problem is illustrated in Figure 1.7.

For now, suppose $g : \mathbb{R}^n \to \mathbb{R}$, so we only have one equality constraint; an example for $n = 2$ is shown in Figure 1.8. We define the set of points satisfying the equality constraint as $S_0 \equiv \{\vec{x} : g(\vec{x}) = 0\}$. Any two $\vec{x}, \vec{y} \in S_0$ satisfy the relationship $g(\vec{y}) - g(\vec{x}) = 0 - 0 = 0$. Applying Taylor's theorem, if $\vec{y} = \vec{x} + \Delta\vec{x}$ for small $\Delta\vec{x}$, then

$$g(\vec{y}) - g(\vec{x}) = \nabla g(\vec{x}) \cdot \Delta\vec{x} + O(\|\Delta\vec{x}\|_2^2).$$

In other words, if $g(\vec{x}) = 0$ and $\nabla g(\vec{x}) \cdot \Delta\vec{x} = 0$, then $g(\vec{x} + \Delta\vec{x}) \approx 0$.

If $\vec{x}$ is a minimum of the constrained optimization problem above, then any small displacement $\vec{x}$ to $\vec{x} + \vec{v}$ still satisfying the constraints should cause an increase from $f(\vec{x})$ to $f(\vec{x} + \vec{v})$. On the infinitesimal scale, since we only care about displacements $\vec{v}$ preserving the $g(\vec{x} + \vec{v}) = c$ constraint, from our argument above we want $\nabla f \cdot \vec{v} = 0$ for all $\vec{v}$ satisfying $\nabla g(\vec{x}) \cdot \vec{v} = 0$. In other words, ∇f and ∇g must be parallel, a condition we can write as $\nabla f = \lambda \nabla g$ for some $\lambda \in \mathbb{R}$, illustrated in Figure 1.8(c).

Define

$$\Lambda(\vec{x}, \lambda) \equiv f(\vec{x}) - \lambda g(\vec{x}).$$

Then, critical points of Λ without constraints satisfy:

$$\frac{\partial \Lambda}{\partial \lambda} = -g(\vec{x}) = 0, \text{ by the constraint } g(\vec{x}) = 0.$$
$$\nabla_{\vec{x}} \Lambda = \nabla f(\vec{x}) - \lambda \nabla g(\vec{x}) = 0, \text{ as argued above.}$$

In other words, critical points of Λ with respect to both λ and $\vec{x}$ satisfy $g(\vec{x}) = 0$ and $\nabla f(\vec{x}) = \lambda \nabla g(\vec{x})$, exactly the optimality conditions we derived!

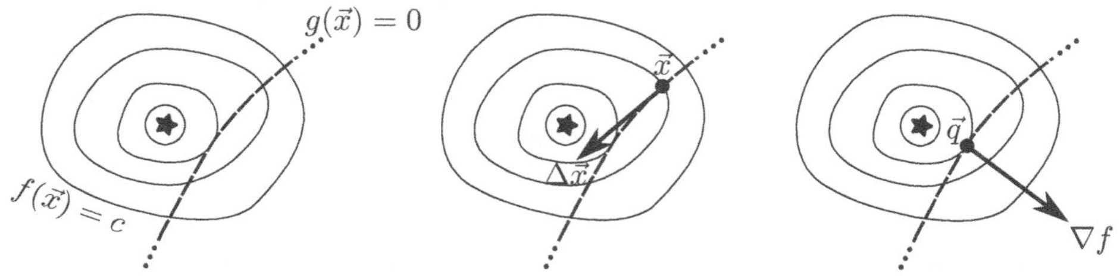

(a) Constrained optimization   (b) Suboptimal $\vec{x}$ (c) Optimal $\vec{q}$

Figure 1.8 (a) An equality-constrained optimization. Without constraints, $f(\vec{x})$ is minimized at the star; solid lines show isocontours $f(\vec{x}) = c$ for increasing c. Minimizing $f(\vec{x})$ subject to $g(\vec{x}) = 0$ forces $\vec{x}$ to be on the dashed curve. (b) The point $\vec{x}$ is suboptimal since moving in the $\Delta\vec{x}$ direction decreases $f(\vec{x})$ while maintaining $g(\vec{x}) = 0$. (c) The point $\vec{q}$ is optimal since decreasing f from $f(\vec{q})$ would require moving in the $-\nabla f$ direction, which is perpendicular to the curve $g(\vec{x}) = 0$.

Extending our argument to $g : \mathbb{R}^n \to \mathbb{R}^k$ yields the following theorem:

Theorem 1.1 (Method of Lagrange multipliers). Critical points of the equality-constrained optimization problem above are (unconstrained) critical points of the Lagrange multiplier function

$$\Lambda(\vec{x}, \vec{\lambda}) \equiv f(\vec{x}) - \vec{\lambda} \cdot g(\vec{x}),$$

with respect to both $\vec{x}$ and $\vec{\lambda}$.

Some treatments of Lagrange multipliers equivalently use the opposite sign for $\vec{\lambda}$; considering $\bar{\Lambda}(\vec{x}, \vec{\lambda}) \equiv f(\vec{x}) + \vec{\lambda} \cdot g(\vec{x})$ leads to an analogous result above.

This theorem provides an analog of the condition $\nabla f(\vec{x}) = \vec{0}$ when equality constraints $g(\vec{x}) = \vec{0}$ are added to an optimization problem and is a cornerstone of variational algorithms we will consider. We conclude with a number of examples applying this theorem; understanding these examples is crucial to our development of numerical methods in future chapters.

Example 1.26 (Maximizing area). Continuing Example 1.25, we define the Lagrange multiplier function $\Lambda(w, h, \lambda) = wh - \lambda(2w + 2h - 1)$. Differentiating Λ with respect to w, h, and λ provides the following optimality conditions:

$$0 = \frac{\partial\Lambda}{\partial w} = h - 2\lambda \qquad 0 = \frac{\partial\Lambda}{\partial h} = w - 2\lambda \qquad 0 = \frac{\partial\Lambda}{\partial\lambda} = 1 - 2w - 2h.$$

So, critical points of the area wh under the constraint $2w + 2h = 1$ satisfy

$$\begin{pmatrix} 0 & 1 & -2 \\ 1 & 0 & -2 \\ 2 & 2 & 0 \end{pmatrix} \begin{pmatrix} w \\ h \\ \lambda \end{pmatrix} = \begin{pmatrix} 0 \\ 0 \\ 1 \end{pmatrix}.$$

Solving the system shows $w = h = 1/4$ (and $\lambda = 1/8$). In other words, for a fixed amount of perimeter, the rectangle with maximal area is a square.

Example 1.27 (Eigenproblems). Suppose that A is a symmetric positive definite matrix, meaning $A^\top = A$ (symmetric) and $\vec{x}^\top A \vec{x} > 0$ for all $\vec{x} \in \mathbb{R}^n \backslash \{\vec{0}\}$ (positive definite). We may wish to minimize $\vec{x}^\top A \vec{x}$ subject to $\|\vec{x}\|_2^2 = 1$ for a given matrix $A \in \mathbb{R}^{n \times n}$; without the constraint the function is minimized at $\vec{x} = \vec{0}$. We define the Lagrange multiplier function

$$\Lambda(\vec{x}, \lambda) = \vec{x}^\top A \vec{x} - \lambda(\|\vec{x}\|_2^2 - 1) = \vec{x}^\top A \vec{x} - \lambda(\vec{x}^\top \vec{x} - 1).$$

Differentiating with respect to $\vec{x}$, we find $0 = \nabla_{\vec{x}} \Lambda = 2A\vec{x} - 2\lambda\vec{x}$. In other words, critical points of $\vec{x}$ are exactly the *eigenvectors* of the matrix A:

$$A\vec{x} = \lambda\vec{x}, \text{ with } \|\vec{x}\|_2^2 = 1.$$

At these critical points, we can evaluate the objective function as $\vec{x}^\top A \vec{x} = \vec{x}^\top \lambda \vec{x} = \lambda\|\vec{x}\|_2^2 = \lambda$. Hence, the minimizer of $\vec{x}^\top A \vec{x}$ subject to $\|\vec{x}\|_2^2 = 1$ is the eigenvector $\vec{x}$ with minimum eigenvalue λ; we will provide practical applications and solution techniques for this optimization problem in detail in Chapter 6.

1.5 EXERCISES

SC 1.1 Illustrate the gradients of $f(x, y) = x^2 + y^2$ and $g(x, y) = \sqrt{x^2 + y^2}$ on the plane, and show that $\|\nabla g(x, y)\|_2$ is constant away from the origin.

DH 1.2 Compute the dimensions of each of the following sets:

(a) $\mathrm{col} \begin{pmatrix} 1 & 0 & 0 \\ 0 & 1 & 0 \\ 0 & 0 & 0 \end{pmatrix}$

(b) $\mathrm{span}\, \{(1, 1, 1), (1, -1, 1), (-1, 1, 1), (1, 1, -1)\}$

(c) $\mathrm{span}\, \{(2, 7, 9), (3, 5, 1), (0, 1, 0)\}$

(d) $\mathrm{col} \begin{pmatrix} 1 & 1 & 0 \\ 1 & 1 & 0 \\ 0 & 0 & 1 \end{pmatrix}$

1.3 Which of the following functions is linear? Why?

(a) $f(x, y, z) = 0$

(b) $f(x, y, z) = 1$

(c) $f(x, y, z) = (1 + x, 2z)$

(d) $f(x) = (x, 2x)$

(e) $f(x, y) = (2x + 3y, x, 0)$

1.4 Suppose that $\mathcal{U}_1$ and $\mathcal{U}_2$ are subspaces of vector space $\mathcal{V}$. Show that $\mathcal{U}_1 \cap \mathcal{U}_2$ is a subspace of $\mathcal{V}$. Is $\mathcal{U}_1 \cup \mathcal{U}_2$ always a subspace of $\mathcal{V}$?

1.5 Suppose $A, B \in \mathbb{R}^{n \times n}$ and $\vec{a}, \vec{b} \in \mathbb{R}^n$. Find a (nontrivial) linear system of equations satisfied by any $\vec{x}$ minimizing the energy $\|A\vec{x} - \vec{a}\|_2^2 + \|B\vec{x} - \vec{b}\|_2^2$.

1.6 Take $C^1(\mathbb{R})$ to be the set of continuously differentiable functions $f : \mathbb{R} \to \mathbb{R}$. Why is $C^1(\mathbb{R})$ a vector space? Show that $C^1(\mathbb{R})$ has dimension ∞.

1.7 Suppose the rows of $A \in \mathbb{R}^{m \times n}$ are given by the transposes of $\vec{r}_1, \dots, \vec{r}_m \in \mathbb{R}^n$ and the columns of $A \in \mathbb{R}^{m \times n}$ are given by $\vec{c}_1, \dots, \vec{c}_n \in \mathbb{R}^m$. That is,

$$A = \begin{pmatrix} - & \vec{r}_1^\top & - \\ - & \vec{r}_2^\top & - \\ & \vdots & \\ - & \vec{r}_m^\top & - \end{pmatrix} = \begin{pmatrix} | & | & & | \\ \vec{c}_1 & \vec{c}_2 & \cdots & \vec{c}_n \\ | & | & & | \end{pmatrix}.$$

Give expressions for the elements of $A^\top A$ and $A A^\top$ in terms of these vectors.

1.8 Give a linear system of equations satisfied by minima of the energy $f(\vec{x}) = \|A\vec{x} - \vec{b}\|_2$ with respect to $\vec{x}$, for $\vec{x} \in \mathbb{R}^n$, $A \in \mathbb{R}^{m \times n}$, and $\vec{b} \in \mathbb{R}^m$.

1.9 Suppose $A, B \in \mathbb{R}^{n \times n}$. Formulate a condition for vectors $\vec{x} \in \mathbb{R}^n$ to be critical points of $\|A\vec{x}\|_2$ subject to $\|B\vec{x}\|_2 = 1$. Also, give an alternative expression for the value of $\|A\vec{x}\|_2$ at these critical points, in terms a Lagrange multiplier for this optimization problem.

1.10 Fix some vector $\vec{a} \in \mathbb{R}^n \backslash \{\vec{0}\}$ and define $f(\vec{x}) = \vec{a} \cdot \vec{x}$. Give an expression for the maximum of $f(\vec{x})$ subject to $\|\vec{x}\|_2 = 1$.

1.11 Suppose $A \in \mathbb{R}^{n \times n}$ is symmetric, and define the *Rayleigh quotient* function $R(\vec{x})$ as

$$R(\vec{x}) \equiv \frac{\vec{x}^\top A \vec{x}}{\|\vec{x}\|_2^2}.$$

Show that minimizers of $R(\vec{x})$ subject to $\vec{x} \neq \vec{0}$ are eigenvectors of A.

1.12 Show that $(A^\top)^{-1} = (A^{-1})^\top$ when $A \in \mathbb{R}^{n \times n}$ is invertible. If $B \in \mathbb{R}^{n \times n}$ is also invertible, show $(AB)^{-1} = B^{-1} A^{-1}$.

1.13 Suppose $A(t)$ is a function taking a parameter t and returning an invertible square matrix $A(t) \in \mathbb{R}^{n \times n}$; we can write $A : \mathbb{R} \to \mathbb{R}^{n \times n}$. Assuming each element $a_{ij}(t)$ of $A(t)$ is a differentiable function of t, define the derivative matrix $\frac{dA}{dt}(t)$ as the matrix whose elements are $\frac{da_{ij}}{dt}(t)$. Verify the following identity:

$$\frac{d(A^{-1})}{dt} = -A^{-1} \frac{dA}{dt} A^{-1}.$$

Hint: Start from the identity $A^{-1}(t) \cdot A(t) = I_{n \times n}$.

1.14 Derive the following relationship stated in §1.4.2:

$$\frac{d}{dt} f(\vec{x} + t\vec{v})\big|_{t=0} = \nabla f(\vec{x}) \cdot \vec{v}.$$

1.15 A matrix $A \in \mathbb{R}^{n \times n}$ is *idempotent* if it satisfies $A^2 = A$.

(a) Suppose $B \in \mathbb{R}^{m \times k}$ is constructed so that $B^\top B$ is invertible. Show that the matrix $B(B^\top B)^{-1} B^\top$ is idempotent.

(b) If A is idempotent, show that $I_{n \times n} - A$ is also idempotent.

(c) If A is idempotent, show that $\frac{1}{2}I_{n \times n} - A$ is invertible and give an expression for its inverse.

(d) Suppose A is idempotent and that we are given $\vec{x} \neq \vec{0}$ and $\lambda \in \mathbb{R}$ satisfying $A\vec{x} = \lambda\vec{x}$. Show that $\lambda \in \{0, 1\}$.

1.16 Show that it takes at least $O(n^2)$ time to find the product AB of two matrices $A, B \in \mathbb{R}^{n \times n}$. What is the runtime of the algorithms in Figure 1.2? Is there room for improvement?

1.17 ("Laplace approximation," [13]) Suppose $p(\vec{x}) : \mathbb{R}^n \to [0, 1]$ is a *probability distribution*, meaning that $p(\vec{x}) \geq 0$ for all $\vec{x} \in \mathbb{R}^n$ and

$$\int_{\mathbb{R}^n} p(\vec{x}) \, d\vec{x} = 1.$$

In this problem, you can assume $p(\vec{x})$ is infinitely differentiable.

One important type of probability distribution is the *Gaussian distribution*, also known as the normal distribution, which takes the form

$$G_{\Sigma, \vec{\mu}}(\vec{x}) \propto e^{-\frac{1}{2}(\vec{x} - \vec{\mu})^\top \Sigma^{-1} (\vec{x} - \vec{\mu})}.$$

Here, $f(\vec{x}) \propto g(\vec{x})$ denotes that there exists some $c \in \mathbb{R}$ such that $f(\vec{x}) = cg(\vec{x})$ for all $\vec{x} \in \mathbb{R}^n$. The covariance matrix $\Sigma \in \mathbb{R}^{n \times n}$ and mean $\vec{\mu} \in \mathbb{R}^n$ determine the particular bell shape of the Gaussian distribution.

Suppose $\vec{x}^* \in \mathbb{R}^n$ is a mode, or local maximum, of $p(\vec{x})$. Propose a Gaussian approximation of $p(\vec{x})$ in a neighborhood of $\vec{x}^*$.

Hint: Consider the *negative log likelihood function*, given by $\ell(\vec{x}) \equiv -\ln p(\vec{x})$.

CHAPTER 2

Numerics and Error Analysis

CONTENTS

2.1   Storing Numbers with Fractional Parts 27
    2.1.1   Fixed-Point Representations 28
    2.1.2   Floating-Point Representations 29
    2.1.3   More Exotic Options 31
2.2   Understanding Error 32
    2.2.1   Classifying Error 33
    2.2.2   Conditioning, Stability, and Accuracy 35
2.3   Practical Aspects 36
    2.3.1   Computing Vector Norms 37
    2.3.2   Larger-Scale Example: Summation 38

N UMERICAL analysis introduces a shift from working with ints and longs to floats and doubles. This seemingly innocent transition shatters intuition from integer arithmetic, requiring adjustment of how we must think about basic algorithmic design and implementation. Unlike discrete algorithms, numerical algorithms cannot always yield exact solutions even to well-studied and well-posed problems. Operation counting no longer reigns supreme; instead, even basic techniques require careful analysis of the trade-offs among timing, approximation error, and other considerations. In this chapter, we will explore the typical factors affecting the quality of a numerical algorithm. These factors set numerical algorithms apart from their discrete counterparts.

2.1   STORING NUMBERS WITH FRACTIONAL PARTS

Most computers store data in *binary* format. In binary, integers are decomposed into powers of two. For instance, we can convert 463 to binary using the following table:

1	1	1	0	0	1	1	1	1
2^8	2^7	2^6	2^5	2^4	2^3	2^2	2^1	2^0

This table illustrates the fact that 463 has a unique decomposition into powers of two as:

$$463 = 256 + 128 + 64 + 8 + 4 + 2 + 1$$
$$= 2^8 + 2^7 + 2^6 + 2^3 + 2^2 + 2^1 + 2^0.$$

All positive integers can be written in this form. Negative numbers also can be represented either by introducing a leading sign bit (e.g., 1 for "positive" and 0 for "negative") or by using a "two's complement" trick.

The binary system admits an extension to numbers with fractional parts by including *negative* powers of two. For instance, 463.25 can be decomposed by adding two slots:

1	1	1	0	0	1	1	1	1.	0	1
2^8	2^7	2^6	2^5	2^4	2^3	2^2	2^1	2^0	2^{-1}	2^{-2}

Representing fractional parts of numbers this way, however, is not nearly as well-behaved as representing integers. For instance, writing the fraction 1/3 in binary requires infinitely many digits:

$$\frac{1}{3} = 0.0101010101\cdots_2.$$

There exist numbers at all scales that cannot be represented using a finite binary string. In fact, all irrational numbers, like $\pi = 11.00100100001\ldots_2$, have infinitely long expansions regardless of which (integer) base you use!

Since computers have a finite amount of storage capacity, systems processing values in $\mathbb{R}$ instead of $\mathbb{Z}$ are forced to approximate or restrict values that can be processed. This leads to many points of confusion while coding, as in the following snippet of C++ code:

```
double x = 1.0;
double y = x / 3.0;
if (x == y*3.0) cout << "They are equal!";
else cout << "They are NOT equal.";
```

Contrary to intuition, this program prints "They are NOT equal." Why? Since 1/3 cannot be written as a finite-length binary string, the definition of y makes an approximation, rounding to the nearest number representable in the double data type. Thus, y*3.0 is *close to but not exactly* 1. One way to fix this issue is to allow for some tolerance:

```
double x = 1.0;
double y = x / 3.0;
if (fabs(x-y*3.0) < numeric_limits<double>::epsilon)
    cout << "They are equal!";
else cout << "They are NOT equal.";
```

Here, we check that x and y*3.0 are near enough to each other to be reasonably considered identical rather than whether they are exactly equal. The tolerance epsilon expresses how far apart values should be before we are confident they are different. It may need to be adjusted depending on context. This example raises a crucial point:

> **Rarely if ever should the operator == and its equivalents be used on fractional values. Instead, some *tolerance* should be used to check if they are equal.**

There is a trade-off here: the size of the tolerance defines a line between equality and "close-but-not-the-same," which must be chosen carefully for a given application.

The error generated by a numerical algorithm depends on the choice of *representations* for real numbers. Each representation has its own compromise among speed, accuracy, range of representable values, and so on. Keeping the example above and its resolution in mind, we now consider a few options for representing numbers discretely.

2.1.1 Fixed-Point Representations

The most straightforward way to store fractions is to use a *fixed* decimal point. That is, as in the example above, we represent values by storing 0-or-1 coefficients in front of powers of two that range from 2^{-k} to 2^ℓ for some $k, \ell \in \mathbb{Z}$. For instance, representing all nonnegative values between 0 and 127.75 in increments of 1/4 can be accomplished by taking $k = 2$ and $\ell = 7$; in this case, we use 10 binary digits total, of which two occur after the decimal point.

The primary advantage of this representation is that many arithmetic operations can be carried out using the same machinery already in place for integers. For example, if a and b are written in fixed-point format, we can write:

$$a + b = (a \cdot 2^k + b \cdot 2^k) \cdot 2^{-k}.$$

The values $a \cdot 2^k$ and $b \cdot 2^k$ are integers, so the summation on the right-hand side is an integer operation. This observation essentially shows that fixed-point addition can be carried out using integer addition essentially by "ignoring" the decimal point. In this way, rather than needing specialized hardware, the preexisting integer arithmetic logic unit (ALU) can carry out fixed-point mathematics quickly.

Fixed-point arithmetic may be fast, but it suffers from serious precision issues. In particular, it is often the case that the output of a binary operation like multiplication or division can require more bits than the operands. For instance, suppose we include one decimal point of precision and wish to carry out the product $1/2 \cdot 1/2 = 1/4$. We write $0.1_2 \times 0.1_2 = 0.01_2$, which gets truncated to 0. More broadly, it is straightforward to combine fixed-point numbers in a reasonable way and get an unreasonable result.

Due to these drawbacks, most major programming languages do not by default include a fixed-point data type. The speed and regularity of fixed-point arithmetic, however, can be a considerable advantage for systems that favor timing over accuracy. Some lower-end graphics processing units (GPU) implement only fixed-point operations since a few decimal points of precision are sufficient for many graphical applications.

2.1.2 Floating-Point Representations

One of many numerical challenges in scientific computing is the extreme range of scales that can appear. For example, chemists deal with values anywhere between 9.11×10^{-31} (the mass of an electron in kilograms) and 6.022×10^{23} (the Avogadro constant). An operation as innocent as a change of units can cause a sudden transition between scales: The same observation written in kilograms per lightyear will look considerably different in megatons per mile. As numerical analysts, we are charged with writing software that can transition gracefully between these scales without imposing unnatural restrictions on the client.

Scientists deal with similar issues when recording experimental measurements, and their methods can motivate our formats for storing real numbers on a computer. Most prominently, one of the following representations is more compact than the other:

$$6.022 \times 10^{23} = 602,200,000,000,000,000,000,000.$$

Not only does the representation on the left avoid writing an unreasonable number of zeros, but it also reflects the fact that we may not know Avogadro's constant beyond the second 2.

In the absence of exceptional scientific equipment, the difference between 6.022×10^{23} and $6.022 \times 10^{23} + 9.11 \times 10^{-31}$ likely is negligible, in the sense that this tiny perturbation is dwarfed by the error of truncating 6.022 to three decimal points. More formally, we say that 6.022×10^{23} has only four *digits of precision* and probably represents some range of possible measurements $[6.022 \times 10^{23} - \varepsilon, 6.022 \times 10^{23} + \varepsilon]$ for some $\varepsilon \approx 0.001 \times 10^{23}$.

Our first observation allowed us to shorten the representation of 6.022×10^{23} by writing it in *scientific notation*. This number system separates the "interesting" digits of a number from its order of magnitude by writing it in the form $a \times 10^e$ for some $a \sim 1$ and $e \in \mathbb{Z}$. We call this format the *floating-point* form of a number, because unlike the fixed-point setup in

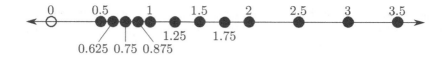

Figure 2.1 The values from Example 2.1 plotted on a number line; typical for floating-point number systems, they are unevenly spaced between the minimum (0.5) and the maximum (3.5).

§2.1.1, the decimal point "floats" so that a is on a reasonable scale. Usually a is called the *significand* and e is called the *exponent*.

Floating-point systems are defined using three parameters:

- The *base* or *radix* $b \in \mathbb{N}$. For scientific notation explained above, the base is $b = 10$; for binary systems the base is $b = 2$.

- The *precision* $p \in \mathbb{N}$ representing the number of digits used to store the significand.

- The range of exponents $[L, U]$ representing the allowable values for e.

The expansion looks like:

$$\underbrace{\pm}_{\text{sign}} \underbrace{(d_0 + d_1 \cdot b^{-1} + d_2 \cdot b^{-2} + \cdots + d_{p-1} \cdot b^{1-p})}_{\text{significand}} \times \underbrace{b^e}_{\text{exponent}},$$

where each digit d_k is in the range $[0, b-1]$ and $e \in [L, U]$. When $b = 2$, an extra bit of precision can be gained by *normalizing* floating-point values and assuming the most significant digit d_0 is one; this change, however, requires special treatment of the value 0.

Floating-point representations have a curious property that can affect software in unexpected ways: Their spacing is uneven. For example, the number of values representable between b and b^2 is the same as that between b^2 and b^3 even though usually $b^3 - b^2 > b^2 - b$. To understand the precision possible with a given number system, we will define the *machine precision* ε_m as the smallest $\varepsilon_m > 0$ such that $1 + \varepsilon_m$ is representable. Numbers like $b + \varepsilon_m$ are not expressible in the number system because ε_m is too small.

Example 2.1 (Floating-point). Suppose we choose $b = 2$, $L = -1$, and $U = 1$. If we choose to use three digits of precision, we might choose to write numbers in the form

$$1.\square\square \times 2^{\square}.$$

Notice this number system does not include 0. The possible significands are $1.00_2 = 1_{10}$, $1.01_2 = 1.25_{10}$, $1.10_2 = 1.5_{10}$, and $1.11_2 = 1.75_{10}$. Since $L = -1$ and $U = 1$, these significands can be scaled by $2^{-1} = 0.5_{10}$, $2^0 = 1_{10}$, and $2^1 = 2_{10}$. With this information in hand, we can list all the possible values in our number system:

Significand	$\times 2^{-1}$	$\times 2^0$	$\times 2^1$
1.00_{10}	0.500_{10}	1.000_{10}	2.000_{10}
1.25_{10}	0.625_{10}	1.250_{10}	2.500_{10}
1.50_{10}	0.750_{10}	1.500_{10}	3.000_{10}
1.75_{10}	0.875_{10}	1.750_{10}	3.500_{10}

These values are plotted in Figure 2.1; as expected, they are unevenly spaced and bunch toward zero. Also, notice the gap between 0 and 0.5 in this sampling of values; some number systems introduce evenly spaced *subnormal* values to fill in this gap, albeit with less precision. Machine precision for this number system is $\varepsilon_m = 0.25$, the smallest displacement possible above 1.

By far the most common format for storing floating-point numbers is provided by the IEEE 754 standard. This standard specifies several classes of floating-point numbers. For instance, a double-precision floating-point number is written in base $b = 2$ (as are all numbers in this format), with a single $\pm$ sign bit, 52 digits for d, and a range of exponents between -1022 and 1023. The standard also specifies how to store $\pm\infty$ and values like NaN, or "not-a-number," reserved for the results of computations like $10/0$.

IEEE 754 also includes agreed-upon conventions for rounding when an operation results in a number not represented in the standard. For instance, a common unbiased strategy for rounding computations is *round to nearest, ties to even,* which breaks equidistant ties by rounding to the nearest floating-point value with an even least-significant (rightmost) bit. There are many equally legitimate strategies for rounding; agreeing upon a single one guarantees that scientific software will work identically on all client machines regardless of their particular processor or compiler.

2.1.3 More Exotic Options

For most of this book, we will assume that fractional values are stored in floating-point format unless otherwise noted. This, however, is not to say that other numerical systems do not exist, and for specific applications an alternative choice might be necessary. We acknowledge some of those situations here.

The headache of inexact arithmetic to account for rounding errors might be unacceptable for some applications. This situation appears in computational geometry, e.g., when the difference between *nearly* and *completely* parallel lines may be a difficult distinction to make. One solution might be to use *arbitrary-precision arithmetic,* that is, to implement fractional arithmetic without rounding or error of any sort.

Arbitrary-precision arithmetic requires a specialized implementation and careful consideration for what types of values you need to represent. For instance, it might be the case that rational numbers $\mathbb{Q}$, which can be written as ratios a/b for $a, b \in \mathbb{Z}$, are sufficient for a given application. Basic arithmetic can be carried out in $\mathbb{Q}$ without any loss in precision, as follows:

$$\frac{a}{b} \times \frac{c}{d} = \frac{ac}{bd} \qquad\qquad \frac{a}{b} \div \frac{c}{d} = \frac{ad}{bc}.$$

Arithmetic in the rationals precludes the existence of a square root operator, since values like $\sqrt{2}$ are irrational. Also, this representation is nonunique since, e.g., $a/b = 5a/5b$, and thus certain operations may require additional routines for simplifying fractions. Even after simplifying, after a few multiplies and adds, the numerator and denominator may require many digits of storage, as in the following sum:

$$\frac{1}{100} + \frac{1}{101} + \frac{1}{102} + \frac{1}{103} + \frac{1}{104} + \frac{1}{105} = \frac{188463347}{3218688200}.$$

In other situations, it may be useful to bracket error by representing values alongside error estimates as a pair $a, \varepsilon \in \mathbb{R}$; we think of the pair (a, ε) as the range $a \pm \varepsilon$. Then, arithmetic operations also update not only the value but also the error estimate, as in

$$(x \pm \varepsilon_1) + (y \pm \varepsilon_2) = (x + y) \pm (\varepsilon_1 + \varepsilon_2 + \text{error}(x + y)),$$

where the final term represents an estimate of the error induced by adding x and y. Maintaining error bars in this fashion keeps track of confidence in a given value, which can be informative for scientific calculations.

2.2 UNDERSTANDING ERROR

With the exception of the arbitrary-precision systems described in §2.1.3, nearly every computerized representation of real numbers with fractional parts is forced to employ rounding and other approximations. Rounding, however, represents one of many sources of error typically encountered in numerical systems:

- *Rounding* or *truncation* error comes from rounding and other approximations used to deal with the fact that we can only represent a finite set of values using most computational number systems. For example, it is impossible to write π exactly as an IEEE 754 floating-point value, so in practice its value is truncated after a finite number of digits.

- *Discretization* error comes from our computerized adaptations of calculus, physics, and other aspects of continuous mathematics. For instance, a numerical system might attempt to approximate the derivative of a function $f(t)$ using *divided differences*:

$$f'(t) \approx \frac{f(t + \varepsilon) - f(t)}{\varepsilon}$$

for some fixed choice of $\varepsilon > 0$. This approximation is a legitimate and useful one that we will study in Chapter 14, but since we must use a finite $\varepsilon > 0$ rather than taking a limit as $\varepsilon \to 0$, the resulting value for $f'(t)$ is only accurate to some number of digits.

- *Modeling* error comes from having incomplete or inaccurate descriptions of the problems we wish to solve. For instance, a simulation predicting weather in Germany may choose to neglect the collective flapping of butterfly wings in Malaysia, although the displacement of air by these butterflies might perturb the weather patterns elsewhere. Furthermore, constants such as the speed of light or acceleration due to gravity might be provided to the system with a limited degree of accuracy.

- *Input* error can come from user-generated approximations of parameters of a given system (and from typos!). Simulation and numerical techniques can help answer "what if" questions, in which exploratory choices of input setups are chosen just to get some idea of how a system behaves. In this case, a highly accurate simulation might be a waste of computational time, since the inputs to the simulation were so rough.

Example 2.2 (Computational physics). Suppose we are designing a system for simulating planets as they revolve around the sun. The system essentially solves Newton's equation $F = ma$ by integrating forces forward in time. Examples of error sources in this system might include:

- *Rounding error:* Rounding the product ma to IEEE floating-point precision

- *Discretization error:* Using divided differences as above to approximate the velocity and acceleration of each planet

- *Modeling error:* Neglecting to simulate the moon's effects on the earth's motion within the planetary system

- *Input error:* Evaluating the cost of sending garbage into space rather than risking a Wall-E style accumulation on Earth, but only guessing the total amount of garbage to jettison monthly

2.2.1 Classifying Error

Given our previous discussion, the following two numbers might be regarded as having the same amount of error:

$$1 \pm 0.01$$
$$10^5 \pm 0.01.$$

Both intervals $[1 - 0.01, 1 + 0.01]$ and $[10^5 - 0.01, 10^5 + 0.01]$ have the same width, but the latter appears to encode a more confident measurement because the error 0.01 is much smaller *relative* to 10^5 than to 1.

The distinction between these two classes of error is described by distinguishing between *absolute* error and *relative* error:

Definition 2.1 (Absolute error). The *absolute error* of a measurement is the difference between the approximate value and its underlying true value.

Definition 2.2 (Relative error). The *relative error* of a measurement is the absolute error divided by the true value.

Absolute error is measured in input units, while relative error is measured as a percentage.

Example 2.3 (Absolute and relative error). Absolute and relative error can be used to express uncertainty in a measurement as follows:

$$\text{Absolute: } 2 \text{ in} \pm 0.02 \text{ in}$$
$$\text{Relative: } 2 \text{ in} \pm 1\%$$

Example 2.4 (Catastrophic cancellation). Suppose we wish to compute the difference $d \equiv 1 - 0.99 = 0.01$. Thanks to an inaccurate representation, we may only know these two values up to ± 0.004. Assuming that we can carry out the subtraction step without error, we are left with the following expression for absolute error:

$$d = 0.01 \pm 0.008.$$

In other words, we know d is somewhere in the range $[0.002, 0.018]$. From an absolute perspective, this error may be fairly small. Suppose we attempt to calculate relative error:

$$\frac{|0.002 - 0.01|}{0.01} = \frac{|0.018 - 0.01|}{0.01} = 80\%.$$

Thus, although 1 and 0.99 are known with relatively small error, the difference has enormous relative error of 80%. This phenomenon, known as *catastrophic cancellation*, is a danger associated with subtracting two nearby values, yielding a result close to zero.

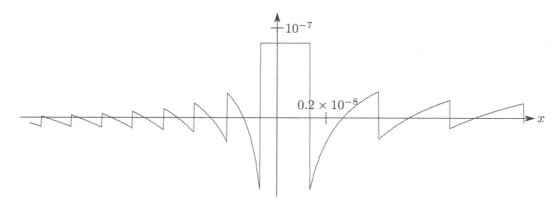

Figure 2.2 Values of $f(x)$ from Example 2.5, computed using IEEE floating-point arithmetic.

Example 2.5 (Loss of precision in practice). Figure 2.2 plots the function

$$f(x) \equiv \frac{e^x - 1}{x} - 1,$$

for evenly spaced inputs $x \in [-10^{-8}, 10^{-8}]$, computed using IEEE floating-point arithmetic. The numerator and denominator approach 0 at approximately the same rate, resulting in loss of precision and vertical jumps up and down near $x = 0$. As $x \to 0$, in theory $f(x) \to 0$, and hence the relative error of these approximate values blows up.

In most applications, the *true* value is unknown; after all, if it were known, there would be no need for an approximation in the first place. Thus, it is difficult to compute relative error in closed form. One possible resolution is to be conservative when carrying out computations: At each step take the largest possible error estimate and propagate these estimates forward as necessary. Such conservative estimates are powerful in that when they are small we can be very confident in our output.

An alternative resolution is to acknowledge *what* you can measure; this resolution requires somewhat more intricate arguments but will appear as a theme in future chapters. For instance, suppose we wish to solve the equation $f(x) = 0$ for x given a function $f : \mathbb{R} \to \mathbb{R}$. Our computational system may yield some x_{est} satisfying $f(x_{\text{est}}) = \varepsilon$ for some ε with $|\varepsilon| \ll 1$. If x_0 is the true root satisfying $f(x_0) = 0$, we may not be able to evaluate the difference $|x_0 - x_{\text{est}}|$ since x_0 is unknown. On the other hand, by evaluating f we can compute $|f(x_{\text{est}}) - f(x_0)| \equiv |f(x_{\text{est}})|$ since $f(x_0) = 0$ by definition. This difference of f values gives a proxy for error that still is zero exactly when $x_{\text{est}} = x_0$.

This example illustrates the distinction between *forward* and *backward* error. Forward error is the most direct definition of error as the difference between the approximated and actual solution, but as we have discussed it is not always computable. Contrastingly, backward error is a calculable proxy for error *correlated* with forward error. We can adjust the definition and interpretation of backward error as we consider different problems, but one suitable—if vague—definition is as follows:

Definition 2.3 (Backward error). The *backward error* of an approximate solution to a numerical problem is the amount by which the problem statement would have to change to make the approximate solution exact.

This definition is somewhat obtuse, so we illustrate its application to a few scenarios.

Example 2.6 (Linear systems). Suppose we wish to solve the $n \times n$ linear system $A\vec{x} = \vec{b}$ for $\vec{x} \in \mathbb{R}^n$. Label the true solution as $\vec{x}_0 \equiv A^{-1}\vec{b}$. In reality, due to rounding error and other issues, our system yields a near-solution $\vec{x}_{\text{est}}$. The forward error of this approximation is the difference $\vec{x}_{\text{est}} - \vec{x}_0$; in practice, this difference is impossible to compute since we do not know $\vec{x}_0$. In reality, $\vec{x}_{\text{est}}$ is the *exact* solution to a modified system $A\vec{x} = \vec{b}_{\text{est}}$ for $\vec{b}_{\text{est}} \equiv A\vec{x}_{\text{est}}$; thus, we might measure backward error in terms of the difference $\vec{b} - \vec{b}_{\text{est}}$. Unlike the forward error, this error is easily computable without inverting A, and $\vec{x}_{\text{est}}$ is a solution to the problem exactly when backward (or forward) error is zero.

Example 2.7 (Solving equations, from [58], Example 1.5). Suppose we write a function for finding square roots of positive numbers that outputs $\sqrt{2} \approx 1.4$. The forward error is $|1.4 - \sqrt{2}| \approx 0.0142$. The backward error is $|1.4^2 - 2| = 0.04$.

These examples demonstrate that backward error can be much easier to compute than forward error. For example, evaluating forward error in Example 2.6 required inverting a matrix A while evaluating backward error required only multiplication by A. Similarly, in Example 2.7, transitioning from forward error to backward error replaced square root computation with multiplication.

2.2.2 Conditioning, Stability, and Accuracy

In nearly any numerical problem, zero backward error implies zero forward error and vice versa. A piece of software designed to solve such a problem surely can terminate if it finds that a candidate solution has zero backward error. But what if backward error is small but nonzero? Does this condition necessarily imply small forward error? We must address such questions to justify replacing forward error with backward error for evaluating the success of a numerical algorithm.

The relationship between forward and backward error can be different for each problem we wish to solve, so in the end we make the following rough classification:

- A problem is *insensitive* or *well-conditioned* when small amounts of backward error imply small amounts of forward error. In other words, a small perturbation to the statement of a well-conditioned problem yields only a small perturbation of the true solution.

- A problem is *sensitive*, *poorly conditioned*, or *stiff* when this is not the case.

Example 2.8 ($ax = b$). Suppose as a toy example that we want to find the solution $x_0 \equiv b/a$ to the linear equation $ax = b$ for $a, x, b \in \mathbb{R}$. Forward error of a potential solution x is given by $|x - x_0|$ while backward error is given by $|b - ax| = |a(x - x_0)|$. So, when $|a| \gg 1$, the problem is well-conditioned since small values of backward error $a(x - x_0)$ imply even smaller values of $x - x_0$; contrastingly, when $|a| \ll 1$ the problem is ill-conditioned, since even if $a(x - x_0)$ is small, the forward error $x - x_0 \equiv 1/a \cdot a(x - x_0)$ may be large given the $1/a$ factor.

We define the *condition number* to be a measure of a problem's sensitivity:

Definition 2.4 (Condition number). The *condition number* of a problem is the ratio of how much its solution changes to the amount its statement changes under small perturbations. Alternatively, it is the ratio of forward to backward error for small changes in the problem statement.

Problems with small condition numbers are well-conditioned, and thus backward error can be used safely to judge success of approximate solution techniques. Contrastingly, much smaller backward error is needed to justify the quality of a candidate solution to a problem with a large condition number.

Example 2.9 ($ax = b$, continued). Continuing Example 2.8, we can compute the condition number exactly:
$$c = \frac{\text{forward error}}{\text{backward error}} = \frac{|x - x_0|}{|a(x - x_0)|} \equiv \frac{1}{|a|}.$$

Computing condition numbers usually is nearly as hard as computing forward error, and thus their exact computation is likely impossible. Even so, many times it is possible to bound or approximate condition numbers to help evaluate how much a solution can be trusted.

Example 2.10 (Root-finding). Suppose that we are given a smooth function $f : \mathbb{R} \to \mathbb{R}$ and want to find roots x with $f(x) = 0$. By Taylor's theorem, $f(x + \varepsilon) \approx f(x) + \varepsilon f'(x)$ when $|\varepsilon|$ is small. Thus, an approximation of the condition number for finding the root x is given by
$$\frac{\text{forward error}}{\text{backward error}} = \frac{|(x + \varepsilon) - x|}{|f(x + \varepsilon) - f(x)|} \approx \frac{|\varepsilon|}{|\varepsilon f'(x)|} = \frac{1}{|f'(x)|}.$$

This approximation generalizes the one in Example 2.9. If we do not know x, we cannot evaluate $f'(x)$, but if we can examine the form of f and *bound* $|f'|$ near x, we have an idea of the worst-case situation.

Forward and backward error measure the *accuracy* of a solution. For the sake of scientific repeatability, we also wish to derive *stable* algorithms that produce self-consistent solutions to a class of problems. For instance, an algorithm that generates accurate solutions only one fifth of the time might not be worth implementing, even if we can use the techniques above to check whether a candidate solution is good. Other numerical methods require the client to tune several unintuitive parameters before they generate usable output and may be unstable or sensitive to changes to any of these options.

2.3 PRACTICAL ASPECTS

The theory of error analysis introduced in §2.2 will allow us to bound the quality of numerical techniques we introduce in future chapters. Before we proceed, however, it is worth noting some more practical oversights and "gotchas" that pervade implementations of numerical methods.

We purposefully introduced the largest offender early in §2.1, which we repeat in a larger font for well-deserved emphasis:

> **Rarely if ever should the operator == and its equivalents be used on fractional values. Instead, some *tolerance* should be used to check if numbers are equal.**

Finding a suitable replacement for == depends on particulars of the situation. Example 2.6 shows that a method for solving $A\vec{x} = \vec{b}$ can terminate when the residual $\vec{b} - A\vec{x}$ is zero; since we do not want to check if A*x==b explicitly, in practice implementations will check norm(A*x-b)<epsilon. This example demonstrates two techniques:

- the use of *backward* error $\vec{b} - A\vec{x}$ rather than forward error to determine when to terminate, and

- checking whether backward error is less than epsilon to avoid the forbidden ==0 predicate.

The parameter epsilon depends on how accurate the desired solution must be as well as the quality of the discrete numerical system.

Based on our discussion of relative error, we can isolate another common cause of bugs in numerical software:

> **Beware of operations that transition between orders of magnitude, like division by small values and subtraction of similar quantities.**

Catastrophic cancellation as in Example 2.4 can cause relative error to explode even if the inputs to an operation are known with near-complete certainty.

2.3.1 Computing Vector Norms

A programmer using floating-point data types and operations must be vigilant when it comes to detecting and preventing poor numerical operations. For example, consider the following code snippet for computing the norm $\|\vec{x}\|_2$ for a vector $\vec{x} \in \mathbb{R}^n$ represented as a 1D array x[]:

```
double normSquared = 0;
for (int i = 0; i < n; i++)
        normSquared += x[i]*x[i];
return sqrt(normSquared);
```

In theory, $\min_i |x_i| \leq \|\vec{x}\|_2/\sqrt{n} \leq \max_i |x_i|$, that is, the norm of $\vec{x}$ is on the order of the values of elements contained in $\vec{x}$. Hidden in the computation of $\|\vec{x}\|_2$, however, is the expression x[i]*x[i]. If there exists i such that x[i] is near DOUBLE_MAX, the product x[i]*x[i] will overflow even though $\|\vec{x}\|_2$ is still within the range of the doubles. Such overflow is preventable by dividing $\vec{x}$ by its maximum value, computing the norm, and multiplying back:

```
double maxElement = epsilon; // don't want to divide by zero!
for (int i = 0; i < n; i++)
        maxElement = max(maxElement, fabs(x[i]));
for (int i = 0; i < n; i++) {
        double scaled = x[i] / maxElement;
        normSquared += scaled*scaled;
}
return sqrt(normSquared) * maxElement;
```

The scaling factor alleviates the overflow problem by ensuring that elements being summed are no larger than 1, at the cost of additional computation time.

This small example shows one of many circumstances in which a single *character* of code can lead to a non-obvious numerical issue, in this case the product *. While our intuition from continuous mathematics is sufficient to formulate many numerical methods, we must always double-check that the operations we employ are valid when transitioning from theory to finite-precision arithmetic.

```
function SIMPLE-SUM(x⃗)
    s ← 0                          ▷ Current total
    for i ← 1, 2, . . . , n : s ← s + xᵢ
    return s
```

(a)

```
function KAHAN-SUM(x⃗)
    s, c ← 0                                    ▷ Current total and compensation
    for i ← 1, 2, . . . , n
        v ← xᵢ + c                     ▷ Try to add xᵢ and compensation c to the sum
        s_next ← s + v                 ▷ Compute the summation result of this iteration
        c ← v − (s_next − s)    ▷ Compute compensation using the Kahan error estimate
        s ← s_next                                              ▷ Update sum
    return s
```

(b)

Figure 2.3 (a) A simplistic method for summing the elements of a vector $\vec{x}$; (b) the Kahan summation algorithm.

2.3.2 Larger-Scale Example: Summation

We now provide an example of a numerical issue caused by finite-precision arithmetic whose resolution involves a more subtle algorithmic trick. Suppose that we wish to sum a list of floating-point values stored in a vector $\vec{x} \in \mathbb{R}^n$, a task required by systems in accounting, machine learning, graphics, and nearly any other field. A simple strategy, iterating over the elements of $\vec{x}$ and incrementally adding each value, is detailed in Figure 2.3(a). For the vast majority of applications, this method is stable and mathematically valid, but in challenging cases it can fail.

What can go wrong? Consider the case where n is large and most of the values x_i are small and positive. Then, as i progresses, the current sum s will become large relative to x_i. Eventually, s could be so large that adding x_i would change only the lowest-order bits of s, and in the extreme case s could be large enough that adding x_i has no effect whatsoever. Put more simply, adding a long list of small numbers can result in a large sum, even if any single term of the sum appears insignificant.

To understand this effect mathematically, suppose that computing a sum $a + b$ can be off by as much as a factor of $\varepsilon > 0$. Then, the method in Figure 2.3(a) can induce error on the order of $n\varepsilon$, which grows linearly with n. If most elements x_i are on the order of ε, then the sum cannot be trusted *whatsoever*! This is a disappointing result: The error can be as large as the sum itself.

Fortunately, there are many ways to do better. For example, adding the smallest values first might make sure they are not deemed insignificant. Methods recursively adding pairs of values from $\vec{x}$ and building up a sum also are more stable, but they can be difficult to implement as efficiently as the **for** loop above. Thankfully, an algorithm by Kahan provides an easily implemented "compensated summation" method that is nearly as fast as iterating over the array [69].

The useful observation to make is that we can approximate the inaccuracy of s as it changes from iteration to iteration. To do so, consider the expression

$$((a + b) - a) - b.$$

Algebraically, this expression equals zero. Numerically, however, this may not be the case. In particular, the sum $(a+b)$ may be rounded to floating-point precision. Subtracting a and b one at a time then yields an approximation of the error of approximating $a+b$. Removing a and b from $a+b$ intuitively transitions *from* large orders of magnitude *to* smaller ones rather than vice versa and hence is less likely to induce rounding error than evaluating the sum $a+b$; this observation explains why the error estimate is not itself as prone to rounding issues as the original operation.

With this observation in mind, the Kahan technique proceeds as in Figure 2.3(b). In addition to maintaining the sum s, now we keep track of a *compensation* value c approximating the difference between s and the true sum at each iteration i. During each iteration, we attempt to add this compensation to s in addition to the current element x_i of $\vec{x}$; then we recompute c to account for the latest error.

Analyzing the Kahan algorithm requires more careful bookkeeping than analyzing the incremental technique in Figure 2.3(a). Although constructing a formal mathematical argument is outside the scope of our discussion, the final mathematical result is that error is on the order $O(\varepsilon + n\varepsilon^2)$, a considerable improvement over $O(n\varepsilon)$ when $0 \le \varepsilon \ll 1$. Intuitively, it makes sense that the $O(n\varepsilon)$ term from Figure 2.3(a) is reduced, since the compensation attempts to represent the small values that were otherwise neglected. Formal arguments for the ε^2 bound are surprisingly involved; one detailed derivation can be found in [49].

Implementing Kahan summation is straightforward but more than doubles the operation count of the resulting program. In this way, there is an implicit trade-off between speed and accuracy that software engineers must make when deciding which technique is most appropriate. More broadly, Kahan's algorithm is one of several methods that bypass the accumulation of numerical error during the course of a computation consisting of more than one operation. Another representative example from the field of computer graphics is Bresenham's algorithm for rasterizing lines [18], which uses only integer arithmetic to draw lines even when they intersect rows and columns of pixels at non-integer locations.

2.4 EXERCISES

2.1 When might it be preferable to use a fixed-point representation of real numbers over floating-point? When might it be preferable to use a floating-point representation of real numbers over fixed-point?

[DH] 2.2 ("Extraterrestrial chemistry") Suppose we are programming a planetary rover to analyze the chemicals in a gas found on a neighboring planet. Our rover is equipped with a flask of volume $0.5\,\mathrm{m}^3$ and also has pressure and temperature sensors. Using the sensor readouts from a given sample, we would like our rover to determine the amount of gas our flask contains.

One of the fundamental physical equations describing a gas is the Ideal Gas Law $PV = nRT$, which states:

$$(P)\text{ressure} \cdot (V)\text{olume} = \text{amou}(n)\text{t of gas} \cdot R \cdot (T)\text{emperature},$$

where R is the ideal gas constant, approximately equal to $8.31\,\mathrm{J \cdot mol^{-1} \cdot K^{-1}}$. Here, P is in pascals, V is in cubic meters, n is in moles, and T is in Kelvin. We will use this equation to approximate n given the other variables.

(a) Describe any forms of rounding, discretization, modeling, and input error that can occur when solving this problem.

(b) Our rover's pressure and temperature sensors do not have perfect accuracy. Suppose the pressure and temperature sensor measurements are accurate to within $\pm \varepsilon_P$ and $\pm \varepsilon_T$, respectively. Assuming V, R, and fundamental arithmetic operations like $+$ and $\times$ induce no errors, bound the relative forward error in computing n, when $0 < \varepsilon_P \ll P$ and $0 < \varepsilon_T \ll T$.

(c) Continuing the previous part, suppose $P = 100\,\mathrm{Pa}$, $T = 300\,\mathrm{K}$, $\varepsilon_P = 1\,\mathrm{Pa}$, and $\varepsilon_T = 0.5\,\mathrm{K}$. Derive upper bounds for the worst absolute and relative errors that we could obtain from a computation of n.

(d) Experiment with perturbing the variables P and T. Based on how much your estimate of n changes between the experiments, suggest when this problem is well-conditioned or ill-conditioned.

^{DH}2.3 In contrast to the "absolute" condition number introduced in this chapter, we can define the "relative" condition number of a problem to be

$$\kappa_{\mathrm{rel}} \equiv \frac{\text{relative forward error}}{\text{relative backward error}}.$$

In some cases, the relative condition number of a problem can yield better insights into its sensitivity.

Suppose we wish to evaluate a function $f : \mathbb{R} \to \mathbb{R}$ at a point $x \in \mathbb{R}$, obtaining $y \equiv f(x)$. Assuming f is smooth, compare the absolute and relative condition numbers of computing y at x. Additionally, provide examples of functions f with large and small relative condition numbers for this problem near $x = 1$.

Hint: Start with the relationship $y + \Delta y = f(x + \Delta x)$, and use Taylor's theorem to write the condition numbers in terms of x, $f(x)$, and $f'(x)$.

2.4 Suppose $f : \mathbb{R} \to \mathbb{R}$ is infinitely differentiable, and we wish to write algorithms for finding x^* minimizing $f(x)$. Our algorithm outputs x_{est}, an approximation of x^*. Assuming that in our context this problem is equivalent to finding roots of $f'(x)$, write expressions for:

(a) Forward error of the approximation

(b) Backward error of the approximation

(c) Conditioning of this minimization problem near x^*

2.5 Suppose we are given a list of floating-point values $x_1, x_2, \ldots, x_n$. The following quantity, known as their "log-sum-exp," appears in many machine learning algorithms:

$$\ell(x_1, \ldots, x_n) \equiv \ln \left[\sum_{k=1}^{n} e^{x_k} \right].$$

(a) The value $p_k \equiv e^{x_k}$ often represents a probability $p_k \in (0, 1]$. In this case, what is the range of possible x_k's?

(b) Suppose many of the x_k's are very negative ($x_k \ll 0$). Explain why evaluating the log-sum-exp formula as written above may cause numerical error in this case.

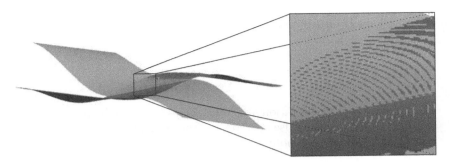

Figure 2.4 z-fighting, for Exercise 2.6; the overlap region is zoomed on the right.

(c) Show that for any $a \in \mathbb{R}$,

$$\ell(x_1, \ldots, x_n) = a + \ln\left[\sum_{k=1}^{n} e^{x_k - a}\right].$$

To avoid the issues you explained in 2.5b, suggest a value of a that may improve the stability of computing $\ell(x_1, \ldots, x_n)$.

2.6 ("z-fighting") A typical pipeline in computer graphics draws three-dimensional surfaces on the screen, one at a time. To avoid rendering a far-away surface on top of a close one, most implementations use a z-buffer, which maintains a double-precision depth value $z(x, y) \geq 0$ representing the depth of the closest object to the camera at each screen coordinate (x, y). A new object is rendered at (x, y) only when its z value is smaller than the one currently in the z-buffer.

A common artifact when rendering using z-buffering known as z-fighting is shown in Figure 2.4. Here, two surfaces overlap at some visible points. Why are there rendering artifacts in this region? Propose a strategy for avoiding this artifact; there are many possible resolutions.

2.7 (Adapted from Stanford CS 205A, 2012) Thanks to floating-point arithmetic, in most implementations of numerical algorithms we cannot expect that computations involving fractional values can be carried out with 100% precision. Instead, every time we do a numerical operation we induce the potential for error. Many models exist for studying how this error affects the quality of a numerical operation; in this problem, we will explore one common model.

Suppose we care about an operation $\diamond$ between two scalars x and y; here $\diamond$ might stand for $+$, $-$, $\times$, $\div$, and so on. As a model for the error that occurs when computing $x \diamond y$, we will say that evaluating $x \diamond y$ on the computer yields a number $(1 + \varepsilon)(x \diamond y)$ for some number ε satisfying $0 \leq |\varepsilon| < \varepsilon_{\max} \ll 1$; we will assume ε can depend on $\diamond$, x, and y.

(a) Why is this a reasonable model for modeling numerical issues in floating-point arithmetic? For example, why does this make more sense than assuming that the output of evaluating $x \diamond y$ is $(x \diamond y) + \varepsilon$?

(b) (Revised by B. Jo) Suppose we are given two vectors $\vec{x}, \vec{y} \in \mathbb{R}^n$ and compute their dot product as s_n via the recurrence:

$$s_0 \equiv 0$$
$$s_k \equiv s_{k-1} + x_k y_k.$$

In practice, both the addition and multiplication steps of computing s_k from s_{k-1} induce numerical error. Use $\hat{s}_k$ to denote the actual value computed incorporating numerical error, and denote $e_k \equiv |\hat{s}_k - s_k|$. Show that

$$|e_n| \le n\varepsilon_{\max}\bar{s}_n + O(n\varepsilon_{\max}^2 \bar{s}_n),$$

where $\bar{s}_n \equiv \sum_{k=1}^n |x_k||y_k|$. You can assume that adding $x_1 y_1$ to zero incurs no error, so $\hat{s}_1 = (1 + \varepsilon^\times)x_1 y_1$, where $\varepsilon^\times$ encodes the error induced by multiplying x_1 and y_1. You also can assume that $n\varepsilon_{\max} < 1$.

2.8 Argue using the error model from the previous problem that the relative error of computing $x - y$ for $x, y > 0$ can be unbounded; assume that there is error in representing x and y in addition to error computing the difference. This phenomenon is known as "catastrophic cancellation" and can cause serious numerical issues.

2.9 In this problem, we continue to explore the conditioning of root-finding. Suppose $f(x)$ and $p(x)$ are smooth functions of $x \in \mathbb{R}$.

(a) Thanks to inaccuracies in how we evaluate or express $f(x)$, we might accidentally compute roots of a perturbation $f(x) + \varepsilon p(x)$. Take x^* to be a root of f, so $f(x^*) = 0$. If $f'(x^*) \ne 0$, for small ε we can write a function $x(\varepsilon)$ such that $f(x(\varepsilon)) + \varepsilon p(x(\varepsilon)) = 0$, with $x(0) = x^*$. Assuming such a function exists and is differentiable, show:

$$\left.\frac{dx}{d\varepsilon}\right|_{\varepsilon=0} = -\frac{p(x^*)}{f'(x^*)}.$$

(b) Assume $f(x)$ is given by Wilkinson's polynomial [131]:

$$f(x) \equiv (x-1) \cdot (x-2) \cdot (x-3) \cdots (x-20).$$

We could have expanded $f(x)$ in the monomial basis as $f(x) = a_0 + a_1 x + a_2 x^2 + \cdots + a_{20}x^{20}$, for appropriate choices of $a_0, \ldots, a_{20}$. If we express the coefficient a_{19} inaccurately, we could use the model from Exercise 2.9a with $p(x) \equiv x^{19}$ to predict how much root-finding will suffer. For these choices of $f(x)$ and $p(x)$, show:

$$\left.\frac{dx}{d\varepsilon}\right|_{\varepsilon=0, x^*=j} = -\prod_{k \ne j} \frac{j}{j-k}.$$

(c) Compare $\frac{dx}{d\varepsilon}$ from the previous part for $x^* = 1$ and $x^* = 20$. Which root is more stable to this perturbation?

2.10 The roots of the quadratic function $ax^2 + bx + c$ are given by the *quadratic equation*

$$x^* \in \frac{-b \pm \sqrt{b^2 - 4ac}}{2a}.$$

(a) Prove the alternative formula

$$x^* \in \frac{-2c}{b \pm \sqrt{b^2 - 4ac}}.$$

(b) Propose a numerically stable algorithm for solving the quadratic equation.

2.11 One technique for tracking uncertainty in a calculation is the use of *interval arithmetic*. In this system, an uncertain value for a variable x is represented as the interval $[x] \equiv [\underline{x}, \overline{x}]$ representing the range of possible values for x, from $\underline{x}$ to $\overline{x}$. Assuming infinite-precision arithmetic, give update rules for the following in terms of $\underline{x}$, $\overline{x}$, $\underline{y}$, and $\overline{y}$:

- $[x] + [y]$
- $[x] - [y]$
- $[x] \times [y]$

- $[x] \div [y]$
- $[x]^{1/2}$

Additionally, propose a conservative modification for finite-precision arithmetic.

2.12 Algorithms for dealing with geometric primitives such as line segments and triangles are notoriously difficult to implement in a numerically stable fashion. Here, we highlight a few ideas from "ε-geometry," a technique built to deal with these issues [55].

(a) Take $\vec{p}, \vec{q}, \vec{r} \in \mathbb{R}^2$. Why might it be difficult to determine whether $\vec{p}$, $\vec{q}$, and $\vec{r}$ are collinear using finite-precision arithmetic?

(b) We will say $\vec{p}$, $\vec{q}$, and $\vec{r}$ are ε-collinear if there exist $\vec{p}'$ with $\|\vec{p} - \vec{p}'\|_2 \le \varepsilon$, $\vec{q}'$ with $\|\vec{q} - \vec{q}'\|_2 \le \varepsilon$, and $\vec{r}'$ with $\|\vec{r} - \vec{r}'\|_2 \le \varepsilon$ such that $\vec{p}'$, $\vec{q}'$, and $\vec{r}'$ are exactly collinear. For fixed $\vec{p}$ and $\vec{q}$, sketch the region $\{\vec{r} \in \mathbb{R}^2 : \vec{p}, \vec{q}, \vec{r} \text{ are } \varepsilon\text{-collinear}\}$. This region is known as the ε-*butterfly* of $\vec{p}$ and $\vec{q}$.

(c) An ordered triplet $(\vec{p}, \vec{q}, \vec{r}) \in \mathbb{R}^2 \times \mathbb{R}^2 \times \mathbb{R}^2$ is ε-clockwise if the three points can be perturbed by at most distance ε so that they form a triangle whose vertices are in clockwise order; we will consider collinear triplets to be both clockwise and counterclockwise. For fixed $\vec{p}$ and $\vec{q}$, sketch the region $\{\vec{r} \in \mathbb{R}^2 : (\vec{p}, \vec{q}, \vec{r}) \text{ is } \varepsilon\text{-clockwise}\}$.

(d) Show a triplet is ε-collinear if and only if it is both ε-clockwise and ε-counterclockwise.

(e) A point $\vec{x} \in \mathbb{R}^2$ is ε-inside the triangle $(\vec{p}, \vec{q}, \vec{r})$ if and only if $\vec{p}$, $\vec{q}$, $\vec{r}$, and $\vec{x}$ can be moved by at most distance ε such that the perturbed $\vec{x}'$ is exactly inside the perturbed triangle $(\vec{p}', \vec{q}', \vec{r}')$. Show that when $\vec{p}$, $\vec{q}$, and $\vec{r}$ are in (exactly) clockwise order, $\vec{x}$ is inside $(\vec{p}, \vec{q}, \vec{r})$ if and only if $(\vec{p}, \vec{q}, \vec{x})$, $(\vec{q}, \vec{r}, \vec{x})$, and $(\vec{r}, \vec{p}, \vec{x})$ are all clockwise. Is the same statement true if we relax to ε-inside and ε-clockwise?

II

Linear Algebra

CHAPTER 3

Linear Systems and the LU Decomposition

CONTENTS

3.1   Solvability of Linear Systems 47
3.2   Ad-Hoc Solution Strategies 49
3.3   Encoding Row Operations 51
      3.3.1   Permutation 51
      3.3.2   Row Scaling 52
      3.3.3   Elimination 52
3.4   Gaussian Elimination 54
      3.4.1   Forward-Substitution 55
      3.4.2   Back-Substitution 56
      3.4.3   Analysis of Gaussian Elimination 56
3.5   LU Factorization 58
      3.5.1   Constructing the Factorization 59
      3.5.2   Using the Factorization 60
      3.5.3   Implementing LU 61

W E commence our discussion of numerical algorithms by deriving ways to solve the linear system of equations $A\vec{x} = \vec{b}$. We will explore applications of these systems in Chapter 4, showing a variety of computational problems that can be approached by constructing appropriate A and $\vec{b}$ and solving for $\vec{x}$. Furthermore, solving a linear system will serve as a basic step in larger methods for optimization, simulation, and other numerical tasks considered in almost all future chapters. For these reasons, a thorough treatment and understanding of linear systems is critical.

3.1 SOLVABILITY OF LINEAR SYSTEMS

As introduced in §1.3.4, systems of linear equations like

$$3x + 2y = 6$$
$$-4x + y = 7$$

can be written in matrix form as in

$$\begin{pmatrix} 3 & 2 \\ -4 & 1 \end{pmatrix} \begin{pmatrix} x \\ y \end{pmatrix} = \begin{pmatrix} 6 \\ 7 \end{pmatrix}.$$

More generally, we can write linear systems in the form $A\vec{x} = \vec{b}$ for $A \in \mathbb{R}^{m \times n}$, $\vec{x} \in \mathbb{R}^n$, and $\vec{b} \in \mathbb{R}^m$.

The solvability of $A\vec{x} = \vec{b}$ must fall into one of three cases:

1. The system may not admit any solutions, as in:

$$\begin{pmatrix} 1 & 0 \\ 1 & 0 \end{pmatrix} \begin{pmatrix} x \\ y \end{pmatrix} = \begin{pmatrix} -1 \\ 1 \end{pmatrix}.$$

   This system enforces two incompatible conditions simultaneously: $x = -1$ and $x = 1$.

2. The system may admit a single solution; for instance, the system at the beginning of this section is solved by $(x, y) = (-8/11, 45/11)$.

3. The system may admit infinitely many solutions, e.g., $0\vec{x} = \vec{0}$. If a system $A\vec{x} = \vec{b}$ admits two distinct solutions $\vec{x}_0$ and $\vec{x}_1$, then it automatically has infinitely many solutions of the form $t\vec{x}_0 + (1 - t)\vec{x}_1$ for all $t \in \mathbb{R}$, since

$$A(t\vec{x}_0 + (1 - t)\vec{x}_1) = tA\vec{x}_0 + (1 - t)A\vec{x}_1 = t\vec{b} + (1 - t)\vec{b} = \vec{b}.$$

   Because it has multiple solutions, this linear system is labeled *underdetermined*.

The solvability of the system $A\vec{x} = \vec{b}$ depends both on A and on $\vec{b}$. For instance, if we modify the unsolvable system above to

$$\begin{pmatrix} 1 & 0 \\ 1 & 0 \end{pmatrix} \begin{pmatrix} x \\ y \end{pmatrix} = \begin{pmatrix} 1 \\ 1 \end{pmatrix},$$

then the system changes from having no solutions to infinitely many of the form $(1, y)$. Every matrix A admits a right-hand side $\vec{b}$ such that $A\vec{x} = \vec{b}$ is solvable, since $A\vec{x} = \vec{0}$ always can be solved by $\vec{x} = \vec{0}$ regardless of A.

For alternative intuition about the solvability of linear systems, recall from §1.3.1 that the matrix-vector product $A\vec{x}$ can be viewed as a linear combination of the columns of A with weights from $\vec{x}$. Thus, as mentioned in §1.3.4, $A\vec{x} = \vec{b}$ is solvable exactly when $\vec{b}$ is in the column space of A.

In a broad way, the shape of the matrix $A \in \mathbb{R}^{m \times n}$ has considerable bearing on the solvability of $A\vec{x} = \vec{b}$. First, consider the case when A is "wide," that is, when it has more columns than rows ($n > m$). Each column is a vector in $\mathbb{R}^m$, so at most the column space can have dimension m. Since $n > m$, the n columns of A must be linearly dependent; this implies that there exists a set of weights $\vec{x}_0 \neq \vec{0}$ such that $A\vec{x}_0 = \vec{0}$. If we can solve $A\vec{x} = \vec{b}$ for $\vec{x}$, then $A(\vec{x} + \alpha\vec{x}_0) = A\vec{x} + \alpha A\vec{x}_0 = \vec{b} + \vec{0} = \vec{b}$, showing that there are actually infinitely many solutions $\vec{x}$ to $A\vec{x} = \vec{b}$. In other words:

> **No wide matrix system admits a unique solution.**

When A is "tall," that is, when it has more rows than columns ($m > n$), then its n columns cannot possibly span the larger-dimensional $\mathbb{R}^m$. For this reason, there exists some vector $\vec{b}_0 \in \mathbb{R}^m \backslash \mathrm{col}\, A$. By definition, this $\vec{b}_0$ cannot satisfy $A\vec{x} = \vec{b}_0$ for *any* $\vec{x}$. That is:

> **For every tall matrix A, there exists a $\vec{b}_0$ such that $A\vec{x} = \vec{b}_0$ is not solvable.**

The situations above are far from favorable for designing numerical algorithms. In the wide case, if a linear system admits many solutions, we must specify *which* solution is desired by the user. After all, the solution $\vec{x} + 10^{31}\vec{x}_0$ might not be as meaningful as $\vec{x} - 0.1\vec{x}_0$. In the tall case, even if $A\vec{x} = \vec{b}$ is solvable for a particular $\vec{b}$, a small perturbation $A\vec{x} = \vec{b} + \varepsilon\vec{b}_0$ may not be solvable. The rounding procedures discussed in the last chapter easily can move a tall system from solvable to unsolvable.

Given these complications, in this chapter we will make some simplifying assumptions:

- We will consider only *square* $A \in \mathbb{R}^{n \times n}$.

- We will assume that A is *nonsingular*, that is, that $A\vec{x} = \vec{b}$ is solvable for any $\vec{b}$.

From §1.3.4, the nonsingularity condition ensures that the columns of A span $\mathbb{R}^n$ and implies the existence of a matrix A^{-1} satisfying $A^{-1}A = AA^{-1} = I_{n \times n}$. We will relax these conditions in subsequent chapters.

A misleading observation is to think that solving $A\vec{x} = \vec{b}$ is equivalent to computing the matrix A^{-1} explicitly and then multiplying to find $\vec{x} \equiv A^{-1}\vec{b}$. While this formula is valid mathematically, it can represent a considerable amount of overkill and potential for numerical instability for several reasons:

- The matrix A^{-1} may contain values that are difficult to express in floating-point precision, in the same way that $1/\varepsilon \to \infty$ as $\varepsilon \to 0$.

- It may be possible to tune the solution strategy both to A and to $\vec{b}$, e.g., by working with the columns of A that are the closest to $\vec{b}$ first. Strategies like these can provide higher numerical stability.

- Even if A is sparse, meaning it contains many zero values that do not need to be stored explicitly, or has other special structure, the same may not be true for A^{-1}.

We highlight this point as a common source of error and inefficiency in numerical software:

> **Avoid computing A^{-1} explicitly unless you have a strong justification for doing so.**

3.2 AD-HOC SOLUTION STRATEGIES

In introductory algebra, we often approach the problem of solving a linear system of equations as a puzzle rather than as a mechanical exercise. The strategy is to "isolate" variables, iteratively simplifying individual equalities until each is of the form $x = \text{const}$. To formulate step-by-step algorithms for solving linear systems, it is instructive to carry out an example of this methodology with an eye for aspects that can be fashioned into a general technique.

We will consider the following system:

$$y - z = -1$$
$$3x - y + z = 4$$
$$x + y - 2z = -3.$$

Alongside each simplification step, we will maintain a matrix system encoding the current state. Rather than writing out $A\vec{x} = \vec{b}$ explicitly, we save space using the augmented matrix

$$\begin{pmatrix} 0 & 1 & -1 & | & -1 \\ 3 & -1 & 1 & | & 4 \\ 1 & 1 & -2 & | & -3 \end{pmatrix}.$$

We can write linear systems this way so long as we agree that variable coefficients remain on the left of the line and the constants on the right.

Perhaps we wish to deal with the variable x first. For convenience, we can *permute* the rows of the system so that the third equation appears first:

$$\begin{aligned} x + y - 2z &= -3 \\ y - z &= -1 \\ 3x - y + z &= 4 \end{aligned} \qquad \left(\begin{array}{ccc|c} 1 & 1 & -2 & -3 \\ 0 & 1 & -1 & -1 \\ 3 & -1 & 1 & 4 \end{array} \right)$$

We then *substitute* the first equation into the third to eliminate the $3x$ term. This is the same as scaling the relationship $x + y - 2z = -3$ by -3 and adding the result to the third equation:

$$\begin{aligned} x + y - 2z &= -3 \\ y - z &= -1 \\ -4y + 7z &= 13 \end{aligned} \qquad \left(\begin{array}{ccc|c} 1 & 1 & -2 & -3 \\ 0 & 1 & -1 & -1 \\ 0 & -4 & 7 & 13 \end{array} \right)$$

Similarly, to eliminate y from the third equation, we scale the second equation by 4 and add the result to the third:

$$\begin{aligned} x + y - 2z &= -3 \\ y - z &= -1 \\ 3z &= 9 \end{aligned} \qquad \left(\begin{array}{ccc|c} 1 & 1 & -2 & -3 \\ 0 & 1 & -1 & -1 \\ 0 & 0 & 3 & 9 \end{array} \right)$$

We have now isolated z! We scale the third row by $1/3$ to yield an expression for z:

$$\begin{aligned} x + y - 2z &= -3 \\ y - z &= -1 \\ z &= 3 \end{aligned} \qquad \left(\begin{array}{ccc|c} 1 & 1 & -2 & -3 \\ 0 & 1 & -1 & -1 \\ 0 & 0 & 1 & 3 \end{array} \right)$$

Now, we substitute $z = 3$ into the other two equations to remove z from all but the final row:

$$\begin{aligned} x + y &= 3 \\ y &= 2 \\ z &= 3 \end{aligned} \qquad \left(\begin{array}{ccc|c} 1 & 1 & 0 & 3 \\ 0 & 1 & 0 & 2 \\ 0 & 0 & 1 & 3 \end{array} \right)$$

Finally, we make a similar substitution for y to reveal the solution:

$$\begin{aligned} x &= 1 \\ y &= 2 \\ z &= 3 \end{aligned} \qquad \left(\begin{array}{ccc|c} 1 & 0 & 0 & 1 \\ 0 & 1 & 0 & 2 \\ 0 & 0 & 1 & 3 \end{array} \right)$$

Revisiting the steps above yields a few observations about how to solve linear systems:

- We wrote successive systems $A_i \vec{x} = \vec{b}_i$ that can be viewed as simplifications of the original $A\vec{x} = \vec{b}$.

- We solved the system without ever writing down A^{-1}.

- We repeatedly used a few elementary operations: scaling, adding, and permuting rows.

- The same operations were applied to A and $\vec{b}$. If we scaled the k-th row of A, we also scaled the k-th row of $\vec{b}$. If we added rows k and ℓ of A, we added rows k and ℓ of $\vec{b}$.

- The steps did not depend on $\vec{b}$. That is, all of our decisions were motivated by eliminating nonzero values in A; $\vec{b}$ just came along for the ride.

- We terminated when we reached the simplified system $I_{n \times n} \vec{x} = \vec{b}$.

We will use all of these general observations about solving linear systems to our advantage.

3.3   ENCODING ROW OPERATIONS

Looking back at the example in §3.2, we see that solving $A\vec{x} = \vec{b}$ only involved three operations: permutation, row scaling, and adding a multiple of one row to another. We can solve *any* linear system this way, so it is worth exploring these operations in more detail.

A pattern we will see for the remainder of this chapter is the use of matrices to express row operations. For example, the following two descriptions of an operation on a matrix A are equivalent:

1. Scale the first row of A by 2.

2. Replace A with $S_2 A$, where S_2 is defined by:

$$S_2 \equiv \begin{pmatrix} 2 & 0 & 0 & \cdots & 0 \\ 0 & 1 & 0 & \cdots & 0 \\ 0 & 0 & 1 & \cdots & 0 \\ \vdots & \vdots & \vdots & \ddots & \vdots \\ 0 & 0 & 0 & \cdots & 1 \end{pmatrix}.$$

When presenting the theory of matrix simplification, it is cumbersome to use words to describe each operation, so when possible we will encode matrix algorithms as a series of pre- and post-multiplications by specially designed matrices like S_2 above.

This description in terms of matrices, however, is a *theoretical* construction. Implementations of algorithms for solving linear systems should not construct matrices like S_2 explicitly. For example, if $A \in \mathbb{R}^{n \times n}$, it should take n steps to scale the first row of A by 2, but explicitly constructing $S_2 \in \mathbb{R}^{n \times n}$ and applying it to A takes n^3 steps! That is, we will show for notational convenience that row operations *can* be encoded using matrix multiplication, but they do not *have* to be encoded this way.

3.3.1   Permutation

Our first step in §3.2 was to swap two of the rows. More generally, we might index the rows of a matrix using the integers $1, \ldots, m$. A *permutation* of those rows can be written as a function $\sigma : \{1, \ldots, m\} \to \{1, \ldots, m\}$ such that $\{\sigma(1), \ldots, \sigma(m)\} = \{1, \ldots, m\}$, that is, σ maps every index to a different target.

If $\vec{e}_k$ is the k-th standard basis vector, the product $\vec{e}_k^\top A$ is the k-th row of the matrix A. We can "stack" or concatenate these row vectors vertically to yield a matrix permuting the rows according to σ:

$$P_\sigma \equiv \begin{pmatrix} - & \vec{e}_{\sigma(1)}^\top & - \\ - & \vec{e}_{\sigma(2)}^\top & - \\ & \vdots & \\ - & \vec{e}_{\sigma(m)}^\top & - \end{pmatrix}.$$

The product $P_\sigma A$ is the matrix A with rows permuted according to σ.

Example 3.1 (Permutation matrices). Suppose we wish to permute rows of a matrix in $\mathbb{R}^{3 \times 3}$ with $\sigma(1) = 2$, $\sigma(2) = 3$, and $\sigma(3) = 1$. According to our formula we have

$$P_\sigma = \begin{pmatrix} 0 & 1 & 0 \\ 0 & 0 & 1 \\ 1 & 0 & 0 \end{pmatrix}.$$

From Example 3.1, P_σ has ones in positions indexed $(k, \sigma(k))$ and zeros elsewhere. Reversing the order of each pair, that is, putting ones in positions indexed $(\sigma(k), k)$ and zeros elsewhere, undoes the effect of the permutation. Hence, the inverse of P_σ must be its transpose $P_\sigma^\top$. Symbolically, we write $P_\sigma^\top P_\sigma = I_{m \times m}$, or equivalently $P_\sigma^{-1} = P_\sigma^\top$.

3.3.2 Row Scaling

Suppose we write down a list of constants $a_1, \ldots, a_m$ and seek to scale the k-th row of A by a_k for each k. This task is accomplished by applying the scaling matrix S_a:

$$S_a \equiv \begin{pmatrix} a_1 & 0 & 0 & \cdots \\ 0 & a_2 & 0 & \cdots \\ \vdots & \vdots & \ddots & \vdots \\ 0 & 0 & \cdots & a_m \end{pmatrix}.$$

Assuming that all the a_k's satisfy $a_k \neq 0$, it is easy to invert S_a by scaling back:

$$S_a^{-1} = S_{1/a} \equiv \begin{pmatrix} 1/a_1 & 0 & 0 & \cdots \\ 0 & 1/a_2 & 0 & \cdots \\ \vdots & \vdots & \ddots & \vdots \\ 0 & 0 & \cdots & 1/a_m \end{pmatrix}.$$

If any a_k equals zero, S_a is not invertible.

3.3.3 Elimination

Finally, suppose we wish to scale row k by a constant c and add the result to row ℓ; we will assume $k \neq \ell$. This operation may seem less natural than the previous two, but actually it is quite practical. In particular, it is the only one we need to combine equations from different rows of the linear system! We will realize this operation using an *elimination matrix* M, such that the product MA is the result of applying this operation to matrix A.

The product $\vec{e}_k^\top A$ picks out the k-th row of A. Pre-multiplying the result by $\vec{e}_\ell$ yields a matrix $\vec{e}_\ell \vec{e}_k^\top A$ that is zero except on its ℓ-th row, which is equal to the k-th row of A.

Example 3.2 (Elimination matrix construction). Take

$$A = \begin{pmatrix} 1 & 2 & 3 \\ 4 & 5 & 6 \\ 7 & 8 & 9 \end{pmatrix}.$$

Suppose we wish to isolate the third row of $A \in \mathbb{R}^{3 \times 3}$ and move it to row two. As discussed above, this operation is accomplished by writing:

$$\begin{aligned} \vec{e}_2 \vec{e}_3^\top A &= \begin{pmatrix} 0 \\ 1 \\ 0 \end{pmatrix} \begin{pmatrix} 0 & 0 & 1 \end{pmatrix} \begin{pmatrix} 1 & 2 & 3 \\ 4 & 5 & 6 \\ 7 & 8 & 9 \end{pmatrix} \\ &= \begin{pmatrix} 0 \\ 1 \\ 0 \end{pmatrix} \begin{pmatrix} 7 & 8 & 9 \end{pmatrix} \\ &= \begin{pmatrix} 0 & 0 & 0 \\ 7 & 8 & 9 \\ 0 & 0 & 0 \end{pmatrix}. \end{aligned}$$

We multiplied right to left above but just as easily could have grouped the product as $(\vec{e}_2\vec{e}_3^\top)A$. Grouping this way involves application of the matrix

$$\vec{e}_2\vec{e}_3^\top = \begin{pmatrix} 0 \\ 1 \\ 0 \end{pmatrix} \begin{pmatrix} 0 & 0 & 1 \end{pmatrix} = \begin{pmatrix} 0 & 0 & 0 \\ 0 & 0 & 1 \\ 0 & 0 & 0 \end{pmatrix}.$$

We have succeeded in isolating row k and moving it to row ℓ. Our original elimination operation was to add c times row k to row ℓ, which we can now carry out using the sum $A + c\vec{e}_\ell\vec{e}_k^\top A = (I_{n\times n} + c\vec{e}_\ell\vec{e}_k^\top)A$. Isolating the coefficient of A, the desired elimination matrix is $M \equiv I_{n\times n} + c\vec{e}_\ell\vec{e}_k^\top$.

The action of M can be reversed: Scale row k by c and *subtract* the result from row ℓ. We can check this formally:

$$(I_{n\times n} - c\vec{e}_\ell\vec{e}_k^\top)(I_{n\times n} + c\vec{e}_\ell\vec{e}_k^\top) = I_{n\times n} + (-c\vec{e}_\ell\vec{e}_k^\top + c\vec{e}_\ell\vec{e}_k^\top) - c^2\vec{e}_\ell\vec{e}_k^\top\vec{e}_\ell\vec{e}_k^\top$$
$$= I_{n\times n} - c^2\vec{e}_\ell(\vec{e}_k^\top\vec{e}_\ell)\vec{e}_k^\top$$
$$= I_{n\times n} \text{ since } \vec{e}_k^\top\vec{e}_\ell = \vec{e}_k \cdot \vec{e}_\ell, \text{ and } k \neq \ell.$$

That is, $M^{-1} = I_{n\times n} - c\vec{e}_\ell\vec{e}_k^\top$.

Example 3.3 (Solving a system). We can now encode each of our operations from Section 3.2 using the matrices we have constructed above:

1. Permute the rows to move the third equation to the first row:

$$P = \begin{pmatrix} 0 & 0 & 1 \\ 1 & 0 & 0 \\ 0 & 1 & 0 \end{pmatrix}.$$

2. Scale row one by -3 and add the result to row three:

$$E_1 = I_{3\times 3} - 3\vec{e}_3\vec{e}_1^\top = \begin{pmatrix} 1 & 0 & 0 \\ 0 & 1 & 0 \\ -3 & 0 & 1 \end{pmatrix}.$$

3. Scale row two by 4 and add the result to row three:

$$E_2 = I_{3\times 3} + 4\vec{e}_3\vec{e}_2^\top = \begin{pmatrix} 1 & 0 & 0 \\ 0 & 1 & 0 \\ 0 & 4 & 1 \end{pmatrix}.$$

4. Scale row three by $1/3$:

$$S = \text{diag}(1, 1, 1/3) = \begin{pmatrix} 1 & 0 & 0 \\ 0 & 1 & 0 \\ 0 & 0 & 1/3 \end{pmatrix}.$$

5. Scale row three by 2 and add it to row one:

$$E_3 = I_{3\times 3} + 2\vec{e}_1\vec{e}_3^\top = \begin{pmatrix} 1 & 0 & 2 \\ 0 & 1 & 0 \\ 0 & 0 & 1 \end{pmatrix}.$$

6. Add row three to row two:

$$E_4 = I_{3\times3} + \vec{e}_2\vec{e}_3^\top = \begin{pmatrix} 1 & 0 & 0 \\ 0 & 1 & 1 \\ 0 & 0 & 1 \end{pmatrix}.$$

7. Scale row two by -1 and add the result to row one:

$$E_5 = I_{3\times3} - \vec{e}_1\vec{e}_3^\top = \begin{pmatrix} 1 & -1 & 0 \\ 0 & 1 & 0 \\ 0 & 0 & 1 \end{pmatrix}.$$

Thus, the inverse of A in Section 3.2 satisfies

$$A^{-1} = E_5 E_4 E_3 S E_2 E_1 P$$
$$= \begin{pmatrix} 1 & -1 & 0 \\ 0 & 1 & 0 \\ 0 & 0 & 1 \end{pmatrix} \begin{pmatrix} 1 & 0 & 0 \\ 0 & 1 & 1 \\ 0 & 0 & 1 \end{pmatrix} \begin{pmatrix} 1 & 0 & 2 \\ 0 & 1 & 0 \\ 0 & 0 & 1 \end{pmatrix} \begin{pmatrix} 1 & 0 & 0 \\ 0 & 1 & 0 \\ 0 & 0 & 1/3 \end{pmatrix}$$
$$\begin{pmatrix} 1 & 0 & 0 \\ 0 & 1 & 0 \\ 0 & 4 & 1 \end{pmatrix} \begin{pmatrix} 1 & 0 & 0 \\ 0 & 1 & 0 \\ -3 & 0 & 1 \end{pmatrix} \begin{pmatrix} 0 & 0 & 1 \\ 1 & 0 & 0 \\ 0 & 1 & 0 \end{pmatrix}$$
$$= \begin{pmatrix} 1/3 & 1/3 & 0 \\ 7/3 & 1/3 & -1 \\ 4/3 & 1/3 & -1 \end{pmatrix}.$$

Make sure you understand why these matrices appear in *reverse* order! As a reminder, we would not normally construct A^{-1} by multiplying the matrices above, since these operations can be implemented more efficiently than generic matrix multiplication. Even so, it is valuable to check that the theoretical operations we have defined are equivalent to the ones we have written in words.

3.4 GAUSSIAN ELIMINATION

The sequence of steps chosen in Section 3.2 was by no means unique: There are many different paths that can lead to the solution of $A\vec{x} = \vec{b}$. Our steps, however, used *Gaussian elimination*, a famous algorithm for solving linear systems of equations.

To introduce this algorithm, let's say our system has the following generic "shape":

$$\begin{pmatrix} A \mid \vec{b} \end{pmatrix} = \left(\begin{array}{cccc|c} \times & \times & \times & \times & \times \\ \times & \times & \times & \times & \times \\ \times & \times & \times & \times & \times \\ \times & \times & \times & \times & \times \end{array} \right).$$

Here, an $\times$ denotes a potentially nonzero value. Gaussian elimination proceeds in phases described below.

3.4.1 Forward-Substitution

Consider the upper-left element of the matrix:

$$(\, A \mid \vec{b} \,) = \begin{pmatrix} \otimes & \times & \times & \times & \times \\ \times & \times & \times & \times & \times \\ \times & \times & \times & \times & \times \\ \times & \times & \times & \times & \times \end{pmatrix}.$$

We will call this element the first *pivot* and will assume it is nonzero; if it is zero we can permute rows so that this is not the case. We first scale the first row by the reciprocal of the pivot so that the value in the pivot position is one:

$$\begin{pmatrix} \textcircled{1} & \times & \times & \times & \times \\ \times & \times & \times & \times & \times \\ \times & \times & \times & \times & \times \\ \times & \times & \times & \times & \times \end{pmatrix}.$$

Now, we use the row containing the pivot to eliminate all other values underneath in the same column using the strategy in §3.3.3:

$$\begin{pmatrix} \textcircled{1} & \times & \times & \times & \times \\ 0 & \times & \times & \times & \times \\ 0 & \times & \times & \times & \times \\ 0 & \times & \times & \times & \times \end{pmatrix}.$$

At this point, the entire first column is zero below the pivot. We change the pivot label to the element in position $(2, 2)$ and repeat a similar series of operations to rescale the pivot row and use it to cancel the values underneath:

$$\begin{pmatrix} 1 & \times & \times & \times & \times \\ 0 & \textcircled{1} & \times & \times & \times \\ 0 & 0 & \times & \times & \times \\ 0 & 0 & \times & \times & \times \end{pmatrix}.$$

Now, our matrix begins to gain some structure. After the first pivot has been eliminated from all other rows, the first column is zero except for the leading one. Thus, any row operation involving rows two to m will not affect the zeros in column one. Similarly, after the second pivot has been processed, operations on rows three to m will not remove the zeros in columns one and two.

We repeat this process until the matrix becomes *upper triangular*:

$$\begin{pmatrix} 1 & \times & \times & \times & \times \\ 0 & 1 & \times & \times & \times \\ 0 & 0 & 1 & \times & \times \\ 0 & 0 & 0 & \textcircled{1} & \times \end{pmatrix}.$$

The method above of making a matrix upper triangular is known as *forward-substitution* and is detailed in Figure 3.1.

---

function FORWARD-SUBSTITUTION$(A, \vec{b})$
   ▷ Converts a system $A\vec{x} = \vec{b}$ to an upper-triangular system $U\vec{x} = \vec{y}$.
   ▷ Assumes invertible $A \in \mathbb{R}^{n \times n}$ and $\vec{b} \in \mathbb{R}^n$.

$U, \vec{y} \leftarrow A, \vec{b}$ ▷ U will be upper triangular at completion
for $p \leftarrow 1, 2, \ldots, n$ ▷ Iterate over current pivot row p
   ▷ Optionally insert pivoting code here

   $s \leftarrow 1/u_{pp}$ ▷ Scale row p to make element at (p, p) equal one
   $y_p \leftarrow s \cdot y_p$
   for $c \leftarrow p, \ldots, n : u_{pc} \leftarrow s \cdot u_{pc}$

   for $r \leftarrow (p+1), \ldots, n$ ▷ Eliminate from future rows
      $s \leftarrow -u_{rp}$ ▷ Scale row p by s and add to row r
      $y_r \leftarrow y_r + s \cdot y_p$
      for $c \leftarrow p, \ldots, n : u_{rc} \leftarrow u_{rc} + s \cdot u_{pc}$
return $U, \vec{y}$

Figure 3.1 Forward-substitution without pivoting; see §3.4.3 for pivoting options.

3.4.2 Back-Substitution

Eliminating the remaining ×'s from the remaining upper-triangular system is an equally straightforward process proceeding in *reverse* order of rows and eliminating backward. After the first set of back-substitution steps, we are left with the following shape:

$$\left(\begin{array}{cccc|c} 1 & \times & \times & 0 & \times \\ 0 & 1 & \times & 0 & \times \\ 0 & 0 & 1 & 0 & \times \\ 0 & 0 & 0 & \boxed{1} & \times \end{array} \right).$$

Similarly, the second iteration yields:

$$\left(\begin{array}{cccc|c} 1 & \times & 0 & 0 & \times \\ 0 & 1 & 0 & 0 & \times \\ 0 & 0 & \boxed{1} & 0 & \times \\ 0 & 0 & 0 & 1 & \times \end{array} \right).$$

After our final elimination step, we are left with our desired form:

$$\left(\begin{array}{cccc|c} \boxed{1} & 0 & 0 & 0 & \times \\ 0 & 1 & 0 & 0 & \times \\ 0 & 0 & 1 & 0 & \times \\ 0 & 0 & 0 & 1 & \times \end{array} \right).$$

The right-hand side now is the solution to the linear system $A\vec{x} = \vec{b}$. Figure 3.2 implements this method of *back-substitution* in more detail.

3.4.3 Analysis of Gaussian Elimination

Each row operation in Gaussian elimination—scaling, elimination, and swapping two rows—takes $O(n)$ time to complete, since they iterate over all n elements of a row (or two) of A.

---

function BACK-SUBSTITUTION$(U, \vec{y})$
   ▷ Solves upper-triangular systems $U\vec{x} = \vec{y}$ for $\vec{x}$.

  $\vec{x} \leftarrow \vec{y}$ ▷ We will start from $U\vec{x} = \vec{y}$ and simplify to $I_{n \times n}\vec{x} = \vec{x}$
  for $p \leftarrow n, n-1, \ldots, 1$ ▷ Iterate backward over pivots
    for $r \leftarrow 1, 2, \ldots, p-1$ ▷ Eliminate values above u_{pp}
      $x_r \leftarrow x_r - u_{rp}x_p/u_{pp}$
  return $\vec{x}$

Figure 3.2 Back-substitution for solving upper-triangular systems; this implementation returns the solution $\vec{x}$ to the system without modifying U.

Once we choose a pivot, we have to do n forward- or back-substitutions into the rows below or above that pivot, respectively; this means the work for a single pivot in total is $O(n^2)$. In total, we choose one pivot per row, adding a final factor of n. Combining these counts, Gaussian elimination runs in $O(n^3)$ time.

One decision that takes place during Gaussian elimination meriting more discussion is the choice of pivots. We can permute rows of the linear system as we see fit before performing forward-substitution. This operation, called *pivoting*, is necessary to be able to deal with all possible matrices A. For example, consider what would happen if we did not use pivoting on the following matrix:

$$A = \begin{pmatrix} \textcircled{0} & 1 \\ 1 & 0 \end{pmatrix}.$$

The circled element is exactly zero, so we cannot scale row one by any value to replace that 0 with a 1. This does *not* mean the system is not solvable—although singular matrices are guaranteed to have this issue—but rather it means we must pivot by swapping the first and second rows.

To highlight a related issue, suppose A looks like:

$$A = \begin{pmatrix} \textcircled{\varepsilon} & 1 \\ 1 & 0 \end{pmatrix},$$

where $0 < \varepsilon \ll 1$. If we do not pivot, then the first iteration of Gaussian elimination yields:

$$\tilde{A} = \begin{pmatrix} \textcircled{1} & 1/\varepsilon \\ 0 & -1/\varepsilon \end{pmatrix}.$$

We have transformed a matrix A that looks nearly like a permutation matrix ($A^{-1} \approx A^{\top}$, a very easy way to solve the system!) into a system with potentially **huge** values of the fraction $1/\varepsilon$. This example is one of many instances in which we should try to avoid dividing by vanishingly small numbers. In this way, there are cases when we may wish to pivot even when Gaussian elimination theoretically could proceed without such a step.

Since Gaussian elimination scales by the reciprocal of the pivot, the most numerically stable option is to have a *large* pivot. Small pivots have large reciprocals, which scale matrix elements to regimes that may lose precision. There are two well-known pivoting strategies:

1. *Partial pivoting* looks through the current column and permutes rows of the matrix so that the element in that column with the largest absolute value appears on the diagonal.

2. *Full pivoting* iterates over the **entire** matrix and permutes rows and columns to place the largest possible value on the diagonal. Permuting columns of a matrix is a valid operation after some added bookkeeping: it corresponds to changing the labeling of the variables in the system, or post-multiplying A by a permutation.

Full pivoting is more expensive computationally than partial pivoting since it requires iterating over the entire matrix (or using a priority queue data structure) to find the largest absolute value, but it results in enhanced numerical stability. Full pivoting is rarely necessary, and it is not enabled by default in common implementations of Gaussian elimination.

Example 3.4 (Pivoting). Suppose after the first iteration of Gaussian elimination we are left with the following matrix:

$$\begin{pmatrix} 1 & 10 & -10 \\ 0 & \boxed{0.1} & 9 \\ 0 & 4 & 6.2 \end{pmatrix}.$$

If we implement partial pivoting, then we will look only in the second column and will swap the second and third rows; we leave the 10 in the first row since that row already has been visited during forward-substitution:

$$\begin{pmatrix} 1 & 10 & -10 \\ 0 & \boxed{4} & 6.2 \\ 0 & 0.1 & 9 \end{pmatrix}.$$

If we implement full pivoting, then we will move the 9:

$$\begin{pmatrix} 1 & -10 & 10 \\ 0 & \boxed{9} & 0.1 \\ 0 & 6.2 & 4 \end{pmatrix}.$$

3.5 LU FACTORIZATION

There are many times when we wish to solve a sequence of problems $A\vec{x}_1 = \vec{b}_1, A\vec{x}_2 = \vec{b}_2, \ldots,$ where in each system the matrix A is the same. For example, in image processing we may apply the same filter encoded in A to a set of images encoded as $\vec{b}_1, \vec{b}_2, \ldots$. As we already have discussed, the steps of Gaussian elimination for solving $A\vec{x}_k = \vec{b}_k$ depend mainly on the structure of A rather than the values in a particular $\vec{b}_k$. Since A is kept constant here, we may wish to cache the steps we took to solve the system so that each time we are presented with a new $\vec{b}_k$ we do not have to start from scratch. Such a caching strategy compromises between restarting Gaussian elimination for each $\vec{b}_i$ and computing the potentially numerically unstable inverse matrix A^{-1}.

Solidifying this suspicion that we can move some of the $O(n^3)$ expense for Gaussian elimination into precomputation time if we wish to reuse A, recall the *upper-triangular* system appearing after forward-substitution:

$$\left(\begin{array}{cccc|c} 1 & \times & \times & \times & \times \\ 0 & 1 & \times & \times & \times \\ 0 & 0 & 1 & \times & \times \\ 0 & 0 & 0 & 1 & \times \end{array} \right).$$

Unlike forward-substitution, solving this system by back-substitution only takes $O(n^2)$ time! Why? As implemented in Figure 3.2, back-substitution can take advantage of the structure of the zeros in the system. For example, consider the circled elements of the initial upper-triangular system:

$$\left(\begin{array}{cccc|c} 1 & \times & \times & \times & \times \\ 0 & 1 & \times & \times & \times \\ 0 & 0 & 1 & \times & \times \\ \textcircled{0} & \textcircled{0} & \textcircled{0} & 1 & \times \end{array} \right).$$

Since we know that the (circled) values to the left of the pivot are zero by definition of an upper-triangular matrix, we do not need to scale them or copy them upward explicitly. If we ignore these zeros completely, this step of backward-substitution only takes n operations rather than the n^2 taken by the corresponding step of forward-substitution.

The next pivot benefits from a similar structure:

$$\left(\begin{array}{cccc|c} 1 & \times & \times & 0 & \times \\ 0 & 1 & \times & 0 & \times \\ \textcircled{0} & \textcircled{0} & 1 & \textcircled{0} & \times \\ 0 & 0 & 0 & 1 & \times \end{array} \right).$$

Again, the zeros on both sides of the one do not need to be copied explicitly.

A nearly identical method can be used to solve *lower*-triangular systems of equations via forward-substitution. Combining these observations, we have shown:

> **While Gaussian elimination takes $O(n^3)$ time, solving triangular systems takes $O(n^2)$ time.**

We will revisit the steps of Gaussian elimination to show that they can be used to factorize the matrix A as $A = LU$, where L is lower triangular and U is upper triangular, so long as pivoting is not needed to solve $A\vec{x} = \vec{b}$. Once the matrices L and U are obtained, solving $A\vec{x} = \vec{b}$ can be carried out by instead solving $LU\vec{x} = \vec{b}$ using forward-substitution followed by backward-substitution; these two steps combined take $O(n^2)$ time rather than the $O(n^3)$ time needed for full Gaussian elimination. This factorization also can be extended to a related and equally useful decomposition when pivoting is desired or necessary.

3.5.1 Constructing the Factorization

Other than full pivoting, from §3.3 we know that all the operations in Gaussian elimination can be thought of as pre-multiplying $A\vec{x} = \vec{b}$ by different matrices M to obtain easier systems $(MA)\vec{x} = M\vec{b}$. As demonstrated in Example 3.3, from this standpoint, each step of Gaussian elimination brings a new system $(M_k \cdots M_2 M_1 A)\vec{x} = M_k \cdots M_2 M_1 \vec{b}$. Explicitly storing these matrices M_k as $n \times n$ objects is overkill, but keeping this interpretation in mind from a theoretical perspective simplifies many of our calculations.

After the forward-substitution phase of Gaussian elimination, we are left with an *upper-triangular* matrix, which we call $U \in \mathbb{R}^{n \times n}$. From the matrix multiplication perspective,

$$M_k \cdots M_1 A = U$$
$$\implies A = (M_k \cdots M_1)^{-1} U$$
$$= (M_1^{-1} M_2^{-1} \cdots M_k^{-1}) U \text{ from the fact } (AB)^{-1} = B^{-1} A^{-1}$$
$$\equiv LU, \text{ if we make the definition } L \equiv M_1^{-1} M_2^{-1} \cdots M_k^{-1}.$$

U is upper triangular by design, but we have not characterized the structure of L; our remaining task is to show that L is lower triangular. To do so, recall that in the absence of pivoting, each matrix M_i is either a scaling matrix or has the structure $M_i = I_{n \times n} + c \vec{e}_\ell \vec{e}_k^\top$, from §3.3.3, where $\ell > k$ since we carried out forward-substitution to obtain U. So, L is the product of scaling matrices and matrices of the form $M_i^{-1} = I_{n \times n} - c \vec{e}_\ell \vec{e}_k^\top$; these matrices are lower triangular since $\ell > k$. Since scaling matrices are diagonal, L is lower triangular by the following proposition:

Proposition 3.1. The product of two or more upper-triangular matrices is upper triangular, and the product of two or more lower-triangular matrices is lower triangular.

Proof. Suppose A and B are upper triangular, and define $C \equiv AB$. By definition of upper-triangular matrices, $a_{ij} = 0$ and $b_{ij} = 0$ when $i > j$. Fix two indices i and j with $i > j$. Then,

$$c_{ij} = \sum_k a_{ik} b_{kj} \text{ by definition of matrix multiplication}$$
$$= a_{i1} b_{1j} + a_{i2} b_{2j} + \cdots + a_{in} b_{nj}.$$

The first $i - 1$ terms of the sum are zero because A is upper triangular, and the last $n - j$ terms are zero because B is upper triangular. Since $i > j$, $(i - 1) + (n - j) > n - 1$ and hence all n terms of the sum over k are zero, as needed.

If A and B are lower triangular, then $A^\top$ and $B^\top$ are upper triangular. By our proof above, $B^\top A^\top = (AB)^\top$ is upper triangular, showing that AB is again lower triangular. $\square$

3.5.2 Using the Factorization

Having factored $A = LU$, we can solve $A \vec{x} = \vec{b}$ in two steps, by writing $(LU)\vec{x} = \vec{b}$, or equivalently $\vec{x} = U^{-1} L^{-1} \vec{b}$:

1. Solve $L \vec{y} = \vec{b}$ for $\vec{y}$, yielding $\vec{y} = L^{-1} \vec{b}$.

2. With $\vec{y}$ now fixed, solve $U \vec{x} = \vec{y}$ for $\vec{x}$.

Checking the validity of $\vec{x}$ as a solution of the system $A \vec{x} = \vec{b}$ comes from the following chain of equalities:

$$\vec{x} = U^{-1} \vec{y} \text{ from the second step}$$
$$= U^{-1}(L^{-1} \vec{b}) \text{ from the first step}$$
$$= (LU)^{-1} \vec{b} \text{ since } (AB)^{-1} = B^{-1} A^{-1}$$
$$= A^{-1} \vec{b} \text{ since we factored } A = LU.$$

Forward- and back-substitution to carry out the two steps above each take $O(n^2)$ time. So, given the LU factorization of A, solving $A \vec{x} = \vec{b}$ can be carried out faster than full $O(n^3)$ Gaussian elimination. When pivoting is necessary, we will modify our factorization to include a permutation matrix P to account for the swapped rows and/or columns, e.g., $A = PLU$ (see Exercise 3.12). This minor change does not affect the asymptotic timing benefits of LU factorization, since $P^{-1} = P^\top$.

3.5.3 Implementing LU

The implementation of Gaussian elimination suggested in Figures 3.1 and 3.2 constructs U but not L. We can make some adjustments to factor $A = LU$ rather than solving a single system $A\vec{x} = \vec{b}$.

Let's examine what happens when we multiply two elimination matrices:

$$(I_{n \times n} - c_\ell \vec{e}_\ell \vec{e}_k^\top)(I_{n \times n} - c_p \vec{e}_p \vec{e}_k^\top) = I_{n \times n} - c_\ell \vec{e}_\ell \vec{e}_k^\top - c_p \vec{e}_p \vec{e}_k^\top.$$

As in the construction of the inverse of an elimination matrix in §3.5.1, the remaining term vanishes by orthogonality of the standard basis vectors $\vec{e}_i$ since $k \neq p$. This formula shows that the product of elimination matrices used to forward-substitute a single pivot after it is scaled to 1 has the form:

$$M = \begin{pmatrix} 1 & 0 & 0 & 0 \\ 0 & \boxed{1} & 0 & 0 \\ 0 & \times & 1 & 0 \\ 0 & \times & 0 & 1 \end{pmatrix},$$

where the values $\times$ are those used for forward-substitutions of the circled pivot. Products of matrices of this form performed in forward-substitution order combine the values below the diagonal, as demonstrated in the following example:

$$\begin{pmatrix} 1 & 0 & 0 & 0 \\ 2 & 1 & 0 & 0 \\ 3 & 0 & 1 & 0 \\ 4 & 0 & 0 & 1 \end{pmatrix} \begin{pmatrix} 1 & 0 & 0 & 0 \\ 0 & 1 & 0 & 0 \\ 0 & 5 & 1 & 0 \\ 0 & 6 & 0 & 1 \end{pmatrix} \begin{pmatrix} 1 & 0 & 0 & 0 \\ 0 & 1 & 0 & 0 \\ 0 & 0 & 1 & 0 \\ 0 & 0 & 7 & 1 \end{pmatrix} = \begin{pmatrix} 1 & 0 & 0 & 0 \\ 2 & 1 & 0 & 0 \\ 3 & 5 & 1 & 0 \\ 4 & 6 & 7 & 1 \end{pmatrix}.$$

We constructed U by pre-multiplying A with a sequence of elimination and scaling matrices. We can construct L simultaneously via a sequence of *post*-multiplies by their inverses, starting from the identity matrix. These post-multiplies can be computed efficiently using the above observations about products of elimination matrices.

For any invertible diagonal matrix D, $(LD)(D^{-1}U)$ provides an alternative factorization of $A = LU$ into lower- and upper-triangular matrices. Thus, by rescaling we can decide to keep the elements along the diagonal of L in the LU factorization equal to 1. With this decision in place, we can compress our storage of *both* L and U into a single $n \times n$ matrix whose upper triangle is U and which is equal to L beneath the diagonal; the missing diagonal elements of L are all 1.

We are now ready to write pseudocode for LU factorization without pivoting, illustrated in Figure 3.3. This method extends the algorithm for forward-substitution by storing the corresponding elements of L under the diagonal rather than zeros. This method has three nested loops and runs in $O(n^3) \approx \frac{2}{3}n^3$ time. After precomputing this factorization, however, solving $A\vec{x} = \vec{b}$ only takes $O(n^2)$ time using forward- and backward-substitution.

3.6 EXERCISES

3.1 Can *all* matrices $A \in \mathbb{R}^{n \times n}$ be factored $A = LU$? Why or why not?

3.2 Solve the following system of equations using Gaussian elimination, writing the corresponding elimination matrix of each step:

$$\begin{pmatrix} 2 & 4 \\ 3 & 5 \end{pmatrix} \begin{pmatrix} x \\ y \end{pmatrix} = \begin{pmatrix} 2 \\ 4 \end{pmatrix}.$$

Factor the matrix on the left-hand side as a product $A = LU$.

---

function LU-FACTORIZATION-COMPACT(A)
   ▷ Factors $A \in \mathbb{R}^{n \times n}$ to $A = LU$ in compact format.
  for $p \leftarrow 1, 2, \ldots, n$ ▷ Choose pivots like in forward-substitution
    for $r \leftarrow p + 1, \ldots, n$ ▷ Forward-substitution row
      $s \leftarrow -a_{rp}/a_{pp}$ ▷ Amount to scale row p for forward-substitution

      $a_{rp} \leftarrow -s$ ▷ L contains $-s$ because it reverses the forward-substitution

      for $c \leftarrow p + 1, \ldots, n$ ▷ Perform forward-substitution
        $a_{rc} \leftarrow a_{rc} + s a_{pc}$
  return A

Figure 3.3 Pseudocode for computing the LU factorization of $A \in \mathbb{R}^{n \times n}$, stored in the compact $n \times n$ format described in §3.5.3. This algorithm will fail if pivoting is needed.

DH 3.3 Factor the following matrix A as a product $A = LU$:

$$\begin{pmatrix} 1 & 2 & 7 \\ 3 & 5 & -1 \\ 6 & 1 & 4 \end{pmatrix}.$$

3.4 Modify the code in Figure 3.1 to include partial pivoting.

3.5 The discussion in §3.4.3 includes an example of a 2×2 matrix A for which Gaussian elimination without pivoting fails. In this case, the issue was resolved by introducing partial pivoting. If exact arithmetic is implemented to alleviate rounding error, does there exist a matrix for which Gaussian elimination fails unless *full* rather than partial pivoting is implemented? Why or why not?

3.6 Numerical algorithms appear in many components of simulation software for quantum physics. The Schrödinger equation and others involve *complex* numbers in $\mathbb{C}$, however, so we must extend the machinery we have developed for solving linear systems of equations to this case. Recall that a complex number $x \in \mathbb{C}$ can be written as $x = a + bi$, where $a, b \in \mathbb{R}$ and $i = \sqrt{-1}$. Suppose we wish to solve $A\vec{x} = \vec{b}$, but now $A \in \mathbb{C}^{n \times n}$ and $\vec{x}, \vec{b} \in \mathbb{C}^n$. Explain how a linear solver that takes only *real-valued* systems can be used to solve this equation.
Hint: Write $A = A_1 + A_2 i$, where $A_1, A_2 \in \mathbb{R}^{n \times n}$. Similarly decompose $\vec{x}$ and $\vec{b}$. In the end you will solve a $2n \times 2n$ real-valued system.

3.7 Suppose $A \in \mathbb{R}^{n \times n}$ is invertible. Show that A^{-1} can be obtained via Gaussian elimination on augmented matrix
$$\left(\, A \mid I_{n \times n} \, \right).$$

3.8 Show that if L is an invertible lower-triangular matrix, none of its diagonal elements can be zero. How does this lemma affect the construction in §3.5.3?

3.9 Show that the inverse of an (invertible) lower-triangular matrix is lower triangular.

3.10 Show that any invertible matrix $A \in \mathbb{R}^{n \times n}$ with $a_{11} = 0$ cannot have a factorization $A = LU$ for lower-triangular L and upper-triangular U.

3.11 Show how the LU factorization of $A \in \mathbb{R}^{n \times n}$ can be used to compute the determinant of A.

3.12 For numerical stability and generality, we incorporated pivoting into our methods for Gaussian elimination. We can modify our construction of the LU factorization somewhat to incorporate pivoting as well.

(a) Argue that following the steps of Gaussian elimination on a matrix $A \in \mathbb{R}^{n \times n}$ with partial pivoting can be used to write $U = L_{n-1} P_{n-1} \cdots L_2 P_2 L_1 P_1 A$, where the P_i's are permutation matrices, the L_i's are lower triangular, and U is upper triangular.

(b) Show that P_i is a permutation matrix that swaps rows i and j for some $j \geq i$. Also, argue that L_i is the product of matrices of the form $I_{n \times n} + c \vec{e}_k \vec{e}_i^\top$ where $k > i$.

(c) Suppose $j, k > i$. Show $P_{jk}(I_{n \times n} + c \vec{e}_k \vec{e}_i^\top) = (I_{n \times n} + c \vec{e}_j \vec{e}_i^\top) P_{jk}$, where P_{jk} is a permutation matrix swapping rows j and k.

(d) Combine the previous two parts to show that

$$L_{n-1} P_{n-1} \cdots L_2 P_2 L_1 P_1 = L_{n-1} L'_{n-2} L'_{n-3} \cdots L'_1 P_{n-1} \cdots P_2 P_1,$$

where $L'_1, \ldots, L'_{n-2}$ are lower triangular.

(e) Conclude that $A = PLU$, where P is a permutation matrix, L is lower triangular, and U is upper triangular.

(f) Extend the method from §3.5.2 for solving $A \vec{x} = \vec{b}$ when we have factored $A = PLU$, without affecting the time complexity compared to factorizations $A = LU$.

3.13 ("Block LU decomposition") Suppose a square matrix $M \in \mathbb{R}^{n \times n}$ is written in block form as

$$M = \begin{pmatrix} A & B \\ C & D \end{pmatrix},$$

where $A \in \mathbb{R}^{k \times k}$ is square and invertible.

(a) Show that we can decompose M as the product

$$M = \begin{pmatrix} I & 0 \\ CA^{-1} & I \end{pmatrix} \begin{pmatrix} A & 0 \\ 0 & D - CA^{-1}B \end{pmatrix} \begin{pmatrix} I & A^{-1}B \\ 0 & I \end{pmatrix}.$$

Here, I denotes an identity matrix of appropriate size.

(b) Suppose we decompose $A = L_1 U_1$ and $D - CA^{-1}B = L_2 U_2$. Show how to construct an LU factorization of M given these additional matrices.

(c) Use this structure to define a recursive algorithm for LU factorization; you can assume $n = 2^\ell$ for some $\ell > 0$. How does the efficiency of your method compare with that of the LU algorithm introduced in this chapter?

3.14 Suppose $A \in \mathbb{R}^{n \times n}$ is *columnwise diagonally dominant*, meaning that for all i, $\sum_{j \neq i} |a_{ji}| < |a_{ii}|$. Show that Gaussian elimination on A can be carried out without pivoting. Is this necessarily a good idea from a numerical standpoint?

3.15 Suppose $A \in \mathbb{R}^{n \times n}$ is invertible and admits a factorization $A = LU$ with ones along the diagonal of L. Show that such a decomposition of A is unique.

CHAPTER 4

Designing and Analyzing Linear Systems

CONTENTS

4.1   Solution of Square Systems 65
    4.1.1   Regression 66
    4.1.2   Least-Squares 68
    4.1.3   Tikhonov Regularization 70
    4.1.4   Image Alignment 71
    4.1.5   Deconvolution 73
    4.1.6   Harmonic Parameterization 74
4.2   Special Properties of Linear Systems 75
    4.2.1   Positive Definite Matrices and the Cholesky Factorization 75
    4.2.2   Sparsity 79
    4.2.3   Additional Special Structures 80
4.3   Sensitivity Analysis 81
    4.3.1   Matrix and Vector Norms 81
    4.3.2   Condition Numbers 84

N OW that we can solve linear systems of equations, we will show how to apply this machinery to several practical problems. The algorithms introduced in the previous chapter can be applied directly to produce the desired output in each case.

While LU factorization and Gaussian elimination are guaranteed to solve each of these problems in polynomial time, a natural question is whether there exist more efficient or stable algorithms if we know more about the structure of a particular linear system. Thus, we will examine the matrices constructed in the initial examples to reveal special properties that some of them have in common. Designing algorithms specifically for these classes of matrices will provide speed and numerical advantages, at the cost of generality.

Finally, we will return to concepts from Chapter 2 to design heuristics evaluating how much we can trust the solution $\vec{x}$ to a linear system $A\vec{x} = \vec{b}$, in the presence of rounding and other sources of error. This aspect of analyzing linear systems must be considered when designing reliable and consistent implementations of numerical algorithms.

4.1   SOLUTION OF SQUARE SYSTEMS

In the previous chapter, we only considered square, invertible matrices A when solving $A\vec{x} = \vec{b}$. While this restriction does preclude some important cases, many if not most

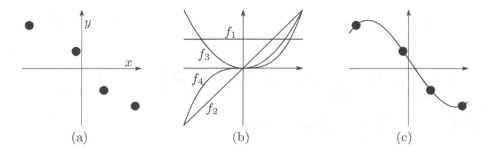

Figure 4.1 (a) The input for regression, a set of $(x^{(k)}, y^{(k)})$ pairs; (b) a set of basis functions $\{f_1, f_2, f_3, f_4\}$; (c) the output of regression, a set of coefficients $c_1, \ldots, c_4$ such that the linear combination $\sum_{k=1}^{4} c_k f_k(x)$ goes through the data points.

applications of linear systems can be posed in terms of square, invertible matrices. We explore a few of these applications below.

4.1.1 Regression

We start with an application from data analysis known as *regression*. Suppose we carry out a scientific experiment and wish to understand the structure of the experimental results. One way to model these results is to write the *independent variables* of a given trial in a vector $\vec{x} \in \mathbb{R}^n$ and to think of the *dependent variable* as a function $f(\vec{x}) : \mathbb{R}^n \to \mathbb{R}$. Given a few $(\vec{x}, f(\vec{x}))$ pairs, our goal is to predict the output of $f(\vec{x})$ for a new $\vec{x}$ without carrying out the full experiment.

Example 4.1 (Biological experiment). Suppose we wish to measure the effects of fertilizer, sunlight, and water on plant growth. We could do a number of experiments applying different amounts of fertilizer (in cm^3), sunlight (in watts), and water (in ml) to a plant and measuring the height of the plant after a few days. Assuming plant height is a direct function of these variables, we can model our observations as samples from a function $f : \mathbb{R}^3 \to \mathbb{R}$ that takes the three parameters we wish to test and outputs the height of the plant at the end of the experimental trial.

In *parametric* regression, we additionally assume that we know the structure of f ahead of time. For example, suppose we assume that f is linear:

$$f(\vec{x}) = a_1 x_1 + a_2 x_2 + \cdots + a_n x_n.$$

Then, our goal becomes more concrete: to estimate the coefficients $a_1, \ldots, a_n$.

We can carry out n experiments to reveal $y^{(k)} \equiv f(\vec{x}^{(k)})$ for samples $\vec{x}^{(k)}$, where $k \in \{1, \ldots, n\}$. For the linear example, plugging into the formula for f shows a set of statements:

$$y^{(1)} = f(\vec{x}^{(1)}) = a_1 x_1^{(1)} + a_2 x_2^{(1)} + \cdots + a_n x_n^{(1)}$$
$$y^{(2)} = f(\vec{x}^{(2)}) = a_1 x_1^{(2)} + a_2 x_2^{(2)} + \cdots + a_n x_n^{(2)}$$
$$\vdots$$

Contrary to our earlier notation $A\vec{x} = \vec{b}$, the unknowns here are the a_i's, *not* the $\vec{x}^{(k)}$'s. With this notational difference in mind, if we make exactly n observations we can write

$$\begin{pmatrix} - & \vec{x}^{(1)\top} & - \\ - & \vec{x}^{(2)\top} & - \\ & \vdots & \\ - & \vec{x}^{(n)\top} & - \end{pmatrix} \begin{pmatrix} a_1 \\ a_2 \\ \vdots \\ a_n \end{pmatrix} = \begin{pmatrix} y^{(1)} \\ y^{(2)} \\ \vdots \\ y^{(n)} \end{pmatrix}.$$

In other words, if we carry out n trials of our experiment and write the independent variables in the columns of a matrix $X \in \mathbb{R}^{n \times n}$ and the dependent variables in a vector $\vec{y} \in \mathbb{R}^n$, then the coefficients $\vec{a}$ can be recovered by solving the linear system $X^\top \vec{a} = \vec{y}$.

We can generalize this method to certain nonlinear forms for the function f using an approach illustrated in Figure 4.1. The key is to write f as a linear combination of *basis functions*. Suppose $f(\vec{x})$ takes the form

$$f(\vec{x}) = a_1 f_1(\vec{x}) + a_2 f_2(\vec{x}) + \cdots + a_m f_m(\vec{x}),$$

where $f_k : \mathbb{R}^n \to \mathbb{R}$ and we wish to estimate the parameters a_k. Then, by a parallel derivation given m observations of the form $\vec{x}^{(k)} \mapsto y^{(k)}$ we can find the parameters by solving:

$$\begin{pmatrix} f_1(\vec{x}^{(1)}) & f_2(\vec{x}^{(1)}) & \cdots & f_m(\vec{x}^{(1)}) \\ f_1(\vec{x}^{(2)}) & f_2(\vec{x}^{(2)}) & \cdots & f_m(\vec{x}^{(2)}) \\ \vdots & \vdots & \cdots & \vdots \\ f_1(\vec{x}^{(m)}) & f_2(\vec{x}^{(m)}) & \cdots & f_m(\vec{x}^{(m)}) \end{pmatrix} \begin{pmatrix} a_1 \\ a_2 \\ \vdots \\ a_m \end{pmatrix} = \begin{pmatrix} y^{(1)} \\ y^{(2)} \\ \vdots \\ y^{(m)} \end{pmatrix}.$$

That is, even if the f's are nonlinear, we can learn weights a_k using purely linear techniques.

Example 4.2 (Linear regression). The system $X^\top \vec{a} = \vec{y}$ from our initial example can be recovered from the general formulation by taking $f_k(\vec{x}) = x_k$.

Example 4.3 (Polynomial regression). As in Figure 4.1, suppose that we observe a function of a single variable $f(x)$ and wish to write it as an $(n-1)$-st degree polynomial

$$f(x) \equiv a_0 + a_1 x + a_2 x^2 + \cdots + a_{n-1} x^{n-1}.$$

Given n pairs $x^{(k)} \mapsto y^{(k)}$, we can solve for the parameters $\vec{a}$ via the system

$$\begin{pmatrix} 1 & x^{(1)} & (x^{(1)})^2 & \cdots & (x^{(1)})^{n-1} \\ 1 & x^{(2)} & (x^{(2)})^2 & \cdots & (x^{(2)})^{n-1} \\ \vdots & \vdots & \vdots & \cdots & \vdots \\ 1 & x^{(n)} & (x^{(n)})^2 & \cdots & (x^{(n)})^{n-1} \end{pmatrix} \begin{pmatrix} a_0 \\ a_1 \\ \vdots \\ a_{n-1} \end{pmatrix} = \begin{pmatrix} y^{(1)} \\ y^{(2)} \\ \vdots \\ y^{(n)} \end{pmatrix}.$$

In other words, we take $f_k(x) = x^{k-1}$ in the general form above. Incidentally, the matrix on the left-hand side of this relationship is known as a Vandermonde matrix.

As an example, suppose we wish to find a parabola $y = ax^2 + bx + c$ going through $(-1, 1)$, $(0, -1)$, and $(2, 7)$. We can write the Vandermonde system in two ways:

$$\left\{ \begin{array}{rl} a(-1)^2 + b(-1) + c & = 1 \\ a(0)^2 + b(0) + c & = -1 \\ a(2)^2 + b(2) + c & = 7 \end{array} \right\} \iff \begin{pmatrix} 1 & -1 & (-1)^2 \\ 1 & 0 & 0^2 \\ 1 & 2 & 2^2 \end{pmatrix} \begin{pmatrix} c \\ b \\ a \end{pmatrix} = \begin{pmatrix} 1 \\ -1 \\ 7 \end{pmatrix}.$$

Gaussian elimination on this system shows $(a, b, c) = (2, 0, -1)$, corresponding to the polynomial $y = 2x^2 - 1$.

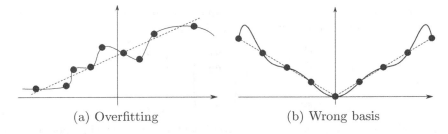

(a) Overfitting (b) Wrong basis

Figure 4.2 Drawbacks of fitting function values exactly: (a) noisy data might be better represented by a simple function rather than a complex curve that touches every data point and (b) the basis functions might not be tuned to the function being sampled. In (b), we fit a polynomial of degree eight to nine samples from $f(x) = |x|$ but would have been more successful using a basis of line segments.

> **Example 4.4** (Oscillation). A foundational notion from signal processing for audio and images is the decomposition of a function into a linear combination of cosine or sine waves at different frequencies. This decomposition of a function defines its *Fourier transform*.
>
> As the simplest possible case, we can try to recover the parameters of a single-frequency wave. Suppose we wish to find parameters a and ϕ of a function $f(x) = a\cos(x + \phi)$ given two (x, y) samples satisfying $y^{(1)} = f(x^{(1)})$ and $y^{(2)} = f(x^{(2)})$. Although this setup as we have written it is nonlinear, we can recover a and ϕ using a linear system after some mathematical transformations.
>
> From trigonometry, any function of the form $g(x) = a_1 \cos x + a_2 \sin x$ can be written $g(x) = a\cos(x + \phi)$ after applying the formulae
>
> $$a = \sqrt{a_1^2 + a_2^2} \qquad\qquad \phi = -\arctan\frac{a_2}{a_1}.$$
>
> We can find $f(x)$ by applying the linear method to compute the coefficients a_1 and a_2 in $g(x)$ and then using these formulas to find a and ϕ. This construction can be extended to fitting functions of the form $f(x) = \sum_k a_k \cos(x + \phi_k)$, giving one way to motivate the discrete Fourier transform of f, explored in Exercise 4.15.

4.1.2 Least-Squares

The techniques in §4.1.1 provide valuable methods for finding a continuous f matching a set of data pairs $\vec{x}_k \mapsto y_k$ *exactly*. For this reason, they are called *interpolation* schemes, which we will explore in detail in Chapter 13. They have two related drawbacks, illustrated in Figure 4.2:

- There might be some error in measuring the values $\vec{x}_k$ and y_k. In this case, a simpler $f(\vec{x})$ satisfying the approximate relationship $f(\vec{x}_k) \approx y_k$ may be acceptable or even preferable to an exact $f(\vec{x}_k) = y_k$ that goes through each data point.

- If there are m functions $f_1, \ldots, f_m$, then we use exactly m observations $\vec{x}_k \mapsto y_k$. Additional observations have to be thrown out, or we have to introduce more f_k's, which can make the resulting function $f(\vec{x})$ increasingly complicated.

Both of these issues are related to the larger problem of *over-fitting*: Fitting a function with n degrees of freedom to n data points leaves no room for measurement error.

More broadly, suppose we wish to solve the linear system $A\vec{x} = \vec{b}$ for $\vec{x}$. If we denote row k of A as $\vec{r}_k^{\top}$, then the system looks like

$$\begin{pmatrix} b_1 \\ b_2 \\ \vdots \\ b_n \end{pmatrix} = \begin{pmatrix} - & \vec{r}_1^{\top} & - \\ - & \vec{r}_2^{\top} & - \\ \vdots & \vdots & \vdots \\ - & \vec{r}_n^{\top} & - \end{pmatrix} \begin{pmatrix} x_1 \\ x_2 \\ \vdots \\ x_n \end{pmatrix} \quad \text{by expanding } A\vec{x}$$

$$= \begin{pmatrix} \vec{r}_1 \cdot \vec{x} \\ \vec{r}_2 \cdot \vec{x} \\ \vdots \\ \vec{r}_n \cdot \vec{x} \end{pmatrix} \quad \text{by definition of matrix multiplication.}$$

From this perspective, each row of the system corresponds to a separate observation of the form $\vec{r}_k \cdot \vec{x} = b_k$. That is, an alternative way to interpret the linear system $A\vec{x} = \vec{b}$ is that it encodes n statements of the form, "The dot product of $\vec{x}$ with $\vec{r}_k$ is b_k."

A tall system $A\vec{x} = \vec{b}$ where $A \in \mathbb{R}^{m \times n}$ and $m > n$ encodes more than n of these dot product observations. When we make more than n observations, however, they may be *incompatible*; as explained §3.1, tall systems do not have to admit a solution.

When we cannot solve $A\vec{x} = \vec{b}$ exactly, we can relax the problem and try to find an approximate solution $\vec{x}$ satisfying $A\vec{x} \approx \vec{b}$. One of the most common ways to solve this problem, known as *least-squares*, is to ask that the residual $\vec{b} - A\vec{x}$ be as small as possible by minimizing the norm $\|\vec{b} - A\vec{x}\|_2$. If there is an exact solution $\vec{x}$ satisfying the tall system $A\vec{x} = \vec{b}$, then the minimum of this energy is zero, since norms are nonnegative and in this case $\|\vec{b} - A\vec{x}\|_2 = \|\vec{b} - \vec{b}\|_2 = 0$.

Minimizing $\|\vec{b} - A\vec{x}\|_2$ is the same as minimizing $\|\vec{b} - A\vec{x}\|_2^2$, which we expanded in Example 1.16 to:

$$\|\vec{b} - A\vec{x}\|_2^2 = \vec{x}^{\top} A^{\top} A \vec{x} - 2\vec{b}^{\top} A\vec{x} + \|\vec{b}\|_2^2.^*$$

The gradient of this expression with respect to $\vec{x}$ must be zero at its minimum, yielding the following system:

$$\vec{0} = 2A^{\top} A\vec{x} - 2A^{\top}\vec{b},$$

or equivalently, $\quad A^{\top} A\vec{x} = A^{\top}\vec{b}.$

This famous relationship is worthy of a theorem:

Theorem 4.1 (Normal equations). Minima of the residual norm $\|\vec{b} - A\vec{x}\|_2$ for $A \in \mathbb{R}^{m \times n}$ (with no restriction on m or n) satisfy $A^{\top} A\vec{x} = A^{\top}\vec{b}.$

The matrix $A^{\top} A$ is sometimes called a *Gram matrix*. If at least n rows of A are linearly independent, then $A^{\top} A \in \mathbb{R}^{n \times n}$ is invertible. In this case, the minimum residual occurs uniquely at $(A^{\top} A)^{-1} A^{\top}\vec{b}$. Put another way:

> **In the overdetermined case, solving the least-squares problem $A\vec{x} \approx \vec{b}$ is equivalent to solving the *square* system $A^{\top} A\vec{x} = A^{\top}\vec{b}$.**

Via the normal equations, we can solve tall systems with $A \in \mathbb{R}^{m \times n}$, $m \geq n$, using algorithms for square matrices.

---

*If this result is not familiar, it may be valuable to return to the material in §1.4 at this point for review.

4.1.3 Tikhonov Regularization

When solving linear systems, the underdetermined case $m < n$ is considerably more difficult to handle due to increased ambiguity. As discussed in §3.1, in this case we lose the possibility of a *unique* solution to $A\vec{x} = \vec{b}$. To choose between the possible solutions, we must make an additional assumption on $\vec{x}$ to obtain a unique solution, e.g., that it has a small norm or that it contains many zeros. Each such *regularizing* assumption leads to a different solution algorithm. The particular choice of a regularizer may be application-dependent, but here we outline a general approach commonly applied in statistics and machine learning; we will introduce an alternative in §7.2.1 after introducing the singular value decomposition (SVD) of a matrix.

When there are multiple vectors $\vec{x}$ that minimize $\|A\vec{x} - \vec{b}\|_2^2$, the least-squares energy function is *insufficient* to isolate a single output. For this reason, for fixed $\alpha > 0$, we might introduce an additional term to the minimization problem:

$$\min_{\vec{x}} \|A\vec{x} - \vec{b}\|_2^2 + \alpha\|\vec{x}\|_2^2.$$

This second term is known as a *Tikhonov regularizer*. When $0 < \alpha \ll 1$, this optimization effectively asks that among the minimizers of $\|A\vec{x} - \vec{b}\|_2$ we would prefer those with small norm $\|\vec{x}\|_2$; as α increases, we prioritize the norm of $\vec{x}$ more. This energy is the product of an "Occam's razor" philosophy: In the absence of more information about $\vec{x}$, we might as well choose an $\vec{x}$ with small entries.

To minimize this new objective, we take the derivative with respect to $\vec{x}$ and set it equal to zero:

$$\vec{0} = 2A^\top A\vec{x} - 2A^\top\vec{b} + 2\alpha\vec{x},$$

or equivalently

$$(A^\top A + \alpha I_{n \times n})\vec{x} = A^\top\vec{b}.$$

So, if we wish to introduce Tikhonov regularization to a linear problem, all we have to do is add α down the diagonal of the Gram matrix $A^\top A$.

When $A\vec{x} = \vec{b}$ is underdetermined, the matrix $A^\top A$ is not invertible. The new Tikhonov term resolves this issue, since for $\vec{x} \neq \vec{0}$,

$$\vec{x}^\top(A^\top A + \alpha I_{n \times n})\vec{x} = \|A\vec{x}\|_2^2 + \alpha\|\vec{x}\|_2^2 > 0.$$

The strict $>$ holds because $\vec{x} \neq \vec{0}$; it implies that $A^\top A + \alpha I_{n \times n}$ cannot have a null space vector $\vec{x}$. Hence, regardless of A, the Tikhonov-regularized system of equations is invertible. In the language we will introduce in §4.2.1, it is *positive definite*.

Tikhonov regularization is effective for dealing with null spaces and numerical issues. When A is poorly conditioned, adding this type of regularization can improve conditioning even when the original system was solvable. We acknowledge two drawbacks, however, that can require more advanced algorithms when they are relevant:

- The solution $\vec{x}$ of the Tikhonov-regularized system no longer satisfies $A\vec{x} = \vec{b}$ exactly.

- When α is small, the matrix $A^\top A + \alpha I_{n \times n}$ is invertible but may be poorly conditioned. Increasing α solves this problem at the cost of less accurate solutions to $A\vec{x} = \vec{b}$.

When the columns of A span $\mathbb{R}^m$, an alternative to Tikhonov regularization is to minimize $\|\vec{x}\|_2$ with the "hard" constraint $A\vec{x} = \vec{b}$. Exercise 4.7 shows that this least-norm solution is given by $\vec{x} = A^\top(AA^\top)^{-1}\vec{b}$, a similar formula to the normal equations for least-squares.

Example 4.5 (Tikhonov regularization). Suppose we pose the following linear system:

$$\begin{pmatrix} 1 & 1 \\ 1 & 1.00001 \end{pmatrix} \vec{x} = \begin{pmatrix} 1 \\ 0.99 \end{pmatrix}.$$

This system is solved by $\vec{x} = (1001, -1000)$.

The scale of this $\vec{x} \in \mathbb{R}^2$, however, is much larger than that of any values in the original problem. We can use Tikhonov regularization to encourage smaller values in $\vec{x}$ that still solve the linear system approximately. In this case, the Tikhonov system is

$$\left[\begin{pmatrix} 1 & 1 \\ 1 & 1.00001 \end{pmatrix}^\top \begin{pmatrix} 1 & 1 \\ 1 & 1.00001 \end{pmatrix} + \alpha I_{2\times2} \right] \vec{x} = \begin{pmatrix} 1 & 1 \\ 1 & 1.00001 \end{pmatrix}^\top \begin{pmatrix} 1 \\ 0.99 \end{pmatrix},$$

or equivalently,

$$\begin{pmatrix} 2 + \alpha & 2.00001 \\ 2.00001 & 2.0000200001 + \alpha \end{pmatrix} \vec{x} = \begin{pmatrix} 1.99 \\ 1.9900099 \end{pmatrix}.$$

As α increases, the regularizer becomes stronger. Some example solutions computed numerically are below:

$$\alpha = 0.00001 \longrightarrow \vec{x} \approx (0.499998, 0.494998)$$
$$\alpha = 0.001 \longrightarrow \vec{x} \approx (0.497398, 0.497351)$$
$$\alpha = 0.1 \longrightarrow \vec{x} \approx (0.485364, 0.485366).$$

Even with a tiny amount of regularization, these solutions approximate the symmetric near-solution $\vec{x} \approx (0.5, 0.5)$, which has much smaller magnitude. If α becomes *too* large, regularization overtakes the system and $\vec{x} \to (0, 0)$.

4.1.4 Image Alignment

Suppose we take two photographs of the same scene from different positions. One common task in computer vision and graphics is to stitch them together to make a single larger image. To do so, the user (or an automatic system) marks p pairs of points $\vec{x}_k, \vec{y}_k \in \mathbb{R}^2$ such that for each k the location $\vec{x}_k$ in image one corresponds to the location $\vec{y}_k$ in image two. Then, the software automatically warps the second image onto the first or vice versa such that the pairs of points are aligned.

When the camera makes a small motion, a reasonable assumption is that there exists some transformation matrix $A \in \mathbb{R}^{2\times2}$ and a translation vector $\vec{b} \in \mathbb{R}^2$ such that for all k,

$$\vec{y}_k \approx A\vec{x}_k + \vec{b}.$$

That is, position $\vec{x}$ on image one should correspond to position $A\vec{x} + \vec{b}$ on image two. Figure 4.3(a) illustrates this notation. With this assumption, given a set of corresponding pairs $(\vec{x}_1, \vec{y}_1), \ldots, (\vec{x}_p, \vec{y}_p)$, our goal is to compute the A and $\vec{b}$ matching these points as closely as possible.

Beyond numerical issues, mistakes may have been made while locating the corresponding points, and we must account for approximation error due to the slightly nonlinear camera projection of real-world lenses. To address this potential for misalignment, rather than

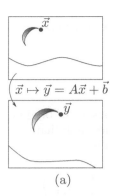

(a)　　　　　　　　(b) Input images with keypoints　　　　(c) Aligned images

Figure 4.3　(a) The image alignment problem attempts to find the parameters A and $\vec{b}$ of a transformation from one image of a scene to another using labeled keypoints $\vec{x}$ on the first image paired with points $\vec{y}$ on the second. As an example, keypoints marked in white on the two images in (b) are used to create (c) the aligned image.

requiring that the marked points match exactly, we can ask that they are matched in a least-squares sense. To do so, we solve the following minimization problem:

$$\min_{A,\vec{b}} \sum_{k=1}^{p} \|(A\vec{x}_k + \vec{b}) - \vec{y}_k\|_2^2.$$

This problem has six unknowns total, the four elements of A and the two elements of $\vec{b}$. Figure 4.3(b,c) shows typical output for this method; five keypoints rather than the required three are used to stabilize the output transformation using least-squares.

This objective is a sum of squared linear expressions in the unknowns A and $\vec{b}$, and we will show that it can be minimized using a linear system. Define

$$f(A,\vec{b}) \equiv \sum_k \|(A\vec{x}_k + \vec{b}) - \vec{y}_k\|_2^2.$$

We can simplify f as follows:

$$f(A,\vec{b}) = \sum_k (A\vec{x}_k + \vec{b} - \vec{y}_k)^\top (A\vec{x}_k + \vec{b} - \vec{y}_k) \text{ since } \|\vec{v}\|_2^2 = \vec{v}^\top \vec{v}$$

$$= \sum_k \left[\vec{x}_k^\top A^\top A \vec{x}_k + 2\vec{x}_k^\top A^\top \vec{b} - 2\vec{x}_k^\top A^\top \vec{y}_k + \vec{b}^\top \vec{b} - 2\vec{b}^\top \vec{y}_k + \vec{y}_k^\top \vec{y}_k \right]$$

where terms with leading 2 apply the fact $\vec{a}^\top \vec{b} = \vec{b}^\top \vec{a}$.

To find where f is minimized, we differentiate it with respect to $\vec{b}$ and with respect to the elements of A, and set these derivatives equal to zero. This leads to the following system:

$$0 = \nabla_{\vec{b}} f(A,\vec{b}) = \sum_k \left[2A\vec{x}_k + 2\vec{b} - 2\vec{y}_k \right]$$

$$0 = \nabla_A f(A,\vec{b}) = \sum_k \left[2A\vec{x}_k \vec{x}_k^\top + 2\vec{b}\vec{x}_k^\top - 2\vec{y}_k \vec{x}_k^\top \right] \text{ by the identities in Exercise 4.3.}$$

In the second equation, we use the gradient $\nabla_A f$ to denote the *matrix* whose entries are $(\nabla_A f)_{ij} \equiv \partial f / \partial A_{ij}$. Simplifying somewhat, if we define $X \equiv \sum_k \vec{x}_k \vec{x}_k^\top$, $\vec{x}_{\text{sum}} \equiv \sum_k \vec{x}_k$,

| (a) Sharp | (b) Blurry | (c) Deconvolved | (d) Difference |

Figure 4.4 Suppose rather than taking (a) the sharp image, we accidentally take (b) a blurry photo; then, deconvolution can be used to recover (c) a sharp approximation of the original image. The difference between (a) and (c) is shown in (d); only high-frequency detail is different between the two images.

$\vec{y}_{\text{sum}} \equiv \sum_k \vec{y}_k$, and $C \equiv \sum_k \vec{y}_k \vec{x}_k^\top$, then the optimal A and $\vec{b}$ satisfy the following linear system of equations:

$$A\vec{x}_{\text{sum}} + p\vec{b} = \vec{y}_{\text{sum}}$$
$$AX + \vec{b}\vec{x}_{\text{sum}}^\top = C.$$

This system is linear in the unknowns A and $\vec{b}$; Exercise 4.4 expands it explicitly using a 6×6 matrix.

This example illustrates a larger pattern in modeling using least-squares. We started by defining a desirable relationship between the unknowns, namely $(A\vec{x} + \vec{b}) - \vec{y} \approx \vec{0}$. Given a number of data points $(\vec{x}_k, \vec{y}_k)$, we designed an objective function f measuring the quality of potential values for the unknowns A and $\vec{b}$ by summing up the squared norms of expressions we wished to equal zero: $\sum_k \|(A\vec{x}_k + \vec{b}) - \vec{y}_k\|_2^2$. Differentiating this sum gave a *linear* system of equations to solve for the best possible choice. This pattern is a common source of optimization problems that can be solved linearly and essentially is a subtle application of the normal equations.

4.1.5 Deconvolution

An artist hastily taking pictures of a scene may accidentally take photographs that are slightly out of focus. While a photo that is completely blurred may be a lost cause, if there is only localized or small-scale blurring, we may be able to recover a sharper image using computational techniques. One strategy is *deconvolution*, explained below; an example test case of the method outlined below is shown in Figure 4.4.

We can think of a grayscale photograph as a point in $\mathbb{R}^p$, where p is the number of pixels it contains; each pixel's intensity is stored in a different dimension. If the photo is in color, we may need red, green, and blue intensities per pixel, yielding a similar representation in $\mathbb{R}^{3p}$. Regardless, most image blurs are linear, including Gaussian convolution or operations averaging a pixel's intensity with those of its neighbors. In image processing, these operators can be encoded using a matrix G taking a sharp image $\vec{x}$ to its blurred counterpart $G\vec{x}$.

Suppose we take a blurry photo $\vec{x}_0 \in \mathbb{R}^p$. Then, we could try to recover the underlying sharp image $\vec{x} \in \mathbb{R}^p$ by solving the least-squares problem

$$\min_{\vec{x} \in \mathbb{R}^p} \|\vec{x}_0 - G\vec{x}\|_2^2.$$

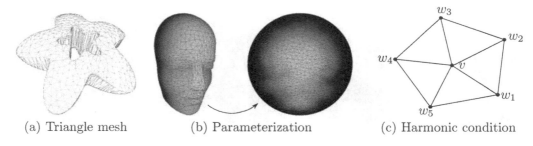

| (a) Triangle mesh | (b) Parameterization | (c) Harmonic condition |

Figure 4.5 (a) An example of a triangle mesh, the typical structure used to represent three-dimensional shapes in computer graphics. (b) In mesh parameterization, we seek a map from a three-dimensional mesh (left) to the two-dimensional image plane (right); the right-hand side shown here was computed using the method suggested in §4.1.6. (c) The harmonic condition is that the position of vertex v is the average of the positions of its neighbors $w_1, \dots, w_5$.

This model assumes that when you blur $\vec{x}$ with G, you get the observed photo $\vec{x}_0$. By the same construction as previous sections, if we know G, then this problem can be solved using linear methods.

In practice, this optimization might be unstable since it is solving a difficult inverse problem. In particular, many pairs of distinct images look very similar after they are blurred, making the reverse operation challenging. One way to stabilize the output of deconvolution is to use Tikhonov regularization, from §4.1.3:

$$\min_{\vec{x} \in \mathbb{R}^p} \|\vec{x}_0 - G\vec{x}\|_2^2 + \alpha \|\vec{x}\|_2^2.$$

More complex versions may constrain $\vec{x} \geq 0$, since negative intensities are not reasonable, but adding such a constraint makes the optimization nonlinear and better solved by the methods we will introduce starting in Chapter 10.

4.1.6 Harmonic Parameterization

Systems for animation often represent geometric objects in a scene using *triangle meshes*, sets of points linked together into triangles as in Figure 4.5(a). To give these meshes fine textures and visual detail, a common practice is to store a detailed color texture as an image or photograph, and to map this texture onto the geometry. Each vertex of the mesh then carries not only its geometric location in space but also *texture coordinates* representing its position on the texture plane.

Mathematically, a mesh can be represented as a collection of n vertices $V \equiv \{v_1, \dots, v_n\}$ linked in pairs by edges $E \subseteq V \times V$. Geometrically, each vertex $v \in V$ is associated with a location $\vec{x}(v)$ in three-dimensional space $\mathbb{R}^3$. Additionally, we will decorate each vertex with a texture coordinate $\vec{t}(v) \in \mathbb{R}^2$ describing its location in the image plane. It is desirable for these positions to be laid out smoothly to avoid squeezing or stretching the texture relative to the geometry of the surface. With this criterion in mind, the problem of *parameterization* is to fill in the positions $\vec{t}(v)$ for all the vertices $v \in V$ given a few positions laid out manually; desirable mesh parameterizations minimize the geometric distortion of the mesh from its configuration in three-dimensional space to the plane. Surprisingly, many state-of-the-art parameterization algorithms involve little more than a linear solve; we will outline one method originally proposed in [123].

For simplicity, suppose that the mesh has disk topology, meaning that it can be mapped to the interior of a circle in the plane, and that we have fixed the location of each vertex on its boundary $B \subseteq V$. The job of the parameterization algorithm then is to fill in positions for the interior vertices of the mesh. This setup and the output of the algorithm outlined below are shown in Figure 4.5(b).

For a vertex $v \in V$, take $N(v)$ to be the set of neighbors of v on the mesh, given by

$$N(v) \equiv \{w \in V : (v, w) \in E\}.$$

Then, for each vertex $v \in V \backslash B$, a reasonable criterion for parameterization quality is that v should be located at the center of its neighbors, illustrated in Figure 4.5(c). Mathematically, this condition is written

$$\vec{t}(v) = \frac{1}{|N(v)|} \sum_{w \in N(v)} \vec{t}(w).$$

Using this expression, we can associate each $v \in V$ with a linear condition either fixing its position on the boundary or asking that its assigned position equals the average of its neighbors' positions. This $|V| \times |V|$ system of equations defines a *harmonic* parameterization.

The final output in Figure 4.5(b) is laid out elastically, evenly distributing vertices on the image plane. Harmonic parameterization has been extended in countless ways to enhance the quality of this result, most prominently by accounting for the lengths of the edges in E as they are realized in three-dimensional space.

4.2 SPECIAL PROPERTIES OF LINEAR SYSTEMS

The examples above provide several contexts in which linear systems of equations are used to model practical computing problems. As derived in the previous chapter, Gaussian elimination solves all of these problems in polynomial time, but it remains to be seen whether this is the fastest or most stable technique. With this question in mind, here we look more closely at the matrices from §4.1 to reveal that they have many properties in common. By deriving solution techniques specific to these classes of matrices, we will design specialized algorithms with better speed and numerical quality.

4.2.1 Positive Definite Matrices and the Cholesky Factorization

As shown in Theorem 4.1, solving the least-squares problem $A\vec{x} \approx \vec{b}$ yields a solution $\vec{x}$ satisfying the square linear system $(A^\top A)\vec{x} = A^\top \vec{b}$. Regardless of A, the matrix $A^\top A$ has a few special properties that distinguish it from arbitrary matrices.

First, $A^\top A$ is symmetric, since by the identities $(AB)^\top = B^\top A^\top$ and $(A^\top)^\top = A$,

$$(A^\top A)^\top = A^\top (A^\top)^\top = A^\top A.$$

We can express this symmetry index-wise by writing $(A^\top A)_{ij} = (A^\top A)_{ji}$ for all indices i, j. This property implies that it is sufficient to store only the values of $A^\top A$ on or above the diagonal, since the rest of the elements can be obtained by symmetry.

Furthermore, $A^\top A$ is a *positive semidefinite* matrix, defined below:

Definition 4.1 (Positive (Semi-)Definite). A matrix $B \in \mathbb{R}^{n \times n}$ is positive semidefinite if for all $\vec{x} \in \mathbb{R}^n$, $\vec{x}^\top B \vec{x} \geq 0$. B is positive definite if $\vec{x}^\top B \vec{x} > 0$ whenever $\vec{x} \neq \vec{0}$.

The following proposition relates this definition to the matrix $A^\top A$:

Proposition 4.1. For any $A \in \mathbb{R}^{m \times n}$, the matrix $A^\top A$ is positive semidefinite. Furthermore, $A^\top A$ is positive definite exactly when the columns of A are linearly independent.

Proof. We first check that $A^\top A$ is *always* positive semidefinite. Take any $\vec{x} \in \mathbb{R}^n$. Then,

$$\vec{x}^\top (A^\top A)\vec{x} = (A\vec{x})^\top (A\vec{x}) = (A\vec{x}) \cdot (A\vec{x}) = \|A\vec{x}\|_2^2 \geq 0.$$

To prove the second statement, first suppose the columns of A are linearly independent. If A were only semidefinite, then there would be an $\vec{x} \neq \vec{0}$ with $\vec{x}^\top A^\top A\vec{x} = 0$, but as shown above, this would imply $\|A\vec{x}\|_2 = 0$, or equivalently $A\vec{x} = \vec{0}$, contradicting the independence of the columns of A. Conversely, if A has linearly *dependent* columns, then there exists a $\vec{y} \neq \vec{0}$ with $A\vec{y} = \vec{0}$. In this case, $\vec{y}^\top A^\top A\vec{y} = \vec{0}^\top \vec{0} = 0$, and hence A is not positive definite. ☐

As a corollary, $A^\top A$ is invertible exactly when A has linearly independent columns, providing a condition to check whether a least-squares problem admits a unique solution.

Given the prevalence of the least-squares system $A^\top A\vec{x} = A^\top \vec{b}$, it is worth considering the possibility of writing faster linear solvers specially designed for this case. In particular, suppose we wish to solve a *symmetric positive definite* (SPD) system $C\vec{x} = \vec{d}$. For least-squares, we could take $C = A^\top A$ and $\vec{d} = A^\top \vec{b}$, but there also exist many systems that naturally are symmetric and positive definite without explicitly coming from a least-squares model. We could solve the system using Gaussian elimination or LU factorization, but given the additional structure on C we can do somewhat better.

Aside 4.1 (Block matrix notation). Our construction in this section will rely on *block matrix* notation. This notation builds larger matrices out of smaller ones. For example, suppose $A \in \mathbb{R}^{m \times n}$, $B \in \mathbb{R}^{m \times k}$, $C \in \mathbb{R}^{p \times n}$, and $D \in \mathbb{R}^{p \times k}$. Then, we could construct a larger matrix by writing:

$$\begin{pmatrix} A & B \\ C & D \end{pmatrix} \in \mathbb{R}^{(m+p) \times (n+k)}.$$

This "block matrix" is constructed by concatenation. Block matrix notation is convenient, but we must be careful to concatenate matrices with dimensions that match. The mechanisms of matrix algebra generally extend to this case, e.g.,

$$\begin{pmatrix} A & B \\ C & D \end{pmatrix} \begin{pmatrix} E & F \\ G & H \end{pmatrix} = \begin{pmatrix} AE + BG & AF + BH \\ CE + DG & CF + DH \end{pmatrix}.$$

We will proceed without checking these identities explicitly, but as an exercise it is worth double-checking that they are true.

We can deconstruct the symmetric positive-definite matrix $C \in \mathbb{R}^{n \times n}$ as a block matrix:

$$C = \begin{pmatrix} c_{11} & \vec{v}^\top \\ \vec{v} & \tilde{C} \end{pmatrix}$$

where $c_{11} \in \mathbb{R}$, $\vec{v} \in \mathbb{R}^{n-1}$, and $\tilde{C} \in \mathbb{R}^{(n-1) \times (n-1)}$. The SPD structure of C provides the following observation:

$$0 < \vec{e}_1^\top C \vec{e}_1 \text{ since } C \text{ is positive definite and } \vec{e}_1 \neq \vec{0}$$

$$= \begin{pmatrix} 1 & 0 & \cdots & 0 \end{pmatrix} \begin{pmatrix} c_{11} & \vec{v}^\top \\ \vec{v} & \tilde{C} \end{pmatrix} \begin{pmatrix} 1 \\ 0 \\ \vdots \\ 0 \end{pmatrix}$$

$$= \begin{pmatrix} 1 & 0 & \cdots & 0 \end{pmatrix} \begin{pmatrix} c_{11} \\ \vec{v} \end{pmatrix}$$

$$= c_{11}.$$

By the strict inequality in the first line, we do not have to use pivoting to guarantee that $c_{11} \neq 0$ in the first step of Gaussian elimination.

Continuing with Gaussian elimination, we can apply a forward-substitution matrix E of the form

$$E = \begin{pmatrix} 1/\sqrt{c_{11}} & \vec{0}^\top \\ \vec{r} & I_{(n-1)\times(n-1)} \end{pmatrix}.$$

Here, the vector $\vec{r} \in \mathbb{R}^{n-1}$ contains forward-substitution scaling factors satisfying $r_{i-1}c_{11} = -c_{i1}$. Unlike our original construction of Gaussian elimination, we scale row 1 by $1/\sqrt{c_{11}}$ for reasons that will become apparent shortly.

By design, after forward-substitution, the form of the product EC is:

$$EC = \begin{pmatrix} \sqrt{c_{11}} & \vec{v}^\top/\sqrt{c_{11}} \\ \vec{0} & D \end{pmatrix},$$

for some $D \in \mathbb{R}^{(n-1)\times(n-1)}$.

Now, we diverge from the derivation of Gaussian elimination. Rather than moving on to the second row, to maintain symmetry, we post-multiply by $E^\top$ to obtain $ECE^\top$:

$$ECE^\top = (EC)E^\top$$

$$= \begin{pmatrix} \sqrt{c_{11}} & \vec{v}^\top/\sqrt{c_{11}} \\ \vec{0} & D \end{pmatrix} \begin{pmatrix} 1/\sqrt{c_{11}} & \vec{r}^\top \\ \vec{0} & I_{(n-1)\times(n-1)} \end{pmatrix}$$

$$= \begin{pmatrix} 1 & \vec{0}^\top \\ \vec{0} & D \end{pmatrix}.$$

The $\vec{0}^\top$ in the upper right follows from the construction of E as an elimination matrix. Alternatively, an easier if less direct argument is that $ECE^\top$ is symmetric, and the lower-left element of the block form for $ECE^\top$ is $\vec{0}$ by block matrix multiplication. Regardless, we have eliminated the first row *and* the first column of C! Furthermore, the remaining submatrix D is also symmetric and positive definite, as suggested in Exercise 4.2.

Example 4.6 (Cholesky factorization, initial step). As a concrete example, consider the following symmetric, positive definite matrix

$$C = \begin{pmatrix} 4 & -2 & 4 \\ -2 & 5 & -4 \\ 4 & -4 & 14 \end{pmatrix}.$$

We can eliminate the first column of C using the elimination matrix E_1 defined as:

$$E_1 = \begin{pmatrix} 1/2 & 0 & 0 \\ 1/2 & 1 & 0 \\ -1 & 0 & 1 \end{pmatrix} \longrightarrow E_1 C = \begin{pmatrix} 2 & -1 & 2 \\ 0 & 4 & -2 \\ 0 & -2 & 10 \end{pmatrix}.$$

We chose the upper left element of E_1 to be $1/2 = 1/\sqrt{4} = 1/\sqrt{c_{11}}$. Following the construction above, we can post-multiply by $E_1^\top$ to obtain:

$$E_1 C E_1^\top = \begin{pmatrix} 1 & 0 & 0 \\ 0 & 4 & -2 \\ 0 & -2 & 10 \end{pmatrix}.$$

The first row *and* column of this product equal the standard basis vector $\vec{e}_1 = (1,0,0)$.

We can repeat this process to eliminate all the rows and columns of C symmetrically. This method is *specific* to symmetric positive-definite matrices, since

- symmetry allowed us to apply the same E to both sides, and

- positive definiteness guaranteed that $c_{11} > 0$, thus implying that $1/\sqrt{c_{11}}$ exists.

Similar to LU factorization, we now obtain a factorization $C = LL^\top$ for a lower-triangular matrix L. This factorization is constructed by applying elimination matrices symmetrically using the process above, until we reach

$$E_k \cdots E_2 E_1 C E_1^\top E_2^\top \cdots E_k^\top = I_{n \times n}.$$

Then, like our construction in §3.5.1, we define L as a product of lower-triangular matrices:

$$L \equiv E_1^{-1} E_2^{-1} \cdots E_k^{-1}.$$

The product $C = LL^\top$ is known as the *Cholesky factorization* of C. If taking the square roots causes numerical issues, a related $LDL^\top$ factorization, where D is a diagonal matrix, avoids this issue and can be derived from the discussion above; see Exercise 4.6.

Example 4.7 (Cholesky factorization, remaining steps). Continuing Example 4.6, we can eliminate the second row and column as follows:

$$E_2 = \begin{pmatrix} 1 & 0 & 0 \\ 0 & 1/2 & 0 \\ 0 & 1/2 & 1 \end{pmatrix} \longrightarrow E_2(E_1 C E_1^\top)E_2^\top = \begin{pmatrix} 1 & 0 & 0 \\ 0 & 1 & 0 \\ 0 & 0 & 9 \end{pmatrix}.$$

Rescaling brings the symmetric product to the identity matrix $I_{3\times 3}$:

$$E_3 = \begin{pmatrix} 1 & 0 & 0 \\ 0 & 1 & 0 \\ 0 & 0 & 1/3 \end{pmatrix} \longrightarrow E_3(E_2 E_1 C E_1^\top E_2^\top)E_3^\top = \begin{pmatrix} 1 & 0 & 0 \\ 0 & 1 & 0 \\ 0 & 0 & 1 \end{pmatrix}.$$

Hence, we have shown $E_3 E_2 E_1 C E_1^\top E_2^\top E_3^\top = I_{3 \times 3}$. As above, define:

$$L = E_1^{-1} E_2^{-1} E_3^{-1} = \begin{pmatrix} 2 & 0 & 0 \\ -1 & 1 & 0 \\ 2 & 0 & 1 \end{pmatrix} \begin{pmatrix} 1 & 0 & 0 \\ 0 & 2 & 0 \\ 0 & -1 & 1 \end{pmatrix} \begin{pmatrix} 1 & 0 & 0 \\ 0 & 1 & 0 \\ 0 & 0 & 3 \end{pmatrix} = \begin{pmatrix} 2 & 0 & 0 \\ -1 & 2 & 0 \\ 2 & -1 & 3 \end{pmatrix}.$$

This matrix L satisfies $LL^\top = C$.

The Cholesky factorization has many practical properties. It takes half the memory to store L from the Cholesky factorization rather than the LU factorization of C. Specifically, L has $n(n+1)/2$ nonzero elements, while the compressed storage of LU factorizations explained in §3.5.3 requires n^2 nonzeros. Furthermore, as with the LU decomposition, solving $C\vec{x} = \vec{d}$ can be accomplished using fast forward- and back-substitution. Finally, the product $LL^\top$ is symmetric and positive semidefinite regardless of L; if we factored $C = LU$ but made rounding and other mistakes, in degenerate cases the computed product $C' \approx LU$ may no longer satisfy these criteria exactly.

Code for Cholesky factorization can be very succinct. To derive a particularly compact form, we can work backward from the factorization $C = LL^\top$ now that we know such an object exists. Suppose we choose an arbitrary $k \in \{1, \ldots, n\}$ and write L in block form isolating the k-th row and column:

$$L = \begin{pmatrix} L_{11} & \vec{0} & 0 \\ \vec{\ell}_k^{\top} & \ell_{kk} & \vec{0}^{\top} \\ L_{31} & \vec{\ell}_k & L_{33} \end{pmatrix}.$$

Here, since L is lower triangular, L_{11} and L_{33} are both lower-triangular square matrices. Applying block matrix algebra to the product $C = LL^{\top}$ shows:

$$C = LL^{\top} = \begin{pmatrix} L_{11} & \vec{0} & 0 \\ \vec{\ell}_k^{\top} & \ell_{kk} & \vec{0}^{\top} \\ L_{31} & \vec{\ell}_k & L_{33} \end{pmatrix} \begin{pmatrix} L_{11}^{\top} & \vec{\ell}_k & L_{31}^{\top} \\ \vec{0}^{\top} & \ell_{kk} & (\vec{\ell}_k)^{\top} \\ 0 & \vec{0} & L_{33}^{\top} \end{pmatrix}$$

$$= \begin{pmatrix} \times & \times & \times \\ \vec{\ell}_k^{\top} L_{11}^{\top} & \vec{\ell}_k^{\top} \vec{\ell}_k + \ell_{kk}^2 & \times \\ \times & \times & \times \end{pmatrix}.$$

We leave out values of the product that are not necessary for our derivation.

Since $C = LL^{\top}$, from the product above we now have $c_{kk} = \vec{\ell}_k^{\top} \vec{\ell}_k + \ell_{kk}^2$, or equivalently

$$\ell_{kk} = \sqrt{c_{kk} - \|\vec{\ell}_k\|_2^2},$$

where $\vec{\ell}_k \in \mathbb{R}^{k-1}$ contains the elements of the k-th row of L to the left of the diagonal. We can choose $\ell_{kk} \geq 0$, since scaling columns of L by -1 has no effect on $C = LL^{\top}$. Furthermore, applying $C = LL^{\top}$ to the middle left element of the product shows $L_{11} \vec{\ell}_k = \vec{c}_k$, where $\vec{c}_k$ contains the elements of C in the same position as $\vec{\ell}_k$. Since L_{11} is lower triangular, this system can be solved by forward-substitution for $\vec{\ell}_k$!

Synthesizing the formulas above reveals an algorithm for computing the Cholesky factorization by iterating $k = 1, 2, \ldots, n$. L_{11} will already be computed by the time we reach row k, so $\vec{\ell}_k$ can be found using forward-substitution. Then, ℓ_{kk} is computed directly using the square root formula. We provide pseudocode in Figure 4.6. As with LU factorization, this algorithm runs in $O(n^3)$ time; more specifically, Cholesky factorization takes approximately $\frac{1}{3}n^3$ operations, half the work needed for LU.

4.2.2 Sparsity

We set out in this section to identify properties of specific linear systems that can make them solvable using more efficient techniques than Gaussian elimination. In addition to positive definiteness, many linear systems of equations naturally enjoy *sparsity*, meaning that most of the entries of A in the system $A\vec{x} = \vec{b}$ are exactly zero. Sparsity can reflect particular structure in a given problem, including the following use cases:

- In image processing (e.g., §4.1.5), systems for photo editing express relationships between the values of pixels and those of their neighbors on the image grid. An image may be a point in $\mathbb{R}^p$ for p pixels, but when solving $A\vec{x} = \vec{b}$ for a new size-p image, $A \in \mathbb{R}^{p \times p}$ may have only $O(p)$ rather than $O(p^2)$ nonzeros since each row only involves a single pixel and its up/down/left/right neighbors.

- In computational geometry (e.g., §4.1.6), shapes are often expressed using collections of triangles linked together into a mesh. Equations for surface smoothing, parameterization, and other tasks link values associated with given vertex with only those at their neighbors in the mesh.

---

function CHOLESKY-FACTORIZATION(C)
   ▷ Factors $C = LL^T$, assuming C is symmetric and positive definite

$L \leftarrow C$ ▷ This algorithm destructively replaces C with L
for $k \leftarrow 1, 2, \ldots, n$
     ▷ Back-substitute to place $\vec{\ell}_k^\top$ at the beginning of row k
     for $i \leftarrow 1, \ldots, k-1$ ▷ Current element i of $\vec{\ell}_k$
         $s \leftarrow 0$
         ▷ Iterate over L_{11}; $j < i$, so the iteration maintains $L_{kj} = (\vec{\ell}_k)_j$.
         for $j \leftarrow 1, \ldots, i-1 : s \leftarrow s + L_{ij}L_{kj}$
         $L_{ki} \leftarrow {(L_{ki}-s)}/{L_{ii}}$

     ▷ Apply the formula for ℓ_{kk}
     $v \leftarrow 0$ ▷ For computing $\|\vec{\ell}_k\|_2^2$
     for $j \leftarrow 1, \ldots, k-1 : v \leftarrow v + L_{kj}^2$
     $L_{kk} \leftarrow \sqrt{L_{kk} - v}$
return L

Figure 4.6 Cholesky factorization for writing $C = LL^\top$, where the input C is symmetric and positive-definite and the output L is lower triangular.

- In machine learning, a *graphical model* uses a graph $G = (V, E)$ to express probability distributions over several variables. Each variable corresponds to a node $v \in V$, and edges $e \in E$ represent probabilistic dependences. Linear systems in this context often have one row per $v \in V$ with nonzeros in columns involving v and its neighbors.

If $A \in \mathbb{R}^{n \times n}$ is sparse to the point that it contains $O(n)$ rather than $O(n^2)$ nonzero values, there is no reason to store A with n^2 values. Instead, *sparse matrix* storage techniques only store the $O(n)$ nonzeros in a more reasonable data structure, e.g., a list of row/column/value triplets. The choice of a matrix data structure involves considering the likely operations that will occur on the matrix, possibly including multiplication, iteration over nonzeros, or iterating over individual rows or columns.

Unfortunately, the LU (and Cholesky) factorizations of a sparse matrix A may not result in sparse L and U matrices; this loss of structure severely limits the applicability of using these methods to solve $A\vec{x} = \vec{b}$ when A is large but sparse. Thankfully, there are many *direct sparse solvers* that produce an LU-like factorization without inducing much *fill*, or additional nonzeros; discussion of these techniques can be found in [32]. Alternatively, *iterative* techniques can obtain approximate solutions to linear systems using only multiplication by A and $A^\top$. We will derive some of these methods in Chapter 11.

4.2.3 Additional Special Structures

Certain matrices are not only sparse but also *structured*. For instance, a *tridiagonal* system of linear equations has the following pattern of nonzero values:

$$
\begin{pmatrix}
\times & \times & & & \\
\times & \times & \times & & \\
& \times & \times & \times & \\
& & \times & \times & \times \\
& & & \times & \times
\end{pmatrix}.
$$

In Exercise 4.8, you will derive a special version of Gaussian elimination for dealing with this *banded* structure.

In other cases, matrices may not be sparse but might admit a sparse representation. For example, consider the *circulant* matrix:

$$\begin{pmatrix} a & b & c & d \\ d & a & b & c \\ c & d & a & b \\ b & c & d & a \end{pmatrix}.$$

This matrix can be stored using only the values a, b, c, d. Specialized techniques for solving systems involving this and other classes of matrices are well-studied and often are more efficient than generic Gaussian elimination.

Broadly speaking, once a problem has been reduced to a linear system $A\vec{x} = \vec{b}$, Gaussian elimination provides only one option for how to find $\vec{x}$. It may be possible to show that the matrix A for the given problem can be solved more easily by identifying special properties like symmetry, positive-definiteness, and sparsity. Interested readers should refer to the discussion in [50] for consideration of numerous cases like the ones above.

4.3   SENSITIVITY ANALYSIS

It is important to examine the matrix of a linear system to find out if it has special properties that can simplify the solution process. Sparsity, positive definiteness, symmetry, and so on provide clues to the proper algorithm to use for a particular problem. Even if a given solution strategy might work in theory, however, it is important to understand how well we can trust the output. For instance, due to rounding and other discrete effects, it might be the case that an implementation of Gaussian elimination for solving $A\vec{x} = \vec{b}$ yields a solution $\vec{x}_0$ such that $0 < \|A\vec{x}_0 - \vec{b}\|_2 \ll 1$; in other words, $\vec{x}_0$ only solves the system approximately.

One general way to understand the likelihood of error is through *sensitivity analysis*. To measure sensitivity, we ask what might happen to $\vec{x}$ if instead of solving $A\vec{x} = \vec{b}$, in reality we solve a *perturbed* system of equations $(A + \delta A)\vec{x} = \vec{b} + \delta\vec{b}$. There are two ways of viewing conclusions made by this type of analysis:

1. We may represent A and $\vec{b}$ inexactly thanks to rounding and other effects. This analysis then shows the best possible accuracy we can expect for $\vec{x}$ given the mistakes made representing the problem.

2. Suppose our solver generates an inexact approximation $\vec{x}_0$ to the solution $\vec{x}$ of $A\vec{x} = \vec{b}$. This vector $\vec{x}_0$ itself is the exact solution of a different system $A\vec{x}_0 = \vec{b}_0$ if we *define* $\vec{b}_0 \equiv A\vec{x}_0$ (be sure you understand why this sentence is not a tautology!). Understanding how changes in $\vec{x}_0$ affect changes in $\vec{b}_0$ show how sensitive the system is to slightly incorrect answers.

The discussion here is motivated by the definitions of forward and backward error in §2.2.1.

4.3.1   Matrix and Vector Norms

Before we can discuss the sensitivity of a linear system, we have to be somewhat careful to define what it means for a change $\delta\vec{x}$ to be "small." Generally, we wish to measure the length, or *norm*, of a vector $\vec{x}$. We have already encountered the two-norm of a vector:

$$\|\vec{x}\|_2 \equiv \sqrt{x_1^2 + x_2^2 + \cdots + x_n^2}$$

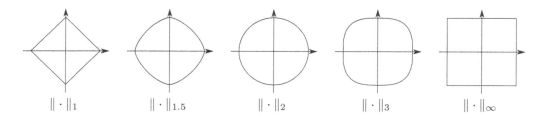

$\|\cdot\|_1$ $\|\cdot\|_{1.5}$ $\|\cdot\|_2$ $\|\cdot\|_3$ $\|\cdot\|_\infty$

Figure 4.7 The set $\{\vec{x} \in \mathbb{R}^2 : \|\vec{x}\| = 1\}$ for different vector norms $\|\cdot\|$.

for $\vec{x} \in \mathbb{R}^n$. This norm is popular thanks to its connection to Euclidean geometry, but it is by no means the only norm on $\mathbb{R}^n$. Most generally, we define a *norm* as follows:

Definition 4.2 (Vector norm). A vector norm is a function $\|\cdot\| : \mathbb{R}^n \to [0, \infty)$ satisfying the following conditions:

- $\|\vec{x}\| = 0$ if and only if $\vec{x} = \vec{0}$ ("$\|\cdot\|$ separates points").

- $\|c\vec{x}\| = |c|\|\vec{x}\|$ for all scalars $c \in \mathbb{R}$ and vectors $\vec{x} \in \mathbb{R}^n$ ("absolute scalability").

- $\|\vec{x} + \vec{y}\| \le \|\vec{x}\| + \|\vec{y}\|$ for all $\vec{x}, \vec{y} \in \mathbb{R}^n$ ("triangle inequality").

Other than $\|\cdot\|_2$, there are many examples of norms:

- The p-norm $\|\vec{x}\|_p$, for $p \ge 1$, is given by

$$\|\vec{x}\|_p \equiv \left(|x_1|^p + |x_2|^p + \cdots + |x_n|^p\right)^{1/p}.$$

  Of particular importance is the 1-norm, also known as the "Manhattan" or "taxicab" norm:

$$\|\vec{x}\|_1 \equiv \sum_{k=1}^n |x_k|.$$

  This norm receives its nickname because it represents the distance a taxicab drives between two points in a city where the roads only run north/south and east/west.

- The ∞-norm $\|\vec{x}\|_\infty$ is given by

$$\|\vec{x}\|_\infty \equiv \max(|x_1|, |x_2|, \cdots, |x_n|).$$

These norms are illustrated in Figure 4.7 by showing the "unit circle" $\{\vec{x} \in \mathbb{R}^2 : \|\vec{x}\| = 1\}$ for different choices of norm $\|\cdot\|$; this visualization shows that $\|\vec{v}\|_p \le \|\vec{v}\|_q$ when $p > q$.

Despite these geometric differences, many norms on $\mathbb{R}^n$ have similar behavior. In particular, suppose we say two norms are *equivalent* when they satisfy the following property:

Definition 4.3 (Equivalent norms). Two norms $\|\cdot\|$ and $\|\cdot\|'$ are *equivalent* if there exist constants c_{low} and c_{high} such that $c_{\text{low}}\|\vec{x}\| \le \|\vec{x}\|' \le c_{\text{high}}\|\vec{x}\|$ for all $\vec{x} \in \mathbb{R}^n$.

This condition guarantees that up to some constant factors, all norms agree on which vectors are "small" and "large." We will state without proof a famous theorem from analysis:

Theorem 4.2 (Equivalence of norms on $\mathbb{R}^n$). *All norms on $\mathbb{R}^n$ are equivalent.*

This somewhat surprising result implies that all vector norms have the same *rough* behavior, but the choice of a norm for analyzing or stating a particular problem still can make a huge difference. For instance, on $\mathbb{R}^3$ the ∞-norm considers the vector $(1000, 1000, 1000)$ to have the same norm as $(1000, 0, 0)$, whereas the 2-norm certainly is affected by the additional nonzero values.

Since we perturb not only vectors but also matrices, we must also be able to take the norm of a matrix. The definition of a matrix norm is nothing more than Definition 4.2 with matrices in place of vectors. For this reason, we can "unroll" any matrix in $\mathbb{R}^{m \times n}$ to a vector in $\mathbb{R}^{nm}$ to adapt any vector norm to matrices. One such norm is the *Frobenius norm*

$$\|A\|_{\mathrm{Fro}} \equiv \sqrt{\sum_{i,j} a_{ij}^2}.$$

Such adaptations of vector norms, however, are not always meaningful. In particular, norms on matrices A constructed this way may not have a clear connection to the *action* of A on vectors. Since we usually use matrices to encode linear transformations, we would prefer a norm that helps us understand what happens when A is multiplied by different vectors $\vec{x}$. With this motivation, we can define the matrix norm *induced* by a vector norm as follows:

Definition 4.4 (Induced norm). The matrix norm on $\mathbb{R}^{m \times n}$ *induced* by a vector norm $\|\cdot\|$ is given by
$$\|A\| \equiv \max\{\|A\vec{x}\| : \|\vec{x}\| = 1\}.$$
That is, the induced norm is the maximum length of the image of a unit vector multiplied by A.

This definition in the case $\|\cdot\| = \|\cdot\|_2$ is illustrated in Figure 4.8. Since vector norms satisfy $\|c\vec{x}\| = |c|\|\vec{x}\|$, this definition is equivalent to requiring

$$\|A\| \equiv \max_{\vec{x} \in \mathbb{R}^n \setminus \{0\}} \frac{\|A\vec{x}\|}{\|\vec{x}\|}.$$

From this standpoint, the norm of A induced by $\|\cdot\|$ is the largest achievable ratio of the norm of $A\vec{x}$ relative to that of the input $\vec{x}$.

This definition in terms of a maximization problem makes it somewhat complicated to compute the norm $\|A\|$ given a matrix A and a choice of $\|\cdot\|$. Fortunately, the matrix norms induced by many popular vector norms can be simplified. Some well-known formulae for matrix norms include the following:

• The induced one-norm of A is the maximum absolute column sum of A:

$$\|A\|_1 = \max_{1 \leq j \leq n} \sum_{i=1}^{m} |a_{ij}|.$$

• The induced ∞-norm of A is the maximum absolute row sum of A:

$$\|A\|_\infty = \max_{1 \leq i \leq m} \sum_{j=1}^{n} |a_{ij}|.$$

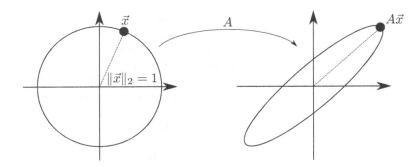

Figure 4.8 The norm $\| \cdot \|_2$ induces a matrix norm measuring the largest distortion of any point on the unit circle after applying A.

- The induced two-norm, or *spectral norm*, of $A \in \mathbb{R}^{n \times n}$ is the square root of the largest eigenvalue of $A^\top A$. That is,

$$\|A\|_2^2 = \max\{\lambda : \text{there exists } \vec{x} \in \mathbb{R}^n \text{ with } A^\top A \vec{x} = \lambda \vec{x}\}.$$

The first two norms are computable directly from the elements of A; the third will require machinery from Chapter 7.

4.3.2   Condition Numbers

Now that we have tools for measuring the action of a matrix, we can define the *condition number* of a linear system by adapting our generic definition of condition numbers from Chapter 2. In this section, we will follow the development presented in [50].

Suppose we are given a perturbation δA of a matrix A and a perturbation $\delta \vec{b}$ of the right-hand side of the linear system $A\vec{x} = \vec{b}$. For small values of ε, ignoring invertibility technicalities we can write a vector-valued function $\vec{x}(\varepsilon)$ as the solution to

$$(A + \varepsilon \cdot \delta A)\vec{x}(\varepsilon) = \vec{b} + \varepsilon \cdot \delta \vec{b}.$$

Differentiating both sides with respect to ε and applying the product rule shows:

$$\delta A \cdot \vec{x}(\varepsilon) + (A + \varepsilon \cdot \delta A)\frac{d\vec{x}(\varepsilon)}{d\varepsilon} = \delta \vec{b}.$$

In particular, when $\varepsilon = 0$ we find

$$\delta A \cdot \vec{x}(0) + A\frac{d\vec{x}}{d\varepsilon}\Big|_{\varepsilon=0} = \delta \vec{b}$$

or, equivalently,

$$\frac{d\vec{x}}{d\varepsilon}\Big|_{\varepsilon=0} = A^{-1}(\delta \vec{b} - \delta A \cdot \vec{x}(0)).$$

Using the Taylor expansion, we can write

$$\vec{x}(\varepsilon) = \vec{x}(0) + \varepsilon \vec{x}'(0) + O(\varepsilon^2),$$

where we define $\vec{x}'(0) = \frac{d\vec{x}}{d\varepsilon}\big|_{\varepsilon=0}$. Thus, we can expand the relative error made by solving the perturbed system:

$$\frac{\|\vec{x}(\varepsilon) - \vec{x}(0)\|}{\|\vec{x}(0)\|} = \frac{\|\varepsilon \vec{x}'(0) + O(\varepsilon^2)\|}{\|\vec{x}(0)\|} \text{ by the Taylor expansion above}$$

$$= \frac{\|\varepsilon A^{-1}(\delta \vec{b} - \delta A \cdot \vec{x}(0)) + O(\varepsilon^2)\|}{\|\vec{x}(0)\|} \quad \text{by the derivative we computed}$$

$$\leq \frac{|\varepsilon|}{\|\vec{x}(0)\|}(\|A^{-1}\delta \vec{b}\| + \|A^{-1}\delta A \cdot \vec{x}(0))\|) + O(\varepsilon^2)$$

$$\text{by the triangle inequality } \|A + B\| \leq \|A\| + \|B\|$$

$$\leq |\varepsilon|\|A^{-1}\| \left(\frac{\|\delta \vec{b}\|}{\|\vec{x}(0)\|} + \|\delta A\| \right) + O(\varepsilon^2) \text{ by the identity } \|AB\| \leq \|A\|\|B\|$$

$$= |\varepsilon|\|A^{-1}\|\|A\| \left(\frac{\|\delta \vec{b}\|}{\|A\|\|\vec{x}(0)\|} + \frac{\|\delta A\|}{\|A\|} \right) + O(\varepsilon^2)$$

$$\leq |\varepsilon|\|A^{-1}\|\|A\| \left(\frac{\|\delta \vec{b}\|}{\|A\vec{x}(0)\|} + \frac{\|\delta A\|}{\|A\|} \right) + O(\varepsilon^2) \text{ since } \|A\vec{x}(0)\| \leq \|A\|\|\vec{x}(0)\|$$

$$= |\varepsilon|\|A^{-1}\|\|A\| \left(\frac{\|\delta \vec{b}\|}{\|\vec{b}\|} + \frac{\|\delta A\|}{\|A\|} \right) + O(\varepsilon^2) \text{ since by definition } A\vec{x}(0) = \vec{b}.$$

Here we have applied some properties of induced matrix norms which follow from corresponding properties for vectors; you will check them explicitly in Exercise 4.12.

The sum $D \equiv \|\delta \vec{b}\|/\|\vec{b}\| + \|\delta A\|/\|A\|$ appearing in the last equality above encodes the magnitudes of the perturbations of δA and $\delta \vec{b}$ relative to the magnitudes of A and $\vec{b}$, respectively. From this standpoint, to first order we have bounded the relative error of perturbing the system by ε in terms of the factor $\kappa \equiv \|A\|\|A^{-1}\|$:

$$\frac{\|\vec{x}(\varepsilon) - \vec{x}(0)\|}{\|\vec{x}(0)\|} \leq |\varepsilon| \cdot D \cdot \kappa + O(\varepsilon^2)$$

Hence, the quantity κ bounds the conditioning of linear systems involving A, inspiring the following definition:

Definition 4.5 (Matrix condition number). The condition number of $A \in \mathbb{R}^{n \times n}$ with respect to a given matrix norm $\|\cdot\|$ is

$$\text{cond } A \equiv \|A\|\|A^{-1}\|.$$

If A is not invertible, we take cond $A \equiv \infty$.

For nearly any matrix norm, cond $A \geq 1$ for all A. Scaling A has no effect on its condition number. Large condition numbers indicate that solutions to $A\vec{x} = \vec{b}$ are unstable under perturbations of A or $\vec{b}$.

If $\|\cdot\|$ is induced by a vector norm and A is invertible, then we have

$$\|A^{-1}\| = \max_{\vec{x} \neq \vec{0}} \frac{\|A^{-1}\vec{x}\|}{\|\vec{x}\|} \quad \text{by definition}$$

$$= \max_{\vec{y} \neq \vec{0}} \frac{\|\vec{y}\|}{\|A\vec{y}\|} \quad \text{by substituting } \vec{y} = A^{-1}\vec{x}$$

$$= \left(\min_{\vec{y} \neq \vec{0}} \frac{\|A\vec{y}\|}{\|\vec{y}\|} \right)^{-1} \quad \text{by taking the reciprocal.}$$

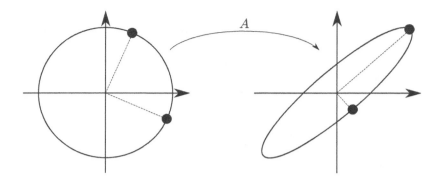

Figure 4.9 The condition number of A measures the ratio of the largest to smallest distortion of any two points on the unit circle mapped under A.

In this case, the condition number of A is given by:

$$\text{cond } A = \left(\max_{\vec{x} \neq \vec{0}} \frac{\|A\vec{x}\|}{\|\vec{x}\|} \right) \left(\min_{\vec{y} \neq \vec{0}} \frac{\|A\vec{y}\|}{\|\vec{y}\|} \right)^{-1}.$$

In other words, cond A measures the ratio of the maximum to the minimum possible stretch of a vector $\vec{x}$ under A; this interpretation is illustrated in Figure 4.9.

A desirable stability property of a system $A\vec{x} = \vec{b}$ is that if A or $\vec{b}$ is perturbed, the solution $\vec{x}$ does not change considerably. Our motivation for cond A shows that when the condition number is small, the change in $\vec{x}$ is small relative to the change in A or $\vec{b}$. Otherwise, a small change in the parameters of the linear system can cause large deviations in $\vec{x}$; this instability can cause linear solvers to make large mistakes in $\vec{x}$ due to rounding and other approximations during the solution process.

In practice, we might wish to evaluate cond A before solving $A\vec{x} = \vec{b}$ to see how successful we can expect to be in this process. Taking the norm $\|A^{-1}\|$, however, can be as difficult as computing the full inverse A^{-1}. A subtle "chicken-and-egg problem" exists here: Do we need to compute the condition number of computing matrix condition numbers? A common way out is to *bound* or *approximate* cond A using expressions that are easier to evaluate. Lower bounds on the condition number represent optimistic bounds that can be used to cull out particularly bad matrices A, while upper bounds guarantee behavior in the worst case. Condition number estimation is itself an area of active research in numerical analysis.

For example, one way to lower-bound the condition number is to apply the identity $\|A^{-1}\vec{x}\| \leq \|A^{-1}\|\|\vec{x}\|$ as in Exercise 4.12. Then, for any $\vec{x} \neq \vec{0}$ we can write $\|A^{-1}\| \geq \|A^{-1}\vec{x}\|/\|\vec{x}\|$. Thus,

$$\text{cond } A = \|A\|\|A^{-1}\| \geq \frac{\|A\|\|A^{-1}\vec{x}\|}{\|\vec{x}\|}.$$

So, we can bound the condition number by solving $A^{-1}\vec{x}$ for some vectors $\vec{x}$. The necessity of a linear solver to find $A^{-1}\vec{x}$ again creates a circular dependence on the condition number to evaluate the quality of the estimate! After considering eigenvalue problems, in future chapters we will provide more reliable estimates when $\| \cdot \|$ is induced by the two-norm.

4.4   EXERCISES

4.1 Give an example of a sparse matrix whose inverse is dense.

4.2 Show that the matrix D introduced in §4.2.1 is symmetric and positive definite.

4.3 ("Matrix calculus") The optimization problem we posed for $A \in \mathbb{R}^{2 \times 2}$ in §4.1.4 is an example of a problem where the unknown is a matrix rather than a vector. These problems appear frequently in machine learning and have inspired an alternative notation for differential calculus better suited to calculations of this sort.

(a) Suppose $f : \mathbb{R}^{n \times m} \to \mathbb{R}$ is a smooth function. Justify why the gradient of f can be thought of as an $n \times m$ matrix. We will use the notation $\frac{\partial f}{\partial A}$ to notate the gradient of $f(A)$ with respect to A.

(b) Take the gradient $\partial/\partial A$ of the following functions, assuming $\vec{x}$ and $\vec{y}$ are constant vectors:
   (i) $\vec{x}^\top A \vec{y}$
   (ii) $\vec{x}^\top A^\top A \vec{x}$
   (iii) $(\vec{x} - A\vec{y})^\top W (\vec{x} - A\vec{y})$ for a constant, symmetric matrix W

(c) Now, suppose $X \in \mathbb{R}^{m \times n}$ is a smooth function of a scalar variable $X(t) : \mathbb{R} \to \mathbb{R}^{m \times n}$. We can notate the *differential* $\partial X \equiv X'(t)$. For matrix functions $X(t)$ and $Y(t)$, justify the following identities:
   (i) $\partial(X + Y) = \partial X + \partial Y$
   (ii) $\partial(X^\top) = (\partial X)^\top$
   (iii) $\partial(XY) = (\partial X)Y + X(\partial Y)$
   (iv) $\partial(X^{-1}) = -X^{-1}(\partial X)X^{-1}$ (see Exercise 1.13)

After establishing a dictionary of identities like the ones above, taking the derivatives of functions involving matrices becomes a far less cumbersome task. See [99] for a comprehensive reference of identities and formulas in matrix calculus.

4.4 The system of equations for A and $\vec{b}$ in §4.1.4 must be "unrolled" if we wish to use standard software for solving linear systems of equations to recover the image transformation. Define

$$A \equiv \begin{pmatrix} a_{11} & a_{12} \\ a_{21} & a_{22} \end{pmatrix} \quad \text{and} \quad \vec{b} \equiv \begin{pmatrix} b_1 \\ b_2 \end{pmatrix}.$$

We can combine all our unknowns into a vector $\vec{u}$ as follows:

$$\vec{u} \equiv \begin{pmatrix} a_{11} \\ a_{12} \\ a_{21} \\ a_{22} \\ b_1 \\ b_2 \end{pmatrix}.$$

Write a matrix $M \in \mathbb{R}^{6 \times 6}$ and vector $\vec{d} \in \mathbb{R}^6$ so that $\vec{u}$—and hence A and $\vec{b}$—can be recovered by solving the system $M\vec{u} = \vec{d}$ for $\vec{u}$; you can use any computable temporary variables to simplify your notation, including $\vec{x}_{\text{sum}}$, $\vec{y}_{\text{sum}}$, X, and C.

4.5 There are many ways to motivate the harmonic parameterization technique from §4.1.6. One alternative is to consider the *Dirichlet energy* of a parameterization

$$E_D[\vec{t}(\cdot)] \equiv \sum_{(v,w)\in E} \|\vec{t}(v) - \vec{t}(w)\|_2^2.$$

Then, we can write an optimization problem given boundary vertex positions $\vec{t}_0(\cdot)$: $B \to \mathbb{R}^2$:

$$\begin{array}{ll} \text{minimize} & E_D[\vec{t}(\cdot)] \\ \text{subject to} & \vec{t}(v) = \vec{t}_0(v) \ \forall v \in B. \end{array}$$

This optimization minimizes the Dirichlet energy $E_D[\cdot]$ over all possible parameterizations $\vec{t}(\cdot)$ with the constraint that the positions of boundary vertices $v \in B$ are fixed. Show that after minimizing this energy, interior vertices $v \in V \backslash B$ satisfy the barycenter property introduced in §4.1.6:

$$\vec{t}(v) = \frac{1}{|N(v)|} \sum_{w\in N(v)} \vec{t}(w).$$

This variational formulation connects the technique to the differential geometry of smooth maps into the plane.

4.6 A more general version of the Cholesky decomposition that does not require the computation of square roots is the LDLT decomposition.

(a) Suppose $A \in \mathbb{R}^{n\times n}$ is symmetric and admits an LU factorization (without pivoting). Show that A can be factored $A = LDL^\top$, where D is diagonal and L is lower triangular.
Hint: Take $D \equiv UL^{-\top}$; you must show that this matrix is diagonal.

(b) Modify the construction of the Cholesky decomposition from §4.2.1 to show how a symmetric, positive-definite matrix A can be factored $A = LDL^\top$ without using any square root operations. Does your algorithm only work when A is positive definite?

4.7 Suppose $A \in \mathbb{R}^{m\times n}$ has full rank, where $m < n$. Show that taking $\vec{x} = A^\top(AA^\top)^{-1}\vec{b}$ solves the following optimization problem:

$$\begin{array}{ll} \min_{\vec{x}} & \|\vec{x}\|_2 \\ \text{subject to} & A\vec{x} = \vec{b}. \end{array}$$

Furthermore, show that taking $\alpha \to 0$ in the Tikhonov-regularized system from §4.1.3 recovers this choice of $\vec{x}$.

4.8 Suppose $A \in \mathbb{R}^{n\times n}$ is *tridiagonal*, meaning it can be written:

$$A = \begin{pmatrix} v_1 & w_1 & & & & \\ u_2 & v_2 & w_2 & & & \\ & u_3 & v_3 & w_3 & & \\ & & \ddots & \ddots & \ddots & \\ & & & u_{n-1} & v_{n-1} & w_{n-1} \\ & & & & u_n & v_n \end{pmatrix}.$$

Show that in this case the system $A\vec{x} = \vec{b}$ can be solved in $O(n)$ time. You can assume that A is *diagonally dominant*, meaning $|v_i| > |u_i| + |w_i|$ for all i.
Hint: Start from Gaussian elimination. This algorithm usually is attributed to [118].

4.9 Show how linear techniques can be used to solve the following optimization problem for $A \in \mathbb{R}^{m \times n}, B \in \mathbb{R}^{k \times n}, \vec{c} \in \mathbb{R}^k$:

$$\text{minimize}_{\vec{x} \in \mathbb{R}^n} \|A\vec{x}\|_2^2$$
$$\text{subject to } B\vec{x} = \vec{c}.$$

4.10 Suppose $A \in \mathbb{R}^{n \times n}$ admits a Cholesky factorization $A = LL^\top$.

   (a) Show that A must be positive semidefinite.

   (b) Use this observation to suggest an algorithm for checking if a matrix is positive semidefinite.

4.11 Are all matrix norms on $\mathbb{R}^{m \times n}$ equivalent? Why or why not?

4.12 For this problem, assume that the matrix norm $\|A\|$ for $A \in \mathbb{R}^{n \times n}$ is induced by a vector norm $\|\vec{v}\|$ for $\vec{v} \in \mathbb{R}^n$ (but it may be the case that $\| \cdot \| \neq \| \cdot \|_2$).

   (a) For $A, B \in \mathbb{R}^{n \times n}$, show $\|A + B\| \leq \|A\| + \|B\|$.

   (b) For $A, B \in \mathbb{R}^{n \times n}$ and $\vec{v} \in \mathbb{R}^n$, show $\|A\vec{v}\| \leq \|A\|\|\vec{v}\|$ and $\|AB\| \leq \|A\|\|B\|$.

   (c) For $k > 0$ and $A \in \mathbb{R}^{n \times n}$, show $\|A^k\|^{1/k} \geq |\lambda|$ for any real eigenvalue λ of A.

   (d) For $A \in \mathbb{R}^{n \times n}$ and $\|\vec{v}\|_1 \equiv \sum_i |v_i|$, show $\|A\|_1 = \max_j \sum_i |a_{ij}|$.

   (e) Prove Gelfand's formula: $\rho(A) = \lim_{k \to \infty} \|A^k\|^{1/k}$, where $\rho(A) \equiv \max\{|\lambda_i|\}$ for eigenvalues $\lambda_1, \ldots, \lambda_m$ of A. In fact, this formula holds for any matrix norm $\| \cdot \|$.

4.13 ("Screened Poisson smoothing") Suppose we sample a function $f(x)$ at n positions $x_1, x_2, \ldots, x_n$, yielding a point $\vec{y} \equiv (f(x_1), f(x_2), \ldots, f(x_n)) \in \mathbb{R}^n$. Our measurements might be noisy, however, so a common task in graphics and statistics is to smooth these values to obtain a new vector $\vec{z} \in \mathbb{R}^n$.

   (a) Provide least-squares energy terms measuring the following:
      (i) The similarity of $\vec{y}$ and $\vec{z}$.
      (ii) The smoothness of $\vec{z}$.
         Hint: We expect $f(x_{i+1}) - f(x_i)$ to be small for smooth f.

   (b) Propose an optimization problem for smoothing $\vec{y}$ using the terms above to obtain $\vec{z}$, and argue that it can be solved using linear techniques.

   (c) Suppose n is very large. What properties of the matrix in 4.13b might be relevant in choosing an effective algorithm to solve the linear system?

4.14 ("Kernel trick") In this chapter, we covered techniques for linear and nonlinear *parametric* regression. Now, we will develop a least-squares technique for *nonparametic* regression that is used commonly in machine learning and vision.

   (a) You can think of the least-squares problem as learning the vector $\vec{a}$ in a function $f(\vec{x}) = \vec{a} \cdot \vec{x}$ given a number of examples $\vec{x}^{(1)} \mapsto y^{(1)}, \ldots, \vec{x}^{(k)} \mapsto y^{(k)}$ and the assumption $f(\vec{x}^{(i)}) \approx y^{(i)}$. Suppose the columns of X are the vectors $\vec{x}^{(i)}$ and that $\vec{y}$ is the vector of values $y^{(i)}$. Provide the normal equations for recovering $\vec{a}$ with Tikhonov regularization.

(b) Show that $\vec{a} \in \text{span}\{\vec{x}^{(1)}, \ldots, \vec{x}^{(k)}\}$ in the Tikhonov-regularized system.

(c) Thus, we can write $\vec{a} = c_1\vec{x}^{(1)} + \cdots + c_k\vec{x}^{(k)}$. Give a $k \times k$ linear system of equations satisfied by $\vec{c}$ assuming $X^\top X$ is invertible.

(d) One way to do nonlinear regression might be to write a function $\phi : \mathbb{R}^n \to \mathbb{R}^m$ and learn $f_\phi(\vec{x}) = \vec{a} \cdot \phi(\vec{x})$, where ϕ may be nonlinear. Define $K(\vec{x}, \vec{y}) = \phi(\vec{x}) \cdot \phi(\vec{y})$. Assuming we continue to use regularized least-squares as in 4.14a, give an alternative form of f_ϕ that can be computed by evaluating K rather than ϕ. *Hint:* What are the elements of $X^\top X$?

(e) Consider the following formula from the Fourier transform of the Gaussian:

$$e^{-\pi(s-t)^2} = \int_{-\infty}^{\infty} e^{-\pi x^2}\left(\sin(2\pi sx)\sin(2\pi tx) + \cos(2\pi sx)\cos(2\pi tx)\right) dx.$$

Suppose we wrote $K(x, y) = e^{-\pi(x-y)^2}$. Explain how this "looks like" $\phi(x) \cdot \phi(y)$ for some ϕ. How does this suggest that the technique from 4.14d can be generalized?

4.15 ("Discrete Fourier transform") This problem deals with complex numbers, so we will take $i \equiv \sqrt{-1}$.

(a) Suppose $\theta \in \mathbb{R}$ and $n \in \mathbb{N}$. Derive *de Moivre's formula* by induction on n:

$$(\cos\theta + i\sin\theta)^n = \cos n\theta + i\sin n\theta.$$

(b) Euler's formula uses "complex exponentials" to define $e^{i\theta} \equiv \cos\theta + i\sin\theta$. Write de Moivre's formula in this notation.

(c) Define the *primitive n-th root of unity* as $\omega_n \equiv e^{-2\pi i/n}$. The *discrete Fourier transform* matrix can be written

$$W_n \equiv \frac{1}{\sqrt{n}}\begin{pmatrix} 1 & 1 & 1 & 1 & \cdots & 1 \\ 1 & \omega_n & \omega_n^2 & \omega_n^3 & \cdots & \omega_n^{n-1} \\ 1 & \omega_n^2 & \omega_n^4 & \omega_n^6 & \cdots & \omega_n^{2(n-1)} \\ 1 & \omega_n^3 & \omega_n^6 & \omega_n^9 & \cdots & \omega_n^{3(n-1)} \\ \vdots & \vdots & \vdots & \vdots & \ddots & \vdots \\ 1 & \omega_n^{n-1} & \omega_n^{2(n-1)} & \omega_n^{3(n-1)} & \cdots & \omega_n^{(n-1)(n-1)} \end{pmatrix}.$$

Show that W_n can be written in terms of a Vandermonde matrix, as defined in Example 4.3.

(d) The *complex conjugate* of $a + bi \in \mathbb{C}$, where $a, b \in \mathbb{R}$, is $\overline{a + bi} \equiv a - bi$. Show that $W_n^{-1} = W_n^*$, where $W_n^* \equiv \overline{W_n}^\top$.

(e) Suppose $n = 2^k$. In this case, show how W_n can be applied to a vector $\vec{x} \in \mathbb{C}^n$ via two applications of $W_{n/2}$ and post-processing that takes $O(n)$ time. *Note:* The *fast Fourier transform* essentially uses this technique recursively to apply W_n in $O(n\log n)$ time.

(f) Suppose that A is circulant, as described in §4.2.3. Show that $W_n^* A W_n$ is diagonal.

CHAPTER 5

Column Spaces and QR

CONTENTS

5.1   The Structure of the Normal Equations 91
5.2   Orthogonality 92
5.3   Strategy for Non-orthogonal Matrices 93
5.4   Gram-Schmidt Orthogonalization 94
    5.4.1   Projections 94
    5.4.2   Gram-Schmidt Algorithm 96
5.5   Householder Transformations 99
5.6   Reduced QR Factorization 103

O NE way to interpret the linear problem $A\vec{x} = \vec{b}$ for $\vec{x}$ is that we wish to write $\vec{b}$ as a linear combination of the columns of A with weights given in $\vec{x}$. This perspective does not change when we allow $A \in \mathbb{R}^{m \times n}$ to be non-square, but the solution may not exist or be unique depending on the structure of the column space of A. For these reasons, some techniques for factoring matrices and analyzing linear systems seek simpler representations of the column space of A to address questions regarding solvability and span more explicitly than row-based factorizations like LU.

5.1   THE STRUCTURE OF THE NORMAL EQUATIONS

As shown in §4.1.2, a necessary and sufficient condition for $\vec{x}$ to be a solution of the least-squares problem $A\vec{x} \approx \vec{b}$ is that $\vec{x}$ must satisfy the normal equations $(A^\top A)\vec{x} = A^\top \vec{b}$. This equation shows that least-squares problems can be solved using linear techniques on the matrix $A^\top A$. Methods like Cholesky factorization use the special structure of this matrix to the solver's advantage.

There is one large problem limiting the use of the normal equations, however. For now, suppose A is square; then we can write:

$$\begin{aligned}
\text{cond } A^\top A &= \|A^\top A\| \|(A^\top A)^{-1}\| \\
&\approx \|A^\top\| \|A\| \|A^{-1}\| \|(A^\top)^{-1}\| \text{ for many choices of } \| \cdot \| \\
&= \|A\|^2 \|A^{-1}\|^2 \\
&= (\text{cond } A)^2.
\end{aligned}$$

That is, the condition number of $A^\top A$ is approximately the **square** of the condition number of A! Thus, while generic linear strategies might work on $A^\top A$ when the least-squares problem is "easy," when the columns of A are nearly linearly dependent these strategies are likely to exhibit considerable error since they do not deal with A directly.

Figure 5.1 The vectors $\vec{a}_1$ and $\vec{a}_2$ nearly coincide; hence, writing $\vec{b}$ in the span of these vectors is difficult since $\vec{v}_1$ can be replaced with $\vec{v}_2$ or vice versa in a linear combination without incurring much error.

Intuitively, a primary reason that cond $A^\top A$ can be large is that columns of A might look "similar," as illustrated in Figure 5.1. Think of each column of A as a vector in $\mathbb{R}^m$. If two columns $\vec{a}_i$ and $\vec{a}_j$ satisfy $\vec{a}_i \approx \vec{a}_j$, then the least-squares residual length $\|\vec{b} - A\vec{x}\|_2$ will not suffer much if we replace multiples of $\vec{a}_i$ with multiples of $\vec{a}_j$ or vice versa. This wide range of nearly—but not completely—equivalent solutions yields poor conditioning. While the resulting vector $\vec{x}$ is unstable, however, the product $A\vec{x}$ remains nearly unchanged. If our goal is to write $\vec{b}$ in the column space of A, either approximate solution suffices. In other words, the backward error of multiple near-optimal $\vec{x}$'s is similar.

To solve such poorly conditioned problems, we will employ an alternative technique with closer attention to the column space of A rather than employing row operations as in Gaussian elimination. This strategy identifies and deals with such near-dependencies *explicitly*, bringing about greater numerical stability.

5.2 ORTHOGONALITY

We have identified why a least-squares problem might be difficult, but we might also ask when it is possible to perform least-squares without suffering from conditioning issues. If we can reduce a system to the straightforward case without inducing conditioning problems along the way, we will have found a stable way around the drawbacks explained in §5.1.

The easiest linear system to solve is $I_{n\times n}\vec{x} = \vec{b}$, where $I_{n\times n}$ is the $n \times n$ identity matrix: The solution is $\vec{x} = \vec{b}$! We are unlikely to bother using a linear solver to invert this particular linear system on purpose, but we may do so accidentally while solving least-squares. Even when $A \neq I_{n\times n}$—A may not even be square—we may, in particularly lucky circumstances, find that the Gram matrix $A^\top A$ satisfies $A^\top A = I_{n\times n}$, making least-squares trivial. To avoid confusion with the general case, we will use the variable Q to represent such a matrix satisfying $Q^\top Q = I_{n\times n}$.

While simply praying that $Q^\top Q = I_{n\times n}$ unlikely will yield a useful algorithm, we can examine this case to see how it becomes so favorable. Write the columns of Q as vectors $\vec{q}_1, \cdots, \vec{q}_n \in \mathbb{R}^m$. Then, the product $Q^\top Q$ has the following structure:

$$Q^\top Q = \begin{pmatrix} - & \vec{q}_1^\top & - \\ - & \vec{q}_2^\top & - \\ & \vdots & \\ - & \vec{q}_n^\top & - \end{pmatrix} \begin{pmatrix} | & | & & | \\ \vec{q}_1 & \vec{q}_2 & \cdots & \vec{q}_n \\ | & | & & | \end{pmatrix} = \begin{pmatrix} \vec{q}_1 \cdot \vec{q}_1 & \vec{q}_1 \cdot \vec{q}_2 & \cdots & \vec{q}_1 \cdot \vec{q}_n \\ \vec{q}_2 \cdot \vec{q}_1 & \vec{q}_2 \cdot \vec{q}_2 & \cdots & \vec{q}_2 \cdot \vec{q}_n \\ \vdots & \vdots & \cdots & \vdots \\ \vec{q}_n \cdot \vec{q}_1 & \vec{q}_n \cdot \vec{q}_2 & \cdots & \vec{q}_n \cdot \vec{q}_n \end{pmatrix}.$$

Setting the expression on the right equal to $I_{n\times n}$ yields the following relationship:

$$\vec{q}_i \cdot \vec{q}_j = \begin{cases} 1 & \text{when } i = j \\ 0 & \text{when } i \neq j. \end{cases}$$

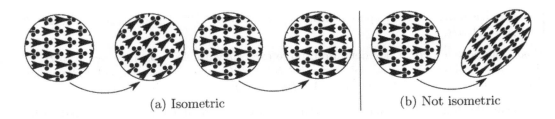

(a) Isometric | (b) Not isometric

Figure 5.2 Isometries can (a) rotate and flip vectors but cannot (b) stretch or shear them.

In other words, the columns of Q are unit-length and orthogonal to one another. We say that they form an *orthonormal basis* for the column space of Q:

Definition 5.1 (Orthonormal; orthogonal matrix). A set of vectors $\{\vec{v}_1, \cdots, \vec{v}_k\}$ is *orthonormal* if $\|\vec{v}_i\|_2 = 1$ for all i and $\vec{v}_i \cdot \vec{v}_j = 0$ for all $i \neq j$. A square matrix whose columns are orthonormal is called an *orthogonal* matrix.

The standard basis $\{\vec{e}_1, \vec{e}_2, \ldots, \vec{e}_n\}$ is an example of an orthonormal basis, and since the columns of the identity matrix $I_{n \times n}$ are these vectors, $I_{n \times n}$ is an orthogonal matrix.

We motivated our discussion by asking when we can expect $Q^\top Q = I_{n \times n}$. Now we know that this condition occurs exactly when the columns of Q are orthonormal. Furthermore, if Q is square and invertible with $Q^\top Q = I_{n \times n}$, then by multiplying both sides of the expression $Q^\top Q = I_{n \times n}$ by Q^{-1} shows $Q^{-1} = Q^\top$. Hence, $Q\vec{x} = \vec{b}$ is equivalent to $\vec{x} = Q^\top \vec{b}$ after multiplying both sides by the transpose $Q^\top$.

Orthonormality has a strong geometric interpretation. Recall from Chapter 1 that we can regard two orthogonal vectors $\vec{a}$ and $\vec{b}$ as being *perpendicular*. So, an orthonormal set of vectors is a set of mutually perpendicular unit vectors in $\mathbb{R}^n$. Furthermore, if Q is orthogonal, then its action does not affect the length of vectors:

$$\|Q\vec{x}\|_2^2 = \vec{x}^\top Q^\top Q\vec{x} = \vec{x}^\top I_{n \times n}\vec{x} = \vec{x} \cdot \vec{x} = \|\vec{x}\|_2^2.$$

Similarly, Q cannot affect the angle between two vectors, since:

$$(Q\vec{x}) \cdot (Q\vec{y}) = \vec{x}^\top Q^\top Q\vec{y} = \vec{x}^\top I_{n \times n}\vec{y} = \vec{x} \cdot \vec{y}.$$

From this standpoint, if Q is orthogonal, then the operation $\vec{x} \mapsto Q\vec{x}$ is an *isometry* of $\mathbb{R}^n$, that is, it preserves lengths and angles. As illustrated in Figure 5.2, Q can rotate or reflect vectors but cannot scale or shear them. From a high level, the linear algebra of orthogonal matrices is easier because their actions do not affect the geometry of the underlying space.

5.3 STRATEGY FOR NON-ORTHOGONAL MATRICES

Most matrices A encountered when solving $A\vec{x} = \vec{b}$ or the least-squares problem $A\vec{x} \approx \vec{b}$ will not be orthogonal, so the machinery of §5.2 does not apply directly. For this reason, we must do some additional computations to connect the general case to the orthogonal one. To this end, we will derive an alternative to LU factorization using orthogonal rather than substitution matrices.

Take a matrix $A \in \mathbb{R}^{m \times n}$, and denote its column space as col A; col A is the span of the columns of A. Now, suppose a matrix $B \in \mathbb{R}^{n \times n}$ is invertible. We make the following observation about the column space of AB relative to that of A:

Proposition 5.1 (Column space invariance). *For any $A \in \mathbb{R}^{m \times n}$ and invertible $B \in \mathbb{R}^{n \times n}$, col $A =$ col AB.*

Proof. Suppose $\vec{b} \in$ col A. By definition, there exists $\vec{x}$ with $A\vec{x} = \vec{b}$. If we take $\vec{y} = B^{-1}\vec{x}$, then $AB\vec{y} = (AB) \cdot (B^{-1}\vec{x}) = A\vec{x} = \vec{b}$, so $\vec{b} \in$ col AB. Conversely, take $\vec{c} \in$ col AB, so there exists $\vec{y}$ with $(AB)\vec{y} = \vec{c}$. In this case, $A \cdot (B\vec{y}) = \vec{c}$, showing that $\vec{c} \in$ col A. $\qquad\square$

Recall the "elimination matrix" description of Gaussian elimination: We started with a matrix A and applied row operation matrices E_i such that the sequence $A, E_1 A, E_2 E_1 A, \ldots$ eventually reduced to more easily solved triangular systems. The proposition above suggests an alternative strategy for situations like least-squares in which we care about the column space of A: Apply *column* operations to A by *post*-multiplication until the columns are orthonormal. So long as these operations are invertible, Proposition 5.1 shows that the column spaces of the modified matrices will be the same as the column space of A.

In the end, we will attempt to find a product $Q = AE_1 E_2 \cdots E_k$ starting from A and applying invertible operation matrices E_i such that Q is orthonormal. As we have argued above, the proposition shows that col $Q =$ col A. Inverting these operations yields a factorization $A = QR$ for $R = E_k^{-1} E_{k-1}^{-1} \cdots E_1^{-1}$. The columns of the matrix Q contain an orthonormal basis for the column space of A, and with careful design we can once again make R upper triangular.

When $A = QR$, by orthogonality of Q we have $A^\top A = R^\top Q^\top QR = R^\top R$. Making this substitution, the normal equations $A^\top A\vec{x} = A^\top \vec{b}$ imply $R^\top R\vec{x} = R^\top Q^\top \vec{b}$, or equivalently $R\vec{x} = Q^\top \vec{b}$. If we design R to be a triangular matrix, then solving the least-squares system $A^\top A\vec{x} = A^\top \vec{b}$ can be carried out efficiently by back-substitution via $R\vec{x} = Q^\top \vec{b}$.

5.4 GRAM-SCHMIDT ORTHOGONALIZATION

Our first algorithm for QR factorization follows naturally from our discussion above but may suffer from numerical issues. We use it here as an initial example of orthogonalization and then will improve upon it with better operations.

5.4.1 Projections

Suppose we have two vectors $\vec{a}$ and $\vec{b}$, with $\vec{a} \neq \vec{0}$. Then, we could easily ask, "Which multiple of $\vec{a}$ is closest to $\vec{b}$?" Mathematically, this task is equivalent to minimizing $\|c\vec{a} - \vec{b}\|_2^2$ over all possible $c \in \mathbb{R}$. If we think of $\vec{a}$ and $\vec{b}$ as $n \times 1$ matrices and c as a 1×1 matrix, then this is nothing more than an unconventional least-squares problem $\vec{a} \cdot c \approx \vec{b}$. In this formulation, the normal equations show $\vec{a}^\top \vec{a} \cdot c = \vec{a}^\top \vec{b}$, or

$$c = \frac{\vec{a} \cdot \vec{b}}{\vec{a} \cdot \vec{a}} = \frac{\vec{a} \cdot \vec{b}}{\|\vec{a}\|_2^2}.$$

We denote the resulting *projection* of $\vec{b}$ onto $\vec{a}$ as:

$$\text{proj}_{\vec{a}}\, \vec{b} \equiv c\vec{a} = \frac{\vec{a} \cdot \vec{b}}{\vec{a} \cdot \vec{a}}\vec{a} = \frac{\vec{a} \cdot \vec{b}}{\|\vec{a}\|_2^2}\vec{a}.$$

By design, $\text{proj}_{\vec{a}}\, \vec{b}$ is parallel to $\vec{a}$. What about the remainder $\vec{b} - \text{proj}_{\vec{a}}\vec{b}$? We can do the following computation to find out:

$$\vec{a} \cdot (\vec{b} - \text{proj}_{\vec{a}}\, \vec{b}) = \vec{a} \cdot \vec{b} - \vec{a} \cdot \left(\frac{\vec{a} \cdot \vec{b}}{\|\vec{a}\|_2^2}\vec{a}\right) \quad \text{by definition of } \text{proj}_{\vec{a}}\, \vec{b}$$

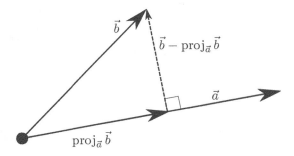

Figure 5.3 The projection $\text{proj}_{\vec{a}}\,\vec{b}$ is parallel to $\vec{a}$, while the remainder $\vec{b} - \text{proj}_{\vec{a}}\,\vec{b}$ is perpendicular to $\vec{a}$.

$$= \vec{a} \cdot \vec{b} - \frac{\vec{a} \cdot \vec{b}}{\|\vec{a}\|_2^2}(\vec{a} \cdot \vec{a}) \text{ by moving the constant outside the dot product}$$

$$= \vec{a} \cdot \vec{b} - \vec{a} \cdot \vec{b} \text{ since } \vec{a} \cdot \vec{a} = \|\vec{a}\|_2^2$$

$$= 0.$$

This simplification shows we have decomposed $\vec{b}$ into a component $\text{proj}_{\vec{a}}\,\vec{b}$ parallel to $\vec{a}$ and another component $\vec{b} - \text{proj}_{\vec{a}}\,\vec{b}$ orthogonal to $\vec{a}$, as illustrated in Figure 5.3.

Now, suppose that $\hat{a}_1, \hat{a}_2, \cdots, \hat{a}_k$ are orthonormal; for clarity, in this section we will put hats over vectors with unit length. For any single i, by the projection formula above

$$\text{proj}_{\hat{a}_i}\,\vec{b} = (\hat{a}_i \cdot \vec{b})\hat{a}_i.$$

The denominator does not appear because $\|\hat{a}_i\|_2 = 1$ by definition. More generally, however, we can project $\vec{b}$ onto span $\{\hat{a}_1, \cdots, \hat{a}_k\}$ by minimizing the following energy function E over $c_1, \ldots, c_k \in \mathbb{R}$:

$$E(c_1, c_2, \ldots, c_k) \equiv \|c_1\hat{a}_1 + c_2\hat{a}_2 + \cdots + c_k\hat{a}_k - \vec{b}\|_2^2$$

$$= \left(\sum_{i=1}^{k}\sum_{j=1}^{k} c_i c_j (\hat{a}_i \cdot \hat{a}_j)\right) - 2\vec{b} \cdot \left(\sum_{i=1}^{k} c_i \hat{a}_i\right) + \vec{b} \cdot \vec{b}$$

$$\text{by applying and expanding } \|\vec{v}\|_2^2 = \vec{v} \cdot \vec{v}$$

$$= \sum_{i=1}^{k}\left(c_i^2 - 2c_i\vec{b} \cdot \hat{a}_i\right) + \|\vec{b}\|_2^2 \text{ since the } \hat{a}_i\text{'s are orthonormal.}$$

The second step here is *only* valid because of orthonormality of the $\hat{a}_i$'s. At a minimum, the derivative of this energy with respect to c_i is zero for every i, yielding the relationship

$$0 = \frac{\partial E}{\partial c_i} = 2c_i - 2\vec{b} \cdot \hat{a}_i \implies c_i = \hat{a}_i \cdot \vec{b}.$$

This argument shows that when $\hat{a}_1, \cdots, \hat{a}_k$ are orthonormal,

$$\text{proj}_{\text{span }\{\hat{a}_1, \cdots, \hat{a}_k\}}\,\vec{b} = (\hat{a}_1 \cdot \vec{b})\hat{a}_1 + \cdots + (\hat{a}_k \cdot \vec{b})\hat{a}_k.$$

This formula extends the formula for $\text{proj}_{\vec{a}}\,\vec{b}$, and by a proof identical to the one above for single-vector projections, we must have

$$\hat{a}_i \cdot (\vec{b} - \text{proj}_{\text{span }\{\hat{a}_1, \cdots, \hat{a}_k\}}\,\vec{b}) = 0.$$

---

function GRAM-SCHMIDT$(\vec{v}_1, \vec{v}_2, \ldots, \vec{v}_k)$
   ▷ Computes an orthonormal basis $\hat{a}_1, \ldots, \hat{a}_k$ for span $\{\vec{v}_1, \ldots, \vec{v}_k\}$
   ▷ Assumes $\vec{v}_1, \ldots, \vec{v}_k$ are linearly independent.
$\hat{a}_1 \leftarrow \vec{v}_1/\|\vec{v}_1\|_2$ ▷ Nothing to project out of the first vector
for $i \leftarrow 2, 3, \ldots, k$
   $\vec{p} \leftarrow \vec{0}$ ▷ Projection of $\vec{v}_i$ onto span $\{\hat{a}_1, \ldots, \hat{a}_{i-1}\}$
   for $j \leftarrow 1, 2, \ldots, i-1$
      $\vec{p} \leftarrow \vec{p} + (\vec{v}_i \cdot \hat{a}_j)\hat{a}_j$ ▷ Projecting onto orthonormal basis
   $\vec{r} \leftarrow \vec{v}_i - \vec{p}$ ▷ Residual is orthogonal to current basis
   $\hat{a}_i \leftarrow \vec{r}/\|\vec{r}\|_2$ ▷ Normalize this residual and add it to the basis
return $\{\hat{a}_1, \ldots, \hat{a}_k\}$

Figure 5.4 The Gram-Schmidt algorithm for orthogonalization. This implementation assumes that the input vectors are linearly independent; in practice, linear dependence can be detected by checking for division by zero.

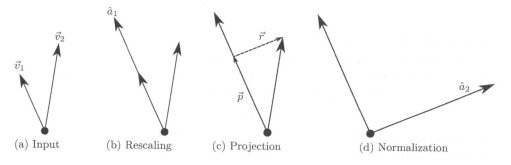

(a) Input   (b) Rescaling   (c) Projection   (d) Normalization

Figure 5.5 Steps of the Gram-Schmidt algorithm on (a) two vectors $\vec{v}_1$ and $\vec{v}_2$: (b) $\hat{a}_1$ is a rescaled version of $\vec{v}_1$; (c) $\vec{v}_2$ is decomposed into a parallel component $\vec{p}$ and a residual $\vec{r}$; (d) $\vec{r}$ is normalized to obtain $\hat{a}_2$.

Once again, we separated $\vec{b}$ into a component parallel to the span of the $\hat{a}_i$'s and a perpendicular residual.

5.4.2   Gram-Schmidt Algorithm

Our observations above lead to an algorithm for *orthogonalization*, or building an orthogonal basis $\{\hat{a}_1, \cdots, \hat{a}_k\}$ whose span is the same as that of a set of linearly independent but not necessarily orthogonal input vectors $\{\vec{v}_1, \cdots, \vec{v}_k\}$.

We add one vector at a time to the basis, starting with $\vec{v}_1$, then $\vec{v}_2$, and so on. When $\vec{v}_i$ is added to the current basis $\{\hat{a}_1, \ldots, \hat{a}_{i-1}\}$, we project out the span of $\hat{a}_1, \ldots, \hat{a}_{i-1}$. By the discussion in §5.4.1 the remaining residual must be orthogonal to the current basis, so we divide this residual by its norm to make it unit-length and add it to the basis. This technique, known as *Gram-Schmidt orthogonalization*, is detailed in Figure 5.4 and illustrated in Figure 5.5.

Example 5.1 (Gram-Schmidt orthogonalization). Suppose we are given $\vec{v}_1 = (1, 0, 0)$, $\vec{v}_2 = (1, 1, 1)$, and $\vec{v}_3 = (1, 1, 0)$. The Gram-Schmidt algorithm proceeds as follows:

1. The first vector $\vec{v}_1$ is already unit-length, so we take $\hat{a}_1 = \vec{v}_1 = (1, 0, 0)$.

2. Now, we remove the span of $\hat{a}_1$ from the second vector $\vec{v}_2$:

$$\vec{v}_2 - \text{proj}_{\hat{a}_1} \vec{v}_2 = \begin{pmatrix} 1 \\ 1 \\ 1 \end{pmatrix} - \left[\begin{pmatrix} 1 \\ 0 \\ 0 \end{pmatrix} \cdot \begin{pmatrix} 1 \\ 1 \\ 1 \end{pmatrix} \right] \begin{pmatrix} 1 \\ 0 \\ 0 \end{pmatrix} = \begin{pmatrix} 0 \\ 1 \\ 1 \end{pmatrix}.$$

Dividing this vector by its norm, we take $\hat{a}_2 = (0, 1/\sqrt{2}, 1/\sqrt{2})$.

3. Finally, we remove span $\{\hat{a}_1, \hat{a}_2\}$ from $\vec{v}_3$:

$$\vec{v}_3 - \text{proj}_{\text{span}\,\{\hat{a}_1, \hat{a}_2\}} \vec{v}_3$$

$$= \begin{pmatrix} 1 \\ 1 \\ 0 \end{pmatrix} - \left[\begin{pmatrix} 1 \\ 0 \\ 0 \end{pmatrix} \cdot \begin{pmatrix} 1 \\ 1 \\ 0 \end{pmatrix} \right] \begin{pmatrix} 1 \\ 0 \\ 0 \end{pmatrix} - \left[\begin{pmatrix} 0 \\ 1/\sqrt{2} \\ 1/\sqrt{2} \end{pmatrix} \cdot \begin{pmatrix} 1 \\ 1 \\ 0 \end{pmatrix} \right] \begin{pmatrix} 0 \\ 1/\sqrt{2} \\ 1/\sqrt{2} \end{pmatrix}$$

$$= \begin{pmatrix} 0 \\ 1/2 \\ -1/2 \end{pmatrix}.$$

Normalizing this vector yields $\hat{a}_3 = (0, 1/\sqrt{2}, -1/\sqrt{2})$.

If we start with a matrix $A \in \mathbb{R}^{m \times n}$ whose columns are $\vec{v}_1, \cdots, \vec{v}_k$, then we can implement Gram-Schmidt using a series of column operations on A. Dividing column i of A by its norm is equivalent to post-multiplying A by a $k \times k$ diagonal matrix. The projection step for column i involves subtracting only multiples of columns j with $j < i$, and thus this operation can be implemented with an upper-triangular elimination matrix. Thus, our discussion in §5.3 applies, and we can use Gram-Schmidt to obtain a factorization $A = QR$. When the columns of A are linearly independent, one way to find R is as a product $R = Q^\top A$; a more stable approach is to keep track of operations as we did for Gaussian elimination.

Example 5.2 (QR factorization). Suppose we construct a matrix whose columns are $\vec{v}_1$, $\vec{v}_2$, and $\vec{v}_3$ from Example 5.1:

$$A \equiv \begin{pmatrix} 1 & 1 & 1 \\ 0 & 1 & 1 \\ 0 & 1 & 0 \end{pmatrix}.$$

The output of Gram-Schmidt orthogonalization can be encoded in the matrix

$$Q \equiv \begin{pmatrix} 1 & 0 & 0 \\ 0 & 1/\sqrt{2} & 1/\sqrt{2} \\ 0 & 1/\sqrt{2} & -1/\sqrt{2} \end{pmatrix}.$$

We can obtain the upper-triangular matrix R in the QR factorization two different ways. First, we can compute R after the fact using a product:

$$R = Q^\top A = \begin{pmatrix} 1 & 0 & 0 \\ 0 & 1/\sqrt{2} & 1/\sqrt{2} \\ 0 & 1/\sqrt{2} & -1/\sqrt{2} \end{pmatrix}^\top \begin{pmatrix} 1 & 1 & 1 \\ 0 & 1 & 1 \\ 0 & 1 & 0 \end{pmatrix} = \begin{pmatrix} 1 & 1 & 1 \\ 0 & \sqrt{2} & 1/\sqrt{2} \\ 0 & 0 & 1/\sqrt{2} \end{pmatrix}.$$

As expected, R is upper triangular.

---

function MODIFIED-GRAM-SCHMIDT($\vec{v}_1, \vec{v}_2, \ldots, \vec{v}_k$)
  ▷ Computes an orthonormal basis $\hat{a}_1, \ldots, \hat{a}_k$ for span $\{\vec{v}_1, \ldots, \vec{v}_k\}$
  ▷ Assumes $\vec{v}_1, \ldots, \vec{v}_k$ are linearly independent.
  for $i \leftarrow 1, 2, \ldots, k$
    $\hat{a}_i \leftarrow \vec{v}_i / \|\vec{v}_i\|_2$ ▷ Normalize the current vector and store in the basis
    for $j \leftarrow i+1, i+2, \ldots, k$
      $\vec{v}_j \leftarrow \vec{v}_j - (\vec{v}_j \cdot \hat{a}_i)\hat{a}_i$ ▷ Project $\hat{a}_i$ out of the remaining vectors
  return $\{\hat{a}_1, \ldots, \hat{a}_k\}$

Figure 5.6 The modified Gram-Schmidt algorithm.

We can also return to the steps of Gram-Schmidt orthogonalization to obtain R from the sequence of elimination matrices. A compact way to write the steps of Gram-Schmidt from Example 5.1 is as follows:

$$\text{Step 1: } Q_0 = \begin{pmatrix} 1 & 1 & 1 \\ 0 & 1 & 1 \\ 0 & 1 & 0 \end{pmatrix}$$

$$\text{Step 2: } Q_1 = Q_0 E_1 = \begin{pmatrix} 1 & 1 & 1 \\ 0 & 1 & 1 \\ 0 & 1 & 0 \end{pmatrix} \begin{pmatrix} 1 & -1/\sqrt{2} & 0 \\ 0 & 1/\sqrt{2} & 0 \\ 0 & 0 & 1 \end{pmatrix} = \begin{pmatrix} 1 & 0 & 1 \\ 0 & 1/\sqrt{2} & 1 \\ 0 & 1/\sqrt{2} & 0 \end{pmatrix}$$

$$\text{Step 3: } Q_2 = Q_1 E_2 = \begin{pmatrix} 1 & 0 & 1 \\ 0 & 1/\sqrt{2} & 1 \\ 0 & 1/\sqrt{2} & 0 \end{pmatrix} \begin{pmatrix} 1 & 0 & -\sqrt{2} \\ 0 & 1 & -1 \\ 0 & 0 & \sqrt{2} \end{pmatrix} = \begin{pmatrix} 1 & 0 & 0 \\ 0 & 1/\sqrt{2} & 1/\sqrt{2} \\ 0 & 1/\sqrt{2} & -1/\sqrt{2} \end{pmatrix}.$$

These steps show $Q = AE_1E_2$, or equivalently $A = QE_2^{-1}E_1^{-1}$. This gives a second way to compute R:

$$R = E_2^{-1}E_1^{-1} = \begin{pmatrix} 1 & 0 & 1 \\ 0 & 1 & 1/\sqrt{2} \\ 0 & 0 & 1/\sqrt{2} \end{pmatrix} \begin{pmatrix} 1 & 1 & 0 \\ 0 & \sqrt{2} & 0 \\ 0 & 0 & 1 \end{pmatrix} = \begin{pmatrix} 1 & 1 & 1 \\ 0 & \sqrt{2} & 1/\sqrt{2} \\ 0 & 0 & 1/\sqrt{2} \end{pmatrix}.$$

The Gram-Schmidt algorithm is well known to be numerically unstable. There are many reasons for this instability that may or may not appear depending on the particular application. For instance, thanks to rounding and other issues, it might be the case that the $\hat{a}_i$'s are not completely orthogonal after the projection step. Our projection formula for finding $\vec{p}$ within the algorithm in Figure 5.4, however, only works when the $\hat{a}_i$'s are orthogonal. For this reason, in the presence of rounding, the projection $\vec{p}$ of $\vec{v}_i$ becomes less accurate.

One way around this issue is the "modified Gram-Schmidt" (MGS) algorithm in Figure 5.6, which has similar running time but makes a subtle change in the way projections are computed. Rather than computing the projection $\vec{p}$ in each iteration i onto span $\{\hat{a}_1, \ldots, \hat{a}_{i-1}\}$, as soon as $\hat{a}_i$ is computed it is projected out of $\vec{v}_{i+1}, \ldots, \vec{v}_k$; subsequently we never have to consider $\hat{a}_i$ again. This way, even if the basis globally is not completely orthogonal due to rounding, the projection step is valid since it only projects onto one $\hat{a}_i$ at a time. In the absence of rounding, modified Gram-Schmidt and classical Gram-Schmidt generate identical output.

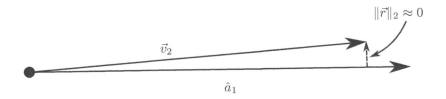

Figure 5.7 A failure mode of the basic and modified Gram-Schmidt algorithms; here $\hat{a}_1$ is nearly parallel to $\vec{v}_2$ and hence the residual $\vec{r}$ is vanishingly small.

A more subtle instability in the Gram-Schmidt algorithm is *not* resolved by MGS and can introduce serious numerical instabilities during the subtraction step. Suppose we provide the vectors $\vec{v}_1 = (1,1)$ and $\vec{v}_2 = (1+\varepsilon, 1)$ as input to Gram-Schmidt for some $0 < \varepsilon \ll 1$. A reasonable basis for span $\{\vec{v}_1, \vec{v}_2\}$ might be $\{(1,0), (0,1)\}$. But, if we apply Gram-Schmidt, we obtain:

$$\hat{a}_1 = \frac{\vec{v}_1}{\|\vec{v}_1\|} = \frac{1}{\sqrt{2}} \begin{pmatrix} 1 \\ 1 \end{pmatrix}$$

$$\vec{p} = \frac{2+\varepsilon}{2} \begin{pmatrix} 1 \\ 1 \end{pmatrix}$$

$$\vec{r} = \vec{v}_2 - \vec{p} = \begin{pmatrix} 1+\varepsilon \\ 1 \end{pmatrix} - \frac{2+\varepsilon}{2} \begin{pmatrix} 1 \\ 1 \end{pmatrix}$$

$$= \frac{1}{2} \begin{pmatrix} \varepsilon \\ -\varepsilon \end{pmatrix}.$$

Taking the norm, $\|\vec{v}_2 - \vec{p}\|_2 = (\sqrt{2}/2) \cdot \varepsilon$, so computing $\hat{a}_2 = (1/\sqrt{2}, -1/\sqrt{2})$ will require division by a scalar on the order of ε. Division by small numbers is an unstable numerical operation that generally should be avoided. A geometric interpretation of this case is shown in Figure 5.7.

5.5 HOUSEHOLDER TRANSFORMATIONS

In §5.3, we motivated the construction of QR factorization through the use of column operations. This construction is reasonable in the context of analyzing column spaces, but as we saw in our derivation of the Gram-Schmidt algorithm, the resulting numerical techniques can be unstable.

Rather than starting with A and post-multiplying by column operations to obtain $Q = AE_1 \cdots E_k$, however, we can also start with A and *pre*-multiply by orthogonal matrices Q_i to obtain $Q_k \cdots Q_1 A = R$. These Q's will act like row operations, eliminating elements of A until the resulting product R is upper triangular. Thanks to orthogonality of the Q's, we can write $A = (Q_1^\top \cdots Q_k^\top)R$, obtaining the QR factorization since products and transposes of orthogonal matrices are orthogonal.

The row operation matrices we used in Gaussian elimination and LU will not suffice for QR factorization since they are not orthogonal. Several alternatives have been suggested; we will introduce a common orthogonal row operation introduced in 1958 by Alston Scott Householder [65].

The space of orthogonal $n \times n$ matrices is very large, so we seek a smaller set of possible Q_i's that is easier to work with while still powerful enough to implement elimination

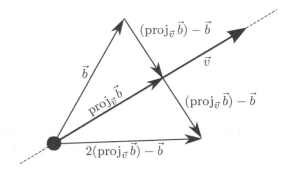

Figure 5.8 Reflecting $\vec{b}$ over $\vec{v}$.

operations. To develop some intuition, from our geometric discussions in §5.2 we know that orthogonal matrices must preserve angles and lengths, so intuitively they only can rotate and reflect vectors. Householder proposed using only reflection operations to reduce A to upper-triangular form. A well-known alternative by Givens uses only rotations to accomplish the same task [48] and is explored in Exercise 5.11.

One way to write an orthogonal reflection matrix is in terms of projections, as illustrated in Figure 5.8. Suppose we have a vector $\vec{b}$ that we wish to reflect over a vector $\vec{v}$. We have shown that the residual $\vec{r} \equiv \vec{b} - \text{proj}_{\vec{v}}\vec{b}$ is perpendicular to $\vec{v}$. Following the reverse of this direction twice shows that the difference $2\text{proj}_{\vec{v}}\vec{b} - \vec{b}$ reflects $\vec{b}$ *over* $\vec{v}$.

We can expand our reflection formula as follows:

$$2\text{proj}_{\vec{v}}\vec{b} - \vec{b} = 2\frac{\vec{v} \cdot \vec{b}}{\vec{v} \cdot \vec{v}}\vec{v} - \vec{b} \text{ by definition of projection}$$

$$= 2\vec{v} \cdot \frac{\vec{v}^\top \vec{b}}{\vec{v}^\top \vec{v}} - \vec{b} \text{ using matrix notation}$$

$$= \left(\frac{2\vec{v}\vec{v}^\top}{\vec{v}^\top \vec{v}} - I_{n \times n}\right)\vec{b}$$

$$\equiv -H_{\vec{v}}\vec{b}, \text{ where we define } H_{\vec{v}} \equiv I_{n \times n} - \frac{2\vec{v}\vec{v}^\top}{\vec{v}^\top \vec{v}}.$$

By this factorization, we can think of reflecting $\vec{b}$ over $\vec{v}$ as applying a matrix $-H_{\vec{v}}$ to $\vec{b}$; $-H_{\vec{v}}$ has no dependence on $\vec{b}$. $H_{\vec{v}}$ without the negative is still orthogonal, and by convention we will use it from now on. Our derivation will parallel that in [58].

Like in forward-substitution, in our first step we wish to pre-multiply A by a matrix that takes the first column of A, which we will denote $\vec{a}$, to some multiple of the first identity vector $\vec{e}_1$. Using reflections rather than forward-substitutions, however, we now need to find some $\vec{v}, c$ such that $H_{\vec{v}}\vec{a} = c\vec{e}_1$. Expanding this relationship,

$$c\vec{e}_1 = H_{\vec{v}}\vec{a}, \text{ as explained above}$$

$$= \left(I_{n \times n} - \frac{2\vec{v}\vec{v}^\top}{\vec{v}^\top \vec{v}}\right)\vec{a}, \text{ by definition of } H_{\vec{v}}$$

$$= \vec{a} - 2\vec{v}\frac{\vec{v}^\top \vec{a}}{\vec{v}^\top \vec{v}}.$$

Moving terms around shows

$$\vec{v} = (\vec{a} - c\vec{e}_1) \cdot \frac{\vec{v}^\top \vec{v}}{2\vec{v}^\top \vec{a}}.$$

In other words, if $H_{\vec{v}}$ accomplishes the desired reflection, then $\vec{v}$ must be parallel to the difference $\vec{a} - c\vec{e}_1$. Scaling $\vec{v}$ does not affect the formula for $H_{\vec{v}}$, so for now assuming such an $H_{\vec{v}}$ exists we can attempt to *choose* $\vec{v} = \vec{a} - c\vec{e}_1$.

If this choice is valid, then substituting $\vec{v} = \vec{a} - c\vec{e}_1$ into the simplified expression shows

$$\vec{v} = \vec{v} \cdot \frac{\vec{v}^\top \vec{v}}{2\vec{v}^\top \vec{a}}.$$

Assuming $\vec{v} \neq \vec{0}$, the coefficient next to $\vec{v}$ on the right-hand side must be 1, showing:

$$1 = \frac{\vec{v}^\top \vec{v}}{2\vec{v}^\top \vec{a}}$$
$$= \frac{\|\vec{a}\|_2^2 - 2c\vec{e}_1 \cdot \vec{a} + c^2}{2(\vec{a} \cdot \vec{a} - c\vec{e}_1 \cdot \vec{a})}$$
$$\text{or, } 0 = \|\vec{a}\|_2^2 - c^2 \implies c = \pm\|\vec{a}\|_2.$$

After choosing $c = \pm\|\vec{a}\|_2$, our steps above are all reversible. We originally set out to find $\vec{v}$ such that $H_{\vec{v}}\vec{a} = c\vec{e}_1$. By taking $\vec{v} = \vec{a} - c\vec{e}_1$ with $c = \pm\|\vec{a}\|_2$, the steps above show:

$$H_{\vec{v}}A = \begin{pmatrix} c & \times & \times & \times \\ 0 & \times & \times & \times \\ \vdots & \vdots & \vdots & \vdots \\ 0 & \times & \times & \times \end{pmatrix}.$$

We have just accomplished a step similar to forward elimination using orthogonal matrices!

Example 5.3 (Householder transformation). Suppose

$$A = \begin{pmatrix} 2 & -1 & 5 \\ 2 & 1 & 2 \\ 1 & 0 & -2 \end{pmatrix}.$$

The first column of A has norm $\sqrt{2^2 + 2^2 + 1^2} = 3$, so if we take $c = 3$ we can write:

$$\vec{v} = \vec{a} - c\vec{e}_1 = \begin{pmatrix} 2 \\ 2 \\ 1 \end{pmatrix} - 3\begin{pmatrix} 1 \\ 0 \\ 0 \end{pmatrix} = \begin{pmatrix} -1 \\ 2 \\ 1 \end{pmatrix}.$$

This choice of $\vec{v}$ gives elimination matrix

$$H_{\vec{v}} = I_{3\times3} - \frac{2\vec{v}\vec{v}^\top}{\vec{v}^\top \vec{v}} = \frac{1}{3}\begin{pmatrix} 2 & 2 & 1 \\ 2 & -1 & -2 \\ 1 & -2 & 2 \end{pmatrix}.$$

As expected, $H_{\vec{v}}^\top H_{\vec{v}} = I_{3\times3}$. Furthermore, $H_{\vec{v}}$ eliminates the first column of A:

$$H_{\vec{v}}A = \frac{1}{3}\begin{pmatrix} 2 & 2 & 1 \\ 2 & -1 & -2 \\ 1 & -2 & 2 \end{pmatrix}\begin{pmatrix} 2 & -1 & 5 \\ 2 & 1 & 2 \\ 1 & 0 & -2 \end{pmatrix} = \begin{pmatrix} 3 & 0 & 4 \\ 0 & -1 & 4 \\ 0 & -1 & -1 \end{pmatrix}.$$

To fully reduce A to upper-triangular form, we must repeat the steps above to eliminate all elements of A below the diagonal. During the k-th step of triangularization, we can take

---

function HOUSEHOLDER-QR(A)
   ▷ Factors $A \in \mathbb{R}^{m \times n}$ as $A = QR$.
   ▷ $Q \in \mathbb{R}^{m \times m}$ is orthogonal and $R \in \mathbb{R}^{m \times n}$ is upper triangular

  $Q \leftarrow I_{m \times m}$
  $R \leftarrow A$
  for $k \leftarrow 1, 2, \ldots, m$
    $\vec{a} \leftarrow R\vec{e}_k$ ▷ Isolate column k of R and store it in $\vec{a}$
    $(\vec{a}_1, \vec{a}_2) \leftarrow$ SPLIT$(\vec{a}, k - 1)$ ▷ Separate off the first $k - 1$ elements of $\vec{a}$

    $c \leftarrow \|\vec{a}_2\|_2$ ▷ Find reflection vector $\vec{v}$ for the Householder matrix $H_{\vec{v}}$
    $\vec{v} \leftarrow \begin{pmatrix} \vec{0} \\ \vec{a}_2 \end{pmatrix} - c\vec{e}_k$

    $R \leftarrow H_{\vec{v}}R$ ▷ Eliminate elements below the diagonal of the k-th column
    $Q \leftarrow QH_{\vec{v}}^{\top}$
  return Q, R

Figure 5.9 Householder QR factorization; the products with $H_{\vec{v}}$ can be carried out in quadratic time after expanding the formula for $H_{\vec{v}}$ in terms of $\vec{v}$ (see Exercise 5.2).

$\vec{a}$ to be the k-th column of $Q_{k-1}Q_{k-2} \cdots Q_1 A$, where the Q_i's are reflection matrices like the one derived above. We can split $\vec{a}$ into two components:

$$\vec{a} = \begin{pmatrix} \vec{a}_1 \\ \vec{a}_2 \end{pmatrix}.$$

Here, $\vec{a}_1 \in \mathbb{R}^{k-1}$ and $\vec{a}_2 \in \mathbb{R}^{m-k+1}$. We wish to find $\vec{v}$ such that

$$H_{\vec{v}}\vec{a} = \begin{pmatrix} \vec{a}_1 \\ c \\ \vec{0} \end{pmatrix}.$$

Following a parallel derivation to the one above for the case $k = 1$ shows that

$$\vec{v} = \begin{pmatrix} \vec{0} \\ \vec{a}_2 \end{pmatrix} - c\vec{e}_k$$

accomplishes exactly this transformation when $c = \pm\|\vec{a}_2\|_2$.

   The algorithm for Householder QR, illustrated in Figure 5.9, applies these formulas iteratively, reducing to triangular form in a manner similar to Gaussian elimination. For each column of A, we compute $\vec{v}$ annihilating the bottom elements of the column and apply $H_{\vec{v}}$ to A. The end result is an upper-triangular matrix $R = H_{\vec{v}_n} \cdots H_{\vec{v}_1} A$. Q is given by the product $H_{\vec{v}_1}^{\top} \cdots H_{\vec{v}_n}^{\top}$. When $m < n$, it may be preferable to store Q implicitly as a list of vectors $\vec{v}$, which fits in the lower triangle that otherwise would be empty in R.

Example 5.4 (Householder QR). Continuing Example 5.3, we split the second column of $H_{\vec{v}}A$ as $\vec{a}_1 = (0) \in \mathbb{R}^1$ and $\vec{a}_2 = (-1, -1) \in \mathbb{R}^2$. We now take $c' = -\|\vec{a}_2\|_2 = -\sqrt{2}$, yielding

$$\vec{v}' = \begin{pmatrix} \vec{0} \\ \vec{a}_2 \end{pmatrix} - c'\vec{e}_2 = \begin{pmatrix} 0 \\ -1 \\ -1 \end{pmatrix} + \sqrt{2}\begin{pmatrix} 0 \\ 1 \\ 0 \end{pmatrix} = \begin{pmatrix} 0 \\ -1 + \sqrt{2} \\ -1 \end{pmatrix}$$

$$\implies H_{\vec{v}'} = \begin{pmatrix} 1 & 0 & 0 \\ 0 & 1/\sqrt{2} & 1/\sqrt{2} \\ 0 & 1/\sqrt{2} & -1/\sqrt{2} \end{pmatrix}.$$

Applying the two Householder steps reveals an upper-triangular matrix:

$$R = H_{\vec{v}'} H_{\vec{v}} A = \begin{pmatrix} 3 & 0 & 4 \\ 0 & -\sqrt{2} & 3/\sqrt{2} \\ 0 & 0 & 5/\sqrt{2} \end{pmatrix}.$$

The corresponding Q is given by $Q = H_{\vec{v}'}^{\top} H_{\vec{v}}^{\top}$.

5.6   REDUCED QR FACTORIZATION

We conclude our discussion by returning to the least-squares problem $A\vec{x} \approx \vec{b}$ when $A \in \mathbb{R}^{m \times n}$ is not square. Both algorithms we have discussed in this chapter can factor non-square matrices A into products QR, but the sizes of Q and R are different depending on the approach:

- When applying Gram-Schmidt, we do column operations on A to obtain Q by orthogonalization. For this reason, the dimension of A is that of Q, yielding $Q \in \mathbb{R}^{m \times n}$ and $R \in \mathbb{R}^{n \times n}$ as a product of elimination matrices.

- When using Householder reflections, we obtain Q as the product of $m \times m$ reflection matrices, leaving $R \in \mathbb{R}^{m \times n}$.

Suppose we are in the typical case for least-squares, for which $m \gg n$. We still prefer to use the Householder method due to its numerical stability, but now the $m \times m$ matrix Q might be too large to store. To save space, we can use the upper-triangular structure of R to our advantage. For instance, consider the structure of a 5×3 matrix R:

$$R = \left(\begin{array}{ccc} \times & \times & \times \\ 0 & \times & \times \\ 0 & 0 & \times \\ \hline 0 & 0 & 0 \\ 0 & 0 & 0 \end{array} \right).$$

Anything below the upper $n \times n$ square of R must be zero, yielding a simplification:

$$A = QR = \begin{pmatrix} Q_1 & Q_2 \end{pmatrix} \begin{pmatrix} R_1 \\ 0 \end{pmatrix} = Q_1 R_1.$$

Here, $Q_1 \in \mathbb{R}^{m \times n}$ and $R_1 \in \mathbb{R}^{n \times n}$ still contains the upper triangle of R. This is called the "reduced" QR factorization of A, since the columns of Q_1 contain a basis for the column space of A rather than for all of $\mathbb{R}^m$; it takes up far less space. The discussion in §5.3 still applies, so the reduced QR factorization can be used for least-squares in a similar fashion.

5.7   EXERCISES

5.1   Use Householder reflections to obtain a QR factorization of the matrix A from Example 5.2. Do you obtain the same QR factorization as the Gram-Schmidt approach?

5.2 Suppose $A \in \mathbb{R}^{n \times n}$ and $\vec{v} \in \mathbb{R}^n$. Provide pseudocode for computing the product $H_{\vec{v}}A$ in $O(n^2)$ time. Explain where this method might be used in implementations of Householder QR factorization.

5.3 (Adapted from Stanford CS 205A, 2012) Suppose $A \in \mathbb{R}^{m \times n}$ is factored $A = QR$. Show that $P_0 = I_{m \times m} - QQ^\top$ is the projection matrix onto the null space of $A^\top$.

5.4 (Adapted from Stanford CS 205A, 2012) Suppose we consider $\vec{a} \in \mathbb{R}^n$ as an $n \times 1$ matrix. Write out its "reduced" QR factorization explicitly.

5.5 Show that the Householder matrix $H_{\vec{v}}$ is *involutary*, meaning $H_{\vec{v}}^2 = I_{n \times n}$. What are the eigenvalues of $H_{\vec{v}}$?

5.6 Propose a method for finding the least-norm projection of a vector $\vec{v}$ onto the column space of $A \in \mathbb{R}^{m \times n}$ with $m > n$.

5.7 Alternatives to the QR factorization:

(a) Can a matrix $A \in \mathbb{R}^{m \times n}$ be factored into $A = RQ$ where R is upper triangular and Q is orthogonal? How?

(b) Can a matrix $A \in \mathbb{R}^{m \times n}$ be factored into $A = QL$ where L is lower triangular?

5.8 Relating QR and Cholesky factorizations:

(a) Take $A \in \mathbb{R}^{m \times n}$ and suppose we apply the Cholesky factorization to obtain $A^\top A = LL^\top$. Define $Q \equiv A(L^\top)^{-1}$. Show that the columns of Q are orthogonal.

(b) Based on the previous part, suggest a relationship between the Cholesky factorization of $A^\top A$ and QR factorization of A.

5.9 Suppose $A \in \mathbb{R}^{m \times n}$ is rank m with $m < n$. Suppose we factor

$$A^\top = Q \begin{pmatrix} R_1 \\ 0 \end{pmatrix}.$$

Provide a solution $\vec{x}$ to the underdetermined system $A\vec{x} = \vec{b}$ in terms of Q and R_1.

Hint: Try the square case $A \in \mathbb{R}^{n \times n}$ first, and use the result to guess a form for $\vec{x}$. Be careful that you multiply matrices of proper size.

5.10 ("Generalized QR," [2]) One way to generalize the QR factorization of a matrix is to consider the possibility of factorizing multiple matrices *simultaneously*.

(a) Suppose $A \in \mathbb{R}^{n \times m}$ and $B \in \mathbb{R}^{n \times p}$, with $m \le n \le p$. Show that there are orthogonal matrices $Q \in \mathbb{R}^{n \times n}$ and $V \in \mathbb{R}^{p \times p}$ as well as a matrix $R \in \mathbb{R}^{n \times m}$ such that the following conditions hold:
   - $Q^\top A = R$.
   - $Q^\top BV = S$, where S can be written

$$S = \begin{pmatrix} 0 & \bar{S} \end{pmatrix},$$

   for upper-triangular $\bar{S} \in \mathbb{R}^{n \times n}$.

- R can be written

$$R = \begin{pmatrix} \bar{R} \\ 0 \end{pmatrix},$$

for upper-triangular $\bar{R} \in \mathbb{R}^{m \times m}$.

Hint: Take $\bar{R}$ to be R_1 from the reduced QR factorization of A. Apply RQ factorization to $Q^\top B$; see Exercise 5.7a.

(b) Show how to solve the following optimization problem for $\vec{x}$ and $\vec{u}$ using the generalized QR factorization:

$$\min_{\vec{x},\vec{u}} \quad \|\vec{u}\|_2$$
$$\text{subject to} \quad A\vec{x} + B\vec{u} = \vec{c}.$$

You can assume $\bar{S}$ and $\bar{R}$ are invertible.

5.11 An alternative algorithm for QR factorization uses *Givens rotations* rather than Householder reflections.

(a) The 2×2 rotation matrix by angle $\theta \in [0, 2\pi)$ is given by

$$R_\theta \equiv \begin{pmatrix} \cos\theta & \sin\theta \\ -\sin\theta & \cos\theta \end{pmatrix}.$$

Show that for a given $\vec{x} \in \mathbb{R}^2$, a θ always exists such that $R_\theta \vec{x} = r\vec{e}_1$, where $r \in \mathbb{R}$ and $\vec{e}_1 = (1, 0)$. Give formulas for $\cos\theta$ and $\sin\theta$ that do not require trigonometric functions.

(b) The *Givens rotation matrix* of rows i and j about angle θ is given by

$$G(i, j, \theta) \equiv \begin{pmatrix} 1 & \cdots & 0 & \cdots & 0 & \cdots & 0 \\ \vdots & \ddots & \vdots & & \vdots & & \vdots \\ 0 & \cdots & c & \cdots & s & \cdots & 0 \\ \vdots & & \vdots & \ddots & \vdots & & \vdots \\ 0 & \cdots & -s & \cdots & c & \cdots & 0 \\ \vdots & & \vdots & & \vdots & \ddots & \vdots \\ 0 & \cdots & 0 & \cdots & 0 & \cdots & 1 \end{pmatrix},$$

where $c \equiv \cos\theta$ and $s \equiv \sin\theta$. In this formula, the c's appear in positions (i, i) and (j, j) while the s's appear in positions (i, j) and (j, i). Provide an $O(n)$ method for finding the product $G(i, j, \theta)A$ for $A \in \mathbb{R}^{n \times n}$; the matrix A can be modified in the process.

(c) Give an $O(n^3)$ time algorithm for overwriting $A \in \mathbb{R}^{n \times n}$ with $Q^\top A = R$, where $Q \in \mathbb{R}^{n \times n}$ is orthogonal and $R \in \mathbb{R}^{n \times n}$ is upper triangular. You do not need to store Q.

(d) Suggest how you might store Q implicitly if you use the QR method you developed in the previous part.

(e) Suggest an $O(n^3)$ method for recovering the matrix Q given A and R.

5.12 (Adapted from [50], §5.1) If $\vec{x}, \vec{y} \in \mathbb{R}^m$ with $\|\vec{x}\|_2 = \|\vec{y}\|_2$, write an algorithm for finding an orthogonal matrix Q such that $Q\vec{x} = \vec{y}$.

5.13 ("TSQR," [28]) The QR factorization algorithms we considered can be challenging to extend to parallel architectures like MapReduce. Here, we consider QR factorization of $A \in \mathbb{R}^{m \times n}$ where $m \gg n$.

    (a) Suppose $A \in \mathbb{R}^{8n \times n}$. Show how to factor $A = Q\bar{R}$, where $Q \in \mathbb{R}^{8n \times 4n}$ has orthogonal columns and $\bar{R} \in \mathbb{R}^{4n \times n}$ contains four $n \times n$ upper-triangular blocks. *Hint:* Write

$$A = \begin{pmatrix} A_1 \\ A_2 \\ A_3 \\ A_4 \end{pmatrix}.$$

    (b) Recursively apply your answer from 5.13a to generate a QR factorization of A.

    (c) Suppose we make the following factorizations:

$$A_1 = Q_1 R_1$$
$$\begin{pmatrix} R_1 \\ A_2 \end{pmatrix} = Q_2 R_2$$
$$\begin{pmatrix} R_2 \\ A_3 \end{pmatrix} = Q_3 R_3$$
$$\begin{pmatrix} R_3 \\ A_4 \end{pmatrix} = Q_4 R_4,$$

    where each of the R_i's are square. Use these matrices to factor $A = QR$.

    (d) Suppose we read A row-by-row. Why might the simplification in 5.13c be useful for QR factorization of A in this case? You can assume we only need R from the QR factorization.

CHAPTER 6

Eigenvectors

CONTENTS

6.1   Motivation 107
    6.1.1   Statistics 108
    6.1.2   Differential Equations 109
    6.1.3   Spectral Embedding 110
6.2   Properties of Eigenvectors 112
    6.2.1   Symmetric and Positive Definite Matrices 114
    6.2.2   Specialized Properties 116
        6.2.2.1   Characteristic Polynomial 116
        6.2.2.2   Jordan Normal Form 116
6.3   Computing a Single Eigenvalue 117
    6.3.1   Power Iteration 117
    6.3.2   Inverse Iteration 118
    6.3.3   Shifting 119
6.4   Finding Multiple Eigenvalues 120
    6.4.1   Deflation 120
    6.4.2   QR Iteration 121
    6.4.3   Krylov Subspace Methods 126
6.5   Sensitivity and Conditioning 126

W E turn our attention now to a *nonlinear* problem about matrices: Finding their eigenvalues and eigenvectors. Eigenvectors $\vec{x}$ and corresponding eigenvalues λ of a square matrix A are determined by the equation $A\vec{x} = \lambda\vec{x}$. There are many ways to see that the eigenvalue problem is nonlinear. For instance, there is a *product* of unknowns λ and $\vec{x}$. Furthermore, to avoid the trivial solution $\vec{x} = \vec{0}$, we constrain $\|\vec{x}\|_2 = 1$; this constraint keeps $\vec{x}$ on the unit sphere, which is not a vector space. Thanks to this structure, algorithms for finding eigenspaces will be considerably different from techniques for solving and analyzing linear systems of equations.

6.1   MOTIVATION

Despite the arbitrary-looking form of the equation $A\vec{x} = \lambda\vec{x}$, the problem of finding eigenvectors and eigenvalues arises naturally in many circumstances. To illustrate this point, before presenting algorithms for finding eigenvectors and eigenvalues we motivate our discussion with a few examples.

It is worth reminding ourselves of one source of eigenvalue problems already considered in Chapter 1. As explained in Example 1.27, the following fact will guide many of our examples:

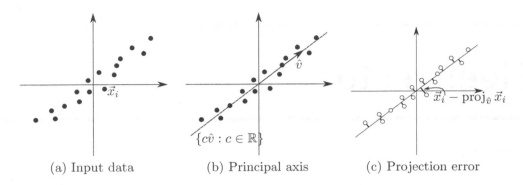

(a) Input data   (b) Principal axis   (c) Projection error

Figure 6.1 (a) A dataset with correlation between the horizontal and vertical axes; (b) we seek the unit vector $\hat{v}$ such that all data points are well-approximated by some point along span $\{\hat{v}\}$; (c) to find $\hat{v}$, we can minimize the sum of squared residual norms $\sum_i \|\vec{x}_i - \text{proj}_{\hat{v}} \vec{x}_i\|_2^2$ with the constraint that $\|\hat{v}\|_2 = 1$.

> **When A is symmetric, the eigenvectors of A are the critical points of $\vec{x}^\top A \vec{x}$ under the constraint $\|\vec{x}\|_2 = 1$.**

Many eigenvalue problems are constructed using this fact as a starting point.

6.1.1 Statistics

Suppose we have machinery for collecting statistical observations about a collection of items. For instance, in a medical study we may collect the age, weight, blood pressure, and heart rate of every patient in a hospital. Each patient i can be represented by a point $\vec{x}_i \in \mathbb{R}^4$ storing these four values.

These statistics may exhibit strong correlations between the different dimensions, as in Figure 6.1(a). For instance, patients with higher blood pressures may be likely to have higher weights or heart rates. For this reason, although we collected our data in $\mathbb{R}^4$, in reality it may—to some approximate degree—live in a lower-dimensional space capturing the relationships between the different dimensions.

For now, suppose that there exists a *one*-dimensional space approximating our dataset, illustrated in Figure 6.1(b). Then, we expect that there exists some vector $\vec{v}$ such that each data point $\vec{x}_i$ can be written as $\vec{x}_i \approx c_i \vec{v}$ for a different $c_i \in \mathbb{R}$. From before, we know that the best approximation of $\vec{x}_i$ parallel to $\vec{v}$ is $\text{proj}_{\vec{v}} \vec{x}_i$. Defining $\hat{v} \equiv \vec{v}/\|\vec{v}\|_2$, we can write

$$\text{proj}_{\vec{v}} \vec{x}_i = \frac{\vec{x}_i \cdot \vec{v}}{\vec{v} \cdot \vec{v}} \vec{v} \text{ by definition}$$
$$= (\vec{x}_i \cdot \hat{v})\hat{v} \text{ since } \vec{v} \cdot \vec{v} = \|\vec{v}\|_2^2.$$

The magnitude of $\vec{v}$ does not matter for the problem at hand, since the projection of $\vec{x}_i$ onto any nonzero multiple of $\hat{v}$ is the same, so it is reasonable to restrict our search to the space of *unit* vectors $\hat{v}$.

Following the pattern of least-squares, we have a new optimization problem:

$$\text{minimize}_{\hat{v}} \sum_i \|\vec{x}_i - \text{proj}_{\hat{v}} \vec{x}_i\|_2^2$$
$$\text{subject to } \|\hat{v}\|_2 = 1.$$

This problem minimizes the sum of squared differences between the data points $\vec{x}_i$ and their best approximation as a multiple of $\hat{v}$, as in Figure 6.1(c). We can simplify our optimization objective using the observations we already have made and some linear algebra:

$$\sum_i \|\vec{x}_i - \text{proj}_{\hat{v}}\, \vec{x}_i\|_2^2 = \sum_i \|\vec{x}_i - (\vec{x}_i \cdot \hat{v})\hat{v}\|_2^2 \text{ as explained above}$$

$$= \sum_i \left(\|\vec{x}_i\|_2^2 - 2(\vec{x}_i \cdot \hat{v})(\vec{x}_i \cdot \hat{v}) + (\vec{x}_i \cdot \hat{v})^2\|\hat{v}\|_2^2\right) \text{ since } \|\vec{w}\|_2^2 = \vec{w} \cdot \vec{w}$$

$$= \sum_i \left(\|\vec{x}_i\|_2^2 - (\vec{x}_i \cdot \hat{v})^2\right) \text{ since } \|\hat{v}\|_2 = 1$$

$$= \text{const.} - \sum_i (\vec{x}_i \cdot \hat{v})^2 \text{ since the unknown here is } \hat{v}$$

$$= \text{const.} - \|X^\top \hat{v}\|_2^2, \text{ where the columns of } X \text{ are the vectors } \vec{x}_i.$$

After removing the negative sign, this derivation shows that we can solve an equivalent maximization problem:

$$\text{maximize } \|X^\top \hat{v}\|_2^2$$
$$\text{subject to } \|\hat{v}\|_2^2 = 1.$$

Statisticians may recognize this equivalence as maximizing variance rather than minimizing approximation error.

We know $\|X^\top \hat{v}\|_2^2 = \hat{v}^\top XX^\top \hat{v}$, so by Example 1.27, $\hat{v}$ is the eigenvector of $XX^\top$ with the highest eigenvalue. The vector $\hat{v}$ is known as the first *principal component* of the dataset.

6.1.2 Differential Equations

Many physical forces can be written as functions of position. For instance, the force exerted by a spring connecting two particles at positions $\vec{x}, \vec{y} \in \mathbb{R}^3$ is $k(\vec{x} - \vec{y})$ by Hooke's Law; such spring forces are used to approximate forces holding cloth together in many simulation systems for computer graphics. Even when forces are not *linear* in position, we often approximate them in a linear fashion. In particular, in a physical system with n particles, we can encode the positions of all the particles simultaneously in a vector $\vec{X} \in \mathbb{R}^{3n}$. Then, the forces in the system might be approximated as $\vec{F} \approx A\vec{X}$ for some matrix $A \in \mathbb{R}^{3n \times 3n}$.

Newton's second law of motion states $F = ma$, or force equals mass times acceleration. In our context, we can write a diagonal *mass matrix* $M \in \mathbb{R}^{3n \times 3n}$ containing the mass of each particle in the system. Then, the second law can be written as $\vec{F} = M\vec{X}''$, where prime denotes differentiation in time. By definition, $\vec{X}'' = (\vec{X}')'$, so after defining $\vec{V} \equiv \vec{X}'$ we have a *first*-order system of equations:

$$\frac{d}{dt}\begin{pmatrix} \vec{X} \\ \vec{V} \end{pmatrix} = \begin{pmatrix} 0 & I_{3n \times 3n} \\ M^{-1}A & 0 \end{pmatrix} \begin{pmatrix} \vec{X} \\ \vec{V} \end{pmatrix}.$$

Here, we simultaneously compute both positions in $\vec{X} \in \mathbb{R}^{3n}$ and velocities $\vec{V} \in \mathbb{R}^{3n}$ of all n particles as functions of time; we will explore this reduction in more detail in Chapter 15.

Beyond this reduction, differential equations of the form $\vec{y}' = B\vec{y}$ for an unknown function $\vec{y}(t)$ and fixed matrix B appear in simulation of cloth, springs, heat, waves, and other

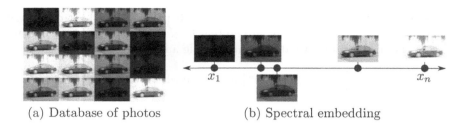

(a) Database of photos   (b) Spectral embedding

Figure 6.2 Suppose we are given (a) an unsorted database of photographs with some matrix W measuring the similarity between image i and image j. (b) The one-dimensional spectral embedding assigns each photograph i a value x_i so that if images i and j are similar, then x_i will be close to x_j (figure generated by D. Hyde).

phenomena. Suppose we know eigenvectors $\vec{y}_1, \ldots, \vec{y}_k$ of B satisfying $B\vec{y}_i = \lambda_i \vec{y}_i$. If we write the initial condition of the differential equation in terms of the eigenvectors as

$$\vec{y}(0) = c_1 \vec{y}_1 + \cdots + c_k \vec{y}_k,$$

then the solution of the differential equation can be written in closed form:

$$\vec{y}(t) = c_1 e^{\lambda_1 t} \vec{y}_1 + \cdots + c_k e^{\lambda_k t} \vec{y}_k.$$

That is, if we expand the initial conditions of this differential equation in the eigenvector basis, then we know the solution for all times $t \geq 0$ for free; you will check this formula in Exercise 6.1. This formula is not the end of the story for simulation: Finding the complete set of eigenvectors of B is expensive, and B may evolve over time.

6.1.3 Spectral Embedding

Suppose we have a collection of n items in a dataset and a measure $w_{ij} \geq 0$ of how similar elements i and j are; we will assume $w_{ij} = w_{ji}$. For instance, maybe we are given a collection of photographs as in Figure 6.2(a) and take w_{ij} to be a measure of the amount of overlap between the distributions of colors in photo i and in photo j.

Given the matrix W of w_{ij} values, we might wish to sort the photographs based on their similarity to simplify viewing and exploring the collection. That is, we could lay them out on a line so that the pair of photos i and j is close when w_{ij} is large, as in Figure 6.2(b). The measurements in w_{ij} may be noisy or inconsistent, however, so it may not be obvious how to sort the n photos directly using the n^2 values in W.

One way to order the collection would be to assign a number x_i to each item i such that similar objects are assigned similar numbers; we can then sort the collection based on the values in $\vec{x}$. We can measure how well an assignment of values in $\vec{x}$ groups similar objects by using the energy function

$$E(\vec{x}) \equiv \sum_{ij} w_{ij}(x_i - x_j)^2.$$

The difference $(x_i - x_j)^2$ is small when x_i and x_j are assigned similar values. Given the weighting w_{ij} next to $(x_i - x_j)^2$, minimizing $E(\vec{x})$ asks that items i and j with high similarity scores w_{ij} get mapped the closest.

Minimizing $E(\vec{x})$ with no constraints gives a minimum $\vec{x}$ with $E(\vec{x}) = 0$: $x_i = \text{const.}$ for all i. Furthermore, adding a constraint $\|\vec{x}\|_2 = 1$ does *not* remove this constant solution: Taking $x_i = 1/\sqrt{n}$ for all i gives $\|\vec{x}\|_2 = 1$ and $E(\vec{x}) = 0$. To obtain a nontrivial output, we must remove this case as well:

$$\text{minimize } E(\vec{x})$$
$$\text{subject to } \|\vec{x}\|_2^2 = 1$$
$$\vec{1} \cdot \vec{x} = 0.$$

Our second constraint requires that the sum of elements in $\vec{x}$ is zero, preventing the choice $x_1 = x_2 = \cdots = x_n$ when combined with the $\|\vec{x}\|_2 = 1$ constraint.

We can simplify the energy in a few steps:

$$E(\vec{x}) = \sum_{ij} w_{ij}(x_i - x_j)^2 \text{ by definition}$$

$$= \sum_{ij} w_{ij}(x_i^2 - 2x_i x_j + x_j^2)$$

$$= \sum_i a_i x_i^2 - 2\sum_{ij} w_{ij} x_i x_j + \sum_j a_j x_j^2 \text{ where } \vec{a} \equiv W\vec{1}, \text{ since } W^\top = W$$

$$= 2\vec{x}^\top(A - W)\vec{x} \text{ where } A \equiv \text{diag}(\vec{a}).$$

We can check that $\vec{1}$ is an eigenvector of $A - W$ with eigenvalue 0:

$$(A - W)\vec{1} = A\vec{1} - W\vec{1} = \vec{a} - \vec{a} = \vec{0}.$$

More interestingly, the eigenvector corresponding to the *second*-smallest eigenvalue is the minimizer for our constrained problem above! One way to see this fact is to write the Lagrange multiplier function corresponding to this optimization:

$$\Lambda \equiv 2\vec{x}^\top(A - W)\vec{x} - \lambda(1 - \|\vec{x}\|_2^2) - \mu(\vec{1} \cdot \vec{x}).$$

Applying Theorem 1.1, at the optimal point we must have:

$$0 = \nabla_{\vec{x}}\Lambda = 4(A - W)\vec{x} + 2\lambda\vec{x} - \mu\vec{1}$$
$$1 = \|\vec{x}\|_2^2$$
$$0 = \vec{1} \cdot \vec{x}.$$

If we take the dot product of both sides of the first expression with $\vec{1}$ shows

$$0 = \vec{1} \cdot [4(A - W)\vec{x} + 2\lambda\vec{x} - \mu\vec{1}]$$
$$= 4\vec{1}^\top(A - W)\vec{x} - \mu n \text{ since } \vec{1} \cdot \vec{x} = 0$$
$$= -\mu n \text{ since } A\vec{1} = W\vec{1} = \vec{a}$$
$$\implies \mu = 0.$$

Substituting this new observation into the Lagrange multiplier condition, we find:

$$2(W - A)\vec{x} = \lambda\vec{x}.$$

We explicitly ignore the eigenvalue $\lambda = 0$ of $W - A$ corresponding to the eigenvector $\vec{1}$, so $\vec{x}$ must be the eigenvector with the *second*-smallest eigenvalue. The resulting $\vec{x}$ is the "spectral embedding" of W onto one dimension, referring to the fact that we call the set of eigenvalues of a matrix its spectrum. Taking more eigenvectors of $A - W$ provides embeddings into higher dimensions.

6.2 PROPERTIES OF EIGENVECTORS

We have established a variety of applications in need of eigenspace computation. Before we can explore algorithms for this purpose, however, we will more closely examine the structure of the eigenvalue problem.

We can begin with a few definitions that likely are evident at this point:

Definition 6.1 (Eigenvalue and eigenvector). An *eigenvector* $\vec{x} \neq \vec{0}$ of a matrix $A \in \mathbb{R}^{n \times n}$ is any vector satisfying $A\vec{x} = \lambda\vec{x}$ for some $\lambda \in \mathbb{R}$; the corresponding λ is known as an *eigenvalue*. *Complex* eigenvalues and eigenvectors satisfy the same relationships with $\lambda \in \mathbb{C}$ and $\vec{x} \in \mathbb{C}^n$.

Definition 6.2 (Spectrum and spectral radius). The *spectrum* of A is the set of eigenvalues of A. The *spectral radius* $\rho(A)$ is the maximum value $|\lambda|$ over all eigenvalues λ of A.

The scale of an eigenvector is not important. In particular, $A(c\vec{x}) = cA\vec{x} = c\lambda\vec{x} = \lambda(c\vec{x})$, so $c\vec{x}$ is an eigenvector with the same eigenvalue. For this reason, we can restrict our search to those eigenvectors $\vec{x}$ with $\|\vec{x}\|_2 = 1$ without losing any nontrivial structure. Adding this constraint does not completely relieve ambiguity, since $\pm\vec{x}$ are both eigenvectors with the same eigenvalue, but this case is easier to detect.

The algebraic properties of eigenvectors and eigenvalues are the subject of many mathematical studies in themselves. Some basic properties will suffice for the discussion at hand, and hence we will mention just a few theorems affecting the design of numerical algorithms. The proofs here parallel the development in [4].

First, we should check that every matrix has at least one eigenvector, so that our search for eigenvectors is not in vain. Our strategy for this and other related problems is to notice that λ is an eigenvalue such that $A\vec{x} = \lambda\vec{x}$ if and only if $(A - \lambda I_{n \times n})\vec{x} = \vec{0}$. That is, λ is an eigenvalue of A exactly when the matrix $A - \lambda I_{n \times n}$ is not full-rank.

Proposition 6.1 ([4], Theorem 2.1). Every matrix $A \in \mathbb{R}^{n \times n}$ has at least one (potentially complex) eigenvector.

Proof. Take any vector $\vec{x} \in \mathbb{R}^n \backslash \{\vec{0}\}$, and assume $A \neq 0$ since this matrix trivially has eigenvalue 0. The set $\{\vec{x}, A\vec{x}, A^2\vec{x}, \cdots, A^n\vec{x}\}$ must be linearly dependent because it contains $n + 1$ vectors in n dimensions. So, there exist constants $c_0, \ldots, c_n \in \mathbb{R}$ not all zero such that $\vec{0} = c_0\vec{x} + c_1 A\vec{x} + \cdots + c_n A^n\vec{x}$. Define a polynomial

$$f(z) \equiv c_0 + c_1 z + \cdots + c_n z^n.$$

By the Fundamental Theorem of Algebra, there exist $m \geq 1$ roots $z_i \in \mathbb{C}$ and $c \neq 0$ such that

$$f(z) = c(z - z_1)(z - z_2) \cdots (z - z_m).$$

Applying this factorization,

$$\begin{aligned}
\vec{0} &= c_0\vec{x} + c_1 A\vec{x} + \cdots + c_n A^n\vec{x} \\
&= (c_0 I_{n \times n} + c_1 A + \cdots + c_n A^n)\vec{x} \\
&= c(A - z_1 I_{n \times n}) \cdots (A - z_m I_{n \times n})\vec{x}.
\end{aligned}$$

In this form, at least one $A - z_i I_{n \times n}$ has a null space, since otherwise each term would be invertible, forcing $\vec{x} = \vec{0}$. If we take $\vec{v}$ to be a nonzero vector in the null space of $A - z_i I_{n \times n}$, then by construction $A\vec{v} = z_i\vec{v}$, as needed. $\square$

There is one additional fact worth checking to motivate our discussion of eigenvector computation. While it can be the case that a single eigenvalue admits more than one corresponding eigenvector, when two eigenvectors have different eigenvalues they cannot be related in the following sense:

Proposition 6.2 ([4], Proposition 2.2). Eigenvectors corresponding to different eigenvalues must be linearly independent.

Proof. Suppose this is not the case. Then there exist eigenvectors $\vec{x}_1, \ldots, \vec{x}_k$ with distinct eigenvalues $\lambda_1, \ldots, \lambda_k$ that are linearly dependent. This implies that there are coefficients $c_1, \ldots, c_k$ not all zero with $\vec{0} = c_1\vec{x}_1 + \cdots + c_k\vec{x}_k$.

For any two indices i and j, since $A\vec{x}_j = \lambda_j\vec{x}_j$, we can simplify the product

$$(A - \lambda_i I_{n\times n})\vec{x}_j = A\vec{x}_j - \lambda_i\vec{x}_j = \lambda_j\vec{x}_j - \lambda_i\vec{x}_j = (\lambda_j - \lambda_i)\vec{x}_j.$$

Pre-multiplying the relationship $\vec{0} = c_1\vec{x}_1 + \cdots + c_k\vec{x}_k$ by the matrix $(A - \lambda_2 I_{n\times n}) \cdots (A - \lambda_k I_{n\times n})$ shows:

$$\vec{0} = (A - \lambda_2 I_{n\times n}) \cdots (A - \lambda_k I_{n\times n})(c_1\vec{x}_1 + \cdots + c_k\vec{x}_k)$$
$$= c_1(\lambda_1 - \lambda_2) \cdots (\lambda_1 - \lambda_k)\vec{x}_1.$$

Since all the λ_i's are distinct, this shows $c_1 = 0$. The same argument shows that the rest of the c_i's have to be zero, contradicting linear dependence. $\square$

This proposition shows that an $n \times n$ matrix can have at most n distinct eigenvalues, since a set of n eigenvalues yields n linearly independent vectors. The maximum number of linearly independent eigenvectors corresponding to an eigenvalue λ is the *geometric multiplicity* of λ. It is not true, however, that a matrix has to have *exactly* n linearly independent eigenvectors. This is the case for many matrices, which we will call *nondefective*:

Definition 6.3 (Nondefective). A matrix $A \in \mathbb{R}^{n\times n}$ is *nondefective* or *diagonalizable* if its eigenvectors span $\mathbb{R}^n$.

Example 6.1 (Defective matrix). The matrix

$$\begin{pmatrix} 5 & 2 \\ 0 & 5 \end{pmatrix}$$

has only one linearly independent eigenvector $(1, 0)$.

We call nondefective matrices *diagonalizable* for the following reason: If a matrix is nondefective, then it has n eigenvectors $\vec{x}_1, \ldots, \vec{x}_n \in \mathbb{R}^n$ with corresponding (possibly nonunique) eigenvalues $\lambda_1, \ldots, \lambda_n$. Take the columns of X to be the vectors $\vec{x}_i$, and define D to be the diagonal matrix with $\lambda_1, \ldots, \lambda_n$ along the diagonal. Then, we have $AX = XD$; this relationship is a "stacked" version of $A\vec{x}_i = \lambda_i\vec{x}_i$. Applying X^{-1} to both sides, $D = X^{-1}AX$, meaning A is diagonalized by a *similarity transformation* $A \mapsto X^{-1}AX$:

Definition 6.4 (Similar matrices). Two matrices A and B are *similar* if there exists T with $B = T^{-1}AT$.

Similar matrices have the same eigenvalues, since if $B\vec{x} = \lambda x$, by substituting $B = T^{-1}AT$ we know $T^{-1}AT\vec{x} = \lambda\vec{x}$. Hence, $A(T\vec{x}) = \lambda(T\vec{x})$, showing $T\vec{x}$ is an eigenvector of A with eigenvalue λ. In other words:

> **We can apply all the similarity transformations we want to a matrix without modifying its set of eigenvalues.**

This observation is the foundation of many eigenvector computation methods, which start with a general matrix A and reduce it to a matrix whose eigenvalues are more obvious by applying similarity transformations. This procedure is analogous to applying row operations to reduce a matrix to triangular form for use in solving linear systems of equations.

6.2.1 Symmetric and Positive Definite Matrices

Unsurprisingly given our special consideration of Gram matrices $A^\top A$ in previous chapters, symmetric and/or positive definite matrices enjoy special eigenvector structure. If we can verify *a priori* that a matrix is symmetric or positive definite, specialized algorithms can be used to extract its eigenvectors more quickly.

Our original definition of eigenvalues allows them to be complex values in $\mathbb{C}$ even if A is a real matrix. We can prove, however, that in the symmetric case we do not need complex arithmetic. To do so, we will generalize symmetric matrices to matrices in $\mathbb{C}^{n \times n}$ by introducing the set of *Hermitian* matrices:

Definition 6.5 (Complex conjugate). The *complex conjugate* of a number $z = a + bi \in \mathbb{C}$, where $a, b \in \mathbb{R}$, is $\bar{z} \equiv a - bi$. The complex conjugate $\bar{A}$ of a matrix $A \in \mathbb{C}^{m \times n}$ is the matrix with elements $\bar{a}_{ij}$.

Definition 6.6 (Conjugate transpose). The *conjugate transpose* of $A \in \mathbb{C}^{m \times n}$ is $A^H \equiv \bar{A}^\top$.

Definition 6.7 (Hermitian matrix). A matrix $A \in \mathbb{C}^{n \times n}$ is *Hermitian* if $A = A^H$.

A symmetric matrix $A \in \mathbb{R}^{n \times n}$ is automatically Hermitian because it has no complex part.

We also can generalize the notion of a dot product to complex vectors by defining an *inner product* as follows:

$$\langle \vec{x}, \vec{y} \rangle \equiv \sum_i x_i \bar{y}_i,$$

where $\vec{x}, \vec{y} \in \mathbb{C}^n$. Once again, this definition coincides with $\vec{x} \cdot \vec{y}$ when $\vec{x}, \vec{y} \in \mathbb{R}^n$; in the complex case, however, dot product symmetry is replaced by the condition $\langle \vec{v}, \vec{w} \rangle = \overline{\langle \vec{w}, \vec{v} \rangle}$.

We now can prove that it is not necessary to search for complex eigenvalues of symmetric or Hermitian matrices:

Proposition 6.3. All eigenvalues of Hermitian matrices are real.

Proof. Suppose $A \in \mathbb{C}^{n \times n}$ is Hermitian with $A\vec{x} = \lambda\vec{x}$. By scaling, we can assume $\|\vec{x}\|_2^2 = \langle \vec{x}, \vec{x} \rangle = 1$. Then:

$$\lambda = \lambda\langle \vec{x}, \vec{x} \rangle \text{ since } \vec{x} \text{ has norm } 1$$
$$= \langle \lambda\vec{x}, \vec{x} \rangle \text{ by linearity of } \langle \cdot, \cdot \rangle$$
$$= \langle A\vec{x}, \vec{x} \rangle \text{ since } A\vec{x} = \lambda\vec{x}$$
$$= (A\vec{x})^\top \vec{x} \text{ by definition of } \langle \cdot, \cdot \rangle$$
$$= \vec{x}^\top \overline{(\bar{A}^\top \vec{x})} \text{ by expanding the product and applying the identity } \overline{ab} = \bar{a}\bar{b}$$
$$= \langle \vec{x}, A^H \vec{x} \rangle \text{ by definition of } A^H \text{ and } \langle \cdot, \cdot \rangle$$

$$= \langle \vec{x}, A\vec{x} \rangle \text{ since } A = A^H$$
$$= \bar{\lambda}\langle \vec{x}, \vec{x} \rangle \text{ since } A\vec{x} = \lambda\vec{x}$$
$$= \bar{\lambda} \text{ since } \vec{x} \text{ has norm } 1.$$

Thus $\lambda = \bar{\lambda}$, which can happen only if $\lambda \in \mathbb{R}$, as needed. $\square$

Not only are the eigenvalues of Hermitian (and symmetric) matrices real, but also their eigenvectors must be orthogonal:

Proposition 6.4. Eigenvectors corresponding to distinct eigenvalues of Hermitian matrices must be orthogonal.

Proof. Suppose $A \in \mathbb{C}^{n \times n}$ is Hermitian, and suppose $\lambda \neq \mu$ with $A\vec{x} = \lambda\vec{x}$ and $A\vec{y} = \mu\vec{y}$. By the previous proposition we know $\lambda, \mu \in \mathbb{R}$. Then, $\langle A\vec{x}, \vec{y} \rangle = \lambda\langle \vec{x}, \vec{y} \rangle$. But since A is Hermitian we can also write $\langle A\vec{x}, \vec{y} \rangle = \langle \vec{x}, A^H\vec{y} \rangle = \langle \vec{x}, A\vec{y} \rangle = \mu\langle \vec{x}, \vec{y} \rangle$. Thus, $\lambda\langle \vec{x}, \vec{y} \rangle = \mu\langle \vec{x}, \vec{y} \rangle$. Since $\lambda \neq \mu$, we must have $\langle \vec{x}, \vec{y} \rangle = 0$. $\square$

Finally, we state (without proof) a crowning result of linear algebra, the Spectral Theorem. This theorem states that all symmetric or Hermitian matrices are non-defective and therefore must have exactly n orthogonal eigenvectors.

Theorem 6.1 (Spectral Theorem). Suppose $A \in \mathbb{C}^{n \times n}$ is Hermitian (if $A \in \mathbb{R}^{n \times n}$, suppose it is symmetric). Then, A has exactly n orthonormal eigenvectors $\vec{x}_1, \cdots, \vec{x}_n$ with (possibly repeated) eigenvalues $\lambda_1, \ldots, \lambda_n$. In other words, there exists an orthogonal matrix X of eigenvectors and diagonal matrix D of eigenvalues such that $D = X^\top A X$.

This theorem implies that any $\vec{y} \in \mathbb{R}^n$ can be decomposed into a linear combination of the eigenvectors of a Hermitian A. Many calculations are easier in this basis, as shown below:

Example 6.2 (Computation using eigenvectors). Take $\vec{x}_1, \ldots, \vec{x}_n \in \mathbb{R}^n$ to be the unit-length eigenvectors of a symmetric invertible matrix $A \in \mathbb{R}^{n \times n}$ with corresponding eigenvalues $\lambda_1, \ldots, \lambda_n \in \mathbb{R}$. Suppose we wish to solve $A\vec{y} = \vec{b}$. By the Spectral Theorem, we can decompose $\vec{b} = c_1\vec{x}_1 + \cdots + c_n\vec{x}_n$, where $c_i = \vec{b} \cdot \vec{x}_i$ by orthonormality. Then,

$$\vec{y} = \frac{c_1}{\lambda_1}\vec{x}_1 + \cdots + \frac{c_n}{\lambda_n}\vec{x}_n.$$

The fastest way to check this formula is to multiply $\vec{y}$ by A and make sure we recover $\vec{b}$:

$$A\vec{y} = A\left(\frac{c_1}{\lambda_1}\vec{x}_1 + \cdots + \frac{c_n}{\lambda_n}\vec{x}_n\right)$$
$$= \frac{c_1}{\lambda_1}A\vec{x}_1 + \cdots + \frac{c_n}{\lambda_n}A\vec{x}_n$$
$$= c_1\vec{x}_1 + \cdots + c_n\vec{x}_n \text{ since } A\vec{x}_k = \lambda_k\vec{x}_k \text{ for all } k$$
$$= \vec{b}, \text{ as desired.}$$

The calculation above has both positive and negative implications. It shows that given the eigenvectors and eigenvalues of symmetric matrix A, operations like inversion become straightforward. On the flip side, this means that finding the full set of eigenvectors of a symmetric matrix A is "at least" as difficult as solving $A\vec{x} = \vec{b}$.

Returning from our foray into the complex numbers, we revisit the real numbers to prove one final useful fact about positive definite matrices:

| **Proposition 6.5.** All eigenvalues of positive definite matrices are positive.

Proof. Take $A \in \mathbb{R}^{n \times n}$ positive definite, and suppose $A\vec{x} = \lambda\vec{x}$ with $\|\vec{x}\|_2 = 1$. By positive definiteness, we know $\vec{x}^\top A\vec{x} > 0$. But, $\vec{x}^\top A\vec{x} = \vec{x}^\top(\lambda\vec{x}) = \lambda\|\vec{x}\|_2^2 = \lambda$, as needed. □

This property is not nearly as remarkable as those associated with symmetric or Hermitian matrices, but it helps *order* the eigenvalues of A. Positive definite matrices enjoy the property that the eigenvalue with smallest absolute value is also the eigenvalue closest to zero, and the eigenvalue with largest absolute value is the one farthest from zero. This property influences methods that seek only a subset of the eigenvalues of a matrix, usually at one of the two ends of its spectrum.

6.2.2 Specialized Properties

We mention some specialized properties of eigenvectors and eigenvalues that influence more advanced methods for their computation. They largely will not figure into our subsequent discussion, so this section can be skipped if readers lack sufficient background.

6.2.2.1 Characteristic Polynomial

The determinant of a matrix $\det A$ satisfies $\det A \neq 0$ if and only if A is invertible. Thus, one way to find eigenvalues of a matrix is to find roots of the *characteristic polynomial*

$$p_A(\lambda) = \det(A - \lambda I_{n \times n}).$$

We have chosen to avoid determinants in our discussion of linear algebra, but simplifying p_A reveals that it is an n-th degree polynomial in λ.

From this construction, we can define the *algebraic multiplicity* of an eigenvalue λ as its multiplicity as a root of p_A. The algebraic multiplicity of any eigenvalue is at least as large as its geometric multiplicity. If the algebraic multiplicity is 1, the root is called *simple*, because it corresponds to a single eigenvector that is linearly independent from any others. Eigenvalues for which the algebraic and geometric multiplicities are not equal are called *defective*, since the corresponding matrix must also be defective in the sense of Definition 6.3.

In numerical analysis, it is common to avoid using the determinant of a matrix. While it is a convenient theoretical construction, its practical applicability is limited. Determinants are difficult to compute. In fact, most eigenvalue algorithms do not attempt to find roots of p_A directly, since doing so would require evaluation of a determinant. Furthermore, the determinant $\det A$ has *nothing* to do with the conditioning of A, so a near-but-not-exactly zero determinant of $\det(A - \lambda I_{n \times n})$ might not show that λ is nearly an eigenvalue of A.

6.2.2.2 Jordan Normal Form

We can only diagonalize a matrix when it has a full eigenspace. All matrices, however, are similar to a matrix in Jordan normal form, a general layout satisfying the following criteria:

- Nonzero values are on the diagonal entries a_{ii} and on the "superdiagonal" $a_{i(i+1)}$.

- Diagonal values are eigenvalues repeated as many times as their algebraic multiplicity; the matrix is block diagonal about these clusters.

- Off-diagonal values are 1 or 0.

Thus, the shape looks something like the following:

$$\begin{pmatrix} \lambda_1 & 1 & & & & & \\ & \lambda_1 & 1 & & & & \\ & & \lambda_1 & & & & \\ & & & \lambda_2 & 1 & & \\ & & & & \lambda_2 & & \\ & & & & & \lambda_3 & \\ & & & & & & \ddots \end{pmatrix}.$$

Jordan normal form is attractive theoretically because it always exists, but the $1/0$ structure is discrete and unstable under numerical perturbation.

6.3 COMPUTING A SINGLE EIGENVALUE

Computing the eigenvalues of a matrix is a well-studied problem with many potential algorithmic approaches. Each is tuned for a different situation, and achieving near-optimal conditioning or speed requires experimentation with several techniques. Here, we cover a few popular algorithms for the eigenvalue problem encountered in practice.

6.3.1 Power Iteration

Assume that $A \in \mathbb{R}^{n \times n}$ is non-defective and nonzero with all real eigenvalues, e.g., A is symmetric. By definition, A has a full set of eigenvectors $\vec{x}_1, \dots, \vec{x}_n \in \mathbb{R}^n$; we sort them such that their corresponding eigenvalues satisfy $|\lambda_1| \geq |\lambda_2| \geq \cdots \geq |\lambda_n|$.

Take an arbitrary vector $\vec{v} \in \mathbb{R}^n$. Since the eigenvectors of A span $\mathbb{R}^n$, we can write $\vec{v}$ in the $\vec{x}_i$ basis as $\vec{v} = c_1 \vec{x}_1 + \cdots + c_n \vec{x}_n$. Applying A to both sides,

$$A\vec{v} = c_1 A\vec{x}_1 + \cdots + c_n A\vec{x}_n$$
$$= c_1 \lambda_1 \vec{x}_1 + \cdots + c_n \lambda_n \vec{x}_n \text{ since } A\vec{x}_i = \lambda_i \vec{x}_i$$
$$= \lambda_1 \left(c_1 \vec{x}_1 + \frac{\lambda_2}{\lambda_1} c_2 \vec{x}_2 + \cdots + \frac{\lambda_n}{\lambda_1} c_n \vec{x}_n \right)$$
$$A^2 \vec{v} = \lambda_1^2 \left(c_1 \vec{x}_1 + \left(\frac{\lambda_2}{\lambda_1}\right)^2 c_2 \vec{x}_2 + \cdots + \left(\frac{\lambda_n}{\lambda_1}\right)^2 c_n \vec{x}_n \right)$$
$$\vdots$$
$$A^k \vec{v} = \lambda_1^k \left(c_1 \vec{x}_1 + \left(\frac{\lambda_2}{\lambda_1}\right)^k c_2 \vec{x}_2 + \cdots + \left(\frac{\lambda_n}{\lambda_1}\right)^k c_n \vec{x}_n \right).$$

As $k \to \infty$, the ratio $(\lambda_i/\lambda_1)^k \to 0$ unless $\lambda_i = \pm\lambda_1$, since λ_1 has the largest magnitude of any eigenvalue by construction. If $\vec{x}$ is the projection of $\vec{v}$ onto the space of eigenvectors with eigenvalues λ_1, then—at least when the absolute values $|\lambda_i|$ are unique—as $k \to \infty$ the following approximation begins to dominate: $A^k \vec{v} \approx \lambda_1^k \vec{x}$.

This argument leads to an exceedingly simple algorithm for computing a single eigenvector $\vec{x}_1$ of A corresponding to its largest-magnitude eigenvalue λ_1:

1. Take $\vec{v}_1 \in \mathbb{R}^n$ to be an arbitrary nonzero vector.

2. Iterate until convergence for increasing k: $\vec{v}_k = A\vec{v}_{k-1}$

```
function POWER-ITERATION(A)
    v⃗ ← ARBITRARY(n)
    for k ← 1, 2, 3, . . .
        v⃗ ← Av⃗
    return v⃗
```

(a)

```
function NORMALIZED-ITERATION(A)
    v⃗ ← ARBITRARY(n)
    for k ← 1, 2, 3, . . .
        w⃗ ← Av⃗
        v⃗ ← w⃗/‖w⃗‖
    return v⃗
```

(b)

Figure 6.3 Power iteration (a) without and (b) with normalization for finding the largest eigenvalue of a matrix.

```
function INVERSE-ITERATION(A)
    v⃗ ← ARBITRARY(n)
    for k ← 1, 2, 3, . . .
        w⃗ ← A⁻¹v⃗
        v⃗ ← w⃗/‖w⃗‖
    return v⃗
```

(a)

```
function INVERSE-ITERATION-LU(A)
    v⃗ ← ARBITRARY(n)
    L, U ← LU-FACTORIZE(A)
    for k ← 1, 2, 3, . . .
        y⃗ ← FORWARD-SUBSTITUTE(L, v⃗)
        w⃗ ← BACK-SUBSTITUTE(U, y⃗)
        v⃗ ← w⃗/‖w⃗‖
    return v⃗
```

(b)

Figure 6.4 Inverse iteration (a) without and (b) with LU factorization.

This algorithm, known as *power iteration* and detailed in Figure 6.3(a), produces vectors $\vec{v}_k$ more and more parallel to the desired $\vec{x}_1$ as $k \to \infty$. Although we have not considered the defective case here, it is still guaranteed to converge; see [98] for a more advanced discussion.

One time that this technique may fail is if we accidentally choose $\vec{v}_1$ such that $c_1 = 0$, but the odds of this peculiarity occurring are vanishingly small. Such a failure mode only occurs when the initial guess has no component parallel to $\vec{x}_1$. Also, while power iteration can succeed in the presence of repeated eigenvalues, it can fail if λ and $-\lambda$ are both eigenvalues of A with the largest magnitude. In the absence of these degeneracies, the rate of convergence for power iteration depends on the decay rate of terms 2 to n in the sum above for $A^k \vec{v}$ and hence is determined by the ratio of the second-largest-magnitude eigenvalue of A to the largest.

If $|\lambda_1| > 1$, however, then $\|\vec{v}_k\| \to \infty$ as $k \to \infty$, an undesirable property for floating-point arithmetic. We only care about the *direction* of the eigenvector rather than its magnitude, so scaling has no effect on the quality of our solution. To avoid dealing with large-magnitude vectors, we can normalize $\vec{v}_k$ at each step, producing the *normalized power iteration* algorithm in Figure 6.3(b). In the algorithm listing, we purposely do not decorate the norm $\| \cdot \|$ with a particular subscript. Mathematically, *any* norm will suffice for preventing $\vec{v}_k$ from going to infinity, since we have shown that all norms on $\mathbb{R}^n$ are equivalent. In practice, we often use the *infinity* norm $\| \cdot \|_\infty$; this choice has the convenient property that during iteration $\|A\vec{v}_k\|_\infty \to |\lambda_1|$.

6.3.2 Inverse Iteration

We now have an iterative algorithm for approximating the *largest*-magnitude eigenvalue λ_1 of a matrix A. Suppose A is invertible, so that we can evaluate $\vec{y} = A^{-1}\vec{v}$ by solving $A\vec{y} = \vec{v}$

```
function RAYLEIGH-QUOTIENT-ITERATION(A, σ)
    v⃗ ← ARBITRARY(n)
    for k ← 1, 2, 3, . . .
        w⃗ ← (A − σI_{n×n})^{−1}v⃗
        v⃗ ← w⃗/∥w⃗∥
        σ ← (v⃗^⊤ A v⃗)/∥v⃗∥²₂
    return v⃗
```

Figure 6.5 Rayleigh quotient iteration for finding an eigenvalue close to an initial guess σ.

using techniques covered in previous chapters. If $A\vec{x} = \lambda\vec{x}$, then $\vec{x} = \lambda A^{-1}\vec{x}$, or equivalently $A^{-1}\vec{x} = \frac{1}{\lambda}\vec{x}$. Thus, $1/\lambda$ is an eigenvalue of A^{-1} with eigenvector $\vec{x}$.

If $|a| \geq |b|$ then $|b|^{-1} \geq |a|^{-1}$, so the smallest-magnitude eigenvalue of A is the *largest-magnitude* eigenvector of A^{-1}. This construction yields an algorithm for finding λ_n rather than λ_1 called *inverse power iteration*, in Figure 6.4(a). This iterative scheme is nothing more than the power method from §6.3.1 applied to A^{-1}.

We repeatedly are solving systems of equations using the same matrix A but different right-hand sides, a perfect application of factorization techniques from previous chapters. For instance, if we write $A = LU$, then we could formulate an equivalent but considerably more efficient version of inverse power iteration illustrated in Figure 6.4(b). With this simplification, each solve for $A^{-1}\vec{v}$ is carried out in two steps, first by solving $L\vec{y} = \vec{v}$ and then by solving $U\vec{w} = \vec{y}$ as suggested in §3.5.1.

6.3.3 Shifting

Suppose λ_2 is the eigenvalue of A with second-largest magnitude. Power iteration converges fastest when $|\lambda_2/\lambda_1|$ is small, since in this case the power $(\lambda_2/\lambda_1)^k$ decays quickly. If this ratio is nearly 1, it may take many iterations before a single eigenvector is isolated.

If the eigenvalues of A are $\lambda_1, \ldots, \lambda_n$ with corresponding eigenvectors $\vec{x}_1, \ldots, \vec{x}_n$, then the eigenvalues of $A - \sigma I_{n \times n}$ are $\lambda_1 - \sigma, \ldots, \lambda_n - \sigma$, since:

$$(A - \sigma I_{n \times n})\vec{x}_i = A\vec{x}_i - \sigma\vec{x}_i = \lambda_i\vec{x}_i - \sigma\vec{x}_i = (\lambda_i - \sigma)\vec{x}_i.$$

With this idea in mind, one way to make power iteration converge quickly is to choose σ such that:

$$\left| \frac{\lambda_2 - \sigma}{\lambda_1 - \sigma} \right| < \left| \frac{\lambda_2}{\lambda_1} \right|.$$

That is, we find eigenvectors of $A - \sigma I_{n \times n}$ rather than A itself, choosing σ to widen the gap between the first and second eigenvalue to improve convergence rates. Guessing a good σ, however, can be an art, since we do not know the eigenvalues of A *a priori*.

More generally, if we think that σ is near an eigenvalue of A, then $A - \sigma I_{n \times n}$ has an eigenvalue close to 0 that we can reveal by inverse iteration. In other words, to use power iteration to target a particular eigenvalue of A rather than its largest or smallest eigenvalue as in previous sections, we shift A so that the eigenvalue we want is close to zero and then can apply inverse iteration to the result.

If our initial guess of σ is inaccurate, we could try to update it from iteration to iteration of the power method. For example, if we have a fixed guess of an eigenvector $\vec{x}$ of A, then by the normal equations the least-squares approximation of the corresponding eigenvalue σ is given by

$$\sigma \approx \frac{\vec{x}^\top A \vec{x}}{\|\vec{x}\|_2^2}.$$

This fraction is known as a Rayleigh quotient. Thus, we can attempt to increase convergence by using *Rayleigh quotient iteration*, in Figure 6.5, which uses this approximation for σ to update the shift in each step.

Rayleigh quotient iteration usually takes fewer steps to converge than power iteration given a good starting guess σ, but the matrix $A - \sigma_k I_{n \times n}$ is different each iteration and cannot be prefactored as in Figure 6.4(b). In other words, fewer iterations are necessary but each iteration takes more time. This trade-off makes the Rayleigh method more or less preferable to power iteration with a fixed shift depending on the particular choice and size of A. As an additional caveat, if σ_k is *too good* an estimate of an eigenvalue, the matrix $A - \sigma_k I_{n \times n}$ can become near-singular, causing conditioning issues during inverse iteration; that said, depending on the linear solver, this ill-conditioning may not be a concern because it occurs in the direction of the eigenvector being computed. In the opposite case, it can be difficult to control which eigenvalue is isolated by Rayleigh quotient iteration, especially if the initial guess is inaccurate.

6.4 FINDING MULTIPLE EIGENVALUES

So far, we have described techniques for finding a single eigenvalue/eigenvector pair: power iteration to find the largest eigenvalue, inverse iteration to find the smallest, and shifting to target values in between. For many applications, however, a single eigenvalue will not suffice. Thankfully, we can modify these techniques to handle this case as well.

6.4.1 Deflation

Recall the high-level structure of power iteration: Choose an arbitrary $\vec{v}_1$, and iteratively multiply it by A until only the largest eigenvalue λ_1 survives. Take $\vec{x}_1$ to be the corresponding eigenvector.

We were quick to dismiss an unlikely failure mode of this algorithm when $\vec{v}_1 \cdot \vec{x}_1 = 0$, that is, when the initial eigenvector guess has no component parallel to $\vec{x}_1$. In this case, no matter how many times we apply A, the result will never have a component parallel to $\vec{x}_1$. The probability of choosing such a $\vec{v}_1$ randomly is vanishingly small, so in all but the most pernicious of cases power iteration is a stable technique.

We can turn this drawback on its head to formulate a method for finding more than one eigenvalue of a symmetric matrix A. Suppose we find $\vec{x}_1$ and λ_1 via power iteration as before. After convergence, we can restart power iteration after projecting $\vec{x}_1$ out of the initial guess $\vec{v}_1$. Since the eigenvectors of A are orthogonal, by the argument in §6.3.1, power iteration after this projection will recover its *second*-largest eigenvalue!

Due to finite-precision arithmetic, applying A to a vector may inadvertently introduce a small component parallel to $\vec{x}_1$. We can avoid this effect by projecting in each iteration. This change yields the algorithm in Figure 6.6 for computing the eigenvalues in order of descending magnitude.

The inner loop of projected iteration is equivalent to power iteration on the matrix AP, where P projects out $\vec{v}_1, \ldots, \vec{v}_{\ell-1}$:

$$P\vec{x} = \vec{x} - \mathrm{proj}_{\mathrm{span}\,\{\vec{v}_1, \ldots, \vec{v}_{\ell-1}\}}\, \vec{x}.$$

```
function PROJECTED-ITERATION(symmetric A,k)
    for ℓ ← 1, 2, ..., k
        v⃗_ℓ ← ARBITRARY(n)
        for p ← 1, 2, 3, ...
            u⃗ ← v⃗_ℓ − proj_span{v⃗_1,...,v⃗_{ℓ-1}} v⃗_ℓ
            w⃗ ← Av⃗
            v⃗_ℓ ← w⃗/‖w⃗‖
    return v⃗_1, ..., v⃗_k
```

Figure 6.6 Projection for finding k eigenvectors of a symmetric matrix A with the largest eigenvalues. If $\vec{u} = \vec{0}$ at any point, the remaining eigenvalues of A are all zero.

AP has the same eigenvectors as A with eigenvalues $0, \ldots, 0, \lambda_\ell, \ldots, \lambda_n$. More generally, the method of *deflation* involves modifying the matrix A so that power iteration reveals an eigenvector that has not already been computed. For instance, AP is a modification of A so that the large eigenvalues we already have computed are zeroed out.

Projection can fail if A is asymmetric. Other deflation formulas, however, can work in its place with similar efficiency. For instance, suppose $A\vec{x}_1 = \lambda_1 \vec{x}_1$ with $\|\vec{x}_1\|_2 = 1$. Take H to be the Householder matrix (see §5.5) such that $H\vec{x}_1 = \vec{e}_1$, the first standard basis vector. From our discussion in §6.2, similarity transforms do not affect the set of eigenvalues, so we safely can conjugate A by H without changing A's eigenvalues. Consider what happens when we multiply $HAH^\top$ by $\vec{e}_1$:

$$
\begin{aligned}
HAH^\top \vec{e}_1 &= HAH\vec{e}_1 \text{ since } H \text{ is symmetric} \\
&= HA\vec{x}_1 \text{ since } H\vec{x}_1 = \vec{e}_1 \text{ and } H^2 = I_{n \times n} \\
&= \lambda_1 H\vec{x}_1 \text{ since } A\vec{x}_1 = \lambda_1 \vec{x}_1 \\
&= \lambda_1 \vec{e}_1 \text{ by definition of } H.
\end{aligned}
$$

From this chain of equalities, the first column of $HAH^\top$ is $\lambda_1 \vec{e}_1$, showing that $HAH^\top$ has the following structure [58]:

$$
HAH^\top = \begin{pmatrix} \lambda_1 & \vec{b}^\top \\ \vec{0} & B \end{pmatrix}.
$$

The matrix $B \in \mathbb{R}^{(n-1) \times (n-1)}$ has eigenvalues $\lambda_2, \ldots, \lambda_n$. Recursively applying this observation, another algorithm for deflation successively generates smaller and smaller B matrices, with each eigenvalue computed using power iteration.

6.4.2 QR Iteration

Deflation has the drawback that each eigenvector must be computed separately, which can be slow and can accumulate error if individual eigenvalues are not accurate. Our remaining algorithms attempt to find more than one eigenvector simultaneously.

Recall that similar matrices A and $B = T^{-1}AT$ have the same eigenvalues for any invertible T. An algorithm seeking the eigenvalues of A can apply similarity transformations to A with abandon in the same way that Gaussian elimination premultiplies by row operations. Applying T^{-1} may be difficult, however, since it would require inverting T, so to make such a strategy practical we seek T's whose inverses are known.

```
function QR-ITERATION(A ∈ ℝ^{n×n})
    for k ← 1, 2, 3, . . .
        Q, R ← QR-FACTORIZE(A)
        A ← RQ
    return diag(R)
```

Figure 6.7 QR iteration for finding all the eigenvalues of A in the non-repeated eigenvalue case.

One of our motivators for the QR factorization in Chapter 5 was that the matrix Q is *orthogonal*, satisfying $Q^{-1} = Q^\top$. Because of this formula, Q and Q^{-1} are equally straightforward to apply, making orthogonal matrices strong choices for similarity transformations. We already applied this observation in §6.4.1 when we deflated using Householder matrices. Conjugating by orthogonal matrices also does not affect the conditioning of the eigenvalue problem.

But if we do not know *any* eigenvectors of A, which orthogonal matrix Q should we choose? Ideally, Q should involve the structure of A while being straightforward to compute. It is less clear how to apply Householder matrices strategically to reveal multiple eigenvalues in parallel (some advanced techniques do exactly this!), but we do know how to generate one orthogonal Q from A by factoring $A = QR$. Then, experimentally we might conjugate A by Q to find:

$$Q^{-1}AQ = Q^\top AQ = Q^\top(QR)Q = (Q^\top Q)RQ = RQ.$$

Amazingly, conjugating $A = QR$ by the orthogonal matrix Q is identical to writing the product RQ!

This matrix $A_2 \equiv RQ$ is *not* equal to $A = QR$, but it has the same eigenvalues. Hence, we can factor $A_2 = Q_2 R_2$ to get a new orthogonal matrix Q_2 and once again conjugate to define $A_3 \equiv R_2 Q_2$. Repeating this process indefinitely generates a sequence of similar matrices $A, A_2, A_3, \ldots$ with the same eigenvalues. Curiously, for many choices of A, as $k \to \infty$, one can check numerically that while iterating QR factorization in this manner, R_k becomes an upper-triangular matrix containing the eigenvalues of A along its diagonal.

Based on this elegant observation, in the 1950s multiple groups of European mathematicians studied the same iterative algorithm for finding the eigenvalues of a matrix A, shown in Figure 6.7:

> **Repeatedly factorize $A = QR$ and replace A with RQ.**

Take A_k to be A after the k-th iteration of this method; that is $A_1 = A = Q_1 R_1$, $A_2 = R_1 Q_1 = Q_2 R_2$, $A_3 = R_2 Q_2 = Q_3 R_3$, and so on. Since they are related via conjugation by a sequence of Q matrices, the matrices A_k all have the same eigenvalues as A. So, our analysis must show (1) when we expect this technique to converge and (2) if and how the limit point reveals eigenvalues of A. We will answer these questions in reverse order, for the case when A is symmetric and invertible with no repeated eigenvalues up to sign; so, if $\lambda \neq 0$ is an eigenvalue of A, then $-\lambda$ is *not* an eigenvalue of A. More advanced analysis and application to asymmetric or defective matrices can be found in [50] and elsewhere.

We begin by proving a proposition that will help characterize limit behavior of the QR iteration algorithm:*

---

*The conditions of this proposition can be relaxed but are sufficient for the discussion at hand.

Proposition 6.6. Take $A, B \in \mathbb{R}^{n \times n}$. Suppose that the eigenvectors of A span $\mathbb{R}^n$ and have distinct eigenvalues. Then, $AB = BA$ if and only if A and B have the same set of eigenvectors (with possibly different eigenvalues).

Proof. Suppose A and B have eigenvectors $\vec{x}_1, \ldots, \vec{x}_n$ with eigenvalues $\lambda_1^A, \ldots, \lambda_n^A$ for A and eigenvalues $\lambda_1^B, \ldots, \lambda_n^B$ for B. Any $\vec{y} \in \mathbb{R}^n$ can be decomposed as $\vec{y} = \sum_i a_i \vec{x}_i$, showing:

$$BA\vec{y} = BA \sum_i a_i \vec{x}_i = B \sum_i \lambda_i^A \vec{x}_i = \sum_i \lambda_i^A \lambda_i^B \vec{x}_i$$

$$AB\vec{y} = AB \sum_i a_i \vec{x}_i = A \sum_i \lambda_i^B \vec{x}_i = \sum_i \lambda_i^A \lambda_i^B \vec{x}_i.$$

So, $AB\vec{y} = BA\vec{y}$ for all $\vec{y} \in \mathbb{R}^n$, or equivalently $AB = BA$.

Now, suppose $AB = BA$, and take $\vec{x}$ to be any eigenvector of A with $A\vec{x} = \lambda\vec{x}$. Then, $A(B\vec{x}) = (AB)\vec{x} = (BA)\vec{x} = B(A\vec{x}) = \lambda(B\vec{x})$. We have two cases:

- If $B\vec{x} \neq \vec{0}$, then $B\vec{x}$ is an eigenvector of A with eigenvalue λ. Since A has no repeated eigenvalues and $\vec{x}$ is also an eigenvector of A with eigenvalue λ, we must have $B\vec{x} = c\vec{x}$ for some $c \neq 0$. In other words, $\vec{x}$ is also an eigenvector of B with eigenvalue c.

- If $B\vec{x} = \vec{0}$, then $\vec{x}$ is an eigenvector of B with eigenvalue 0.

Hence, all of the eigenvectors of A are eigenvectors of B. Since the eigenvectors of A span $\mathbb{R}^n$, A and B have exactly the same set of eigenvectors. □

Returning to QR iteration, suppose $A_k \to A_\infty$ as $k \to \infty$. If we factor $A_\infty = Q_\infty R_\infty$, then since QR iteration converged, $A_\infty = Q_\infty R_\infty = R_\infty Q_\infty$. By the conjugation property, $Q_\infty^\top A_\infty Q_\infty = R_\infty Q_\infty = A_\infty$, or equivalently $A_\infty Q_\infty = Q_\infty A_\infty$. Since A_∞ has a full set of distinct eigenvalues, by Proposition 6.6, Q_∞ has the same eigenvectors as A_∞. The eigenvalues of Q_∞ are ± 1 by orthogonality. Suppose $A_\infty \vec{x} = \lambda\vec{x}$. In this case,

$$\lambda\vec{x} = A_\infty \vec{x} = Q_\infty R_\infty \vec{x} = R_\infty Q_\infty \vec{x} = \pm R_\infty \vec{x},$$

so $R_\infty \vec{x} = \pm\lambda\vec{x}$. Since R_∞ is upper triangular, we now know (Exercise 6.3):

> **The eigenvalues of A_∞—and hence the eigenvalues of A—equal the diagonal elements of R_∞ up to sign.**

We can remove the sign caveat by computing QR using rotations rather than reflections.

The derivation above assumes that there exists A_∞ with $A_k \to A_\infty$ as $k \to \infty$. Although we have not shown it yet, QR iteration is a stable method guaranteed to converge in many situations, and even when it does not converge, the relevant eigenstructure of A often can be computed from R_k as $k \to \infty$ regardless. We will not derive exact convergence conditions here but will provide some intuition for why we might expect this method to converge, at least given our restrictions on A.

To help motivate when we expect QR iteration to converge and yield eigenvalues along the diagonal of R_∞, suppose the columns of A are given by $\vec{a}_1, \ldots, \vec{a}_n$, and consider the matrix A^k for large k. We can write:

$$A^k = A^{k-1} \cdot A = \begin{pmatrix} | & | & & | \\ A^{k-1}\vec{a}_1 & A^{k-1}\vec{a}_2 & \cdots & A^{k-1}\vec{a}_n \\ | & | & & | \end{pmatrix}.$$

By our derivation of power iteration, in the absence of degeneracies, the first column of A^k will become more and more parallel to the eigenvector $\vec{x}_1$ of A with largest magnitude $|\lambda_1|$ as $k \to \infty$, since we took a vector $\vec{a}_1$ and multiplied it by A many times.

Applying intuition from deflation, suppose we project $\vec{x}_1$, which is approximately parallel to the first column of A^k, out of the second column of A^k. By orthogonality of the eigenvectors of A, we equivalently could have projected $\vec{x}_1$ out of $\vec{a}_2$ *initially* and then applied A^{k-1}. For this reason, as in §6.4.1, thanks to the removal of $\vec{x}_1$ the result of either process must be nearly parallel to $\vec{x}_2$, the vector with the *second*-most dominant eigenvalue! Proceeding inductively, when A is symmetric and thus has a full set of orthogonal eigenvectors, factoring $A^k = QR$ yields a set of near-eigenvectors of A in the columns of Q, in order of decreasing eigenvalue magnitude, with the corresponding eigenvalues along the diagonal of R.

Multiplying to find A^k for large k approximately takes the condition number of A to the k-th power, so computing the QR decomposition of A^k explicitly is likely to lead to numerical problems. Since decomposing A^k would reveal the eigenvector structure of A, however, we use this fact to our advantage without paying numerically. To do so, we make the following observation about QR iteration:

$$A = Q_1 R_1 \text{ by definition of QR iteration}$$
$$A^2 = (Q_1 R_1)(Q_1 R_1)$$
$$= Q_1(R_1 Q_1)R_1 \text{ by regrouping}$$
$$= Q_1 Q_2 R_2 R_1 \text{ since } A_2 = R_1 Q_1 = Q_2 R_2$$
$$\vdots$$
$$A^k = Q_1 Q_2 \cdots Q_k R_k R_{k-1} \cdots R_1 \text{ by induction.}$$

Grouping the Q_i variables and the R_i variables separately provides a QR factorization of A^k. In other words, we can use the Q_k's and R_k's constructed during each step of QR iteration to construct a factorization of A^k, and thus we expect the columns of the product $Q_1 \cdots Q_k$ to converge to the eigenvectors of A.

By a similar argument, we show a related fact about the iterates $A_1, A_2, \ldots$ from QR iteration. Since $A_k = Q_k R_k$, we substitute $R_k = Q_k^\top A_k$ inductively to show:

$$A_1 = A$$
$$A_2 = R_1 Q_1 \text{ by our construction of QR iteration}$$
$$= Q_1^\top A Q_1 \text{ since } R_1 = Q_1^\top A_1$$
$$A_3 = R_2 Q_2$$
$$= Q_2^\top A_2 Q_2$$
$$= Q_2^\top Q_1^\top A Q_1 Q_2 \text{ from the previous step}$$
$$\vdots$$
$$A_{k+1} = Q_k^\top \cdots Q_1^\top A Q_1 \cdots Q_k \text{ inductively}$$
$$= (Q_1 \cdots Q_k)^\top A(Q_1 \cdots Q_k),$$

where A_k is the k-th matrix from QR iteration. Thus, A_{k+1} is the matrix A conjugated by the product $\bar{Q}_k \equiv Q_1 \cdots Q_k$. We argued earlier that the columns of $\bar{Q}_k$ converge to the eigenvectors of A. Since conjugating by the matrix of eigenvectors yields a diagonal matrix of eigenvalues, we know $A_{k+1} = \bar{Q}_k^\top A \bar{Q}$ will have approximate eigenvalues of A along its diagonal as $k \to \infty$, at least when eigenvalues are not repeated.

In the case of symmetric matrices without repeated eigenvalues, we have shown that both A_k and R_k will converge unconditionally to diagonal matrices containing the eigenvalues of

A, while the product of the Q_k's will converge to a matrix of the corresponding eigenvectors. This case is but one example of the power of QR iteration, which is applied to many problems in which more than a few eigenvectors are needed of a given matrix A.

In practice, a few simplifying steps are usually applied before commencing QR iteration. QR factorization of a full matrix is relatively expensive computationally, so each iteration of the algorithm as we have described it is costly for large matrices. One way to avoid this cost for symmetric A is first to *tridiagonalize* A, systematically conjugating it by orthogonal matrices until entries not on or immediately adjacent to the diagonal are zero; tridiagonalization can be carried out using Householder matrices in $O(n^3)$ time for $A \in \mathbb{R}^{n \times n}$ [22]. QR factorization of symmetric tridiagonal matrices is much more efficient than the general case [92].

Example 6.3 (QR iteration). To illustrate typical behavior of QR iteration, we apply the algorithm to the matrix

$$A = \begin{pmatrix} 2 & 3 \\ 3 & 2 \end{pmatrix}.$$

The first few iterations, computed numerically, are shown below:

$$A_1 = \begin{pmatrix} 2.000 & 3.000 \\ 3.000 & 2.000 \end{pmatrix} = \underbrace{\begin{pmatrix} -0.555 & 0.832 \\ -0.832 & -0.555 \end{pmatrix}}_{Q_1} \underbrace{\begin{pmatrix} -3.606 & -3.328 \\ 0.000 & 1.387 \end{pmatrix}}_{R_1}$$

$$\implies A_2 = R_1 Q_1 = \begin{pmatrix} 4.769 & -1.154 \\ -1.154 & -0.769 \end{pmatrix}$$

$$A_2 = \begin{pmatrix} 4.769 & -1.154 \\ -1.154 & -0.769 \end{pmatrix} = \underbrace{\begin{pmatrix} -0.972 & -0.235 \\ 0.235 & -0.972 \end{pmatrix}}_{Q_2} \underbrace{\begin{pmatrix} -4.907 & 0.941 \\ 0.000 & 1.019 \end{pmatrix}}_{R_2}$$

$$\implies A_3 = R_2 Q_2 = \begin{pmatrix} 4.990 & 0.240 \\ 0.240 & -0.990 \end{pmatrix}$$

$$A_3 = \begin{pmatrix} 4.990 & 0.240 \\ 0.240 & -0.990 \end{pmatrix} = \underbrace{\begin{pmatrix} -0.999 & 0.048 \\ -0.048 & -0.999 \end{pmatrix}}_{Q_3} \underbrace{\begin{pmatrix} -4.996 & -0.192 \\ 0.000 & 1.001 \end{pmatrix}}_{R_3}$$

$$\implies A_4 = R_3 Q_3 = \begin{pmatrix} 5.000 & -0.048 \\ -0.048 & -1.000 \end{pmatrix}$$

$$A_4 = \begin{pmatrix} 5.000 & -0.048 \\ -0.048 & -1.000 \end{pmatrix} = \underbrace{\begin{pmatrix} -1.000 & -0.010 \\ 0.010 & -1.000 \end{pmatrix}}_{Q_4} \underbrace{\begin{pmatrix} -5.000 & 0.038 \\ 0.000 & 1.000 \end{pmatrix}}_{R_4}$$

$$\implies A_5 = R_4 Q_4 = \begin{pmatrix} 5.000 & 0.010 \\ 0.010 & -1.000 \end{pmatrix}$$

$$A_5 = \begin{pmatrix} 5.000 & 0.010 \\ 0.010 & -1.000 \end{pmatrix} = \underbrace{\begin{pmatrix} -1.000 & 0.002 \\ -0.002 & -1.000 \end{pmatrix}}_{Q_5} \underbrace{\begin{pmatrix} -5.000 & -0.008 \\ 0.000 & 1.000 \end{pmatrix}}_{R_5}$$

$$\implies A_6 = R_5 Q_5 = \begin{pmatrix} 5.000 & -0.002 \\ -0.002 & -1.000 \end{pmatrix}$$

$$A_6 = \begin{pmatrix} 5.000 & -0.002 \\ -0.002 & -1.000 \end{pmatrix} = \underbrace{\begin{pmatrix} -1.000 & -0.000 \\ 0.000 & -1.000 \end{pmatrix}}_{Q_6} \underbrace{\begin{pmatrix} -5.000 & 0.002 \\ 0.000 & 1.000 \end{pmatrix}}_{R_6}$$

$$\implies A_7 = R_6 Q_6 = \begin{pmatrix} 5.000 & 0.000 \\ 0.000 & -1.000 \end{pmatrix}$$

The diagonal elements of A_k converge to the eigenvalues 5 and -1 of A, as expected.

6.4.3 Krylov Subspace Methods

Our justification for QR iteration involved analyzing the columns of A^k as $k \to \infty$, applying observations we already made about power iteration in §6.3.1. More generally, for a vector $\vec{b} \in \mathbb{R}^n$, we can examine the so-called *Krylov matrix*

$$K_k \equiv \begin{pmatrix} | & | & | & & | \\ \vec{b} & A\vec{b} & A^2\vec{b} & \cdots & A^{k-1}\vec{b} \\ | & | & | & & | \end{pmatrix}.$$

Methods analyzing K_k to find eigenvectors and eigenvalues generally are classified as *Krylov subspace methods*. For instance, the *Arnoldi iteration* algorithm uses Gram-Schmidt orthogonalization to maintain an orthogonal basis $\{\vec{q}_1, \ldots, \vec{q}_k\}$ for the column space of K_k:

1. Begin by taking $\vec{q}_1$ to be an arbitrary unit-norm vector.

2. For $k = 2, 3, \ldots$

    (a) Take $\vec{a}_k = A\vec{q}_{k-1}$.

    (b) Project out the $\vec{q}$'s you already have computed:

    $$\vec{b}_k = \vec{a}_k - \text{proj}_{\text{span}\{\vec{q}_1, \ldots, \vec{q}_{k-1}\}} \vec{a}_k.$$

    (c) Renormalize to find the next $\vec{q}_k = \vec{b}_k / \|\vec{b}_k\|_2$.

The matrix Q_k whose columns are the vectors found above is an orthogonal matrix with the same column space as K_k, and eigenvalue estimates can be recovered from the structure of $Q_k^\top A Q_k$.

The use of Gram-Schmidt makes this technique unstable, and its timing gets progressively worse as k increases. So, extensions are needed to make it feasible. For instance, one approach involves running some iterations of the Arnoldi algorithm, using the output to generate a better guess for the initial $\vec{q}_1$, and restarting [80]. Methods in this class are suited for problems requiring multiple eigenvectors at the ends of the spectrum of A without computing the complete set. They also can be applied to designing iterative methods for solving linear systems of equations, as we will explore in Chapter 11.

6.5 SENSITIVITY AND CONDITIONING

We have only outlined a few eigenvalue techniques out of a rich and long-standing literature. Almost any algorithmic technique has been experimented with for finding spectra, from iterative methods to root-finding on the characteristic polynomial to methods that divide matrices into blocks for parallel processing.

As with linear solvers, we can evaluate the conditioning of an eigenvalue problem independently of the solution technique. This analysis can help understand whether a simplistic iterative algorithm will be successful at finding the eigenvectors of a given matrix or if more complex stabilized methods are necessary. To do so, we will derive a condition number for the problem of finding eigenvalues for a given matrix A. Before proceeding, we should highlight that the conditioning of an eigenvalue problem is *not* the same as the condition number of the matrix for solving linear systems.

Suppose a matrix A has an eigenvector $\vec{x}$ with eigenvalue λ. Analyzing the conditioning of the eigenvalue problem involves analyzing the stability of $\vec{x}$ and λ to perturbations in A. To this end, we might perturb A by a small matrix δA, thus changing the set of eigenvectors.

We can write eigenvectors of $A + \delta A$ as perturbations of eigenvectors of A by solving the problem

$$(A + \delta A)(\vec{x} + \delta \vec{x}) = (\lambda + \delta \lambda)(\vec{x} + \delta \vec{x}).$$

Expanding both sides yields:

$$A\vec{x} + A\delta\vec{x} + \delta A \cdot \vec{x} + \delta A \cdot \delta \vec{x} = \lambda \vec{x} + \lambda \delta \vec{x} + \delta \lambda \cdot \vec{x} + \delta \lambda \cdot \delta \vec{x}.$$

Since δA is small, we will assume that $\delta \vec{x}$ and $\delta \lambda$ also are small (this assumption should be checked in a more rigorous treatment!). Products between these variables then are negligible, yielding the following approximation:

$$A\vec{x} + A\delta\vec{x} + \delta A \cdot \vec{x} \approx \lambda \vec{x} + \lambda \delta \vec{x} + \delta \lambda \cdot \vec{x}.$$

Since $A\vec{x} = \lambda\vec{x}$, we can subtract this vector from both sides to find:

$$A\delta\vec{x} + \delta A \cdot \vec{x} \approx \lambda \delta \vec{x} + \delta \lambda \cdot \vec{x}.$$

We now apply an analytical trick to complete our derivation. Since $A\vec{x} = \lambda\vec{x}$, we know $(A - \lambda I_{n \times n})\vec{x} = \vec{0}$, so $A - \lambda I_{n \times n}$ is not full rank. The transpose of a matrix is full-rank only if the matrix is full-rank, so we know $(A - \lambda I_{n \times n})^{\top} = A^{\top} - \lambda I_{n \times n}$ also has a null space vector $\vec{y}$, with $A^{\top}\vec{y} = \lambda\vec{y}$. We call $\vec{y}$ a *left* eigenvector corresponding to $\vec{x}$. Left-multiplying our perturbation estimate above by $\vec{y}^{\top}$ shows

$$\vec{y}^{\top}(A\delta\vec{x} + \delta A \cdot \vec{x}) \approx \vec{y}^{\top}(\lambda \delta \vec{x} + \delta \lambda \cdot \vec{x}).$$

Since $A^{\top}\vec{y} = \lambda\vec{y}$, we can simplify:

$$\vec{y}^{\top}\delta A \cdot \vec{x} \approx \delta\lambda\vec{y}^{\top}\vec{x}.$$

Rearranging yields:

$$\delta\lambda \approx \frac{\vec{y}^{\top}(\delta A)\vec{x}}{\vec{y}^{\top}\vec{x}}.$$

Finally, assume $\|\vec{x}\|_2 = 1$ and $\|\vec{y}\|_2 = 1$. Then, taking norms on both sides shows:

$$|\delta\lambda| \lesssim \frac{\|\delta A\|_2}{|\vec{y} \cdot \vec{x}|}.$$

This expression shows that conditioning of the eigenvalue problem roughly depends directly on the size of the perturbation δA and inversely on the angle between the left and right eigenvectors $\vec{x}$ and $\vec{y}$.

Based on this derivation, we can use $1/|\vec{x} \cdot \vec{y}|$ as an approximate condition number for finding the eigenvalue λ corresponding to eigenvector $\vec{x}$ of A. Symmetric matrices have the same left and right eigenvectors, so $\vec{x} = \vec{y}$, yielding a condition number of 1. This strong conditioning reflects the fact that the eigenvectors of symmetric matrices are orthogonal and thus maximally separated.

6.6 EXERCISES

6.1 Verify the solution $\vec{y}(t)$ given in §6.1.2 to the ODE $\vec{y}' = B\vec{y}$.

6.2 Define
$$A \equiv \begin{pmatrix} 0 & 1 \\ 1 & 0 \end{pmatrix}.$$

Can power iteration find eigenvalues of this matrix? Why or why not?

6.3 Show that the eigenvalues of upper-triangular matrices $U \in \mathbb{R}^{n \times n}$ are exactly their diagonal elements.

6.4 Extending Exercise 6.3, if we assume that the eigenvectors of U are $\vec{v}_k$ satisfying $U\vec{v}_k = u_{kk}\vec{v}_k$, characterize span $\{\vec{v}_1, \ldots, \vec{v}_k\}$ for $1 \leq k \leq n$ when the diagonal values u_{kk} of U are distinct.

6.5 We showed that the Rayleigh quotient iteration method can converge more quickly than power iteration. Why, however, might it still be more efficient to use the power method in some cases?

6.6 (Suggested by J. Yeo) Suppose $\vec{u}$ and $\vec{v}$ are vectors in $\mathbb{R}^n$ such that $\vec{u}^\top \vec{v} = 1$, and define $A \equiv \vec{u}\vec{v}^\top$.

   (a) What are the eigenvalues of A?

   (b) How many iterations does power iteration take to converge to the dominant eigenvalue of A?

6.7 (Suggested by J. Yeo) Suppose $B \in \mathbb{R}^{n \times n}$ is diagonalizable with eigenvalues λ_i satisfying $0 < \lambda_1 = \lambda_2 < \lambda_3 < \cdots < \lambda_n$. Let $\vec{v}_i$ be the eigenvector corresponding to λ_i. Show that the inverse power method applied to B converges to a linear combination of $\vec{v}_1$ and $\vec{v}_2$.

6.8 ("Mini-Riesz Representation Theorem") We will say $\langle \cdot, \cdot \rangle$ is an *inner product* on $\mathbb{R}^n$ if it satisfies:

   1. $\langle \vec{x}, \vec{y} \rangle = \langle \vec{y}, \vec{x} \rangle \, \forall \vec{x}, \vec{y} \in \mathbb{R}^n$,

   2. $\langle \alpha\vec{x}, \vec{y} \rangle = \alpha\langle \vec{x}, \vec{y} \rangle \, \forall \vec{x}, \vec{y} \in \mathbb{R}^n, \alpha \in \mathbb{R}$,

   3. $\langle \vec{x} + \vec{y}, \vec{z} \rangle = \langle \vec{x}, \vec{z} \rangle + \langle \vec{y}, \vec{z} \rangle \, \forall \vec{x}, \vec{y}, \vec{z} \in \mathbb{R}^n$, and

   4. $\langle \vec{x}, \vec{x} \rangle \geq 0$ with equality if and only if $\vec{x} = \vec{0}$.

   (a) Given an inner product $\langle \cdot, \cdot \rangle$, show that there exists a matrix $A \in \mathbb{R}^{n \times n}$ (depending on $\langle \cdot, \cdot \rangle$) such that $\langle \vec{x}, \vec{y} \rangle = \vec{x}^\top A\vec{y}$ for all $\vec{x}, \vec{y} \in \mathbb{R}^n$. Also, show that there exists a matrix $M \in \mathbb{R}^{n \times n}$ such that $\langle \vec{x}, \vec{y} \rangle = (M\vec{x}) \cdot (M\vec{y})$ for all $\vec{x}, \vec{y} \in \mathbb{R}^n$. [This shows that all inner products are dot products after suitable rotation, stretching, and shearing of $\mathbb{R}^n$!]

   (b) A *Mahalanobis metric* on $\mathbb{R}^n$ is a distance function of the form $d(\vec{x}, \vec{y}) = \sqrt{\langle \vec{x} - \vec{y}, \vec{x} - \vec{y} \rangle}$ for a fixed inner product $\langle \cdot, \cdot \rangle$. Use Exercise 6.8a to write Mahalanobis metrics in terms of matrices M, and show that $d(\vec{x}, \vec{y})^2$ is a quadratic function in $\vec{x}$ and $\vec{y}$ jointly.

   (c) Suppose we are given several pairs $(\vec{x}_i, \vec{y}_i) \in \mathbb{R}^n \times \mathbb{R}^n$. A typical "metric learning" problem involves finding a nontrivial Mahalanobis metric such that each $\vec{x}_i$ is close to each $\vec{y}_i$ with respect to that metric. Propose an optimization problem for this task that can be solved using eigenvector computation.
Note: Make sure that your optimal Mahalanobis distance is not identically zero, but it is acceptable if your optimization allows *pseudometrics*; that is, there can exist some $\vec{x} \neq \vec{y}$ with $d(\vec{x}, \vec{y}) = 0$.

6.9 ("Shifted QR iteration") A widely used generalization of the QR iteration algorithm for finding eigenvectors and eigenvalues of $A \in \mathbb{R}^{n \times n}$ uses a shift in each iteration:

$$A_0 = A$$
$$A_k - \sigma_k I_{n \times n} = Q_k R_k$$
$$A_{k+1} = R_k Q_k + \sigma_k I_{n \times n}.$$

Uniformly choosing $\sigma_k \equiv 0$ recovers basic QR iteration. Different variants of this method propose heuristics for choosing $\sigma_k \neq 0$ to encourage convergence or numerical stability.

(a) Show that A_k is similar to A for all $k \geq 0$.

(b) Propose a heuristic for choosing σ_k based on the construction of Rayleigh quotient iteration. Explain when you expect your method to converge faster than basic QR iteration.

6.10 Suppose $A, B \in \mathbb{R}^{n \times n}$ are symmetric and positive definite.

(a) Define a matrix $\sqrt{A} \in \mathbb{R}^{n \times n}$ and show that $(\sqrt{A})^2 = A$. Generally speaking, $\sqrt{A}$ is not the same as L in the Cholesky factorization $A = LL^\top$.

(b) Do most matrices have unique square roots? Why or why not?

(c) We can define the *exponential* of A as $e^A \equiv \sum_{k=0}^{\infty} \frac{1}{k!} A^k$; this sum is unconditionally convergent (you do not have to prove this!). Write an alternative expression for e^A in terms of the eigenvectors and eigenvalues of A.

(d) If $AB = BA$, show $e^{A+B} = e^A e^B$.

(e) Show that the ordinary differential equation $\vec{y}'(t) = -A\vec{y}$ with $\vec{y}(0) = \vec{y}_0$ for some $\vec{y}_0 \in \mathbb{R}^n$ is solved by $\vec{y}(t) = e^{-At}\vec{y}_0$. What happens as $t \to \infty$?

6.11 ("Epidemiology") Suppose $\vec{x}_0 \in \mathbb{R}^n$ contains sizes of different populations carrying a particular infection in year 0; for example, when tracking malaria we might take x_{01} to be the number of humans with malaria and x_{02} to be the number of mosquitoes carrying the disease. By writing relationships like "The average mosquito infects two humans," we can write a matrix M such that $\vec{x}_1 \equiv M\vec{x}_0$ predicts populations in year 1, $\vec{x}_2 \equiv M^2\vec{x}_0$ predicts populations in year 2, and so on.

(a) The spectral radius $\rho(M)$ is given by $\max_i |\lambda_i|$, where the eigenvalues of M are $\lambda_1, \ldots, \lambda_k$. Epidemiologists call this number the "reproduction number" $\mathcal{R}_0$ of M. Explain the difference between the cases $\mathcal{R}_0 < 1$ and $\mathcal{R}_0 > 1$ in terms of the spread of disease. Which case is more dangerous?

(b) Suppose we only care about proportions. For instance, we might use $M \in \mathbb{R}^{50 \times 50}$ to model transmission of diseases between residents in each of the 50 states of the USA, and we only care about the fraction of the total people with a disease who live in each state. If $\vec{y}_0$ holds these proportions in year 0, give an iterative scheme to predict proportions in future years. Characterize behavior as time goes to infinity.

Note: Those readers concerned about computer graphics applications of this material should know that the reproduction number $\mathcal{R}_0$ is referenced in the 2011 thriller *Contagion*.

6.12 ("Normalized cuts," [110]) Similar to spectral embedding (§6.1.3), suppose we have a collection of n objects and a symmetric matrix $W \in (\mathbb{R}^+)^{n \times n}$ whose entries w_{ij} measure the similarity between object i and object j. Rather than computing an embedding, however, now we would like to *cluster* the objects into two groups. This machinery is used to mark photos as day or night and to classify pixels in an image as foreground or background.

(a) Suppose we cluster $\{1, \ldots, n\}$ into two disjoint sets A and B; this clustering defines a *cut* of the collection. We define the *cut score* of (A, B) as follows:

$$C(A, B) \equiv \sum_{\substack{i \in A \\ j \in B}} w_{ij}.$$

This score is large if objects in A and B are similar. Efficiency aside, why is it inadvisable to minimize $C(A, B)$ with respect to A and B?

(b) Define the *volume* of a set A as $V(A) \equiv \sum_{i \in A} \sum_{j=1}^{n} w_{ij}$. To alleviate issues with minimizing the cut score directly, instead we will attempt minimize the *normalized cut* score $N(A, B) \equiv C(A, B)(V(A)^{-1} + V(B)^{-1})$. What does this score measure?

(c) For a fixed choice of A and B, define $\vec{x} \in \mathbb{R}^n$ as follows:

$$x_i \equiv \begin{cases} V(A)^{-1} & \text{if } i \in A \\ -V(B)^{-1} & \text{if } i \in B. \end{cases}$$

Explain how to construct matrices L and D from W such that

$$\vec{x}^\top L \vec{x} = \sum_{\substack{i \in A \\ j \in B}} w_{ij} \left(V(A)^{-1} + V(B)^{-1} \right)^2$$

$$\vec{x}^\top D \vec{x} = V(A)^{-1} + V(B)^{-1}.$$

Conclude that $N(A, B) = \frac{\vec{x}^\top L \vec{x}}{\vec{x}^\top D \vec{x}}$.

(d) Show that $\vec{x}^\top D \vec{1} = 0$.

(e) The *normalized cuts algorithm* computes A and B by optimizing for $\vec{x}$. Argue that the result of the following optimization lower-bounds the minimum normalized cut score of any partition (A, B) :

$$\min_{\vec{x}} \quad \frac{\vec{x}^\top L \vec{x}}{\vec{x}^\top D \vec{x}}$$
$$\text{subject to} \quad \vec{x}^\top D \vec{1} = 0.$$

Assuming D is invertible, show that this relaxed $\vec{x}$ can be computed using an eigenvalue problem.

CHAPTER 7

Singular Value Decomposition

CONTENTS

7.1   Deriving the SVD 131
       7.1.1   Computing the SVD 133
7.2   Applications of the SVD 134
       7.2.1   Solving Linear Systems and the Pseudoinverse 134
       7.2.2   Decomposition into Outer Products and Low-Rank
                Approximations 135
       7.2.3   Matrix Norms 136
       7.2.4   The Procrustes Problem and Point Cloud Alignment 137
       7.2.5   Principal Component Analysis (PCA) 139
       7.2.6   Eigenfaces 140

$\mathbb{C}$ HAPTER 6 derived a number of algorithms for computing the eigenvalues and eigenvectors of matrices $A \in \mathbb{R}^{n \times n}$. Using this machinery, we complete our initial discussion of numerical linear algebra by deriving and making use of one final matrix factorization that exists for *any* matrix $A \in \mathbb{R}^{m \times n}$, even if it is not symmetric or square: the singular value decomposition (SVD).

7.1   DERIVING THE SVD

For $A \in \mathbb{R}^{m \times n}$, we can think of the function $\vec{v} \mapsto A\vec{v}$ as a map taking points $\vec{v} \in \mathbb{R}^n$ to points $A\vec{v} \in \mathbb{R}^m$. From this perspective, we might ask what happens to the geometry of $\mathbb{R}^n$ in the process, and in particular the effect A has on lengths of and angles between vectors.

Applying our usual starting point for eigenvalue problems, we examine the effect that A has on the lengths of vectors by examining critical points of the ratio

$$R(\vec{v}) = \frac{\|A\vec{v}\|_2}{\|\vec{v}\|_2}$$

over various vectors $\vec{v} \in \mathbb{R}^n \backslash \{\vec{0}\}$. This quotient measures relative shrinkage or growth of $\vec{v}$ under the action of A. Scaling $\vec{v}$ does not matter, since

$$R(\alpha\vec{v}) = \frac{\|A \cdot \alpha\vec{v}\|_2}{\|\alpha\vec{v}\|_2} = \frac{|\alpha|}{|\alpha|} \cdot \frac{\|A\vec{v}\|_2}{\|\vec{v}\|_2} = \frac{\|A\vec{v}\|_2}{\|\vec{v}\|_2} = R(\vec{v}).$$

Thus, we can restrict our search to $\vec{v}$ with $\|\vec{v}\|_2 = 1$. Furthermore, since $R(\vec{v}) \geq 0$, we can instead find critical points of $[R(\vec{v})]^2 = \|A\vec{v}\|_2^2 = \vec{v}^\top A^\top A \vec{v}$. As we have shown in previous chapters, critical points of $\vec{v}^\top A^\top A\vec{v}$ subject to $\|\vec{v}\|_2 = 1$ are exactly the eigenvectors $\vec{v}_i$ satisfying $A^\top A\vec{v}_i = \lambda_i \vec{v}_i$; we know $\lambda_i \geq 0$ and $\vec{v}_i \cdot \vec{v}_j = 0$ when $i \neq j$ since $A^\top A$ is symmetric and positive semidefinite.

Based on our use of the function R, the $\{\vec{v}_i\}$ basis is a reasonable one for studying the effects of A on $\mathbb{R}^n$. Returning to the original goal of characterizing the action of A from a geometric standpoint, define $\vec{u}_i \equiv A\vec{v}_i$. We can make an observation about $\vec{u}_i$ revealing a second eigenvalue structure:

$$\lambda_i \vec{u}_i = \lambda_i \cdot A\vec{v}_i \text{ by definition of } \vec{u}_i$$
$$= A(\lambda_i \vec{v}_i)$$
$$= A(A^\top A\vec{v}_i) \text{ since } \vec{v}_i \text{ is an eigenvector of } A^\top A$$
$$= (AA^\top)(A\vec{v}_i) \text{ by associativity}$$
$$= (AA^\top)\vec{u}_i.$$

Taking norms shows $\|\vec{u}_i\|_2 = \|A\vec{v}_i\|_2 = \sqrt{\|A\vec{v}_i\|_2^2} = \sqrt{\vec{v}_i^\top A^\top A\vec{v}_i} = \sqrt{\lambda_i}\|\vec{v}_i\|_2$. This formula leads to one of two conclusions:

1. Suppose $\vec{u}_i \neq \vec{0}$. In this case, $\vec{u}_i = A\vec{v}_i$ is a *corresponding* eigenvector of $AA^\top$ with $\|\vec{u}_i\|_2 = \sqrt{\lambda_i}\|\vec{v}_i\|_2$.

2. Otherwise, $\vec{u}_i = \vec{0}$.

An identical proof shows that if $\vec{u}$ is an eigenvector of $AA^\top$, then $\vec{v} \equiv A^\top\vec{u}$ is either zero or an eigenvector of $A^\top A$ with the same eigenvalue.

Take k to be the number of strictly positive eigenvalues $\lambda_i > 0$ for $i \in \{1, \ldots, k\}$. By our construction above, we can take $\vec{v}_1, \ldots, \vec{v}_k \in \mathbb{R}^n$ to be eigenvectors of $A^\top A$ and corresponding eigenvectors $\vec{u}_1, \ldots, \vec{u}_k \in \mathbb{R}^m$ of $AA^\top$ such that

$$A^\top A\vec{v}_i = \lambda_i \vec{v}_i$$
$$AA^\top \vec{u}_i = \lambda_i \vec{u}_i$$

for eigenvalues $\lambda_i > 0$; here, we normalize such that $\|\vec{v}_i\|_2 = \|\vec{u}_i\|_2 = 1$ for all i. Define matrices $\bar{V} \in \mathbb{R}^{n \times k}$ and $\bar{U} \in \mathbb{R}^{m \times k}$ whose columns are $\vec{v}_i$'s and $\vec{u}_i$'s, respectively. By construction, $\bar{U}$ contains an orthogonal basis for the column space of A, and $\bar{V}$ contains an orthogonal basis for the row space of A.

We can examine the effect of these new basis matrices on A. Take $\vec{e}_i$ to be the i-th standard basis vector. Then,

$$\bar{U}^\top A\bar{V}\vec{e}_i = \bar{U}^\top A\vec{v}_i \text{ by definition of } \bar{V}$$
$$= \frac{1}{\lambda_i}\bar{U}^\top A(\lambda_i \vec{v}_i) \text{ since we assumed } \lambda_i > 0$$
$$= \frac{1}{\lambda_i}\bar{U}^\top A(A^\top A\vec{v}_i) \text{ since } \vec{v}_i \text{ is an eigenvector of } A^\top A$$
$$= \frac{1}{\lambda_i}\bar{U}^\top (AA^\top)A\vec{v}_i \text{ by associativity}$$
$$= \frac{1}{\sqrt{\lambda_i}}\bar{U}^\top (AA^\top)\vec{u}_i \text{ since we rescaled so that } \|\vec{u}_i\|_2 = 1$$
$$= \sqrt{\lambda_i}\bar{U}^\top \vec{u}_i \text{ since } AA^\top \vec{u}_i = \lambda_i \vec{u}_i$$
$$= \sqrt{\lambda_i}\vec{e}_i.$$

Take $\bar{\Sigma} = \text{diag}(\sqrt{\lambda_1}, \ldots, \sqrt{\lambda_k})$. Then, the derivation above shows that $\bar{U}^\top A\bar{V} = \bar{\Sigma}$.

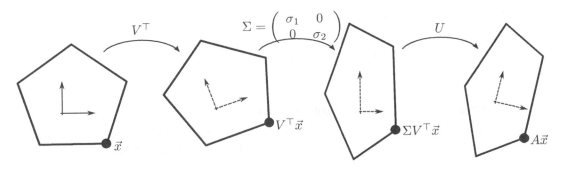

Figure 7.1 Geometric interpretation for the singular value decomposition $A = U\Sigma V^\top$. The matrices U and $V^\top$ are orthogonal and hence preserve lengths and angles. The diagonal matrix Σ scales the horizontal and vertical axes independently.

Complete the columns of $\bar{U}$ and $\bar{V}$ to $U \in \mathbb{R}^{m \times m}$ and $V \in \mathbb{R}^{n \times n}$ by adding orthonormal null space vectors $\vec{v}_i$ and $\vec{u}_i$ with $A^\top A \vec{v}_i = \vec{0}$ and $AA^\top \vec{u}_i = \vec{0}$, respectively. After this extension, $U^\top A V \vec{e}_i = \vec{0}$ and/or $\vec{e}_i^\top U^\top A V = \vec{0}^\top$ for $i > k$. If we take

$$\Sigma_{ij} \equiv \begin{cases} \sqrt{\lambda_i} & i = j \text{ and } i \leq k \\ 0 & \text{otherwise,} \end{cases}$$

then we can extend our previous relationship to show $U^\top A V = \Sigma$, or, by orthogonality of U and V,

$$A = U\Sigma V^\top.$$

This factorization is the *singular value decomposition* (SVD) of A. The columns of U are called the *left singular vectors*, and the columns of V are called the *right singular vectors*. The diagonal elements σ_i of Σ are the *singular values* of A; usually they are sorted such that $\sigma_1 \geq \sigma_2 \geq \cdots \geq 0$. Both U and V are orthogonal matrices; the columns of U and V corresponding to $\sigma_i \neq 0$ span the column and row spaces of A, respectively.

The SVD provides a complete geometric characterization of the action of A. Since U and V are orthogonal, they have no effect on lengths and angles; as a diagonal matrix, Σ scales individual coordinate axes. Since the SVD always exists, *all* matrices $A \in \mathbb{R}^{m \times n}$ are a composition of an isometry, a scale in each coordinate, and a second isometry. This sequence of operations is illustrated in Figure 7.1.

7.1.1 Computing the SVD

The columns of V are the eigenvectors of $A^\top A$, so they can be computed using algorithms discussed in the previous chapter. Rewriting $A = U\Sigma V^\top$ as $AV = U\Sigma$, the columns of U corresponding to nonzero singular values in Σ are normalized columns of AV. The remaining columns satisfy $AA^\top \vec{u}_i = \vec{0}$ and can be computed using the LU factorization.

This is by no means the most efficient or stable way to compute the SVD, but it works reasonably well for many applications. We omit more specialized algorithms for finding the SVD, but many of them are extensions of power iteration and other algorithms we already have covered that avoid forming $A^\top A$ or $AA^\top$ explicitly.

7.2   APPLICATIONS OF THE SVD

We devote the remainder of this chapter to introducing applications of the SVD. The SVD appears countless times in both the theory and practice of numerical linear algebra, and its importance hardly can be exaggerated.

7.2.1   Solving Linear Systems and the Pseudoinverse

In the special case where $A \in \mathbb{R}^{n \times n}$ is square and invertible, the SVD can be used to solve the linear problem $A\vec{x} = \vec{b}$. By substituting $A = U\Sigma V^\top$, we have $U\Sigma V^\top \vec{x} = \vec{b}$, or by orthogonality of U and V,

$$\vec{x} = V\Sigma^{-1}U^\top \vec{b}.$$

Σ is a square diagonal matrix, so Σ^{-1} is the matrix with diagonal entries $1/\sigma_i$.

Computing the SVD is far more expensive than most of the linear solution techniques we introduced in Chapter 3, so this initial observation mostly is of theoretical rather than practical interest. More generally, however, suppose we wish to find a least-squares solution to $A\vec{x} \approx \vec{b}$, where $A \in \mathbb{R}^{m \times n}$ is not necessarily square. From our discussion of the normal equations, we know that $\vec{x}$ must satisfy $A^\top A\vec{x} = A^\top \vec{b}$. But when A is "short" or "underdetermined," that is, when A has more columns than rows ($m < n$) or has linearly dependent columns, the solution to the normal equations might not be unique.

To cover the under-, completely-, and overdetermined cases simultaneously without resorting to regularization (see §4.1.3), we can solve an optimization problem of the following form:

$$\text{minimize} \quad \|\vec{x}\|_2^2$$
$$\text{subject to} \quad A^\top A\vec{x} = A^\top \vec{b}.$$

This optimization chooses the vector $\vec{x} \in \mathbb{R}^n$ with least norm that satisfies the normal equations $A^\top A\vec{x} = A^\top \vec{b}$. When $A^\top A$ is invertible, meaning the least-squares problem is completely- or overdetermined, there is only one $\vec{x}$ satisfying the constraint. Otherwise, of all the feasible vectors $\vec{x}$, we choose the one with minimal $\|\vec{x}\|_2$. That is, we seek the smallest possible least-square solution of $A\vec{x} \approx \vec{b}$, when multiple $\vec{x}$'s minimize $\|A\vec{x} - \vec{b}\|_2$.

Write $A = U\Sigma V^\top$. Then,

$$A^\top A = (U\Sigma V^\top)^\top (U\Sigma V^\top)$$
$$= V\Sigma^\top U^\top U\Sigma V^\top \text{ since } (AB)^\top = B^\top A^\top$$
$$= V\Sigma^\top \Sigma V^\top \text{ since } U \text{ is orthogonal.}$$

Using this expression, the constraint $A^\top A\vec{x} = A^\top \vec{b}$ can be written

$$V\Sigma^\top \Sigma V^\top \vec{x} = V\Sigma^\top U^\top \vec{b},$$

or equivalently, $\Sigma^\top \Sigma \vec{y} = \Sigma^\top \vec{d}$,

after taking $\vec{d} \equiv U^\top \vec{b}$ and $\vec{y} \equiv V^\top \vec{x}$.

Since V is orthogonal, $\|\vec{y}\|_2 = \|\vec{x}\|_2$ and our optimization becomes:

$$\text{minimize} \quad \|\vec{y}\|_2^2$$
$$\text{subject to} \quad \Sigma^\top \Sigma \vec{y} = \Sigma^\top \vec{d}.$$

Since Σ is diagonal, the condition $\Sigma^\top \Sigma \vec{y} = \Sigma^\top \vec{d}$ can be written $\sigma_i^2 y_i = \sigma_i d_i$. So, whenever $\sigma_i \neq 0$ we must have $y_i = d_i/\sigma_i$. When $\sigma_i = 0$, there is *no* constraint on y_i. Since we are minimizing $\|\vec{y}\|_2^2$ we might as well take $y_i = 0$. In other words, the solution to this optimization is $\vec{y} = \Sigma^+ \vec{d}$, where $\Sigma^+ \in \mathbb{R}^{n \times m}$ has the form:

$$\Sigma_{ij}^+ \equiv \begin{cases} 1/\sigma_i & i = j \text{ and } \sigma_i \neq 0 \\ 0 & \text{otherwise.} \end{cases}$$

Undoing the change of variables, this result in turn yields $\vec{x} = V\vec{y} = V\Sigma^+ \vec{d} = V\Sigma^+ U^\top \vec{b}$.

With this motivation, we make the following definition:

Definition 7.1 (Pseudoinverse). The *pseudoinverse* of $A = U\Sigma V^\top \in \mathbb{R}^{m \times n}$ is $A^+ \equiv V\Sigma^+ U^\top \in \mathbb{R}^{n \times m}$.

Our derivation above shows that the pseudoinverse of A enjoys the following properties:

- When A is square and invertible, $A^+ = A^{-1}$.

- When A is overdetermined, $A^+ \vec{b}$ gives the least-squares solution to $A\vec{x} \approx \vec{b}$.

- When A is underdetermined, $A^+ \vec{b}$ gives the least-squares solution to $A\vec{x} \approx \vec{b}$ with minimal (Euclidean) norm.

This construction from the SVD unifies solutions of the underdetermined, fully determined, and overdetermined cases of $A\vec{x} \approx \vec{b}$.

7.2.2 Decomposition into Outer Products and Low-Rank Approximations

If we expand the product $A = U\Sigma V^\top$ column by column, an equivalent formula is the following:

$$A = \sum_{i=1}^{\ell} \sigma_i \vec{u}_i \vec{v}_i^\top,$$

where $\ell \equiv \min\{m, n\}$ and $\vec{u}_i$ and $\vec{v}_i$ are the i-th columns of U and V, respectively. The sum only goes to ℓ since the remaining columns of U or V will be zeroed out by Σ.

This expression shows that any matrix can be decomposed as the sum of *outer products* of vectors:

Definition 7.2 (Outer product). The *outer product* of $\vec{u} \in \mathbb{R}^m$ and $\vec{v} \in \mathbb{R}^n$ is the matrix $\vec{u} \otimes \vec{v} \equiv \vec{u}\vec{v}^\top \in \mathbb{R}^{m \times n}$.

This alternative formula for the SVD provides a new way to compute the product $A\vec{x}$:

$$A\vec{x} = \left(\sum_{i=1}^{\ell} \sigma_i \vec{u}_i \vec{v}_i^\top\right)\vec{x} = \sum_{i=1}^{\ell} \sigma_i \vec{u}_i(\vec{v}_i^\top \vec{x}) = \sum_{i=1}^{\ell} \sigma_i(\vec{v}_i \cdot \vec{x})\vec{u}_i, \text{ since } \vec{x} \cdot \vec{y} = \vec{x}^\top \vec{y}.$$

In words, applying A to $\vec{x}$ is the same as linearly combining the $\vec{u}_i$ vectors with weights $\sigma_i(\vec{v}_i \cdot \vec{x})$. This formula provides savings when the number of nonzero σ_i values is relatively small. More importantly, we can round small values of σ_i to zero, truncating this sum to *approximate* $A\vec{x}$ with fewer terms.

Similarly, from §7.2.1 we can write the pseudoinverse of A as:

$$A^+ = \sum_{\sigma_i \neq 0} \frac{\vec{v}_i \vec{u}_i^\top}{\sigma_i}.$$

With this formula, we can apply the same truncation trick to compute $A^+ \vec{x}$ and can approximate $A^+ \vec{x}$ by only evaluating those terms in the sum for which σ_i is relatively *small*.

In practice, we compute the singular values σ_i as square roots of eigenvalues of $A^\top A$ or $AA^\top$, and methods like power iteration can be used to reveal a partial rather than full set of eigenvalues. If we are satisfied with approximating $A^+ \vec{x}$, we can compute a few of the smallest σ_i values and truncate the formula above rather than finding A^+ completely. This also avoids ever having to compute or store the full A^+ matrix and can be accurate when A has a wide range of singular values.

Returning to our original notation $A = U\Sigma V^\top$, our argument above shows that a useful approximation of A is $\tilde{A} \equiv U\tilde{\Sigma}V^\top$, where $\tilde{\Sigma}$ rounds small values of Σ to zero. The column space of $\tilde{A}$ has dimension equal to the number of nonzero values on the diagonal of $\tilde{\Sigma}$. This approximation is not an *ad hoc* estimate but rather solves a difficult optimization problem posed by the following famous theorem (stated without proof):

Theorem 7.1 (Eckart-Young, 1936). Suppose $\tilde{A}$ is obtained from $A = U\Sigma V^\top$ by truncating all but the k largest singular values σ_i of A to zero. Then, $\tilde{A}$ minimizes both $\|A - \tilde{A}\|_{\mathrm{Fro}}$ and $\|A - \tilde{A}\|_2$ subject to the constraint that the column space of $\tilde{A}$ has at most dimension k.

7.2.3 Matrix Norms

Constructing the SVD also enables us to return to our discussion of matrix norms from §4.3.1. For example, recall that the *Frobenius* norm of A is

$$\|A\|_{\mathrm{Fro}}^2 \equiv \sum_{ij} a_{ij}^2.$$

If we write $A = U\Sigma V^\top$, we can simplify this expression:

$$\|A\|_{\mathrm{Fro}}^2 = \sum_j \|A\vec{e}_j\|_2^2 \text{ since the product } A\vec{e}_j \text{ is the } j\text{-th column of } A$$

$$= \sum_j \|U\Sigma V^\top \vec{e}_j\|_2^2, \text{ substituting the SVD}$$

$$= \sum_j \vec{e}_j^\top V\Sigma^2 V^\top \vec{e}_j \text{ since } \|\vec{x}\|_2^2 = \vec{x}^\top \vec{x} \text{ and } U \text{ is orthogonal}$$

$$= \|\Sigma V^\top\|_{\mathrm{Fro}}^2 \text{ by reversing the steps above}$$

$$= \|V\Sigma\|_{\mathrm{Fro}}^2 \text{ since a matrix and its transpose have the same Frobenius norm}$$

$$= \sum_j \|V\Sigma\vec{e}_j\|_2^2 = \sum_j \sigma_j^2 \|V\vec{e}_j\|_2^2 \text{ since } \Sigma \text{ is a diagonal matrix}$$

$$= \sum_j \sigma_j^2 \text{ since } V \text{ is orthogonal.}$$

Thus, the squared Frobenius norm of $A \in \mathbb{R}^{m \times n}$ is the sum of the squares of its singular values.

This result is of theoretical interest, but it is easier to evaluate the Frobenius norm of A by summing the squares of its elements rather than finding its SVD. More interestingly, recall that the induced two-norm of A is given by

$$\|A\|_2^2 = \max\{\lambda : \text{there exists } \vec{x} \in \mathbb{R}^n \text{ with } A^\top A\vec{x} = \lambda \vec{x}\}.$$

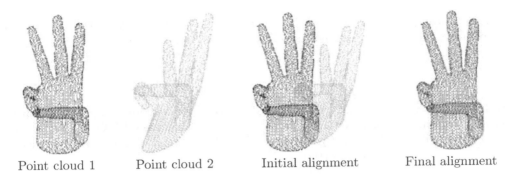

Point cloud 1   Point cloud 2   Initial alignment   Final alignment

Figure 7.2 If we scan a three-dimensional object from two angles, the end result is two point clouds that are not aligned. The approach explained in §7.2.4 aligns the two clouds, serving as the first step in combining the scans. (Figure generated by S. Chung.)

In the language of the SVD, this value is the square root of the largest eigenvalue of $A^\top A$, or equivalently

$$\|A\|_2 = \max\{\sigma_i\}.$$

In other words, the induced two-norm of A can be read directly from its singular values.

Similarly, recall that the condition number of an invertible matrix A is given by cond $A = \|A\|_2\|A^{-1}\|_2$. By our derivation of A^+, the singular values of A^{-1} must be the reciprocals of the singular values of A. Combining this with the formula above for $\|A\|_2$ yields:

$$\text{cond } A = \frac{\sigma_{\max}}{\sigma_{\min}}.$$

This expression provides a new formula for evaluating the conditioning of A.

There is one caveat that prevents this formula for the condition number from being used universally. In some cases, algorithms for computing $\sigma_{\min}$ may involve solving systems $A\vec{x} = \vec{b}$, a process which in itself may suffer from poor conditioning of A. Hence, we cannot always trust values of $\sigma_{\min}$. If this is an issue, condition numbers can be bounded or approximated using various inequalities involving the singular values of A. Also, alternative iterative algorithms similar to QR iteration can be applied to computing $\sigma_{\min}$.

7.2.4 The Procrustes Problem and Point Cloud Alignment

Many techniques in computer vision involve the alignment of three-dimensional shapes. For instance, suppose we have a laser scanner that collects two point clouds of the same rigid object from different views. A typical task is to align these two point clouds into a single coordinate frame, as illustrated in Figure 7.2.

Since the object is rigid, we expect there to be some orthogonal matrix R and translation $\vec{t} \in \mathbb{R}^3$ such that rotating the first point cloud by R and then translating by $\vec{t}$ aligns the two data sets. Our job is to estimate $\vec{t}$ and R.

If the two scans overlap, the user or an automated system may mark n points that correspond between the two scans; we can store these in two matrices $X_1, X_2 \in \mathbb{R}^{3 \times n}$. Then, for each column $\vec{x}_{1i}$ of X_1 and $\vec{x}_{2i}$ of X_2, we expect $R\vec{x}_{1i} + \vec{t} = \vec{x}_{2i}$. To account for error in measuring X_1 and X_2, rather than expecting exact equality, we will minimize an objective function that measures how much this relationship holds true:

$$E(R, \vec{t}) \equiv \sum_i \|R\vec{x}_{1i} + \vec{t} - \vec{x}_{2i}\|_2^2.$$

If we fix R and only consider $\vec{t}$, minimizing E becomes a least-squares problem. On the other hand, optimizing for R with $\vec{t}$ fixed is the same as minimizing $\|RX_1 - X_2^t\|_{\text{Fro}}^2$, where the columns of X_2^t are those of X_2 translated by $\vec{t}$. This second optimization is subject to the constraint that R is a 3×3 orthogonal matrix, that is, that $R^\top R = I_{3\times 3}$. It is known as the *orthogonal Procrustes problem*.

To solve this problem using the SVD, we will introduce the *trace* of a square matrix as follows:

Definition 7.3 (Trace). The *trace* of $A \in \mathbb{R}^{n \times n}$ is the sum of its diagonal elements:

$$\text{tr}(A) \equiv \sum_i a_{ii}.$$

In Exercise 7.2, you will check that $\|A\|_{\text{Fro}}^2 = \text{tr}(A^\top A)$. Starting from this identity, E can be simplified as follows:

$$
\begin{aligned}
\|RX_1 - X_2^t\|_{\text{Fro}}^2 &= \text{tr}((RX_1 - X_2^t)^\top (RX_1 - X_2^t)) \\
&= \text{tr}(X_1^\top X_1 - X_1^\top R^\top X_2^t - X_2^{t\top} RX_1 + X_2^{t\top} X_2) \\
&= \text{const.} - 2\text{tr}(X_2^{t\top} RX_1), \\
&\qquad \text{since } \text{tr}(A+B) = \text{tr}\,A + \text{tr}\,B \text{ and } \text{tr}(A^\top) = \text{tr}(A).
\end{aligned}
$$

This argument shows that we wish to maximize $\text{tr}(X_2^{t\top} RX_1)$ with $R^\top R = I_{3\times 3}$. From Exercise 7.2, $\text{tr}(AB) = \text{tr}(BA)$. Applying this identity, the objective simplifies to $\text{tr}(RC)$ with $C \equiv X_1 X_2^{t\top}$. If we decompose $C = U\Sigma V^\top$ then:

$$
\begin{aligned}
\text{tr}(RC) &= \text{tr}(RU\Sigma V^\top) \text{ by definition} \\
&= \text{tr}((V^\top RU)\Sigma) \text{ since } \text{tr}(AB) = \text{tr}(BA) \\
&= \text{tr}(\tilde{R}\Sigma) \text{ if we define } \tilde{R} = V^\top RU, \text{ which is orthogonal} \\
&= \sum_i \sigma_i \tilde{r}_{ii} \text{ since } \Sigma \text{ is diagonal.}
\end{aligned}
$$

Since $\tilde{R}$ is orthogonal, its columns all have unit length. This implies that $|\tilde{r}_{ii}| \leq 1$ for all i, since otherwise the norm of column i would be too big. Since $\sigma_i \geq 0$ for all i, this argument shows that $\text{tr}(RC)$ is maximized by taking $\tilde{R} = I_{3\times 3}$, which achieves that upper bound. Undoing our substitutions shows $R = V\tilde{R}U^\top = VU^\top$.

Changing notation slightly, we have derived the following fact:

Theorem 7.2 (Orthogonal Procrustes). The orthogonal matrix R minimizing $\|RX - Y\|_{\text{Fro}}^2$ is given by $VU^\top$, where SVD is applied to factor $XY^\top = U\Sigma V^\top$.

Returning to the alignment problem, one typical strategy employs *alternation*:

1. Fix R and minimize E with respect to $\vec{t}$.

2. Fix the resulting $\vec{t}$ and minimize E with respect to R subject to $R^\top R = I_{3\times 3}$.

3. Return to step 1.

The energy E decreases with each step and thus converges to a local minimum. Since we never optimize $\vec{t}$ and R simultaneously, we cannot guarantee that the result is the smallest possible value of E, but in practice this method works well. Alternatively, in some cases it is possible to work out an explicit formula for $\vec{t}$, circumventing the least-squares step.

7.2.5 Principal Component Analysis (PCA)

Recall the setup from §6.1.1: We wish to find a low-dimensional approximation of a set of data points stored in the columns of a matrix $X \in \mathbb{R}^{n\times k}$, for k observations in n dimensions. Previously, we showed that if we wish to project onto a single dimension, the best possible axis is given by the dominant eigenvector of $XX^\top$. With the SVD in hand, we can consider more complicated datasets that need more than one projection axis.

Suppose that we wish to choose d vectors whose span best contains the data points in X (we considered $d = 1$ in §6.1.1); we will assume $d \leq \min\{k, n\}$. These vectors can be written in the columns of an $n \times d$ matrix C. The column space of C is preserved when we orthogonalize its columns. Rather than orthogonalizing a $posteriori$, however, we can safely restrict our search to matrices C whose columns are orthonormal, satisfying $C^\top C = I_{d\times d}$. Then, the projection of X onto the column space of C is given by $CC^\top X$.

Paralleling our earlier development, we will minimize $\|X - CC^\top X\|_{\mathrm{Fro}}$ subject to $C^\top C = I_{d\times d}$. The objective can be simplified using trace identities:

$$\|X - CC^\top X\|_{\mathrm{Fro}}^2 = \mathrm{tr}((X - CC^\top X)^\top(X - CC^\top X)) \text{ since } \|A\|_{\mathrm{Fro}}^2 = \mathrm{tr}(A^\top A)$$
$$= \mathrm{tr}(X^\top X - 2X^\top CC^\top X + X^\top CC^\top CC^\top X)$$
$$= \mathrm{const.} - \mathrm{tr}(X^\top CC^\top X) \text{ since } C^\top C = I_{d\times d}$$
$$= -\|C^\top X\|_{\mathrm{Fro}}^2 + \mathrm{const.}$$

By this chain of equalities, an equivalent problem to the minimization posed above is to maximize $\|C^\top X\|_{\mathrm{Fro}}^2$. For statisticians, when the rows of X have mean zero, this shows that we wish to maximize the variance of the projection $C^\top X$.

Now, introduce the SVD to factor $X = U\Sigma V^\top$. Taking $\tilde{C} \equiv U^\top C$, we are maximizing $\|C^\top U\Sigma V^\top\|_{\mathrm{Fro}} = \|\Sigma^\top \tilde{C}\|_{\mathrm{Fro}}$ by orthogonality of V. If the elements of $\tilde{C}$ are $\tilde{c}_{ij}$, then expanding the formula for the Frobenius norm shows

$$\|\Sigma^\top \tilde{C}\|_{\mathrm{Fro}}^2 = \sum_i \sigma_i^2 \sum_j \tilde{c}_{ij}^2.$$

By orthogonality of the columns of $\tilde{C}$, $\sum_i \tilde{c}_{ij}^2 = 1$ for all j, and, taking into account the fact that $\tilde{C}$ may have fewer than n columns, $\sum_j \tilde{c}_{ij}^2 \leq 1$. Hence, the coefficient next to σ_i^2 is at most 1 in the sum above, and if we sort such that $\sigma_1 \geq \sigma_2 \geq \cdots$, then the maximum is achieved by taking the columns of $\tilde{C}$ to be $\vec{e}_1, \ldots, \vec{e}_d$. Undoing our change of coordinates, we see that our choice of C should be the first d columns of U.

We have shown that the SVD of X can be used to solve such a $principal$ $component$ $analysis$ (PCA) problem. In practice, the rows of X usually are shifted to have mean zero before carrying out the SVD.

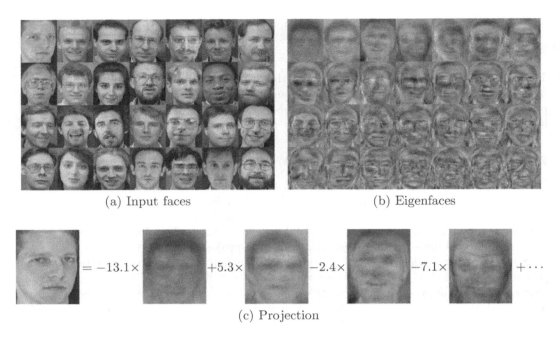

(a) Input faces · (b) Eigenfaces

(c) Projection

Figure 7.3 The "eigenface" technique [122] performs PCA on (a) a database of face images to extract (b) their most common modes of variation. For clustering, recognition, and other tasks, face images are written as (c) linear combinations of the eigenfaces, and the resulting coefficients are compared. (Figure generated by D. Hyde; images from the AT&T Database of Faces, AT&T Laboratories Cambridge.)

7.2.6 Eigenfaces*

One application of PCA in computer vision is the eigenfaces technique for face recognition, originally introduced in [122]. This popular method works by applying PCA to the images in a database of faces. Projecting new input faces onto the small PCA basis encodes a face image using just a few basis coefficients without sacrificing too much accuracy, a benefit that the method inherits from PCA.

For simplicity, suppose we have a set of k photographs of faces with similar lighting and alignment, as in Figure 7.3(a). After resizing, we can assume the photos are all of size $m \times n$, so they are representable as vectors in $\mathbb{R}^{mn}$ containing one pixel intensity per dimension. As in §7.2.5, we will store our entire database of faces in a "training matrix" $X \in \mathbb{R}^{mn \times k}$. By convention, we subtract the average face image from each column, so $X\vec{1} = \vec{0}$.

Applying PCA to X, as explained in the previous section, yields a set of "eigenface" images in the basis matrix C representing the common modes of variation between faces. One set of eigenfaces ordered by decreasing singular value is shown in Figure 7.3(b); the first few eigenfaces capture common changes in face shape, prominent features, and so on. Intuitively, PCA in this context searches for the most common distinguishing features that make a given face different from average.

The eigenface basis $C \in \mathbb{R}^{mn \times d}$ can be applied to face recognition. Suppose we take a new photo $\vec{x} \in \mathbb{R}^{mn}$ and wish to find the closest match in the database of faces. The

---

*Written with assistance by D. Hyde.

projection of $\vec{x}$ onto the eigenface basis is $\vec{y} \equiv C^\top \vec{x}$. The best matching face is then the closest column of $C^\top X$ to $\vec{y}$.

There are two primary advantages of eigenfaces for practical face recognition. First, usually $d \ll mn$, reducing the dimensionality of the search problem. More importantly, PCA helps separate the *relevant* modes of variation between faces from noise. Differencing the mn pixels of face images independently does not search for important facial features, while the PCA axes in C are tuned to the differences observed in the columns of X.

Many modifications, improvements, and extensions have been proposed to augment the original eigenfaces technique. For example, we can set a minimum threshold so that if the weights of a new image do not closely match any of the database weights, we report that no match was found. PCA also can be modified to be more sensitive to differences between identity rather than between lighting or pose. Even so, a rudimentary implementation is surprisingly effective. In our example, we train eigenfaces using photos of 40 subjects and then test using 40 *different* photos of the same subjects; the basic method described achieves 80% recognition accuracy.

7.3 EXERCISES

7.1 Suppose $A \in \mathbb{R}^{n \times n}$. Show that condition number of $A^\top A$ with respect to $\| \cdot \|_2$ is the square of the condition number of A

7.2 Suppose $A \in \mathbb{R}^{m \times n}$ and $B \in \mathbb{R}^{n \times m}$. Show $\|A\|_{\text{Fro}}^2 = \text{tr}(A^\top A)$ and $\text{tr}(AB) = \text{tr}(BA)$.

7.3 Provide the SVD and condition number with respect to $\| \cdot \|_2$ of the following matrices.

(a) $\begin{pmatrix} 0 & 0 & 1 \\ 0 & \sqrt{2} & 0 \\ \sqrt{3} & 0 & 0 \end{pmatrix}$

(b) $\begin{pmatrix} -5 \\ 3 \end{pmatrix}$

7.4 (Suggested by Y. Zhao.) Show that $\|A\|_2 = \|\Sigma\|_2$, where $A = U\Sigma V^T$ is the singular value decomposition of A.

7.5 Show that adding a row to a matrix cannot decrease its largest singular value.

7.6 (Suggested by Y. Zhao.) Show that the null space of a matrix $A \in \mathbb{R}^{n \times n}$ is spanned by columns of V corresponding to zero singular values, where $A = U\Sigma V^\top$ is the singular value decomposition of A.

7.7 Take $\sigma_i(A)$ to be the i-th singular value of the square matrix $A \in \mathbb{R}^{n \times n}$. Define the *nuclear norm* of A to be

$$\|A\|_* \equiv \sum_{i=1}^{n} \sigma_i(A).$$

Note: What follows is a tricky problem. Apply the mantra from this chapter: "If a linear algebra problem is hard, substitute the SVD."

(a) Show $\|A\|_* = \text{tr}(\sqrt{A^\top A})$, where trace of a matrix $\text{tr}(A)$ is the sum $\sum_i a_{ii}$ of its diagonal elements. For this problem, we will define the square root of a symmetric, positive semidefinite matrix M to be $\sqrt{M} \equiv XD^{1/2}X^\top$, where $D^{1/2}$ is the diagonal matrix containing (nonnegative) square roots of the eigenvalues of M and X contains the eigenvectors of $M = XDX^\top$.

Hint (to get started): Write $A = U\Sigma V^\top$ and argue $\Sigma^\top = \Sigma$ in this case.

(b) Show $\|A\|_* = \max_{C^\top C=I} \text{tr}(AC)$.
   Hint: Substitute the SVD of A and apply Exercise 7.2.

(c) Show that $\|A + B\|_* \leq \|A\|_* + \|B\|_*$.
   Hint: Use Exercise 7.7b.

(d) Minimizing $\|A\vec{x} - \vec{b}\|_2^2 + \|\vec{x}\|_1$ provides an alternative to Tikhonov regularization that can yield *sparse* vectors $\vec{x}$ under certain conditions. Assuming this is the case, explain informally why minimizing $\|A - A_0\|_{\text{Fro}}^2 + \|A\|_*$ over A for a fixed $A_0 \in \mathbb{R}^{n \times n}$ might yield a *low-rank* approximation of A_0.

(e) Provide an application of solutions to the "low-rank matrix completion" problem; 7.7d provides an optimization approach to this problem.

7.8 ("Polar decomposition") In this problem we will add one more matrix factorization to our linear algebra toolbox and derive an algorithm by N. Higham for its computation [61]. The decomposition has been used in animation applications interpolating between motions of a rigid object while projecting out undesirable shearing artifacts [111].

(a) Show that any matrix $A \in \mathbb{R}^{n \times n}$ can be factored $A = WP$, where W is orthogonal and P is symmetric and positive semidefinite. This factorization is known as the polar decomposition.
   Hint: Write $A = U\Sigma V^\top$ and show $V\Sigma V^\top$ is positive semidefinite.

(b) The polar decomposition of an invertible $A \in \mathbb{R}^{n \times n}$ can be computed using an iterative scheme:

$$X_0 \equiv A \qquad\qquad X_{k+1} = \frac{1}{2}(X_k + (X_k^{-1})^\top)$$

We will prove this in a few steps:

(i) Use the SVD to write $A = U\Sigma V^\top$, and define $D_k = U^\top X_k V$. Show $D_0 = \Sigma$ and $D_{k+1} = \frac{1}{2}(D_k + (D_k^{-1})^\top)$.

(ii) From (i), each D_k is diagonal. If d_{ki} is the i-th diagonal element of D_k, show

$$d_{(k+1)i} = \frac{1}{2}\left(d_{ki} + \frac{1}{d_{ki}}\right).$$

(iii) Assume $d_{ki} \to c_i$ as $k \to \infty$ (this convergence assumption requires proof!). Show $c_i = 1$.

(iv) Use 7.8(b)iii to show $X_k \to UV^\top$.

7.9 ("Derivative of SVD," [95]) In this problem, we will continue to use the notation of Exercise 4.3. Our goal is to differentiate the SVD of a matrix A with respect to changes in A. Such derivatives are used to simulate the dynamics of elastic objects; see [6] for one application.

(a) Suppose $Q(t)$ is an orthogonal matrix for all $t \in \mathbb{R}$. If we define $\Omega_Q \equiv Q^\top \partial Q$, show that Ω_Q is *antisymmetric*, that is, $\Omega_Q^\top = -\Omega_Q$. What are the diagonal elements of Ω_Q?

(b) Suppose for a matrix-valued function $A(t)$ we use SVD to decompose $A(t) = U(t)\Sigma(t)V(t)^\top$. Derive the following formula:

$$U^\top(\partial A)V = \Omega_U\Sigma + \partial\Sigma - \Sigma\Omega_V.$$

(c) Show how to compute $\partial\Sigma$ directly from ∂A and the SVD of A.

(d) Provide a method for finding Ω_U and Ω_V from ∂A and the SVD of A using a sequence of 2×2 solves. Conclude with formulas for ∂U and ∂V in terms of the Ω's.

Hint: It is sufficient to compute the elements of Ω_U and Ω_V above the diagonal.

7.10 ("Latent semantic analysis," [35]) In this problem, we explore the basics of *latent semantic analysis*, used in natural language processing to analyze collections of documents.

(a) Suppose we have a dictionary of m words and a collection of n documents. We can write an *occurrence matrix* $X \in \mathbb{R}^{m \times n}$ whose entries x_{ij} are equal to the number of times word i appears in document j. Propose interpretations of the entries of $XX^\top$ and $X^\top X$.

(b) Each document in X is represented using a point in $\mathbb{R}^m$, where m is potentially large. Suppose for efficiency and robustness to noise, we would prefer to use representations in $\mathbb{R}^k$, for some $k \ll \min\{m, n\}$. Apply Theorem 7.1 to propose a set of k vectors in $\mathbb{R}^m$ that best approximates the full space of documents with respect to the Frobenius norm.

(c) In *cross-language* applications, we might have a collection of n documents translated into two different languages, with m_1 and m_2 words, respectively. Then, we can write two occurrence matrices $X_1 \in \mathbb{R}^{m_1 \times n}$ and $X_2 \in \mathbb{R}^{m_2 \times n}$. Since we do not know which words in the first language correspond to which words in the second, the columns of these matrices are in correspondence but the rows are not.

One way to find similar phrases in the two languages is to find vectors $\vec{v}_1 \in \mathbb{R}^{m_1}$ and $\vec{v}_2 \in \mathbb{R}^{m_2}$ such that $X_1^\top\vec{v}_1$ and $X_2^\top\vec{v}_2$ are similar. To do so, we can solve a *canonical correlation* problem:

$$\max_{\vec{v}_1, \vec{v}_2} \frac{(X_1^\top\vec{v}_1) \cdot (X_2^\top\vec{v}_2)}{\|\vec{v}_1\|_2 \|\vec{v}_2\|_2}.$$

Show how this maximization can be solved using SVD machinery.

7.11 ("Stable rank," [121]) The *stable rank* of $A \in \mathbb{R}^{n \times n}$ is defined as

$$\text{STABLE-RANK}(A) \equiv \frac{\|A\|_{\text{Fro}}^2}{\|A\|_2^2}.$$

It is used in research on low-rank matrix factorization as a proxy for the rank (dimension of the column space) of A.

(a) Show that if all n columns of A are the same vector $\vec{v} \in \mathbb{R}^n\backslash\{\vec{0}\}$, then $\text{STABLE-RANK}(A) = 1$.

(b) Show that when the columns of A are orthonormal, STABLE-RANK$(A) = n$.

(c) More generally, show $1 \le$ STABLE-RANK$(A) \le n$.

(d) Show STABLE-RANK$(A) \le$ RANK(A).

III

Nonlinear Techniques

Nonlinear Systems

CONTENTS

8.1   Root-Finding in a Single Variable 147
     8.1.1   Characterizing Problems 147
     8.1.2   Continuity and Bisection 148
     8.1.3   Fixed Point Iteration 149
     8.1.4   Newton's Method 151
     8.1.5   Secant Method 153
     8.1.6   Hybrid Techniques 155
     8.1.7   Single-Variable Case: Summary 155
8.2   Multivariable Problems 156
     8.2.1   Newton's Method 156
     8.2.2   Making Newton Faster: Quasi-Newton and Broyden 156
8.3   Conditioning 158

TRY as we might, it is not possible to express all systems of equations in the linear framework we have developed over the last several chapters. Logarithms, exponentials, trigonometric functions, absolute values, polynomials, and so on are commonplace in practical problems, but none of these functions is linear. When these functions appear, we must employ a more general—but often less efficient—toolbox for nonlinear problems.

8.1 ROOT-FINDING IN A SINGLE VARIABLE

We begin by considering methods for root-finding in a single scalar variable. Given a function $f(x) : \mathbb{R} \to \mathbb{R}$, we wish to develop algorithms for finding points $x^* \in \mathbb{R}$ subject to $f(x^*) = 0$; we call x^* a *root* or *zero* of f. Single-variable problems in linear algebra are not particularly interesting; after all we can solve the equation $ax - b = 0$ in closed form as $x^* = {}^b\!/_a$. Roots of a nonlinear equation like $y^2 + e^{\cos y} - 3 = 0$, however, are less easily calculated.

8.1.1 Characterizing Problems

We no longer assume f is linear, but without *any* information about its structure, we are unlikely to make headway on finding its roots. For instance, root-finding is guaranteed to fail on

$$f(x) = \begin{cases} -1 & x \leq 0 \\ 1 & x > 0 \end{cases}$$

or even more deviously (recall $\mathbb{Q}$ denotes the set of rational numbers):

$$f(x) = \begin{cases} -1 & x \in \mathbb{Q} \\ 1 & \text{otherwise.} \end{cases}$$

These examples are trivial in the sense that any reasonable client of root-finding software would be unlikely to expect it to succeed in this case, but more subtle examples are not much more difficult to construct.

For this reason, we must add some "regularizing" assumptions about f to make the root-finding problem well-posed. Typical assumptions include the following:

- *Continuity:* A function f is *continuous* if it can be drawn without lifting up a pen; more formally, f is continuous if the difference $f(x) - f(y)$ vanishes as $x \to y$.

- *Lipschitz:* A function f is *Lipschitz continuous* if there exists a constant c such that $|f(x) - f(y)| \leq c|x - y|$; Lipschitz functions need not be differentiable but are limited in their rates of change.

- *Differentiability:* A function f is *differentiable* if its derivative f' exists for all x.

- C^k: A function is C^k if it is differentiable k times and each of those k derivatives is continuous; C^∞ indicates that all derivatives of f exist and are continuous.

Example 8.1 (Classifying functions). The function $f(x) = \cos x$ is C^∞ and Lipschitz on $\mathbb{R}$. The function $g(x) = x^2$ as a function on $\mathbb{R}$ is C^∞ but *not* Lipschitz. In particular, $|g(x) - g(0)| = x^2$, which cannot be bounded by any linear function of x as $x \to \infty$. When restricted to the unit interval $[0, 1]$, however, $g(x) = x^2$ can be considered Lipschitz since its slope is bounded by 2 in this interval; we say f is "locally Lipschitz" since this property holds on any interval $[a, b]$. The function $h(x) = |x|$ is continuous—or C^0—and Lipschitz but not differentiable thanks to its singularity at $x = 0$.

When our assumptions about f are stronger, we can design more effective algorithms to solve $f(x^*) = 0$. We will illustrate the spectrum trading off between generality and efficiency by considering a few algorithms below.

8.1.2 Continuity and Bisection

Suppose that all we know about f is that it is continuous. This is enough to state an intuitive theorem from single-variable calculus:

Theorem 8.1 (Intermediate Value Theorem). Suppose that $f : [a, b] \to \mathbb{R}$ is continuous and that $f(a) < u < f(b)$ or $f(b) < u < f(a)$. Then, there exists $z \in (a, b)$ such that $f(z) = u$.

In other words, in the space between a and b, the function f must achieve every value between $f(a)$ and $f(b)$.

Suppose we are given as input a continuous function $f(x)$ as well as two values ℓ and r such that $f(\ell) \cdot f(r) < 0$; that is, $f(\ell)$ and $f(r)$ have opposite sign. Then, by the Intermediate Value Theorem, somewhere between ℓ and r there is a root of f. Similar to binary search, this property suggests a bisection algorithm for finding x^*, shown in Figure 8.1. This algorithm divides the interval $[\ell, r]$ in half recursively, each time keeping the side in which a root is known to exist by the Intermediate Value Theorem. It converges *unconditionally*, in the sense that ℓ and r are guaranteed to become arbitrarily close to one another and converge to a root x^* of $f(x)$.

Bisection is the simplest but not necessarily the fastest technique for root-finding. As with eigenvalue methods, bisection inherently is iterative and may never provide an *exact* solution x^*; this property is true for nearly any root-finding algorithm unless we put strong assumptions on the class of f. We can ask, however, how close the value c_k of the center

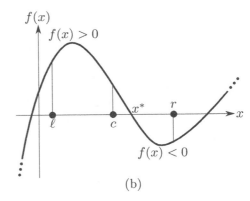

```
function BISECTION(f(x), ℓ, r)
    for k ← 1, 2, 3, …
        c ← ℓ+r/2
        if |f(c)| < ε_f or |r − ℓ| < ε_x then
            return x* ≈ c
        else if f(ℓ) · f(c) < 0 then
            r ← c
        else
            ℓ ← c
```

(a)   (b)

Figure 8.1 (a) Pseudocode and (b) an illustration of the bisection algorithm for finding roots of continuous $f(x)$ given endpoints $\ell, r \in \mathbb{R}$ with $f(\ell) \cdot f(r) < 0$. The interval $[c, r]$ contains a root x^* because $f(c)$ and $f(r)$ have opposite sign.

point c between ℓ_k and r_k in the k-th iteration is to the root x^* that we hope to compute. This analysis will provide a baseline for comparison to other methods.

More broadly, suppose we can establish an error bound E_k such that the estimate x_k of the root x^* during the k-th iteration of root-finding satisfies $|x_k - x^*| < E_k$. Any algorithm with $E_k \to 0$ is *convergent*. Assuming a root-finding algorithm is convergent, however, the primary property of interest is the *convergence rate*, characterizing the rate at which E_k shrinks.

For bisection, since during each iteration c_k and x^* are in the interval $[\ell_k, r_k]$, an upper bound of error is given by $E_k \equiv |r_k - \ell_k|$. Since we divide the interval in half each iteration, we can reduce our error bound by half in each iteration: $E_{k+1} = 1/2 E_k$. Since E_{k+1} is linear in E_k, we say that bisection exhibits *linear* convergence.

In exchange for unconditional linear convergence, bisection requires initial estimates of ℓ and r bracketing a root. While some heuristic search methods exist for finding a bracketing interval, unless more is known about the form of f, finding this pair may be nearly as difficult as computing a root! In this case, bisection might be thought of as a method for *refining* a root estimate rather than for global search.

8.1.3 Fixed Point Iteration

Bisection is guaranteed to converge to a root of any continuous function f, but if we know more about f we can formulate algorithms that converge more quickly.

As an example, suppose we wish to find x^* satisfying $g(x^*) = x^*$; this setup is equivalent to root-finding since solving $g(x^*) = x^*$ is the same as solving $g(x^*) - x^* = 0$. As an additional piece of information, however, we also might know that g is Lipschitz with constant $0 \le c < 1$ (see §8.1.1). This condition defines g as a *contraction*, since $|g(x) - g(y)| < |x - y|$ for any x, y.

The system $g(x) = x$ suggests a potential solution method:

1. Take x_0 to be an initial guess of x^*.

2. Iterate $x_k = g(x_{k-1})$.

If this iteration converges, the result is a *fixed point* of g satisfying the criteria above.

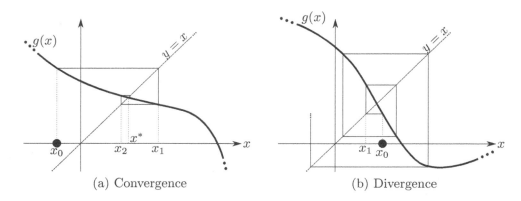

(a) Convergence　　　　　　　(b) Divergence

Figure 8.2 Convergence of fixed point iteration. Fixed point iteration searches for the intersection of $g(x)$ with the line $y = x$ by iterating $x_k = g(x_{k-1})$. One way to visualize this method on the graph of $g(x)$ visualized above is that it alternates between moving horizontally to the line $y = x$ and vertically to the position $g(x)$. Fixed point iteration (a) converges when the slope of $g(x)$ is small and (b) diverges otherwise.

When $c < 1$, the Lipschitz property ensures convergence to a root if one exists. To verify this statement, if $E_k = |x_k - x^*|$, then we have the following property:

$$\begin{aligned} E_k &= |x_k - x^*| \\ &= |g(x_{k-1}) - g(x^*)| \text{ by design of the iterative scheme and definition of } x^* \\ &\leq c|x_{k-1} - x^*| \text{ since } g \text{ is Lipschitz} \\ &= cE_{k-1}. \end{aligned}$$

Applying this statement inductively shows $E_k \leq c^k E_0 \to 0$ as $k \to \infty$.

If g is Lipschitz with constant $c < 1$ in a *neighborhood* $[x^* - \delta, x^* + \delta]$, then so long as x_0 is chosen in this interval, fixed point iteration will converge. This is true since our expression for E_k above shows that it shrinks each iteration. When the Lipschitz constant is too large—or equivalently, when g has large slope—fixed point iteration diverges. Figure 8.2 visualizes the two possibilities.

One important case occurs when g is C^1 and $|g'(x^*)| < 1$. By continuity of g' in this case, there are values $\varepsilon, \delta > 0$ such that $|g'(x)| < 1 - \varepsilon$ for any $x \in (x^* - \delta, x^* + \delta)$. (This statement is hard to parse: Make sure you understand it!) Take any $x, y \in (x^* - \delta, x^* + \delta)$. Then,

$$\begin{aligned} |g(x) - g(y)| &= |g'(\theta)| \cdot |x - y| \text{ by the Mean Value Theorem, for some } \theta \in [x, y] \\ &< (1 - \varepsilon)|x - y|. \end{aligned}$$

This argument shows that g is Lipschitz with constant $1-\varepsilon < 1$ in the interval $(x^*-\delta, x^*+\delta)$. Applying our earlier discussion, when g is continuously differentiable and $g'(x^*) < 1$, fixed point iteration will converge to x^* when the initial guess x_0 is close by.

So far, we have little reason to use fixed point iteration: We have shown it is guaranteed to converge only when g is Lipschitz, and our argument about the E_k's shows linear convergence, like bisection. There is one case, however, in which fixed point iteration provides an advantage.

Suppose g is differentiable with $g'(x^*) = 0$. Then, the first-order term vanishes in the Taylor series for g, leaving behind:

$$g(x_k) = g(x^*) + \frac{1}{2}g''(x^*)(x_k - x^*)^2 + O\left((x_k - x^*)^3\right).$$

In this case,

$$
\begin{aligned}
E_k &= |x_k - x^*| \\
&= |g(x_{k-1}) - g(x^*)| \text{ as before} \\
&= \frac{1}{2}|g''(x^*)|(x_{k-1} - x^*)^2 + O((x_{k-1} - x^*)^3) \text{ from the Taylor argument} \\
&\leq \frac{1}{2}(|g''(x^*)| + \varepsilon)(x_{k-1} - x^*)^2 \text{ for some } \varepsilon \text{ so long as } x_{k-1} \text{ is close to } x^* \\
&= \frac{1}{2}(|g''(x^*)| + \varepsilon)E_{k-1}^2.
\end{aligned}
$$

By this chain of inequalities, in this case E_k is *quadratic* in E_{k-1}, so we say fixed point iteration can have *quadratic convergence*. This implies that $E_k \to 0$ much faster, needing fewer iterations to reach a reasonable root approximation.

Example 8.2 (Fixed point iteration). We can apply fixed point iteration to solving $x = \cos x$ by iterating $x_{k+1} = \cos x_k$. A numerical example starting from $x_0 = 0$ proceeds as follows:

k	0	1	2	3	4	5	6	7	8	9
x_k	0	1.000	0.540	0.858	0.654	0.793	0.701	0.764	0.722	0.750

In this case, fixed point iteration converges linearly to the root $x^* \approx 0.739085$.

The root-finding problem $x = \sin x^2$ satisfies the condition for quadratic convergence near $x^* = 0$. For this reason, fixed point iteration $x_{k+1} = \sin x_k^2$ starting at $x_0 = 1$ converges more quickly to the root:

k	0	1	2	3	4	5	6	7	8	9
x_k	1	0.841	0.650	0.410	0.168	0.028	0.001	0.000	0.000	0.000

Finally, the roots of $x = e^x + e^{-x} - 5$ do *not* satisfy convergence criteria for fixed point iteration. Iterates of the failed fixed point scheme $x_{k+1} = e^{x_k} + e^{-x_k} - 5$ starting at $x_0 = 1$ are shown below:

k	0	1	2	3	4	5	6	7
x_k	1	-1.914	1.927	2.012	2.609	8.660	5760.375	$\cdots$

8.1.4 Newton's Method

We tighten our class of functions once more to derive a root-finding algorithm based more fundamentally on a differentiability assumption, this time with consistent quadratic convergence. We will attempt to solve $f(x^*) = 0$ rather than finding fixed points, with the assumption that $f \in C^1$—a slightly tighter condition than Lipschitz.

Since f is differentiable, it can be approximated near $x_k \in \mathbb{R}$ using a tangent line:

$$f(x) \approx f(x_k) + f'(x_k)(x - x_k).$$

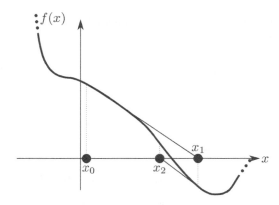

Figure 8.3 Newton's method iteratively approximates $f(x)$ with tangent lines to find roots of a differentiable function $f(x)$.

Setting the expression on the right equal to zero and solving for x provides an approximation x_{k+1} of the root:

$$x_{k+1} = x_k - \frac{f(x_k)}{f'(x_k)}.$$

In reality, x_{k+1} may not satisfy $f(x_{k+1}) = 0$, but since it is the root of an approximation of f we might hope that it is closer to x^* than x_k. If this is true, then iterating this formula should give x_k's that get closer and closer to x^*. This technique is known as *Newton's method* for root-finding, and it amounts to repeatedly solving linear approximations of the original nonlinear problem. It is illustrated in Figure 8.3.

If we define

$$g(x) = x - \frac{f(x)}{f'(x)},$$

then Newton's method amounts to fixed point iteration on g. Differentiating,

$$g'(x) = 1 - \frac{f'(x)^2 - f(x)f''(x)}{f'(x)^2} \quad \text{by the quotient rule}$$

$$= \frac{f(x)f''(x)}{f'(x)^2} \quad \text{after simplification.}$$

Suppose x^* is a *simple* root of $f(x)$, meaning $f'(x^*) \neq 0$. Using this formula, $g'(x^*) = 0$, and by our analysis of fixed point iteration in §8.1.3, Newton's method must converge *quadratically* to x^* when starting from a sufficiently close x_0. When x^* is not simple, however, convergence of Newton's method can be linear or worse.

The derivation of Newton's method via linear approximation suggests other methods using more terms in the Taylor series. For instance, "Halley's method" also makes use of f'' via quadratic approximation, and more general "Householder methods" can include an arbitrary number of derivatives. These techniques offer higher-order convergence at the cost of having to evaluate many derivatives and the possibility of more exotic failure modes. Other methods replace Taylor series with alternative approximations; for example, "linear fractional interpolation" uses rational functions to better approximate functions with asymptotes.

Example 8.3 (Newton's method). The last part of Example 8.2 can be expressed as a root-finding problem on $f(x) = e^x + e^{-x} - 5 - x$. The derivative of $f(x)$ in this case is $f'(x) = e^x - e^{-x} - 1$, so Newton's method can be written

$$x_{k+1} = x_k - \frac{e^{x_k} + e^{-x_k} - 5 - x_k}{e^{x_k} - e^{-x_k} - 1}.$$

This iteration quickly converges to a root starting from $x_0 = 2$:

k	0	1	2	3	4
x_k	2	1.9161473	1.9115868	1.9115740	1.9115740

Example 8.4 (Newton's method failure). Suppose $f(x) = x^5 - 3x^4 + 25$. Newton's method applied to this function gives the iteration

$$x_{k+1} = x_k - \frac{x_k^5 - 3x_k^4 + 25}{5x_k^4 - 12x_k^3}.$$

These iterations converge when x_0 is sufficiently close to the root $x^* \approx -1.5325$. For instance, the iterates starting from $x_0 = -2$ are shown below:

k	0	1	2	3	4
x_k	-2	-1.687500	-1.555013	-1.533047	-1.532501

Farther away from this root, however, Newton's method can fail. For instance, starting from $x_0 = 0.25$ gives a divergent set of iterates:

k	0	1	2	3	4
x_k	0.25	149.023256	119.340569	95.594918	76.599025

8.1.5 Secant Method

One concern about Newton's method is the cost of evaluating f and its derivative f'. If f is complicated, we may wish to minimize the number of times we have to evaluate either of these functions. Higher orders of convergence for root-finding alleviate this problem by reducing the number of iterations needed to approximate x^*, but we also can design numerical methods that explicitly avoid evaluating costly derivatives.

Example 8.5 (Rocket design). Suppose we are designing a rocket and wish to know how much fuel to add to the engine. For a given number of gallons x, we can write a function $f(x)$ giving the maximum height of the rocket during flight; our engineers have specified that the rocket should reach a height h, so we need to solve $f(x) = h$. Evaluating $f(x)$ involves simulating a rocket as it takes off and monitoring its fuel consumption, which is an expensive proposition. Even if f is differentiable, we might not be able to evaluate f' in a practical amount of time.

One strategy for designing lower-impact methods is to reuse data as much as possible. For instance, we could approximate the derivative f' appearing in Newton's method as follows:

$$f'(x_k) \approx \frac{f(x_k) - f(x_{k-1})}{x_k - x_{k-1}}.$$

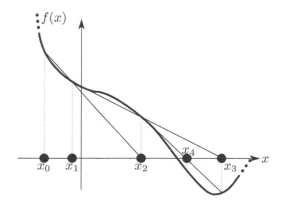

Figure 8.4 The secant method is similar to Newton's method (Figure 8.3) but approximates tangents to $f(x)$ as the lines through previous iterates. It requires both x_0 and x_1 for initialization.

Since we had to compute $f(x_{k-1})$ in the previous iteration anyway, we reuse this value to approximate the derivative for the next one. This approximation works well when x_k's are near convergence and close to one another. Plugging it into Newton's method results in a new scheme known as the *secant method*, illustrated in Figure 8.4:

$$x_{k+1} = x_k - \frac{f(x_k)(x_k - x_{k-1})}{f(x_k) - f(x_{k-1})}.$$

The user must provide two initial guesses x_0 and x_1 or can run a single iteration of Newton to get it started.

Analyzing the secant method is more involved than the other methods we have considered because it uses both $f(x_k)$ and $f(x_{k-1})$; proof of its convergence is outside the scope of our discussion. Error analysis reveals that the secant method decreases error at a rate of $(1+\sqrt{5})/2$ (the "Golden Ratio"), which is between linear and quadratic. Since convergence is *close* to that of Newton's method without the need for evaluating f', the secant method is a strong alternative.

Example 8.6 (Secant method). Suppose $f(x) = x^4 - 2x^2 - 4$. Iterates of Newton's method for this function are given by

$$x_{k+1} = x_k - \frac{x_k^4 - 2x_k^2 - 4}{4x_k^3 - 4x_k}.$$

Contrastingly, iterates of the secant method for the same function are given by

$$x_{k+1} = x_k - \frac{(x_k^4 - 2x_k^2 - 4)(x_k - x_{k-1})}{(x_k^4 - 2x_k^2 - 4) - (x_{k-1}^4 - 2x_{k-1}^2 - 4)}.$$

By construction, a less expensive way to compute these iterates is to save and reuse $f(x_{k-1})$ from the previous iteration. We can compare the two methods starting from $x_0 = 3$; for the secant method we also choose $x_{-1} = 2$:

k	0	1	2	3	4	5	6
x_k (Newton)	3	2.385417	2.005592	1.835058	1.800257	1.798909	1.798907
x_k (secant)	3	1.927273	1.882421	1.809063	1.799771	1.798917	1.798907

The two methods exhibit similar convergence on this example.

8.1.6 Hybrid Techniques

With additional engineering, we can combine the advantages of different root-finding algorithms. For instance, we might make the following observations:

- *Bisection* is guaranteed to converge, but only at a linear rate.

- The *secant method* has a faster rate of convergence, but it may not converge at all if the initial guess x_0 is far from the root x^*.

Suppose we have bracketed a root of $f(x)$ in the interval $[\ell_k, r_k]$. Given the iterates x_k and x_{k-1}, we could take the next estimate x_{k+1} to be either of the following:

- The next secant method iterate, if it is contained in (ℓ_k, r_k).

- The midpoint $\ell_k + r_k/2$ otherwise.

This combination of the secant method and bisection guarantees that $x_{k+1} \in (\ell_k, r_k)$. Regardless of the choice above, we can update the bracket containing the root to $[\ell_{k+1}, r_{k+1}]$ by examining the sign of $f(x_{k+1})$.

The algorithm above, called "Dekker's method," attempts to combine the unconditional convergence of bisection with the stronger root estimates of the secant method. In many cases it is successful, but its convergence rate is somewhat difficult to analyze. Specialized failure modes can reduce this method to linear convergence or worse: In some cases, bisection can converge *more* quickly! Other techniques, e.g., "Brent's method," make bisection steps more often to strengthen convergence and can exhibit guaranteed behavior at the cost of a more complex implementation.

8.1.7 Single-Variable Case: Summary

We only have scratched the surface of the one-dimensional root-finding problem. Many other iterative schemes for root-finding exist, with different guarantees, convergence rates, and caveats. Starting from the methods above, we can make a number of broader observations:

- To support arbitrary functions f that may not have closed-form solutions to $f(x^*) = 0$, we use iterative algorithms generating approximations that get closer and closer to the desired root.

- We wish for the sequence x_k of root estimates to reach x^* as quickly as possible. If E_k is an error bound with $E_k \to 0$ as $k \to \infty$, then we can characterize the order of convergence using classifications like the following:

  1. Linear convergence: $E_{k+1} \leq CE_k$ for some $C < 1$.
  2. Superlinear convergence: $E_{k+1} \leq CE_k^r$ for $r > 1$; we do not require $C < 1$ since if E_k is small enough, the r-th power of E_k can cancel the effects of C.
  3. Quadratic convergence: $E_{k+1} \leq CE_k^2$.
  4. Cubic convergence: $E_{k+1} \leq CE_k^3$ (and so on).

- A method might converge quickly, needing fewer iterations to get sufficiently close to x^*, but each individual iteration may require additional computation time. In this case, it may be preferable to do more iterations of a simpler method than fewer iterations of a more complex one. This idea is further explored in Exercise 8.1.

8.2   MULTIVARIABLE PROBLEMS

Some applications may require solving the multivariable problem $f(\vec{x}) = \vec{0}$ given a function $f : \mathbb{R}^n \to \mathbb{R}^m$. We have already seen one instance of this problem when solving $A\vec{x} = \vec{b}$, which is equivalent to finding roots of $f(\vec{x}) \equiv A\vec{x} - \vec{b}$, but the general case is considerably more difficult. Strategies like bisection are challenging to extend since we now must guarantee that m different functions all equal zero *simultaneously*.

8.2.1   Newton's Method

One of our single-variable strategies extends in a straightforward way. Recall from §1.4.2 that for a differentiable function $f : \mathbb{R}^n \to \mathbb{R}^m$ we can define the *Jacobian* matrix giving the derivative of each component of f in each of the coordinate directions:

$$(Df)_{ij} \equiv \frac{\partial f_i}{\partial x_j}.$$

We can use the Jacobian of f to extend our derivation of Newton's method to multiple dimensions. In more than one dimension, a first-order approximation of f is given by

$$f(\vec{x}) \approx f(\vec{x}_k) + Df(\vec{x}_k) \cdot (\vec{x} - \vec{x}_k).$$

Substituting the desired condition $f(\vec{x}) = \vec{0}$ yields the following linear system determining the next iterate $\vec{x}_{k+1}$:

$$Df(\vec{x}_k) \cdot (\vec{x}_{k+1} - \vec{x}_k) = -f(\vec{x}_k).$$

When Df is square and invertible, requiring $n = m$, we obtain the iterative formula for a multidimensional version of Newton's method:

$$\vec{x}_{k+1} = \vec{x}_k - [Df(\vec{x}_k)]^{-1} f(\vec{x}_k),$$

where as always we do not explicitly compute the matrix $[Df(\vec{x}_k)]^{-1}$ but rather solve a linear system, e.g., using the techniques from Chapter 3. When $m < n$, this equation can be solved using the pseudoinverse to find one of potentially many roots of f; when $m > n$, one can attempt least-squares, but the existence of a root and convergence of this technique are both unlikely.

An analogous multidimensional argument to that in §8.1.3 shows that fixed-point methods like Newton's method iterating $\vec{x}_{k+1} = g(\vec{x}_k)$ converge when the largest-magnitude eigenvalue of Dg has absolute value less than 1 (Exercise 8.2). A derivation identical to the one-dimensional case in §8.1.4 then shows that Newton's method in multiple variables can have quadratic convergence near roots $\vec{x}^*$ for which $Df(\vec{x}^*)$ is nonsingular.

8.2.2   Making Newton Faster: Quasi-Newton and Broyden

As m and n increase, Newton's method becomes very expensive. For each iteration, a *different* matrix $Df(\vec{x}_k)$ must be inverted. Since it changes in each iteration, factoring $Df(\vec{x}_k) = L_k U_k$ does not help.

Quasi-Newton algorithms apply various approximations to reduce the cost of individual iterations. One approach extends the secant method beyond one dimension. Just as the secant method contains the same division operation as Newton's method, such secant-like approximations will not necessarily alleviate the need to invert a matrix. Instead, they make it possible to carry out root-finding without explicitly calculating the Jacobian Df.

An extension of the secant method to multiple dimensions will require careful adjustment, however, since divided differences yield a single value rather than a full approximate Jacobian matrix.

The directional derivative of f in the direction $\vec{v}$ is given by $D_{\vec{v}} f = Df \cdot \vec{v}$. To imitate the secant method, we can use this scalar value to our advantage by requiring that the Jacobian approximation J satisfies

$$J_k \cdot (\vec{x}_k - \vec{x}_{k-1}) = f(\vec{x}_k) - f(\vec{x}_{k-1}).$$

This formula does not determine the action of J on any vector perpendicular to $\vec{x}_k - \vec{x}_{k-1}$, so we need additional approximation assumptions to describe a complete root-finding algorithm.

One algorithm using the approximation above is *Broyden's method*, which maintains not only an estimate $\vec{x}_k$ of $\vec{x}^*$ but also a full matrix J_k estimating a Jacobian at $\vec{x}_k$ that satisfies the condition above. Initial estimates J_0 and $\vec{x}_0$ both must be supplied by the user; commonly, we approximate $J_0 = I_{n \times n}$ in the absence of more information.

Suppose we have an estimate J_{k-1} of the Jacobian at $\vec{x}_{k-1}$ left over from the previous iteration. We now have a new data point $\vec{x}_k$ at which we have evaluated $f(\vec{x}_k)$, so we would like to update J_{k-1} to a new matrix J_k taking into account this new piece of information. Broyden's method applies the directional derivative approximation above to finding J_k while keeping it as similar as possible to J_{k-1} by solving the following optimization problem:

$$\begin{aligned} &\text{minimize}_{J_k} &&\|J_k - J_{k-1}\|_{\text{Fro}}^2 \\ &\text{subject to} &&J_k \cdot (\vec{x}_k - \vec{x}_{k-1}) = f(\vec{x}_k) - f(\vec{x}_{k-1}). \end{aligned}$$

To solve this problem, define $\Delta J \equiv J_k - J_{k-1}$, $\Delta \vec{x} \equiv \vec{x}_k - \vec{x}_{k-1}$, and $\vec{d} \equiv f(\vec{x}_k) - f(\vec{x}_{k-1}) - J_{k-1} \cdot \Delta \vec{x}$. Making these substitutions provides an alternative optimization problem:

$$\begin{aligned} &\text{minimize}_{\Delta J} &&\|\Delta J\|_{\text{Fro}}^2 \\ &\text{subject to} &&\Delta J \cdot \Delta \vec{x} = \vec{d}. \end{aligned}$$

If we take $\vec{\lambda}$ to be a Lagrange multiplier, this minimization is equivalent to finding critical points of the Lagrangian Λ:

$$\Lambda = \|\Delta J\|_{\text{Fro}}^2 + \vec{\lambda}^\top (\Delta J \cdot \Delta \vec{x} - \vec{d}).$$

Differentiating with respect to an unknown element $(\Delta J)_{ij}$ shows:

$$0 = \frac{\partial \Lambda}{\partial (\Delta J)_{ij}} = 2(\Delta J)_{ij} + \lambda_i (\Delta \vec{x})_j \implies \Delta J = -\frac{1}{2} \vec{\lambda} (\Delta \vec{x})^\top.$$

Substituting into $\Delta J \cdot \Delta \vec{x} = \vec{d}$ shows $\vec{\lambda} (\Delta \vec{x})^\top (\Delta \vec{x}) = -2\vec{d}$, or equivalently $\vec{\lambda} = -2\vec{d}/\|\Delta \vec{x}\|_2^2$. Finally, we substitute into the Lagrange multiplier expression to find:

$$\Delta J = -\frac{1}{2} \vec{\lambda} (\Delta \vec{x})^\top = \frac{\vec{d} (\Delta \vec{x})^\top}{\|\Delta \vec{x}\|_2^2}.$$

Expanding back to the original notation shows:

$$\begin{aligned} J_k &= J_{k-1} + \Delta J \\ &= J_{k-1} + \frac{\vec{d} (\Delta \vec{x})^\top}{\|\Delta \vec{x}\|_2^2} \\ &= J_{k-1} + \frac{(f(\vec{x}_k) - f(\vec{x}_{k-1}) - J_{k-1} \cdot \Delta \vec{x})}{\|\vec{x}_k - \vec{x}_{k-1}\|_2^2} (\vec{x}_k - \vec{x}_{k-1})^\top. \end{aligned}$$

$$
\boxed{
\begin{array}{l}
\textbf{function } \textsc{Broyden}(f(\vec{x}), \vec{x}_0, J_0) \\
\quad J \leftarrow J_0 \quad \triangleright \text{ Can default to } I_{n \times n} \\
\quad \vec{x} \leftarrow \vec{x}_0 \\
\quad \textbf{for } k \leftarrow 1, 2, 3, \ldots \\
\qquad \Delta \vec{x} \leftarrow -J^{-1} f(\vec{x}) \quad \triangleright \text{ Linear} \\
\qquad \Delta f \leftarrow f(\vec{x} + \Delta x) - f(\vec{x}) \\
\qquad \vec{x} \leftarrow \vec{x} + \Delta \vec{x} \\
\qquad J \leftarrow J + \frac{(\Delta f - J \Delta \vec{x})}{\|\Delta \vec{x}\|_2^2} (\Delta x)^\top \\
\quad \textbf{return } \vec{x}
\end{array}
}
$$

(a)

$$
\boxed{
\begin{array}{l}
\textbf{function } \textsc{Broyden-Inverted}(f(\vec{x}), \vec{x}_0, J_0^{-1}) \\
\quad J^{-1} \leftarrow J_0^{-1} \qquad \triangleright \text{ Can default to } I_{n \times n} \\
\quad \vec{x} \leftarrow \vec{x}_0 \\
\quad \textbf{for } k \leftarrow 1, 2, 3, \ldots \\
\qquad \Delta \vec{x} \leftarrow -J^{-1} f(\vec{x}) \quad \triangleright \text{ Matrix multiply} \\
\qquad \Delta f \leftarrow f(\vec{x} + \Delta x) - f(\vec{x}) \\
\qquad \vec{x} \leftarrow \vec{x} + \Delta \vec{x} \\
\qquad J^{-1} \leftarrow J^{-1} + \frac{\Delta \vec{x} - J^{-1} \Delta f}{\Delta \vec{x}^\top J^{-1} \Delta f} \Delta \vec{x}^\top J^{-1} \\
\quad \textbf{return } \vec{x}
\end{array}
}
$$

(b)

Figure 8.5 (a) Broyden's method as described in §8.2.2 requires solving a linear system of equations, but the formula from Exercise 8.7 yields (b) an equivalent method using only matrix multiplication by updating the inverse matrix J^{-1} directly instead of J.

Broyden's method alternates between this update and the corresponding Newton step $\vec{x}_{k+1} = \vec{x}_k - J_k^{-1} f(\vec{x}_k)$.

Additional efficiency in some cases can be gained by keeping track of the matrix J_k^{-1} explicitly rather than the matrix J_k, which can be updated using a similar formula and avoids the need to solve any linear systems of equations. This possibility is explored via the Sherman-Morrison update formula in Exercise 8.7. Both versions of the algorithm are shown in Figure 8.5.

8.3 CONDITIONING

We already showed in Example 2.10 that the condition number of root-finding in a single variable is:

$$
\text{cond}_{x^*} f = \frac{1}{|f'(x^*)|}.
$$

As shown in Figure 8.6, this condition number shows that the best possible situation for root-finding occurs when f is changing rapidly near x^*, since in this case perturbing x^* will make f take values far from 0.

Applying an identical argument when f is multidimensional gives a condition number of $\|Df(\vec{x}^*)\|^{-1}$. When Df is not invertible, the condition number is *infinite*. This degeneracy occurs because perturbing $\vec{x}^*$ preserves $f(\vec{x}) = \vec{0}$ to first order, and indeed such a condition can create challenging root-finding cases similar to that shown in Figure 8.6(b).

8.4 EXERCISES

8.1 Suppose it takes processor time t to evaluate $f(x)$ or $f'(x)$ given $x \in \mathbb{R}$. So, computing the pair $(f(x), f'(x))$ takes time $2t$. For this problem, assume that individual arithmetic operations take negligible amounts of processor time compared to t.

   (a) Approximately how much time does it take to carry out k iterations of Newton's method on $f(x)$? Approximately how much time does it take to carry out k iterations of the secant method on $f(x)$?

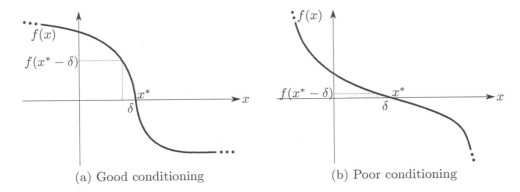

(a) Good conditioning (b) Poor conditioning

Figure 8.6 Intuition for the conditioning of finding roots of a function $f(x)$. (a) When the slope at the root x^* is large, the problem is well-conditioned because moving a small distance δ away from x^* makes the value of f change by a large amount. (b) When the slope at x^* is smaller, values of $f(x)$ remain close to zero as we move away from the root, making it harder to pinpoint the exact location of x^*.

(b) Why might the secant method be preferable in this case?

DH 8.2 Recall from §8.1.3 the proof of conditions under which single-variable fixed point iteration converges. Consider now the multivariable fixed point iteration scheme $\vec{x}_{k+1} \equiv g(\vec{x}_k)$ for $g : \mathbb{R}^n \to \mathbb{R}^n$.

   (a) Suppose that $g \in C^1$ and that $\vec{x}_k$ is within a small neighborhood of a fixed point $\vec{x}^*$ of g. Suggest a condition on the Jacobian Dg of g that guarantees g is Lipschitz in this neighborhood.

   (b) Using the previous result, derive a bound for the error of $\vec{x}_{k+1}$ in terms of the error of $\vec{x}_k$ and the Jacobian of g.

   (c) Show a condition on the eigenvalues of Dg that guarantees convergence of multivariable fixed point iteration.

   (d) How does the rate of convergence change if $Dg(\vec{x}^*) = 0$?

DH 8.3 Which method would you recommend for finding the root of $f : \mathbb{R} \to \mathbb{R}$ if all you know about f is that:

   (a) $f \in C^1$ and f' is inexpensive to evaluate;

   (b) f is Lipschitz with constant c satisfying $0 \leq c \leq 1$;

   (c) $f \in C^1$ and f' is costly to evaluate; or

   (d) $f \in C^0 \backslash C^1$, the continuous but non-differentiable functions.

DH 8.4 Provide an example of root-finding problems that satisfy the following criteria:

   (a) Can be solved by bisection but not by fixed point iteration

   (b) Can be solved using fixed point iteration, but not using Newton's method

8.5 Is Newton's method guaranteed to have quadratic convergence? Why?

DH 8.6 Suppose we wish to compute $\sqrt[p]{y}$ for a given $y > 0$. Using the techniques from this chapter, derive a quadratically convergent iterative method that finds this root given a sufficiently close initial guess.

8.7 In this problem, we show how to carry out Broyden's method for finding roots without solving linear systems of equations.

(a) Verify the Sherman-Morrison formula, for invertible $A \in \mathbb{R}^{n \times n}$ and vectors $\vec{u}, \vec{v} \in \mathbb{R}^n$:
$$(A + \vec{u}\vec{v}^\top)^{-1} = A^{-1} - \frac{A^{-1}\vec{u}\vec{v}^\top A^{-1}}{1 + \vec{v}^\top A^{-1}\vec{u}}.$$

(b) Use this formula to show that the algorithm in Figure 8.5(b) is equivalent to Broyden's method as described in §8.2.2.

8.8 In this problem, we will derive a technique known as Newton-Raphson division. Thanks to its fast convergence, it is often implemented in hardware for IEEE-754 floating-point arithmetic.

(a) Show how the reciprocal $\frac{1}{a}$ of $a \in \mathbb{R}$ can be computed iteratively using Newton's method. Write your iterative formula in a way that requires at most two multiplications, one addition or subtraction, and no divisions.

(b) Take x_k to be the estimate of $\frac{1}{a}$ during the k-th iteration of Newton's method. If we define $\varepsilon_k \equiv ax_k - 1$, show that $\varepsilon_{k+1} = -\varepsilon_k^2$.

(c) Approximately how many iterations of Newton's method are needed to compute $\frac{1}{a}$ within d binary decimal points? Write your answer in terms of ε_0 and d, and assume $|\varepsilon_0| < 1$.

(d) Is this method always convergent regardless of the initial guess of $\frac{1}{a}$?

8.9 (LSQI, [50]) In this problem, we will develop a method for solving least-squares with a quadratic inequality constraint:
$$\min_{\|\vec{x}\|_2 \leq 1} \|A\vec{x} - \vec{b}\|_2.$$

You can assume the least-squares system $A\vec{x} \approx \vec{b}$, where $A \in \mathbb{R}^{m \times n}$ with $m > n$, is overdetermined.

(a) The optimal $\vec{x}$ either satisfies $\|\vec{x}\|_2 < 1$ or $\|\vec{x}\|_2 = 1$. Explain how to distinguish between the two cases, and give a formula for $\vec{x}$ when $\|\vec{x}\|_2 < 1$.

(b) Suppose we are in the $\|\vec{x}\|_2 = 1$ case. Show that there exists $\lambda \in \mathbb{R}$ such that $(A^\top A + \lambda I_{n \times n})\vec{x} = A^\top \vec{b}$.

(c) Define $f(\lambda) \equiv \|\vec{x}(\lambda)\|_2^2 - 1$, where $\vec{x}(\lambda)$ is the solution to the system $(A^\top A + \lambda I_{n \times n})\vec{x} = A^\top \vec{b}$ for fixed $\lambda \geq 0$. Assuming that the optimal $\vec{x}$ for the original optimization problem satisfies $\|\vec{x}\|_2 = 1$, show $f(0) \geq 0$ and that $f(\lambda) < 0$ for sufficiently large $\lambda > 0$.

(d) Propose a strategy for the $\|\vec{x}\|_2 = 1$ case using root-finding.

8.10 (Proposed by A. Nguyen.) Suppose we have a polynomial $p(x) = a_k x^k + \cdots + a_1 x + a_0$. You can assume $a_k \neq 0$ and $k \geq 1$.

    (a) Suppose the derivative $p'(x)$ has no roots in (a, b). How many roots can $p(x)$ have in this interval?

    (b) Using the result of Exercise 8.10a, propose a recursive algorithm for estimating all the real roots of $p(x)$. Assume we know that the roots of $p(x)$ are at least ε apart and that they are contained with an interval $[a, b]$.

8.11 Root-finding for complex- or real-valued polynomials is closely linked to the eigenvalue problem considered in Chapter 6.

    (a) Give a matrix A whose eigenvalues are the roots of a given polynomial $p(x) = a_k x^k + \cdots + a_1 x + a_0$; you can assume $p(x)$ has no repeated roots.

    (b) Show that the eigenvalues of a matrix $A \in \mathbb{R}^{n \times n}$ are the roots of a polynomial function. Is it advisable to use root-finding algorithms from this chapter for the eigenvalue problem?

CHAPTER 9

Unconstrained Optimization

CONTENTS

9.1 Unconstrained Optimization: Motivation 163
9.2 Optimality 165
    9.2.1 Differential Optimality 166
    9.2.2 Alternative Conditions for Optimality 168
9.3 One-Dimensional Strategies 169
    9.3.1 Newton's Method 170
    9.3.2 Golden Section Search 170
9.4 Multivariable Strategies 173
    9.4.1 Gradient Descent 173
    9.4.2 Newton's Method in Multiple Variables 174
    9.4.3 Optimization without Hessians: BFGS 175

P REVIOUS chapters have taken a largely *variational* approach to deriving numerical algorithms. That is, we define an *objective function* or *energy* $E(\vec{x})$, possibly with constraints, and pose our algorithms as approaches to a corresponding minimization or maximization problem. A sampling of problems that we solved this way is listed below:

Problem	§	Objective	Constraints
Least-squares	4.1.2	$E(\vec{x}) = \|A\vec{x} - \vec{b}\|_2^2$	None
Project $\vec{b}$ onto $\vec{a}$	5.4.1	$E(c) = \|c\vec{a} - \vec{b}\|_2^2$	None
Eigenvectors of symmetric A	6.1	$E(\vec{x}) = \vec{x}^\top A \vec{x}$	$\|\vec{x}\|_2 = 1$
Pseudoinverse	7.2.1	$E(\vec{x}) = \|\vec{x}\|_2^2$	$A^\top A \vec{x} = A^\top \vec{b}$
Principal component analysis	7.2.5	$E(C) = \|X - CC^\top X\|_{\text{Fro}}$	$C^\top C = I_{d \times d}$
Broyden step	8.2.2	$E(J_k) = \|J_k - J_{k-1}\|_{\text{Fro}}^2$	$J_k \cdot \Delta \vec{x}_k = \Delta f_k$

The formulation of numerical problems in variational language is a powerful and general technique. To make it applicable to a larger class of nonlinear problems, we will design algorithms that can perform minimization or maximization in the absence of a special form for the energy E.

9.1 UNCONSTRAINED OPTIMIZATION: MOTIVATION

In this chapter, we will consider *unconstrained* problems, that is, problems that can be posed as minimizing or maximizing a function $f : \mathbb{R}^n \to \mathbb{R}$ without any constraints on the input $\vec{x}$. It is not difficult to encounter such problems in practice; we explore a few examples below.

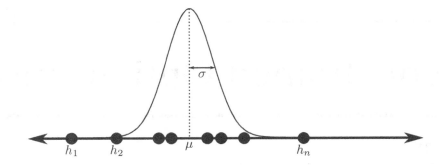

Figure 9.1 Illustration for Example 9.2. Given the heights $h_1, h_2, \ldots, h_n$ of students in a class, we may wish to estimate the mean μ and standard deviation σ of the most likely normal distribution explaining the observed heights.

Example 9.1 (Nonlinear least-squares). Suppose we are given a number of pairs (x_i, y_i) such that $f(x_i) \approx y_i$ and wish to find the best approximating f within a particular class. For instance, if we expect that f is exponential, we should be able to write $f(x) = ce^{ax}$ for some $c, a \in \mathbb{R}$; our job is to find the parameters a and c that best fit the data. One strategy we already developed in Chapter 4 is to minimize the following energy function:

$$E(a, c) = \sum_i (y_i - ce^{ax_i})^2.$$

This form for E is not quadratic in a, so the linear least-squares methods from §4.1.2 do not apply to this minimization problem. Hence, we must employ alternative methods to minimize E.

Example 9.2 (Maximum likelihood estimation). In machine learning, the problem of *parameter estimation* involves examining the results of a randomized experiment and trying to summarize them using a probability distribution of a particular form. For example, we might measure the height of every student in a class to obtain a list of heights h_i for each student i. If we have a lot of students, we can model the distribution of student heights using a *normal distribution*:

$$g(h; \mu, \sigma) = \frac{1}{\sigma\sqrt{2\pi}} e^{-(h-\mu)^2/2\sigma^2},$$

where μ is the mean of the distribution and σ is the standard deviation of the standard "bell curve" shape. This notation is illustrated in Figure 9.1.

Under this normal distribution, the likelihood that we observe height h_i for student i is given by $g(h_i; \mu, \sigma)$, and under the (reasonable) assumption that the height of student i is probabilistically independent of that of student j, the likelihood of observing the entire set of heights observed is proportional to the product

$$P(\{h_1, \ldots, h_n\}; \mu, \sigma) = \prod_i g(h_i; \mu, \sigma).$$

A common method for estimating the parameters μ and σ of g is to maximize P viewed as a function of μ and σ with $\{h_i\}$ fixed; this is called the *maximum-likelihood estimate* of μ and

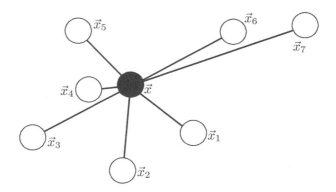

Figure 9.2 The geometric median problem seeks a point $\vec{x}$ minimizing the total (non-squared) distance to a set of data points $\vec{x}_1, \ldots, \vec{x}_k$.

σ. In practice, we usually optimize the *log likelihood* $\ell(\mu, \sigma) \equiv \log P(\{h_1, \ldots, h_n\}; \mu, \sigma)$. This function has the same maxima but enjoys better numerical and mathematical properties.

Example 9.3 (Geometric problems). Many geometric problems encountered in computer graphics and vision do not reduce to least-squares energies. For instance, suppose we have a number of points $\vec{x}_1, \ldots, \vec{x}_k \in \mathbb{R}^n$. If we wish to *cluster* these points, we might wish to summarize them with a single $\vec{x}$ minimizing

$$E(\vec{x}) \equiv \sum_i \|\vec{x} - \vec{x}_i\|_2.$$

The $\vec{x}$ minimizing E is known as the *geometric median* of $\{\vec{x}_1, \ldots, \vec{x}_k\}$, as illustrated in Figure 9.2. Since the norm of the difference $\vec{x} - \vec{x}_i$ in E is not squared, the energy is no longer quadratic in the components of $\vec{x}$.

Example 9.4 (Physical equilibria, adapted from [58]). Suppose we attach an object to a set of springs; each spring is anchored at point $\vec{x}_i \in \mathbb{R}^3$ with natural length L_i and constant k_i. In the absence of gravity, if our object is located at position $\vec{p} \in \mathbb{R}^3$, the network of springs has potential energy

$$E(\vec{p}) = \frac{1}{2} \sum_i k_i \left(\|\vec{p} - \vec{x}_i\|_2 - L_i \right)^2.$$

Equilibria of this system are given by local minima of E and represent points $\vec{p}$ at which the spring forces are all balanced. Extensions of this problem are used to visualize graphs $G = (V, E)$, by attaching vertices in V with springs for each pair in E.

9.2 OPTIMALITY

Before discussing how to minimize or maximize a function, we should characterize properties of the maxima and minima we are seeking. With this goal in mind, for a particular $f : \mathbb{R}^n \to \mathbb{R}$ and $\vec{x}^* \in \mathbb{R}^n$, we will derive *optimality conditions* that verify whether $\vec{x}^*$ has the optimal

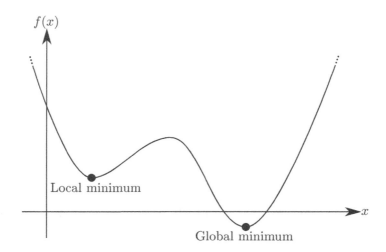

Figure 9.3 A function $f(x)$ with two local minima but only one global minimum.

value $f(\vec{x}^*)$. Maximizing f is the same as minimizing $-f$, so from this section onward the minimization problem is sufficient for our consideration.

In most situations, we ideally would like to find *global* minima of f:

Definition 9.1 (Global minimum). The point $\vec{x}^* \in \mathbb{R}^n$ is a *global minimum* of $f : \mathbb{R}^n \to \mathbb{R}$ if $f(\vec{x}^*) \leq f(\vec{x})$ for all $\vec{x} \in \mathbb{R}^n$.

Finding a global minimum of $f(\vec{x})$ without any bounds on $\vec{x}$ or information about the structure of f effectively requires searching in the dark. For instance, suppose an optimization algorithm identifies the left local minimum in the function in Figure 9.3. It is nearly impossible to realize that there is a second, lower minimum by guessing x values—and for all we know, there may be a third even lower minimum of f miles to the right!

To relax these difficulties, in many cases we are satisfied if we can find a *local* minimum:

Definition 9.2 (Local minimum). The point $\vec{x}^* \in \mathbb{R}^n$ is a *local minimum* of $f : \mathbb{R}^n \to \mathbb{R}$ if there exists some $\varepsilon > 0$ such that $f(\vec{x}^*) \leq f(\vec{x})$ for all $\vec{x} \in \mathbb{R}^n$ satisfying $\|\vec{x} - \vec{x}^*\|_2 < \varepsilon$.

This definition requires that $\vec{x}^*$ attains the smallest value in some *neighborhood* defined by the radius ε. Local optimization algorithms have the severe limitation that they may not find the lowest possible value of f, as in the left local minimum in Figure 9.3. To mitigate these issues, many strategies, heuristic and otherwise, are applied to explore the landscape of possible $\vec{x}$'s to help gain confidence that a local minimum has the best possible value.

9.2.1 Differential Optimality

A familiar story from single- and multi-variable calculus is that finding potential minima and maxima of a function $f : \mathbb{R}^n \to \mathbb{R}$ is more straightforward when f is differentiable. In this case, the gradient vector $\nabla f = (\partial f / \partial x_1, \dots, \partial f / \partial x_n)$ at $\vec{x}$ points in the direction moving from $\vec{x}$ in which f increases at the fastest rate; the vector $-\nabla f$ points in the direction of greatest decrease. One way to see this is to approximate $f(\vec{x})$ linearly near a point $\vec{x}_0 \in \mathbb{R}^n$:

$$f(\vec{x}) \approx f(\vec{x}_0) + \nabla f(\vec{x}_0) \cdot (\vec{x} - \vec{x}_0).$$

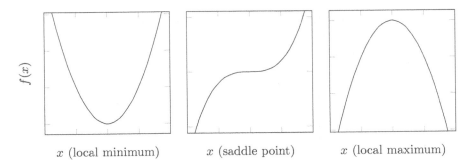

x (local minimum)   x (saddle point)   x (local maximum)

Figure 9.4 Different types of critical points.

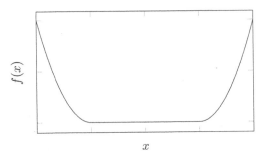

Figure 9.5 A function with many stationary points.

If we take $\vec{x} - \vec{x}_0 = \alpha \nabla f(\vec{x}_0)$, then

$$f(\vec{x}_0 + \alpha \nabla f(\vec{x}_0)) \approx f(\vec{x}_0) + \alpha \|\nabla f(\vec{x}_0)\|_2^2.$$

The value $\|\nabla f(\vec{x}_0)\|_2^2$ is *always* nonnegative, so when $\|\nabla f(\vec{x}_0)\|_2 > 0$, the sign of α determines whether f increases or decreases locally.

By the above argument, if $\vec{x}_0$ is a local minimum, then $\nabla f(\vec{x}_0) = \vec{0}$. This condition is *necessary* but not *sufficient*: Maxima and saddle points also have $\nabla f(\vec{x}_0) = \vec{0}$ as shown in Figure 9.4. Even so, this observation about minima of differentiable functions yields a high-level approach to optimization:

1. Find points $\vec{x}_i$ satisfying $\nabla f(\vec{x}_i) = \vec{0}$.

2. Check which of these points is a local minimum as opposed to a maximum or saddle point.

Given their role in optimization, we give the points $\vec{x}_i$ a special name:

Definition 9.3 (Stationary point). A *stationary point* of $f : \mathbb{R}^n \to \mathbb{R}$ is a point $\vec{x} \in \mathbb{R}^n$ satisfying $\nabla f(\vec{x}) = \vec{0}$.

Our methods for minimization mostly will find stationary points of f and subsequently eliminate those that are not minima.

It is imperative to keep in mind when we can expect minimization algorithms to succeed. In most cases, such as those in Figure 9.4, the stationary points of f are *isolated*, meaning we can write them in a discrete list $\{\vec{x}_0, \vec{x}_1, \ldots\}$. A degenerate case, however, is shown in Figure 9.5; here, an entire interval of values x is composed of stationary points, making it impossible to consider them individually. For the most part, we will ignore such issues as unlikely, poorly conditioned degeneracies.

Suppose we identify a point $\vec{x} \in \mathbb{R}$ as a stationary point of f and wish to check if it is a local minimum. If f is twice-differentiable, we can use its *Hessian* matrix

$$H_f(\vec{x}) = \begin{pmatrix} \frac{\partial^2 f}{\partial x_1^2} & \frac{\partial^2 f}{\partial x_1 \partial x_2} & \cdots & \frac{\partial^2 f}{\partial x_1 \partial x_n} \\ \frac{\partial^2 f}{\partial x_2 \partial x_1} & \frac{\partial^2 f}{\partial^2 x_2} & \cdots & \frac{\partial^2 f}{\partial x_2 \partial x_n} \\ \vdots & \vdots & \cdots & \vdots \\ \frac{\partial^2 f}{\partial x_n \partial x_1} & \frac{\partial^2 f}{\partial x_n \partial x_2} & \cdots & \frac{\partial^2 f}{\partial^2 x_n} \end{pmatrix}.$$

Adding a term to the linearization of f reveals the role of H_f:

$$f(\vec{x}) \approx f(\vec{x}_0) + \nabla f(\vec{x}_0) \cdot (\vec{x} - \vec{x}_0) + \frac{1}{2}(\vec{x} - \vec{x}_0)^\top H_f(\vec{x} - \vec{x}_0).$$

If we substitute a stationary point $\vec{x}^*$, then since $\nabla f(\vec{x}^*) = \vec{0}$,

$$f(\vec{x}) \approx f(\vec{x}^*) + \frac{1}{2}(\vec{x} - \vec{x}^*)^\top H_f(\vec{x} - \vec{x}^*).$$

If H_f is positive definite, then this expression shows $f(\vec{x}) \geq f(\vec{x}^*)$ near $\vec{x}^*$, and thus $\vec{x}^*$ is a local minimum. More generally, a few situations can occur:

- If H_f is *positive definite*, then $\vec{x}^*$ is a local minimum of f.

- If H_f is *negative definite*, then $\vec{x}^*$ is a local maximum of f.

- If H_f is *indefinite*, then $\vec{x}^*$ is a saddle point of f.

- If H_f is *not invertible*, then oddities such as the function in Figure 9.5 can occur; this includes the case where H_f is *semidefinite*.

Checking if a Hessian matrix is positive definite can be accomplished by checking if its Cholesky factorization exists or—more slowly—by verifying that all its eigenvalues are positive. So, when f is sufficiently smooth and the Hessian of f is known, we can check stationary points for optimality using the list above. Many optimization algorithms including the ones we will discuss ignore the non-invertible case and notify the user, since again it is relatively unlikely.

9.2.2 Alternative Conditions for Optimality

If we know more information about $f : \mathbb{R}^n \to \mathbb{R}$, we can provide optimality conditions that are stronger or easier to check than the ones above. These conditions also can help when f is not differentiable but has other geometric properties that make it possible to find a minimum.

One property of f that has strong implications for optimization is *convexity*, illustrated in Figure 9.6(a):

Definition 9.4 (Convex). A function $f : \mathbb{R}^n \to \mathbb{R}$ is *convex* when for all $\vec{x}, \vec{y} \in \mathbb{R}^n$ and $\alpha \in (0, 1)$ the following relationship holds:

$$f((1 - \alpha)\vec{x} + \alpha\vec{y}) \leq (1 - \alpha)f(\vec{x}) + \alpha f(\vec{y}).$$

When the inequality is strict (replace $\leq$ with $<$), the function is *strictly convex*.

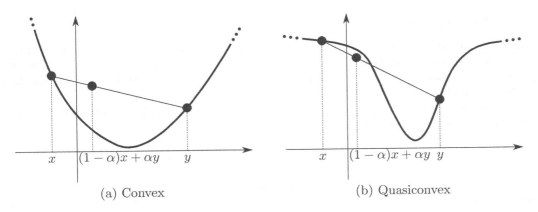

(a) Convex   (b) Quasiconvex

Figure 9.6 (a) Convex functions must be bowl-shaped, while (b) quasiconvex functions can have more complicated features.

Convexity implies that if you connect two points in $\mathbb{R}^n$ with a line, the values of f along the line are less than or equal to those you would obtain by linear interpolation.

Convex functions enjoy many strong properties, the most basic of which is the following:

Proposition 9.1. A local minimum of a convex function $f : \mathbb{R}^n \to \mathbb{R}$ is necessarily a global minimum.

Proof. Take $\vec{x}$ to be such a local minimum and suppose there exists $\vec{x}^*$ with $f(\vec{x}^*) < f(\vec{x})$. Then, for sufficiently small $\alpha \in (0, 1)$,

$$f(\vec{x}) \leq f(\vec{x} + \alpha(\vec{x}^* - \vec{x})) \text{ since } \vec{x} \text{ is a local minimum}$$
$$\leq (1 - \alpha)f(\vec{x}) + \alpha f(\vec{x}^*) \text{ by convexity.}$$

Moving terms in the inequality $f(\vec{x}) \leq (1 - \alpha)f(\vec{x}) + \alpha f(\vec{x}^*)$ shows $f(\vec{x}) \leq f(\vec{x}^*)$. This contradicts our assumption that $f(\vec{x}^*) < f(\vec{x})$, so $\vec{x}$ must minimize f globally. □

This proposition and related observations show that it is possible to check if you have reached a *global* minimum of a convex function by applying first-order optimality. Thus, it is valuable to check by hand if a function being optimized happens to be convex, a situation occurring surprisingly often in scientific computing; one sufficient condition that can be easier to check when f is twice-differentiable is that H_f is positive definite *everywhere*.

Other optimization techniques have guarantees under weaker assumptions about f. For example, one relaxation of convexity is *quasi*-convexity, achieved when

$$f((1 - \alpha)\vec{x} + \alpha\vec{y}) \leq \max(f(\vec{x}), f(\vec{y})).$$

An example of a quasiconvex function is shown in Figure 9.6(b). Although it does not have the characteristic "bowl" shape of a convex function, its local minimizers are necessarily global minimizers.

9.3 ONE-DIMENSIONAL STRATEGIES

As in the last chapter, we will start by studying optimization for functions $f : \mathbb{R} \to \mathbb{R}$ of one variable and then expand to more general functions $f : \mathbb{R}^n \to \mathbb{R}$.

9.3.1 Newton's Method

Our principal strategy for minimizing differentiable functions $f : \mathbb{R}^n \to \mathbb{R}$ will be to find stationary points $\vec{x}^*$ satisfying $\nabla f(\vec{x}^*) = 0$. Assuming we can check whether stationary points are maxima, minima, or saddle points as a post-processing step, we will focus on the problem of finding the stationary points $\vec{x}^*$.

To this end, suppose $f : \mathbb{R} \to \mathbb{R}$ is twice-differentiable. Then, following our derivation of Newton's method for root-finding in §8.1.4, we can approximate:

$$f(x) \approx f(x_k) + f'(x_k)(x - x_k) + \frac{1}{2}f''(x_k)(x - x_k)^2.$$

We need to include second-order terms since linear functions have no nontrivial minima or maxima. The approximation on the right-hand side is a parabola whose vertex is located at $x_k - f'(x_k)/f''(x_k)$.

In reality, f may not be a parabola, so its vertex will not necessarily give a critical point of f directly. So, Newton's method for minimization iteratively minimizes and adjusts the parabolic approximation:

$$x_{k+1} = x_k - \frac{f'(x_k)}{f''(x_k)}.$$

This technique is easily analyzed given the work we put into understanding Newton's method in the previous chapter. Specifically, an alternative way to derive the iterative formula above comes from applying Newton's method for root-finding to $f'(x)$, since stationary points x of $f(x)$ satisfy $f'(x) = 0$. Applying results about convergence to a root, in most cases Newton's method for optimization exhibits quadratic convergence, provided the initial guess x_0 is sufficiently close to x^*.

A natural question is whether the secant method can be similarly adapted to minimization. Our derivation of Newton's method above finds roots of f', so the secant method could be used to eliminate f'' but not f' from the optimization formula. One-dimensional situations in which f' is known but not f'' are relatively rare. A more suitable parallel is to replace line segments through the last two iterates, used to approximate f in the secant method for root-finding, with parabolas through the last three iterates. The resulting algorithm, known as *successive parabolic interpolation*, also minimizes a quadratic approximation of f at each iteration, but rather than using $f(x_k)$, $f'(x_k)$, and $f''(x_k)$ to construct the approximation, it uses $f(x_k)$, $f(x_{k-1})$, and $f(x_{k-2})$. This technique can converge superlinearly; in practice, however, it can have drawbacks that make other methods discussed in this chapter more preferable. We explore its design in Exercise 9.3.

9.3.2 Golden Section Search

Since Newton's method for optimization is so closely linked to root-finding, we might ask whether a similar adaptation can be applied to bisection. Unfortunately, this transition is not obvious. A primary reason for using bisection is that it employs the weakest assumption on f needed to find roots: continuity. Continuity is enough to prove the Intermediate Value Theorem, which justifies convergence of bisection. The Intermediate Value Theorem does not apply to extrema of a function in any intuitive way, so it appears that directly using bisection to minimize a function is not so straightforward.

It is valuable, however, to have at least one minimization algorithm available that does not require differentiability of f as an underlying assumption. After all, there are non-differentiable functions that have clear minima, like $f(x) \equiv |x|$ at $x = 0$. To this end, one alternative assumption might be that f is *unimodular*:

```
function GOLDEN-SECTION-SEARCH(f(x), a, b)
    τ ← ½(√5 − 1)
    x₀ ← a + (1 − τ)(b − a)          ▷ Initial division of interval a < x₀ < x₁ < b
    x₁ ← a + τ(b − a)
    f₀ ← f(x₀)                        ▷ Function values at x₀ and x₁
    f₁ ← f(x₁)
    for k ← 1, 2, 3, . . .
        if |b − a| < ε then           ▷ Golden section search converged
            return x* = ½(a + b)
        else if f₀ ≥ f₁ then          ▷ Remove the interval [a, x₀]
            a ← x₀                                    ▷ Move left side
            x₀ ← x₁                         ▷ Reuse previous iteration
            f₀ ← f₁
            x₁ ← a + τ(b − a)                    ▷ Generate new sample
            f₁ ← f(x₁)
        else if f₁ > f₀ then          ▷ Remove the interval [x₁, b]
            b ← x₁                                    ▷ Move right side
            x₁ ← x₀                         ▷ Reuse previous iteration
            f₁ ← f₀
            x₀ ← a + (1 − τ)(b − a)              ▷ Generate new sample
            f₀ ← f(x₀)
```

Figure 9.7 The golden section search algorithm finds minima of unimodular functions $f(x)$ on the interval $[a, b]$ even if they are not differentiable.

Definition 9.5 (Unimodular). A function $f : [a, b] \to \mathbb{R}$ is *unimodular* if there exists $x^* \in [a, b]$ such that f is decreasing (or non-increasing) for $x \in [a, x^*]$ and increasing (or non-decreasing) for $x \in [x^*, b]$.

In other words, a unimodular function decreases for some time, and then begins increasing; no localized minima are allowed. Functions like $|x|$ are not differentiable but still are unimodular.

Suppose we have two values x_0 and x_1 such that $a < x_0 < x_1 < b$. We can make two observations that will help us formulate an optimization technique for a unimodular function $f(x)$:

- If $f(x_0) \geq f(x_1)$, then $f(x) \geq f(x_1)$ for all $x \in [a, x_0]$. Thus, the interval $[a, x_0]$ can be discarded in a search for the minimum of f.

- If $f(x_1) \geq f(x_0)$, then $f(x) \geq f(x_0)$ for all $x \in [x_1, b]$, and we can discard the interval $[x_1, b]$.

This structure suggests a bisection-like minimization algorithm beginning with the interval $[a, b]$ and iteratively removing pieces according to the rules above. In such an algorithm, we could remove a *third* of the interval each iteration. This requires two evaluations of f, at $x_0 = 2a/3 + b/3$ and $x_1 = a/3 + 2b/3$. If evaluating f is expensive, however, we may attempt to reduce the number of evaluations per iteration to one.

To design such a method reducing the computational load, we will focus on the case when $a = 0$ and $b = 1$; the strategies we derive below eventually will work more generally by shifting and scaling. In the absence of more information about f, we will make a symmetric

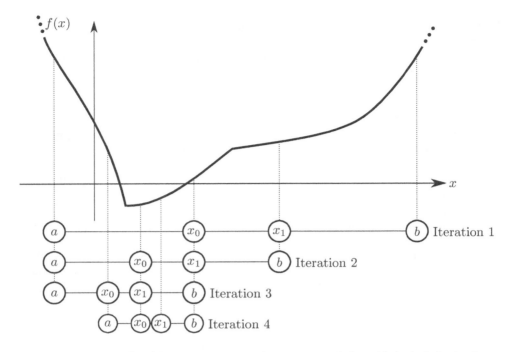

Figure 9.8 Iterations of golden section search on unimodular $f(x)$ shrink the interval $[a, b]$ by eliminating the left segment $[a, x_0]$ or the right segment $[x_1, b]$; each iteration reuses either $f(x_0)$ or $f(x_1)$ via the construction in §9.3.2. In this illustration, each horizontal line represents an iteration of golden section search, with the values a, x_0, x_1, and b labeled in the circles.

choice $x_0 = \alpha$ and $x_1 = 1 - \alpha$ for some $\alpha \in (0, 1/2)$; taking $\alpha = 1/3$ recovers the evenly divided technique suggested above.

Now, suppose that during minimization we can eliminate the rightmost interval $[x_1, b]$ by the rules listed above. In the next iteration, the search interval shrinks to $[0, 1 - \alpha]$, with $x_0 = \alpha(1 - \alpha)$ and $x_1 = (1 - \alpha)^2$. To reuse $f(\alpha)$, we could set $(1 - \alpha)^2 = \alpha$, yielding:

$$\alpha = \frac{1}{2}(3 - \sqrt{5})$$

$$1 - \alpha = \frac{1}{2}(\sqrt{5} - 1).$$

The value $1 - \alpha \equiv \tau$ above is the *golden ratio*! A symmetric argument shows that the same choice of α works if we had removed the left interval instead of the right one. In short, "trisection" algorithms minimizing unimodular functions $f(x)$ dividing intervals into segments with length determined using this ratio can reuse a function evaluation from one iteration to the next.

The *golden section search* algorithm, documented in Figure 9.7 and illustrated in Figure 9.8, makes use of this construction to minimize a unimodular function $f(x)$ on the interval $[a, b]$ via subdivision with one evaluation of $f(x)$ per iteration. It converges unconditionally and linearly, since a fraction α of the interval $[a, b]$ bracketing the minimum is removed in each step.

---

function GRADIENT-DESCENT$(f(\vec{x}), \vec{x}_0)$
    $\vec{x} \leftarrow \vec{x}_0$
    for $k \leftarrow 1, 2, 3, \ldots$
        DEFINE-FUNCTION$(g(t) \equiv f(\vec{x} - t\nabla f(\vec{x})))$
        $t^* \leftarrow$ LINE-SEARCH$(g(t), t \geq 0)$
        $\vec{x} \leftarrow \vec{x} - t^*\nabla f(\vec{x})$ ▷ Update estimate of minimum
        if $\|\nabla f(\vec{x})\|_2 < \varepsilon$ **then**
            return $x^* = \vec{x}$

Figure 9.9 The gradient descent algorithm iteratively minimizes $f : \mathbb{R}^n \to \mathbb{R}$ by solving one-dimensional minimizations through the gradient direction. LINE-SEARCH can be one of the methods from §9.3 for minimization in one dimension. In faster, more advanced techniques, this method can find suboptimal $t^* > 0$ that still decreases $g(t)$ sufficiently to make sure the optimization does not get stuck.

When f is not globally unimodular, golden section search does not apply unless we can find some $[a, b]$ such that f is unimodular on that interval. In some cases, $[a, b]$ can be guessed by attempting to bracket a local minimum of f. For example, [101] suggests stepping farther and farther away from some starting point $x_0 \in \mathbb{R}$, moving downhill from $f(x_0)$ until f increases again, indicating the presence of a local minimum.

9.4 MULTIVARIABLE STRATEGIES

We continue to parallel our discussion of root-finding by expanding from single-variable to multivariable problems. As with root-finding, multivariable optimization problems are considerably more difficult than optimization in a single variable, but they appear so many times in practice that they are worth careful consideration.

Here, we will consider only the case that $f : \mathbb{R}^n \to \mathbb{R}$ is twice-differentiable. Optimization methods similar to golden section search for non-differentiable functions are less common and are difficult to formulate. See, e.g., [74, 17] for consideration of non-differentiable optimization, subgradients, and related concepts.

9.4.1 Gradient Descent

From our previous discussion, $\nabla f(\vec{x})$ points in the direction of "steepest ascent" of f at $\vec{x}$ and $-\nabla f(\vec{x})$ points in the direction of "steepest descent." If nothing else, these properties suggest that when $\nabla f(\vec{x}) \neq \vec{0}$, for small $\alpha > 0$, $f(\vec{x} - \alpha\nabla f(\vec{x})) \leq f(\vec{x})$.

Suppose our current estimate of the minimizer of f is $\vec{x}_k$. A reasonable iterative minimization strategy should seek the next iterate $\vec{x}_{k+1}$ so that $f(\vec{x}_{k+1}) < f(\vec{x}_k)$. Since we do not expect to find a global minimum in one shot, we can make restrictions to simplify the search for $\vec{x}_{k+1}$. A typical simplification is to use a one-variable algorithm from §9.3 on f restricted to a line through $\vec{x}_k$; once we solve the one-dimensional problem for $\vec{x}_{k+1}$, we choose a new line through $\vec{x}_{k+1}$ and repeat.

Consider the function $g_k(t) \equiv f(\vec{x}_k - t\nabla f(\vec{x}_k))$, which restricts f to the line through $\vec{x}_k$ parallel to $-\nabla f(\vec{x}_k)$. We have shown that when $\nabla f(\vec{x}_k) \neq \vec{0}$, $g(t) < g(0)$ for small $t > 0$. Hence, this is a reasonable direction for a restricted search for the new iterate. The resulting *gradient descent* algorithm shown in Figure 9.9 and illustrated in Figure 9.10 iteratively solves one-dimensional problems to improve $\vec{x}_k$.

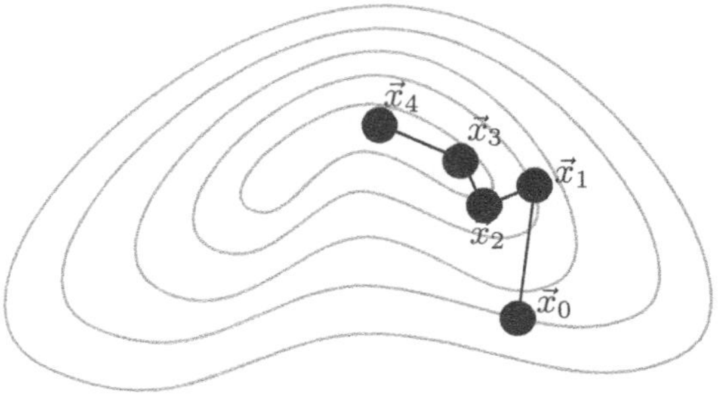

Figure 9.10 Gradient descent on a function $f : \mathbb{R}^2 \to \mathbb{R}$, whose level sets are shown in gray. The gradient $\nabla f(\vec{x})$ points perpendicular to the level sets of f, as in Figure 1.6; gradient descent iteratively minimizes f along the line through this direction.

Each iteration of gradient descent decreases $f(\vec{x}_k)$, so these values converge assuming they are bounded below. The approximations $\vec{x}_k$ only stop changing when $\nabla f(\vec{x}_k) \approx \vec{0}$, showing that gradient descent must at least reach a local minimum; convergence can be slow for some functions f, however.

Rather than solving the one-variable problem exactly in each step, line search can be replaced by a method that finds points along the line that decrease the objective a non-negligible if suboptimal amount. It is more difficult to guarantee convergence in this case, since each step may not reach a local minimum on the line, but the computational savings can be considerable since full one-dimensional minimization is avoided; see [90] for details.

Taking the more limited line search strategy to an extreme, sometimes a fixed $t > 0$ is used for *all* iterations to avoid line search altogether. This choice of t is known in machine learning as the *learning rate* and trades off between taking large minimization steps and potentially skipping over a minimum. Gradient descent with a constant step is unlikely to converge to a minimum in this case, but depending on f it may settle in some neighborhood of the optimal point; see Exercise 9.7 for an error bound of this method in one case.

9.4.2 Newton's Method in Multiple Variables

Paralleling our derivation of the single-variable case in §9.3.1, we can write a Taylor series approximation of $f : \mathbb{R}^n \to \mathbb{R}$ using its Hessian matrix H_f:

$$f(\vec{x}) \approx f(\vec{x}_k) + \nabla f(\vec{x}_k)^\top \cdot (\vec{x} - \vec{x}_k) + \frac{1}{2}(\vec{x} - \vec{x}_k)^\top \cdot H_f(\vec{x}_k) \cdot (\vec{x} - \vec{x}_k).$$

Differentiating with respect to $\vec{x}$ and setting the result equal to zero yields the following iterative scheme:

$$\vec{x}_{k+1} = \vec{x}_k - [H_f(\vec{x}_k)]^{-1} \nabla f(\vec{x}_k).$$

This expression generalizes Newton's method from §9.3.1, and once again it converges quadratically when $\vec{x}_0$ is near a minimum.

Newton's method can be more efficient than gradient descent depending on the objective f since it makes use of both first- and second-order information. Gradient descent has no knowledge of H_f; it proceeds analogously to walking downhill by looking only at your feet. By using H_f, Newton's method has a larger picture of the shape of f nearby.

Each iteration of gradient descent potentially requires many evaluations of f during line search. On the other hand, we must evaluate and invert the Hessian H_f during each iteration of Newton's method. These implementation differences do not affect the number of iterations to convergence but do affect the computational time taken per iteration of the two methods.

When H_f is nearly singular, Newton's method can take very large steps away from the current estimate of the minimum. These large steps are a good idea if the second-order approximation of f is accurate, but as the step becomes large the quality of this approximation can degenerate. One way to take more conservative steps is to "dampen" the change in $\vec{x}$ using a small multiplier $\gamma > 0$:

$$\vec{x}_{k+1} = \vec{x}_k - \gamma [H_f(\vec{x}_k)]^{-1} \nabla f(\vec{x}_k).$$

A more expensive but safer strategy is to do line search from $\vec{x}_k$ along the direction $-[H_f(\vec{x}_k)]^{-1} \nabla f(\vec{x}_k)$.

When H_f is not positive definite, the objective locally might look like a saddle or peak rather than a bowl. In this case, jumping to an approximate stationary point might not make sense. To address this issue, adaptive techniques check if H_f is positive definite before applying a Newton step; if it is not positive definite, the methods revert to gradient descent to find a better approximation of the minimum. Alternatively, they can modify H_f, for example, by projecting onto the closest positive definite matrix (see Exercise 9.8).

9.4.3 Optimization without Hessians: BFGS

Newton's method can be difficult to apply to complicated or high-dimensional functions $f : \mathbb{R}^n \to \mathbb{R}$. The Hessian of f is often more expensive to evaluate than f or ∇f, and each Hessian H_f is used to solve only one linear system of equations, eliminating potential savings from LU or QR factorization. Additionally, H_f has size $n \times n$, requiring $O(n^2)$ space, which might be too large. Since Newton's method deals with *approximations* of f in each iteration anyway, we might attempt to formulate less expensive second-order approximations that still outperform gradient descent.

As in our discussion of root-finding in §8.2.2, techniques for minimization that imitate Newton's method but use approximate derivatives are called *quasi-Newton methods*. They can have similarly strong convergence properties without the need for explicit re-evaluation and even inversion of the Hessian at each iteration. Here, we will follow the development of [90] to motivate one modern technique for quasi-Newton optimization.

Suppose we wish to minimize $f : \mathbb{R}^n \to \mathbb{R}$ iteratively. Near the current estimate $\vec{x}_k$ of the minimizer, we might estimate f with a quadratic function:

$$f(\vec{x}_k + \delta\vec{x}) \approx f(\vec{x}_k) + \nabla f(\vec{x}_k) \cdot \delta\vec{x} + \frac{1}{2}(\delta\vec{x})^\top B_k(\delta\vec{x}).$$

Here, we require that our approximation agrees with f to first order at $\vec{x}_k$, but we will allow the estimate of the Hessian B_k to differ from the actual Hessian of f.

Slightly generalizing Newton's method in §9.4.2, this quadratic approximation is minimized by taking $\delta\vec{x} = -B_k^{-1}\nabla f(\vec{x}_k)$. In case $\|\delta\vec{x}\|_2$ is large and we do not wish to take such a large step, we will allow ourselves to scale this difference by a step size α_k determined, e.g., using a line search procedure, yielding the iteration

$$\vec{x}_{k+1} = \vec{x}_k - \alpha_k B_k^{-1} \nabla f(\vec{x}_k).$$

Our goal is to estimate B_{k+1} by updating B_k, so that we can repeat this process.

---

function BFGS($f(\vec{x}), \vec{x}_0$)
  $H \leftarrow I_{n \times n}$
  $\vec{x} \leftarrow \vec{x}_0$
  for $k \leftarrow 1, 2, 3, \ldots$
    if $\|\nabla f(\vec{x})\| < \varepsilon$ **then**
      return $x^* = \vec{x}$
    $\vec{p} \leftarrow -H_k \nabla f(\vec{x})$ ▷ Next search direction
    $\alpha \leftarrow$ COMPUTE-ALPHA($f, \vec{p}, \vec{x}, \vec{y}$)   ▷ Satisfy positive definite condition
    $\vec{s} \leftarrow \alpha \vec{p}$ ▷ Displacement of $\vec{x}$
    $\vec{x} \leftarrow \vec{x} + \vec{s}$ ▷ Update estimate
    $\vec{y} \leftarrow \nabla f(\vec{x} + \vec{s}) - \nabla f(\vec{x})$ ▷ Change in gradient

    $\rho \leftarrow 1/\vec{y} \cdot \vec{s}$ ▷ Apply BFGS update to inverse Hessian approximation
    $H \leftarrow (I_{n \times n} - \rho \vec{s} \vec{y}^\top) H (I_{n \times n} - \rho \vec{y} \vec{s}^\top) + \rho \vec{s} \vec{s}^\top$

Figure 9.11 The BFGS algorithm for finding a local minimum of differentiable $f(\vec{x})$ without its Hessian. The function COMPUTE-ALPHA finds large $\alpha > 0$ satisfying $\vec{y} \cdot \vec{s} > 0$, where $\vec{y} = \nabla f(\vec{x} + \vec{s}) - \nabla f(\vec{x})$ and $\vec{s} = \alpha \vec{p}$.

The Hessian of f is nothing more than the derivative of ∇f, so like Broyden's method we can use previous iterates to impose a secant-style condition on B_{k+1}:

$$B_{k+1}(\vec{x}_{k+1} - \vec{x}_k) = \nabla f(\vec{x}_{k+1}) - \nabla f(\vec{x}_k).$$

For convenience of notation, we will define $\vec{s}_k \equiv \vec{x}_{k+1} - \vec{x}_k$ and $\vec{y}_k \equiv \nabla f(\vec{x}_{k+1}) - \nabla f(\vec{x}_k)$, simplifying this condition to $B_{k+1} \vec{s}_k = \vec{y}_k$.

Given the optimization at hand, we wish for B_k to have two properties:

- B_k should be a symmetric matrix, like the Hessian H_f.

- B_k should be positive (semi-)definite, so that we are seeking minima of f rather than maxima or saddle points.

These conditions eliminate the possibility of using the Broyden estimate we developed in the previous chapter.

The positive definite constraint implicitly puts a condition on the relationship between $\vec{s}_k$ and $\vec{y}_k$. Pre-multiplying the relationship $B_{k+1} \vec{s}_k = \vec{y}_k$ by $\vec{s}_k^\top$ shows $\vec{s}_k^\top B_{k+1} \vec{s}_k = \vec{s}_k^\top \vec{y}_k$. For B_{k+1} to be positive definite, we must then have $\vec{s}_k \cdot \vec{y}_k > 0$. This observation can guide our choice of α_k; it must hold for sufficiently small $\alpha_k > 0$.

Assume that $\vec{s}_k$ and $\vec{y}_k$ satisfy the positive definite compatibility condition. Then, we can write down a Broyden-style optimization problem leading to an updated Hessian approximation B_{k+1}:

$$\begin{aligned} \text{minimize}_{B_{k+1}} \quad & \|B_{k+1} - B_k\| \\ \text{subject to} \quad & B_{k+1}^\top = B_{k+1} \\ & B_{k+1} \vec{s}_k = \vec{y}_k. \end{aligned}$$

For appropriate choice of norms $\|\cdot\|$, this optimization yields the well-known DFP (Davidon-Fletcher-Powell) iterative scheme.

Rather than working out the details of the DFP scheme, we derive a more popular method known as the BFGS (Broyden-Fletcher-Goldfarb-Shanno) algorithm, in Figure 9.11. The BFGS algorithm is motivated by reconsidering the construction of B_{k+1} in DFP. We use B_k when minimizing the second-order approximation, taking $\delta \vec{x} = -B_k^{-1} \nabla f(\vec{x}_k)$. Based on this formula, the behavior of our iterative minimizer is dictated by the *inverse* matrix B_k^{-1}. Asking that $\|B_{k+1} - B_k\|$ is small can still imply relatively large differences between B_k^{-1} and B_{k+1}^{-1}!

With this observation in mind, BFGS makes a small alteration to the optimization for B_k. Rather than updating B_k in each iteration, we can compute its inverse $H_k \equiv B_k^{-1}$ directly. We choose to use standard notation for BFGS in this section, but a common point of confusion is that H now represents an approximate *inverse* Hessian; this is the **not** the same as the Hessian H_f in §9.4.2 and elsewhere.

Now, the condition $B_{k+1}\vec{s}_k = \vec{y}_k$ gets reversed to $\vec{s}_k = H_{k+1}\vec{y}_k$; the condition that B_k is symmetric is the same as the condition that H_k is symmetric. After these changes, the BFGS algorithm updates H_k by solving an optimization problem

$$\begin{aligned} \text{minimize}_{H_{k+1}} \quad & \|H_{k+1} - H_k\| \\ \text{subject to} \quad & H_{k+1}^\top = H_{k+1} \\ & \vec{s}_k = H_{k+1}\vec{y}_k. \end{aligned}$$

This construction has the convenient side benefit of not requiring matrix inversion to compute $\delta \vec{x} = -H_k \nabla f(\vec{x}_k)$.

To derive a formula for H_{k+1}, we must decide on a matrix norm $\|\cdot\|$. The *Frobenius* norm looks closest to least-squares optimization, making it likely we can generate a closed-form expression for H_{k+1}. This norm, however, has one serious drawback for modeling Hessian matrices and their inverses. The Hessian matrix has entries $(H_f)_{ij} = \partial^2 f / \partial x_i \partial x_j$. Often, the quantities x_i for different i can have different *units*. Consider maximizing the profit (in dollars) made by selling a cheeseburger of radius r (in inches) and price p (in dollars), a function $f : (\text{inches}, \text{dollars}) \to \text{dollars}$. Squaring quantities in different units and adding them up does not make sense.

Suppose we find a symmetric positive definite matrix W so that $W\vec{s}_k = \vec{y}_k$; we will check in the exercises that such a matrix exists. This matrix takes the units of $\vec{s}_k = \vec{x}_{k+1} - \vec{x}_k$ to those of $\vec{y}_k = \nabla f(\vec{x}_{k+1}) - \nabla f(\vec{x}_k)$. Taking inspiration from the expression $\|A\|_{\text{Fro}}^2 = \text{Tr}(A^\top A)$, we can define a *weighted Frobenius norm* of a matrix A as

$$\|A\|_W^2 \equiv \text{Tr}(A^\top W^\top A W).$$

Unlike the Frobenius norm of H_{k+1}, this expression has consistent units when applied to the optimization for H_{k+1}.

When both W and A are symmetric with columns $\vec{w}_i$ and $\vec{a}_i$, respectively, expanding the expression above shows:

$$\|A\|_W^2 = \sum_{ij} (\vec{w}_i \cdot \vec{a}_j)(\vec{w}_j \cdot \vec{a}_i).$$

This choice of norm combined with the choice of W yields a particularly clean formula for H_{k+1} given H_k, $\vec{s}_k$, and $\vec{y}_k$:

$$H_{k+1} = (I_{n \times n} - \rho_k \vec{s}_k \vec{y}_k^\top) H_k (I_{n \times n} - \rho_k \vec{y}_k \vec{s}_k^\top) + \rho_k \vec{s}_k \vec{s}_k^\top,$$

where $\rho_k \equiv 1/\vec{y}_k \cdot \vec{s}_k$. We show in the appendix to this chapter how to derive this formula, which remarkably has no W dependence. The proof requires a number of algebraic steps but conceptually is no more difficult than direct application of Lagrange multipliers for constrained optimization (see Theorem 1.1).

The BFGS algorithm avoids the need to compute and invert a Hessian matrix for f, but it still requires $O(n^2)$ storage for H_k. The L-BFGS ("Limited-Memory BFGS") variant avoids this issue by keeping a limited history of vectors $\vec{y}_k$ and $\vec{s}_k$ and using these to apply H_k by expanding its formula recursively. L-BFGS can have *better* convergence than BFGS despite its compact use of space, since old vectors $\vec{y}_k$ and $\vec{s}_k$ may no longer be relevant and *should* be ignored. Exercise 9.11 derives this technique.

9.5 EXERCISES

9.1 Suppose $A \in \mathbb{R}^{n \times n}$. Show that $f(\vec{x}) = \|A\vec{x} - \vec{b}\|_2^2$ is a convex function. When is $g(\vec{x}) = \vec{x}^\top A\vec{x} + \vec{b}^\top \vec{x} + c$ convex?

9.2 Some observations about convex and quasiconvex functions:

(a) Show that every convex function is quasiconvex, but that some quasiconvex functions are not convex.

(b) Show that any local minimum of a continuous, strictly quasiconvex function $f : \mathbb{R}^n \to \mathbb{R}$ is also a global minimum of f. Here, *strict* quasiconvexity replaces the $\leq$ in the definition of quasiconvex functions with $<$.

(c) Show that the sum of two convex functions is convex, but give a counterexample showing that the sum of two quasiconvex functions may not be quasiconvex.

(d) Suppose $f(x)$ and $g(x)$ are quasiconvex. Show that $h(x) = \max(f(x), g(x))$ is quasiconvex.

9.3 In §9.3.1, we suggested the possibility of using parabolas rather than secants to minimize a function $f : \mathbb{R} \to \mathbb{R}$ without knowing any of its derivatives. Here, we outline the design of such an algorithm:

(a) Suppose we are given three points $(x_1, y_1), (x_2, y_2), (x_3, y_3)$ with distinct x values. Show that the vertex of the parabola $y = ax^2 + bx + c$ through these points is given by:
$$x = x_2 - \frac{(x_2 - x_1)^2(y_2 - y_3) - (x_2 - x_3)^2(y_2 - y_1)}{2(x_2 - x_1)(y_2 - y_3) - (x_2 - x_3)(y_2 - y_1)}.$$

(b) Use this formula to propose an iterative technique for minimizing a function of one variable without using any of its derivatives.

(c) What happens when the three points in Exercise 9.3a are collinear? Does this suggest a failure mode of successive parabolic interpolation?

(d) Does the formula in Exercise 9.3a distinguish between maxima and minima of parabolas? Does this suggest a second failure mode?

9.4 Show that a strictly convex function $f : [a, b] \to \mathbb{R}$ is unimodular.

9.5 We might ask how well we can expect methods like golden section search can work after introducing finite precision arithmetic. We step through a few analytical steps from [101]:

(a) Suppose we have bracketed a local minimum x^* of differentiable $f(x)$ in a small interval. Justify the following approximation in this interval:

$$f(x) \approx f(x^*) + \frac{1}{2}f''(x^*)(x - x^*)^2.$$

(b) Suppose we wish to refine the interval containing the minimum until the second term in this approximation is negligible. Show that if we wish to upper-bound the absolute value of the ratio of the two terms in Exercise 9.5a by ε, we should enforce

$$|x - x^*| < \sqrt{\frac{2\varepsilon|f(x^*)|}{|f''(x^*)|}}.$$

(c) By taking ε to be machine precision as in §2.1.2, conclude that the size of the interval in which $f(x)$ and $f(x^*)$ are indistinguishable numerically grows like $\sqrt{\varepsilon}$. Based on this observation, can golden section search bracket a minimizer within machine precision?
Hint: For small $\varepsilon > 0$, $\sqrt{\varepsilon} \gg \varepsilon$.

DH 9.6 For a convex function $f : U \to \mathbb{R}^n$, where $U \subseteq \mathbb{R}^n$ is convex and open, define a *subgradient* of f at $\vec{x}_0 \in U$ to be any vector $\vec{s} \in \mathbb{R}^n$ such that

$$f(\vec{x}) - f(\vec{x}_0) \geq \vec{s} \cdot (\vec{x} - \vec{x}_0)$$

for all $\vec{x} \in U$ [112]. The subgradient is a plausible choice for generalizing the notion of a gradient at a point where f is not differentiable. The *subdifferential* $\partial f(\vec{x}_0)$ is the set of all subgradients of f at $\vec{x}_0$.

For the remainder of this question, assume that f is convex and continuous:

(a) What is $\partial f(0)$ for the function $f(x) = |x|$?

(b) Suppose we wish to minimize (convex and continuous) $f : \mathbb{R}^n \to \mathbb{R}$, which may not be differentiable everywhere. Propose an optimality condition involving sub-differentials for a point $\vec{x}^*$ to be a minimizer of f. Show that your condition holds if and only if $\vec{x}^*$ globally minimizes f.

DH 9.7 Continuing the previous problem, the *subgradient method* extends gradient descent to a wider class of functions. Analogously to gradient descent, the subgradient method performs the iteration

$$\vec{x}_{k+1} \equiv \vec{x}_k - \alpha_k \vec{g}_k,$$

where α_k is a step size and g_k is *any* subgradient of f at $\vec{x}_k$. This method might not decrease f in each iteration, so instead we keep track of the best iterate we have seen so far, $\vec{x}_k^{\text{best}}$. We will use $\vec{x}^*$ to denote the minimizer of f on U.

In the following parts, assume that we fix $\alpha > 0$ to be a constant with no dependence on k, that f is Lipschitz continuous with constant $C > 0$, and that $\|\vec{x}_1 - \vec{x}^*\|_2 \leq B$ for some $B > 0$. Under these assumptions, we will show that

$$\lim_{k \to \infty} f(\vec{x}_k^{\text{best}}) \leq f(\vec{x}^*) + \frac{C^2}{2}\alpha,$$

a bound characterizing convergence of the subgradient method.

(a) Derive an upper bound for the error $\|\vec{x}_{k+1} - \vec{x}^*\|_2^2$ of $\vec{x}_{k+1}$ in terms of $\|\vec{x}_k - \vec{x}^*\|_2^2$, $\vec{g}_k$, α, $f(\vec{x}_k)$, and $f(\vec{x}^*)$.

(b) By recursively applying the result from Exercise 9.7a, provide an upper bound for the squared error of $\vec{x}_{k+1}$ in terms of B, α, the subgradients, and evaluations of f.

(c) Incorporate $f(\vec{x}_k^{\text{best}})$ and the bounds given at the beginning of the problem into your result, and take a limit as $k \to \infty$ to obtain the desired conclusion.

(d) Suppose we are willing to run subgradient descent for exactly k steps. Suggest a choice of α for this case; your formula for α can and should involve k.

^{SC}9.8 This problem will demonstrate how to project a Hessian onto the nearest positive definite matrix. Some optimization techniques use this operation to avoid attempting to minimize in directions where a function is not bowl-shaped.

(a) Suppose $M, U \in \mathbb{R}^{n \times n}$, where M is symmetric and U is orthogonal. Show that $\|UMU^\top\|_{\text{Fro}} = \|M\|_{\text{Fro}}$.

(b) Decompose $M = Q\Lambda Q^\top$, where Λ is a diagonal matrix of eigenvalues and Q is an orthogonal matrix of eigenvectors. Using the result of the previous part, explain how the positive semidefinite matrix $\bar{M}$ closest to M with respect to the Frobenius norm can be constructed by clamping the negative eigenvalues in Λ to zero.

9.9 Our derivation of the BFGS algorithm in §9.4.3 depended on the existence of a symmetric positive definite matrix W satisfying $W\vec{s}_k = \vec{y}_k$. Show that one such matrix is $W \equiv \bar{G}_k$, where $\bar{G}_k$ is the *average Hessian* [90]:

$$\bar{G}_k \equiv \int_0^1 H_f(\vec{x}_k + \tau\vec{s}_k)\, d\tau.$$

Do we ever have to compute W in the course of running BFGS?

9.10 Derive an explicit update formula for obtaining B_{k+1} from B_k in the Davidon-Fletcher-Powell scheme mentioned in §9.4.3. Use the $\|\cdot\|_W$ norm introduced in the derivation of BFGS, but with the reversed assumption $W\vec{y}_k = \vec{s}_k$.

9.11 The matrix H used in the BFGS algorithm generally is dense, requiring $O(n^2)$ storage for $f : \mathbb{R}^n \to \mathbb{R}$. This scaling may be infeasible for large n.

(a) Provide an alternative approach to storing H requiring $O(nk)$ storage in iteration k of BFGS.
Hint: Your algorithm may have to "remember" data from previous iterations.

(b) If we need to run for many iterations, the storage from the previous part can exceed the $O(n^2)$ limit we were attempting to avoid. Propose an approximation to H that uses no more than $O(nk_{\text{max}})$ storage, for a user-specified constant k_{max}.

9.12 The BFGS and DFP algorithms update (inverse) Hessian approximations using matrices of rank two. For simplicity, the *symmetric-rank-1* (SR1) update restricts changes to be rank one instead [90].

(a) Suppose $B_{k+1} = B_k + \sigma \vec{v}\vec{v}^\top$, where $|\sigma| = 1$ and $\vec{y}_k = B_{k+1}\vec{s}_k$. Show that under these conditions we must have

$$B_{k+1} = B_k + \frac{(\vec{y}_k - B_k\vec{s}_k)(\vec{y}_k - B_k\vec{s}_k)^\top}{(\vec{y}_k - B_k\vec{s}_k)^\top \vec{s}_k}.$$

(b) Suppose $H_k \equiv B_k^{-1}$. Show that H_k can be updated as

$$H_{k+1} = H_k + \frac{(\vec{s}_k - H_k\vec{y}_k)(\vec{s}_k - H_k\vec{y}_k)^\top}{(\vec{s}_k - H_k\vec{y}_k)^\top \vec{y}_k}.$$

Hint: Use the result of Exercise 8.7.

9.13 Here we examine some changes to the gradient descent algorithm for unconstrained optimization on a function f.

(a) In machine learning, the *stochastic gradient descent* algorithm can be used to optimize many common objective functions:

   (i) Give an example of a practical optimization problem with an objective taking the form $f(\vec{x}) = \frac{1}{N}\sum_{i=1}^{N} g(\vec{x}_i - \vec{x})$ for some function $g : \mathbb{R}^n \to \mathbb{R}$.

   (ii) Propose a randomized approximation of ∇f summing no more than k terms (for some $k \ll N$) assuming the $\vec{x}_i$'s are similar to one another. Discuss advantages and drawbacks of using such an approximation.

(b) The "line search" part of gradient descent must be considered carefully:

   (i) Suppose an iterative optimization routine gives a sequence of estimates $\vec{x}_1, \vec{x}_2, \ldots$ of the position $\vec{x}^*$ of the minimum of f. Is it enough to assume $f(\vec{x}_k) < f(\vec{x}_{k-1})$ to guarantee that the $\vec{x}_k$'s converge to a local minimum? Why?

   (ii) Suppose we run gradient descent. If we suppose $f(\vec{x}) \geq 0$ for all $\vec{x}$ and that we are able to find t^* exactly in each iteration, show that $f(\vec{x}_k)$ converges as $k \to \infty$.

   (iii) Explain how the optimization in 9.13(b)ii for t^* can be overkill. In particular, explain how the Wolfe conditions (you will have to look these up!) relax the assumption that we can find t^*.

9.14 Sometimes we are greedy and wish to optimize multiple objectives simultaneously. For example, we might want to fire a rocket to reach an optimal point in time *and* space. It may not be possible to carry out both tasks simultaneously, but some theories attempt to reconcile multiple optimization objectives.

Suppose we are given functions $f_1(\vec{x}), f_2(\vec{x}), \ldots, f_k(\vec{x})$. A point $\vec{y}$ is said to *Pareto dominate* another point $\vec{x}$ if $f_i(\vec{y}) \leq f_i(\vec{x})$ for all i and $f_j(\vec{y}) < f_j(\vec{x})$ for some $j \in \{1, \ldots, k\}$. A point $\vec{x}^*$ is *Pareto optimal* if it is not dominated by any point $\vec{y}$. Assume $f_1, \ldots, f_k$ are strictly convex functions on a closed, convex set $S \subset \mathbb{R}^n$ (in particular, assume each f_i is minimized at a unique point $\vec{x}_i^*$).

(a) Show that the set of Pareto optimal points is nonempty in this case.

(b) Suppose $\sum_i \gamma_i = 1$ and $\gamma_i > 0$ for all i. Show that the minimizer $\vec{x}^*$ of $g(\vec{x}) \equiv \sum_i \gamma_i f_i(\vec{x})$ is Pareto optimal.
   Note: One strategy for multi-objective optimization is to promote $\vec{\gamma}$ to a variable with constraints $\vec{\gamma} \geq \vec{0}$ and $\sum_i \gamma_i = 1$.

(c) Suppose $\vec{x}_i^*$ minimizes $f_i(\vec{x})$ over all possible $\vec{x}$. Write vector $\vec{z} \in \mathbb{R}^k$ with components $z_i = f_i(\vec{x}_i^*)$. Show that the minimizer $\vec{x}^*$ of $h(\vec{x}) \equiv \sum_i (f_i(\vec{x}) - z_i)^2$ is Pareto optimal.

Note: This part and the previous part represent two possible *scalarizations* of the multi-objective optimization problem that can be used to find Pareto optimal points.

9.6 APPENDIX: DERIVATION OF BFGS UPDATE

In this optional appendix, we derive in detail the BFGS update from §9.4.3.* Our optimization for H_{k+1} has the following Lagrange multiplier expression (for ease of notation we take $H_{k+1} \equiv H$ and $H_k = H^*$):

$$\Lambda \equiv \sum_{ij}(\vec{w}_i \cdot (\vec{h}_j - \vec{h}_j^*))(\vec{w}_j \cdot (\vec{h}_i - \vec{h}_i^*)) - \sum_{i<j}\alpha_{ij}(H_{ij} - H_{ji}) - \vec{\lambda}^\top(H\vec{y}_k - \vec{s}_k)$$

$$= \sum_{ij}(\vec{w}_i \cdot (\vec{h}_j - \vec{h}_j^*))(\vec{w}_j \cdot (\vec{h}_i - \vec{h}_i^*)) - \sum_{ij}\alpha_{ij}H_{ij} - \vec{\lambda}^\top(H\vec{y}_k - \vec{s}_k) \text{ if we define } \alpha_{ij} = -\alpha_{ji}$$

Taking derivatives to find critical points shows (for $\vec{y} \equiv \vec{y}_k, \vec{s} \equiv \vec{s}_k$):

$$0 = \frac{\partial\Lambda}{\partial H_{ij}} = \sum_\ell 2w_{i\ell}(\vec{w}_j \cdot (\vec{h}_\ell - \vec{h}_\ell^*)) - \alpha_{ij} - \lambda_i y_j$$

$$= 2\sum_\ell w_{i\ell}(W^\top(H - H^*))_{j\ell} - \alpha_{ij} - \lambda_i y_j$$

$$= 2\sum_\ell (W^\top(H - H^*))_{j\ell}w_{\ell i} - \alpha_{ij} - \lambda_i y_j \text{ by symmetry of } W$$

$$= 2(W^\top(H - H^*)W)_{ji} - \alpha_{ij} - \lambda_i y_j$$

$$= 2(W(H - H^*)W)_{ij} - \alpha_{ij} - \lambda_i y_j \text{ by symmetry of } W \text{ and } H.$$

So, in matrix form we have the following list of facts:

$$0 = 2W(H - H^*)W - A - \vec{\lambda}\vec{y}^\top, \text{ where } A_{ij} = \alpha_{ij}$$
$$A^\top = -A$$
$$W^\top = W$$
$$H^\top = H$$
$$(H^*)^\top = H^*$$
$$H\vec{y} = \vec{s}$$
$$W\vec{s} = \vec{y}.$$

We can achieve a pair of relationships using transposition combined with symmetry of H and W and asymmetry of A:

$$0 = 2W(H - H^*)W - A - \vec{\lambda}\vec{y}^\top$$
$$0 = 2W(H - H^*)W + A - \vec{y}\vec{\lambda}^\top$$
$$\implies 0 = 4W(H - H^*)W - \vec{\lambda}\vec{y}^\top - \vec{y}\vec{\lambda}^\top.$$

---

*Special thanks to Tao Du for debugging several parts of this derivation.

Post-multiplying this relationship by $\vec{s}$ shows:

$$\vec{0} = 4(\vec{y} - WH^*\vec{y}) - \vec{\lambda}(\vec{y} \cdot \vec{s}) - \vec{y}(\vec{\lambda} \cdot \vec{s}).$$

Now, take the dot product with $\vec{s}$:

$$0 = 4(\vec{y} \cdot \vec{s}) - 4(\vec{y}^\top H^*\vec{y}) - 2(\vec{y} \cdot \vec{s})(\vec{\lambda} \cdot \vec{s}).$$

This shows:

$$\vec{\lambda} \cdot \vec{s} = 2\rho\vec{y}^\top(\vec{s} - H^*\vec{y}), \text{ for } \rho \equiv 1/\vec{y}\cdot\vec{s}.$$

Now, we substitute this into our vector equality:

$$\vec{0} = 4(\vec{y} - WH^*\vec{y}) - \vec{\lambda}(\vec{y} \cdot \vec{s}) - \vec{y}(\vec{\lambda} \cdot \vec{s}) \text{ from before}$$
$$= 4(\vec{y} - WH^*\vec{y}) - \vec{\lambda}(\vec{y} \cdot \vec{s}) - \vec{y}[2\rho\vec{y}^\top(\vec{s} - H^*\vec{y})] \text{ from our simplification}$$
$$\implies \vec{\lambda} = 4\rho(\vec{y} - WH^*\vec{y}) - 2\rho^2[\vec{y}^\top(\vec{s} - H^*\vec{y})]\vec{y}.$$

Post-multiplying by $\vec{y}^\top$ shows:

$$\vec{\lambda}\vec{y}^\top = 4\rho(\vec{y} - WH^*\vec{y})\vec{y}^\top - 2\rho^2[\vec{y}^\top(\vec{s} - H^*\vec{y})]\vec{y}\vec{y}^\top.$$

Taking the transpose,

$$\vec{y}\vec{\lambda}^\top = 4\rho\vec{y}(\vec{y}^\top - \vec{y}^\top H^*W) - 2\rho^2[\vec{y}^\top(\vec{s} - H^*\vec{y})]\vec{y}\vec{y}^\top.$$

Combining these results and dividing by four shows:

$$\frac{1}{4}(\vec{\lambda}\vec{y}^\top + \vec{y}\vec{\lambda}^\top) = \rho(2\vec{y}\vec{y}^\top - WH^*\vec{y}\vec{y}^\top - \vec{y}\vec{y}^\top H^*W) - \rho^2[\vec{y}^\top(\vec{s} - H^*\vec{y})]\vec{y}\vec{y}^\top.$$

Now, we will pre- and post-multiply by W^{-1}. Since $W\vec{s} = \vec{y}$, we can equivalently write $\vec{s} = W^{-1}\vec{y}$. Furthermore, by symmetry of W we then know $\vec{y}^\top W^{-1} = \vec{s}^\top$. Applying these identities to the expression above shows:

$$\frac{1}{4}W^{-1}(\vec{\lambda}\vec{y}^\top + \vec{y}\vec{\lambda}^\top)W^{-1} = 2\rho\vec{s}\vec{s}^\top - \rho H^*\vec{y}\vec{s}^\top - \rho\vec{s}\vec{y}^\top H^* - \rho^2(\vec{y}^\top\vec{s})\vec{s}\vec{s}^\top + \rho^2(\vec{y}^\top H^*\vec{y})\vec{s}\vec{s}^\top$$
$$= 2\rho\vec{s}\vec{s}^\top - \rho H^*\vec{y}\vec{s}^\top - \rho\vec{s}\vec{y}^\top H^* - \rho\vec{s}\vec{s}^\top + \vec{s}\rho^2(\vec{y}^\top H^*\vec{y})\vec{s}^\top$$
$$\text{by definition of } \rho$$
$$= \rho\vec{s}\vec{s}^\top - \rho H^*\vec{y}\vec{s}^\top - \rho\vec{s}\vec{y}^\top H^* + \vec{s}\rho^2(\vec{y}^\top H^*\vec{y})\vec{s}^\top.$$

Finally, we can conclude our derivation of the BFGS step as follows:

$$0 = 4W(H - H^*)W - \vec{\lambda}\vec{y}^\top - \vec{y}\vec{\lambda}^\top \text{ from before}$$
$$\implies H = \frac{1}{4}W^{-1}(\vec{\lambda}\vec{y}^\top + \vec{y}\vec{\lambda}^\top)W^{-1} + H^*$$
$$= \rho\vec{s}\vec{s}^\top - \rho H^*\vec{y}\vec{s}^\top - \rho\vec{s}\vec{y}^\top H^* + \vec{s}\rho^2(\vec{y}^\top H^*\vec{y})\vec{s}^\top + H^* \text{ from the last paragraph}$$
$$= H^*(I - \rho\vec{y}\vec{s}^\top) + \rho\vec{s}\vec{s}^\top - \rho\vec{s}\vec{y}^\top H^* + (\rho\vec{s}\vec{y}^\top)H^*(\rho\vec{y}\vec{s}^\top)$$
$$= H^*(I - \rho\vec{y}\vec{s}^\top) + \rho\vec{s}\vec{s}^\top - \rho\vec{s}\vec{y}^\top H^*(I - \rho\vec{y}\vec{s}^\top)$$
$$= \rho\vec{s}\vec{s}^\top + (I - \rho\vec{s}\vec{y}^\top)H^*(I - \rho\vec{y}\vec{s}^\top).$$

This final expression is exactly the BFGS step introduced in the chapter.

CHAPTER 10

Constrained Optimization

CONTENTS

10.1   Motivation 186
10.2   Theory of Constrained Optimization 189
        10.2.1 Optimality 189
        10.2.2 KKT Conditions 189
10.3   Optimization Algorithms 192
        10.3.1 Sequential Quadratic Programming (SQP) 193
                10.3.1.1   Equality Constraints 193
                10.3.1.2   Inequality Constraints 193
        10.3.2 Barrier Methods 194
10.4   Convex Programming 194
        10.4.1 Linear Programming 196
        10.4.2 Second-Order Cone Programming 197
        10.4.3 Semidefinite Programming 199
        10.4.4 Integer Programs and Relaxations 200

W E continue our consideration of optimization problems by studying the *constrained* case. These problems take the following general form:

$$\text{minimize } f(\vec{x})$$
$$\text{subject to } g(\vec{x}) = \vec{0}$$
$$h(\vec{x}) \geq \vec{0}.$$

Here, $f : \mathbb{R}^n \to \mathbb{R}$, $g : \mathbb{R}^n \to \mathbb{R}^m$, and $h : \mathbb{R}^n \to \mathbb{R}^p$; we call f the *objective function* and the expressions $g(\vec{x}) = \vec{0}, h(\vec{x}) \geq \vec{0}$ the *constraints*.

This form is extremely generic, so algorithms for solving such problems in the absence of additional assumptions on f, g, or h are subject to degeneracies such as local minima and lack of convergence. In fact, this general problem encodes other problems we already have considered. If we take $f(\vec{x}) = h(\vec{x}) \equiv 0$, then this constrained optimization becomes root-finding on g (Chapter 8), while if we take $g(\vec{x}) = h(\vec{x}) \equiv \vec{0}$, it reduces to unconstrained optimization on f (Chapter 9).

Despite this bleak outlook, optimization methods handling the general constrained problem can be valuable even when f, g, and h do not have strong structure. In many cases, especially when f is heuristic anyway, finding a feasible $\vec{x}$ for which $f(\vec{x}) < f(\vec{x}_0)$ starting from an initial guess $\vec{x}_0$ still represents an improvement from the starting point. One application of this philosophy would be an economic system in which f measures costs; since we wish to minimize costs, *any* $\vec{x}$ decreasing f is a useful—and profitable—output.

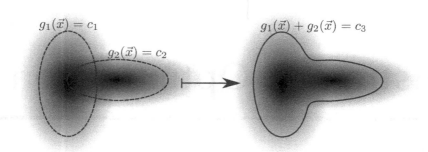

$g_1(\vec{x}) = c_1$

$g_2(\vec{x}) = c_2$

$g_1(\vec{x}) + g_2(\vec{x}) = c_3$

Figure 10.1 "Blobby" shapes are constructed as level sets of a linear combination of functions.

10.1 MOTIVATION

Constrained optimization problems appear in nearly any area of applied math, engineering, and computer science. We already listed many applications of constrained optimization when we discussed eigenvectors and eigenvalues in Chapter 6, since this problem for symmetric matrices $A \in \mathbb{R}^{n \times n}$ can be posed as finding critical points of $\vec{x}^\top A \vec{x}$ subject to $\|\vec{x}\|_2 = 1$. The particular case of eigenvalue computation admits special algorithms that make it a simpler problem. Here, however, we list other optimization problems that do not enjoy the unique structure of eigenvalue problems:

Example 10.1 (Geometric projection). Many shapes S in $\mathbb{R}^n$ can be written *implicitly* in the form $g(\vec{x}) = 0$ for some g. For example, the unit sphere results from taking $g(\vec{x}) \equiv \|\vec{x}\|_2^2 - 1$, while a cube can be constructed by taking $g(\vec{x}) = \|\vec{x}\|_1 - 1$. Some 3D modeling environments allow users to specify "blobby" objects, as in Figure 10.1, as zero-value level sets of $g(\vec{x})$ given by

$$g(\vec{x}) \equiv c + \sum_i a_i e^{-b_i \|\vec{x} - \vec{x}_i\|_2^2}.$$

Suppose we are given a point $\vec{y} \in \mathbb{R}^3$ and wish to find the closest point $\vec{x} \in S$ to $\vec{y}$. This problem is solved by using the following constrained minimization:

$$\text{minimize}_{\vec{x}} \ \|\vec{x} - \vec{y}\|_2$$
$$\text{subject to } g(\vec{x}) = 0.$$

Example 10.2 (Manufacturing). Suppose you have m different materials; you have s_i units of each material i in stock. You can manufacture k different products; product j gives you profit p_j and uses c_{ij} of material i to make. To maximize profits, you can solve the following optimization for the amount x_j you should manufacture of each item j:

$$\text{maximize}_{\vec{x}} \ \sum_{j=1}^{k} p_j x_j$$
$$\text{subject to } x_j \geq 0 \, \forall j \in \{1, \ldots, k\}$$
$$\sum_{j=1}^{k} c_{ij} x_j \leq s_i \, \forall i \in \{1, \ldots, m\}.$$

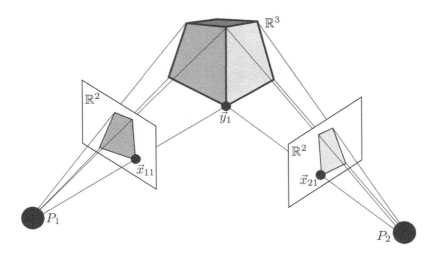

Figure 10.2 Notation for bundle adjustment with two images. Given corresponding points $\vec{x}_{ij}$ marked on images, bundle adjustment simultaneously optimizes for camera parameters encoded in P_i and three-dimensional positions $\vec{y}_j$.

The first constraint ensures that you do not make negative amounts of any product, and the second ensures that you do not use more than your stock of each material. This optimization is an example of a *linear program*, because the objective and constraints are all linear functions. Linear programs allow for inequality constraints, so they cannot always be solved using Gaussian elimination.

Example 10.3 (Nonnegative least-squares). We already have seen numerous examples of least-squares problems, but sometimes negative values in the solution vector might not make sense. For example, in computer graphics, an animated model can be expressed as a deforming bone structure plus a meshed "skin"; for each point on the skin a list of weights can be computed to approximate the influence of the positions of the bone joints on the position of the skin vertices [67]. Such weights should be constrained to be nonnegative to avoid degenerate behavior while the surface deforms. In such a case, we can solve the "nonnegative least-squares" problem:

$$\text{minimize}_{\vec{x}} \; \|A\vec{x} - \vec{b}\|_2$$
$$\text{subject to } x_i \geq 0 \; \forall i.$$

Some machine learning methods leverage the *sparsity* of nonnegative least-squares solutions, which often lead to optimal vectors $\vec{x}$ with $x_i = 0$ for many indices i [113].

Example 10.4 (Bundle adjustment). In computer vision, suppose we take pictures of an object from several angles. A natural task is to reconstruct the three-dimensional shape of the object from these pictures. To do so, we might mark a corresponding set of points on each image; we can take $\vec{x}_{ij} \in \mathbb{R}^2$ to be the position of feature point j on image i, as in Figure 10.2. In reality, each feature point has a position $\vec{y}_j \in \mathbb{R}^3$ in space, which we would like to compute. Additionally, we must find the positions of the cameras themselves, which we can represent as unknown projection matrices P_i.

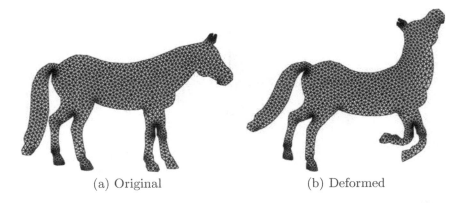

(a) Original   (b) Deformed

Figure 10.3 As-rigid-as-possible (ARAP) optimization generates the deformed mesh on the right from the original mesh on the left given target positions for a few points on the head, feet, and torso.

The problem of estimating the $\vec{y}_j$'s and P_i's, known as *bundle adjustment*, can be posed as an optimization:

$$\text{minimize}_{\vec{y}_j, P_i} \sum_{ij} \|P_i \vec{y}_j - \vec{x}_{ij}\|_2^2$$

such that P_i is orthogonal $\forall i$.

The orthogonality constraint ensures that the camera transformations could have come from a typical lens.

Example 10.5 (As-rigid-as-possible deformation). The "as-rigid-as-possible" (ARAP) modeling technique is used in computer graphics to deform two- and three-dimensional shapes in real time for modeling and animation software [116]. In the planar setting, suppose we are given a two-dimensional triangle mesh, as in Figure 10.3(a). This mesh consists of a collection of vertices V connected into triangles by edges $E \subseteq V \times V$; we will assume each vertex $v \in V$ is associated with a position $\vec{x}_v \in \mathbb{R}^2$. Furthermore, assume the user manually moves a subset of vertices $V_0 \subset V$ to target positions $\vec{y}_v \in \mathbb{R}^2$ for $v \in V_0$ to specify a potential deformation of the shape. The goal of ARAP is to deform the remainder $V \backslash V_0$ of the mesh vertices elastically, as in Figure 10.3(b), yielding a set of new positions $\vec{y}_v \in \mathbb{R}^2$ for each $v \in V$ with $\vec{y}_v$ fixed by the user when $v \in V_0$.

The least-distorting deformation of the mesh is a *rigid* motion, meaning it rotates and translates but does not stretch or shear. In this case, there exists an *orthogonal* matrix $R \in \mathbb{R}^{2 \times 2}$ so that the deformation satisfies $\vec{y}_v - \vec{y}_w = R(\vec{x}_v - \vec{x}_w)$ for any edge $(v, w) \in E$. But, if the user wishes to stretch or bend part of the shape, there might not exist a single R rotating the entire mesh to satisfy the position constraints in V_0.

To loosen the single-rotation assumption, ARAP asks that a deformation is *approximately* or *locally* rigid. Specifically, no single vertex on the mesh should experience more than a little stretch or shear, so in a neighborhood of each vertex $v \in V$ there should exist an orthogonal matrix R_v satisfying $\vec{y}_v - \vec{y}_w \approx R_v(\vec{x}_v - \vec{x}_w)$ for any $(v, w) \in E$. Once again applying least-squares, we define the as-rigid-as-possible deformation of the mesh to be the one mapping $\vec{x}_v \mapsto \vec{y}_v$ for all $v \in V$ by solving the following optimization problem:

$$\text{minimize}_{R_v, \vec{y}_v} \sum_{v \in V} \sum_{(v,w) \in E} \| R_v(\vec{x}_v - \vec{x}_w) - (\vec{y}_v - \vec{y}_w) \|_2^2$$
$$\text{subject to } R_v^\top R_v = I_{2 \times 2} \ \forall v \in V$$
$$\vec{y}_v \text{ fixed } \forall v \in V_0.$$

We will suggest one way to solve this optimization problem in Example 12.5.

10.2 THEORY OF CONSTRAINED OPTIMIZATION

In our discussion, we will assume that f, g, and h are differentiable. Some methods exist that only make weak continuity or Lipschitz assumptions, but these techniques are quite specialized and require advanced analytical consideration.

10.2.1 Optimality

Although we have not yet developed algorithms for general constrained optimization, we have made use of the *theory* of these problems. Specifically, recall the method of Lagrange multipliers, introduced in Theorem 1.1. In this technique, critical points of $f(\vec{x})$ subject to $g(\vec{x}) = \vec{0}$ are given by critical points of the *unconstrained* Lagrange multiplier function

$$\Lambda(\vec{x}, \vec{\lambda}) \equiv f(\vec{x}) - \vec{\lambda} \cdot \vec{g}(\vec{x})$$

with respect to both $\vec{\lambda}$ and $\vec{x}$ simultaneously. This theorem allowed us to provide variational interpretations of eigenvalue problems; more generally, it gives an alternative criterion for $\vec{x}$ to be a critical point of an *equality-constrained* optimization.

As we saw in Chapter 8, even finding a feasible $\vec{x}$ satisfying the constraint $g(\vec{x}) = \vec{0}$ can be a considerable challenge even before attempting to minimize $f(\vec{x})$. We can separate these issues by making a few definitions:

Definition 10.1 (Feasible point and feasible set). A *feasible point* of a constrained optimization problem is any point $\vec{x}$ satisfying $g(\vec{x}) = \vec{0}$ and $h(\vec{x}) \geq \vec{0}$. The *feasible set* is the set of all points $\vec{x}$ satisfying these constraints.

Definition 10.2 (Critical point of constrained optimization). A critical point of a constrained optimization satisfies the constraints and is also a local maximum, minimum, or saddle point of f within the feasible set.

10.2.2 KKT Conditions

Constrained optimizations are difficult because they simultaneously solve root-finding problems (the $g(\vec{x}) = \vec{0}$ constraint), satisfiability problems (the $h(\vec{x}) \geq \vec{0}$ constraint), and minimization (on the function f). As stated in Theorem 1.1, Lagrange multipliers allow us to turn equality-constrained minimization problems into root-finding problems on Λ. To push our differential techniques to complete generality, we must find a way to add inequality constraints $h(\vec{x}) \geq \vec{0}$ to the Lagrange multiplier system.

Suppose we have found a local minimum subject to the constraints, denoted $\vec{x}^*$. For each inequality constraint $h_i(\vec{x}^*) \geq 0$, we have two options:

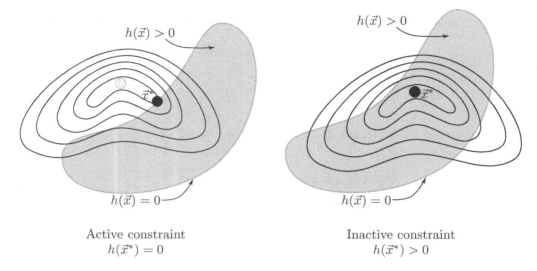

Active constraint
$h(\vec{x}^*) = 0$

Inactive constraint
$h(\vec{x}^*) > 0$

Figure 10.4 Active and inactive constraints $h(\vec{x}) \geq 0$ for minimizing a function whose level sets are shown in black; the region $h(\vec{x}) \geq 0$ is shown in gray. When the $h(\vec{x}) \geq 0$ constraint is active, the optimal point $\vec{x}^*$ is on the border of the feasible domain and would move if the constraint were removed. When the constraint is inactive, $\vec{x}^*$ is in the *interior* of the feasible set, so the constraint $h(\vec{x}) \geq 0$ has no effect on the position of the $\vec{x}^*$ locally.

- $h_i(\vec{x}^*) = 0$: Such a constraint is *active*, likely indicating that if the constraint were removed $\vec{x}^*$ would no longer be optimal.

- $h_i(\vec{x}^*) > 0$: Such a constraint is *inactive*, meaning in a neighborhood of $\vec{x}^*$ if we had removed this constraint we still would have reached the same minimum.

These two cases are illustrated in Figure 10.4. While this classification will prove valuable, we do not know *a priori* which constraints will be active or inactive at $\vec{x}^*$ until we solve the optimization problem and find $\vec{x}^*$.

If all of our constraints were active, then we could change the constraint $h(\vec{x}) \geq \vec{0}$ to an equality constraint $h(\vec{x}) = \vec{0}$ without affecting the outcome of the optimization. Then, applying the equality-constrained Lagrange multiplier conditions, we could find critical points of the following Lagrange multiplier expression:

$$\Lambda(\vec{x}, \vec{\lambda}, \vec{\mu}) \equiv f(\vec{x}) - \vec{\lambda} \cdot g(\vec{x}) - \vec{\mu} \cdot h(x).$$

In reality, we no longer can say that $\vec{x}^*$ is a critical point of Λ, because inactive inequality constraints would remove terms above. Ignoring this (important!) issue for the time being, we could proceed blindly and ask for critical points of this new Λ with respect to $\vec{x}$, which satisfy the following:

$$\vec{0} = \nabla f(\vec{x}) - \sum_i \lambda_i \nabla g_i(\vec{x}) - \sum_j \mu_j \nabla h_j(\vec{x}).$$

Here, we have separated out the individual components of g and h and treated them as scalar functions to avoid complex notation.

A clever trick can extend this (currently incorrect) optimality condition to include inequality constraints. If we *define* $\mu_j \equiv 0$ whenever h_j is inactive, then the irrelevant terms are removed from the optimality conditions. In other words, we can *add* a constraint on the Lagrange multiplier above:

$$\mu_j h_j(\vec{x}) = 0.$$

With this constraint in place, we know that at least one of μ_j and $h_j(\vec{x})$ must be zero; when the constraint $h_j(\vec{x}) \geq 0$ is inactive, then μ_j must equal zero to compensate. Our first-order optimality condition still holds at critical points of the inequality-constrained problem—after adding this extra constraint.

So far, our construction has not distinguished between the constraint $h_j(\vec{x}) \geq 0$ and the constraint $h_j(\vec{x}) \leq 0$. If the constraint is inactive, it could have been dropped without affecting the outcome of the optimization locally, so we consider the case when the constraint is active. Intuitively,* in this case we expect there to be a way to decrease f by violating the constraint. Locally, the direction in which f decreases is $-\nabla f(\vec{x}^*)$ and the direction in which h_j decreases is $-\nabla h_j(\vec{x}^*)$. Thus, starting at $\vec{x}^*$ we can decrease f even more by violating the constraint $h_j(\vec{x}) \geq 0$ when $\nabla f(\vec{x}^*) \cdot \nabla h_j(\vec{x}^*) > 0$.

Products of gradients of f and h_j are difficult to manipulate. At $\vec{x}^*$, however, our first-order optimality condition tells us:

$$\nabla f(\vec{x}^*) = \sum_i \lambda_i^* \nabla g_i(\vec{x}^*) + \sum_{j \text{ active}} \mu_j^* \nabla h_j(\vec{x}^*).$$

The inactive μ_j values are zero and can be removed. We removed the $g(\vec{x}) = 0$ constraints by adding inequality constraints $g(\vec{x}) \geq \vec{0}$ and $g(\vec{x}) \leq \vec{0}$ to h; this is a mathematical convenience rather than a numerically wise maneuver.

Taking dot products with ∇h_k for any fixed k shows:

$$\sum_{j \text{ active}} \mu_j^* \nabla h_j(\vec{x}^*) \cdot \nabla h_k(\vec{x}^*) = \nabla f(\vec{x}^*) \cdot \nabla h_k(\vec{x}^*) \geq 0.$$

Vectorizing this expression shows $Dh(\vec{x}^*)Dh(\vec{x}^*)^\top \vec{\mu}^* \geq \vec{0}$. Since $Dh(\vec{x}^*)Dh(x^*)^\top$ is positive semidefinite, this implies $\vec{\mu}^* \geq \vec{0}$. Thus, the $\nabla f(\vec{x}^*) \cdot \nabla h_j(\vec{x}^*) \geq 0$ observation is equivalent to the much easier condition $\mu_j \geq 0$.

These observations can be combined and formalized to prove a first-order optimality condition for inequality-constrained minimization problems:

Theorem 10.1 (Karush-Kuhn-Tucker (KKT) conditions). The vector $\vec{x}^* \in \mathbb{R}^n$ is a critical point for minimizing f subject to $g(\vec{x}) = \vec{0}$ and $h(\vec{x}) \geq \vec{0}$ when there exists $\vec{\lambda} \in \mathbb{R}^m$ and $\vec{\mu} \in \mathbb{R}^p$ such that:

- $\vec{0} = \nabla f(\vec{x}^*) - \sum_i \lambda_i \nabla g_i(\vec{x}^*) - \sum_j \mu_j \nabla h_j(\vec{x}^*)$ ("stationarity")

- $g(\vec{x}^*) = \vec{0}$ and $h(\vec{x}^*) \geq \vec{0}$ ("primal feasibility")

- $\mu_j h_j(\vec{x}^*) = 0$ for all j ("complementary slackness")

- $\mu_j \geq 0$ for all j ("dual feasibility")

When h is removed, this theorem reduces to the Lagrange multiplier criterion.

---

*You should not consider this discussion a formal proof, since we do not consider many boundary cases.

Example 10.6 (KKT conditions). Suppose we wish to solve the following optimization (proposed by R. Israel, UBC Math 340, Fall 2006):

$$\text{maximize } xy$$
$$\text{subject to } x + y^2 \leq 2$$
$$x, y \geq 0.$$

In this case we will have no λ's and three μ's. We take $f(x, y) = -xy$, $h_1(x, y) \equiv 2 - x - y^2$, $h_2(x, y) = x$, and $h_3(x, y) = y$. The KKT conditions are:

$$\text{Stationarity: } 0 = -y + \mu_1 - \mu_2$$
$$0 = -x + 2\mu_1 y - \mu_3$$
$$\text{Primal feasibility: } x + y^2 \leq 2$$
$$x, y \geq 0$$
$$\text{Complementary slackness: } \mu_1(2 - x - y^2) = 0$$
$$\mu_2 x = 0$$
$$\mu_3 y = 0$$
$$\text{Dual feasibility: } \mu_1, \mu_2, \mu_3 \geq 0$$

Example 10.7 (Linear programming). Consider the optimization:

$$\text{minimize}_{\vec{x}} \ \vec{b} \cdot \vec{x}$$
$$\text{subject to } A\vec{x} \geq \vec{c}.$$

Example 10.2 can be written this way. The KKT conditions for this problem are:

$$\text{Stationarity: } A^\top \vec{\mu} = \vec{b}$$
$$\text{Primal feasibility: } A\vec{x} \geq \vec{c}$$
$$\text{Complementary slackness: } \mu_i(\vec{a}_i \cdot \vec{x} - c_i) = 0 \ \forall i, \text{ where } \vec{a}_i^\top \text{ is row } i \text{ of } A$$
$$\text{Dual feasibility: } \vec{\mu} \geq \vec{0}$$

As with Lagrange multipliers, we cannot assume that any $\vec{x}^*$ satisfying the KKT conditions automatically minimizes f subject to the constraints, even locally. One way to check for local optimality is to examine the Hessian of f restricted to the subspace of $\mathbb{R}^n$ in which $\vec{x}$ can move without violating the constraints. If this "reduced" Hessian is positive definite, then the optimization has reached a local minimum.

10.3 OPTIMIZATION ALGORITHMS

A careful consideration of algorithms for constrained optimization is out of the scope of our discussion. Thankfully, many stable implementations of these techniques exist, and much can be accomplished as a "client" of this software rather than rewriting it from scratch. Even so, it is useful to sketch common approaches to gain some intuition for how these libraries work.

10.3.1 Sequential Quadratic Programming (SQP)

Similar to BFGS and other methods we considered in Chapter 9, one typical strategy for constrained optimization is to approximate f, g, and h with simpler functions, solve the approximate optimization, adjust the approximation based on the latest function evaluation, and repeat.

Suppose we have a guess $\vec{x}_k$ of the solution to the constrained optimization problem. We could apply a second-order Taylor expansion to f and first-order approximation to g and h to define a next iterate as the following:

$$\vec{x}_{k+1} \equiv \vec{x}_k + \arg \min_{\vec{d}} \left[\frac{1}{2} \vec{d}^\top H_f(\vec{x}_k) \vec{d} + \nabla f(\vec{x}_k) \cdot \vec{d} + f(\vec{x}_k) \right]$$
$$\text{subject to } g_i(\vec{x}_k) + \nabla g_i(\vec{x}_k) \cdot \vec{d} = 0$$
$$h_i(\vec{x}_k) + \nabla h_i(\vec{x}_k) \cdot \vec{d} \geq 0.$$

The optimization to find $\vec{d}$ has a quadratic objective with linear constraints, which can be solved using one of many specialized algorithms; it is known as a *quadratic program*. This Taylor approximation, however, only works in a neighborhood of the optimal point. When a good initial guess $\vec{x}_0$ is unavailable, these strategies may fail.

10.3.1.1 Equality Constraints

When the only constraints are equalities and h is removed, the quadratic program for $\vec{d}$ has Lagrange multiplier optimality conditions derived as follows:

$$\Lambda(\vec{d}, \vec{\lambda}) \equiv \frac{1}{2} \vec{d}^\top H_f(\vec{x}_k) \vec{d} + \nabla f(\vec{x}_k) \cdot \vec{d} + f(\vec{x}_k) + \vec{\lambda}^\top (g(\vec{x}_k) + Dg(\vec{x}_k) \vec{d})$$
$$\implies \vec{0} = \nabla_{\vec{d}} \Lambda = H_f(\vec{x}_k) \vec{d} + \nabla f(\vec{x}_k) + [Dg(\vec{x}_k)]^\top \vec{\lambda}.$$

Combining this expression with the linearized equality constraint yields a symmetric linear system for $\vec{d}$ and $\vec{\lambda}$:

$$\begin{pmatrix} H_f(\vec{x}_k) & [Dg(\vec{x}_k)]^\top \\ Dg(\vec{x}_k) & 0 \end{pmatrix} \begin{pmatrix} \vec{d} \\ \vec{\lambda} \end{pmatrix} = \begin{pmatrix} -\nabla f(\vec{x}_k) \\ -g(\vec{x}_k) \end{pmatrix}.$$

Each iteration of sequential quadratic programming in the presence of only equality constraints can be implemented by solving this linear system to get $\vec{x}_{k+1} \equiv \vec{x}_k + \vec{d}$. This linear system is *not* positive definite, so on a large scale it can be difficult to solve. Extensions operate like BFGS for unconstrained optimization by approximating the Hessian H_f. Stability also can be improved by limiting the distance that $\vec{x}$ can move during any single iteration.

10.3.1.2 Inequality Constraints

Specialized algorithms exist for solving quadratic programs rather than general nonlinear programs that can be used for steps of SQP. One notable strategy is to keep an "active set" of constraints that are active at the minimum with respect to $\vec{d}$. The equality-constrained methods above can be applied by ignoring inactive constraints. Iterations of active-set optimization update the active set by adding violated constraints and removing those inequality constraints h_j for which $\nabla f \cdot \nabla h_j \leq 0$ as in §10.2.2.

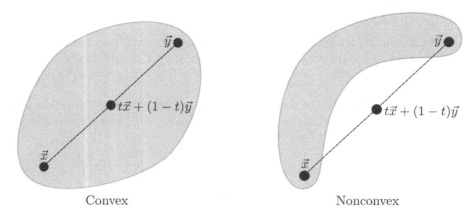

Figure 10.5 Convex and nonconvex shapes on the plane.

10.3.2 Barrier Methods

Another option for constrained minimization is to change the constraints to energy terms. For example, in the equality constrained case we could minimize an "augmented" objective as follows:

$$f_\rho(\vec{x}) = f(\vec{x}) + \rho\|g(\vec{x})\|_2^2.$$

Taking $\rho \to \infty$ will force $\|g(\vec{x})\|_2$ to be as small as possible, eventually reaching $g(\vec{x}) \approx \vec{0}$.

Barrier methods for constrained optimization apply iterative *unconstrained* optimization to f_ρ and check how well the constraints are satisfied; if they are not within a given tolerance, ρ is increased and the optimization continues using the previous iterate as a starting point. Barrier methods are simple to implement and use, but they can exhibit some pernicious failure modes. In particular, as ρ increases, the influence of f on the objective function diminishes and the Hessian of f_ρ becomes more and more poorly conditioned.

Barrier methods be constructed for inequality constraints as well as equality constraints. In this case, we must ensure that $h_i(\vec{x}) \geq 0$ for all i. Typical choices of barrier functions for inequality constraints include $1/h_i(\vec{x})$ (the "inverse barrier") and $-\log h_i(\vec{x})$ (the "logarithmic barrier").

10.4 CONVEX PROGRAMMING

The methods we have described for constrained optimization come with few guarantees on the quality of the output. Certainly they are unable to obtain global minima without a good initial guess $\vec{x}_0$, and in some cases, e.g., when Hessians near $\vec{x}^*$ are not positive definite, they may not converge at all.

There is a notable exception to this rule, which appears in many well-known optimization problems: *convex programming*. The idea here is that when f is a convex function and the feasible set itself is convex, then the optimization problem possesses a unique minimum. We considered convex functions in Definition 9.4 and now expand the class of convex problems to those containing convex constraint sets:

Definition 10.3 (Convex set). A set $S \subseteq \mathbb{R}^n$ is *convex* if for any $\vec{x}, \vec{y} \in S$, the point $t\vec{x} + (1-t)\vec{y}$ is also in S for any $t \in [0, 1]$.

Intuitively, a set is convex if its boundary does not bend inward, as shown in Figure 10.5.

Example 10.8 (Circles). The disc $\{\vec{x} \in \mathbb{R}^n : \|\vec{x}\|_2 \leq 1\}$ is convex, while the unit circle $\{\vec{x} \in \mathbb{R}^n : \|\vec{x}\|_2 = 1\}$ is not.

A nearly identical proof to that of Proposition 9.1 shows:

> **A convex function cannot have suboptimal local minima even when it is restricted to a convex domain.**

If a convex objective function has two local minima, then the line of points between those minima must yield objective values less than or equal to those on the endpoints; by Definition 10.3 this entire line is feasible, completing the proof.

Strong convergence guarantees are available for convex optimization methods that guarantee finding a *global* minimum so long as f is convex and the constraints on g and h make a convex feasible set. A valuable exercise for any optimization problem is to check if it is convex, since this property can increase confidence in the output quality and the chances of success by a large factor.

A new field called *disciplined convex programming* attempts to chain together rules about convexity to generate convex optimization problems. The end user is allowed to combine convex energy terms and constraints so long as they do not violate the convexity of the final problem; the resulting objective and constraints are then provided automatically to an appropriate solver. Useful statements about convexity that can be used to construct convex programs from smaller convex building blocks include the following:

- The intersection of convex sets is convex; thus, enforcing more than one convex constraint is allowable.

- The sum of convex functions is convex.

- If f and g are convex, so is $h(\vec{x}) \equiv \max\{f(\vec{x}), g(\vec{x})\}$.

- If f is a convex function, the set $\{\vec{x} : f(\vec{x}) \leq c\}$ is convex for fixed $c \in \mathbb{R}$.

Tools such as the CVX library help separate implementation of convex programs from the mechanics of minimization algorithms [51, 52].

Example 10.9 (Convex programming).

- The nonnegative least-squares problem in Example 10.3 is convex because $\|A\vec{x} - \vec{b}\|_2$ is a convex function of $\vec{x}$ and the set $\{\vec{x} \in \mathbb{R}^n : \vec{x} \geq \vec{0}\}$ is convex.

- Linear programs, introduced in Example 10.7, are convex because they have linear objectives and linear constraints.

- We can include $\|\vec{x}\|_1$ in a convex optimization objective, if $\vec{x}$ is an optimization variable. To do so, introduce a variable $\vec{y}$ and add constraints $y_i \geq x_i$ and $y_i \geq -x_i$ for each i. Then, $\|\vec{x}\|_1$ can be written as $\sum_i y_i$. At the minimum, we must have $y_i = |x_i|$ since we have constrained $y_i \geq |x_i|$ and might as well minimize the elements of $\vec{y}$. "Disciplined" convex libraries do such operations behind the scenes without exposing substitutions and helper variables to the end user.

Convex programming has much in common with areas of computer science theory involving *reductions* of algorithmic problems to one another. Rather than verifying NP-completeness, however, in this context we wish to use a generic solver to optimize a given objective, just like we reduced assorted problems to a linear solve in Chapter 4. There is a

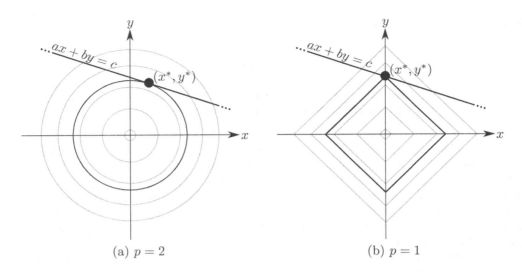

(a) $p = 2$ (b) $p = 1$

Figure 10.6 On the (x, y) plane, the optimization minimizing $\|(x, y)\|_p$ subject to $ax + by = c$ has considerably different output depending on whether we choose (a) $p = 2$ or (b) $p = 1$. Level sets $\{(x, y) : \|(x, y)\|_p = c\}$ are shown in gray.

formidable pantheon of industrial-scale convex programming tools that can handle different classes of problems with varying efficiency and generality; below, we discuss some common classes. See [15, 84] for larger discussions of related topics.

10.4.1 Linear Programming

A well-studied example of convex optimization is *linear programing*, introduced in Example 10.7. Exercise 10.4 will walk through the derivation of some properties making linear programs attractive both theoretically and from an algorithmic design standpoint.

The famous *simplex algorithm,* which can be considered an active set method as in §10.3.1.2, updates the estimate of $\vec{x}^*$ using a linear solve, and checks if the active set must be updated. No Taylor approximations are needed because the objective and constraints are linear. *Interior point* linear programming algorithms such as the barrier method in §10.3.2 also are successful for these problems. Linear programs can be solved on a *huge* scale—up to millions or billions of variables!—and often appear in problems like scheduling or pricing.

One popular application of linear programming inspired by Example 10.9 provides an alternative to using pseudoinverse for underdetermined linear systems (§7.2.1). When a matrix A is underdetermined, there are many vectors $\vec{x}$ that satisfy $A\vec{x} = \vec{b}$ for a given vector $\vec{b}$. In this case, the pseudoinverse A^+ applied to $\vec{b}$ solves the following problem:

$$\text{Pseudoinverse} \begin{cases} \text{minimize}_{\vec{x}} & \|\vec{x}\|_2 \\ \text{subject to} & A\vec{x} = \vec{b}. \end{cases}$$

Using linear programs, we can solve a slightly different system:

$$L_1 \text{ minimization} \begin{cases} \text{minimize}_{\vec{x}} & \|\vec{x}\|_1 \\ \text{subject to} & A\vec{x} = \vec{b}. \end{cases}$$

All we have done here is replace the norm $\| \cdot \|_2$ with a different norm $\| \cdot \|_1$.

Why does this one-character change make a significant difference in the output $\vec{x}$? Consider the two-dimensional instance of this problem shown in Figure 10.6, which minimizes

$\|(x,y)\|_p$ for $p = 2$ (pseudoinverse) and $p = 1$ (linear program). In the $p = 2$ case (a), we are minimizing $x^2 + y^2$, which has circular level sets; the optimal (x^*, y^*) subject to the constraints is in the interior of the first quadrant. In the $p = 1$ case (b), we are minimizing $|x| + |y|$, which has diamond-shaped level sets; this makes $x^* = 0$ since the outer points of the diamond align with the x and y axes, a more *sparse* solution.

More generally, the use of the norm $\|\vec{x}\|_2$ indicates that no single element x_i of $\vec{x}$ should have a large value; this regularization tends to favor vectors $\vec{x}$ with lots of small nonzero values. On the other hand, $\|\vec{x}\|_1$ does not care if a single element of $\vec{x}$ has a large value so long as the sum of all the elements' absolute values is small. As we have illustrated in the two-dimensional case, this type of regularization can produce *sparse* vectors $\vec{x}$, with elements that are exactly zero.

This type of regularization using $\|\cdot\|_1$ is fundamental in the field of *compressed sensing*, which solves underdetermined signal processing problems with the additional assumption that the output should be sparse. This assumption makes sense in many contexts where sparse solutions of $A\vec{x} = \vec{b}$ imply that many columns of A are irrelevant [37].

A minor extension of linear programming is to keep using linear inequality constraints but introduce convex quadratic terms to the objective, changing the optimization in Example 10.7 to:

$$\text{minimize}_{\vec{x}} \ \vec{b} \cdot \vec{x} + \vec{x}^\top M \vec{x}$$
$$\text{subject to } A\vec{x} \geq \vec{c}.$$

Here, M is an $n \times n$ positive semidefinite matrix. With this machinery, we can provide an alternative to Tikhonov regularization from §4.1.3:

$$\min_{\vec{x}} \|A\vec{x} - \vec{b}\|_2^2 + \alpha\|\vec{x}\|_1.$$

This "lasso" regularizer also promotes sparsity in $\vec{x}$ while solving $A\vec{x} \approx \vec{b}$, but it does not enforce $A\vec{x} = \vec{b}$ exactly. It is useful when A or $\vec{b}$ is noisy and we prefer sparsity of $\vec{x}$ over solving the system exactly [119].

10.4.2 Second-Order Cone Programming

A *second-order cone program* (SOCP) is a convex optimization problem taking the following form [15]:

$$\text{minimize}_{\vec{x}} \ \vec{b} \cdot \vec{x}$$
$$\text{subject to } \|A_i\vec{x} - \vec{b}_i\|_2 \leq d_i + \vec{c}_i \cdot \vec{x} \text{ for all } i = 1, \ldots, k.$$

Here, we use matrices $A_1, \ldots, A_k$, vectors $\vec{b}_1, \ldots, \vec{b}_k$, vectors $\vec{c}_1, \ldots, \vec{c}_k$, and scalars $d_1, \ldots, d_k$ to specify the k constraints. These "cone constraints" will allow us to pose a broader set of convex optimization problems.

One non-obvious application of second-order cone programming explained in [83] appears when we wish to solve the least-squares problem $A\vec{x} \approx \vec{b}$, but we do not know the elements of A exactly. For instance, A might have been constructed from data we have measured experimentally (see §4.1.2 for an example in least-squares regression).

Take $\vec{a}_i^\top$ to be the i-th row of A. Then, the least-squares problem $A\vec{x} \approx \vec{b}$ can be understood as minimizing $\sum_i (\vec{a}_i \cdot \vec{x} - b_i)^2$ over $\vec{x}$. If we do not know A exactly, however, we might allow each $\vec{a}_i$ to vary somewhat before solving least-squares. In particular, maybe we think that $\vec{a}_i$ is an approximation of some unknown $\vec{a}_i^0$ satisfying $\|\vec{a}_i^0 - \vec{a}_i\|_2 \leq \varepsilon$ for some fixed $\varepsilon > 0$.

To make least-squares robust to this model of error, we can choose $\vec{x}$ to thwart an adversary picking the worst possible $\vec{a}_i^0$. Formally, we solve the following "minimax" problem:

$$\text{minimize}_{\vec{x}} \left[\begin{array}{ll} \max_{\{\vec{a}_i^0\}} & \sum_i (\vec{a}_i^0 \cdot \vec{x} - b_i)^2 \\ \text{subject to} & \|\vec{a}_i^0 - \vec{a}_i\|_2 \leq \varepsilon \text{ for all } i \end{array} \right].$$

That is, we want to choose $\vec{x}$ so that the least-squares energy with the *worst* possible unknowns $\vec{a}_i^0$ satisfying $\|\vec{a}_i^0 - \vec{a}_i\|_2 \leq \varepsilon$ still is small. It is far from evident that this complicated optimization problem is solvable using SOCP machinery, but after some simplification we will manage to write it in the standard SOCP form above.

If we define $\delta\vec{a}_i \equiv \vec{a}_i - \vec{a}_i^0$, then our optimization becomes:

$$\text{minimize}_{\vec{x}} \left[\begin{array}{ll} \max_{\{\delta\vec{a}_i\}} & \sum_i (\vec{a}_i \cdot \vec{x} + \delta\vec{a}_i \cdot \vec{x} - b_i)^2 \\ \text{subject to} & \|\delta\vec{a}_i\|_2 \leq \varepsilon \text{ for all } i \end{array} \right].$$

When maximizing over $\delta\vec{a}_i$, each term of the sum over i is independent. Hence, we can solve the inner maximization for one $\delta\vec{a}_i$ at a time. Peculiarly, if we maximize an absolute value rather than a sum (usually we go in the other direction!), we can find a closed-form solution to the optimization for $\delta\vec{a}_i$ for a single fixed i:

$$\max_{\|\delta\vec{a}_i\|_2 \leq \varepsilon} |\vec{a}_i \cdot \vec{x} + \delta\vec{a}_i \cdot \vec{x} - b_i| = \max_{\|\delta\vec{a}_i\|_2 \leq \varepsilon} \max\{\vec{a}_i \cdot \vec{x} + \delta\vec{a}_i \cdot \vec{x} - b_i, -\vec{a}_i \cdot \vec{x} - \delta\vec{a}_i \cdot \vec{x} + b_i\}$$

$$\text{since } |x| = \max\{x, -x\}$$

$$= \max \left\{ \max_{\|\delta\vec{a}_i\|_2 \leq \varepsilon} [\vec{a}_i \cdot \vec{x} + \delta\vec{a}_i \cdot \vec{x} - b_i], \right.$$

$$\left. \max_{\|\delta\vec{a}_i\|_2 \leq \varepsilon} [-\vec{a}_i \cdot \vec{x} - \delta\vec{a}_i \cdot \vec{x} + b_i] \right\}$$

after changing the order of the maxima

$$= \max\{\vec{a}_i \cdot \vec{x} + \varepsilon\|\vec{x}\|_2 - b_i, -\vec{a}_i \cdot \vec{x} + \varepsilon\|\vec{x}\|_2 + b_i\}$$

$$= |\vec{a}_i \cdot \vec{x} - b_i| + \varepsilon\|\vec{x}\|_2.$$

After this simplification, our optimization for $\vec{x}$ becomes:

$$\text{minimize}_{\vec{x}} \sum_i (|\vec{a}_i \cdot \vec{x} - b_i| + \varepsilon\|\vec{x}\|_2)^2.$$

This minimization can be written as a second-order cone problem:

$$\begin{array}{ll} \text{minimize}_{s, \vec{t}, \vec{x}} & s \\ \text{subject to} & \|\vec{t}\|_2 \leq s \\ & (\vec{a}_i \cdot \vec{x} - b_i) + \varepsilon\|\vec{x}\|_2 \leq t_i \; \forall i \\ & -(\vec{a}_i \cdot \vec{x} - b_i) + \varepsilon\|\vec{x}\|_2 \leq t_i \; \forall i. \end{array}$$

In this optimization, we have introduced two extra variables s and $\vec{t}$. Since we wish to minimize s with the constraint $\|\vec{t}\|_2 \leq s$, we are effectively minimizing the norm of $\vec{t}$. The last two constraints ensure that each element of $\vec{t}$ satisfies $t_i = |\vec{a}_i \cdot \vec{x} - b_i| + \varepsilon\|\vec{x}\|_2$.

This type of regularization provides yet another variant of least-squares. In this case, rather than being robust to near-singularity of A, we have incorporated an error model directly into our formulation allowing for mistakes in measuring rows of A. The parameter ε controls sensitivity to the elements of A in a similar fashion to the weight α of Tikhonov or L_1 regularization.

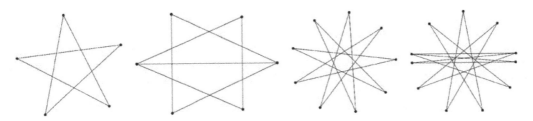

Figure 10.7 Examples of graphs laid out via semidefinite embedding.

10.4.3 Semidefinite Programming

Suppose A and B are $n \times n$ positive semidefinite matrices; we will notate this as $A, B \succeq 0$. Take $t \in [0,1]$. Then, for any $\vec{x} \in \mathbb{R}^n$ we have:

$$\vec{x}^\top (tA + (1-t)B)\vec{x} = t\vec{x}^\top A\vec{x} + (1-t)\vec{x}^\top B\vec{x} \geq 0,$$

where the inequality holds by semidefiniteness of A and B. This proof verifies a surprisingly useful fact:

> **The set of positive semidefinite matrices is convex.**

Hence, if we are solving optimization problems for a matrix A, we safely can add constraints $A \succeq 0$ without affecting convexity.

Algorithms for *semidefinite programming* optimize convex objectives with the ability to add constraints that matrix-valued variables must be positive (or negative) semidefinite. More generally, semidefinite programming machinery can include *linear matrix inequality* (LMI) constraints of the form:

$$x_1 A_1 + x_2 A_2 + \cdots + x_k A_k \succeq 0,$$

where $\vec{x} \in \mathbb{R}^k$ is an optimization variable and the matrices A_i are fixed.

As an example of semidefinite programming, we will sketch a technique known as *semidefinite embedding* from graph layout and manifold learning [130]. Suppose we are given a graph (V, E) consisting of a set of vertices $V = \{v_1, \ldots, v_k\}$ and a set of edges $E \subseteq V \times V$. For some fixed n, the semidefinite embedding method computes positions $\vec{x}_1, \ldots, \vec{x}_k \in \mathbb{R}^n$ for the vertices, so that vertices connected by edges are nearby in the embedding with respect to Euclidean distance $\|\cdot\|_2$; some examples are shown in Figure 10.7.

If we already have computed $\vec{x}_1, \ldots, \vec{x}_k$, we can construct a Gram matrix $G \in \mathbb{R}^{k \times k}$ satisfying $G_{ij} = \vec{x}_i \cdot \vec{x}_j$. G is a matrix of inner products and hence is symmetric and positive semidefinite. We can measure the squared distance from $\vec{x}_i$ to $\vec{x}_j$ using G:

$$\begin{aligned}
\|\vec{x}_i - \vec{x}_j\|_2^2 &= (\vec{x}_i - \vec{x}_j) \cdot (\vec{x}_i - \vec{x}_j) \\
&= \|\vec{x}_i\|_2^2 - 2\vec{x}_i \cdot \vec{x}_j + \|\vec{x}_j\|_2^2 \\
&= G_{ii} - 2G_{ij} + G_{jj}.
\end{aligned}$$

Similarly, suppose we wish the center of mass $\frac{1}{k}\sum_i \vec{x}_i$ to be $\vec{0}$, since shifting the embedding of the graph does not have a significant effect on its layout. We alternatively can write $\|\sum_i \vec{x}_i\|_2^2 = 0$ and can express this condition in terms of G:

$$0 = \left\| \sum_i \vec{x}_i \right\|_2^2 = \left(\sum_i \vec{x}_i \right) \cdot \left(\sum_i \vec{x}_i \right) = \sum_{ij} \vec{x}_i \cdot \vec{x}_j = \sum_{ij} G_{ij}.$$

Finally, we might wish that our embedding of the graph is relatively compact or small. One way to do this would be to minimize $\sum_i \|\vec{x}_i\|_2^2 = \sum_i G_{ii} = \text{Tr}(G)$.

The semidefinite embedding technique turns these observations on their head, optimizing for the Gram matrix G directly rather than the positions $\vec{x}_i$ of the vertices. Making use of the observations above, semidefinite embedding solves the following optimization problem:

$$\begin{array}{ll} \text{minimize}_{G \in \mathbb{R}^{k \times k}} & \text{Tr}(G) \\ \text{subject to} & G = G^\top \\ & G \succeq 0 \\ & G_{ii} - 2G_{ij} + G_{jj} = 1 \ \forall (v_i, v_j) \in E \\ & \sum_{ij} G_{ij} = 0. \end{array}$$

This optimization for G is motivated as follows:

- The objective asks that the embedding of the graph is compact by minimizing the sum of squared norms $\sum_i \|\vec{x}_i\|_2^2$.

- The first two constraints require that the Gram matrix is symmetric and positive definite.

- The third constraint requires that the embeddings of any two adjacent vertices in the graph have distance one.

- The final constraint centers the full embedding about the origin.

We can use semidefinite programming to solve this optimization problem for G. Then, since G is symmetric and positive semidefinite, we can use the Cholesky factorization (§4.2.1) or the eigenvector decomposition (§6.2) of G to write $G = X^\top X$ for some matrix $X \in \mathbb{R}^{k \times k}$. Based on the discussion above, the columns of X are an embedding of the vertices of the graph into $\mathbb{R}^k$ where all the edges in the graph have length one, the center of mass is the origin, and the total square norm of the positions is minimized.

We set out to embed the graph into $\mathbb{R}^n$ rather than $\mathbb{R}^k$, and generally $n \leq k$. To compute a lower-dimensional embedding that *approximately* satisfies the constraints, we can decompose $G = X^\top X$ using its eigenvectors; then, we remove $k - n$ eigenvectors with eigenvalues closest to zero. This operation is exactly the low-rank approximation of G via SVD given in §7.2.2. This final step provides an embedding of the graph into $\mathbb{R}^n$.

A legitimate question about the semidefinite embedding is how the optimization for G interacts with the low-rank eigenvector approximation applied in post-processing. In many well-known cases, the solution of semidefinite optimizations like the one above yield *low-rank* or nearly low-rank matrices whose lower-dimensional approximations are close to the original; a formalized version of this observation justifies the approximation. We already explored such a justification in Exercise 7.7, since the nuclear norm of a symmetric positive semidefinite matrix is its trace.

10.4.4 Integer Programs and Relaxations

Our final application of convex optimization is—surprisingly—to a class of *highly* non-convex problems: Ones with integer variables. In particular, an *integer program* is an optimization in which one or more variables is constrained to be an integer rather than a real number. Within this class, two well-known subproblems are *mixed-integer programming*, in which some variables are continuous while others are integers, and *zero-one programming*, where the variables take Boolean values in $\{0, 1\}$.

Example 10.10 (3-SAT). We can define the following operations from Boolean algebra for binary variables $U, V \in \{0, 1\}$:

U	V	$\neg U$ ("not U")	$\neg V$ ("not V")	$U \wedge V$ ("U and V")	$U \vee V$ ("U or V")
0	0	1	1	0	0
0	1	1	0	0	1
1	0	0	1	0	1
1	1	0	0	1	1

We can convert Boolean satisfiability problems into integer programs using a few steps. For example, we can express the "not" operation algebraically using $\neg U = 1 - U$. Similarly, suppose we wish to find U, V satisfying $(U \vee \neg V) \wedge (\neg U \vee V)$. Then, U and V as integers satisfy the following constraints:

$$
\begin{aligned}
U + (1 - V) &\geq 1 & (U \vee \neg V) \\
(1 - U) + V &\geq 1 & (\neg U \vee V) \\
U, V &\in \mathbb{Z} & \text{(integer constraint)} \\
0 \leq U, V &\leq 1 & \text{(Boolean variables)}
\end{aligned}
$$

As demonstrated in Example 10.10, integer programs encode a wide class of discrete problems, including many that are known to be NP-hard. For this reason, we cannot expect to solve them exactly with convex optimization; doing so would settle a long-standing question of theoretical computer science by showing "$P = NP$." We can, however, use convex optimization to find approximate solutions to integer programs.

If we write a discrete problem like Example 10.10 as an optimization, we can *relax* the constraint keeping variables in $\mathbb{Z}$ and allow them to be in $\mathbb{R}$ instead. Such a relaxation can yield invalid solutions, e.g., Boolean variables that take on values like 0.75. So, after solving the relaxed problem, one of many strategies can be used to generate an integer approximation of the solution. For example, non-integral variables can be *rounded* to the closest integer, at the risk of generating outputs that are suboptimal or violate the constraints. Alternatively, a slower but potentially more effective method iteratively rounds one variable at a time, adds a constraint fixing the value of that variable, and re-optimizes the objective subject to the new constraint.

Many difficult discrete problems can be reduced to integer programs, from satisfiability problems like the one in Example 10.10 to the traveling salesman problem. These reductions should indicate that the design of effective integer programming algorithms is challenging even in the approximate case. State-of-the-art convex relaxation methods for integer programming, however, are fairly effective for a large class of problems, providing a remarkably general piece of machinery for approximating solutions to problems for which it may be difficult or impossible to design a discrete algorithm. Many open research problems involve designing effective integer programming methods and understanding potential relaxations; this work provides a valuable and attractive link between continuous and discrete mathematics.

10.5 EXERCISES

10.1   Prove the following statement from §10.4: If f is a convex function, the set $\{\vec{x} : f(\vec{x}) \leq c\}$ is convex.

10.2 The standard deviation of k values $x_1, \ldots, x_k$ is

$$\sigma(x_1, \ldots, x_k) \equiv \sqrt{\frac{1}{k} \sum_{i=1}^{k} (x_i - \mu)^2},$$

where $\mu \equiv \frac{1}{k} \sum_i x_i$. Show that σ is a convex function of $x_1, \ldots, x_k$.

10.3 Some properties of second-order cone programming:

(a) Show that the *Lorentz cone* $\{\vec{x} \in \mathbb{R}^n, c \in \mathbb{R} : \|\vec{x}\|_2 \leq c\}$ is convex.

(b) Use this fact to show that the second-order cone program in §10.4.2 is convex.

(c) Show that second-order cone programming can be used to solve linear programs.

10.4 In this problem we will study *linear programming* in more detail.

(a) A linear program in "standard form" is given by:

$$\begin{aligned} \text{minimize}_{\vec{x}} \quad & \vec{c}^\top \vec{x} \\ \text{subject to} \quad & A\vec{x} = \vec{b} \\ & \vec{x} \geq \vec{0}. \end{aligned}$$

Here, the optimization is over $\vec{x} \in \mathbb{R}^n$; the remaining variables are constants $A \in \mathbb{R}^{m \times n}$, $\vec{b} \in \mathbb{R}^m$, and $\vec{c} \in \mathbb{R}^n$. Find the KKT conditions of this system.

(b) Suppose we add a constraint of the form $\vec{v}^\top \vec{x} \leq d$ for some fixed $\vec{v} \in \mathbb{R}^n$ and $d \in \mathbb{R}$. Explain how such a constraint can be added while keeping a linear program in standard form.

(c) The "dual" of this linear program is another optimization:

$$\begin{aligned} \text{maximize}_{\vec{y}} \quad & \vec{b}^\top \vec{y} \\ \text{subject to} \quad & A^\top \vec{y} \leq \vec{c}. \end{aligned}$$

Assuming that the primal and dual have exactly one stationary point, show that the optimal value of the primal and dual objectives coincide.
Hint: Show that the KKT multipliers of one problem can be used to solve the other.
Note: This property is called "strict duality." The famous simplex algorithm for solving linear programs maintains estimates of $\vec{x}$ and $\vec{y}$, terminating when $\vec{c}^\top \vec{x}^* - \vec{b}^\top \vec{y}^* = 0$.

10.5 Suppose we take a grayscale photograph of size $n \times m$ and represent it as a vector $\vec{v} \in \mathbb{R}^{nm}$ of values in $[0, 1]$. We used the wrong lens, however, and our photo is blurry! We wish to use *deconvolution* machinery to undo this effect.

(a) Find the KKT conditions for the following optimization problem:

$$\begin{aligned} \text{minimize}_{\vec{x} \in \mathbb{R}^{nm}} \quad & \|A\vec{x} - \vec{b}\|_2^2 \\ \text{subject to} \quad & 0 \leq x_i \leq 1 \; \forall i \in \{1, \ldots, nm\}. \end{aligned}$$

(b) Suppose we are given a matrix $G \in \mathbb{R}^{nm \times nm}$ taking sharp images to blurry ones. Propose an optimization in the form of (a) for recovering a sharp image from our blurry $\vec{v}$.

(c) We do not know the operator G, making the model in (b) difficult to use. Suppose, however, that for each $r \geq 0$ we can write a matrix $G_r \in \mathbb{R}^{nm \times nm}$ approximating a blur with radius r. Using the same camera, we now take k *pairs* of photos $(\vec{v}_1, \vec{w}_1), \ldots, (\vec{v}_k, \vec{w}_k)$, where $\vec{v}_i$ and $\vec{w}_i$ are of the same scene but $\vec{v}_i$ is blurry (taken using the same lens as our original bad photo) and $\vec{w}_i$ is sharp. Propose a nonlinear optimization for approximating r using this data.

DH 10.6 ("Fenchel duality," adapted from [10]) Let $f(\vec{x})$ be a convex function on $\mathbb{R}^n$ that is *proper*. This means that f accepts vectors from $\mathbb{R}^n$ or whose coordinates may (individually) be $\pm\infty$ and returns a real scalar in $\mathbb{R} \cup \{\infty\}$ with at least one $f(\vec{x}_0)$ taking a non-infinite value. Under these assumptions, the *Fenchel dual* of f at $\vec{y} \in \mathbb{R}^n$ is defined to be the function

$$f^*(\vec{y}) \equiv \sup_{\vec{x} \in \mathbb{R}^n} (\vec{x} \cdot \vec{y} - f(\vec{x})).$$

Fenchel duals are used to study properties of convex optimization problems in theory and practice.

(a) Show that f^* is convex.

(b) Derive the *Fenchel-Young inequality*:

$$f(\vec{x}) + f^*(\vec{y}) \geq \vec{x} \cdot \vec{y}.$$

(c) The *indicator function* of a subset $A \in \mathbb{R}^n$ is given by

$$\chi_A(\vec{x}) \equiv \begin{cases} 0 & \text{if } \vec{x} \in A \\ \infty & \text{otherwise.} \end{cases}$$

With this definition in mind, determine the Fenchel dual of $f(\vec{x}) = \vec{c} \cdot \vec{x}$, where $\vec{c} \in \mathbb{R}^n$.

(d) What is the Fenchel dual of the linear function $f(x) = ax + b$?

(e) Show that $f(\vec{x}) = \frac{1}{2}\|\vec{x}\|_2^2$ is *self-dual*, meaning $f = f^*$.

(f) Suppose $p, q \in (1, \infty)$ satisfy $\frac{1}{p} + \frac{1}{q} = 1$. Show that the Fenchel dual of $f(x) = \frac{1}{p}|x|^p$ is $f^*(y) = \frac{1}{q}|y|^q$. Use this result along with previous parts of this problem to derive Hölder's inequality

$$\sum_k |u_k v_k| \leq \left(\sum_k |u_k|^p \right)^{1/p} \left(\sum_k |v_k|^q \right)^{1/q},$$

for all $\vec{u}, \vec{v} \in \mathbb{R}^n$.

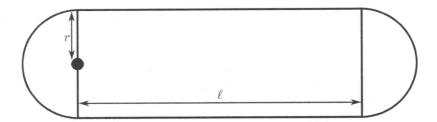

Figure 10.8 Notation for Exercise 10.7.

SC 10.7 A monomial is a function of the form $f(\vec{x}) = cx_1^{a_1} x_2^{a_2} \cdots x_n^{a_n}$, where each $a_i \in \mathbb{R}$ and $c > 0$. We define a *posynomial* as a sum of one or more monomials:

$$f(\vec{x}) = \sum_{k=1}^{K} c_k x_1^{a_{k1}} x_2^{a_{k2}} \cdots x_n^{a_{kn}}.$$

Geometric programs are optimization problems taking the following form:

$$\begin{aligned}
\text{minimize}_{\vec{x}} \quad & f_0(\vec{x}) \\
\text{subject to} \quad & f_i(\vec{x}) \leq 1 \; \forall i \in \{1, \ldots, m\} \\
& g_i(\vec{x}) = 1 \; \forall i \in \{1, \ldots, p\},
\end{aligned}$$

where the functions f_i are posynomials and the functions g_i are monomials.

(a) Suppose you are designing a slow-dissolving medicinal capsule. The capsule looks like a cylinder with hemispherical ends, illustrated in Figure 10.8. To ensure that the capsule dissolves slowly, you need to minimize its surface area.

The cylindrical portion of the capsule must have volume larger than or equal to V to ensure that it can hold the proper amount of medicine. Also, because the capsule is manufactured as two halves that slide together, to ensure that the capsule will not break, the length ℓ of its cylindrical portion must be at least $\ell_{\min}$. Finally, due to packaging limitations, the total length of the capsule must be no larger than C.

Write the corresponding minimization problem and argue that it is a geometric program.

(b) Transform the problem from Exercise 10.7a into a convex programming problem. *Hint:* Consider the substitution $y_i = \log x_i$.

10.8 The *cardinality function* $\|\cdot\|_0$ computes the number of nonzero elements of $\vec{x} \in \mathbb{R}^n$:

$$\|\vec{x}\|_0 = \sum_{i=1}^{n} \begin{cases} 1 & x_i \neq 0 \\ 0 & \text{otherwise.} \end{cases}$$

(a) Show that $\|\cdot\|_0$ is *not* a norm on $\mathbb{R}^n$, but that it is connected to L_p norms by the relationship

$$\|\vec{x}\|_0 = \lim_{p \to 0^+} \sum_{i=1}^{n} |x_i|^p.$$

(b) Suppose we wish to solve an underdetermined system of equations $A\vec{x} = \vec{b}$. One alternative to SVD-based approaches or Tikhonov regularizations is *cardinality minimization*:

$$\min_{\vec{x} \in \mathbb{R}^n} \quad \|\vec{x}\|_0$$
$$\text{subject to} \quad A\vec{x} = \vec{b}$$
$$\|\vec{x}\|_\infty \le R.$$

Rewrite this optimization in the form

$$\min_{\vec{x}, \vec{z}} \quad \|\vec{z}\|_1$$
$$\text{subject to} \quad \vec{z} \in \{0, 1\}^n$$
$$\vec{x}, \vec{z} \in \mathcal{C},$$

where $\mathcal{C}$ is some convex set [15].

(c) Show that relaxing the constraint $\vec{z} \in \{0, 1\}^n$ to $\vec{z} \in [0, 1]^n$ lower-bounds the original problem. Propose a heuristic for the $\{0, 1\}$ problem based on this relaxation.

10.9 ("Grasping force optimization;" adapted from [83]) Suppose we are writing code to control a robot hand with n fingers grasping a rigid object. Each finger i is controlled by a motor that outputs nonnegative torque t_i.

The force $\vec{F}_i$ imparted by each finger onto the object can be decomposed into two orthogonal parts as $\vec{F}_i = \vec{F}_{ni} + \vec{F}_{si}$, a normal force $\vec{F}_{ni}$ and a tangential friction force $\vec{F}_{si}$:

Normal force: $\vec{F}_{ni} = c_i t_i \vec{v}_i = (\vec{v}_i^\top \vec{F}_i) \vec{v}_i$

Friction force: $\vec{F}_{si} = (I_{3 \times 3} - \vec{v}_i \vec{v}_i^\top) \vec{F}_i$, where $\|\vec{F}_{si}\|_2 \le \mu \|\vec{F}_{ni}\|_2$

Here, $\vec{v}_i$ is a (fixed) unit vector normal to the surface at the point of contact of finger i. The value c_i is a constant associated with finger i. Additionally, the object experiences a gravitational force in the downward direction given by $\vec{F}_g = m\vec{g}$.

For the object to be grasped firmly in place, the sum of the forces exerted by all fingers must be $\vec{0}$. Show how to minimize the total torque outputted by the motors while firmly grasping the object using a second-order cone program.

10.10 Show that when $\vec{c}_i = \vec{0}$ for all i in the second-order cone program of §10.4.2, the optimization problem can be solved as a convex quadratic program with quadratic constraints.

10.11 (Suggested by Q. Huang) Suppose we know

$$\begin{pmatrix} 1 & 1 & 1 \\ 1 & 1 & x \\ 1 & x & 1 \end{pmatrix} \succeq 0.$$

What can we say about x?

^{SC}10.12 We can modify the gradient descent algorithm for minimizing $f(\vec{x})$ to account for linear equality constraints $A\vec{x} = \vec{b}$.

(a) Assuming we choose $\vec{x}_0$ satisfying the equality constraint, propose a modification to gradient descent so that each iterate $\vec{x}_k$ satisfies $A\vec{x}_k = \vec{b}$.
Hint: The gradient $\nabla f(\vec{x})$ may point in a direction that could violate the constraint.

(b) Briefly justify why the modified gradient descent algorithm should reach a local minimum of the constrained optimization problem.

(c) Suppose rather than $A\vec{x} = \vec{b}$ we have a nonlinear constraint $g(\vec{x}) = \vec{0}$. Propose a modification of your strategy from Exercise 10.12a maintaining this new constraint approximately. How is the modification affected by the choice of step sizes?

10.13 Show that linear programming and second-order cone programming are special cases of semidefinite programming.

CHAPTER 11

Iterative Linear Solvers

CONTENTS

11.1   Gradient Descent 208
      11.1.1   Gradient Descent for Linear Systems 208
      11.1.2   Convergence 209
11.2   Conjugate Gradients 211
      11.2.1   Motivation 212
      11.2.2   Suboptimality of Gradient Descent 214
      11.2.3   Generating A-Conjugate Directions 215
      11.2.4   Formulating the Conjugate Gradients Algorithm 217
      11.2.5   Convergence and Stopping Conditions 219
11.3   Preconditioning 219
      11.3.1   CG with Preconditioning 220
      11.3.2   Common Preconditioners 221
11.4   Other Iterative Algorithms 222

IN the previous two chapters, we developed general algorithms for minimizing a function $f(\vec{x})$ with or without constraints on $\vec{x}$. In doing so, we relaxed our viewpoint from numerical linear algebra that we must find an *exact* solution to a system of equations and instead designed iterative methods that successively produce better approximations of the minimizer. Even if we never find the position $\vec{x}^*$ of a local minimum exactly, such methods generate $\vec{x}_k$ with smaller and smaller $f(\vec{x}_k)$, in many cases getting arbitrarily close to the desired optimum.

We now revisit our favorite problem from numerical linear algebra, solving $A\vec{x} = \vec{b}$ for $\vec{x}$, but apply an *iterative* approach rather than seeking a solution in closed form. This adjustment reveals a new class of linear solvers that can find reliable approximations of $\vec{x}$ in remarkably few iterations. To formulate these methods, we will view solving $A\vec{x} = \vec{b}$ not as a system of equations but rather as a minimization problem, e.g., on energies like $\|A\vec{x} - \vec{b}\|_2^2$.

Why bother deriving yet another class of linear solvers? So far, most of our direct solvers require us to represent A as a full $n \times n$ matrix, and algorithms such as LU, QR, and Cholesky factorization all take around $O(n^3)$ time. Two cases motivate the need for iterative methods:

- When A is sparse, Gaussian elimination tends to induce *fill*, meaning that even if A contains $O(n)$ nonzero values, intermediate steps of elimination may fill in the remaining $O(n^2)$ empty positions. Storing a matrix in sparse format dramatically reduces the space it takes in memory, but fill during elimination can rapidly undo these savings. Contrastingly, the algorithms in this chapter require only *application A* to vectors (that is, computation of the product $A\vec{v}$ for any $\vec{v}$), which does not induce fill and can be carried out in time proportional to the number of nonzeros.

- We may wish to defeat the $O(n^3)$ runtime of standard matrix factorization techniques. If an iterative scheme can uncover a fairly, if not completely, accurate solution to $A\vec{x} = \vec{b}$ in a few steps, we may halt the method early in favor of speed over accuracy of the output.

Newton's method and other nonlinear optimization algorithms solve a linear system in each iteration. Formulating the fastest possible solver can make a huge difference in efficiency when implementing these methods for large-scale problems. An inaccurate but fast linear solve may be sufficient, since it feeds into a larger iterative technique anyway.

Although our discussion in this chapter benefits from intuition and formalism developed in previous chapters, our approach to deriving iterative linear methods owes much to the classic extended treatment in [109].

11.1   GRADIENT DESCENT

We will focus our discussion on solving $A\vec{x} = \vec{b}$ where A has three properties:

1. $A \in \mathbb{R}^{n \times n}$ is square.

2. A is symmetric, that is, $A^\top = A$.

3. A is positive definite, that is, for all $\vec{x} \neq \vec{0}$, $\vec{x}^\top A \vec{x} > 0$.

Toward the end of this chapter we will relax these assumptions. Of course, we always can replace $A\vec{x} = \vec{b}$—at least when A is invertible or overdetermined—with the normal equations $A^\top A \vec{x} = A^\top \vec{b}$ to satisfy these criteria, although as discussed in §5.1, this substitution can create conditioning issues.

11.1.1   Gradient Descent for Linear Systems

Under the restrictions above, solutions of $A\vec{x} = \vec{b}$ are minima of the function $f(\vec{x})$ given by the *quadratic form*

$$f(\vec{x}) \equiv \frac{1}{2}\vec{x}^\top A \vec{x} - \vec{b}^\top \vec{x} + c$$

for any $c \in \mathbb{R}$. To see this connection, when A is symmetric, taking the derivative of f shows

$$\nabla f(\vec{x}) = A\vec{x} - \vec{b},$$

and setting $\nabla f(\vec{x}) = \vec{0}$ yields the desired result.

Solving $\nabla f(\vec{x}) = \vec{0}$ directly amounts to performing Gaussian elimination on A. Instead, suppose we apply gradient descent to this minimization problem. Recall the basic gradient descent algorithm:

1. Compute the search direction $\vec{d}_k \equiv -\nabla f(\vec{x}_{k-1}) = \vec{b} - A\vec{x}_{k-1}$.

2. Define $\vec{x}_k \equiv \vec{x}_{k-1} + \alpha_k \vec{d}_k$, where α_k is chosen such that $f(\vec{x}_k) < f(\vec{x}_{k-1})$.

3. Repeat.

For a generic function f, deciding on the value of α_k can be a difficult one-dimensional "line search" problem, boiling down to minimizing $f(\vec{x}_{k-1} + \alpha_k \vec{d}_k)$ as a function of a single

```
function LINEAR-GRADIENT-DESCENT(A, b⃗)
    x⃗ ← 0⃗
    for k ← 1, 2, 3, . . .
        d⃗ ← b⃗ − Ax⃗                    ▷ Search direction is residual
        α ← ‖d⃗‖²₂ / d⃗ᵀAd⃗              ▷ Line search formula
        x⃗ ← x⃗ + αd⃗                    ▷ Update solution vector x⃗
```

Figure 11.1 Gradient descent algorithm for solving $A\vec{x} = \vec{b}$ for symmetric and positive definite A, by iteratively decreasing the energy $f(\vec{x}) = \frac{1}{2}\vec{x}^\top A\vec{x} - \vec{b}^\top \vec{x} + c$.

variable $\alpha_k \geq 0$. For the quadratic form $f(\vec{x}) = \frac{1}{2}\vec{x}^\top A\vec{x} - \vec{b}^\top \vec{x} + c$, however, we can choose α_k optimally using a closed-form formula. To do so, define

$$
\begin{aligned}
g(\alpha) &\equiv f(\vec{x} + \alpha\vec{d}) \\
&= \frac{1}{2}(\vec{x} + \alpha\vec{d})^\top A(\vec{x} + \alpha\vec{d}) - \vec{b}^\top(\vec{x} + \alpha\vec{d}) + c \text{ by definition of } f \\
&= \frac{1}{2}(\vec{x}^\top A\vec{x} + 2\alpha\vec{x}^\top A\vec{d} + \alpha^2\vec{d}^\top A\vec{d}) - \vec{b}^\top\vec{x} - \alpha\vec{b}^\top\vec{d} + c \\
&\quad \text{after expanding the product} \\
&= \frac{1}{2}\alpha^2\vec{d}^\top A\vec{d} + \alpha(\vec{x}^\top A\vec{d} - \vec{b}^\top\vec{d}) + \text{const.} \\
\implies \frac{dg}{d\alpha}(\alpha) &= \alpha\vec{d}^\top A\vec{d} + \vec{d}^\top(A\vec{x} - \vec{b}) \text{ by symmetry of } A.
\end{aligned}
$$

With this simplification, to minimize g with respect to α, we solve $dg/d\alpha = 0$ to find

$$
\alpha = \frac{\vec{d}^\top(\vec{b} - A\vec{x})}{\vec{d}^\top A\vec{d}}.
$$

For gradient descent, we chose $\vec{d}_k = \vec{b} - A\vec{x}_k$, so α_k takes the form

$$
\alpha_k = \frac{\|\vec{d}_k\|_2^2}{\vec{d}_k^\top A\vec{d}_k}.
$$

Since A is positive definite, $\alpha_k > 0$ by definition. This formula leads to the iterative gradient descent algorithm for solving $A\vec{x} = \vec{b}$ shown in Figure 11.1. Unlike generic line search, for this problem the choice of α in each iteration is optimal.

11.1.2 Convergence

By construction, gradient descent decreases $f(\vec{x}_k)$ in each step. Even so, we have not shown that the algorithm approaches the minimum possible $f(\vec{x}_k)$, nor we have been able to characterize how many iterations we should run to reach a reasonable level of confidence that $A\vec{x}_k \approx \vec{b}$. One way to understand the convergence of the gradient descent algorithm for our choice of f is to examine the change in backward error from iteration to iteration; we will follow the argument in [38] and elsewhere.

Suppose $\vec{x}^*$ satisfies $A\vec{x}^* = \vec{b}$ exactly. Then, the change in backward error in iteration k is given by

$$R_k \equiv \frac{f(\vec{x}_k) - f(\vec{x}^*)}{f(\vec{x}_{k-1}) - f(\vec{x}^*)}.$$

Bounding $R_k < \beta < 1$ for some fixed β (possibly depending on A) would imply $f(\vec{x}_k) - f(\vec{x}^*) \to 0$ as $k \to \infty$, showing that the gradient descent algorithm converges.

For convenience, we can expand $f(\vec{x}_k)$:

$$f(\vec{x}_k) = f(\vec{x}_{k-1} + \alpha_k \vec{d}_k) \text{ by our iterative scheme}$$

$$= \frac{1}{2}(\vec{x}_{k-1} + \alpha_k \vec{d}_k)^\top A(\vec{x}_{k-1} + \alpha_k \vec{d}_k) - \vec{b}^\top (\vec{x}_{k-1} + \alpha_k \vec{d}_k) + c$$

$$= f(\vec{x}_{k-1}) + \alpha_k \vec{d}_k^\top A \vec{x}_{k-1} + \frac{1}{2}\alpha_k^2 \vec{d}_k^\top A \vec{d}_k - \alpha_k \vec{b}^\top \vec{d}_k \text{ by definition of } f$$

$$= f(\vec{x}_{k-1}) + \alpha_k \vec{d}_k^\top (\vec{b} - \vec{d}_k) + \frac{1}{2}\alpha_k^2 \vec{d}_k^\top A \vec{d}_k - \alpha_k \vec{b}^\top \vec{d}_k \text{ since } \vec{d}_k = \vec{b} - A\vec{x}_{k-1}$$

$$= f(\vec{x}_{k-1}) - \alpha_k \vec{d}_k^\top \vec{d}_k + \frac{1}{2}\alpha_k^2 \vec{d}_k^\top A \vec{d}_k \text{ since the remaining terms cancel}$$

$$= f(\vec{x}_{k-1}) - \frac{\vec{d}_k^\top \vec{d}_k}{\vec{d}_k^\top A \vec{d}_k}(\vec{d}_k^\top \vec{d}_k) + \frac{1}{2}\left(\frac{\vec{d}_k^\top \vec{d}_k}{\vec{d}_k^\top A \vec{d}_k}\right)^2 \vec{d}_k^\top A \vec{d}_k \text{ by definition of } \alpha_k$$

$$= f(\vec{x}_{k-1}) - \frac{(\vec{d}_k^\top \vec{d}_k)^2}{2\vec{d}_k^\top A \vec{d}_k}.$$

We can use this formula to find an alternative expression for the backward error R_k:

$$R_k = \frac{f(\vec{x}_{k-1}) - \frac{(\vec{d}_k^\top \vec{d}_k)^2}{2\vec{d}_k^\top A \vec{d}_k} - f(\vec{x}^*)}{f(\vec{x}_{k-1}) - f(\vec{x}^*)} \text{ by the expansion of } f(\vec{x}_k)$$

$$= 1 - \frac{(\vec{d}_k^\top \vec{d}_k)^2}{2\vec{d}_k^\top A \vec{d}_k (f(\vec{x}_{k-1}) - f(\vec{x}^*))}.$$

To simplify the difference in the denominator, we can use $\vec{x}^* = A^{-1}\vec{b}$ to write:

$$f(\vec{x}_{k-1}) - f(\vec{x}^*) = \left[\frac{1}{2}\vec{x}_{k-1}^\top A\vec{x}_{k-1} - \vec{b}^\top \vec{x}_{k-1} + c\right] - \left[\frac{1}{2}(\vec{x}^*)^\top \vec{b} - \vec{b}^\top \vec{x}^* + c\right]$$

$$= \frac{1}{2}\vec{x}_{k-1}^\top A\vec{x}_{k-1} - \vec{b}^\top \vec{x}_{k-1} + \frac{1}{2}\vec{b}^\top A^{-1}\vec{b} \text{ again since } \vec{x}^* = A^{-1}\vec{b}$$

$$= \frac{1}{2}(A\vec{x}_{k-1} - \vec{b})^\top A^{-1}(A\vec{x}_{k-1} - \vec{b}) \text{ by symmetry of } A$$

$$= \frac{1}{2}\vec{d}_k^\top A^{-1}\vec{d}_k \text{ by definition of } \vec{d}_k.$$

Plugging this expression into our simplified formula for R_k shows:

$$R_k = 1 - \frac{(\vec{d}_k^\top \vec{d}_k)^2}{\vec{d}_k^\top A \vec{d}_k \cdot \vec{d}_k^\top A^{-1}\vec{d}_k}$$

$$= 1 - \frac{\vec{d}_k^\top \vec{d}_k}{\vec{d}_k^\top A \vec{d}_k} \cdot \frac{\vec{d}_k^\top \vec{d}_k}{\vec{d}_k^\top A^{-1}\vec{d}_k}$$

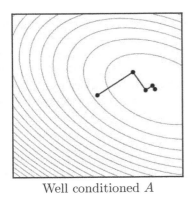

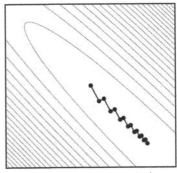

Well conditioned A Poorly conditioned A

Figure 11.2 Gradient descent starting from the origin $\vec{0}$ (at the center) on $f(\vec{x}) = \frac{1}{2}\vec{x}^\top A\vec{x} - \vec{b}^\top \vec{x} + c$ for two choices of A. Each figure shows level sets of $f(\vec{x})$ as well as iterates of gradient descent connected by line segments.

$$\leq 1 - \left(\min_{\|\vec{d}\|=1} \frac{1}{\vec{d}^\top A\vec{d}} \right) \left(\min_{\|\vec{d}\|=1} \frac{1}{\vec{d}^\top A^{-1}\vec{d}} \right) \text{ since this makes the second term smaller}$$

$$= 1 - \left(\max_{\|\vec{d}\|=1} \vec{d}^\top A\vec{d} \right)^{-1} \left(\max_{\|\vec{d}\|=1} \vec{d}^\top A^{-1}\vec{d} \right)^{-1}$$

$$= 1 - \frac{\sigma_{\min}}{\sigma_{\max}} \text{ where } \sigma_{\min}, \sigma_{\max} \text{ are the minimum/maximum singular values of } A$$

$$= 1 - \frac{1}{\text{cond } A}.$$

Here, we assume the condition number $\text{cond } A$ is computed with respect to the two-norm of A. It took a considerable amount of algebra, but we proved an important fact:

Convergence of gradient descent on f depends on the conditioning of A.

That is, the better conditioned A is, the faster gradient descent will converge. Additionally, since $\text{cond } A \geq 1$, we know that gradient descent converges *unconditionally* to $\vec{x}^*$, although convergence can be slow when A is poorly conditioned.

Figure 11.2 illustrates the behavior of gradient descent for well and poorly conditioned matrices A. When the eigenvalues of A have a wide spread, A is poorly conditioned and gradient descent struggles to find the minimum of our quadratic function f, zig-zagging along the energy landscape.

11.2 CONJUGATE GRADIENTS

Solving $A\vec{x} = \vec{b}$ for dense $A \in \mathbb{R}^{n \times n}$ takes $O(n^3)$ time using Gaussian elimination. Reexamining gradient descent from §11.1.1 above, we see that in the dense case each iteration takes $O(n^2)$ time, since we must compute matrix-vector products between A and $\vec{x}_{k-1}, \vec{d}_k$. So, if gradient descent takes more than n iterations, from a timing standpoint we might as well have used Gaussian elimination, which would have recovered the *exact* solution in the same amount of time. Unfortunately, gradient descent may never reach the exact solution $\vec{x}^*$ in a finite number of iterations, and in poorly conditioned cases it can take a huge number of iterations to approximate $\vec{x}^*$ well.

For this reason, we will design the *conjugate gradients* (CG) algorithm, which is *guaranteed* to converge in at most n steps, preserving $O(n^3)$ worst-case timing for solving linear systems. We also will find that this algorithm exhibits better convergence properties overall, often making it preferable to gradient descent even if we do not run it to completion.

11.2.1 Motivation

Our derivation of the conjugate gradients algorithm is motivated by writing the energy functional $f(\vec{x})$ in an alternative form. Suppose we knew the solution $\vec{x}^*$ to $A\vec{x}^* = \vec{b}$. Then, we could write:

$$f(\vec{x}) = \frac{1}{2}\vec{x}^\top A\vec{x} - \vec{b}^\top \vec{x} + c \text{ by definition}$$

$$= \frac{1}{2}(\vec{x} - \vec{x}^*)^\top A(\vec{x} - \vec{x}^*) + \vec{x}^\top A\vec{x}^* - \frac{1}{2}(\vec{x}^*)^\top A\vec{x}^* - \vec{b}^\top \vec{x} + c$$

$$\text{by adding and subtracting the same terms}$$

$$= \frac{1}{2}(\vec{x} - \vec{x}^*)^\top A(\vec{x} - \vec{x}^*) + \vec{x}^\top \vec{b} - \frac{1}{2}(\vec{x}^*)^\top \vec{b} - \vec{b}^\top \vec{x} + c \text{ since } A\vec{x}^* = \vec{b}$$

$$= \frac{1}{2}(\vec{x} - \vec{x}^*)^\top A(\vec{x} - \vec{x}^*) + \text{const. since the } \vec{x}^\top \vec{b} \text{ terms cancel.}$$

Thus, up to a constant shift, f is the same as the product $\frac{1}{2}(\vec{x} - \vec{x}^*)^\top A(\vec{x} - \vec{x}^*)$. In practice, we do not know $\vec{x}^*$, but this observation shows us the nature of f: It measures the distance from $\vec{x}$ to $\vec{x}^*$ with respect to the "A-norm" $\|\vec{v}\|_A^2 \equiv \vec{v}^\top A\vec{v}$.

Since A is symmetric and positive definite, even if it might be slow to compute algorithmically, we know from §4.2.1 that A admits a Cholesky factorization $A = LL^\top$. With this factorization, f takes a nicer form:

$$f(\vec{x}) = \frac{1}{2}\|L^\top(\vec{x} - \vec{x}^*)\|_2^2 + \text{const.}$$

From this form of $f(\vec{x})$, we now know that the A-norm truly measures a distance between $\vec{x}$ and $\vec{x}^*$.

Define $\vec{y} \equiv L^\top \vec{x}$ and $\vec{y}^* \equiv L^\top \vec{x}^*$. After this change of variables, we are minimizing $\bar{f}(\vec{y}) \equiv \|\vec{y} - \vec{y}^*\|_2^2$. Optimizing $\bar{f}$ would be easy if we knew L and $\vec{y}^*$ (take $\vec{y} = \vec{y}^*$), but to eventually remove the need for L we consider the possibility of minimizing $\bar{f}$ using only line searches derived in §11.1.1; from this point on, we will assume that we use the optimal step α for this search rather than any other procedure.

We make an observation about minimizing our simplified function $\bar{f}$ using line searches, illustrated in Figure 11.3:

Proposition 11.1. Suppose $\{\vec{w}_1, \ldots, \vec{w}_n\}$ are orthogonal in $\mathbb{R}^n$. Then, $\bar{f}$ is minimized in at most n steps by line searching in direction $\vec{w}_1$, then direction $\vec{w}_2$, and so on.

Proof. Take the columns of $Q \in \mathbb{R}^{n \times n}$ to be the vectors $\vec{w}_i$; Q is an orthogonal matrix. Since Q is orthogonal, we can write $\bar{f}(\vec{y}) = \|\vec{y} - \vec{y}^*\|_2^2 = \|Q^\top \vec{y} - Q^\top \vec{y}^*\|_2^2$; in other words, we rotate so that $\vec{w}_1$ is the first standard basis vector, $\vec{w}_2$ is the second, and so on. If we write $\vec{z} \equiv Q^\top \vec{y}$ and $\vec{z}^* \equiv Q^\top \vec{y}^*$, then after the first iteration we must have $z_1 = z_1^*$, after the second iteration $z_2 = z_2^*$, and so on. After n steps we reach $z_n = z_n^*$, yielding the desired result. □

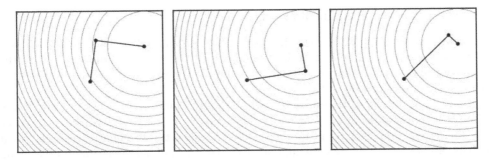

Figure 11.3 Searching along *any* two orthogonal directions minimizes $\bar{f}(\vec{y}) = \|\vec{y} - \vec{y}^*\|_2^2$ over $\vec{y} \in \mathbb{R}^2$. Each example in this figure has the same starting point but searches along a different pair of orthogonal directions; in the end they all reach the same optimal point.

So, optimizing $\bar{f}$ can be accomplished via n line searches so long as those searches are in *orthogonal* directions.

All we did to pass from f to $\bar{f}$ is change coordinates using $L^\top$. Linear transformations take straight lines to straight lines, so line search on $\bar{f}$ along some vector $\vec{w}$ is equivalent to line search along $(L^\top)^{-1}\vec{w}$ on the original quadratic function f. Conversely, if we do n line searches on f in directions $\vec{v}_i$ such that $L^\top \vec{v}_i \equiv \vec{w}_i$ are orthogonal, then by Proposition 11.1 we must have found $\vec{x}^*$. The condition $\vec{w}_i \cdot \vec{w}_j = 0$ can be simplified:

$$0 = \vec{w}_i \cdot \vec{w}_j = (L^\top \vec{v}_i)^\top (L^\top \vec{v}_j) = \vec{v}_i^\top (LL^\top)\vec{v}_j = \vec{v}_i^\top A\vec{v}_j.$$

We have just argued a corollary to Proposition 11.1. Define *conjugate* vectors as follows:

Definition 11.1 (*A*-conjugate vectors). Two vectors $\vec{v}, \vec{w}$ are *A-conjugate* if $\vec{v}^\top A\vec{w} = 0$.

Then, we have shown how to use Proposition 11.1 to optimize f rather than $\bar{f}$:

Proposition 11.2. Suppose $\{\vec{v}_1, \ldots, \vec{v}_n\}$ are *A*-conjugate. Then, f is minimized in at most n steps by line search in direction $\vec{v}_1$, then direction $\vec{v}_2$, and so on.

Inspired by this proposition, the conjugate gradients algorithm generates and searches along *A*-conjugate directions rather than moving along $-\nabla f$. This change might appear somewhat counterintuitive: Conjugate gradients does not necessarily move along the steepest descent direction in each iteration, but rather constructs a *set* of search directions satisfying a global criterion to avoid repeating work. This setup guarantees convergence in a finite number of iterations and acknowledges the structure of f in terms of $\bar{f}$ discussed above.

We motivated the use of *A*-conjugate directions by their orthogonality after applying $L^\top$ from the factorization $A = LL^\top$. From this standpoint, we are dealing with two dot products: $\vec{x}_i \cdot \vec{x}_j$ and $\vec{y}_i \cdot \vec{y}_j \equiv (L^\top \vec{x}_i) \cdot (L^\top \vec{x}_j) = x_i^\top LL^\top \vec{x}_j = \vec{x}_i^\top A\vec{x}_j$. These two products will figure into our subsequent discussion, so for clarity we will denote the "*A*-inner product" as

$$\langle \vec{u}, \vec{v} \rangle_A \equiv (L^\top \vec{u}) \cdot (L^\top \vec{v}) = \vec{u}^\top A\vec{v}.$$

11.2.2 Suboptimality of Gradient Descent

If we can find n A-conjugate search directions, then we can solve $A\vec{x} = \vec{b}$ in n steps via line searches along these directions. What remains is to uncover a formula for finding these directions efficiently. To do so, we will examine one more property of gradient descent that will inspire a more refined algorithm.

Suppose we are at $\vec{x}_k$ during an iterative line search method on $f(\vec{x})$; we will call the direction of steepest descent of f at $\vec{x}_k$ the *residual* $\vec{r}_k \equiv \vec{b} - A\vec{x}_k$. We may not decide to do a line search along $\vec{r}_k$ as in gradient descent, since the gradient directions are not necessarily A-conjugate. So, generalizing slightly, we will find $\vec{x}_{k+1}$ via line search along a yet-undetermined direction $\vec{v}_{k+1}$.

From our derivation of gradient descent in §11.1.1, even if $\vec{v}_{k+1} \neq \vec{r}_k$, we should choose $\vec{x}_{k+1} = \vec{x}_k + \alpha_{k+1}\vec{v}_{k+1}$, where

$$\alpha_{k+1} = \frac{\vec{v}_{k+1}^\top \vec{r}_k}{\vec{v}_{k+1}^\top A\vec{v}_{k+1}}.$$

Applying this expansion of $\vec{x}_{k+1}$, we can write an update formula for the residual:

$$\vec{r}_{k+1} = \vec{b} - A\vec{x}_{k+1}$$
$$= \vec{b} - A(\vec{x}_k + \alpha_{k+1}\vec{v}_{k+1}) \text{ by definition of } \vec{x}_{k+1}$$
$$= (\vec{b} - A\vec{x}_k) - \alpha_{k+1}A\vec{v}_{k+1}$$
$$= \vec{r}_k - \alpha_{k+1}A\vec{v}_{k+1} \text{ by definition of } \vec{r}_k.$$

This formula holds regardless of our choice of $\vec{v}_{k+1}$ and can be applied to any iterative line search method on f.

In the case of gradient descent, we chose $\vec{v}_{k+1} \equiv \vec{r}_k$, giving a recurrence relation $\vec{r}_{k+1} = \vec{r}_k - \alpha_{k+1}A\vec{r}_k$. This formula inspires an instructive proposition:

Proposition 11.3. When performing gradient descent on f, $\text{span}\{\vec{r}_0, \ldots, \vec{r}_k\} = \text{span}\{\vec{r}_0, A\vec{r}_0, \ldots, A^k\vec{r}_0\}$.

Proof. This statement follows inductively from our formula for $\vec{r}_{k+1}$ above. □

The structure we are uncovering is beginning to look a lot like the Krylov subspace methods mentioned in Chapter 6: This is not a coincidence!

Gradient descent gets to $\vec{x}_k$ by moving along $\vec{r}_0$, then $\vec{r}_1$, and so on through $\vec{r}_k$. In the end we know that the iterate $\vec{x}_k$ of gradient descent on f lies somewhere in the plane $\vec{x}_0 + \text{span}\{\vec{r}_0, \vec{r}_1, \ldots, \vec{r}_{k-1}\} = \vec{x}_0 + \text{span}\{\vec{r}_0, A\vec{r}_0, \ldots, A^{k-1}\vec{r}_0\}$, by Proposition 11.3. Unfortunately, it is *not* true that if we run gradient descent, the iterate $\vec{x}_k$ is optimal in this subspace. In other words, it can be the case that

$$\vec{x}_k - \vec{x}_0 \neq \underset{\vec{v} \in \text{span}\{\vec{r}_0, A\vec{r}_0, \ldots, A^{k-1}\vec{r}_0\}}{\arg\min} f(\vec{x}_0 + \vec{v}).$$

Ideally, switching this inequality to an equality would make sure that generating $\vec{x}_{k+1}$ from $\vec{x}_k$ does not "cancel out" any work done during iterations 1 to $k-1$.

If we reexamine our proof of Proposition 11.1 from this perspective, we can make an observation suggesting how we might use conjugacy to improve gradient descent. Once z_i switches to z_i^*, it never changes in a future iteration. After rotating back from $\vec{z}$ to $\vec{x}$ the following proposition holds:

Proposition 11.4. Take $\vec{x}_k$ to be the k-th iterate of the process from Proposition 11.1 after searching along $\vec{v}_k$. Then,

$$\vec{x}_k - \vec{x}_0 = \underset{\vec{v} \in \operatorname{span}\{\vec{v}_1, \ldots, \vec{v}_k\}}{\arg\min} f(\vec{x}_0 + \vec{v}).$$

In the best of all possible worlds and in an attempt to outdo gradient descent, we might hope to find A-conjugate directions $\{\vec{v}_1, \ldots, \vec{v}_n\}$ such that $\operatorname{span}\{\vec{v}_1, \ldots, \vec{v}_k\} = \operatorname{span}\{\vec{r}_0, A\vec{r}_0, \ldots, A^{k-1}\vec{r}_0\}$ for each k. By the previous two propositions, the resulting iterative scheme would be guaranteed to do no worse than gradient descent even if it is halted early. But, we wish to do so without incurring significant memory demand or computation time. Amazingly, the conjugate gradient algorithm satisfies all these criteria.

11.2.3 Generating A-Conjugate Directions

Given any set of directions spanning $\mathbb{R}^n$, we can make them A-orthogonal using Gram-Schmidt orthogonalization. Explicitly orthogonalizing $\{\vec{r}_0, A\vec{r}_0, A^2\vec{r}_0, \ldots\}$ to find the set of search directions, however, is expensive and would require us to maintain a complete list of directions in memory; this construction likely would exceed the time and memory requirements even of Gaussian elimination. Alternatively, we will reveal one final observation *about* Gram-Schmidt that makes conjugate gradients tractable by generating conjugate directions without an expensive orthogonalization process.

To start, we might write a "method of conjugate directions" using the following iterations:

$$
\begin{array}{ll}
\vec{v}_k \leftarrow A^{k-1}\vec{r}_0 - \sum_{i<k} \frac{\langle A^{k-1}\vec{r}_0, \vec{v}_i \rangle_A}{\langle \vec{v}_i, \vec{v}_i \rangle_A} \vec{v}_i & \triangleright \text{ Explicit Gram-Schmidt} \\
\alpha_k \leftarrow \frac{\vec{v}_k^\top \vec{r}_{k-1}}{\vec{v}_k^\top A \vec{v}_k} & \triangleright \text{ Line search} \\
\vec{x}_k \leftarrow \vec{x}_{k-1} + \alpha_k \vec{v}_k & \triangleright \text{ Update estimate} \\
\vec{r}_k \leftarrow \vec{r}_{k-1} - \alpha_k A \vec{v}_k & \triangleright \text{ Update residual}
\end{array}
$$

Here, we compute the k-th search direction $\vec{v}_k$ by projecting $\vec{v}_1, \ldots, \vec{v}_{k-1}$ out of the vector $A^{k-1}\vec{r}_0$ using the Gram-Schmidt algorithm. This algorithm has the property $\operatorname{span}\{\vec{v}_1, \ldots, \vec{v}_k\} = \operatorname{span}\{\vec{r}_0, A\vec{r}_0, \ldots, A^{k-1}\vec{r}_0\}$ suggested in §11.2.2, but it has two issues:

1. Similar to power iteration for eigenvectors, the power $A^{k-1}\vec{r}_0$ is likely to look mostly like the first eigenvector of A, making projection poorly conditioned when k is large.

2. We have to store $\vec{v}_1, \ldots, \vec{v}_{k-1}$ to compute $\vec{v}_k$, so each iteration needs more memory and time than the last.

We can fix the first issue in a relatively straightforward manner. Right now, we project the previous search directions out of $A^{k-1}\vec{r}_0$, but in reality we can project out previous directions from *any* vector $\vec{w}$ so long as

$$\vec{w} \in \operatorname{span}\{\vec{r}_0, A\vec{r}_0, \ldots, A^{k-1}\vec{r}_0\} \backslash \operatorname{span}\{\vec{r}_0, A\vec{r}_0, \ldots, A^{k-2}\vec{r}_0\},$$

that is, as long as $\vec{w}$ has some component in the new part of the space.

An alternative choice of $\vec{w}$ in this span is the residual $\vec{r}_{k-1}$. We can check this using the residual update $\vec{r}_k = \vec{r}_{k-1} - \alpha_k A \vec{v}_k$; in this expression, we multiply $\vec{v}_k$ by A, introducing the new power of A that we need. This choice also more closely mimics the gradient descent algorithm, which took $\vec{v}_k = \vec{r}_{k-1}$. We can update our algorithm to use this improved choice:

$$\vec{v}_k \leftarrow \vec{r}_{k-1} - \sum_{i<k} \frac{\langle \vec{r}_{k-1}, \vec{v}_i \rangle_A}{\langle \vec{v}_i, \vec{v}_i \rangle_A} \vec{v}_i \qquad \qquad \triangleright \text{ Gram-Schmidt on residual}$$

$$\alpha_k \leftarrow \frac{\vec{v}_k^\top \vec{r}_{k-1}}{\vec{v}_k^\top A \vec{v}_k} \qquad \qquad \triangleright \text{ Line search}$$

$$\vec{x}_k \leftarrow \vec{x}_{k-1} + \alpha_k \vec{v}_k \qquad \qquad \triangleright \text{ Update estimate}$$

$$\vec{r}_k \leftarrow \vec{r}_{k-1} - \alpha_k A \vec{v}_k \qquad \qquad \triangleright \text{ Update residual}$$

Now we do not do arithmetic with the poorly conditioned vector $A^{k-1}\vec{r}_0$ but still have the "memory" problem above since the sum in the first step is over $k-1$ vectors.

A surprising observation about the residual Gram-Schmidt projection above is that most terms in the sum are exactly zero! This observation allows each iteration of conjugate gradients to be carried out without increasing memory requirements. We memorialize this result in a proposition:

Proposition 11.5. In the second "conjugate direction" method above, $\langle \vec{r}_k, \vec{v}_\ell \rangle_A = 0$ for all $\ell < k$.

Proof. We proceed inductively. There is nothing to prove for the base case $k = 1$, so assume $k > 1$ and that the result holds for all $k' < k$. By the residual update formula,

$$\langle \vec{r}_k, \vec{v}_\ell \rangle_A = \langle \vec{r}_{k-1}, \vec{v}_\ell \rangle_A - \alpha_k \langle A \vec{v}_k, \vec{v}_\ell \rangle_A = \langle \vec{r}_{k-1}, \vec{v}_\ell \rangle_A - \alpha_k \langle \vec{v}_k, A \vec{v}_\ell \rangle_A,$$

where the second equality follows from symmetry of A.

First, suppose $\ell < k - 1$. Then the first term of the difference above is zero by induction. Furthermore, by construction $A \vec{v}_\ell \in \text{span}\{\vec{v}_1, \ldots, \vec{v}_{\ell+1}\}$, so since we have constructed our search directions to be A-conjugate, the second term must be zero as well.

To conclude the proof, we consider the case $\ell = k - 1$. By the residual update formula,

$$A \vec{v}_{k-1} = \frac{1}{\alpha_{k-1}} (\vec{r}_{k-2} - \vec{r}_{k-1}).$$

Pre-multiplying by $\vec{r}_k^\top$ shows

$$\langle \vec{r}_k, \vec{v}_{k-1} \rangle_A = \frac{1}{\alpha_{k-1}} \vec{r}_k^\top (\vec{r}_{k-2} - \vec{r}_{k-1}).$$

The difference $\vec{r}_{k-2} - \vec{r}_{k-1}$ is in the subspace $\text{span}\{\vec{r}_0, A\vec{r}_0, \ldots, A^{k-1}\vec{r}_0\}$, by the residual update formula. Proposition 11.4 shows that $\vec{x}_k$ is optimal in this subspace. Since $\vec{r}_k = -\nabla f(\vec{x}_k)$, this implies that we must have $\vec{r}_k \perp \text{span}\{\vec{r}_0, A\vec{r}_0, \ldots, A^{k-1}\vec{r}_0\}$, since otherwise there would exist a direction in the subspace to move from $\vec{x}_k$ to decrease f. In particular, this shows the inner product above $\langle \vec{r}_k, \vec{v}_{k-1} \rangle_A = 0$, as desired. □

Our proof above shows that we can find a new direction $\vec{v}_k$ as follows:

$$\vec{v}_k = \vec{r}_{k-1} - \sum_{i<k} \frac{\langle \vec{r}_{k-1}, \vec{v}_i \rangle_A}{\langle \vec{v}_i, \vec{v}_i \rangle_A} \vec{v}_i \quad \text{by the Gram-Schmidt formula}$$

$$= \vec{r}_{k-1} - \frac{\langle \vec{r}_{k-1}, \vec{v}_{k-1} \rangle_A}{\langle \vec{v}_{k-1}, \vec{v}_{k-1} \rangle_A} \vec{v}_{k-1} \quad \text{because the remaining terms vanish.}$$

Since the summation over i disappears, the cost of computing $\vec{v}_k$ has no dependence on k.

11.2.4   Formulating the Conjugate Gradients Algorithm

Now that we can obtain A-conjugate search directions with relatively little computational effort, we apply this strategy to formulate the conjugate gradients algorithm, with full pseudocode in Figure 11.4(a):

$$
\begin{aligned}
&\vec{v}_k \leftarrow \vec{r}_{k-1} - \frac{\langle \vec{r}_{k-1}, \vec{v}_{k-1} \rangle_A}{\langle \vec{v}_{k-1}, \vec{v}_{k-1} \rangle_A} \vec{v}_{k-1} && \triangleright \text{ Update search direction} \\
&\alpha_k \leftarrow \frac{\vec{v}_k^\top \vec{r}_{k-1}}{\vec{v}_k^\top A \vec{v}_k} && \triangleright \text{ Line search} \\
&\vec{x}_k \leftarrow \vec{x}_{k-1} + \alpha_k \vec{v}_k && \triangleright \text{ Update estimate} \\
&\vec{r}_k \leftarrow \vec{r}_{k-1} - \alpha_k A \vec{v}_k && \triangleright \text{ Update residual}
\end{aligned}
$$

This iterative scheme is only a minor adjustment to the gradient descent algorithm but has many desirable properties by construction:

- $f(\vec{x}_k)$ is upper-bounded by that of the k-th iterate of gradient descent.

- The algorithm converges to $\vec{x}^*$ in at most n steps, as illustrated in Figure 11.5.

- At each step, the iterate $\vec{x}_k$ is optimal in the subspace spanned by the first k search directions.

In the interests of squeezing maximal numerical quality out of conjugate gradients, we can simplify the numerics of the formulation in Figure 11.4(a). For instance, if we plug the search direction update into the formula for α_k, by orthogonality we know

$$
\alpha_k = \frac{\vec{r}_{k-1}^\top \vec{r}_{k-1}}{\vec{v}_k^\top A \vec{v}_k}.
$$

The numerator of this fraction now is guaranteed to be nonnegative even when using finite-precision arithmetic.

Similarly, we can define a constant β_k to split the search direction update into two steps:

$$
\beta_k \equiv -\frac{\langle \vec{r}_{k-1}, \vec{v}_{k-1} \rangle_A}{\langle \vec{v}_{k-1}, \vec{v}_{k-1} \rangle_A}
$$

$$
\vec{v}_k = \vec{r}_{k-1} + \beta_k \vec{v}_{k-1}.
$$

We can simplify the formula for β_k:

$$
\begin{aligned}
\beta_k &= -\frac{\vec{r}_{k-1} A \vec{v}_{k-1}}{\vec{v}_{k-1}^\top A \vec{v}_{k-1}} && \text{by definition of } \langle \cdot, \cdot \rangle_A \\
&= -\frac{\vec{r}_{k-1}^\top (\vec{r}_{k-2} - \vec{r}_{k-1})}{\alpha_{k-1} \vec{v}_{k-1}^\top A \vec{v}_{k-1}} && \text{since } \vec{r}_k = \vec{r}_{k-1} - \alpha_k A \vec{v}_k \\
&= \frac{\vec{r}_{k-1}^\top \vec{r}_{k-1}}{\alpha_{k-1} \vec{v}_{k-1}^\top A \vec{v}_{k-1}} && \text{by a calculation below} \\
&= \frac{\vec{r}_{k-1}^\top \vec{r}_{k-1}}{\vec{r}_{k-2}^\top \vec{r}_{k-2}} && \text{by our last formula for } \alpha_k.
\end{aligned}
$$

This expression guarantees that $\beta_k \geq 0$, a property that might not have held after rounding using the original formula. We have one remaining calculation below:

$$
\vec{r}_{k-2}^\top \vec{r}_{k-1} = \vec{r}_{k-2}^\top (\vec{r}_{k-2} - \alpha_{k-1} A \vec{v}_{k-1}) \quad \text{by the residual update formula}
$$

function Conjugate-Grad-1$(A, \vec{b}, \vec{x}_0)$
$\quad \vec{x} \leftarrow \vec{x}_0$
$\quad \vec{r} \leftarrow \vec{b} - A\vec{x}$
$\quad \vec{v} \leftarrow \vec{r}$
$\quad$**for** $k \leftarrow 1, 2, 3, \ldots$
$\qquad \alpha \leftarrow \frac{\vec{v}^\top \vec{r}}{\vec{v}^\top A \vec{v}}$ $\qquad$ ▷ Line search
$\qquad \vec{x} \leftarrow \vec{x} + \alpha \vec{v}$ $\qquad$ ▷ Update estimate
$\qquad \vec{r} \leftarrow \vec{r} - \alpha A \vec{v}$ $\qquad$ ▷ Update residual
$\qquad$**if** $\|\vec{r}\|_2^2 < \varepsilon \|\vec{r}_0\|_2^2$ **then**
$\qquad\quad$**return** $x^* = \vec{x}$
$\qquad \vec{v} \leftarrow \vec{r} - \frac{\langle \vec{r}, \vec{v} \rangle_A}{\langle \vec{v}, \vec{v} \rangle_A} \vec{v}$ $\quad$ ▷ Search direction

function Conjugate-Grad-2$(A, \vec{b}, \vec{x}_0)$
$\quad \vec{x} \leftarrow \vec{x}_0$
$\quad \vec{r} \leftarrow \vec{b} - A\vec{x}$
$\quad \vec{v} \leftarrow \vec{r}$
$\quad \beta \leftarrow 0$
$\quad$**for** $k \leftarrow 1, 2, 3, \ldots$
$\qquad \vec{v} \leftarrow \vec{r} + \beta \vec{v}$ $\qquad$ ▷ Search direction
$\qquad \alpha \leftarrow \frac{\|\vec{r}\|_2^2}{\vec{v}^\top A \vec{v}}$ $\qquad$ ▷ Line search
$\qquad \vec{x} \leftarrow \vec{x} + \alpha \vec{v}$ $\qquad$ ▷ Update estimate
$\qquad \vec{r}_{\text{old}} \leftarrow \vec{r}$ $\qquad$ ▷ Save old residual
$\qquad \vec{r} \leftarrow \vec{r} - \alpha A \vec{v}$ $\qquad$ ▷ Update residual
$\qquad$**if** $\|\vec{r}\|_2^2 < \varepsilon \|\vec{r}_0\|_2^2$ **then**
$\qquad\quad$**return** $x^* = \vec{x}$
$\qquad \beta \leftarrow \|\vec{r}\|_2^2 / \|\vec{r}_{\text{old}}\|_2^2$ $\quad$ ▷ Direction step

Figure 11.4 Two equivalent formulations of the conjugate gradients algorithm for solving $A\vec{x} = \vec{b}$ when A is symmetric and positive definite. The initial guess $\vec{x}_0$ can be $\vec{0}$ in the absence of a better estimate.

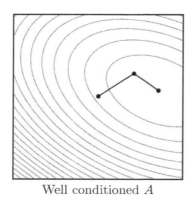
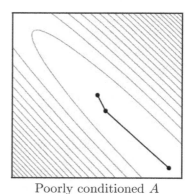

Well conditioned A $\qquad\qquad$ Poorly conditioned A

Figure 11.5 The conjugate gradients algorithm solves both linear systems in Figure 11.2 in two steps.

$$= \vec{r}_{k-2}^{\top}\vec{r}_{k-2} - \frac{\vec{r}_{k-2}^{\top}\vec{r}_{k-2}}{\vec{v}_{k-1}^{\top}A\vec{v}_{k-1}}\vec{r}_{k-2}^{\top}A\vec{v}_{k-1} \text{ by our formula for } \alpha_k$$

$$= \vec{r}_{k-2}^{\top}\vec{r}_{k-2} - \frac{\vec{r}_{k-2}^{\top}\vec{r}_{k-2}}{\vec{v}_{k-1}^{\top}A\vec{v}_{k-1}}\vec{v}_{k-1}^{\top}A\vec{v}_{k-1}$$

by the update for $\vec{v}_k$ and A-conjugacy of the $\vec{v}_k$'s

$$= 0, \text{ as needed.}$$

Our new observations about the iterates of CG provide an alternative but equivalent formulation that can have better numerical properties; it is shown in Figure 11.4(b). Also for numerical reasons, occasionally rather than using the update formula for $\vec{r}_k$ it is advisable to use the residual formula $\vec{r}_k = \vec{b} - A\vec{x}_k$. This requires an extra matrix-vector multiply but repairs numerical "drift" caused by finite-precision rounding. There is no need to store a long list of previous residuals or search directions; conjugate gradients takes a constant amount of space from iteration to iteration.

11.2.5 Convergence and Stopping Conditions

By construction, the conjugate gradients (CG) algorithm is guaranteed to converge as fast as gradient descent on f, while being no harder to implement and having a number of other favorable properties. A detailed discussion of CG convergence is out of the scope of our treatment, but in general the algorithm behaves best on matrices with eigenvalues evenly distributed over a small range.

One rough bound paralleling the estimate in §11.1.2 shows that the CG algorithm satisfies:

$$\frac{f(\vec{x}_k) - f(\vec{x}^*)}{f(\vec{x}_0) - f(\vec{x}^*)} \leq 2\left(\frac{\sqrt{\kappa} - 1}{\sqrt{\kappa} + 1}\right)^k$$

where $\kappa \equiv \text{cond } A$. Broadly speaking, the number of iterations needed for conjugate gradient to reach a given error level usually can be bounded by a function of $\sqrt{\kappa}$, whereas bounds for convergence of gradient descent are proportional to κ.

Conjugate gradients is guaranteed to converge to $\vec{x}^*$ exactly in n steps—m steps if A has $m < n$ unique eigenvalues—but when n is large it may be preferable to stop earlier. The formula for β_k will divide by zero when the residual gets very short, which can cause numerical precision issues near the minimum of f. Thus, in practice CG usually is halted when the ratio $\|\vec{r}_k\|/\|\vec{r}_0\|$ is sufficiently small.

11.3 PRECONDITIONING

We now have two powerful iterative algorithms for solving $A\vec{x} = \vec{b}$ when A is symmetric and positive definite: gradient descent and conjugate gradients. Both converge *unconditionally*, meaning that regardless of the initial guess $\vec{x}_0$, with enough iterations they will get arbitrarily close to the true solution $\vec{x}^*$; conjugate gradients reaches $\vec{x}^*$ exactly in a finite number of iterations. The "clock time" taken to solve $A\vec{x} = \vec{b}$ for both of these methods is proportional to the number of iterations needed to reach $\vec{x}^*$ within an acceptable tolerance, so it makes sense to minimize the number of iterations until convergence.

We characterized the convergence rates of both algorithms in terms of the condition number $\text{cond } A$. The smaller the value of $\text{cond } A$, the less time it should take to solve $A\vec{x} = \vec{b}$. This situation contrasts with Gaussian elimination, which takes the same number of steps regardless of A; what is new here is that the conditioning of A affects not only the quality of the output of iterative methods but also the speed at which $\vec{x}^*$ is approached.

For any invertible matrix P, solving $PA\vec{x} = P\vec{b}$ is equivalent to solving $A\vec{x} = \vec{b}$. The condition number of PA, however, does *not* need to be the same as that of A. In the extreme, if we took $P = A^{-1}$, then conditioning issues would be removed altogether! More generally, suppose $P \approx A^{-1}$. Then, we expect $\operatorname{cond} PA \ll \operatorname{cond} A$, making it advisable to apply P before solving the linear system using iterative methods. In this case, we will call P a *preconditioner*.

While the idea of preconditioning appears attractive, two issues remain:

1. While A may be symmetric and positive definite, the product PA in general will not enjoy these properties.

2. We need to find $P \approx A^{-1}$ that is easier to compute than A^{-1} itself.

We address these issues in the sections below.

11.3.1   CG with Preconditioning

We will focus our discussion of preconditioning on conjugate gradients since it has better convergence properties than gradient descent, although most of our constructions can be paralleled to precondition other iterative linear methods.

Starting from the steps in §11.2.1, the construction of CG fundamentally depended on both the symmetry and positive definiteness of A. Hence, running CG on PA usually will not converge, since it may violate these assumptions. Suppose, however, that the preconditioner P is itself symmetric and positive definite. This is a reasonable assumption since the inverse A^{-1} of a symmetric, positive definite matrix A is itself symmetric and positive definite. Under this assumption, we can write a Cholesky factorization of the inverse $P^{-1} = EE^\top$. Then, $E^{-1}AE^{-\top} \approx E^{-1}P^{-1}E^{-\top} = E^{-1}EE^\top E^{-\top} = I_{n \times n}$. In words, we expect $E^{-1}AE^{-\top}$ to be well-conditioned when PA is well-conditioned. This intuition is partially confirmed by the following observation:

┃ **Proposition 11.6.** PA and $E^{-1}AE^{-\top}$ have the same eigenvalues.

Proof. Suppose $E^{-1}AE^{-\top}\vec{x} = \lambda\vec{x}$; notice the vectors $\vec{x}$ span $\mathbb{R}^n$ because $E^{-1}AE^{-\top}$ is symmetric. By construction, $P^{-1} = EE^\top$, so $P = E^{-\top}E^{-1}$. If we pre-multiply both sides of the eigenvector expression by $E^{-\top}$, we find $PAE^{-\top}\vec{x} = \lambda E^{-\top}\vec{x}$. Defining $\vec{y} \equiv E^{-\top}\vec{x}$ shows $PA\vec{y} = \lambda\vec{y}$. Hence, each eigenvector $\vec{x}$ of $E^{-1}AE^{-\top}$ provides a corresponding eigenvector $\vec{y}$ of PA, showing that PA and $E^{-1}AE^{-\top}$ both have full eigenspaces and identical eigenvalues. □

This proposition implies that if we do CG on the symmetric positive definite matrix $E^{-1}AE^{-\top}$, we will receive similar conditioning benefits enjoyed by PA. Imitating the construction in Proposition 11.6 above, we can carry out our new solve for $\vec{y} = E^\top\vec{x}$ in two steps:

1. Solve $E^{-1}AE^{-\top}\vec{y} = E^{-1}\vec{b}$ for $\vec{y}$ using the CG algorithm.

2. Multiply to find $\vec{x} = E^{-\top}\vec{y}$.

Evaluating E and its inverse would be integral to this strategy, but doing so can induce fill and take too much time. By modifying the steps of CG for the first step above, however, we can make this factorization unnecessary.

If we had computed E, we could perform step 1 using CG as follows:

$$\beta_k \leftarrow \frac{\vec{r}_{k-1}^{\top}\vec{r}_{k-1}}{\vec{r}_{k-2}^{\top}\vec{r}_{k-2}} \qquad\qquad \triangleright \text{ Update search direction}$$

$$\vec{v}_k \leftarrow \vec{r}_{k-1} + \beta_k \vec{v}_{k-1}$$

$$\alpha_k \leftarrow \frac{\vec{r}_{k-1}^{\top}\vec{r}_{k-1}}{\vec{v}_k^{\top}E^{-1}AE^{-\top}\vec{v}_k} \qquad\qquad \triangleright \text{ Line search}$$

$$\vec{y}_k \leftarrow \vec{y}_{k-1} + \alpha_k \vec{v}_k \qquad\qquad \triangleright \text{ Update estimate}$$

$$\vec{r}_k \leftarrow \vec{r}_{k-1} - \alpha_k E^{-1}AE^{-\top}\vec{v}_k \qquad\qquad \triangleright \text{ Update residual}$$

This iteration will converge according to the conditioning of $E^{-1}AE^{-\top}$.

Define $\tilde{r}_k \equiv E\vec{r}_k$, $\tilde{v}_k \equiv E^{-\top}\vec{v}_k$, and $\vec{x}_k \equiv E^{-\top}\vec{y}_k$. By the relationship $P = E^{-\top}E^{-1}$, we can rewrite our preconditioned conjugate gradients iteration completely in terms of these new variables:

$$\beta_k \leftarrow \frac{\tilde{r}_{k-1}^{\top}P\tilde{r}_{k-1}}{\tilde{r}_{k-2}^{\top}P\tilde{r}_{k-2}} \qquad\qquad \triangleright \text{ Update search direction}$$

$$\tilde{v}_k \leftarrow P\tilde{r}_{k-1} + \beta_k \tilde{v}_{k-1}$$

$$\alpha_k \leftarrow \frac{\tilde{r}_{k-1}^{\top}P\tilde{r}_{k-1}}{\tilde{v}_k^{\top}A\tilde{v}_k} \qquad\qquad \triangleright \text{ Line search}$$

$$\vec{x}_k \leftarrow \vec{x}_{k-1} + \alpha_k \tilde{v}_k \qquad\qquad \triangleright \text{ Update estimate}$$

$$\tilde{r}_k \leftarrow \tilde{r}_{k-1} - \alpha_k A\tilde{v}_k \qquad\qquad \triangleright \text{ Update residual}$$

This iteration does not depend on the Cholesky factorization of P^{-1}, but instead can be carried out using only P and A. By the substitutions above, $\vec{x}_k \to \vec{x}^*$, and this scheme enjoys the benefits of preconditioning without needing to compute the Cholesky factorization of P.

As a side note, more general preconditioning can be carried out by replacing A with PAQ for a second matrix Q, although this second matrix will require additional computations to apply. This extension presents a common trade-off: If a preconditioner takes too long to apply in each iteration of CG, it may not be worth the reduced number of iterations.

11.3.2 Common Preconditioners

Finding good preconditioners in practice is as much an art as it is a science. Finding an effective approximation P of A^{-1} depends on the structure of A, the particular application at hand, and so on. Even rough approximations, however, can help convergence, so rarely do applications of CG appear that do *not* use a preconditioner.

The best strategy for finding P often is application-specific, and generally it is necessary to test a few possibilities for P before settling on the most effective option. A few common generic preconditioners include the following:

- A *diagonal* (or "*Jacobi*") preconditioner takes P to be the matrix obtained by inverting diagonal elements of A; that is, P is the diagonal matrix with entries $1/a_{ii}$. This preconditioner can alleviate nonuniform scaling from row to row, which is a common cause of poor conditioning.

- The *sparse approximate inverse* preconditioner is formulated by solving a subproblem $\min_{P \in S} \|AP - I\|_{\text{Fro}}$, where P is restricted to be in a set S of matrices over which it is less difficult to optimize such an objective. For instance, a common constraint is to prescribe a sparsity pattern for P, e.g., that it only has nonzeros on its diagonal or where A has nonzeros.

- The *incomplete Cholesky* preconditioner factors $A \approx L_* L_*^\top$ and then approximates A^{-1} by carrying out forward- and back-substitution. For instance, a popular heuristic involves going through the steps of Cholesky factorization but only saving the parts of L in positions (i, j) where $a_{ij} \neq 0$.

- The nonzero values in A can be used to construct a graph with edge (i, j) whenever $a_{ij} \neq 0$. Removing edges in the graph or grouping nodes may disconnect assorted components; the resulting system is block-diagonal after permuting rows and columns and thus can be solved using a sequence of smaller solves. Such a *domain decomposition* can be effective for linear systems arising from differential equations like those considered in Chapter 16.

Some preconditioners come with bounds describing changes to the conditioning of A after replacing it with PA, but for the most part these are heuristic strategies that should be tested and refined.

11.4 OTHER ITERATIVE ALGORITHMS

The algorithms we have developed in this chapter apply to solving $A\vec{x} = \vec{b}$ when A is square, symmetric, and positive definite. We have focused on this case because it appears so often in practice, but there are cases when A is asymmetric, indefinite, or even rectangular. It is out of the scope of our discussion to derive iterative algorithms in each case, since many require some specialized analysis or advanced development (see, e.g., [7, 50, 56, 105]), but we summarize some techniques here:

- *Splitting* methods decompose $A = M - N$ and use the fact that $A\vec{x} = \vec{b}$ is equivalent to $M\vec{x} = N\vec{x} + \vec{b}$. If M is easy to invert, then a fixed-point scheme can be derived by writing $M\vec{x}_k = N\vec{x}_{k-1} + \vec{b}$; these techniques are easy to implement but have convergence depending on the spectrum of the matrix $G = M^{-1}N$ and in particular can diverge when the spectral radius of G is greater than one. One popular choice of M is the diagonal of A. Methods such as *successive over-relaxation* (SOR) weight these two terms for better convergence.

- The *conjugate gradient normal equation residual* (CGNR) method applies the CG algorithm to the normal equations $A^\top A\vec{x} = A^\top \vec{b}$. This method is guaranteed to converge so long as A is full-rank, but convergence can be slow thanks to poor conditioning of $A^\top A$ as in §5.1.

- The *conjugate gradient normal equation error* (CGNE) method similarly solves $AA^\top \vec{y} = \vec{b}$; then, the solution of $A\vec{x} = \vec{b}$ is $A^\top \vec{y}$.

- Methods such as MINRES and SYMMLQ apply to all symmetric matrices A by replacing the quadratic form $f(\vec{x})$ with $g(\vec{x}) \equiv \|\vec{b} - A\vec{x}\|_2^2$ [93]; this function g is minimized at solutions to $A\vec{x} = \vec{b}$ regardless of the definiteness of A.

- Given the poor conditioning of CGNR and CGNE, the LSQR and LSMR algorithms also minimize $g(\vec{x})$ with fewer assumptions on A, in particular allowing for solution of least-squares systems [94, 42].

- Generalized methods including GMRES, QMR, BiCG, CGS, and BiCGStab solve $A\vec{x} = \vec{b}$ with the only caveat that A is square and invertible [106, 44, 40, 115, 126]. They optimize similar energies but often have to store more information about previous iterations and may have to factor intermediate matrices to guarantee convergence with such generality.

- Finally, methods like the *Fletcher-Reeves, Hestenes-Stiefel, Polak-Ribière,* and *Dai-Yuan* algorithms return to the more general problem of minimizing a non-quadratic function f, applying conjugate gradient steps to finding new line search directions [30, 41, 59, 100]. Functions f that are well-approximated by quadratics can be minimized very effectively using these strategies, even though they do not necessarily make use of the Hessian. For instance, the Fletcher-Reeves method replaces the residual in CG iterations with the negative gradient $-\nabla f$.

Most of these algorithms are nearly as easy to implement as CG or gradient descent. Pre-packaged implementations are readily available that only require A and $\vec{b}$ as input; they typically require the end user to implement subroutines for multiplying vectors by A and by $A^\top$, which can be a technical challenge in some cases when A is only known implicitly.

As a rule of thumb, the more general a method is—that is, the fewer the assumptions a method makes on the structure of the matrix A—the more iterations it is likely to need to compensate for this lack of assumptions. This said, there are no hard-and-fast rules that can be applied by examining the elements of A for guessing the most successful iterative scheme.

11.5 EXERCISES

11.1 If we use infinite-precision arithmetic (so rounding is not an issue), can the conjugate gradients algorithm be used to recover *exact* solutions to $A\vec{x} = \vec{b}$ for symmetric positive definite matrices A? Why or why not?

11.2 Suppose $A \in \mathbb{R}^{n \times n}$ is invertible but not symmetric or positive definite.

   (a) Show that $A^\top A$ is symmetric and positive definite.

   (b) Propose a strategy for solving $A\vec{x} = \vec{b}$ using the conjugate gradients algorithm based on your observation in (a).

   (c) How quickly do you expect conjugate gradients to converge in this case? Why?

11.3 Propose a method for preconditioning the gradient descent algorithm from §11.1.1, paralleling the derivation in §11.3.

11.4 In this problem we will derive an iterative method of solving $A\vec{x} = \vec{b}$ via *splitting* [50].

   (a) Suppose we decompose $A = M - N$, where M is invertible. Show that the iterative scheme $\vec{x}_k = M^{-1}(N\vec{x}_{k-1} + \vec{b})$ converges to $A^{-1}\vec{b}$ when $\max\{|\lambda| : \lambda$ is an eigenvalue of $M^{-1}N\} < 1$.
   Hint: Define $\vec{x}^* = A^{-1}\vec{b}$ and take $\vec{e}_k = \vec{x}_k - \vec{x}^*$. Show that $\vec{e}_k = G^k\vec{e}_0$, where $G = M^{-1}N$. For this problem, you can assume that the eigenvectors of G span $\mathbb{R}^n$ (it is possible to prove this statement without the assumption but doing so requires more analysis than we have covered).

(b) Suppose A is strictly diagonally dominant, that is, for each i it satisfies

$$\sum_{j \neq i} |a_{ij}| < |a_{ii}|.$$

Suppose we define M to be the diagonal part of A and $N = M - A$. Show that the iterative scheme from Exercise 11.4a converges in this case. You can assume the statement from Exercise 11.4a holds regardless of the eigenspace of G.

11.5 As introduced in §10.4.3, a graph is a data structure $G = (V, E)$ consisting of n vertices in a set $V = \{1, \ldots, n\}$ and a set of edges $E \subseteq V \times V$. A common problem is *graph layout*, where we choose positions of the vertices in V on the plane $\mathbb{R}^2$ respecting the connectivity of G. For this problem we will assume $(i, i) \notin E$ for all $i \in V$.

(a) Take $\vec{v}_1, \ldots, \vec{v}_n \in \mathbb{R}^2$ to be the positions of the vertices in V; these are the unknowns in graph layout. The Dirichlet energy of a layout is

$$E(\vec{v}_1, \ldots, \vec{v}_n) = \sum_{(i,j) \in E} \|\vec{v}_i - \vec{v}_j\|_2^2.$$

Suppose an artist specifies positions of vertices in a nonempty subset $V_0 \subseteq V$. We will label these positions as $\vec{v}_k^0$ for $k \in V_0$. Derive two $(n - |V_0|) \times (n - |V_0|)$ linear systems of equations satisfied by the x and y components of the unknown $\vec{v}_i$'s solving the following minimization problem:

$$\text{minimize } E(\vec{v}_1, \ldots, \vec{v}_n)$$
$$\text{subject to } \vec{v}_k = \vec{v}_k^0 \; \forall k \in V_0.$$

Hint: Your answer can be written as two independent linear systems $A\vec{x} = \vec{b}_x$ and $A\vec{y} = \vec{b}_y$.

(b) Show that your systems from the previous part are symmetric and positive definite.

(c) Implement both gradient descent and conjugate gradients for solving this system, updating a display of the graph layout after each iteration. Compare the number of iterations needed to reach a reasonable solution using both strategies.

(d) Implement preconditioned conjugate gradients using a preconditioner of your choice. How much does convergence improve?

DH 11.6 The *successive over-relaxation* (SOR) method is an example of an iterative splitting method for solving $A\vec{x} = \vec{b}$, for $A \in \mathbb{R}^{n \times n}$. Suppose we decompose $A = D + L + U$, where D, L, and U are the diagonal, strictly lower-triangular, and strictly upper-triangular parts of A, respectively. Then, the SOR iteration is given by:

$$(\omega^{-1}D + L)\vec{x}_{k+1} = ((\omega^{-1} - 1)D - U)\vec{x}_k + \vec{b},$$

for some constant $\omega \in \mathbb{R}$. We will show that if A is symmetric and positive definite and $\omega \in (0, 2)$, then the SOR method converges.

(a) Show how SOR is an instance of the splitting method in Exercise 11.4 by defining matrices M and N appropriately. Hence, using this problem we now only need to show that $\rho(G) < 1$ for $G = M^{-1}N$ to establish convergence of SOR.

(b) Define $Q \equiv (\omega^{-1}D + L)$ and let $\vec{y} = (I_{n \times n} - G)\vec{x}$ for an arbitrary eigenvector $\vec{x} \in \mathbb{C}^n$ of G with corresponding eigenvalue $\lambda \in \mathbb{C}$. Derive expressions for $Q\vec{y}$ and $(Q - A)\vec{y}$ in terms of A, $\vec{x}$, and λ.

(c) Show that $d_{ii} > 0$ for all i. This expression shows that all the possibly nonzero elements of the diagonal matrix D are positive.

(d) Substitute the definition of Q into your relationships from Exercise 11.6b and simplify to show that:

$$\omega^{-1}\langle \vec{y}, \vec{y} \rangle_D + \langle \vec{y}, \vec{y} \rangle_L = (1 - \bar{\lambda})\langle \vec{x}, \vec{x} \rangle_A$$
$$(\omega^{-1} - 1)\langle \vec{y}, \vec{y} \rangle_D - \langle \vec{y}, \vec{y} \rangle_{U^\top} = (1 - \lambda)\bar{\lambda}\langle \vec{x}, \vec{x} \rangle_A.$$

Note: We are dealing with complex values here, so inner products in this problem are given by $\langle \vec{x}, \vec{y} \rangle_A \equiv (A\vec{x})^\top \text{conjugate}(\vec{y})$.

(e) Recalling our assumptions on A, write a relationship between L and U. Use this and the previous part to conclude that

$$(2\omega^{-1} - 1)\langle \vec{y}, \vec{y} \rangle_D = (1 - |\lambda|^2)\langle \vec{x}, \vec{x} \rangle_A.$$

(f) Justify why, under the given assumptions and results of the previous parts, each of $(2\omega^{-1} - 1)$, $\langle \vec{y}, \vec{y} \rangle_D$, and $\langle \vec{x}, \vec{x} \rangle_A$ must be positive. What does this imply about $|\lambda|$? Conclude that the SOR method converges under our assumptions.

DH 11.7 ("Gradient domain painting," [86]) Let $I : S \to \mathbb{R}$ be a monochromatic image, where $S \subset \mathbb{R}^2$ is a rectangle. We know I on a collection of square pixels tiling S.

Suppose an artist is editing I in the gradient domain. This means the artist edits the x and y derivatives g_x and g_y of I rather than values in I. After editing g_x and g_y, we need to recover a new image $\tilde{I}$ that has the edited gradients, at least approximately.

(a) For the artist to paint in the gradient domain, we first have to calculate discrete approximations of g_x and g_y using the values of I on different pixels. How might you estimate the derivatives of I in the x and y directions from a pixel using the values of I at one or both of the two horizontally adjacent pixels?

(b) Describe matrices A_x and A_y such that $A_x I = g_x$ and $A_y I = g_y$, where in this case we have written I as a vector $I = [I_{1,1}, I_{1,2}, ..., I_{1,n}, I_{2,1}, ..., I_{m,n}]^T$ and $I_{i,j}$ is the value of I at pixel (i, j). Assume the image I is m pixels tall and n pixels wide.

(c) Give an example of a function $g : \mathbb{R}^2 \to \mathbb{R}^2$ that is not a gradient, that is, g admits no f such that $\nabla f = g$. Justify your answer.

(d) In light of the fact that $\nabla \tilde{I} = g$ may not be solvable exactly, propose an optimization problem whose solution is the "best" approximate solution (in the L_2 norm) to this equation. Describe the advantage of using conjugate gradients to solve such a system.

11.8 The locally optimal block preconditioned conjugate gradient (LOBPCG) algorithm applies conjugate gradients to finding generalized eigenvectors $\vec{x}$ of matrices A and B satisfying $A\vec{x} = \lambda B\vec{x}$ [75, 76]. Assume $A, B \in \mathbb{R}^{n \times n}$ are symmetric and positive definite.

(a) Define the *generalized Rayleigh quotient* $\rho(\vec{x})$ as the function

$$\rho(\vec{x}) \equiv \frac{\vec{x}^\top A \vec{x}}{\vec{x}^\top B \vec{x}}.$$

Show that $\nabla \rho$ is parallel to $A\vec{x} - \rho(\vec{x})B\vec{x}$.

(b) Show that critical points of $\rho(\vec{x})$ with $\vec{x} \neq \vec{0}$ are the generalized eigenvectors of (A, B). Argue that the largest and smallest generalized eigenvalues come from maximizing and minimizing $\rho(\vec{x})$, respectively.

(c) Suppose we wish to find the generalized eigenvector with the largest eigenvalue. If we search in the gradient direction from the current iterate $\vec{x}$, we must solve the following line search problem:

$$\max_{\alpha \in \mathbb{R}} \rho(\vec{x} + \alpha \vec{r}(\vec{x})),$$

where $r(\vec{x}) \equiv A\vec{x} - \rho(\vec{x})B\vec{x}$. Show that α can be found by computing roots of a low-degree polynomial.

(d) Based on our construction above, propose an iteration for finding $\vec{x}$. When $B = I_{n \times n}$, is this method the same as the power method?

CHAPTER 12

Specialized Optimization Methods

CONTENTS

12.1	Nonlinear Least-Squares	227
	12.1.1 Gauss-Newton	228
	12.1.2 Levenberg-Marquardt	229
12.2	Iteratively Reweighted Least-Squares	230
12.3	Coordinate Descent and Alternation	231
	12.3.1 Identifying Candidates for Alternation	231
	12.3.2 Augmented Lagrangians and ADMM	235
12.4	Global Optimization	240
	12.4.1 Graduated Optimization	241
	12.4.2 Randomized Global Optimization	243
12.5	Online Optimization	244

OPTIMIZATION algorithms like Newton's method are completely generic approaches to minimizing a function $f(\vec{x})$, with or without constraints on $\vec{x}$. These algorithms make few assumptions about the form of f or the constraints. Contrastingly, by designing the conjugate gradient algorithm specifically for minimizing the objective $f(\vec{x}) \equiv \frac{1}{2}\vec{x}^\top A\vec{x} - \vec{b}^\top \vec{x} + c$, we were able to guarantee more reliable and efficient behavior than general algorithms.

In this chapter, we continue to exploit special structure to solve optimization problems, this time for more complex nonlinear objectives. Replacing monolithic generic algorithms with ones tailored to a given problem can make optimization faster and easier to troubleshoot, although doing so requires more implementation effort than calling a pre-packaged solver.

12.1 NONLINEAR LEAST-SQUARES

Recall the nonlinear regression problem posed in Example 9.1. If we wish to fit a function $y = ce^{ax}$ to a set of data points $(x_1, y_1), \ldots, (x_k, y_k)$, an optimization mimicking linear least-squares is to minimize the function

$$E(a, c) \equiv \sum_i (y_i - ce^{ax_i})^2.$$

This energy reflects the fact that we wish $y_i - ce^{ax_i} \approx 0$ for all i.

More generally, suppose we are given a set of functions $f_1(\vec{x}), \ldots, f_k(\vec{x})$ for $\vec{x} \in \mathbb{R}^n$. If we want $f_i(\vec{x}) \approx 0$ for all i, then a reasonable objective trading off between these terms is

$$E_{\text{NLS}}(\vec{x}) \equiv \frac{1}{2} \sum_i [f_i(\vec{x})]^2.$$

Objective functions of this form are known as *nonlinear least-squares* problems. For the exponential regression problem above, we would take $f_i(a, c) \equiv y_i - ce^{ax_i}$.

12.1.1 Gauss-Newton

When we run Newton's method to minimize a function $f(\vec{x})$, we must know the gradient *and* Hessian of f. Knowing only the gradient of f is not enough, since approximating functions with planes provides no information about their extrema. The BFGS algorithm carries out optimization without Hessians, but its approximate Hessians depend on the sequence of iterations and hence are not local to the current iterate.

Contrastingly, the Gauss-Newton algorithm for nonlinear least-squares makes the observation that approximating each f_i with a linear function yields a nontrivial curved approximation of E_{NLS} since each term in the sum is squared. The main feature of this approach is that it requires only *first-order* approximation of the f_i's rather than Hessians.

Suppose we write

$$f_i(\vec{x}) \approx f_i(\vec{x}_0) + [\nabla f_i(\vec{x}_0)] \cdot (\vec{x} - \vec{x}_0).$$

Then, we can approximate E_{NLS} with E^0_{NLS} given by

$$E^0_{\text{NLS}}(\vec{x}) = \frac{1}{2} \sum_i \left(f_i(\vec{x}_0) + [\nabla f_i(\vec{x}_0)] \cdot (\vec{x} - \vec{x}_0) \right)^2.$$

Define $F(\vec{x}) \equiv (f_1(\vec{x}), f_2(\vec{x}), \ldots, f_k(\vec{x}))$ by stacking the f_i's into a column vector. Then,

$$E^0_{\text{NLS}}(\vec{x}) = \frac{1}{2} \|F(\vec{x}_0) + DF(\vec{x}_0)(\vec{x} - \vec{x}_0)\|_2^2,$$

where DF is the Jacobian of F. Minimizing $E^0_{\text{NLS}}(\vec{x})$ is a *linear* least-squares problem $-F(\vec{x}_0) \approx DF(\vec{x}_0)(\vec{x} - \vec{x}_0)$ that can be solved via the normal equations:

$$\vec{x} = \vec{x}_0 - (DF(\vec{x}_0)^\top DF(\vec{x}_0))^{-1} DF(\vec{x}_0)^\top F(\vec{x}_0).$$

More practically, as we have discussed, the system can be solved using the QR factorization of $DF(\vec{x}_0)$ or—in higher dimensions—using conjugate gradients and related methods.

We can view $\vec{x}$ from minimizing $E^0_{\text{NLS}}(\vec{x})$ as an improved approximation of the minimum of $E_{\text{NLS}}(\vec{x})$ starting from $\vec{x}_0$. The Gauss-Newton algorithm iterates this formula to solve nonlinear least-squares:

$$\vec{x}_{k+1} = \vec{x}_k - (DF(\vec{x}_k)^\top DF(\vec{x}_k))^{-1} DF(\vec{x}_k)^\top F(\vec{x}_k).$$

This iteration is not guaranteed to converge in all situations. Given an initial guess sufficiently close to the minimum of the nonlinear least-squares problem, however, the approximation above behaves similarly to Newton's method and even can have quadratic convergence. Given the nature of the Gauss-Newton approximation, the algorithm works best when the optimal objective value $E_{\text{NLS}}(\vec{x}^*)$ is small; convergence can suffer when the optimal value is relatively large.

12.1.2 Levenberg-Marquardt

The Gauss-Newton algorithm uses an approximation $E_{\mathrm{NLS}}^0(\vec{x})$ of the nonlinear least-squares energy as a proxy for $E_{\mathrm{NLS}}(\vec{x})$ that is easier to minimize. In practice, this approximation is likely to fail as $\vec{x}$ moves farther from $\vec{x}_0$, so we might modify the Gauss-Newton step to include a step size limitation:

$$\min_{\vec{x}} \quad E_{\mathrm{NLS}}^0(\vec{x})$$
$$\text{subject to} \quad \|\vec{x} - \vec{x}_0\|_2^2 \leq \Delta.$$

That is, we now restrict our change in $\vec{x}$ to have norm less than some user-provided value Δ; the Δ neighborhood about $\vec{x}_0$ is called a *trust region*. Denote $H \equiv DF(\vec{x}_0)^\top DF(\vec{x}_0)$ and $\delta\vec{x} \equiv \vec{x} - \vec{x}_0$. Then, we can solve:

$$\min_{\delta\vec{x}} \quad \tfrac{1}{2}\delta\vec{x}^\top H \delta\vec{x} + F(\vec{x}_0)^\top DF(\vec{x}_0)\delta\vec{x}$$
$$\text{subject to} \quad \|\delta\vec{x}\|_2^2 \leq \Delta.$$

That is, we displace $\vec{x}$ by minimizing the Gauss-Newton approximation after imposing the step size restriction. This problem has the following KKT conditions (see §10.2.2):

$$\text{Stationarity: } \vec{0} = H\delta\vec{x} + DF(\vec{x}_0)^\top F(\vec{x}_0) + 2\mu\delta\vec{x}$$

$$\text{Primal feasibility: } \|\delta\vec{x}\|_2^2 \leq \Delta$$

$$\text{Complementary slackness: } \mu(\Delta - \|\delta\vec{x}\|_2^2) = 0$$

$$\text{Dual feasibility: } \mu \geq 0.$$

Define $\lambda \equiv 2\mu$. Then, the stationarity condition can be written as follows:

$$(H + \lambda I_{n \times n})\delta\vec{x} = -DF(\vec{x}_0)^\top F(\vec{x}_0).$$

Assume the constraint $\|\delta\vec{x}\|_2^2 \leq \Delta$ is active, that is, $\|\delta\vec{x}\|_2^2 = \Delta$. Then, except in degenerate cases $\lambda > 0$; combining this inequality with the fact that H is positive semidefinite, $H + \lambda I_{n \times n}$ must be positive definite.

The Levenberg-Marquardt algorithm *starts* from this stationarity formula, taking the following step derived from a user-supplied parameter $\lambda > 0$ [82, 85]:

$$\vec{x} = \vec{x}_0 - (DF(\vec{x}_0)^\top DF(\vec{x}_0) + \lambda I_{n \times n})^{-1} DF(\vec{x}_0)^\top F(\vec{x}_0).$$

This linear system also can be derived by applying Tikhonov regularization to the Gauss-Newton linear system. When λ is small, it behaves similarly to the Gauss-Newton algorithm, while large λ results in a gradient descent step for E_{NLS}.

Rather than specifying Δ as introduced above, Levenberg-Marquardt steps fix $\lambda > 0$ directly. By the KKT conditions, *a posteriori* we know this choice corresponds to having taken $\Delta = \|\vec{x} - \vec{x}_0\|_2^2$. As $\lambda \to \infty$, the step from Levenberg-Marquardt satisfies $\|\vec{x} - \vec{x}_0\|_2 \to 0$; so, we can regard Δ and λ as approximately inversely proportional.

Typical approaches adaptively adjust the *damping parameter* λ during each iteration:

$$\vec{x}_{k+1} = \vec{x}_k - (DF(\vec{x}_k)^\top DF(\vec{x}_k) + \lambda_k I_{n \times n})^{-1} DF(\vec{x}_0)^\top F(\vec{x}_k).$$

For instance, we can scale up λ_k when the step in $E_{\mathrm{NLS}}(\vec{x})$ agrees well with the approximate value predicted by $E_{\mathrm{NLS}}^0(\vec{x})$, since this corresponds to increasing the size of the neighborhood in which the Gauss-Newton approximation is effective.

12.2   ITERATIVELY REWEIGHTED LEAST-SQUARES

Continuing in our consideration of least-squares problems, suppose we wish to minimize a function of the form:

$$E_{\text{IRLS}}(\vec{x}) \equiv \sum_i f_i(\vec{x})[g_i(\vec{x})]^2.$$

We can think of $f_i(\vec{x})$ as a *weight* on the least-squares term $g_i(\vec{x})$.

Example 12.1 (L^p optimization). Similar to the compressed sensing problems in §10.4.1, given $A \in \mathbb{R}^{m \times n}$ and $\vec{b} \in \mathbb{R}^m$ we can generalize least-squares by minimizing

$$E_p(\vec{x}) \equiv \|A\vec{x} - \vec{b}\|_p^p.$$

Choosing $p = 1$ can promote sparsity in the residual $\vec{b} - A\vec{x}$. We can write this function in an alternative form:

$$E_p(\vec{x}) = \sum_i (\vec{a}_i \cdot \vec{x} - b_i)^{p-2} (\vec{a}_i \cdot \vec{x} - b_i)^2.$$

Here, we denote the rows of A as $\vec{a}_i^\top$. Then, $E_p = E_{\text{IRLS}}$ after defining:

$$f_i(\vec{x}) = (\vec{a}_i \cdot \vec{x} - b_i)^{p-2}$$
$$g_i(\vec{x}) = \vec{a}_i \cdot \vec{x} - b_i.$$

The *iteratively reweighted least-squares* (IRLS) algorithm makes use of the following fixed point iteration:

$$\vec{x}_{k+1} = \min_{\vec{x}_{k+1}} \sum_i f_i(\vec{x}_k)[g_i(\vec{x}_{k+1})]^2.$$

In the minimization, $\vec{x}_k$ is fixed, so the optimization is a least-squares problem over the g_i's. When g_i is linear, the minimization can be carried out via linear least-squares; otherwise we can use the nonlinear least-squares techniques in §12.1.

Example 12.2 (L^1 optimization). Continuing Example 12.1, suppose we take $p = 1$. Then,

$$E_1(\vec{x}) = \sum_i |\vec{a}_i \cdot \vec{x} - b_i| = \sum_i \frac{1}{|\vec{a}_i \cdot \vec{x} - b_i|} (\vec{a}_i \cdot \vec{x} - b_i)^2.$$

This functional leads to the following IRLS iteration, after adjustment for numerical issues:

$w_i \leftarrow [\max(|\vec{a}_i \cdot \vec{x} - b_i|, \delta)]^{-1}$	▷ Recompute weights
$\vec{x} \leftarrow \min_{\vec{x}} \sum_i w_i (\vec{a}_i \cdot \vec{x} - b_i)^2$	▷ Linear least-squares

The parameter $\delta > 0$ avoids division by zero; large values of δ make better-conditioned linear systems but worse approximations of the original $\|\cdot\|_1$ problem.

Example 12.3 (Weiszfeld algorithm). Recall the geometric median problem from Example 9.3. In this problem, given $\vec{x}_1, \ldots, \vec{x}_k \in \mathbb{R}^n$, we wish to minimize

$$E(\vec{x}) \equiv \sum_i \|\vec{x} - \vec{x}_i\|_2.$$

Similar to the L^1 problem in Example 12.2, we can write this function like a weighted least-squares problem:

$$E(\vec{x}) \equiv \sum_i \frac{1}{\|\vec{x} - \vec{x}_i\|_2} \|\vec{x} - \vec{x}_i\|_2^2.$$

Then, IRLS provides the *Weiszfeld algorithm* for geometric median problems:

> $w_i \leftarrow [\max(\|\vec{x} - \vec{x}_i\|_2, \delta)]^{-1}$ ▷ Recompute weights
> $\vec{x} \leftarrow \min_{\vec{x}} \sum_i w_i (\vec{x} - \vec{x}_i)^2$ ▷ Linear least-squares

We can solve for the second step of the Weiszfeld algorithm in closed form. Differentiating the objective with respect to $\vec{x}$ shows

$$\vec{0} = \sum_i 2 w_i (\vec{x} - \vec{x}_i) \implies \vec{x} = \frac{\sum_i w_i \vec{x}_i}{\sum_i w_i}.$$

Thus, the two alternating steps of Weiszfeld's algorithm can be carried out efficiently as:

> $w_i \leftarrow [\max(\|\vec{x} - \vec{x}_i\|_2, \delta)]^{-1}$ ▷ Recompute weights
> $\vec{x} \leftarrow \frac{\sum_i w_i \vec{x}_i}{\sum_i w_i}$ ▷ Weighted centroid

IRLS algorithms are straightforward to formulate, so they are worth trying if an optimization can be written in the form of E_{IRLS}. When g_i is linear for all i as in Example 12.2, each iteration of IRLS can be carried out quickly using Cholesky factorization, QR, conjugate gradients, and so on, avoiding line search and other more generic strategies.

It is difficult to formulate general conditions under which IRLS will reach the minimum of E_{IRLS}. Often, iterates must be approximated somewhat as in the introduction of δ to Example 12.2 to avoid division by zero and other degeneracies. In the case of L^1 optimization, however, IRLS can be shown with small modification to converge to the optimal point [31].

12.3 COORDINATE DESCENT AND ALTERNATION

Suppose we wish to minimize a function $f : \mathbb{R}^{n+m} \to \mathbb{R}$. Rather than viewing the input as a single variable $\vec{x} \in \mathbb{R}^{n+m}$, we might write f in an alternative form as $f(\vec{x}, \vec{y})$, for $\vec{x} \in \mathbb{R}^n$ and $\vec{y} \in \mathbb{R}^m$. One strategy for optimization is to fix $\vec{y}$ and minimize f with respect to $\vec{x}$, fix $\vec{x}$ and minimize f with respect to $\vec{y}$, and repeat:

> **for** $i \leftarrow 1, 2, \ldots$
> $\vec{x}_{i+1} \leftarrow \min_{\vec{x}} f(\vec{x}, \vec{y}_i)$ ▷ Optimize $\vec{x}$ with $\vec{y}$ fixed
> $\vec{y}_{i+1} \leftarrow \min_{\vec{y}} f(\vec{x}_{i+1}, \vec{y})$ ▷ Optimize $\vec{y}$ with $\vec{x}$ fixed

In this *alternating* approach, the value of $f(\vec{x}_i, \vec{y}_i)$ decreases monotonically as i increases since a minimization is carried out at each step. We cannot prove that alternation always reaches a global or even local minimum, but in many cases it can be an efficient option for otherwise challenging problems.

12.3.1 Identifying Candidates for Alternation

There are a few reasons why we might wish to perform alternating optimization:

- The individual problems over $\vec{x}$ and $\vec{y}$ are optimizations in a lower dimension and may converge more quickly.

- We may be able to split the variables in such a way that the individual $\vec{x}$ and $\vec{y}$ steps are far more efficient than optimizing both variables jointly.

Below we provide a few examples of alternating optimization in practice.

Example 12.4 (Generalized PCA). In the PCA problem from §7.2.5, we are given a data matrix $X \in \mathbb{R}^{n \times k}$ whose columns are k data points in $\mathbb{R}^n$. We seek a basis in $\mathbb{R}^n$ of size d such that the projection of the data points onto the basis introduces minimal approximation error; we will store this basis in the columns of $C \in \mathbb{R}^{n \times d}$. Classical PCA minimizes $\|X - CY\|_{\text{Fro}}^2$ over both C and Y, where the columns of $Y \in \mathbb{R}^{d \times k}$ are the coefficients of the data points in the C basis. If C is constrained to be orthogonal, then $Y = C^\top X$, recovering the formula in our previous discussion.

The Frobenius norm in PCA is somewhat arbitrary: The relevant relationship is $X - CY \approx 0$. Alternative PCA models minimize $\mu(X - CY)$ over C and Y, for some other energy function $\mu : \mathbb{R}^{n \times k} \to \mathbb{R}$ favoring matrices with entries near zero; μ can provide enhanced robustness to noise or encode application-specific assumptions. Taking $\mu(M) \equiv \|M\|_{\text{Fro}}^2$ recovers classical PCA; another popular choice is *robust PCA* [71], which takes $\mu(M) \equiv \sum_{ij} |M_{ij}|$.

The product CY in $\mu(X - CY)$ makes the energy nonlinear and nonconvex. A typical minimization routine for this problem uses alternation: First optimize C with Y fixed, then optimize Y with C fixed, and repeat. Whereas optimizing the energy with respect to C and Y jointly might require a generic large-scale method, the individual alternating C and Y steps can be easier:

- When $\mu(M) = \|M\|_{\text{Fro}}^2$, both the Y and C alternations are least-squares problems, leading to the *alternating least-squares* (ALS) algorithm for classical PCA.

- When $\mu(M) \equiv \sum_{ij} |M_{ij}|$, the Y and C alternations are linear programs, which can be optimized using the techniques mentioned in §10.4.1.

Example 12.5 (ARAP). Recall the planar "as-rigid-as-possible" (ARAP) problem introduced in Example 10.5:

$$\text{minimize}_{R_v, \vec{y}_v} \sum_{v \in V} \sum_{(v,w) \in E} \|R_v(\vec{x}_v - \vec{x}_w) - (\vec{y}_v - \vec{y}_w)\|_2^2$$

$$\text{subject to } R_v^\top R_v = I_{2 \times 2} \ \forall v \in V$$

$$\vec{y}_v \text{ fixed } \forall v \in V_0.$$

Solving for the matrices $R_v \in \mathbb{R}^{2 \times 2}$ and vertex positions $\vec{y}_v \in \mathbb{R}^2$ simultaneously is a highly nonlinear and nonconvex task, especially given the orthogonality constraint $R_v^\top R_v = I_{2 \times 2}$. There is one $\vec{y}_v$ and one R_v for each vertex v of a triangle mesh with potentially thousands or even millions of vertices, so such a direct optimization using quasi-Newton methods requires a large-scale linear solve per iteration and still is prone to finding local minima.

Instead, [116] suggests alternating between the following two steps:

1. Fixing the R_v matrices and optimizing only for the positions $\vec{y}_v$:

$$\text{minimize}_{\vec{y}_v} \sum_{v \in V} \sum_{(v,w) \in E} \|R_v(\vec{x}_v - \vec{x}_w) - (\vec{y}_v - \vec{y}_w)\|_2^2$$

$$\text{subject to } \vec{y}_v \text{ fixed } \forall v \in V_0.$$

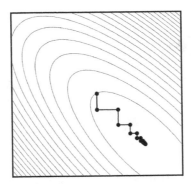

Figure 12.1 Coordinate descent in two dimensions alternates between minimizing in the horizontal and vertical axis directions.

This least-squares problem can be solved using a sparse, positive-definite linear system of equations.

2. Fixing the $\vec{y}_v$'s and optimizing for the R_v's. No energy terms or constraints couple any pair R_v, R_w for $v, w \in V$, so we can solve for each matrix R_v independently. That is, rather than solving for $4|V|$ unknowns simultaneously, we loop over $v \in V$, solving the following optimization for each $R_v \in \mathbb{R}^{2 \times 2}$:

$$\text{minimize}_{R_v} \sum_{(v,w) \in E} \| R_v(\vec{x}_v - \vec{x}_w) - (\vec{y}_v - \vec{y}_w) \|_2^2$$
$$\text{subject to } R_v^\top R_v = I_{2 \times 2}.$$

This optimization problem is an instance of the Procrustes problem from §7.2.4 and can be solved in closed-form using a 2×2 SVD. We have replaced a large-scale minimization with the application of a formula that can be evaluated in parallel for each vertex, a massive computational savings.

Alternating between optimizing for the $\vec{y}_v$'s with the R_v's fixed and vice versa decreases the energy using two efficient pieces of machinery, sparse linear solvers and 2×2 SVD factorization. This can be far more efficient than considering the $\vec{y}_v$'s and R_v's simultaneously, and in practice a few iterations can be sufficient to generate elastic deformations like the one shown in Figure 10.3. Extensions of ARAP even run in real time, optimizing fast enough to provide interactive feedback to artists editing two- and three-dimensional shapes.

Example 12.6 (Coordinate descent). Taking the philosophy of alternating optimization to an extreme, rather than splitting the inputs of $f : \mathbb{R}^n \to \mathbb{R}$ into two variables, we could view f as a function of several variables $f(x_1, x_2, \ldots, x_n)$. Then, we could cycle through each input x_i, performing a one-dimensional optimization in each step. This lightweight algorithm, illustrated in Figure 12.1, is known as *coordinate descent*.

For instance, suppose we wish to solve the least-squares problem $A\vec{x} \approx \vec{b}$ by minimizing $\|A\vec{x} - \vec{b}\|_2^2$. As in Chapter 11, line search over any single x_i can be solved in closed form. If the columns of A are vectors $\vec{a}_1, \ldots, \vec{a}_n$, then as shown in §1.3.1 we can write $A\vec{x} - \vec{b} =$

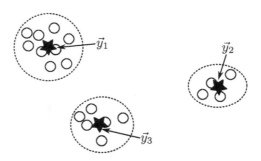

Figure 12.2 The k-means algorithm seeks cluster centers $\vec{y}_i$ that partition a set of data points $\vec{x}_1, \ldots, \vec{x}_m$ based on their closest center.

$x_1 \vec{a}_1 + \cdots + x_n \vec{a}_n - \vec{b}$. By this expansion,

$$0 = \frac{\partial}{\partial x_i} \|x_1 \vec{a}_1 + \cdots + x_n \vec{a}_n - \vec{b}\|_2^2 = 2(A\vec{x} - \vec{b}) \cdot \vec{a}_i = \sum_j \left[\left(\sum_k a_{ji} a_{jk} x_k \right) - a_{ji} b_j \right].$$

Solving this equation for x_i yields the following coordinate descent update for x_i:

$$x_i \leftarrow \frac{\vec{a}_i \cdot \vec{b} - \sum_{k \neq i} x_k (\vec{a}_i \cdot \vec{a}_k)}{\|\vec{a}_i\|_2^2}.$$

Coordinate descent for least-squares iterates this formula over $i = 1, 2, \ldots, n$ repeatedly until convergence. This approach has efficient localized updates and appears in machine learning methods where A has many more rows than columns, sampled from a data distribution. We have traded a global method for one that locally updates the solution $\vec{x}$ by solving extremely simple subproblems.

Example 12.7 (k-means clustering). Suppose we are given a set of data points $\vec{x}_1, \ldots, \vec{x}_m \in \mathbb{R}^n$ and wish to group these points into k clusters based on distance, as in Figure 12.2. Take $\vec{y}_1, \ldots, \vec{y}_k \in \mathbb{R}^n$ to be the centers of clusters $1, \ldots, k$, respectively. To cluster the data by assigning each point $\vec{x}_i$ to a single cluster centered at $\vec{y}_c$, the k-means technique optimizes the following energy:

$$E(\vec{y}_1, \ldots, \vec{y}_k) \equiv \sum_{i=1}^m \min_{c \in \{1, \ldots, k\}} \|\vec{x}_i - \vec{y}_c\|_2^2.$$

In words, E measures the total squared distance of the data points $\vec{x}_i$ to their closest cluster center $\vec{y}_c$.

Define $c_i \equiv \arg\min_{c \in \{1, \ldots, k\}} \|\vec{x}_i - \vec{y}_c\|_2^2$; that is, c_i is the index of the cluster center $\vec{y}_{c_i}$ closest to $\vec{x}_i$. Using this substitution, we can write an expanded formulation of the k-means objective as follows:

$$E(\vec{y}_1, \ldots, \vec{y}_k; c_1, \ldots, c_m) \equiv \sum_{i=1}^m \|\vec{x}_i - \vec{y}_{c_i}\|_2^2.$$

The variables c_i are integers, but we can optimize them jointly with the $\vec{y}$'s using alternation:

- When the c_i's are fixed, the optimization for the $\vec{y}_j$'s is a least-squares problem whose solution can be written in closed form as

$$\vec{y}_j = \frac{\sum_{c_i=j} \vec{x}_i}{|\{c_i = j\}|}.$$

That is, $\vec{y}_j$ is the average of the points $\vec{x}_i$ assigned to cluster j.

- The optimization for c_i also can be carried out in closed form using the expression $c_i \equiv \arg\min_{c \in \{1,\ldots,k\}} \|\vec{x}_i - \vec{y}_c\|_2^2$ by iterating from 1 to k for each i. This iteration just assigns each $\vec{x}_i$ to its closest cluster center.

This alternation is known as the k-means algorithm and is a popular method for clustering. One drawback of this method is that it is sensitive to the initial guesses of $\vec{y}_1, \ldots, \vec{y}_k$. In practice, k-means is often run several times with different initial guesses, and only the best output is preserved. Alternatively, methods like "k-means++" specifically design initial guesses of the $\vec{y}_i$'s to encourage convergence to a better local minimum [3].

12.3.2 Augmented Lagrangians and ADMM

Nonlinear constrained problems are often the most challenging optimization tasks. While the general algorithms in §10.3 are applicable, they can be sensitive to the initial guess of the minimizer, slow to iterate due to large linear solves, and slow to converge in the absence of more information about the problems at hand. Using these methods is easy from an engineering perspective since they require providing only a function and its derivatives, but with some additional work on paper, certain objective functions can be tackled using faster techniques, many of which can be parallelized on multiprocessor machines. It is worth checking if a problem can be solved via one of these strategies, especially when the dimensionality is high or the objective has a number of similar or repeated terms.

In this section, we consider an alternating approach to equality-constrained optimization that has gained considerable attention in recent literature. While it can be used out-of-the-box as yet another generic optimization algorithm, its primary value appears to be in the decomposition of complex minimization problems into simpler steps that can be iterated, often in parallel. In large part we will follow the development of [14], which contains many examples of applications of this class of techniques.

As considered in Chapter 10, the equality-constrained optimization problem can be stated as follows:

$$\text{minimize } f(\vec{x})$$
$$\text{subject to } g(\vec{x}) = \vec{0}.$$

One incarnation of the barrier method suggested in §10.3.2 optimizes an unconstrained objective with a quadratic penalty:

$$f_\rho(\vec{x}) = f(\vec{x}) + \frac{1}{2}\rho\|g(\vec{x})\|_2^2.$$

As $\rho \to \infty$, critical points of f_ρ satisfy the $g(\vec{x}) = \vec{0}$ constraint more and more closely. The trade-off for this method, however, is that the optimization becomes poorly conditioned as

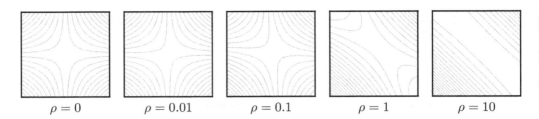

| $\rho = 0$ | $\rho = 0.01$ | $\rho = 0.1$ | $\rho = 1$ | $\rho = 10$ |

Figure 12.3 We can optimize $f(x, y) \equiv xy$ subject to $x + y = 1$ approximately by minimizing the penalized version $f_\rho(x, y) = xy + \rho(x + y - 1)^2$. As ρ increases, however, level sets of xy get obscured in favor of enforcing the constraint.

ρ becomes large. This effect is illustrated in Figure 12.3; when ρ is large, the level sets of f_ρ mostly are dedicated to enforcing the constraint rather than minimizing the objective $f(\vec{x})$, making it difficult to distinguish between $\vec{x}$'s that all satisfy the constraint.

Alternatively, by the method of Lagrange multipliers (Theorem 1.1), we can seek first-order optima of this problem as the critical points of $\Lambda(\vec{x}, \vec{\lambda})$ given by

$$\Lambda(\vec{x}, \vec{\lambda}) \equiv f(\vec{x}) - \vec{\lambda}^\top g(\vec{x}).$$

This Lagrangian does not suffer from conditioning issues that affect the quadratic penalty method. On the other hand, it replaces a minimization problem—which can be solved by moving "downhill"—with a more challenging saddle point problem in which critical points should be minima of Λ with respect to $\vec{x}$ and maxima of Λ with respect to $\vec{\lambda}$. Optimizing by alternatively minimizing with respect to $\vec{x}$ and maximizing with respect to $\vec{\lambda}$ can be unstable; intuitively this makes some sense since it is unclear whether Λ should be small or large.

The *augmented Lagrangian* method for equality-constrained optimization combines the quadratic penalty and Lagrangian strategies, using the penalty to "soften" individual iterations of the alternation for optimizing Λ described above. It replaces the original equality-constrained optimization problem with the following equivalent augmented problem:

$$\text{minimize } f(\vec{x}) + \frac{1}{2}\rho\|g(\vec{x})\|_2^2$$
$$\text{subject to } g(\vec{x}) = \vec{0}.$$

Any $\vec{x}$ satisfying the $g(\vec{x}) = \vec{0}$ constraint makes the second objective term vanish. But, when the constraint is not exactly satisfied, the second energy term biases the objective toward points $\vec{x}$ that approximately satisfy the equality constraint. In other words, during iterations of augmented Lagrangian optimization, the $\rho\|g(\vec{x})\|_2^2$ acts like a rubber band pulling $\vec{x}$ closer to the constraint set even during the minimization step.

This modified problem has a new Lagrangian given by

$$\Lambda_\rho(\vec{x}, \vec{\lambda}) \equiv f(\vec{x}) + \frac{1}{2}\rho\|g(\vec{x})\|_2^2 - \vec{\lambda}^\top g(\vec{x}).$$

Hence, the augmented Lagrangian method optimizes this objective by alternating as follows:

> **for** $i \leftarrow 1, 2, \ldots$
> $\quad \vec{\lambda}_{i+1} \leftarrow \vec{\lambda}_i - \rho g(\vec{x}_i)$ ▷ Dual update
> $\quad \vec{x}_i \leftarrow \min_{\vec{x}} \Lambda_\rho(\vec{x}, \vec{\lambda}_{i+1})$ ▷ Primal update

The dual update step can be thought of as a gradient ascent step for $\vec{\lambda}$. The parameter ρ here no longer has to approach infinity for exact constraint satisfaction, since the Lagrange multiplier enforces the constraint regardless. Instead, the quadratic penalty serves to make sure the output of the $\vec{x}$ iteration does not violate the constraints too strongly.

Augmented Lagrangian optimization has the advantage that it alternates between applying a formula to update $\vec{\lambda}$ and solving an *unconstrained* minimization problem for $\vec{x}$. For many optimization problems, however, the unconstrained objective still may be nondifferentiable or difficult to optimize. A few special cases, e.g., Uzawa iteration for dual decomposition [124], can be effective for optimization but in many circumstances quasi-Newton algorithms outperform this approach with respect to speed and convergence.

A small alteration to general augmented Lagrangian minimization, however, yields the *alternating direction method of multipliers* (ADMM) for optimizing slightly more specific objectives of the form

$$\text{minimize } f(\vec{x}) + h(\vec{z})$$
$$\text{subject to } A\vec{x} + B\vec{z} = \vec{c}.$$

Here, the optimization variables are both $\vec{x}$ and $\vec{z}$, where $f, h : \mathbb{R}^n \to \mathbb{R}$ are given functions and the equality constraint is linear. As we will show, this form encapsulates many important optimization problems. We will design an algorithm that carries out alternation between the two primal variables $\vec{x}$ and $\vec{z}$, as well as between primal and dual optimization.

The augmented Lagrangian in this case is

$$\Lambda_\rho(\vec{x}, \vec{z}, \vec{\lambda}) \equiv f(\vec{x}) + h(\vec{z}) + \frac{1}{2}\rho\|A\vec{x} + B\vec{z} - \vec{c}\|_2^2 + \vec{\lambda}^\top(A\vec{x} + B\vec{z} - \vec{c}).$$

Alternating in three steps between optimizing $\vec{x}$, $\vec{z}$, and $\vec{\lambda}$ suggests a modification of the augmented Lagrangian method:

$$
\begin{array}{ll}
\textbf{for } i \leftarrow 1, 2, \ldots & \\
\quad \vec{x}_{i+1} \leftarrow \arg\min_{\vec{x}} \Lambda_\rho(\vec{x}, \vec{z}_i, \vec{\lambda}_i) & \triangleright \ \vec{x} \text{ update} \\
\quad \vec{z}_{i+1} \leftarrow \arg\min_{\vec{z}} \Lambda_\rho(\vec{x}_{i+1}, \vec{z}, \vec{\lambda}_i) & \triangleright \ \vec{z} \text{ update} \\
\quad \vec{\lambda}_{i+1} \leftarrow \vec{\lambda}_i + \rho(A\vec{x}_{i+1} + B\vec{z}_{i+1} - \vec{c}) & \triangleright \ \text{Dual update}
\end{array}
$$

In this algorithm, $\vec{x}$ and $\vec{z}$ are optimized one at a time; the augmented Lagrangian method would optimize them jointly. Although this splitting can require more iterations for convergence, clever choices of $\vec{x}$ and $\vec{z}$ lead to powerful division-of-labor strategies for breaking down difficult problems. Each individual iteration will take *far* less time, even though more iterations may be needed for convergence. In a sense, ADMM is a "meta-algorithm" used to design optimization techniques. Rather than calling a generic package to minimize Λ_ρ with respect to $\vec{x}$ and $\vec{z}$, we will find choices of $\vec{x}$ and $\vec{z}$ that make individual steps fast.

Before working out examples of ADMM in action, it is worth noting that it is guaranteed to converge to a critical point of the objective under fairly weak conditions. For instance, ADMM reaches a global minimum when f and h are convex and Λ_ρ has a saddle point. ADMM has also been observed to converge even for nonconvex problems, although current theoretical understanding in this case is limited. In practice, ADMM tends to be quick to generate *approximate* minima of the objective but can require a long tail of iterations to squeeze out the last decimal points of accuracy; for this reason, some systems use ADMM to do initial large-scale steps and transition to other algorithms for localized optimization.

We dedicate the remainder of this section to working out examples of ADMM in practice. The general pattern is to split the optimization variables into $\vec{x}$ and $\vec{z}$ in such a way that the two primal update steps each can be carried out efficiently, preferably in closed form or decoupling so that parallelized computations can be used to solve many subproblems at once. This makes individual iterations of ADMM inexpensive.

Example 12.8 (Nonnegative least-squares). Suppose we wish to minimize $\|A\vec{x} - \vec{b}\|_2^2$ with respect to $\vec{x}$ subject to the constraint $\vec{x} \geq \vec{0}$. The $\vec{x} \geq 0$ constraint rules out using Gaussian elimination, but ADMM provides one way to bypass this issue.

Consider solving the following equivalent problem:

$$\text{minimize } \|A\vec{x} - \vec{b}\|_2^2 + h(\vec{z})$$
$$\text{subject to } \vec{x} = \vec{z}.$$

Here, we define the new function $h(\vec{z})$ as follows:

$$h(\vec{z}) = \begin{cases} 0 & \vec{z} \geq \vec{0} \\ \infty & \text{otherwise.} \end{cases}$$

The function $h(\vec{z})$ is discontinuous, but it is convex. This equivalent form of nonnegative least-squares may be harder to read, but it provides an effective ADMM splitting.

For this optimization, the augmented Lagrangian is

$$\Lambda_\rho(\vec{x}, \vec{z}, \vec{\lambda}) = \|A\vec{x} - \vec{b}\|_2^2 + h(\vec{z}) + \frac{1}{2}\rho\|\vec{x} - \vec{z}\|_2^2 + \vec{\lambda}^\top(\vec{x} - \vec{z}).$$

For fixed $\vec{z}$ with $z_i \neq \infty$ for all i, then Λ_ρ is differentiable with respect to $\vec{x}$. Hence, we can carry out the $\vec{x}$ step of ADMM by setting the gradient with respect to $\vec{x}$ equal to $\vec{0}$:

$$\vec{0} = \nabla_{\vec{x}}\Lambda_\rho(\vec{x}, \vec{z}, \vec{\lambda})$$
$$= 2A^\top A\vec{x} - 2A^\top\vec{b} + \rho(\vec{x} - \vec{z}) + \vec{\lambda}$$
$$= (2A^\top A + \rho I_{n \times n})\vec{x} + (\vec{\lambda} - 2A^\top\vec{b} - \rho\vec{z})$$
$$\implies \vec{x} = (2A^\top A + \rho I_{n \times n})^{-1}(2A^\top\vec{b} + \rho\vec{z} - \vec{\lambda}).$$

This linear solve is a Tikhonov-regularized least-squares problem. For extra speed, the Cholesky factorization of $2A^\top A + \rho I_{n \times n}$ can be computed before commencing ADMM and used to find $\vec{x}$ in each iteration.

Minimizing Λ_ρ with respect to $\vec{z}$ can be carried out in closed form. Any objective function involving h effectively constrains each component of $\vec{z}$ to be nonnegative, so we can find $\vec{z}$ using the following optimization:

$$\text{minimize}_{\vec{z}} \frac{1}{2}\rho\|\vec{x} - \vec{z}\|_2^2 + \vec{\lambda}^\top(\vec{x} - \vec{z})$$
$$\text{subject to } \vec{z} \geq \vec{0}.$$

The $\|A\vec{x} - \vec{b}\|_2^2$ term in the full objective is removed because it has no $\vec{z}$ dependence. This problem *decouples* over the components of $\vec{z}$ since no energy terms involve more than one dimension of $\vec{z}$ at a time. So, we can solve many instances of the following one-dimensional problem:

$$\text{minimize}_{z_i} \frac{1}{2}\rho(x_i - z_i)^2 + \lambda_i(x_i - z_i)$$
$$\text{subject to } z_i \geq 0.$$

In the absence of the $z_i \geq 0$ constraint, the objective is minimized when $0 = \rho(z_i - x_i) - \lambda_i \implies z_i = x_i + \lambda_i/\rho$; when this value is negative, we fix $z_i = 0$.

Hence, the ADMM algorithm for nonnegative least-squares is:

> **for** $i \leftarrow 1, 2, \ldots$
> $\quad \vec{x}_{i+1} \leftarrow (2A^\top A + \rho I_{n \times n})^{-1} (2A^\top \vec{b} + \rho \vec{z}_i - \vec{\lambda}_i)$ ▷ $\vec{x}$ update; least-squares
> $\quad \vec{z}^0 \leftarrow \vec{\lambda}_i / \rho + \vec{x}_{i+1}$ ▷ Unconstrained $\vec{z}$ formula
> $\quad \vec{z}_{i+1} \leftarrow \text{ELEMENTWISE-MAX}(\vec{z}^0, \vec{0})$ ▷ Enforce $\vec{z} \geq \vec{0}$
> $\quad \vec{\lambda}_{i+1} \leftarrow \vec{\lambda}_i + \rho(\vec{x}_{i+1} - \vec{z}_{i+1})$ ▷ Dual update

This algorithm for nonnegative least-squares took our original problem—a quadratic program that could require difficult constrained optimization techniques—and replaced it with an alternation between a linear solve for $\vec{x}$, a formula for $\vec{z}$, and a formula for $\vec{\lambda}$. These individual steps are straightforward to implement and efficient computationally.

Example 12.9 (ADMM for geometric median). Returning to Example 12.3, we can reconsider the energy $E(\vec{x})$ for the geometric median problem using the machinery of ADMM:

$$E(\vec{x}) \equiv \sum_{i=1}^{N} \|\vec{x} - \vec{x}_i\|_2.$$

This time, we will split the problem into two unknowns $\vec{z}_i, \vec{x}$:

$$\text{minimize} \sum_i \|\vec{z}_i\|_2$$
$$\text{subject to } \vec{z}_i + \vec{x} = \vec{x}_i \; \forall i.$$

The augmented Lagrangian for this problem is:

$$\Lambda_\rho = \sum_i \left[\|\vec{z}_i\|_2 + \frac{1}{2}\rho \|\vec{z}_i + \vec{x} - \vec{x}_i\|_2^2 + \vec{\lambda}_i^\top (\vec{z}_i + \vec{x} - \vec{x}_i) \right].$$

As a function of $\vec{x}$, the augmented Lagrangian is differentiable and hence to find the $\vec{x}$ iteration we write:

$$\vec{0} = \nabla_{\vec{x}} \Lambda_\rho = \sum_i \left[\rho(\vec{x} - \vec{x}_i + \vec{z}_i) + \vec{\lambda}_i \right]$$
$$\implies \vec{x} = \frac{1}{N} \sum_i \left[\vec{x}_i - \vec{z}_i - \frac{1}{\rho}\vec{\lambda}_i \right].$$

The optimization for the $\vec{z}_i$'s decouples over i when $\vec{x}$ is fixed, so after removing constant terms we minimize $\|\vec{z}_i\|_2 + \frac{1}{2}\rho \|\vec{z}_i + \vec{x} - \vec{x}_i\|_2^2 + \vec{\lambda}_i^\top \vec{z}_i$ for each $\vec{z}_i$ separately. We can combine the second and third terms by "completing the square" as follows:

$$\frac{1}{2}\rho \|\vec{z}_i + \vec{x} - \vec{x}_i\|_2^2 + \vec{\lambda}_i^\top \vec{z}_i = \frac{1}{2}\rho \|\vec{z}_i\|_2^2 + \rho \vec{z}_i^\top \left(\frac{1}{\rho}\vec{\lambda}_i + \vec{x} - \vec{x}_i \right) + \text{const.}$$
$$= \frac{1}{2}\rho \left\| \vec{z}_i + \frac{1}{\rho}\vec{\lambda}_i + \vec{x} - \vec{x}_i \right\|_2^2 + \text{const.}$$

The constant terms can have $\vec{x}$ dependence since it is fixed in the $\vec{z}_i$ iteration. Defining $\vec{z}^0 \equiv -\frac{1}{\rho}\vec{\lambda}_i - \vec{x} + \vec{x}_i$, in the $\vec{z}_i$ iteration we have shown that we can solve:

$$\min_{\vec{z}_i} \left[\|\vec{z}_i\|_2 + \frac{1}{2}\rho \|\vec{z}_i - \vec{z}^0\|_2^2 \right].$$

Written in this form, it is clear that the optimal $\vec{z}_i$ satisfies $\vec{z}_i = t\vec{z}^0$ for some $t \in [0, 1]$, since the two terms of the objective balance the distance of $\vec{z}_i$ to $\vec{0}$ and to $\vec{z}^0$. After dividing by $\|\vec{z}^0\|_2$, we can solve:

$$\min_{t \geq 0} \left[t + \frac{1}{2}\rho\|\vec{z}^0\|_2(t-1)^2 \right].$$

Using elementary calculus techniques we find:

$$t = \begin{cases} 1 - 1/\rho\|\vec{z}^0\|_2 & \text{when } \rho\|\vec{z}^0\|_2 \geq 1 \\ 0 & \text{otherwise.} \end{cases}$$

Taking $\vec{z}_i = t\vec{z}_0$ finishes the $\vec{z}$ iteration of ADMM.

In summary, the ADMM algorithm for geometric medians is as follows:

---

for $i \leftarrow 1, 2, \ldots$

$\quad \vec{x} \leftarrow \frac{1}{N}\sum_i \left[\vec{x}_i - \vec{z}_i - \frac{1}{\rho}\vec{\lambda}_i \right]$ ▷ $\vec{x}$ update

$\quad$ **for** $j \leftarrow 1, 2, \ldots, N$ ▷ Can parallelize

$\quad\quad \vec{z}^0 \leftarrow -\frac{1}{\rho}\vec{\lambda}_i - \vec{x} + \vec{x}_i$

$\quad\quad t \leftarrow \begin{cases} 1 - 1/\rho\|\vec{z}^0\|_2 & \text{when } \rho\|\vec{z}^0\|_2 \geq 1 \\ 0 & \text{otherwise} \end{cases}$

$\quad\quad \vec{z}_j \leftarrow t\vec{z}^0$ ▷ $\vec{z}$ update

$\quad\quad \vec{\lambda}_j \leftarrow \vec{\lambda}_j + \rho(\vec{z}_i + \vec{x} - \vec{x}_i)$ ▷ Dual update

---

The examples above show the typical ADMM strategy, in which a difficult nonlinear problem is split into two subproblems that can be carried out in closed form or via more efficient operations. The art of posing a problem in terms of $\vec{x}$ and $\vec{z}$ to get these savings requires practice and careful study of individual problems.

The parameter $\rho > 0$ often does not affect whether or not ADMM will eventually converge, but an intelligent choice of ρ can help this technique reach the optimal point faster. Some experimentation can be required, or ρ can be adjusted from iteration to iteration depending on whether the primal or dual variables are converging more quickly [127]. In some cases, ADMM provably converges faster when $\rho \to \infty$ as the iterations proceed [104].

12.4 GLOBAL OPTIMIZATION

Nonlinear least-squares, IRLS, and alternation are lightweight approaches for nonlinear objectives that can be optimized quickly after simplification. On the other side of the spectrum, some minimization problems not only do not readily admit fast specialized algorithms but also are failure modes for Newton's method and other generic solvers. Convergence guarantees for Newton's method and other algorithms based on the Taylor approximation assume that we have a strong initial guess of the minimum that we wish to refine. When we lack such an initial guess or a simplifying assumption like convexity, we must solve a *global optimization* problem searching over the entire space of feasible output.

As discussed briefly in §9.2, global optimization is a challenging, nearly ill-posed problem. For example, in the unconstrained case it is difficult to know whether $\vec{x}^*$ yields the minimum possible $f(\vec{x})$ *anywhere*, since this is a statement over an infinitude of points $\vec{x}$. Hence, global optimization methods use one or more strategies to improve the odds of finding a minimum:

- Initially approximate the objective $f(\vec{x})$ with an easier function to minimize to get a better starting point for the original problem.

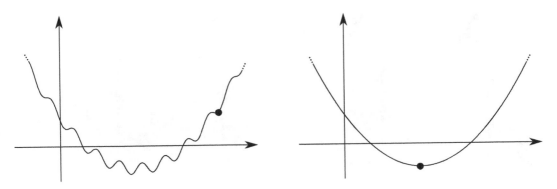

Figure 12.4 Newton's method can get caught in any number of local minima in the function on the left; smoothing this function, however, can generate a stronger initial guess of the global optimum.

- Sample the space of possible inputs $\vec{x}$ to get a better idea of the behavior of f over a large domain.

These and other strategies are *heuristic*, meaning that they usually cannot be used to guarantee that the output of such a minimization is globally optimal. In this section, we mention a few common techniques for global optimization as pointers to more specialized literature.

12.4.1   Graduated Optimization

Consider the optimization objective illustrated in Figure 12.4. Locally, this objective wiggles up and down, but at a larger scale, a more global pattern emerges. Newton's method seeks *any* critical point of $f(x)$ and easily can get caught in one of its local minima. To avoid this suboptimal output, we might attempt to minimize a smoothed version of $f(x)$ to generate an initial guess for the minimum of the more involved optimization problem.

Graduated optimization techniques solve progressively harder optimization problems with the hope that the coarse initial iterations will generate better initial guesses for the more accurate but sensitive later steps. In particular, suppose we wish to minimize some function $f(\vec{x})$ over $\vec{x} \in \mathbb{R}^n$ with many local optima as in Figure 12.4. Graduated methods generate a sequence of functions $f_1(\vec{x}), f_2(\vec{x}), \ldots, f_k(\vec{x})$ with $f_k(\vec{x}) = f(\vec{x})$, using critical points of f_i as initial guesses for minima of f_{i+1}.

Example 12.10 (Image alignment). A common task making use of graduated optimization is photograph alignment as introduced in §4.1.4. Consider the images in Figure 12.5. Aligning the original two images can be challenging because they have lots of high-frequency detail; for instance, the stones on the wall all look similar and easily could be misidentified. By *blurring* the input images, a better initial guess of the alignment can be obtained, because high-frequency details are suppressed.

The art of graduated optimization lies in finding an appropriate sequence of f_i's to help reach a global optimum. In signal and image processing, like in Example 12.10, a typical approach is to use the same optimization objective in each iteration but blur the underlying data to reveal larger-scale patterns. *Scale space* methods like [81] blur the objective itself,

Original　　　　　　　　　Blurred

Figure 12.5 The photos on the left can be hard to align using automatic methods because they have lots of high-frequency detail that can obscure larger alignment patterns; by blurring the photos we can align larger features before refining the alignment using texture and other detail.

for instance by defining f_i to be $f(\vec{x}) * g_{\sigma_i}(\vec{x})$, the result of blurring $f(\vec{x})$ using a Gaussian of width σ_i, with $\sigma_i \to 0$ as $i \to \infty$.

A related set of algorithms known as *homotopy continuation methods* continuously changes the optimization objective by leveraging intuition from topology. These algorithms make use of the following notion from classical mathematics:

Definition 12.1 (Homotopic functions). *Two continuous functions $f(\vec{x})$ and $g(\vec{x})$ are* homotopic *if there exists continuous function $H(\vec{x}, s)$ with*

$$H(\vec{x}, 0) = f(\vec{x}) \quad \text{and} \quad H(\vec{x}, 1) = g(\vec{x})$$

for all $\vec{x}$.

The idea of homotopy is illustrated in Figure 12.6.

Similar to graduated methods, homotopy optimizations minimize $f(\vec{x})$ by defining a new function $H(\vec{x}, s)$ where $H(\vec{x}, 0)$ is easy to optimize and $H(\vec{x}, 1) = f(\vec{x})$. Taking $\vec{x}_0^*$ to be the minimum of $H(\vec{x}, 0)$ with respect to $\vec{x}$, basic homotopy methods incrementally increase s, each time updating to a new $\vec{x}_s^*$. Assuming H is continuous, we expect the minimum $\vec{x}_s^*$ to trace a continuous path in $\mathbb{R}^n$ as s increases; hence, the solve for each $\vec{x}_s^*$ after increasing s differentially has a strong initial guess from the previous iteration.

Example 12.11 (Homotopy methods, [45]). Homotopy methods also apply to root-finding. As a small example, suppose we wish to find points x satisfying $\arctan(x) = 0$. Applying the formula from §8.1.4, Newton's method for finding such a root iterates

$$x_{k+1} = x_k - (1 + x_k^2) \arctan(x).$$

If we provide an initial guess $x_0 = 4$, however, this iteration diverges. Instead, we can define a homotopy function as

$$H(x, s) \equiv \arctan(x) + (s - 1) \arctan(4).$$

We know $H(x, 0) = \arctan(x) - \arctan(4)$ has a root at the initial guess $x_0 = 4$. Stepping s by increments of $1/10$ from 0 to 1, each time minimizing $H(x, s_i)$ with initial guess x_{i-1}^* via Newton's method yields a sequence of convergent problems reaching $x^* = 0$.

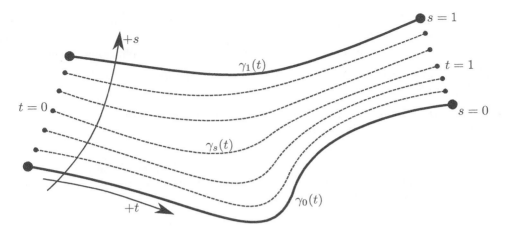

Figure 12.6 The curves $\gamma_0(t)$ and $\gamma_1(t)$ are homotopic because there exists a continuously varying set of curves $\gamma_s(t)$ for $s \in [0, 1]$ coinciding with γ_0 at $s = 0$ and γ_1 at $s = 1$.

More generally, we can think of a *solution path* as a curve of points $(\vec{x}(t), s(t))$ such that $s(0) = 0$, $s(1) = 1$, and at each time t, $\vec{x}(t)$ is a local minimizer of $H(\vec{x}, s(t))$ over $\vec{x}$. Our initial description of homotopy optimization would take $s(t) = t$, but now we can allow $s(t)$ to be non-monotonic as a function of t as long as it eventually reaches $s = 1$. Advanced homotopy continuation methods view $(\vec{x}(t), s(t))$ as a curve satisfying certain ordinary differential equations, which you will derive in Exercise 12.6; these equations can be solved using the techniques we will define in Chapter 15.

12.4.2 Randomized Global Optimization

When smoothing the objective function is impractical or fails to remove local minima from $f(\vec{x})$, it makes sense to sample the space of possible inputs $\vec{x}$ to get some idea of the energy landscape. Newton's method, gradient descent, and others all have strong dependence on the initial guess of the location of the minimum, so trying more than one starting point increases the chances of success.

If the objective f is sufficiently noisy, we may wish to remove dependence on differential estimates altogether. Without gradients, we do not know which directions locally point downhill, but via sampling we can find such patterns on a larger scale. Heuristics for global optimization at this scale commonly draw inspiration from the natural world and the idea of *swarm intelligence*, that complex natural processes can arise from individual actors following simple rules, often in the presence of stochasticity, or randomness. For instance, optimization routines have been designed to mimic ant colonies transporting food [26], thermodynamic energy in "annealing" processes [73], and evolution of DNA and genetic material [87]. These methods usually are considered heuristics without convergence guarantees but can help guide a large-scale search for optima.

As one example of a method well-tuned to continuous problems, we consider the *particle swarm* method introduced in [72] as an optimization technique inspired by social behavior in bird flocks and fish schools. Many variations of this technique have been proposed, but we explore one of the original versions introduced in [36].

Suppose we have a set of candidate minima $\vec{x}_1, \ldots, \vec{x}_k$. We will think of these points as particles moving around the possible space of $\vec{x}$ values, and hence they will also be assigned velocities $\vec{v}_1, \ldots, \vec{v}_k$. The particle swarm method maintains a few additional variables:

- $\vec{p}_1, \ldots, \vec{p}_k$, the position over all iterations so far of the lowest value $f(\vec{p}_i)$ observed by each particle i.

- The position $\vec{g} \in \{\vec{p}_1, \ldots, \vec{p}_k\}$ with the smallest objective value; this position is the *globally* best solution observed so far.

This notation is illustrated in Figure 12.7.

In each iteration of particle swarm optimization, the velocities of the particles are updated to guide them toward likely minima. Each particle is attracted to its own best observed minimum as well as to the global best position so far:

$$\vec{v}_i \leftarrow \vec{v}_i + \alpha(\vec{p}_i - \vec{x}_i) + \beta(\vec{g} - \vec{x}_i).$$

The parameters $\alpha, \beta \geq 0$ determine the amount of force felt from $\vec{x}_i$ to move toward these two positions; larger α, β values will push particles toward minima faster at the cost of more limited exploration of the space of possible minima. Once velocities have been updated, the particles move along their velocity vectors:

$$\vec{x}_i \leftarrow \vec{x}_i + \vec{v}_i.$$

Then, the process repeats. This algorithm is not guaranteed to converge, but it can be terminated at any point, with $\vec{g}$ as the best observed minimum. The final method is documented in Figure 12.8.

12.5 ONLINE OPTIMIZATION

We briefly consider a class of optimization problems from machine learning, game theory, and related fields in which the objective itself is allowed to change from iteration to iteration. These problems, known as *online optimization* problems, reflect a world in which evolving input parameters, priorities, and desired outcomes can make the output of an optimization irrelevant soon after it is generated. Hence, techniques in this domain must adaptively react to the changing objective in the presence of noise. Our discussion will introduce a few basic ideas from [107]; we refer the reader to that survey article for a more detailed treatment.

Example 12.12 (Stock market). Suppose we run a financial institution and wish to maintain an optimal portfolio of investments. On the morning of day t, in a highly simplified model we might choose how much of each stock $1, \ldots, n$ to buy, represented by a vector $\vec{x}_t \in (\mathbb{R}^+)^n$. At the end of the day, based on fluctuations of the market, we will know a function f_t so that $f_t(\vec{x})$ gives us our total profit or loss based on the decision $\vec{x}$ made in the morning. The function f_t can be different every day, so we must attempt to design a policy that predicts the objective function and/or its optimal point every day.

Problems in this class often can be formalized as *online convex optimization* problems. In the unconstrained case, online convex optimization algorithms are designed for the following feedback loop:

for $t = 1, 2, \ldots$ ▷ At each time t
   ▷ Predict $\vec{x}_t \in U$
   ▷ Receive loss function $f_t : U \to \mathbb{R}$
   ▷ Suffer loss $f_t(\vec{x}_t)$

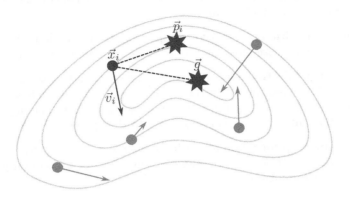

Figure 12.7 The particle swarm navigates the landscape of $f(\vec{x})$ by maintaining positions and velocities for a set of potential minima $\vec{x}_i$; each $\vec{x}_i$ is attracted to the position $\vec{p}_i$ at which it has observed the smallest value of $f(\vec{x}_i)$ as well as to the minimum $\vec{g}$ observed thus far by any particle.

---

function Particle-Swarm$(f(\vec{x}), k, \alpha, \beta, \vec{x}_{\min}, \vec{x}_{\max}, \vec{v}_{\min}, \vec{v}_{\max})$

$\quad f_{\min} \leftarrow \infty$

$\quad$**for** $i \leftarrow 1, 2, \ldots, k$

$\quad\quad \vec{x}_i \leftarrow$ Random-Position$(\vec{x}_{\min}, \vec{x}_{\max})$ $\qquad$ ▷ Initialize positions randomly

$\quad\quad \vec{v}_i \leftarrow$ Random-Velocity$(\vec{v}_{\min}, \vec{v}_{\max})$ $\qquad$ ▷ Initialize velocities randomly

$\quad\quad f_i \leftarrow f(\vec{x}_i)$ $\qquad\qquad\qquad\qquad\qquad\qquad$ ▷ Evaluate f

$\quad\quad \vec{p}_i \leftarrow \vec{x}_i$ $\qquad\qquad\qquad\qquad\qquad$ ▷ Current particle optimum

$\quad\quad$**if** $f_i < f_{\min}$ **then** $\qquad\qquad\qquad$ ▷ Check if it is global optimum

$\quad\quad\quad f_{\min} \leftarrow f_i$ $\qquad\qquad\qquad\qquad\qquad$ ▷ Update optimal value

$\quad\quad\quad \vec{g} \leftarrow \vec{x}_i$ $\qquad\qquad\qquad\qquad\qquad$ ▷ Set global optimum

$\quad$**for** $j \leftarrow 1, 2, \ldots$ $\qquad\qquad\qquad$ ▷ Stop when satisfied with $\vec{g}$

$\quad\quad$**for** $i \leftarrow 1, 2, \ldots, k$

$\quad\quad\quad \vec{v}_i \leftarrow \vec{v}_i + \alpha(\vec{p}_i - \vec{x}_i) + \beta(\vec{g} - \vec{x}_i)$ $\qquad$ ▷ Update velocity

$\quad\quad\quad \vec{x}_i \leftarrow \vec{x}_i + \vec{v}_i$ $\qquad\qquad\qquad\qquad$ ▷ Update position

$\quad\quad$**for** $i \leftarrow 1, 2, \ldots, k$

$\quad\quad\quad$**if** $f(\vec{x}_i) < f_i$ **then** $\qquad\qquad$ ▷ Better minimum for particle i

$\quad\quad\quad\quad \vec{p}_i \leftarrow \vec{x}_i$ $\qquad\qquad\qquad\qquad$ ▷ Update particle optimum

$\quad\quad\quad\quad f_i \leftarrow f(\vec{x}_i)$ $\qquad\qquad\qquad\qquad$ ▷ Store objective value

$\quad\quad\quad\quad$**if** $f_i < f_{\min}$ **then** $\qquad$ ▷ Check if it is a global optimum

$\quad\quad\quad\quad\quad f_{\min} \leftarrow f_i$ $\qquad\qquad\qquad\qquad$ ▷ Update optimal value

$\quad\quad\quad\quad\quad \vec{g} \leftarrow \vec{x}_i$ $\qquad\qquad\qquad\qquad\qquad$ ▷ Global optimum

---

Figure 12.8 Particle swarm optimization attempts to minimize $f(\vec{x})$ by simulating a collection of particles $\vec{x}_1, \ldots, \vec{x}_k$ moving in the space of potential inputs $\vec{x}$.

We will assume the f_t's are convex and that $U \subseteq \mathbb{R}^n$ is a convex set. There are a few features of this setup worth highlighting:

- To stay consistent with our discussion of optimization in previous chapters, we phrase the problem as *minimizing loss* rather than, e.g., maximizing profit.

- The optimization objective can change at each time t, and we do not get to know the objective f_t before choosing $\vec{x}_t$. In the stock market example, this feature reflects the fact that we do not know the price of a stock on day t until the day is over, and we must decide how much to buy before getting to that point.

- The online convex optimization algorithm can choose to store $f_1, \ldots, f_{t-1}$ to inform its choice of $\vec{x}_t$. For stock investment, we can use the stock prices on previous days to predict them for the future.

Since online convex optimization algorithms do not know f_t before predicting $\vec{x}_t$, we cannot expect them to perform perfectly. An "adversarial" client might wait for $\vec{x}_t$ and purposefully choose a loss function f_t to make $\vec{x}_t$ look bad! For this reason, metrics like *cumulative loss* $\sum_{t=1}^{T} f_t(\vec{x}_t)$ are unfair measures for the quality of an online optimization method at time T. In some sense, we must lower our standards for success.

One model for online convex optimization is minimization of *regret*, which compares performance to that of a fixed expert benefiting from hindsight:

> **Definition 12.2** (Regret). The *regret* of an online optimization algorithm at time T over a set U is given by
> $$R_T \equiv \max_{\vec{u} \in U} \left[\sum_{t=1}^{T} (f_t(\vec{x}_t) - f_t(\vec{u})) \right].$$

The regret R_T measures the difference between how well our algorithm has performed over time—as measured by summing $f_t(\vec{x}_t)$ over t—and the performance of any constant point $\vec{u}$ that must remain the same over all t. For the stock example, regret compares the profits lost by using our algorithm and the loss of using any single stock portfolio over all time. Ideally, the ratio R_T/T measuring average regret over time should decrease as $T \to \infty$.

The most obvious approach to online optimization is the "follow the leader" (FTL) strategy, which chooses $\vec{x}_t$ based on how it would have performed at times $1, \ldots, t-1$:

$$\textbf{Follow the leader: } \vec{x}_t \equiv \arg\min_{\vec{x} \in U} \sum_{s=1}^{t-1} f_s(\vec{x}).$$

FTL is a reasonable heuristic if we assume past performance has some bearing on future results. After all, if we do not know f_t we might as well hope that it is similar to the objectives $f_1, \ldots, f_{t-1}$ we have observed in the past.

For many classes of functions f_t, FTL is an effective approach that makes increasingly well-informed choices of $\vec{x}_t$ as t progresses. It can experience some serious drawbacks, however, as illustrated in the following example:

> **Example 12.13** (Failure of FTL, [107] §2.2). Suppose $U = [0, 1]$ and we generate a sequence of functions as follows:
> $$f_t(x) = \begin{cases} -x/2 & \text{if } t = 1 \\ x & \text{if } t \text{ is even} \\ -x & \text{otherwise.} \end{cases}$$

FTL minimizes the sum over all previous objective functions, giving the following series of outputs:

$$
\begin{aligned}
\mathbf{t} = \mathbf{1}: &\quad x \text{ arbitrary } \in [0,1] \\
\mathbf{t} = \mathbf{2}: &\quad x_2 = \arg\min_{x \in [0,1]} -x/2 = 1 \\
\mathbf{t} = \mathbf{3}: &\quad x_3 = \arg\min_{x \in [0,1]} x/2 = 0 \\
\mathbf{t} = \mathbf{4}: &\quad x_4 = \arg\min_{x \in [0,1]} -x/2 = 1 \\
\mathbf{t} = \mathbf{5}: &\quad x_5 = \arg\min_{x \in [0,1]} x/2 = 0 \\
&\quad \vdots
\end{aligned}
$$

From the above calculation, we find that in every iteration except $t = 1$, FTL incurs loss 1, while fixing $x = 0$ for all time would incur zero loss. For this example, FTL has regret growing proportionally to t.

This example illustrates the type of analysis and reasoning typically needed to design online learning methods. To bound regret, we must consider the *worst* possible adversary, who generates functions f_t specifically designed to take advantage of the weaknesses of a given technique.

FTL failed because it was too strongly sensitive to the fluctuations of f_t from iteration to iteration. To resolve this issue, we can take inspiration from Tikhonov regularization (§4.1.3), L^1 regularization (§10.4.1), and other methods that dampen the output of numerical methods by adding an energy term punishing irregular or large output vectors. To do so, we define the "follow the regularized leader" (FTRL) strategy:

$$
\textbf{Follow the regularized leader: } \vec{x}_t \equiv \arg\min_{\vec{x} \in U} \left[r(\vec{x}) + \sum_{s=1}^{t-1} f_s(\vec{x}) \right].
$$

Here, $r(\vec{x})$ is a convex regularization function, such as $\|\vec{x}\|_2^2$ (Tikhonov regularization), $\|\vec{x}\|_1$ (L^1 regularization), or $\sum_i x_i \log x_i$ when U includes only $\vec{x} \geq \vec{0}$ (entropic regularization).

Just as regularization improves the conditioning of a linear problem when it is close to singular, in this case the change from FTL to FTRL avoids fluctuation issues illustrated in Example 12.13. For instance, suppose $r(\vec{x})$ is *strongly convex* as defined below for differentiable r:

Definition 12.3 (Strongly convex). A differentiable regularizer $r(\vec{x})$ is σ-*strongly convex* with respect to a norm $\| \cdot \|$ if for any $\vec{x}, \vec{y}$ the following relationship holds:

$$
(\nabla r(\vec{x}) - \nabla r(\vec{y})) \cdot (\vec{x} - \vec{y}) \geq \sigma \|\vec{x} - \vec{y}\|_2^2.
$$

Intuitively, a strongly convex regularizer not only is bowl-shaped but has a lower bound for the curvature of that bowl. Then, we can prove the following statement:

Proposition 12.1 ([107], Theorem 2.11). Assume $r(\vec{x})$ is σ-strongly convex and that each f_t is convex and L-Lipschitz (see §8.1.1). Then, the regret is bounded as follows:

$$
R_T \leq \left[\max_{\vec{u} \in U} r(\vec{u}) \right] - \left[\min_{\vec{v} \in U} r(\vec{v}) \right] + \frac{TL^2}{\sigma}.
$$

The proof of this proposition uses techniques well within the scope of this book but due to its length is omitted from our discussion.

Proposition 12.1 can be somewhat hard to interpret, but it is a strong result about the effectiveness of the FTRL technique given an appropriate choice of r. In particular, the max and min terms as well as σ are properties of $r(\vec{x})$ that should guide which regularizer to use for a particular problem. The value σ contributes to both terms in competing ways:

- The difference between the maximum and minimum values of r is its range of possible outputs. Increasing σ has the potential to increase this difference, since it is bounded below by a "steeper" bowl. So, minimizing this term in our regret bound prefers *small* σ.

- Minimizing TL^2/σ prefers *large* σ.

Practically speaking, we can decide what range of T we care about and choose a regularizer accordingly:

Example 12.14 (FTRL choice of regularizers)**.** Consider the regularizer $r_\sigma(\vec{x}) \equiv \frac{1}{2}\sigma\|\vec{x}\|_2^2$. It has gradient $\nabla r_\sigma(\vec{x}) = \sigma\vec{x}$, so by direct application of Definition 12.3, it is σ-strongly convex. Suppose $U = \{\vec{x} \in \mathbb{R}^n : \|\vec{x}\|_2 \leq 1\}$ and that we expect to run our optimization for T time steps. If we take $\sigma = \sqrt{T}$, then the regret bound from Proposition 12.1 shows:

$$R_T \leq (1 + L^2)\sqrt{T}.$$

For large T, this value is small relative to T, compared to the linear growth for FTL in Example 12.13.

Online optimization is a rich area of research that continues to be explored. Beyond FTRL, we can define algorithms with better or more usable regret bounds, especially if we know more about the class of functions f_t we expect to observe. FTRL also has the drawback that it has to solve a potentially complex optimization problem at each iteration, which may not be practical for systems that have to make decisions quickly. Surprisingly, even easy-to-solve linearizations can behave fairly well for convex objectives, as illustrated in Exercise 12.14. Popular online optimization techniques like [34] have been applied to a variety of learning problems in the presence of huge amounts of noisy data.

12.6 EXERCISES

12.1 An alternative derivation of the Gauss-Newton algorithm shows that it can be thought of as an approximation of Newton's method for unconstrained optimization.

    (a) Write an expression for the Hessian of $E_{\mathrm{NLS}}(\vec{x})$ (defined in §12.1) in terms of the derivatives of the f_i's.

    (b) Show that the Gauss-Newton algorithm on E_{NLS} is equivalent to Newton's method (§9.4.2) after removing second derivative terms from the Hessian.

    (c) When is such an approximation of the Hessian reasonable?

12.2 Motivate the Levenberg-Marquardt algorithm by applying Tikhonov regularization to the Gauss-Newton algorithm.

12.3 Derive steps of an alternating least-squares (ALS) iterative algorithm for minimizing $\|X - CY\|_{\mathrm{Fro}}$ with respect to $C \in \mathbb{R}^{n \times d}$ and $Y \in \mathbb{R}^{d \times k}$, given a fixed matrix $X \in \mathbb{R}^{n \times k}$. Explain how the output of your algorithm depends on the initial guesses of C and Y. Provide an extension of your algorithm that orthogonalizes the columns of C in each iteration using its reduced QR factorization, and argue why the energy still decreases in each iteration.

12.4 Incorporate matrix factorization into the nonnegative least-squares algorithm in Example 12.8 to make the $\vec{x}$ step more efficient. When do you expect this modification to improve the speed of the algorithm?

12.5 For a fixed parameter $\delta > 0$, the *Huber loss function* $L_\delta(x)$ is defined as:

$$L_\delta(x) \equiv \begin{cases} x^2/2, & \text{when } |x| \le \delta \\ \delta(|x| - \delta/2), & \text{otherwise.} \end{cases}$$

This function "softens" the non-differentiable singularity of $|x|$ at $x = 0$.

(a) Illustrate the effect of choosing different values of δ on the shape of $L_\delta(x)$.

(b) Recall that we can find an $\vec{x}$ nearly satisfying the overdetermined system $A\vec{x} \approx \vec{b}$ by minimizing $\|A\vec{x} - \vec{b}\|_2$ (least-squares) or $\|A\vec{x} - \vec{b}\|_1$ (compressive sensing). Propose a similar optimization compromising between these two methods using L_δ.

(c) Propose an IRLS algorithm for optimizing your objective from Exercise 12.5b. You can assume $A^\top A$ is invertible.

(d) Propose an ADMM algorithm for optimizing your objective from Exercise 12.5b. Again, assume $A^\top A$ is invertible.
   Hint: Introduce a variable $\vec{z} = A\vec{x} - \vec{b}$.

DH 12.6 (From notes by P. Blomgren) In §12.4.1, we introduced homotopy continuation methods for optimization. These methods begin by minimizing a simple objective $H(\vec{x}, 0) = f_0(\vec{x})$ and then smoothly modify the objective and minimizer simultaneously until a minimum of $H(\vec{x}, 1) = f(\vec{x})$—the original objective—is found.

Suppose that $s(t)$ is a function of $t \ge 0$ such that $s(0) = 0$; we will assume that $s(t) \ge 0$ for all $t \ge 0$ and that $s(t)$ eventually reaches $s(t) = 1$. Our goal is to produce a path $\vec{x}(t)$ such that each $\vec{x}(t)$ minimizes $H(\vec{x}, s(t))$ with respect to $\vec{x}$.

(a) To maintain optimality of $\vec{x}(t)$, what relationship does $\nabla_{\vec{x}} H(\vec{x}, s)$ satisfy for all $t \ge 0$ at points $(\vec{x}(t), s(t))$ on the solution path?

(b) Differentiate this equation with respect to t. Write one side as a matrix-vector product.

(c) Provide a geometric interpretation of the vector $\vec{g}(t) \equiv (\vec{x}'(t), s'(t))$ in terms of the solution path $(\vec{x}(t), s(t))$.

(d) We will impose the restriction that $\|\vec{g}(t)\|_2 = 1 \ \forall t \ge 0$, i.e., that $\vec{g}(t)$ has unit length. In this case, what is the geometric interpretation of t in terms of the solution path?

(e) Combine Exercises 12.6b and 12.6d to propose an ordinary differential equation (ODE) for computing $(\vec{x}'(t), s'(t))$ from $(\vec{x}(t), s(t))$, so that the resulting solution path maintains our design constraints.
   Note: Using this formula, numerical ODE solvers like the ones we will propose in Chapter 15 can calculate a solution path for homotopy continuation optimization. This derivation provides a connection between topology, optimization, and differential equations.

12.7 ("Least absolute deviations") Instead of solving least-squares, to take advantage of methods from compressive sensing we might wish to minimize $\|A\vec{x} - \vec{b}\|_1$ with $\vec{x}$ unconstrained. Propose an ADMM-style splitting of this optimization and give the alternating steps of the optimization technique in this case.

^{DH} 12.8 Suppose we have two convex sets $S, T \subseteq \mathbb{R}^n$. The *alternating projection* method discussed in [9] and elsewhere is used to find a point $\vec{x} \in S \cap T$. For any initial guess $\vec{x}_0$, alternating projection performs the iteration

$$\vec{x}_{k+1} = \mathcal{P}_S \left(\mathcal{P}_T \left(\vec{x}_k \right) \right),$$

where $\mathcal{P}_S$ and $\mathcal{P}_T$ are operators that project onto the nearest point in S or T with respect to $\|\cdot\|_2$, respectively. As long as $S \cap T \neq \emptyset$, this iterative procedure is guaranteed to converge to an $\vec{x} \in S \cap T$, though this convergence may be impractically slow [23]. Instead of this algorithm, we will consider finding a point in the intersection of convex sets using ADMM.

(a) Propose an unconstrained optimization problem whose solution is a point $\vec{x} \in S \cap T$, assuming $S \cap T \neq \emptyset$.
Hint: Use indicator functions.

(b) Write this problem in a form that is amenable to ADMM, using $\vec{x}$ and $\vec{z}$ as your variables.

(c) Explicitly write the ADMM iterations for updating $\vec{x}$, $\vec{z}$, and any dual variables. Your expressions can use $\mathcal{P}_S$ and $\mathcal{P}_T$.

^{DH} 12.9 A popular technique for global optimization is *simulated annealing* [73], a method motivated by ideas from statistical physics. The term *annealing* refers to the process in metallurgy whereby a metal is heated and then cooled so its constituent particles arrange in a minimum energy state. In this thermodynamic process, atoms may move considerably at higher temperatures but become restricted in motion as the temperature decreases. Borrowing from this analogy in the context of global optimization, we could let a potential optimal point take large, random steps early on in a search to explore the space of outputs, eventually taking smaller steps as the number of iterations gets large, to obtain a more refined output. Pseudocode for the resulting simulated annealing algorithm is provided in the following box.

```
function SIMULATED-ANNEALING(f(x⃗), x⃗₀)
    T₀ ← High temperature
    Tᵢ ← Cooling schedule, e.g., Tᵢ = αTᵢ₋₁ for some α < 1
    x⃗ ← x⃗₀                              ▷ Current model initialized to the input x⃗₀
    for i ← 1, 2, 3, . . .
        y⃗ ← RANDOM-MODEL                        ▷ Random guess of output
        Δf ← f(y⃗) − f(x⃗)                        ▷ Compute change in objective
        if Δf < 0 then                          ▷ Objective improved at y⃗
            x⃗ ← y⃗
        else if UNIFORM(0,1)< e^(−Δf/Tᵢ) then   ▷ True with probability e^(−Δf/Tᵢ)
            x⃗ ← y⃗                               ▷ Randomly keep suboptimal output
```

Simulated annealing randomly guesses a solution to the optimization problem in each iteration. If the new solution achieves a lower objective value than the current solution, the algorithm keeps the new solution. If the new solution is less optimal, however, it is not necessarily rejected. Instead, the suboptimal point is accepted with exponentially small probability as temperature decreases. The hope of this construction is that local minima will be avoided early on in favor of global minima due to the significant amount of exploration during the first few iterations, while some form of convergence is still obtained as the iterates stabilize at lower temperatures.

Consider the Euclidean traveling salesman problem (TSP): Given a set of points $\vec{x}_1, \ldots, \vec{x}_n \in \mathbb{R}^2$ representing the positions of cities on a map, we wish to visit each city exactly once while minimizing the total distance traveled. While Euclidean TSP is NP-hard, simulated annealing provides a practical way to approximate its solution.

(a) Phrase Euclidean TSP as a global optimization problem. It is acceptable to have variables that are discrete rather than continuous.

(b) Propose a method for generating random tours that reach each city exactly once. What f should you use to evaluate the quality of a tour?

(c) Implement your simulated annealing solution to Euclidean TSP and explore the trade-off between solution quality and runtime when the initial temperature T_0 is changed. Also, experiment with different cooling schedules, either by varying α in the example T_i or by proposing your own cooling schedule.

(d) Choose another global optimization algorithm and explain how to use it to solve Euclidean TSP. Analyze how its efficiency compares to that of simulated annealing.

(e) Rather than generating a completely new tour in each iteration of simulated annealing, propose a method that perturbs tours slightly to generate new ones. What would be the advantages and/or disadvantages of using this technique in place of totally random models?

SC 12.10 Recall the setup from Exercise 10.7 for designing a slow-dissolving medicinal capsule shaped as a cylinder with hemispherical ends.

(a) Suppose we are unhappy with the results of the optimization proposed in Exercise 10.7 and want to ensure that the volume of the *entire* capsule (including the ends) is at least V. Explain why the resulting problem cannot be solved using geometric programming methods.

(b) Propose an alternating optimization method for this problem. Is it necessary to solve a geometric program in either alternation?

12.11 The mean shift algorithm, originally proposed in [27], is an iterative clustering technique appearing in literature on nonparametric machine learning and image processing. Given n data points $\vec{x}_i \in \mathbb{R}^d$, the algorithm groups points together based on their closest maxima in a smoothed density function approximating the distribution of data points.

(a) Take $k(x) : \mathbb{R} \to \mathbb{R}^+$ to be a nonnegative function. For a fixed bandwidth parameter $h > 0$, define the *kernel density estimator* $\hat{f}(\vec{x})$ to be

$$\hat{f}_k(\vec{x}) \equiv \frac{c_{k,d}}{nh^d} \sum_{i=1}^{n} k\left(\left\|\frac{\vec{x} - \vec{x}_i}{h}\right\|_2^2\right).$$

If $k(x)$ is peaked at $x = 0$, explain how $\hat{f}_k(\vec{x})$ encodes the density of data points $\vec{x}_i$. What is the effect of increasing the parameter h?

Note: The constant $c_{k,d}$ is chosen so that $\int_{\mathbb{R}^d} \hat{f}(\vec{x})\, d\vec{x} = 1$. Choosing $k(x) \equiv e^{-x/2}$ makes $\hat{f}$ a sum of Gaussians.

(b) Define $g(x) \equiv -k'(x)$ and take $m(\vec{x})$ to be the *mean shift* vector given by

$$m(\vec{x}) \equiv \frac{\sum_i \vec{x}_i g\left(\left\|\frac{\vec{x}-\vec{x}_i}{h}\right\|_2^2\right)}{\sum_i g\left(\left\|\frac{\vec{x}-\vec{x}_i}{h}\right\|_2^2\right)} - \vec{x}.$$

Show that $\nabla \hat{f}_k(\vec{x})$ can be factored as follows:

$$\nabla \hat{f}_k(\vec{x}) = \frac{\alpha}{h^2} \cdot \hat{f}_g(\vec{x}) \cdot m(\vec{x}),$$

for some constant α.

(c) Suppose $\vec{y}_0$ is a guess of the location of a peak of $\hat{f}_k$. Using your answer from Exercise 12.11b, motivate the *mean shift* algorithm for finding a peak of $\hat{f}_k(\vec{x})$, which iterates the formula

$$\vec{y}_{k+1} \equiv \frac{\sum_i \vec{x}_i g\left(\left\|\frac{\vec{y}_k-\vec{x}_i}{h}\right\|_2^2\right)}{\sum_i g\left(\left\|\frac{\vec{y}_k-\vec{x}_i}{h}\right\|_2^2\right)}.$$

Note: This algorithm is guaranteed to converge under mild conditions on k. Mean shift clustering runs this method to convergence starting from $\vec{y}_0 = \vec{x}_i$ for each i in parallel; $\vec{x}_i$ and $\vec{x}_j$ are assigned to the same cluster if mean shift iteration yields the same output (within some tolerance) for starting points $\vec{y}_0 = \vec{x}_i$ and $\vec{y}_0 = \vec{x}_j$.

(d) Suppose we represent a grayscale image as a set of pairs $(\vec{p}_i, q_i)$, where $\vec{p}_i$ is the center of pixel i (typically laid out on a grid), and $q_i \in [0, 1]$ is the intensity of pixel i. The *bilateral filter* [120] for blurring images while preserving their sharp edges is given by:

$$\hat{q}_i \equiv \frac{\sum_j q_j k_1(\|\vec{p}_j - \vec{p}_i\|_2) k_2(|q_j - q_i|)}{\sum_j k_1(\|\vec{p}_j - \vec{p}_i\|_2) k_2(|q_j - q_i|)},$$

where k_1, k_2 are Gaussian kernels given by $k_i(x) \equiv e^{-a_i x^2}$. Fast algorithms have been developed in the computer graphics community for evaluating the bilateral filter and its variants [97].

Propose an algorithm for clustering the pixels in an image using iterated calls to a modified version of the bilateral filter; the resulting method is called the "local mode filter" [125, 96].

12.12 The *iterative shrinkage-thresholding algorithm* (ISTA) is another technique relevant to large-scale optimization applicable to common objectives from machine learning. Extensions such as [11] have led to renewed interest in this technique. We follow the development of [20].

(a) Show that the iteration from gradient descent

$$\vec{x}_{k+1} = \vec{x}_k - \alpha \nabla f(\vec{x}_k)$$

can be rewritten in *proximal form* as

$$\vec{x}_{k+1} = \arg\min_{\vec{x}} \left[f(\vec{x}_k) + \nabla f(\vec{x}_k)^\top (\vec{x} - \vec{x}_k) + \frac{1}{2\alpha} \|\vec{x} - \vec{x}_k\|_2^2 \right].$$

(b) Suppose we wish to minimize a sum $f(\vec{x}) + g(\vec{x})$. Based on the previous part, ISTA attempts to combine exact optimization for g with gradient descent on f:

$$\vec{x}_{k+1} \equiv \arg\min_{\vec{x}} \left[f(\vec{x}_k) + \nabla f(\vec{x}_k)^\top (\vec{x} - \vec{x}_k) + \frac{1}{2\alpha} \|\vec{x} - \vec{x}_k\|_2^2 + g(\vec{x}) \right].$$

Derive the alternative form

$$\vec{x}_{k+1} = \arg\min_{\vec{x}} \left[g(\vec{x}) + \frac{1}{2\alpha} \|\vec{x} - (\vec{x}_k - \alpha \nabla f(\vec{x}_k))\|_2^2 \right].$$

(c) Derive a formula for ISTA iterations when $g(\vec{x}) = \lambda \|\vec{x}\|_1$, where $\lambda > 0$.
Hint: This case reduces to solving a set of single-variable problems.

12.13 Suppose $\mathcal{D}$ is a bounded, convex, and closed domain in $\mathbb{R}^n$ and $f(\vec{x})$ is a convex, differentiable objective function. The *Frank-Wolfe* algorithm for minimizing $f(\vec{x})$ subject to $\vec{x} \in \mathcal{D}$ is as follows [43]:

$$\vec{s}_k \leftarrow \arg\min_{\vec{s} \in \mathcal{D}} [\vec{s} \cdot \nabla f(\vec{x}_{k-1})]$$

$$\gamma_k \leftarrow \frac{2}{k+2}$$

$$\vec{x}_k \leftarrow (1 - \gamma_k)\vec{x}_{k-1} + \gamma_k \vec{s}_k.$$

A starting point $\vec{x}_0 \in \mathcal{D}$ must be provided. This algorithm has gained renewed attention for large-scale optimization in machine learning in the presence of sparsity and other specialized structure [66].

(a) Argue that $\vec{s}_k$ minimizes a linearized version of f subject to the constraints. Also, show that if $\mathcal{D} = \{\vec{x} : A\vec{x} \leq \vec{b}\}$ for fixed $A \in \mathbb{R}^{m \times n}$ and $\vec{b} \in \mathbb{R}^m$, then each iteration of the Frank-Wolfe algorithm solves a linear program.

(b) Show that $\vec{x}_k \in \mathcal{D}$ for all $k > 0$.

(c) Assume $\nabla f(\vec{x})$ is L-Lipschitz on $\mathcal{D}$, meaning $\|\nabla f(\vec{x}) - \nabla f(\vec{y})\|_2 \leq L\|\vec{x} - \vec{y}\|_2$, for all $\vec{x}, \vec{y} \in \mathcal{D}$. Derive the bound (proposed in [88]):

$$|f(\vec{y}) - f(\vec{x}) - (\vec{y} - \vec{x}) \cdot \nabla f(\vec{x})| \leq \frac{L}{2} \|\vec{y} - \vec{x}\|_2^2.$$

Hint: By the Fundamental Theorem of Calculus, $f(\vec{y}) = f(\vec{x}) + \int_0^1 (\vec{y} - \vec{x}) \cdot \nabla f(\vec{x} + \tau(\vec{y} - \vec{x})) \, d\tau$.

(d) Define the *diameter* of $\mathcal{D}$ to be $d \equiv \max_{\vec{x}, \vec{y} \in \mathcal{D}} \|\vec{x} - \vec{y}\|_2$. Furthermore, assume $\nabla f(\vec{x})$ is L-Lipschitz on $\mathcal{D}$. Show that

$$\frac{2}{\gamma^2}(f(\vec{y}) - f(\vec{x}) - (\vec{y} - \vec{x}) \cdot \nabla f(\vec{x})) \le d^2 L,$$

for all $\vec{x}, \vec{y}, \vec{s} \in \mathcal{D}$ with $\vec{y} = \vec{x} + \gamma(\vec{s} - \vec{x})$ and $\gamma \in [0, 1]$. Conclude that

$$f(\vec{y}) \le f(\vec{x}) + \gamma(\vec{s} - \vec{x}) \cdot \nabla f(\vec{x}) + \frac{\gamma^2 d^2 L}{2}.$$

(e) Define the *duality gap* $g(\vec{x}) \equiv \max_{\vec{s} \in \mathcal{D}}(\vec{x} - \vec{s}) \cdot \nabla f(\vec{x})$. For the Frank-Wolfe algorithm, show that

$$f(\vec{x}_k) \le f(\vec{x}_{k-1}) - \gamma g(\vec{x}_{k-1}) + \frac{\gamma_k^2 d^2 L}{2}.$$

(f) Take $\vec{x}^*$ to be the location of the minimum for the optimization problem, and define $h(\vec{x}) \equiv f(\vec{x}) - f(\vec{x}^*)$. Show $g(\vec{x}) \ge h(\vec{x})$, and using the previous part conclude

$$h(\vec{x}_k) \le (1 - \gamma_k)h(\vec{x}_{k-1}) + \frac{\gamma_k^2 d^2 L}{2}.$$

(g) Conclude $h(\vec{x}_k) \to 0$ as $k \to \infty$. What does this imply about the Frank-Wolfe algorithm?

12.14 The FTRL algorithm from §12.5 can be expensive when the f_t's are difficult to minimize. In this problem, we derive a linearized alternative with similar performance guarantees.

(a) Suppose we make the following assumptions about an instance of FTRL:
   - $U = \{\vec{x} \in \mathbb{R}^n : \|\vec{x}\|_2 \le 1\}$.
   - All of the objectives f_t provided to FTRL are of the form $f_t(\vec{x}) = \vec{z}_t \cdot \vec{x}$ for $\|\vec{z}_t\|_2 \le 1$.
   - $r(\vec{x}) \equiv \frac{1}{2}\sigma\|\vec{x}\|_2^2$.

   Provide an explicit formula for the iterates $\vec{x}_t$ in this case, and specialize the bound from Proposition 12.1.

(b) We wish to apply the bound from 12.14a to more general f_t's. To do so, suppose we replace FTRL with a linearized objective for $\vec{x}_t$:

$$\vec{x}_t \equiv \arg\min_{\vec{x} \in U} \left[r(\vec{x}) + \sum_{s=1}^{t-1} (f_s(\vec{x}_s) + \nabla f_s(\vec{x}_s) \cdot (\vec{x} - \vec{x}_s)) \right].$$

   Provide an explicit formula for $\vec{x}_t$ in this case, assuming the same choice of U and r.

(c) Propose a regret bound for the linearized method in 12.14b.
   Hint: Apply convexity of the f_t's and the result of 12.14a.

IV

Functions, Derivatives, and Integrals

CHAPTER 13

Interpolation

CONTENTS

13.1   Interpolation in a Single Variable 258
        13.1.1   Polynomial Interpolation 258
        13.1.2   Alternative Bases 262
        13.1.3   Piecewise Interpolation 263
13.2   Multivariable Interpolation 265
        13.2.1   Nearest-Neighbor Interpolation 265
        13.2.2   Barycentric Interpolation 266
        13.2.3   Grid-Based Interpolation 268
13.3   Theory of Interpolation 269
        13.3.1   Linear Algebra of Functions 269
        13.3.2   Approximation via Piecewise Polynomials 272

S O far we have derived methods for *analyzing* functions f, e.g., finding their minima and roots. Evaluating $f(\vec{x})$ at a particular $\vec{x} \in \mathbb{R}^n$ might be expensive, but a fundamental assumption of the methods we developed in previous chapters is that we can obtain $f(\vec{x})$ when we want it, regardless of $\vec{x}$.

There are many contexts in which this assumption is unrealistic. For instance, if we take a photograph with a digital camera, we receive an $n \times m$ grid of pixel color values sampling the continuum of light coming into the camera lens. We might think of a photograph as a continuous function from image position (x, y) to color (r, g, b), but in reality we only know the image value at nm separated locations on the image plane. Similarly, in machine learning and statistics, often we only are given samples of a function at points where we collected data, and we must interpolate to have values elsewhere; in a medical setting we may monitor a patient's response to different dosages of a drug but must predict what will happen at a dosage we have not tried explicitly.

In these cases, before we can minimize a function, find its roots, or even compute values $f(\vec{x})$ at arbitrary locations $\vec{x}$, we need a model for interpolating $f(\vec{x})$ to all of $\mathbb{R}^n$ (or some subset thereof) given a collection of samples $f(\vec{x}_i)$. Techniques for this *interpolation* problem are inherently approximate, since we do not know the true values of f, so instead we seek for the interpolated function to be smooth and serve as a reasonable prediction of function values. Mathematically, the definition of "reasonable" will depend on the particular application. If we want to evaluate $f(\vec{x})$ directly, we may choose an interpolant and sample positions $\vec{x}_i$ so that the distance of the interpolated $f(\vec{x})$ from the true values can be bounded above given smoothness assumptions on f; future chapters will estimate derivatives, integrals, and other properties of f from samples and may choose an interpolant designed to make these approximations accurate or stable.

In this chapter, we will assume that the values $f(\vec{x}_i)$ are known with complete certainty; in this case, we can think of the problem as extending f to the remainder of the domain without perturbing the value at any of the input locations. To contrast, the *regression* problem considered in §4.1.1 and elsewhere may forgo matching $f(\vec{x}_i)$ exactly in favor of making f more smooth.

13.1 INTERPOLATION IN A SINGLE VARIABLE

Before considering the general case, we will design methods for interpolating functions of a single variable $f : \mathbb{R} \to \mathbb{R}$. As input, we will take a set of k pairs (x_i, y_i) with the assumption $f(x_i) = y_i$; our job is to predict $f(x)$ for $x \notin \{x_1, \ldots, x_k\}$. Desirable *interpolants* $f(x)$ should be smooth and should interpolate the data points faithfully without adding extra features like spurious local minima and maxima.

We will take inspiration from linear algebra by writing $f(x)$ in a *basis*. The set of all possible functions $f : \mathbb{R} \to \mathbb{R}$ is far too large to work with and includes many functions that are not practical in a computational setting. Thus, we simplify the search space by forcing f to be written as a linear combination of building block basis functions. This formulation is familiar from calculus: The Taylor expansion writes functions in the basis of polynomials, while Fourier series use sine and cosine.

The construction and analysis of interpolation bases is a classical topic that has been studied for centuries. We will focus on practical aspects of choosing and using interpolation bases, with a brief consideration of theoretical aspects in §13.3. Detailed aspects of error analysis can be found in [117] and other advanced texts.

13.1.1 Polynomial Interpolation

Perhaps the most straightforward class of interpolation formulas assumes that $f(x)$ is in $\mathbb{R}[x]$, the set of polynomials. Polynomials are smooth, and we already have explored linear methods for finding a degree $k - 1$ polynomial through k sample points in Chapter 4.

Example 4.3 worked out the details of such an interpolation technique. As a reminder, suppose we wish to find $f(x) \equiv a_0 + a_1 x + a_2 x^2 + \cdots + a_{k-1} x^{k-1}$ through the points $(x_1, y_1), \ldots, (x_k, y_k)$; here our unknowns are the values $a_0, \ldots, a_{k-1}$. Plugging in the expression $y_i = f(x_i)$ for each i shows that the vector $\vec{a}$ satisfies the $k \times k$ *Vandermonde* system:

$$\begin{pmatrix} 1 & x_1 & x_1^2 & \cdots & x_1^{k-1} \\ 1 & x_2 & x_2^2 & \cdots & x_2^{k-1} \\ \vdots & \vdots & \vdots & \cdots & \vdots \\ 1 & x_k & x_k^2 & \cdots & x_k^{k-1} \end{pmatrix} \begin{pmatrix} a_0 \\ a_1 \\ \vdots \\ a_{k-1} \end{pmatrix} = \begin{pmatrix} y_0 \\ y_1 \\ \vdots \\ y_k \end{pmatrix}.$$

By this construction, degree $k - 1$ polynomial interpolation can be accomplished using a $k \times k$ linear solve for $\vec{a}$ using the linear algorithms in Chapter 3. This method, however, is far from optimal for many applications.

As mentioned above, one way to think about the space of polynomials is that it can be spanned by a basis of functions. Just like writing vectors in $\mathbb{R}^n$ as linear combinations of linearly independent vectors $\vec{v}_1, \ldots, \vec{v}_n \in \mathbb{R}^n$, in our derivation of the Vandermonde matrix, we wrote polynomials in the *monomial basis* $\{1, x, x^2, \ldots, x^{k-1}\}$ for polynomials of degree $k - 1$. Although monomials may be an obvious basis for $\mathbb{R}[x]$, they have limited properties useful for simplifying the polynomial interpolation problem. One way to visualize this issue is to plot the sequence of functions $1, x, x^2, x^3, \ldots$ for $x \in [0, 1]$; in this interval, as shown in

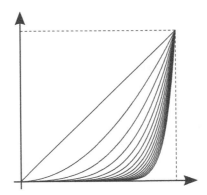

Figure 13.1 As k increases, the monomials x^k on $[0, 1]$ begin to look more and more similar. This similarity creates poor conditioning for monomial basis problems like solving the Vandermonde system.

Figure 13.1, the functions x^k all start looking similar as k increases. As we know from our consideration of projection problems in Chapter 5, projection onto a set of similar-looking basis vectors can be unstable.

We may choose to write polynomials in a basis that is better suited to the problem at hand. Recall that we are given k pairs $(x_1, y_1), \ldots, (x_k, y_k)$. We can use these (fixed) points to define the *Lagrange interpolation* basis $\phi_1, \ldots, \phi_k$ by writing:

$$\phi_i(x) \equiv \frac{\prod_{j \neq i}(x - x_j)}{\prod_{j \neq i}(x_i - x_j)}.$$

Example 13.1 (Lagrange basis). Suppose $x_1 = 0$, $x_2 = 2$, $x_3 = 3$, and $x_4 = 4$. The Lagrange basis for this set of x_i's is:

$$\phi_1(x) = \frac{(x-2)(x-3)(x-4)}{-2 \cdot -3 \cdot -4} = \frac{1}{24}(-x^3 + 9x^2 - 26x + 24)$$

$$\phi_2(x) = \frac{x(x-3)(x-4)}{2 \cdot (2-3)(2-4)} = \frac{1}{4}(x^3 - 7x^2 + 12x)$$

$$\phi_3(x) = \frac{x(x-2)(x-4)}{3 \cdot (3-2) \cdot (3-4)} = \frac{1}{3}(-x^3 + 6x^2 - 8x)$$

$$\phi_4(x) = \frac{x(x-2)(x-3)}{4 \cdot (4-2) \cdot (4-3)} = \frac{1}{8}(x^3 - 5x^2 + 6x).$$

This basis is shown in Figure 13.2.

As shown in this example, although we did not define it explicitly in the monomial basis $\{1, x, x^2, \ldots, x^{k-1}\}$, each ϕ_i is still a polynomial of degree $k-1$. Furthermore, the Lagrange basis has the following desirable property:

$$\phi_i(x_\ell) = \begin{cases} 1 & \text{when } \ell = i \\ 0 & \text{otherwise.} \end{cases}$$

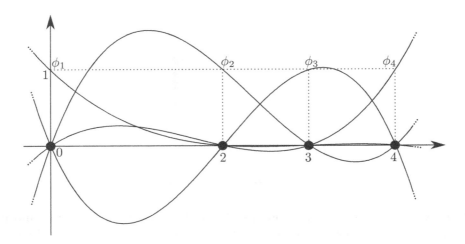

Figure 13.2 The Lagrange basis for $x_1 = 0, x_2 = 2, x_3 = 3, x_4 = 4$. Each ϕ_i satisfies $\phi_i(x_i) = 1$ and $\phi_i(x_j) = 0$ for all $i \neq j$.

Using this formula, finding the unique degree $k - 1$ polynomial fitting our (x_i, y_i) pairs is formulaic in the Lagrange basis:

$$f(x) \equiv \sum_i y_i \phi_i(x).$$

To check, if we substitute $x = x_j$ we find:

$$f(x_j) = \sum_i y_i \phi_i(x_j)$$

$$= y_j \text{ since } \phi_i(x_j) = 0 \text{ when } i \neq j.$$

We have shown that in the Lagrange basis we can write a closed formula for $f(x)$ that does not require solving the Vandermonde system; in other words, we have replaced the Vandermonde matrix with the identity matrix. The drawback, however, is that each $\phi_i(x)$ takes $O(k)$ time to evaluate using the formula above, so computing $f(x)$ takes $O(k^2)$ time total; contrastingly, if we find the coefficients a_i from the Vandermonde system explicitly, the evaluation time for interpolation subsequently becomes $O(k)$.

Computation time aside, the Lagrange basis has an additional numerical drawback, in that the denominator is the product of a potentially large number of terms. If the x_i's are close together, then this product may include many terms close to zero; the end result is division by a small number when evaluating $\phi_i(x)$. As we have seen, this operation can create numerical instabilities that we wish to avoid.

A third basis for polynomials of degree $k - 1$ that attempts to compromise between the numerical quality of the monomials and the efficiency of the Lagrange basis is the *Newton* basis, defined as

$$\psi_i(x) = \prod_{j=1}^{i-1}(x - x_j).$$

This product has no terms when $i = 1$, so we define $\psi_1(x) \equiv 1$. Then, for all indices i, the function $\psi_i(x)$ is a degree $i - 1$ polynomial.

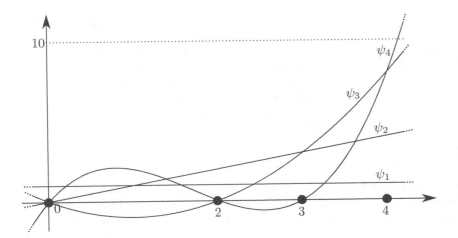

Figure 13.3 The Newton basis for $x_1 = 0, x_2 = 2, x_3 = 3, x_4 = 4$. Each ψ_i satisfies $\psi_i(x_j) = 0$ when $j < i$.

Example 13.2 (Newton basis). Continuing from Example 13.1, again suppose $x_1 = 0$, $x_2 = 2$, $x_3 = 3$, and $x_4 = 4$. The corresponding Newton basis is:

$$\psi_1(x) = 1$$
$$\psi_2(x) = x$$
$$\psi_3(x) = x(x - 2) = x^2 - 2x$$
$$\psi_4(x) = x(x - 2)(x - 3) = x^3 - 5x^2 + 6x.$$

This basis is illustrated in Figure 13.3.

By definition of ψ_i, $\psi_i(x_\ell) = 0$ for all $\ell < i$. If we wish to write $f(x) = \sum_i c_i \psi_i(x)$ and write out this observation more explicitly, we find:

$$f(x_1) = c_1 \psi_1(x_1)$$
$$f(x_2) = c_1 \psi_1(x_2) + c_2 \psi_2(x_2)$$
$$f(x_3) = c_1 \psi_1(x_3) + c_2 \psi_2(x_3) + c_3 \psi_3(x_3)$$
$$\vdots \quad \vdots$$

These expressions provide the following lower-triangular system for $\vec{c}$:

$$\begin{pmatrix} \psi_1(x_1) & 0 & 0 & \cdots & 0 \\ \psi_1(x_2) & \psi_2(x_2) & 0 & \cdots & 0 \\ \psi_1(x_3) & \psi_2(x_3) & \psi_3(x_3) & \cdots & 0 \\ \vdots & \vdots & \vdots & \cdots & \vdots \\ \psi_1(x_k) & \psi_2(x_k) & \psi_3(x_k) & \cdots & \psi_k(x_k) \end{pmatrix} \begin{pmatrix} c_1 \\ c_2 \\ \vdots \\ c_k \end{pmatrix} = \begin{pmatrix} y_1 \\ y_2 \\ \vdots \\ y_k \end{pmatrix}.$$

This system can be solved in $O(k^2)$ time using forward-substitution, rather than the $O(k^3)$ time needed to solve the Vandermonde system using Gaussian elimination.* Evaluation time

---

*For completeness, we should mention that $O(k^2)$ Vandermonde solvers can be formulated; see [62] for discussion of these specialized techniques.

is similar to that of the Lagrange basis, but since there is no denominator, numerical issues are less likely to appear.

We now have three strategies of interpolating k data points using a degree $k - 1$ polynomial by writing it in the monomial, Lagrange, and Newton bases. All three represent different compromises between numerical quality and speed, but the resulting interpolated function $f(x)$ is the *same* in each case. More explicitly, there is exactly one polynomial of degree $k - 1$ going through a set of k points, so since all our interpolants are degree $k - 1$ they must have the same output.

13.1.2 Alternative Bases

Although polynomial functions are particularly amenable to mathematical analysis, there is no fundamental reason why an interpolation basis cannot consist of different types of functions. For example, a crowning result of Fourier analysis implies that many functions are well-approximated by linear combinations of trigonometric functions $\cos(kx)$ and $\sin(kx)$ for $k \in \mathbb{N}$. A construction like the Vandermonde matrix still applies in this case, and the fast Fourier transform algorithm (which merits a larger discussion) solves the resulting linear system with remarkable efficiency.

A smaller extension of the development in §13.1.1 is to *rational* functions of the form:

$$f(x) \equiv \frac{p_0 + p_1 x + p_2 x^2 + \cdots + p_m x^m}{q_0 + q_1 x + q_2 x^2 + \cdots + q_n x^n}.$$

If we are given k pairs (x_i, y_i), then we will need $m + n + 1 = k$ for this function to be well-defined. One degree of freedom must be fixed to account for the fact that the same rational function can be expressed multiple ways by simultaneously scaling the numerator and the denominator.

Rational functions can have asymptotes and other features not achievable using only polynomials, so they can be desirable interpolants for functions that change quickly or have poles. Once m and n are fixed, the coefficients p_i and q_i still can be found using linear techniques by multiplying both sides by the denominator:

$$y_i(q_0 + q_1 x_i + q_2 x_i^2 + \cdots + q_n x_i^n) = p_0 + p_1 x_i + p_2 x_i^2 + \cdots + p_m x_i^m.$$

For interpolation, the unknowns in this expression are the p's and q's.

The flexibility of rational functions, however, can cause some issues. For instance, consider the following example:

Example 13.3 (Failure of rational interpolation, [117] §2.2). Suppose we wish to find a rational function $f(x)$ interpolating the following data points: $(0, 1)$, $(1, 2)$, $(2, 2)$. If we choose $m = n = 1$, then the linear system for finding the unknown coefficients is:

$$q_0 = p_0$$
$$2(q_0 + q_1) = p_0 + p_1$$
$$2(q_0 + 2q_1) = p_0 + 2p_1.$$

One nontrivial solution to this system is:

$$p_0 = 0 \qquad q_0 = 0$$
$$p_1 = 2 \qquad q_1 = 1.$$

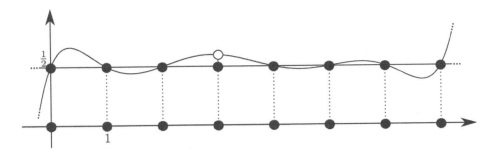

Figure 13.4 Interpolating eight samples of the function $f(x) \equiv 1/2$ using a seventh-degree polynomial yields a straight line, but perturbing a single data point at $x = 3$ creates an interpolant that oscillates far away from the infinitesimal vertical displacement.

This implies the following form for $f(x)$:

$$f(x) = \frac{2x}{x}.$$

This function has a degeneracy at $x = 0$, and canceling the x in the numerator and denominator does not yield $f(0) = 1$ as we might desire.

This example illustrates a larger phenomenon. The linear system for finding the p's and q's can run into issues when the resulting denominator $\sum_\ell p_\ell x^\ell$ has a root at any of the fixed x_i's. It can be shown that when this is the case, no rational function exists with the fixed choice of m and n interpolating the given values. A typical partial resolution in this case is presented in [117], which suggests incrementing m and n alternatively until a nontrivial solution exists. From a practical standpoint, however, the specialized nature of these methods indicates that alternative interpolation strategies may be preferable when the basic rational methods fail.

13.1.3 Piecewise Interpolation

So far, we have constructed interpolation bases out of elementary functions defined on all of $\mathbb{R}$. When the number k of data points becomes high, however, many degeneracies become apparent. For example, Figure 13.4 illustrates how polynomial interpolation is *nonlocal*, meaning that changing any single value y_i in the input data can change the behavior of f for all x, even those that are far away from x_i. This property is undesirable for most applications: We usually expect only the input data near a given x to affect the value of the interpolated function $f(x)$, especially when there is a large cloud of input points. While the Weierstrass Approximation Theorem from real analysis guarantees that any smooth function $f(x)$ on an interval $x \in [a, b]$ can be approximated arbitrarily well using polynomials, achieving a quality interpolation in practice requires choosing many carefully placed sample points.

As an alternative to global interpolation bases, when we design a set of basis functions $\phi_1, \ldots, \phi_k$, a desirable property we have not yet considered is *compact support*:

Definition 13.1 (Compact support). A function $g(\vec{x})$ has *compact support* if there exists $C \in \mathbb{R}$ such that $g(\vec{x}) = 0$ for any $\vec{x}$ with $\|\vec{x}\|_2 > C$.

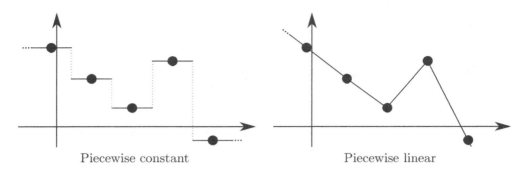

Piecewise constant   Piecewise linear

Figure 13.5 Two piecewise interpolation strategies.

That is, compactly supported functions only have a finite range of points in which they can take nonzero values.

Piecewise formulas provide one technique for constructing interpolatory bases with compact support. Most prominently, methods in computer graphics and many other fields make use of *piecewise polynomials*, which are defined by breaking $\mathbb{R}$ into a set of intervals and writing a different polynomial in each interval. To do so, we will order the data points so that $x_1 < x_2 < \cdots < x_k$. Then, two examples of piecewise interpolants are the following, illustrated in Figure 13.5:

- Piecewise constant interpolation: For a given $x \in \mathbb{R}$, find the data point x_i minimizing $|x - x_i|$ and define $f(x) = y_i$.

- Piecewise linear interpolation: If $x < x_1$ take $f(x) = y_1$, and if $x > x_k$ take $f(x) = y_k$. Otherwise, find the interval with $x \in [x_i, x_{i+1}]$ and define

$$f(x) = y_{i+1} \cdot \frac{x - x_i}{x_{i+1} - x_i} + y_i \cdot \left(1 - \frac{x - x_i}{x_{i+1} - x_i}\right).$$

Notice our pattern so far: Piecewise constant polynomials are discontinuous, while piecewise linear functions are continuous. Piecewise quadratics can be C^1, piecewise cubics can be C^2, and so on. This increased continuity and differentiability occurs even though each y_i has local support; this theory is worked out in detail in constructing "splines," or curves interpolating between points given function values and tangents.

Increased continuity, however, has its drawbacks. With each additional degree of differentiability, we put a stronger smoothness assumption on f. This assumption can be unrealistic: Many physical phenomena truly are noisy or discontinuous, and increased smoothness can negatively affect interpolatory results. One domain in which this effect is particularly clear is when interpolation is used in conjunction with physical simulation algorithms. Simulating turbulent fluid flows with excessively smooth functions inadvertently can remove discontinuous phenomena like shock waves.

These issues aside, piecewise polynomials still can be written as linear combinations of basis functions. For instance, the following functions serve as a basis for the piecewise constant functions:

$$\phi_i(x) = \begin{cases} 1 & \text{when } \frac{x_{i-1}+x_i}{2} \le x < \frac{x_i+x_{i+1}}{2} \\ 0 & \text{otherwise.} \end{cases}$$

This basis puts the constant 1 near x_i and 0 elsewhere; the piecewise constant interpolation of a set of points (x_i, y_i) is written as $f(x) = \sum_i y_i \phi_i(x)$. Similarly, the so-called "hat" basis

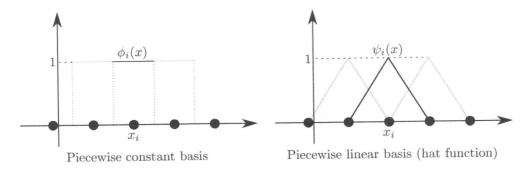

Figure 13.6 Basis functions corresponding to the piecewise interpolation strategies in Figure 13.5.

spans the set of piecewise linear functions with sharp edges at the data points x_i:

$$\psi_i(x) = \begin{cases} \frac{x - x_{i-1}}{x_i - x_{i-1}} & \text{when } x_{i-1} < x \leq x_i \\ \frac{x_{i+1} - x}{x_{i+1} - x_i} & \text{when } x_i < x \leq x_{i+1} \\ 0 & \text{otherwise.} \end{cases}$$

Once again, by construction, the piecewise linear interpolation of the given data points is $f(x) = \sum_i y_i \psi_i(x)$. Examples of both bases are shown in Figure 13.6.

13.2 MULTIVARIABLE INTERPOLATION

It is possible to extend the strategies above to the case of interpolating a function given data points $(\vec{x}_i, y_i)$ where $\vec{x}_i \in \mathbb{R}^n$ now can be multidimensional. Interpolation algorithms in this general case are challenging to formulate, however, because it is less obvious how to partition $\mathbb{R}^n$ into a small number of regions around the source points $\vec{x}_i$.

13.2.1 Nearest-Neighbor Interpolation

Given the complication of interpolation on $\mathbb{R}^n$, a common pattern is to interpolate using many *low-order* functions rather than fewer smooth functions, that is, to favor simplistic and efficient interpolants over ones that output C^∞ functions. For example, if all we are given is a set of pairs $(\vec{x}_i, y_i)$, then one piecewise constant strategy for interpolation is to use *nearest-neighbor interpolation*. In this case, $f(\vec{x})$ takes the value y_i corresponding to $\vec{x}_i$ minimizing $\|\vec{x} - \vec{x}_i\|_2$. Simple implementations iterate over all i to find the closest $\vec{x}_i$ to $\vec{x}$, and data structures like k-d trees can find nearest neighbors more quickly.

Just as piecewise constant interpolants on $\mathbb{R}$ take constant values on intervals about the data points x_i, nearest-neighbor interpolation yields a function that is piecewise-constant on *Voronoi cells*:

Definition 13.2 (Voronoi cell). Given a set of points $S = \{\vec{x}_1, \vec{x}_2, \ldots, \vec{x}_k\} \subseteq \mathbb{R}^n$, the *Voronoi cell* corresponding to a specific $\vec{x}_i \in S$ is the set $V_i \equiv \{\vec{x} : \|\vec{x} - \vec{x}_i\|_2 < \|\vec{x} - \vec{x}_j\|_2$ for all $j \neq i\}$. That is, V_i is the set of points closer to $\vec{x}_i$ than to any other $\vec{x}_j$ in S.

Figure 13.7 shows an example of the Voronoi cells about a set of points in $\mathbb{R}^2$. These cells have many favorable properties; for example, they are convex polygons and are localized

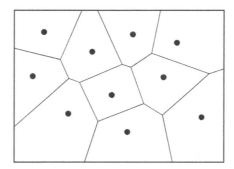

Figure 13.7 Voronoi cells associated with ten points in a rectangle.

about each $\vec{x}_i$. The adjacency of Voronoi cells is a well-studied problem in computational geometry leading to the construction of the celebrated Delaunay triangulation [33].

In many cases, however, it is desirable for the interpolant $f(\vec{x})$ to be continuous or differentiable. There are many options for continuous interpolation in $\mathbb{R}^n$, each with its own advantages and disadvantages. If we wish to extend the nearest-neighbor formula, we could compute multiple nearest neighbors $\vec{x}_1, \ldots, \vec{x}_k$ of $\vec{x}$ and interpolate $f(\vec{x})$ by averaging the corresponding $y_1, \ldots, y_k$ with distance-based weights; Exercise 13.4 explores one such weighting. Certain "k-nearest neighbor" data structures also can accelerate queries searching for multiple points in a dataset closest to a given $\vec{x}$.

13.2.2 Barycentric Interpolation

Another continuous multi-dimensional interpolant appearing frequently in the computer graphics literature is *barycentric* interpolation. Suppose we have exactly $n+1$ sample points $(\vec{x}_1, y_1), \ldots, (\vec{x}_{n+1}, y_{n+1})$, where $\vec{x}_i \in \mathbb{R}^n$, and we wish to interpolate the y_i's to all of $\mathbb{R}^n$; on the plane $\mathbb{R}^2$, we would be given three values associated with the vertices of a triangle. In the absence of degeneracies (e.g., three of the $\vec{x}_i$'s coinciding on the same line), any $\vec{x} \in \mathbb{R}^n$ can be written uniquely as a linear combination $\vec{x} = \sum_{i=1}^{n+1} a_i \vec{x}_i$ where $\sum_i a_i = 1$. This formula expresses $\vec{x}$ as a weighted average of the $\vec{x}_i$'s with weights a_i. For fixed $\vec{x}_1, \ldots, \vec{x}_{n+1}$, the weights a_i can be thought of as components of a function $\vec{a}(\vec{x})$ taking points $\vec{x}$ to their corresponding coefficients. Barycentric interpolation then defines $f(\vec{x}) \equiv \sum_i a_i(\vec{x}) y_i$.

On the plane, barycentric interpolation has a straightforward geometric interpretation involving triangle areas, illustrated in Figure 13.8(a). Regardless of dimension, however, the barycentric interpolant $f(\vec{x})$ is *affine*, meaning it can be written $f(\vec{x}) = c + \vec{d} \cdot x$ for some $c \in \mathbb{R}$ and $\vec{d} \in \mathbb{R}^n$. Counting degrees of freedom, the $n+1$ sample points are accounted for via n unknowns in $\vec{d}$ and one unknown in c.

The system of equations to find $\vec{a}(\vec{x})$ corresponding to some $\vec{x} \in \mathbb{R}^n$ is:

$$\sum_i a_i \vec{x}_i = \vec{x} \qquad\qquad \sum_i a_i = 1$$

This system usually is invertible when there are $n+1$ points $\vec{x}_i$. In the presence of additional $\vec{x}_i$'s, however, it becomes *underdetermined*. This implies that there are multiple ways of writing $\vec{x}$ as a weighted average of the $\vec{x}_i$'s, making room for additional design decisions during barycentric interpolation, encoded in the particular choice of $\vec{a}(\vec{x})$.

One resolution of this non-uniqueness is to add more linear or nonlinear constraints on the weights $\vec{a}$. These yield different *generalized barycentric coordinates*. Typical constraints

(a)   (b)

Figure 13.8 (a) The barycentric coordinates of $\vec{p}$ $\in$ $\mathbb{R}^2$ relative to the points $\vec{p}_1$, $\vec{p}_2$, and $\vec{p}_3$, respectively, are $(A_1/A, A_2/A, A_3/A)$, where $A \equiv A_1 + A_2 + A_3$ and A_i is the area of triangle i; (b) the barycentric deformation method [129] uses a generalized version of barycentric coordinates to deform planar shapes according to motions of a polygon with more than three vertices.

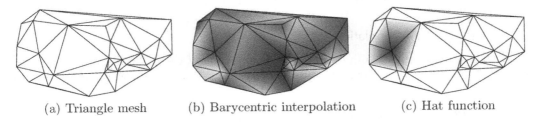

(a) Triangle mesh   (b) Barycentric interpolation   (c) Hat function

Figure 13.9 (a) A collection of points on $\mathbb{R}^2$ can be triangulated into a triangle mesh; (b) using this mesh, a per-point function can be interpolated to the interior using per-triangle barycentric interpolation; (c) a single "hat" basis function takes value one on a single vertex and is interpolated using barycentric coordinates to the remainder of the domain.

on $\vec{a}$ ask that it is smooth as a function of $\vec{x}$ on $\mathbb{R}^n$ and nonnegative on the interior of the polygon or polyhedron bordered by the $\vec{x}_i$'s. Figure 13.8(b) shows an example of image deformation using a recent generalized barycentric coordinates algorithm; the particular method shown makes use of complex-valued coordinates to take advantage of geometric properties of the complex plane [129].

Another way to carry out barycentric interpolation with more than $n + 1$ data points employs *piecewise* affine functions for interpolation; we will restrict our discussion to $\vec{x}_i \in \mathbb{R}^2$ for simplicity, although extensions to higher dimensions are possible. Suppose we are given not only a set of points $\vec{x}_i \in \mathbb{R}^2$ but also a triangulation linking those points together, as in Figure 13.9(a). If the triangulation is not known *a priori*, it can be computed using well-known geometric techniques [33]. Then, we can interpolate values from the vertices of each triangle to its interior using barycentric interpolation.

Example 13.4 (Shading). A typical representation of three-dimensional shapes in computer graphics is a set of triangles linked into a mesh. In the *per-vertex* shading model, one color is computed for each vertex on the mesh using lighting of the scene, material properties, and so on. Then, to render the shape on-screen, those per-vertex colors are interpolated using barycentric interpolation to the interiors of the triangles. Similar strategies are used for texturing and other common tasks. Figure 13.9(b) shows an example of this technique.

As an aside, one pertinent issue specific to computer graphics is the interplay between perspective transformations and interpolation. Barycentric interpolation of color along a triangulated 3D surface and then projection of that color onto the image plane is not the same as projecting triangles to the image plane and subsequently interpolating color along the projected two-dimensional triangles. Algorithms in this domain must use *perspective-corrected* interpolation strategies to account for this discrepancy during the rendering process.

Interpolation using a triangulation parallels the use of a piecewise-linear hat basis for one-dimensional functions, introduced in §13.1.3. Now, we can think of $f(\vec{x})$ as a linear combination $\sum_i y_i \phi_i(\vec{x})$, where each $\phi_i(\vec{x})$ is the piecewise affine function obtained by putting a 1 on $\vec{x}_i$ and 0 everywhere else, as in Figure 13.9(c).

Given a set of points in $\mathbb{R}^2$, the problem of triangulation is far from trivial, and analogous constructions in higher dimensions can scale poorly. When $n > 3$, methods that do not require explicitly partitioning the domain usually are preferable.

13.2.3 Grid-Based Interpolation

Rather than using triangles, an alternative decomposition of the domain of f occurs when the points $\vec{x}_i$ occur on a regular grid. The following examples illustrate situations when this is the case:

Example 13.5 (Image processing). A typical digital photograph is represented as an $m \times n$ grid of red, green, and blue color intensities. We can think of these values as living on the lattice $\mathbb{Z} \times \mathbb{Z} \subset \mathbb{R} \times \mathbb{R}$. Suppose we wish to rotate the image by an angle that is not a multiple of 90°. Then, we must look up color values at potentially non-integer positions, requiring the interpolation of the image to $\mathbb{R} \times \mathbb{R}$.

Example 13.6 (Medical imaging). The output of a magnetic resonance imaging (MRI) device is an $m \times n \times p$ grid of values representing the density of tissue at different points; a theoretical model for this data is as a function $f : \mathbb{R}^3 \to \mathbb{R}$. We can extract the outer surface of a particular organ by finding the level set $\{\vec{x} : f(\vec{x}) = c\}$ for some c. Finding this level set requires us to extend f to the entire voxel grid to find exactly where it crosses c.

Grid-based interpolation applies the one-dimensional formulae from §13.1.3 one dimension at a time. For example, *bilinear* interpolation in $\mathbb{R}^2$ applies linear interpolation in x_1 and then x_2 (or vice versa):

Example 13.7 (Bilinear interpolation). Suppose f takes on the following values:

$$f(0,0) = 1 \qquad f(0,1) = -3 \qquad f(1,0) = 5 \qquad f(1,1) = -11$$

and that in between f is obtained by bilinear interpolation. To find $f(\frac{1}{4}, \frac{1}{2})$, we first interpolate in x_1 to find:

$$f\left(\frac{1}{4}, 0\right) = \frac{3}{4}f(0,0) + \frac{1}{4}f(1,0) = 2$$

$$f\left(\frac{1}{4}, 1\right) = \frac{3}{4}f(0,1) + \frac{1}{4}f(1,1) = -5.$$

Next, we interpolate in x_2:

$$f\left(\frac{1}{4}, \frac{1}{2}\right) = \frac{1}{2}f\left(\frac{1}{4}, 0\right) + \frac{1}{2}f\left(\frac{1}{4}, 1\right) = -\frac{3}{2}.$$

We receive the same output interpolating first in x_2 and second in x_1.

Higher-order methods like bicubic and Lanczos interpolation use more polynomial terms but are slower to evaluate. For example, bicubic interpolation requires values from more grid points than just the four closest to $\vec{x}$ needed for bilinear interpolation. This additional expense can slow down image processing tools for which every lookup in memory incurs significant computation time.

13.3   THEORY OF INTERPOLATION

Our treatment of interpolation has been fairly heuristic. While relying on our intuition for what a "reasonable" interpolation for a set of function values for the most part is acceptable, subtle issues can arise with different interpolation methods that should be acknowledged.

13.3.1   Linear Algebra of Functions

We began our discussion by posing interpolation strategies using different bases for the set of functions $f : \mathbb{R} \to \mathbb{R}$. This analogy to vector spaces extends to a complete linear-algebraic theory of functions, and in many ways the field of *functional analysis* essentially extends the geometry of $\mathbb{R}^n$ to sets of functions. Here, we will discuss functions of one variable, although many aspects of the extension to more general functions are easy to carry out.

Just as we can define notions of span and linear combination for functions, for fixed $a, b \in \mathbb{R}$ we can define an *inner product* of functions $f(x)$ and $g(x)$ as follows:

$$\langle f, g \rangle \equiv \int_a^b f(x)g(x)\, dx.$$

We then can define the norm of a function $f(x)$ to be $\|f\|_2 \equiv \sqrt{\langle f, f \rangle}$. These constructions parallel the corresponding constructions on $\mathbb{R}^n$; both the dot product $\vec{x} \cdot \vec{y}$ and the inner product $\langle f, g \rangle$ are obtained by multiplying the "elements" of the two multiplicands and summing—or integrating.

Example 13.8 (Functional inner product). Take $p_n(x) = x^n$ to be the n-th monomial. Then, for $a = 0$ and $b = 1$,

$$\langle p_n, p_m \rangle = \int_0^1 x^n \cdot x^m\, dx = \int_0^1 x^{n+m}\, dx = \frac{1}{n+m+1}.$$

This shows:

$$\left\langle \frac{p_n}{\|p_n\|}, \frac{p_m}{\|p_m\|} \right\rangle = \frac{\langle p_n, p_m \rangle}{\|p_n\|\|p_m\|}$$
$$= \frac{\sqrt{(2n+1)(2m+1)}}{n+m+1}.$$

This value is approximately 1 when $n \approx m$ but $n \neq m$, substantiating our earlier claim illustrated in Figure 13.1 that the monomials "overlap" considerably on $[0, 1]$.

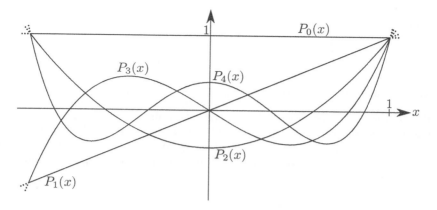

Figure 13.10 The first five Legendre polynomials, notated $P_0(x), \ldots, P_4(x)$.

Given this inner product, we can apply the Gram-Schmidt algorithm to find an orthogonal basis for the set of polynomials, as we did in §5.4 to orthogonalize a set of vectors. If we take $a = -1$ and $b = 1$, applying Gram-Schmidt to the monomial basis yields the Legendre polynomials, plotted in Figure 13.10:

$$P_0(x) = 1$$
$$P_1(x) = x$$
$$P_2(x) = \frac{1}{2}(3x^2 - 1)$$
$$P_3(x) = \frac{1}{2}(5x^3 - 3x)$$
$$P_4(x) = \frac{1}{8}(35x^4 - 30x^2 + 3)$$
$$\vdots \qquad \vdots$$

These polynomials have many useful properties thanks to their orthogonality. For example, suppose we wish to approximate $f(x)$ with a sum $\sum_i a_i P_i(x)$. If we wish to minimize $\|f - \sum_i a_i P_i\|_2$ in the functional norm, this is a *least-squares* problem! By orthogonality of the Legendre basis for $\mathbb{R}[x]$, our formula from Chapter 5 for projection onto an orthogonal basis shows:

$$a_i = \frac{\langle f, P_i \rangle}{\langle P_i, P_i \rangle}.$$

Thus, approximating f using polynomials can be accomplished by integrating f against the members of the Legendre basis. In the next chapter, we will learn how this integral can be carried out numerically.

Given a positive function $w(x)$, we can define a more general inner product $\langle \cdot, \cdot \rangle_w$ as

$$\langle f, g \rangle_w \equiv \int_a^b w(x) f(x) g(x) \, dx.$$

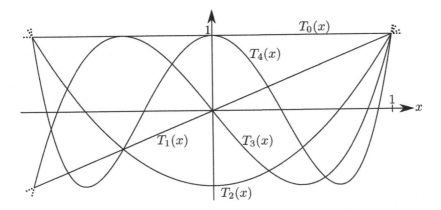

Figure 13.11 The first five Chebyshev polynomials, notated $T_0(x), \ldots, T_4(x)$.

If we take $w(x) = \frac{1}{\sqrt{1-x^2}}$ with $a = -1$ and $b = 1$, then Gram-Schmidt on the monomials yields the *Chebyshev* polynomials, shown in Figure 13.11:

$$T_0(x) = 1$$
$$T_1(x) = x$$
$$T_2(x) = 2x^2 - 1$$
$$T_3(x) = 4x^3 - 3x$$
$$T_4(x) = 8x^4 - 8x^2 + 1$$
$$\vdots \qquad \vdots$$

A surprising identity holds for these polynomials:

$$T_k(x) = \cos(k \arccos(x)).$$

This formula can be checked by explicitly verifying it for T_0 and T_1, and then inductively applying the observation:

$$
\begin{aligned}
T_{k+1}(x) &= \cos((k+1)\arccos(x)) \\
&= 2x \cos(k \arccos(x)) - \cos((k-1)\arccos(x)) \text{ by the identity} \\
&\qquad \cos((k+1)\theta) = 2\cos(k\theta)\cos(\theta) - \cos((k-1)\theta) \\
&= 2x T_k(x) - T_{k-1}(x).
\end{aligned}
$$

This three-term recurrence formula also gives a way to generate explicit expressions for the Chebyshev polynomials in the monomial basis.

Thanks to this trigonometric characterization of the Chebyshev polynomials, the minima and maxima of T_k oscillate between $+1$ and -1. Furthermore, these extrema are located at $x = \cos(i\pi/k)$ (the *Chebyshev points*) for i from 0 to k. This even distribution of extrema avoids oscillatory phenomena like that shown in Figure 13.4 when using a finite number of polynomial terms to approximate a function. More technical treatments of polynomial interpolation recommend placing samples x_i for interpolation near Chebyshev points to obtain smooth output.

13.3.2 Approximation via Piecewise Polynomials

Suppose we wish to approximate a function $f(x)$ with a polynomial of degree n on an interval $[a, b]$. Define Δx to be the spacing $b - a$. One measure of the error of an approximation is as a function of Δx. If we approximate f with piecewise polynomials, this type of analysis tells us how far apart we should space the sample points to achieve a desired level of approximation.

Suppose we approximate $f(x)$ with a constant $c = f(\frac{a+b}{2})$, as in piecewise constant interpolation. If we assume $|f'(x)| < M$ for all $x \in [a, b]$, we have:

$$\max_{x \in [a,b]} |f(x) - c| \leq \Delta x \max_{x \in [a,b]} M \text{ by the mean value theorem}$$

$$\leq M \Delta x.$$

Thus, we expect $O(\Delta x)$ error when using piecewise constant interpolation.

Suppose instead we approximate f using piecewise linear interpolation, that is, by taking

$$\tilde{f}(x) = \frac{b - x}{b - a} f(a) + \frac{x - a}{b - a} f(b).$$

We can use the Taylor expansion about x to write expressions for $f(a)$ and $f(b)$:

$$f(a) = f(x) + (a - x)f'(x) + \frac{1}{2}(a - x)^2 f''(x) + O(\Delta x^3)$$

$$f(b) = f(x) + (b - x)f'(x) + \frac{1}{2}(b - x)^2 f''(x) + O(\Delta x^3).$$

Substituting these expansions into the formula for $\tilde{f}(x)$ shows

$$\tilde{f}(x) = f(x) + \frac{1}{2\Delta x}((x - a)(b - x)^2 + (b - x)(x - a)^2)f''(x) + O(\Delta x^3)$$

$$= f(x) + \frac{1}{2}(x - a)(x - b)f''(x) + O(\Delta x^3) \text{ after simplification.}$$

This expression shows that linear interpolation holds up to $O(\Delta x^2)$, assuming f'' is bounded. Furthermore, for all $x \in [a, b]$ we have the bound $|x - a||x - b| \leq \Delta x^2/4$, implying an error bound proportional to $\Delta x^2/8$ for the second term.

Generalizing this argument shows that approximation with a degree-n polynomial generates $O(\Delta x^{n+1})$ error. In particular, if $f(x)$ is sampled at $x_0, x_1, \ldots, x_n$ to generate a degree-n polynomial p_n, then assuming $x_0 < x_1 < \cdots < x_n$, the error of such an approximation can be bounded as

$$|f(x) - p_n(x)| \leq \frac{1}{(n + 1)!} \left[\max_{x \in [x_0, x_n]} \prod_k |x - x_k| \right] \cdot \left[\max_{x \in [x_0, x_n]} |f^{(n+1)}(x)| \right],$$

for any $x \in [x_0, x_n]$.

13.4 EXERCISES

13.1 Write the degree-three polynomial interpolating between the data points $(-2, 15)$, $(0, -1)$, $(1, 0)$, and $(3, -2)$.

Hint: Your answer does not have to be written in the monomial basis.

13.2 Show that the interpolation from Example 13.7 yields the same result regardless of whether x_1 or x_2 is interpolated first.

13.3 ("Runge function") Consider the function

$$f(x) \equiv \frac{1}{1 + 25x^2}.$$

Suppose we approximate $f(x)$ using a degree-k polynomial $p_k(x)$ through $k+1$ points $x_0, \ldots, x_k$ with $x_i = 2i/k - 1$.

(a) Plot $p_k(x)$ for a few samples of k. Does increasing k improve the quality of the approximation?

(b) Specialize the bound at the end of §13.3.2 to show

$$\max_{x \in [-1,1]} |f(x) - p_k(x)| \leq \frac{1}{(k+1)!} \left[\max_{x \in [-1,1]} \prod_i |x - x_i| \right] \cdot \left[\max_{x \in [-1,1]} |f^{(k+1)}(x)| \right].$$

Does this bound get tighter as k increases?

(c) Suggest a way to fix this problem assuming we cannot move the x_i's.

(d) Suggest an alternative way to fix this problem by moving the x_i's.

13.4 ("Inverse distance weighting") Suppose we are given a set of distinct points $\vec{x}_1, \ldots, \vec{x}_k \in \mathbb{R}^n$ with labels $y_1, \ldots, y_k \in \mathbb{R}$. Then, one interpolation strategy defines an interpolant $f(\vec{x})$ as follows [108]:

$$f(\vec{x}) \equiv \begin{cases} y_i & \text{if } \vec{x} = \vec{x}_i \text{ for some } i \\ \frac{\sum_i w_i(\vec{x}) y_i}{\sum_i w_i(\vec{x})} & \text{otherwise,} \end{cases}$$

where $w_i(\vec{x}) \equiv \|\vec{x} - \vec{x}_i\|_2^{-p}$ for some fixed $p \geq 1$.

(a) Argue that as $p \to \infty$, the interpolant $f(\vec{x})$ becomes piecewise constant on the Voronoi cells of the $\vec{x}_i$'s.

(b) Define the function

$$\phi(\vec{x}, y) \equiv \left(\sum_i \frac{(y - y_i)^2}{\|\vec{x} - \vec{x}_i\|_2^p} \right)^{1/p}.$$

Show that for fixed $\vec{x} \in \mathbb{R}^n \setminus \{\vec{x}_1, \ldots, \vec{x}_k\}$, the value $f(\vec{x})$ is the minimum of $\phi(\vec{x}, y)$ over all y.

(c) Evaluating the sum in this formula can be expensive when k is large. Propose a modification to the w_i's that avoids this issue; there are many possible techniques here.

13.5 ("Barycentric Lagrange interpolation," [12]) Suppose we are given k pairs $(x_1, y_1), \ldots, (x_k, y_k)$.

(a) Define $\ell(x) \equiv \prod_{j=1}^{k} (x - x_j)$. Show that the Lagrange basis satisfies

$$\phi_i(x) = \frac{w_i \ell(x)}{x - x_i},$$

for some weight w_i depending on $x_1, \ldots, x_n$. The value w_i is known as the *barycentric weight* of x_i.

(b) Suppose $f(x)$ is the degree $k - 1$ polynomial through the given (x_i, y_i) pairs. Assuming you have precomputed the w_i's, use the result of the previous part to give a formula for Lagrange interpolation that takes $O(k)$ time to evaluate.

(c) Use the result of 13.5b to write a formula for the constant function $g(x) \equiv 1$.

(d) Combine the results of the previous two parts to provide a third formula for $f(x)$ that does not involve $\ell(x)$.
Hint: $f(x)/1 = f(x)$.

13.6 ("Cubic Hermite interpolation") In computer graphics, a common approach to drawing curves is to use cubic interpolation. Typically, artists design curves by specifying their endpoints as well as the tangents to the curves at the endpoints.

(a) Suppose $P(t)$ is the cubic polynomial:

$$P(t) = at^3 + bt^2 + ct + d.$$

Write a set of linear conditions on a, b, c, and d such that $P(t)$ satisfies the following conditions for fixed values of h_0, h_1, h_2, and h_3:

$$\begin{aligned} P(0) &= h_0 & P'(0) &= h_2 \\ P(1) &= h_1 & P'(1) &= h_3. \end{aligned}$$

(b) Write the *cubic Hermite* basis for cubic polynomials $\{\phi_0(t), \phi_1(t), \phi_2(t), \phi_3(t)\}$ such that $P(t)$ satisfying the conditions from 13.6a can be written

$$P(t) = h_0\phi_0(t) + h_1\phi_1(t) + h_2\phi_2(t) + h_3\phi_3(t).$$

13.7 ("Cubic blossom") We continue to explore interpolation techniques suggested in the previous problem.

(a) Given $P(t) = at^3 + bt^2 + ct + d$, define a *cubic blossom function* $F(t_1, t_2, t_3)$ in terms of $\{a, b, c, d\}$ satisfying the following properties [102]:
  Symmetric: $F(t_1, t_2, t_3) = F(t_i, t_j, t_k)$
  for any permutation (i, j, k) of $\{1, 2, 3\}$
  Affine: $F(\alpha u + (1 - \alpha)v, t_2, t_3) = \alpha F(u, t_2, t_3) + (1 - \alpha)F(v, t_2, t_3)$
  Diagonal: $f(t) = F(t, t, t)$

(b) Now, define

$$\begin{aligned} p &= F(0, 0, 0) & q &= F(0, 0, 1) \\ r &= F(0, 1, 1) & s &= F(1, 1, 1). \end{aligned}$$

Write expressions for $f(0)$, $f(1)$, $f'(0)$, and $f'(1)$ in terms of p, q, r, and s.

(c) Write a basis $\{B_0(t), B_1(t), B_2(t), B_3(t)\}$ for cubic polynomials such that given a cubic blossom $F(t_1, t_2, t_3)$ of $f(t)$ we can write

$$f(t) = F(0, 0, 0)B_0(t) + F(0, 0, 1)B_1(t) + F(0, 1, 1)B_2(t) + F(1, 1, 1)B_3(t).$$

The functions $B_i(t)$ are known as the cubic Bernstein basis.

(d) Suppose $F_1(t_1, t_2, t_3)$ and $F_2(t_1, t_2, t_3)$ are the cubic blossoms of functions $f_1(t)$ and $f_2(t)$, respectively, and define $\vec{F}(t_1, t_2, t_3) \equiv (F_1(t_1, t_2, t_3), F_2(t_1, t_2, t_3))$. Consider the four points shown in Figure 13.12. By bisecting line segments and drawing new ones, show how to construct $\vec{F}(1/2, 1/2, 1/2)$.

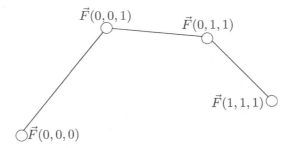

Figure 13.12 Diagram for Exercise 13.7d.

DH 13.8 Consider the polynomial $p(x) = a_0 + a_1 x + a_2 x^2 + \cdots + a_{n-1} x^{n-1}$. Alternatively, we can write $p(x)$ in the Newton basis relative to $x_1, \ldots, x_n$ as

$$p(x) = c_1 + c_2 (x - x_1) + c_3 (x - x_1)(x - x_2) + \cdots + c_n \prod_{i=1}^{n-1} (x - x_i),$$

where $x_1, \ldots, x_n$ are fixed constants.

(a) Argue why we can write any $(n-1)$-st degree $p(x)$ in this form.

(b) Find explicit expressions for c_1, c_2, and c_3 in terms of x_1, x_2, and evaluations of $p(\cdot)$. Based on these expressions (and computing more terms if needed), propose a pattern for finding c_k.

(c) Use function evaluation to define the *zeroth divided difference* of p as $p[x_1] = p(x_1)$. Furthermore, define the *first divided difference* of p as

$$p[x_1, x_2] = \frac{p[x_1] - p[x_2]}{x_1 - x_2}.$$

Finally, define the *second divided difference* as

$$p[x_1, x_2, x_3] = \frac{p[x_1, x_2] - p[x_2, x_3]}{x_1 - x_3}.$$

Based on this pattern and the pattern you observed in the previous part, define $p[x_i, x_{i+1}, \ldots, x_j]$ and use it to provide a formula for the coefficients c_k.

(d) Suppose we add another point (x_{n+1}, y_{n+1}) and wish to recompute the Newton interpolant. How many Newton coefficients need to be recomputed? Why?

13.9 ("Horner's rule") Consider the polynomial $p(x) \equiv a_0 + a_1 x + a_2 x^2 + \cdots + a_k x^k$. For fixed $x_0 \in \mathbb{R}$, define $c_0, \ldots, c_k \in \mathbb{R}$ recursively as follows:

$$c_k \equiv a_k$$
$$c_i \equiv a_i + c_{i+1} x_0 \; \forall i < k.$$

Show $c_0 = p(x_0)$, and compare the number of multiplication and addition operations needed to compute $p(x_0)$ using this method versus the formula in terms of the a_i's.

DH 13.10 Consider the L_2 distance between polynomials f, g on $[-1, 1]$, given by

$$\|f - g\|_2 \equiv \left[\int_{-1}^{1} (f(x) - g(x))^2 \, dx \right]^{1/2},$$

which arises from the inner product $\langle f, g \rangle = \int_{-1}^{1} f(x)g(x) \, dx$. Let $\mathcal{P}_n$ be the vector space of polynomials of degree no more than n, endowed with this inner product. As we have discussed, polynomials $\{p_i\}_{i=1}^{m}$ are *orthogonal* with respect to this inner product if for all $i \neq j$, $\langle p_i, p_j \rangle = 0$; we can systematically obtain a set of orthonormal polynomials using the Gram-Schmidt process.

(a) Derive constant multiples of the first three Legendre polynomials via Gram-Schmidt orthogonalization on the monomials 1, x, and x^2.

(b) Suppose we wish to approximate a function f with a degree-n polynomial g. To do so, we can find the $g \in \mathcal{P}_n$ that is the best least-squares fit for f in the norm above. Write an optimization problem for finding g.

(c) Suppose we construct the Gram matrix G with entries $g_{ij} \equiv \langle p_i, p_j \rangle$ for a basis of polynomials $p_1, \ldots, p_n \in \mathcal{P}_n$. How is G involved in solving Exercise 13.10b? What is the structure of G when $p_1, \ldots, p_n$ are the first n Legendre polynomials?

DH 13.11 For a given n, the *Chebyshev points* are given by $x_k = \cos\left(\frac{k\pi}{n}\right)$, where $k \in \{0, \ldots, n\}$.

(a) Show that the Chebyshev points are the projections onto the x axis of n *evenly spaced* points on the upper half of the unit circle.

(b) Suppose that we *define* the Chebyshev polynomials using the expression $T_k(x) \equiv \cos(k \arccos(x))$. Starting from this expression, compute the first four Chebyshev polynomials in the monomial basis.

(c) Show that the Chebyshev polynomials you computed in the previous part are orthogonal with respect to the inner product $\langle f, g \rangle \equiv \int_{-1}^{1} \frac{f(x)g(x)}{\sqrt{1-x^2}} \, dx$.

(d) Show that the extrema of T_n are located at Chebyshev points x_k.

13.12 We can use interpolation strategies to formulate methods for root-finding in one or more variables.

(a) Show how to recover the parameters a, b, c of the *linear fractional transformation*

$$f(x) \equiv \frac{x + a}{bx + c}$$

going through the points (x_0, y_0), (x_1, y_1), and (x_2, y_2), either in closed form or by posing a 3×3 linear system of equations.

(b) Find x_4 such that $f(x_4) = 0$.

(c) Suppose we are given a function $f(x)$ and wish to find a root x^* with $f(x^*) = 0$. Suggest an algorithm for root-finding using the construction in Exercise 13.12b.

CHAPTER 14

Integration and Differentiation

CONTENTS

14.1   Motivation 278
14.2   Quadrature 279
       14.2.1 Interpolatory Quadrature 280
       14.2.2 Quadrature Rules 281
       14.2.3 Newton-Cotes Quadrature 282
       14.2.4 Gaussian Quadrature 286
       14.2.5 Adaptive Quadrature 287
       14.2.6 Multiple Variables 289
       14.2.7 Conditioning 290
14.3   Differentiation 290
       14.3.1 Differentiating Basis Functions 291
       14.3.2 Finite Differences 291
       14.3.3 Richardson Extrapolation 293
       14.3.4 Choosing the Step Size 294
       14.3.5 Automatic Differentiation 295
       14.3.6 Integrated Quantities and Structure Preservation 296

THE previous chapter developed tools for predicting values of a function $f(\vec{x})$ given a sampling of points $(\vec{x}_i, f(\vec{x}_i))$ in the domain of f. Such methods are useful in themselves for completing functions that are known to be continuous or differentiable but whose values only are sampled at a set of isolated points, but in some cases we instead wish to compute "derived quantities" from the sampled function. Most commonly, many applications must approximate the integral or derivatives of f rather than its values.

There are many applications in which numerical integration and differentiation play key roles for computation. In the most straightforward instance, some well-known functions are *defined* as integrals. For instance, the "error function" given by the cumulative distribution of a bell curve is defined as:

$$\operatorname{erf}(x) \equiv \frac{2}{\sqrt{\pi}} \int_0^x e^{-t^2} \, dt.$$

Approximations of $\operatorname{erf}(x)$ are needed in statistical methods, and one reasonable approach to finding these values is to compute the integral above numerically.

Other times, numerical approximations of derivatives and integrals are part of a larger system. For example, methods we will develop in future chapters for approximating solutions to differential equations will depend strongly on discretizations of derivatives. In computational electrodynamics, *integral equations* for an unknown function $\phi(\vec{y})$ given a kernel $K(\vec{x}, \vec{y})$ and function $f(\vec{x})$ are expressed as the relationship

$$f(\vec{x}) = \int_{\mathbb{R}^n} K(\vec{x}, \vec{y}) \phi(\vec{y}) \, d\vec{y}.$$

Equations in this form are solved for ϕ to estimate electric and magnetic fields, but unless the ϕ and K are very special we cannot hope to work with such an integral in closed form. Hence, these methods typically discretize ϕ and the integral using a set of samples and then solve the resulting discrete system of equations.

In this chapter, we will develop methods for numerical integration and differentiation given a sampling of function values. We also will suggest strategies to evaluate how well we can expect approximations of derivatives and integrals to perform, helping formalize intuition for their relative quality and efficiency in different circumstances or applications.

14.1 MOTIVATION

It is not hard to encounter applications of numerical integration and differentiation, given how often the tools of calculus appear in physics, statistics, and other fields. Well-known formulas aside, here we suggest a few less obvious places requiring algorithms for integration and differentiation.

Example 14.1 (Sampling from a distribution). Suppose we are given a probability distribution $p(t)$ on the interval $[0, 1]$; that is, if we randomly sample values according to this distribution, we expect $p(t)$ to be proportional to the number of times we draw a value near t. A common task is to generate random numbers distributed like $p(t)$.

Rather than develop a specialized sampling method every time we receive a new $p(t)$, it is possible to leverage a single uniform sampling tool to sample from nearly any distribution on $[0, 1]$. We define the *cumulative distribution function* (CDF) of p to be

$$F(t) = \int_0^t p(x) \, dx.$$

If X is a random number distributed evenly in $[0, 1]$, one can show that $F^{-1}(X)$ is distributed like p, where F^{-1} is the inverse of F. That is, if we can approximate F or F^{-1}, we can generate random numbers according to an arbitrary distribution p.

Example 14.2 (Optimization). Most of our methods for minimizing and finding roots of a function $f(\vec{x})$ require computing not only values $f(\vec{x})$ but also gradients $\nabla f(\vec{x})$ and even Hessians $H_f(\vec{x})$. BFGS and Broyden's method build up rough approximations of derivatives of f during optimization. When f changes rapidly in small neighborhoods, however, it may be better to approximate ∇f directly near the current iterate $\vec{x}_k$ rather than using values from potentially far-away iterates $\vec{x}_\ell$ for $\ell < k$, which can happen as BFGS or Broyden slowly build up derivative matrices.

Example 14.3 (Rendering). The *rendering equation* from computer graphics and ray tracing is an integral equation expressing conservation of light energy [70]. As it was originally presented, the rendering equation states:

$$I(\vec{x}, \vec{y}) = g(\vec{x}, \vec{y}) \left[\varepsilon(\vec{x}, \vec{y}) + \int_S \rho(\vec{x}, \vec{y}, \vec{z}) I(\vec{y}, \vec{z}) \, d\vec{z} \right].$$

Here $I(\vec{x}, \vec{y})$ is proportional to the intensity of light going from point $\vec{y}$ to point $\vec{x}$ in a scene. The functions on the right-hand side are:

$$g(\vec{x}, \vec{y}) \quad \text{A } \textit{geometry term} \text{ accounting, e.g., for objects occluding the path from } \vec{x} \text{ to } \vec{y}$$

$$\varepsilon(\vec{x}, \vec{y}) \quad \text{The } \textit{light emitted} \text{ directly from } \vec{x} \text{ to } \vec{y}$$

$$\rho(\vec{x}, \vec{y}, \vec{z}) \quad \text{A } \textit{scattering} \text{ term giving the amount of light scattered to point } \vec{x} \text{ by a patch of surface at location } \vec{z} \text{ from light located at } \vec{z}$$

$$S = \cup_i S_i \quad \text{The set of surfaces } S_i \text{ in the scene}$$

Many rendering algorithms can be described as approximate strategies for solving this integral equation.

Example 14.4 (Image processing). Suppose we think of an image or photograph as a function of two variables $I(x, y)$ giving the brightness of the image at each position (x, y). Many classical image processing filters can be thought of as *convolutions*, given by

$$(I * g)(x, y) = \iint_{\mathbb{R}^2} I(u, v) g(x - u, y - v) \, du \, dv.$$

For example, to blur an image we can take g to be a Gaussian or bell curve; in this case $(I * g)(x, y)$ is a weighted average of the colors of I near the point (x, y). In practice, images are sampled on discrete grids of pixels, so this integral must be approximated.

Example 14.5 (Bayes' Rule). Suppose X and Y are continuously valued random variables; we can use $P(X)$ and $P(Y)$ to express the probabilities that X and Y take particular values. Sometimes, knowing X may affect our knowledge of Y. For instance, if X is a patient's blood pressure and Y is a patient's weight, then knowing a patient has high weight may suggest that he or she also has high blood pressure. In this situation, we can write *conditional* probability distributions $P(X|Y)$ (read "the probability of X given Y") expressing such relationships.

A foundation of modern probability theory states that $P(X|Y)$ and $P(Y|X)$ are related by *Bayes' rule*

$$P(X|Y) = \frac{P(Y|X)P(X)}{\int P(Y|X)P(X) \, dX}.$$

Estimating the integral in the denominator can be a serious problem in machine learning algorithms where the probability distributions take complex forms. Approximate and often randomized integration schemes are needed for algorithms in parameter selection that use this value as part of a larger optimization technique [63].

14.2 QUADRATURE

We will begin by considering the problem of numerical integration, or *quadrature*. This problem—in a single variable—can be expressed as: "Given a sampling of n points from some function $f(x)$, find an approximation of $\int_a^b f(x) \, dx$." In the previous section, we presented some applications that reduce to exactly this problem.

There are a few variations of this setup that require slightly different treatment or adaptation:

- The endpoints a and b may be fixed, or we may wish to find a quadrature scheme that efficiently can approximate integrals for many (a, b) pairs.

- We may be able to query $f(x)$ at any x but wish to approximate the integral using relatively few samples, or we may be given a list of precomputed pairs $(x_i, f(x_i))$ and are constrained to using these data points in our approximation.

These considerations should be kept in mind as we design assorted quadrature techniques.

14.2.1 Interpolatory Quadrature

Many of the interpolation strategies developed in the previous chapter can be extended to methods for quadrature. Suppose we write a function $f(x)$ in terms of a set of basis functions $\phi_i(x)$:

$$f(x) = \sum_i a_i \phi_i(x).$$

Then, we can find the integral of f as follows:

$$\int_a^b f(x)\, dx = \int_a^b \left[\sum_i a_i \phi_i(x) \right] dx \text{ by definition of } f$$

$$= \sum_i a_i \left[\int_a^b \phi_i(x)\, dx \right] \text{ by swapping the sum and the integral}$$

$$= \sum_i c_i a_i \text{ if we make the definition } c_i \equiv \int_a^b \phi_i(x)\, dx.$$

In other words, the integral of $f(x)$ written in a basis is a weighted sum of the integrals of the basis functions making up f.

Example 14.6 (Monomials). Suppose we write $f(x) = \sum_k a_k x^k$. We know

$$\int_0^1 x^k\, dx = \frac{1}{k+1}.$$

Applying the formula above, we can write

$$\int_0^1 f(x)\, dx = \sum_k \frac{a_k}{k+1}.$$

In the more general notation above, we have taken $c_k = \frac{1}{k+1}$. This formula shows that the integral of $f(x)$ in the monomial basis can be computed directly via a weighted sum of the coefficients a_k.

Integration schemes derived using interpolatory basis functions are known as *interpolatory quadrature* rules; nearly all the methods we will present below can be written this way. We can encounter a chicken-and-egg problem if the integral $\int \phi_i(x)\, dx$ itself is not known in closed form. Certain methods in higher-order finite elements deal with this problem by putting extra computational time into making a high-quality numerical approximation of the integral of a single ϕ_i. Then, since all the ϕ's have similar form, these methods apply change-of-coordinates formulas to compute integrals of the remaining basis functions. The canonical integral can be approximated offline using a high-accuracy scheme and then reused during computations where timing matters.

14.2.2   Quadrature Rules

Our discussion above suggests the following form for a *quadrature rule* approximating the integral of f on some interval given a set of sample locations x_i:

$$Q[f] \equiv \sum_i w_i f(x_i).$$

Different weights w_i yield different approximations of the integral, which we hope become increasingly similar as the x_i's are sampled more densely. From this perspective, the choices of $\{x_i\}$ and $\{w_i\}$ determine a quadrature rule.

The classical theory of integration suggests that this formula is a reasonable starting point. For example, the *Riemann integral* presented in introductory calculus takes the form

$$\int_a^b f(x)\,dx \equiv \lim_{\Delta x_k \to 0} \sum_k f(\tilde{x}_k)(x_{k+1} - x_k).$$

Here, the interval $[a, b]$ is partitioned into pieces $a = x_1 < x_2 < \cdots < x_n = b$, where $\Delta x_k = x_{k+1} - x_k$, and $\tilde{x}_k$ is any point in $[x_k, x_{k+1}]$. For a fixed set of x_k's before taking the limit, this integral is in the $Q[f]$ form above.

There are many ways to choose the form of $Q[\cdot]$, as we will see in the coming section and as we already have seen for interpolatory quadrature. If we can query f for its values anywhere, then the x_i's *and* w_i's can be chosen strategically to sample f in a near-optimal way, but even if the x_i's are fixed, there exist many ways to choose the weights w_i with different advantages and disadvantages.

Example 14.7 (Method of undetermined coefficients). Suppose we fix $x_1, \ldots, x_n$ and wish to find a reasonable set of weights w_i so that $\sum_i w_i f(x_i)$ approximates the integral of f for reasonably smooth $f : [a, b] \to \mathbb{R}$. An alternative to interpolatory quadrature is the *method of undetermined coefficients*. In this strategy, we choose n functions $f_1(x), \ldots, f_n(x)$ whose integrals are known, and require that the quadrature rule recovers the integrals of these functions exactly:

$$\int_a^b f_1(x)\,dx = w_1 f_1(x_1) + w_2 f_1(x_2) + \cdots + w_n f_1(x_n)$$

$$\int_a^b f_2(x)\,dx = w_1 f_2(x_1) + w_2 f_2(x_2) + \cdots + w_n f_2(x_n)$$

$$\vdots \qquad \vdots$$

$$\int_a^b f_n(x)\,dx = w_1 f_n(x_1) + w_2 f_n(x_2) + \cdots + w_n f_n(x_n).$$

The n expressions above create an $n \times n$ linear system of equations for the unknown w_i's.

One common choice is to take $f_k(x) \equiv x^{k-1}$, that is, to make sure that the quadrature scheme recovers the integrals of low-order polynomials. As in Example 14.6,

$$\int_a^b x^k\,dx = \frac{b^{k+1} - a^{k+1}}{k+1}.$$

Figure 14.1 Closed and open Newton-Cotes quadrature schemes differ by where they place the samples x_i on the interval $[a, b]$; here we show the two samplings for $n = 8$.

Thus, we solve the following linear system of equations for the w_i's:

$$w_1 + w_2 + \cdots + w_n = b - a$$

$$x_1 w_1 + x_2 w_2 + \cdots + x_n w_n = \frac{b^2 - a^2}{2}$$

$$x_1^2 w_1 + x_2^2 w_2 + \cdots + x_n^2 w_n = \frac{b^3 - a^3}{3}$$

$$\vdots \qquad \vdots$$

$$x_1^{n-1} w_1 + x_2^{n-1} w_2 + \cdots + x_n^{n-1} w_n = \frac{b^n - a^n}{n}.$$

In matrix form, this system is

$$
\begin{pmatrix}
1 & 1 & \cdots & 1 \\
x_1 & x_2 & \cdots & x_n \\
x_1^2 & x_2^2 & \cdots & x_n^2 \\
\vdots & \vdots & \ddots & \vdots \\
x_1^{n-1} & x_2^{n-1} & \cdots & x_n^{n-1}
\end{pmatrix}
\begin{pmatrix}
w_1 \\
w_2 \\
\vdots \\
w_n
\end{pmatrix}
=
\begin{pmatrix}
b - a \\
\frac{1}{2}(b^2 - a^2) \\
\frac{1}{3}(b^3 - a^3) \\
\vdots \\
\frac{1}{n}(b^n - a^n)
\end{pmatrix}.
$$

This is the transpose of the Vandermonde system discussed in §13.1.1.

14.2.3 Newton-Cotes Quadrature

Quadrature rules that integrate the result of polynomial interpolation when the $x_i's$ are evenly spaced in $[a, b]$ are known as *Newton-Cotes* quadrature rules. As illustrated in Figure 14.1, there are two reasonable choices of evenly spaced samples:

- *Closed* Newton-Cotes quadrature places x_i's at a and b. In particular, for $k \in \{1, \ldots, n\}$ we take

$$x_k \equiv a + \frac{(k - 1)(b - a)}{n - 1}.$$

- *Open* Newton-Cotes quadrature does not place an x_i at a or b:

$$x_k \equiv a + \frac{k(b - a)}{n + 1}.$$

The Newton-Cotes formulae compute the integral of the polynomial interpolant approximating the function on a to b through these points; the degree of the polynomial must be $n - 1$ to keep the quadrature rule well-defined. There is no inherent advantage to using

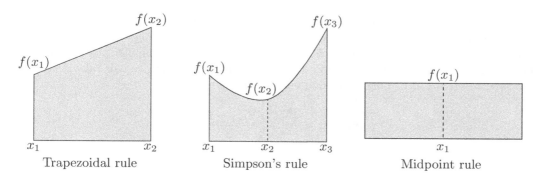

Figure 14.2 Newton-Cotes quadrature schemes; the approximated integral based on the $(x_i, f(x_i))$ pairs shown is given by the area of the gray region.

closed versus open Newton-Cotes rules; the choice between these options generally depends on which set of samples is available.

We illustrate the integration rules below in Figure 14.2. We will keep n relatively small to avoid oscillation and noise sensitivity that occur when fitting high-degree polynomials to a set of data points. Then, as in piecewise polynomial interpolation, we will then chain together small pieces into *composite* rules when integrating over a large interval $[a, b]$.

Closed rules. Closed Newton-Cotes quadrature strategies require $n \geq 2$ to avoid dividing by zero. The two lowest-order closed integrators are the most common:

- The *trapezoidal* rule for $n = 2$ (so $x_1 = a$ and $x_2 = b$) is constructed by linearly interpolating from $f(a)$ to $f(b)$. It effectively computes the area of a trapezoid via the formula

$$\int_a^b f(x)\, dx \approx (b - a)\frac{f(a) + f(b)}{2}.$$

- *Simpson's rule* is used for $n = 3$, with sample points

$$x_1 = a$$
$$x_2 = \frac{a + b}{2}$$
$$x_3 = b.$$

Integrating the parabola that goes through these three points yields

$$\int_a^b f(x)\, dx \approx \frac{b - a}{6}\left(f(a) + 4f\left(\frac{a + b}{2}\right) + f(b)\right).$$

Open rules. By far the most common rule for open quadrature is the *midpoint rule*, which takes $n = 1$ and approximates an integral with the signed area of a rectangle through the midpoint of the integration interval $[a, b]$:

$$\int_a^b f(x)\, dx \approx (b - a)f\left(\frac{a + b}{2}\right).$$

Larger values of n yield formulas similar to Simpson's rule and the trapezoidal rule.

Composite integration. We usually wish to integrate $f(x)$ with more than one, two, or three sample points x_i. To do so, we can construct a composite rule out of the midpoint or trapezoidal rules, as illustrated in Figure 14.3, by summing up smaller pieces along each interval. For example, if we subdivide $[a, b]$ into k intervals, then we can take $\Delta x \equiv \frac{b-a}{k}$ and $x_i \equiv a + (i-1)\Delta x$. Then, the composite midpoint rule is

$$\int_a^b f(x)\, dx \approx \sum_{i=1}^{k} f\left(\frac{x_{i+1} + x_i}{2}\right) \Delta x.$$

Similarly, the composite trapezoidal rule is

$$\int_a^b f(x)\, dx \approx \sum_{i=1}^{k} \left(\frac{f(x_i) + f(x_{i+1})}{2}\right) \Delta x$$

$$= \Delta x \left(\frac{1}{2} f(a) + f(x_2) + f(x_3) + \cdots + f(x_k) + \frac{1}{2} f(b)\right)$$

after reorganizing the sum.

An alternative derivation of the composite midpoint rule applies the interpolatory quadrature formula from §14.2.1 to piecewise constant interpolation; the composite version of the trapezoidal rule comes from piecewise linear interpolation.

The composite version of Simpson's rule, also illustrated in Figure 14.3, chains together three points at a time to make parabolic approximations. Adjacent parabolas meet at every other x_i and may not share tangents. After combining terms, this quadrature rule becomes:

$$\int_a^b f(x)\, dx \approx \frac{\Delta x}{6} \left[f(a) + 4f(x_2) + 2f(x_3) + 4f(x_4) + 2f(x_5) + \cdots + 4f(x_k) + f(b) \right].$$

Accuracy. We have developed a number of quadrature rules that combine the same set of $f(x_i)$'s with different weights to obtain potentially unequal approximations of the integral of f. Each approximation is based on a different interpolatory construction, so it is unclear that any of these rules is better than any other. Thus, we need to compute error estimates characterizing their respective behavior. We will study the basic Newton-Cotes integrators above to show how such comparisons might be carried out.

First, consider the midpoint quadrature rule on a single interval $[a, b]$. Define $c \equiv \frac{1}{2}(a+b)$. The Taylor series of f about c is:

$$f(x) = f(c) + f'(c)(x - c) + \frac{1}{2} f''(c)(x - c)^2 + \frac{1}{6} f'''(c)(x - c)^3 + \frac{1}{24} f''''(c)(x - c)^4 + \cdots$$

After integration, by symmetry about c, the odd-numbered derivatives drop out:

$$\int_a^b f(x)\, dx = (b - a)f(c) + \frac{1}{24} f''(c)(b - a)^3 + \frac{1}{1920} f''''(c)(b - a)^5 + \cdots$$

The first term of this sum is exactly the estimate of $\int_a^b f(x)\, dx$ provided by the midpoint rule, so based on this formula we can conclude that this rule is accurate up to $O(\Delta x^3)$.

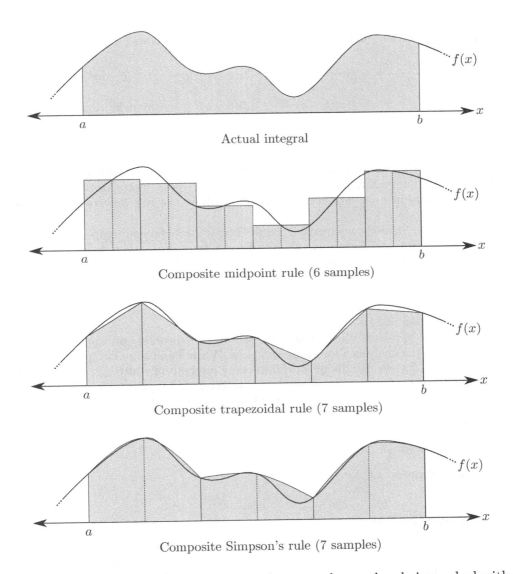

Figure 14.3 Composite Newton-Cotes quadrature rules; each rule is marked with the number of samples $(x_i, f(x_i))$ used to approximate the integral over six subintervals.

Continuing, plugging a and b into the Taylor series for $f(x)$ about c shows:

$$f(a) = f(c) + f'(c)(a - c) + \frac{1}{2}f''(c)(a - c)^2 + \frac{1}{6}f'''(c)(a - c)^3 + \cdots$$

$$f(b) = f(c) + f'(c)(b - c) + \frac{1}{2}f''(c)(b - c)^2 + \frac{1}{6}f'''(c)(b - c)^3 + \cdots$$

Adding these together and multiplying both sides by $\frac{1}{2}(b - a)$ shows:

$$(b - a)\frac{f(a) + f(b)}{2} = f(c)(b - a) + \frac{1}{4}f''(c)(b - a)((a - c)^2 + (b - c)^2) + \cdots$$

$$= f(c)(b - a) + \frac{1}{8}f''(c)(b - a)^3 + \cdots \text{ by definition of } c.$$

The $f'(c)$ term vanishes for the first line by substituting $c = \frac{1}{2}(a + b)$. Now, the left-hand side is the trapezoidal rule integral estimate, and the right-hand side agrees with the Taylor series for $\int_a^b f(x)\,dx$ up to the cubic term. Hence, the trapezoidal rule is also $O(\Delta x^3)$ accurate in a single interval. A similar argument provides error estimate for Simpson's rule; after somewhat more involved algebra, one can show Simpson's rule has error scaling like $O(\Delta x^5)$.

We pause here to highlight a surprising result: The trapezoidal and midpoint rules have the same order of accuracy! Examining the third-order term shows that the midpoint rule is approximately two times more accurate than the trapezoidal rule, making it marginally preferable for many calculations. This observation seems counterintuitive, since the trapezoidal rule uses a linear approximation while the midpoint rule uses a constant approximation. As you will see in Exercise 14.1, however, the midpoint rule recovers the integrals of linear functions, explaining its extra degree of accuracy.

A notable caveat applies to this sort of analysis. Taylor's theorem only applies when Δx is *small*; otherwise, the analysis above is meaningless. When a and b are far apart, to return to the case of small Δx, we can divide $[a, b]$ into many intervals of width Δx and apply the composite quadrature rules. The total number of intervals is $b-a/\Delta x$, so we must multiply error estimates by $1/\Delta x$ in this case. Hence, the following orders of accuracy hold:

- Composite midpoint: $O(\Delta x^2)$

- Composite trapezoid: $O(\Delta x^2)$

- Composite Simpson: $O(\Delta x^4)$

14.2.4 Gaussian Quadrature

In some applications, we can choose the locations x_i where f is sampled. In this case, we can optimize not only the weights for the quadrature rule but also the locations x_i to get the highest quality. This observation leads to challenging but theoretically appealing quadrature rules, such as the Gaussian quadrature technique explored below.

The details of this technique are outside the scope of our discussion, but we provide one path to its derivation. Generalizing Example 14.7, suppose that we wish to optimize $x_1, \ldots, x_n$ and $w_1, \ldots, w_n$ simultaneously to increase the order of an integration scheme. Now we have $2n$ instead of n unknowns, so we can enforce equality for $2n$ examples:

$$\int_a^b f_1(x)\,dx = w_1 f_1(x_1) + w_2 f_1(x_2) + \cdots + w_n f_1(x_n)$$

$$\int_a^b f_2(x)\,dx = w_1 f_2(x_1) + w_2 f_2(x_2) + \cdots + w_n f_2(x_n)$$

$$\vdots \qquad \vdots$$

$$\int_a^b f_{2n}(x)\,dx = w_1 f_{2n}(x_1) + w_2 f_{2n}(x_2) + \cdots + w_n f_{2n}(x_n).$$

Since both the x_i's and the w_i's are unknown, this system of equations is not linear and must be solved using more involved methods.

Example 14.8 (Gaussian quadrature). If we wish to optimize weights and sample locations for polynomials on the interval $[-1, 1]$, we would have to solve the following system of polynomials [58]:

$$w_1 + w_2 = \int_{-1}^1 1\,dx = 2$$

$$w_1 x_1 + w_2 x_2 = \int_{-1}^1 x\,dx = 0$$

$$w_1 x_1^2 + w_2 x_2^2 = \int_{-1}^1 x^2\,dx = \frac{2}{3}$$

$$w_1 x_1^3 + w_2 x_2^3 = \int_{-1}^1 x^3\,dx = 0.$$

Systems like this can have multiple roots and other degeneracies that depend not only on the f_i's (typically polynomials) but also on the interval over which the integral is approximated. These rules are not *progressive*, in that the x_i's chosen to integrate using n data points have little in common with those used to integrate using k data points when $k \neq n$. So, it is difficult to reuse data to achieve a better estimate with this quadrature rule. On the other hand, Gaussian quadrature has the highest possible degree of accuracy for fixed n. *Kronrod* quadrature rules adapt Gaussian points to the progressive case but no longer have the highest possible order of accuracy.

14.2.5 Adaptive Quadrature

Our discussion of Gaussian quadrature suggests that the placement of the x_i's can affect the quality of a quadrature scheme. There still is one piece of information we have not used, however: the function values $f(x_i)$. That is, different classes or shapes of functions may require different integration methods, but so far our algorithms have not attempted to detect this structure into account in any serious way.

With this situation in mind, *adaptive* quadrature strategies examine the current estimate of an integral and generate new x_i's where the integrand appears to be undersampled. Strategies for adaptive integration often compare the output of multiple quadrature techniques, e.g., trapezoid and midpoint, with the assumption that they agree where sampling of f is sufficient, as illustrated in Figure 14.4. If they do not agree to some tolerance on a given interval, an additional sample point is generated and the integral estimates are updated.

Figure 14.5 outlines a bisection technique for adaptive quadrature. The idea is to subdivide intervals in which the integral estimate appears to be inaccurate recursively. This method must be accompanied with special consideration when the level of recursion is too deep, accounting for the case of a function $f(x)$ that is noisy even at tiny scale.

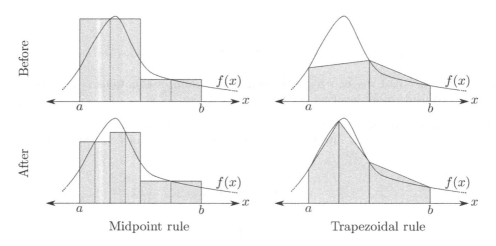

Figure 14.4 The trapezoidal and midpoint rules disagree considerably on the left subinterval (top), so adaptive quadrature methods subdivide in that region to get better accuracy (bottom).

---

function RECURSIVE-QUADRATURE($f(x), a, b, \varepsilon_0$)
  $I \leftarrow$ QUADRATURE-RULE($f(x), a, b$)
  $E \leftarrow$ ERROR-ESTIMATE($f(x), I, a, b$)
  if $E < \varepsilon_0$ **then**
    return I
  else
    $c \leftarrow \frac{1}{2}(a + b)$
    $I_1 \leftarrow$ RECURSIVE-QUADRATURE($f(x), a, c, \varepsilon_0$)
    $I_2 \leftarrow$ RECURSIVE-QUADRATURE($f(x), c, b, \varepsilon_0$)
    return $I_1 + I_2$

Figure 14.5 An outline for recursive quadrature via bisection. This method can use any of the quadrature rules discussed in this chapter; error estimates can be constructed, e.g., by evaluating the difference between using different quadrature rules for the same interval. The parameter ε_0 is a tolerance for the quality of the quadrature rule.

```
function MONTE-CARLO-INTEGRAL(f(x⃗), Ω ⊆ [a, b]ⁿ, p)
    c, d ← 0              ▷ Number of points inside Ω and average value
    for k ← 1, 2, . . . , p          ▷ Sample p points
        x⃗ ← UNIFORM-RANDOM([a, b]ⁿ)
        if INSIDE(x⃗, Ω) then          ▷ Otherwise reject
            c ← c + 1
            d ← d + f(x⃗)
    v ← c/p (b − a)ⁿ          ▷ Estimate of |Ω|
    y ← d/c                   ▷ Average observed f(x⃗)
    return vy
```

Figure 14.6 Pseudocode for Monte Carlo integration of a function $f(\vec{x}) : \Omega \rightarrow \mathbb{R}$.

14.2.6 Multiple Variables

Many times we wish to integrate functions $f(\vec{x})$ where $\vec{x} \in \mathbb{R}^n$. For example, when $n = 2$ we might integrate over a rectangle by computing

$$\int_a^b \int_c^d f(x, y)\, dx\, dy.$$

More generally, we might wish to find an integral $\int_\Omega f(\vec{x})\, d\vec{x}$, where Ω is some subset of $\mathbb{R}^n$.

A "curse of dimensionality" makes integration more difficult as the dimension increases. The number of sample locations $\vec{x}_i$ of $f(\vec{x})$ needed to achieve comparable quadrature accuracy for an integral in $\mathbb{R}^n$ increases exponentially in n. This observation may be disheartening but is somewhat reasonable: The more input dimensions for f, the more samples are needed to understand its behavior in all dimensions.

This issue aside, one way to extend single-variable integration to $\mathbb{R}^k$ is via the *iterated integral*. For example, if $f(x, y)$ is a function of two variables, suppose we wish to find $\int_a^b \int_c^d f(x, y)\, dx\, dy$. For fixed y, we can approximate the inner integral over x using a one-dimensional quadrature rule; then, we integrate these values over y using another quadrature rule. The inner and outer integrals both induce some error, so we may need to sample the $\vec{x}_i$'s more densely than in one dimension to achieve desired output quality.

Alternatively, just as we subdivided $[a, b]$ into intervals, we can subdivide Ω into triangles and rectangles in 2D, polyhedra or boxes in 3D, and so on and use interpolatory quadrature rules in each piece. For instance, one popular option is to integrate barycentric interpolants (§13.2.2), since this integral is known in closed form.

When n is high, however, it is not practical to divide the domain as suggested. In this case, we can use the randomized *Monte Carlo method*. In the most basic version of this method, we generate k random points $\vec{x}_i \in \Omega$ with uniform probability. Averaging the values $f(\vec{x}_i)$ and scaling the result by the volume $|\Omega|$ of Ω yields an approximation of $\int_\Omega f(\vec{x})\, d\vec{x}$:

$$\int_\Omega f(\vec{x})\, d\vec{x} \approx \frac{|\Omega|}{k} \sum_{i=1}^k f(\vec{x}_i).$$

This approximation converges like $1/\sqrt{k}$ as more sample points are added—independent of the dimension of Ω! So, in large dimensions the Monte Carlo estimate is preferable to the deterministic quadrature methods above. A proof of convergence requires some notions from probability theory, so we refer the reader to [103] or a similar reference for discussion.

One advantage of Monte Carlo techniques is that they are easily implemented and extended. Figure 14.6 provides a pseudocode implementation of Monte Carlo integration over a region $\Omega \subseteq [a, b]^n$. Even if we do not have a method for producing uniform samples in Ω directly, the more general integral can be carried out by sampling in the box $[a, b]^n$ and rejecting those samples outside Ω. This sampling is inappropriate when Ω is small relative to the bounding box $[a, b]^n$, since the odds of randomly drawing a point in Ω decrease in this case. To improve conditioning of this case, more advanced techniques *bias* their samples of $[a, b]^n$ based on evidence of where Ω takes the most space and where $f(\vec{x})$ is nontrivial.

Iterated integration can be effective for low-dimensional problems, and Monte Carlo methods show the greatest advantage in high dimensions. In between these two regimes, the choice of integrators is less clear. One compromise that samples less densely than iterated integration without resorting to randomization is the *sparse grid* or *Smolyak grid* method, designed to reduce the effect of the curse of dimensionality on numerical quadrature. We refer the reader to [114, 47] for discussion of this advanced technique.

14.2.7 Conditioning

We have evaluated the quality of a quadrature method by bounding its accuracy like $O(\Delta x^k)$ for small Δx. By this metric, a set of quadrature weights with large k is preferable. Another measure discussed in [58] and elsewhere, however, balances out the accuracy measurements obtained using Taylor arguments by considering the *stability* of a quadrature method under perturbations of the function being integrated.

Consider the quadrature rule $Q[f] \equiv \sum_i w_i f(x_i)$. Suppose we perturb f to some other $\hat{f}$. Define $\|f - \hat{f}\|_\infty \equiv \max_{x \in [a,b]} |f(x) - \hat{f}(x)|$. Then,

$$
\frac{|Q[f] - Q[\hat{f}]|}{\|f - \hat{f}\|_\infty} = \frac{|\sum_i w_i(f(x_i) - \hat{f}(x_i))|}{\|f - \hat{f}\|_\infty}
$$

$$
\leq \frac{\sum_i |w_i||f(x_i) - \hat{f}(x_i)|}{\|f - \hat{f}\|_\infty} \quad \text{by the triangle inequality}
$$

$$
\leq \|\vec{w}\|_\infty \quad \text{since } |f(x_i) - \hat{f}(x_i)| \leq \|f - \hat{f}\|_\infty \text{ by definition.}
$$

According to this bound, the most *stable* quadrature rules are those with small weights $\vec{w}$.

If we increase the order of quadrature accuracy by augmenting the degree of the polynomial used in Newton-Cotes quadrature, the conditioning bound $\|\vec{w}\|_\infty$ generally becomes less favorable. In degenerate circumstances, the w_i's even can take *negative* values, echoing the degeneracies of high-order polynomial interpolation. Thus, in practice we usually prefer composite quadrature rules summing simple estimates from many small subintervals to quadrature from higher-order interpolants, which can be unstable under numerical perturbation.

14.3 DIFFERENTIATION

Numerical integration is a relatively stable problem, in that the influence of any single value $f(x)$ on $\int_a^b f(x) \, dx$ shrinks to zero as a and b become far apart. Approximating the derivative of a function $f'(x)$, on the other hand, has no such property. From the Fourier analysis perspective, one can show that the integral $\int f(x) \, dx$ generally has lower frequencies than f, while differentiating to produce f' amplifies the frequency content of f, making sampling constraints, conditioning, and stability particularly challenging for approximating f'.

Despite the challenging circumstances, approximations of derivatives usually are relatively easy to implement and can be stable under sufficient smoothness assumptions. For

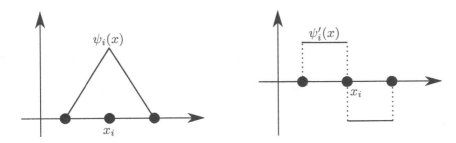

Figure 14.7 If a function is written in the basis of piecewise-linear "hat" functions $\psi_i(x)$, then its derivative can be written in the basis of piecewise constant functions $\psi_i'(x)$.

example, while developing the secant rule, Broyden's method, and so on we used approximations of derivatives and gradients to help guide optimization routines with success on a variety of objectives.

Here, we will focus on approximating f' for $f : \mathbb{R} \to \mathbb{R}$. Finding gradients and Jacobians usually is carried out by differentiating in one dimension at a time, effectively reducing to the one-dimensional problem.

14.3.1 Differentiating Basis Functions

From a mathematical perspective, perhaps the simplest use case for numerical differentiation involves functions that are constructed using interpolation formulas. As in §14.2.1, if $f(x) = \sum_i a_i \phi_i(x)$, then by linearity

$$f'(x) = \sum_i a_i \phi_i'(x).$$

In other words, the functions ϕ_i' form a *basis* for derivatives of functions written in the ϕ_i basis!

This phenomenon often connects different interpolatory schemes, as in Figure 14.7. For example, piecewise linear functions have piecewise constant derivatives, polynomial functions have polynomial derivatives of lower degree, and so on. In future chapters, we will see that this structure strongly influences discretizations of differential equations.

14.3.2 Finite Differences

A more common situation is that we have a function $f(x)$ that we can query but whose derivatives are unknown. This often happens when f takes on a complex form or when a user provides $f(x)$ as a subroutine without analytical information about its structure.

The definition of the derivative suggests a reasonable approximation

$$f'(x) \equiv \lim_{h \to 0} \frac{f(x+h) - f(x)}{h}.$$

As we might expect, for a finite $h > 0$ with small $|h|$ the expression in the limit provides an approximation of $f'(x)$.

To substantiate this intuition, use Taylor series to write

$$f(x + h) = f(x) + f'(x)h + \frac{1}{2}f''(x)h^2 + \cdots.$$

Rearranging this expression shows

$$f'(x) = \frac{f(x+h) - f(x)}{h} + O(h).$$

Thus, the following *forward difference approximation* of f' has linear convergence:

$$f'(x) \approx \frac{f(x+h) - f(x)}{h}.$$

Similarly, flipping the sign of h shows that *backward differences* also have linear convergence:

$$f'(x) \approx \frac{f(x) - f(x-h)}{h}.$$

We can improve this approximation by combining the forward and backward estimates. By Taylor's theorem,

$$f(x+h) = f(x) + f'(x)h + \frac{1}{2}f''(x)h^2 + \frac{1}{6}f'''(x)h^3 + \cdots$$

$$f(x-h) = f(x) - f'(x)h + \frac{1}{2}f''(x)h^2 - \frac{1}{6}f'''(x)h^3 + \cdots$$

$$\implies f(x+h) - f(x-h) = 2f'(x)h + \frac{1}{3}f'''(x)h^3 + \cdots$$

$$\implies \frac{f(x+h) - f(x-h)}{2h} = f'(x) + O(h^2).$$

Hence, *centered differences* approximate $f'(x)$ with quadratic convergence; this is the highest order of convergence we can expect to achieve with a single divided difference. We can, however, achieve more accuracy by evaluating f at other points, e.g., $x + 2h$, at the cost of additional computation time, as explored in §14.3.3.

Approximations of higher-order derivatives can be derived via similar constructions. If we add together the Taylor expansions of $f(x+h)$ and $f(x-h)$, then

$$f(x+h) + f(x-h) = 2f(x) + f''(x)h^2 + O(h^3)$$

$$\implies \frac{f(x+h) - 2f(x) + f(x-h)}{h^2} = f''(x) + O(h).$$

To construct similar combinations for higher derivatives, one trick is to notice that our second derivative formula can be factored differently:

$$\frac{f(x+h) - 2f(x) + f(x-h)}{h^2} = \frac{\frac{f(x+h)-f(x)}{h} - \frac{f(x)-f(x-h)}{h}}{h}.$$

That is, the second derivative approximation is a "finite difference of finite differences." One way to interpret this formula is shown in Figure 14.8. When we compute the forward difference approximation of f' between x and $x + h$, we can think of this slope as living at $x + h/2$; we similarly can use backward differences to place a slope at $x - h/2$. Finding the slope between these values puts the approximation back on x.

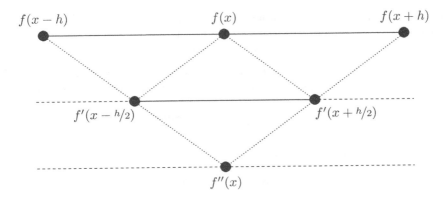

Figure 14.8 Computing the second derivative $f''(x)$ by divided differences can be thought of as applying the same divided difference rule once to approximate f' and a second time to approximate f''.

14.3.3 Richardson Extrapolation

One way to improve convergence of the approximations above is *Richardson extrapolation*. As an example of a more general pattern, suppose we wish to use forward differences to approximate $f'(x)$. For fixed $x \in \mathbb{R}$, define

$$D(h) \equiv \frac{f(x+h) - f(x)}{h}.$$

We have argued that $D(h)$ approaches $f'(x)$ as $h \to 0$. Furthermore, the difference between $D(h)$ and $f'(x)$ scales like $O(h)$.

More specifically, from our discussion in §14.3.2, $D(h)$ takes the form

$$D(h) = f'(x) + \frac{1}{2}f''(x)h + O(h^2).$$

Suppose we know $D(h)$ and $D(\alpha h)$ for some $0 < \alpha < 1$. Then,

$$D(\alpha h) = f'(x) + \frac{1}{2}f''(x)\alpha h + O(h^2).$$

We can combine these two relationships in matrix form as

$$\begin{pmatrix} 1 & \frac{1}{2}h \\ 1 & \frac{1}{2}\alpha h \end{pmatrix} \begin{pmatrix} f'(x) \\ f''(x) \end{pmatrix} = \begin{pmatrix} D(h) \\ D(\alpha h) \end{pmatrix} + O(h^2).$$

Applying the inverse of the 2×2 matrix on the left,

$$\begin{pmatrix} f'(x) \\ f''(x) \end{pmatrix} = \begin{pmatrix} 1 & \frac{1}{2}h \\ 1 & \frac{1}{2}\alpha h \end{pmatrix}^{-1} \left[\begin{pmatrix} D(h) \\ D(\alpha h) \end{pmatrix} + O(h^2) \right]$$

$$= \frac{1}{1-\alpha} \begin{pmatrix} -\alpha & 1 \\ \frac{2}{h} & -\frac{2}{h} \end{pmatrix} \left[\begin{pmatrix} D(h) \\ D(\alpha h) \end{pmatrix} + O(h^2) \right]$$

$$= \frac{1}{1-\alpha} \begin{pmatrix} -\alpha & 1 \\ \frac{2}{h} & -\frac{2}{h} \end{pmatrix} \begin{pmatrix} D(h) \\ D(\alpha h) \end{pmatrix} + \begin{pmatrix} O(h^2) \\ O(h) \end{pmatrix}.$$

Focusing on the first row, we took two $O(h)$ approximations of $f'(x)$ using $D(h)$ and combined them to make an $O(h^2)$ approximation! This clever technique is a method for *sequence acceleration*, improving the order of convergence of the approximation $D(h)$. The same method is applicable to many other problems including numerical integration, as explored in Exercise 14.9. Richardson extrapolation even can be applied recursively to make higher and higher order approximations of the same quantity.

> **Example 14.9** (Richardson extrapolation). Suppose we wish to approximate $f'(1)$ for $f(x) = \sin x^2$. To carry out Richardson extrapolation, we will use the function
>
> $$D(h) = \frac{\sin(1+h)^2 - \sin 1^2}{h}.$$
>
> If we take $h = 0.1$ and $\alpha = 0.5$, then
>
> $$D(0.1) = 0.941450167\ldots$$
> $$D(0.1 \cdot 0.5) = 1.017351587\ldots$$
>
> These approximations both hold up to $O(h)$. The $O(h^2)$ Richardson approximation is
>
> $$\frac{1}{1 - 0.5}(-0.5D(0.5) + D(0.1 \cdot 0.5)) = 1.0932530067\ldots$$
>
> This approximation is a closer match to the ground truth value $f'(1) \approx 1.0806046117\ldots$.

14.3.4 Choosing the Step Size

We showed that the error of Richardson extrapolation shrinks more quickly as $h \to 0$ than the error of divided differences. We have not justified, however, why this scaling matters. The Richardson extrapolation derivative formula requires *more* arithmetic than divided differences, so at first glance it may seem to be of limited interest. That is, in theory we can avoid depleting a fixed error budget in computing numerical derivatives equally well with both formulas, even though divided differences will need a far smaller h.

More broadly, unlike quadrature, numerical differentiation has a curious property. It appears that any formula above can be arbitrarily accurate without extra computational cost by choosing a sufficiently small h. This observation is appealing from the perspective that we can achieve higher-quality approximations without additional computation time.

The catch, however, is that implementations of arithmetic operations usually are inexact. The smaller the value of h, the more similar the values $f(x)$ and $f(x + h)$ become, to the point that they are indistinguishable in finite-precision arithmetic. Dividing by very small $h > 0$ induces additional numerical instability. Thus, there is a range of h values that are not large enough to induce significant discretization error and not small enough to generate numerical problems. Figure 14.9 shows an example for differentiating a simple function in IEEE floating-point arithmetic.

Similarly, suppose as in §14.2.7 that due to noise, rather than evaluating $f(x)$, we receive perturbed values from a function $\hat{f}(x)$ satisfying $\|f - \hat{f}\|_\infty \le \varepsilon$. Then, we can bound the error of computing a difference quotient:

$$\left| \frac{\hat{f}(x+h) - \hat{f}(x)}{h} - f'(x) \right| \le \left| \frac{\hat{f}(x+h) - \hat{f}(x)}{h} - \frac{f(x+h) - f(x)}{h} \right| + O(h)$$

by our previous bound

$$\le \left| \frac{(\hat{f}(x+h) - f(x+h)) - (\hat{f}(x) - f(x))}{h} \right| + O(h)$$

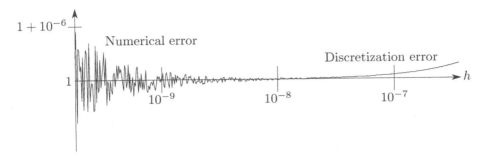

Figure 14.9 The finite difference $1/h(f(x+h)-f(x))$ as a function of h for $f(x) = x^2/2$, computed using IEEE floating-point arithmetic; when h is too small, the approximation suffers from numerical issues, while large h yields discretization error. The horizontal axis is on a logarithmic scale, and the vertical axis scales linearly.

$$\leq \frac{2\varepsilon}{h} + O(h) \text{ since } \|f - \hat{f}\|_\infty \leq \varepsilon.$$

For fixed $\varepsilon > 0$, this bound *degrades* if we take $h \to 0$. Instead, we should choose h to balance the $2\varepsilon/h$ and $O(h)$ terms to get minimal error. That is, if we cannot compute values of $f(x)$ exactly, taking larger $h > 0$ can actually *improve* the quality of the estimate of $f'(x)$. Exercise 14.6f has a similar conclusion about a method for numerical integration.

14.3.5 Automatic Differentiation

As we have seen, typical algorithms for numerical differentiation are relatively fast since they involve little more than computing a difference quotient. Their main drawback is numerical, in that finite-precision arithmetic and/or inexact evaluation of functions fundamentally limit the quality of the output. Noisy or rapidly varying functions are thus difficult to differentiate numerically with any confidence.

On the other end of the spectrum between computational efficiency and numerical quality lies the technique of *automatic differentiation* ("autodiff"), which is not subject to any discretization error [8]. Instead, this technique takes advantage of the chain rule and other properties of derivatives to compute them exactly.

"Forward" automatic differentiation is particularly straightforward to implement. Suppose we have two variables u and v, stored using floating-point values. We store alongside these variables additional values $u' \equiv du/dt$ and $v' \equiv dv/dt$ for some independent variable t; in some programming languages, we alternatively can define a new data type holding pairs of values $[u, u']$ and $[v, v']$. We can define an algebra on these pairs that encodes typical operations:

$$[u, u'] + [v, v'] \equiv [u + v, u' + v']$$
$$c[u, u'] \equiv [cu, cu']$$
$$[u, u'] \cdot [v, v'] \equiv [uv, uv' + u'v]$$
$$[u, u'] \div [v, v'] \equiv \left[\frac{u}{v}, \frac{vu' - uv'}{v^2}\right]$$
$$\exp([u, u']) \equiv [e^u, u'e^u]$$

$$\ln([u, u']) \equiv \left[\ln u, \frac{u'}{u} \right]$$

$$\cos([u, u']) \equiv [\cos u, -u' \sin u]$$

$$\vdots \quad \vdots$$

Starting with the pair $t \equiv [t_0, 1]$—since $dt/dt = 1$—we can evaluate a function $f(t)$ and its derivative $f'(t)$ simultaneously using these rules. If they are implemented in a programming language supporting operator overloading, the additional derivative computations can be completely transparent to the implementer.

The method we just described builds up the derivative $f'(t)$ in parallel with building $y = f(t)$. "Backward" automatic differentiation is an alternative algorithm that can require fewer function evaluations in exchange for more memory usage and a more complex implementation. This technique constructs a graph representing the steps of computing $f(t)$ as a sequence of elementary operations. Then, rather than starting from the fact $dt/dt = 1$ and working forward to dy/dt, backward automatic differentiation starts with $dy/dy = 1$ and works backward from the same rules to replace the denominator with dt. Backward automatic differentiation can avoid unnecessary computations, particularly when y is a function of multiple variables. For instance, suppose we can write $f(t_1, t_2) = f_1(t_1) + f_2(t_2)$; in this case, backward automatic differentiation does not need to differentiate f_1 with respect to t_2 or f_2 with respect to t_1. The *backpropagation* method for neural networks in machine learning is a special case of backward automatic differentiation.

Automatic differentiation is widely regarded as an under-appreciated numerical technique, yielding *exact* derivatives of functions with minimal implementation effort. It is particularly valuable when prototyping software making use of optimization methods requiring derivatives or Hessians, avoiding having to recompute derivatives by hand every time an objective function is adjusted. The cost of this convenience, however, is computational efficiency, since in effect automatic differentiation methods do not simplify expressions for derivatives but rather apply the most obvious rules.

14.3.6 Integrated Quantities and Structure Preservation

Continuing in our consideration of alternatives to numerical differentiation, we outline an approach that has gained popularity in the geometry and computer graphics communities for dealing with curvature and other differential measures of shape.

As we have seen, a typical pattern from numerical analysis is to prove that properties of approximated derivatives hold as $\Delta x \to 0$ for some measure of spacing Δx. While this type of analysis provides intuition relating discrete computations to continuous notions from calculus, it neglects a key fact: In reality, we must fix $\Delta x > 0$. Understanding what happens in the $\Delta x > 0$ regime can be equally important to the $\Delta x \to 0$ limit, especially when taking coarse approximations. For example, in computational geometry, it may be desirable to link measures like curvature of smooth shape directly to discrete values like lengths and angles that can be computed on complexes of polygons.

With this new view, some techniques involving derivatives, integrals, and other quantities are designed with *structure preservation* in mind, yielding "discrete" rather than "discretized" analogs of continuous quantities [53]. That is, rather than asking that structure from continuous calculus emerges as $\Delta x \to 0$, we design differentiators and integrators for which certain theorems from continuous mathematics hold exactly.

One central technique in this domain is the use of *integrated quantities* to encode derivatives. As a basic example, suppose we are sampling $f(t)$ and have computed

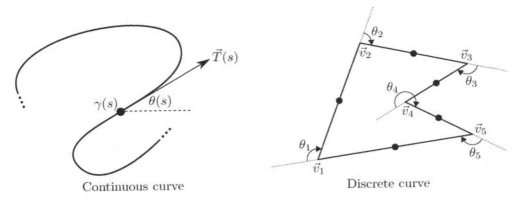

Figure 14.10 Notation for Example 14.10; each curve segment Γ_i is the union of the two half-segments adjacent to $\vec{v}_i$, bounded by the marked midpoints.

$f(t_1), f(t_2), \ldots, f(t_k)$ for some discrete set of times $t_1 < t_2 < \cdots < t_k$. Rather than using divided differences to approximate the derivative f', we can use the Fundamental Theorem of Calculus to show

$$\int_{t_i}^{t_{i+1}} f'(t) \, dt = f(t_{i+1}) - f(t_i).$$

This formula may not appear remarkable beyond first-year calculus, but it encodes a deep idea. The difference $f(t_{i+1}) - f(t_i)$ on the right side is computable *exactly* from the samples $f(t_1), f(t_2), \ldots, f(t_k)$, while the quantity on the left is an averaged version of the derivative f'. By substituting integrated versions of f' into computations whenever possible, we can carry out discrete analogs of continuous calculus for which certain theorems and properties hold exactly rather than in the limit.

Example 14.10 (Curvature of a 2D curve, [53]). In the continuous theory of differential geometry, a smooth curve Γ on the two-dimensional plane can be parameterized as a function $\gamma(s) : \mathbb{R} \to \mathbb{R}^2$ satisfying $\gamma'(s) \neq \vec{0}$ for all s. Assume that $\|\gamma'(s)\|_2 = 1$ for all s; such an arc length parameterization is always possible by moving along the curve with constant speed. Then, Γ has unit tangent vector $\vec{T}(s) \equiv \gamma'(s)$. If we write $\vec{T}(s) \equiv (\cos\theta(s), \sin\theta(s))$ for angle $\theta(s)$, then the *curvature* of $\gamma(s)$ is given by the derivative $\kappa(s) \equiv \theta'(s)$. This notation is illustrated in Figure 14.10 alongside notation for the discretization below.

Suppose Γ is closed, that is, $\gamma(s_0) = \gamma(s_1)$ for some $s_0, s_1 \in \mathbb{R}$. In this case, the *turning number theorem* from topology states

$$\int_{s_0}^{s_1} \kappa(s) \, ds = 2\pi k,$$

for some integer k. Intuitively, this theorem represents the fact that $\vec{T}(s_0) = \vec{T}(s_1)$, and hence θ took some number of loops around the full circle.

A typical discretization of a two-dimensional curve is as a sequence of line segments $\vec{v}_i \leftrightarrow \vec{v}_{i+1}$. Approximating $\kappa(s)$ on such a curve can be challenging, since κ is related to the second derivative γ''. Instead, suppose at each joint $\vec{v}_i$ we define the *integrated curvature* over the two half-segments around $\vec{v}_i$ to be the turning angle θ_i given by the π minus the angle between the two segments adjacent to $\vec{v}_i$.

Partition the discretization of Γ into pairs of half-segments Γ_i. Then, if Γ is closed,

$$\int_\Gamma \kappa\, ds = \sum_i \int_{\Gamma_i} \kappa\, ds \text{ by breaking into individual terms}$$

$$= \sum_i \theta_i \text{ by definition of integrated curvature}$$

$$= 2\pi k,$$

where the final equality comes from the fact that the discrete Γ is a polygon, and we are summing its exterior angles. That is, for this choice of discrete curvature, the turning number theorem holds *exactly* even for coarse approximations of Γ, rather than becoming closer and closer to true as the lengths $|\Gamma_i| \to 0$. In this sense, the integrated turning-angle curvature has more properties in common with the continuous curvature of a curve $\gamma(s)$ than an inexact but convergent discretization coming from divided differences.

The example above shows a typical structure-preserving treatment of a derivative quantity, in this case the curvature of a two-dimensional curve, accompanied by a discrete structure—the turning number theorem—holding without taking any limit as $\Delta x \to 0$. We have not shown, however, that the value θ_i—or more precisely some non-integrated pointwise approximation like $\theta_i/|\Gamma_i|$—actually converges to the curvature of Γ. This type of convergence does *not* always hold, and in some cases it is impossible to preserve structure exactly and converge as $\Delta x \to 0$ simultaneously [128]. Such issues are the topic of active research at the intersection of numerical methods and geometry processing.

14.4 EXERCISES

14.1 Show that the midpoint rule is exact for the function $f(x) = mx + c$ along any interval $x \in [a, b]$.

14.2 (Suggested by Y. Zhao) Derive α, β, and x_1 such that the following quadrature rule holds exactly for polynomials of degree ≤ 2 :

$$\int_0^2 f(x)\, dx \approx \alpha f(0) + \beta f(x_1).$$

14.3 Suppose we are given a quadrature rule of the form $\int_0^1 f(x)\, dx \approx af(0) + bf(1)$ for some $a, b \in \mathbb{R}$. Propose a corresponding composite rule for approximating $\int_0^1 f(x)\, dx$ given $n + 1$ closed sample points $y_0 \equiv f(0), y_1 \equiv f(1/n), y_2 \equiv f(2/n), \ldots, y_n \equiv f(1)$.

14.4 Some quadrature problems can be solved by applying a suitable change of variables:

(a) Our strategies for quadrature break down when the interval of integration is not of finite length. Derive the following relationships for $f : \mathbb{R} \to \mathbb{R}$:

$$\int_{-\infty}^\infty f(x)\, dx = \int_{-1}^1 f\left(\frac{t}{1-t^2}\right) \frac{1+t^2}{(1-t^2)^2}\, dt$$

$$\int_0^\infty f(x)\, dx = \int_0^1 \frac{f(-\ln t)}{t}\, dt$$

$$\int_c^\infty f(x)\, dx = \int_0^1 f\left(c + \frac{t}{1-t}\right) \cdot \frac{1}{(1-t)^2}\, dt.$$

How can these formulas be used to integrate over intervals of infinite length? What might be a drawback of evenly spacing t samples?

(b) Suppose $f : [-1, 1] \to \mathbb{R}$ can be written:

$$f(\cos \theta) = \frac{a_0}{2} + \sum_{k=1}^{\infty} a_k \cos(k\theta).$$

Then, show:

$$\int_{-1}^{1} f(x) \, dx = a_0 + \sum_{k=1}^{\infty} \frac{2a_{2k}}{1 - (2k)^2}.$$

This formula provides a way to integrate a function given its Fourier series [25].

14.5 The methods in this chapter for differentiation were limited to single-valued functions $f : \mathbb{R} \to \mathbb{R}$. Suppose $g : \mathbb{R}^n \to \mathbb{R}^m$. How would you use these techniques to approximate the Jacobian Dg? How does the timing of your approach scale with m and n?

14.6 ("Lanczos differentiator," [77]) Suppose $f(t)$ is a smooth function.

(a) Suppose we sample $f(t)$ at $t = kh$ for $k \in \{-n, -n+1, \ldots, 0, \ldots, n\}$, yielding samples $y_{-n} = f(-nh), y_{-n+1} = f((-n+1)h), \ldots, y_n = f(nh)$. Show that the parabola $p(t) = at^2 + bt + c$ optimally fitting these data points via least-squares satisfies

$$p'(0) = \frac{\sum_k k y_k}{h \sum_k k^2}.$$

(b) Use this formula to propose approximations of $f'(0)$ when $n = 1, 2, 3$.

(c) Motivate the following formula for "differentiation by integration":

$$f'(0) = \lim_{h \to 0} \frac{3}{2h^3} \int_{-h}^{h} tf(t) \, dt.$$

This formula provides one connection between numerical methods for integration and differentiation.

(d) Show that when $h > 0$,

$$\frac{3}{2h^3} \int_{-h}^{h} tf(t) \, dt = f'(0) + O(h^2).$$

(e) Denote $D_h f \equiv \frac{3}{2h^3} \int_{-h}^{h} tf(t) \, dt$. Suppose thanks to noise we actually observe $f^\varepsilon(t)$ satisfying $|f(t) - f^\varepsilon(t)| \le \varepsilon$ for all t. Show the following relationship:

$$|D_h f^\varepsilon - f'(0)| \le \frac{3\varepsilon}{2h} + O(h^2).$$

(f) Suppose the second term in Exercise 14.6e is bounded above by $Mh^2/10$; this is the case when $|f'''(t)| \le M$ everywhere [54]. Show that with the right choice of h, the integral approximation from Exercise 14.6e is within $O(\varepsilon^{2/3})$ of $f'(0)$.
Note: Your choice of h effectively trades off between numerical approximation error from using the "differentiation by integration" formula and noise approximating f with f^ε. This property makes the Lanczos approximation effective for certain noisy functions.

14.7 Propose an extension of forward automatic differentiation to maintaining first and second derivatives in triplets $[u, u', u'']$. Provide analogous formulas for the operations listed in §14.3.5 given $[u, u', u'']$ and $[v, v', v'']$.

14.8 The problem of numerical differentiation is challenging for noisy functions. One way to stabilize such a calculation is to consider multiple samples simultaneously [1]. For this problem, assume $f : [0, 1] \to \mathbb{R}$ is differentiable.

(a) By the Fundamental Theorem of Calculus, there exists $c \in \mathbb{R}$ such that

$$f(x) = c + \int_0^x f'(\bar{x}) \, d\bar{x}.$$

Suppose we sample $f(x)$ at evenly spaced points $x_0 = 0, x_1 = h, x_2 = 2h, \ldots, x_n = 1$ and wish to approximate the first derivative $f'(x)$ at $x_1 - h/2, x_2 - h/2, \ldots, x_n - h/2$. If we label our samples of $f'(x)$ as $a_1, \ldots, a_n$, write a least-squares problem in the a_i's and an additional unknown c approximating this integral relationship.

(b) Propose a Tikhonov regularizer for this problem.

(c) We also could have written

$$f(x) = \tilde{c} - \int_x^1 f'(\bar{x}) \, d\bar{x}.$$

Does your approximation of $f'(\bar{x})$ change if you use this formula?

14.9 The *Romberg* quadrature rules are derived by applying Richardson extrapolation (§14.3.3) to numerical integration. Here, we will derive Romberg integration for $f : [a, b] \to \mathbb{R}$.

(a) Suppose we divide $[a, b]$ into 2^k subintervals for $k \geq 0$. Denote by $T_{k,0}$ the result of applying the composite trapezoidal rule to $f(x)$ to this subdivision. Show that there exists a constant C dependent on f but not k such that:

$$\int_a^b f(x) \, dx = T_{k,0} + Ch^2 + O(h^4),$$

where $h(k) = (b-a)/2^k$. For this problem, you may assume that f is infinitely differentiable and that the Taylor series for f centered at any $c \in [a, b]$ is convergent.

(b) Use Richardson extrapolation to derive an estimate $T_{k,1}$ of the integral that is accurate up to $O(h^4)$.
Hint: Combine $T_{k,0}$ and $T_{k-1,0}$.

(c) Assume that the error expansion for the trapezoidal rule continues in a similar fashion:

$$\int_a^b f(x) \, dx = T_{k,0} + C_2 h^2 + C_4 h^4 + C_6 h^6 + \cdots.$$

By iteratively applying Richardson extrapolation, propose values $T_{k,j}$ for $j \leq k$ that can be used to achieve arbitrarily high-order estimates of the desired integral.
Hint: You should be able to define $T_{k,j}$ as a linear combination of $T_{k,j-1}$ and $T_{k-1,j-1}$.

14.10 Give examples of closed and open Newton-Cotes quadrature rules with negative coefficients for integrating $f(x)$ on $[0, 1]$. What unnatural properties can be exhibited by these approximations?

14.11 Provide a sequence of differentiable functions $f_k : [0, 1] \to \mathbb{R}$ and a function $f : [0, 1] \to \mathbb{R}$ such that $\max_{x \in [0,1]} |f_k(x) - f(x)| \to 0$ as $k \to \infty$ but $\max_{x \in [0,1]} |f_k'(x) - f'(x)| \to \infty$. What does this example imply about numerical differentiation when function values are noisy? Is a similar counterexample possible for integration when f and the f_k's are differentiable?

CHAPTER 15

Ordinary Differential Equations

CONTENTS

15.1	Motivation	304
15.2	Theory of ODEs	305
	15.2.1 Basic Notions	305
	15.2.2 Existence and Uniqueness	307
	15.2.3 Model Equations	309
15.3	Time-Stepping Schemes	311
	15.3.1 Forward Euler	311
	15.3.2 Backward Euler	313
	15.3.3 Trapezoidal Method	314
	15.3.4 Runge-Kutta Methods	315
	15.3.5 Exponential Integrators	316
15.4	Multivalue Methods	318
	15.4.1 Newmark Integrators	318
	15.4.2 Staggered Grid and Leapfrog	321
15.5	Comparison of Integrators	322

$\mathcal{C}$ HAPTER 13 motivated the problem of interpolation by transitioning from *analyzing* functions to *finding* functions. In problems like interpolation and regression, the unknown is a entire function $f(\vec{x})$, and the job of the algorithm is to fill in $f(\vec{x})$ at positions $\vec{x}$ where it is unknown.

In this chapter and the next, our unknown will continue to be a function f, but rather than filling in missing values we will solve more complex design problems like the following:

- Find f approximating some other function f_0 but satisfying additional criteria (smoothness, continuity, boundedness, etc.).

- Simulate some dynamical or physical relationship as $f(t)$ where t is time.

- Find f with similar values to f_0 but certain properties in common with a different function g_0.

In each of these cases, our unknown is a function f, but our criterion for success is more involved than "matches a given set of data points."

The theories of ordinary differential equations (ODEs) and partial differential equations (PDEs) involve the case where we wish to find a function $f(\vec{x})$ based on information about or relationships between its derivatives. We inadvertently solved one problem in this class while studying quadrature: Given $f'(t)$, quadrature approximates $f(t)$ using integration.

In this chapter, we will consider *ordinary* differential equations and in particular *initial value problems*. In these problems, the unknown is a function $f(t) : \mathbb{R} \to \mathbb{R}^n$, given $f(0)$ and an equation satisfied by f and its derivatives. Our goal is to predict $f(t)$ for $t > 0$. We will provide examples of ODEs appearing in practice and then will describe common solution techniques.

15.1 MOTIVATION

ODEs appear in nearly every branch of science, and hence it is not difficult to identify target applications of solution techniques. We choose a few representative examples both from the computational and scientific literatures:

Example 15.1 (Newton's Second Law). Continuing from §6.1.2, recall that Newton's Second Law of Motion states $\vec{F} = m\vec{a}$, that is, the total force on an object is equal to its mass times its acceleration. If we simulate n particles simultaneously as they move in three-dimensional space, we can combine all their positions into a single vector $\vec{x}(t) \in \mathbb{R}^{3n}$. Similarly, we can write a function $\vec{F}(t, \vec{x}, \vec{x}') \in \mathbb{R}^{3n}$ taking the current time, the positions of the particles, and their velocities and returning the total force on each particle divided by its mass. This function can take into account interrelationships between particles (e.g., gravitational forces, springs, or intermolecular bonds), external effects like wind resistance (which depends on $\vec{x}'$), external forces varying with time t, and so on. To find the positions of all the particles as functions of time, we can integrate Newton's second law forward in time by solving the equation $\vec{x}'' = \vec{F}(t, \vec{x}, \vec{x}')$. We usually are given the positions and velocities of all the particles at time $t = 0$ as a starting condition.

Example 15.2 (Protein folding). On a small scale, the equations governing motions of molecules stem from Newton's laws or—at even smaller scales—the Schrödinger equation of quantum mechanics. One challenging case is that of *protein folding*, in which the geometric structure of a protein is predicted by simulating intermolecular forces over time. These forces take many nonlinear forms that continue to challenge researchers in computational biology due in large part to a variety of *time scales*: The same forces that cause protein folding and related phenomena also can make molecules vibrate rapidly, and the disparate time scales of these two different behaviors makes them difficult to capture simultaneously.

Example 15.3 (Gradient descent). Suppose we wish to minimize an objective function $E(\vec{x})$ over all $\vec{x}$. Especially if E is a convex function, the most straightforward option for minimization from Chapter 9 is gradient descent with a constant step size or "learning rate." Since $-\nabla E(\vec{x})$ points in the direction along which E decreases the most from a given $\vec{x}$, we can iterate:

$$\vec{x}_{i+i} \equiv \vec{x}_i - h\nabla E(\vec{x}_i),$$

for fixed $h > 0$. We can rewrite this relationship as

$$\frac{\vec{x}_{i+1} - \vec{x}_i}{h} = -\nabla E(\vec{x}_i).$$

In the style of §14.3, we might think of $\vec{x}_k$ as a sample of a function $\vec{x}(t)$ at $t = hk$. Heuristically, taking $h \to 0$ motivates an ordinary differential equation

$$\vec{x}'(t) = -\nabla E(\vec{x}).$$

If we take $\vec{x}(0)$ to be an initial guess of the location where $E(\vec{x})$ is minimized, then this ODE is a continuous model of gradient descent. It can be thought of as the equation of a path smoothly walking "downhill" along a landscape provided by E.

For example, suppose we wish to solve $A\vec{x} = \vec{b}$ for symmetric positive definite A. From §11.1.1, this is equivalent to minimizing $E(\vec{x}) \equiv \frac{1}{2}\vec{x}^\top A\vec{x} - \vec{b}^\top \vec{x} + c$. Using the continuous model of gradient descent, we can instead solve the ODE $\vec{x}' = -\nabla E(\vec{x}) = \vec{b} - A\vec{x}$. As $t \to \infty$, we expect $\vec{x}(t)$ to better and better satisfy the linear system.

Example 15.4 (Crowd simulation). Suppose we are writing video game software requiring realistic simulation of virtual crowds of humans, animals, spaceships, and the like. One way to generate plausible motion is to use differential equations. In this technique, the velocity of a member of the crowd is determined as a function of its environment; for example, in human crowds, the proximity of other humans, distance to obstacles, and so on can affect the direction a given agent is moving. These rules can be simple, but in the aggregate their interaction becomes complex. Stable integrators for differential equations underlie crowd simulation to avoid noticeably unrealistic or unphysical behavior.

15.2   THEORY OF ODES

A full treatment of the theory of ordinary differential equations is outside the scope of our discussion, and we refer the reader to [64] or any other basic text for details from this classical theory. We highlight relevant results here for development in future sections.

15.2.1   Basic Notions

The most general initial value problem takes the following form:

$$
\begin{array}{ll}
\text{Find} & f(t) : \mathbb{R}^+ \to \mathbb{R}^n \\
\text{satisfying} & F[t, f(t), f'(t), f''(t), \ldots, f^{(k)}(t)] = \vec{0} \\
\text{given} & f(0), f'(0), f''(0), \ldots, f^{(k-1)}(0).
\end{array}
$$

Here, F is some relationship between f and all its derivatives; we use $f^{(\ell)}$ to denote the ℓ-th derivative of f. The functions f and F can be *multidimensional*, taking on values in $\mathbb{R}^n$ rather than $\mathbb{R}$, but by convention and for convenience of notation we will omit the vector sign. We also will use the notation $\vec{y} \equiv f(t)$ as an alternative to writing $f(t)$ when the t dependence is implicit; in this case, derivatives will be notated $\vec{y}' \equiv f'(t)$, $\vec{y}'' \equiv f''(t)$, and so on.

Example 15.5 (Canonical ODE form). Suppose we wish to solve the ODE $y'' = ty' \cos y$. In the general form above, the ODE can be written $F[t, y, y', y''] = 0$, where $F[t, a, b, c] \equiv tb \cos a - c$.

ODEs determine the *evolution* of f over time t; we know f and its derivatives at time $t = 0$ and wish to predict these quantities moving forward. They can take many forms even in a single variable. For instance, denote $y = f(t)$ for $y \in \mathbb{R}^1$. Then, examples of ODEs include the following:

Example ODE	Distinguishing properties
$y' = 1 + \cos t$	Can be solved by integrating both sides with respect to t; can be solved discretely using quadrature
$y' = ay$	Linear in y, no dependence on time t
$y' = ay + e^t$	Time- and value-dependent
$y'' + 3y' - y = t$	Involves multiple derivatives of y
$y'' \sin y = e^{ty'}$	Nonlinear in y and t

We will restrict most of our discussion to the case of *explicit* ODEs, in which the highest-order derivative can be isolated:

Definition 15.1 (Explicit ODE). An ODE is *explicit* if can be written in the form

$$f^{(k)}(t) = F[t, f(t), f'(t), f''(t), \ldots, f^{(k-1)}(t)].$$

Certain *implicit* ODEs can be converted to explicit form by solving a root-finding problem, for example, using the machinery introduced in Chapter 8, but this approach can fail in the presence of multiple roots.

Generalizing a trick first introduced in §6.1.2, any explicit ODE can be converted to a first-order equation $f'(t) = F[t, f(t)]$ by adding to the dimensionality of f. This construction implies that it will be enough for us to consider algorithms for solving (multivariable) ODEs containing only a single time derivative. As a reminder of this construction for the second-order ODE $y'' = F[t, y, y']$, recall that

$$\frac{d^2 y}{dt^2} = \frac{d}{dt}\left(\frac{dy}{dt}\right).$$

Defining an intermediate variable $z \equiv dy/dt$, we can expand to the following first-order system:

$$\frac{d}{dt}\begin{pmatrix} y \\ z \end{pmatrix} = \begin{pmatrix} z \\ F[t, y, z] \end{pmatrix}.$$

More generally, if we wish to solve the explicit problem

$$f^{(k)}(t) = F[t, f(t), f'(t), f''(t), \ldots, f^{(k-1)}(t)]$$

for $f : \mathbb{R}^+ \to \mathbb{R}^n$, then instead we can solve the first-order ODE in dimension $n(k+1)$:

$$\frac{d}{dt}\begin{pmatrix} f_0(t) \\ f_1(t) \\ f_2(t) \\ \vdots \\ f_{k-1}(t) \end{pmatrix} = \begin{pmatrix} f_1(t) \\ f_2(t) \\ f_3(t) \\ \vdots \\ F[t, f_0(t), f_1(t), \ldots, f_{k-1}(t)] \end{pmatrix}.$$

Here, we denote $f_i(t) : \mathbb{R} \to \mathbb{R}^n$ as the i-th derivative of $f_0(t)$, which satisfies the original ODE. To check, our expanded system above implies $f_1(t) = f_0'(t)$, $f_2(t) = f_1'(t) = f_0''(t)$, and so on; the final row encodes the original ODE.

This trick simplifies notation and allows us to emphasize first-order ODEs, but some care should be taken to understand that it does come with a cost. The expansion above replaces ODEs with potentially many derivatives with ODEs containing just one derivative but with much higher dimensionality. We will return to this trade-off between dimensionality and number of derivatives when designing methods specifically for second-order ODEs in §15.4.2.

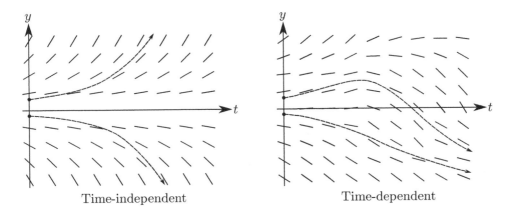

Time-independent   Time-dependent

Figure 15.1 First-order ODEs in one variable $y' = F[t, y]$ can be visualized using *slope fields* on the (t, y) plane. Here, short line segments show the slope $F[t, y]$ at each sampled point; solution curves $y(t)$ shown as dotted lines start at $(0, y(0))$ and follow the slope field as their tangents. We show an example of a time-independent ("autonomous") ODE $y' = F[y]$ and an example of a time-dependent ODE $y' = F[t, y]$.

Example 15.6 (ODE expansion). Suppose we wish to solve $y''' = 3y'' - 2y' + y$ where $y(t) : \mathbb{R}^+ \to \mathbb{R}$. This equation is equivalent to:

$$\frac{d}{dt}\begin{pmatrix} y \\ z \\ w \end{pmatrix} = \begin{pmatrix} 0 & 1 & 0 \\ 0 & 0 & 1 \\ 1 & -2 & 3 \end{pmatrix}\begin{pmatrix} y \\ z \\ w \end{pmatrix}.$$

In the interests of making our canonical ODE problem as simple as possible, we can further restrict our consideration to *autonomous* ODEs. These equations are of the form $f'(t) = F[f(t)]$, that is, F has no dependence on t (or on higher-order derivatives of f, removed above). To reduce an ODE to this form, we use the fact $d/dt(t) = 1$. After defining a trivial function $g(t) = t$, the ODE $f'(t) = F[t, f(t)]$ can be rewritten as the autonomous equation

$$\frac{d}{dt}\begin{pmatrix} g(t) \\ f(t) \end{pmatrix} = \begin{pmatrix} 1 \\ F[g(t), f(t)] \end{pmatrix},$$

with an additional initial condition $g(0) = 0$.

It is possible to visualize the behavior and classification of low-dimensional ODEs in many ways. If the unknown $f(t)$ is a function of a single variable, then $F[f(t)]$ provides the slope of $f(t)$, as shown in Figure 15.1. For higher-order ODEs, it can be useful to plot $f(t)$ and its derivatives, shown for the equation of motion for a pendulum in Figure 15.2. In higher dimensions, it may be possible only to show example solution paths, as in Figure 15.3.

15.2.2 Existence and Uniqueness

Before we discretize the initial value ODE problem, we should acknowledge that not all differential equations are solvable, while others admit infinitely many solutions. Existence and uniqueness of ODE solutions can be challenging to prove, but without these properties

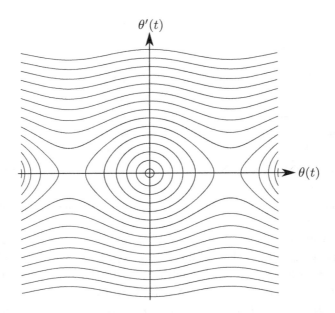

Figure 15.2 The *phase space diagram* of a pendulum, which satisfies the ODE $\theta'' = -\sin\theta$. Here, the horizontal axis shows position θ of the pendulum as it swings (as an angle from vertical), and the vertical axis shows the angular velocity θ'. Each path represents the motion of a pendulum with different starting conditions; the time t is not depicted. Rings indicate a swinging pendulum, while waves indicate that the pendulum is doing complete revolutions.

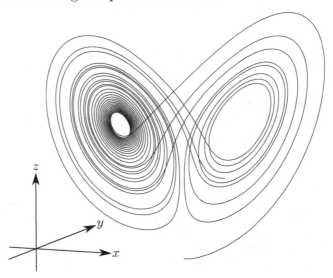

Figure 15.3 The *trace* of an ODE solution $(x(t), y(t), z(t))$ shows typical behavior without showing the velocity of the path or dependence on time t; here we show a solution to the *Lorenz equations* (known as a "Lorenz attractor") $x' = \sigma(y-x), y' = x(\rho - z) - y, z' = xy - \beta z$ integrated numerically ($\rho = 28, \sigma = 10, \beta = 8/3$).

we cannot hold numerical methods responsible for failure to recover a reasonable solution. Numerical ODE solvers can be thought of as filling the gap between knowing that a solution to a differential equation exists and being able to write this solution in closed form; checking existence and uniqueness is largely a function of how an ODE is written *before* discretization and usually is checked theoretically rather than algorithmically.

Example 15.7 (Unsolvable ODE). Consider the equation $y' = 2y/t$, with $y(0) \neq 0$ given; the $1/t$ factor does not divide by zero because the ODE only has to hold for $t > 0$. Rewriting as

$$\frac{1}{y}\frac{dy}{dt} = \frac{2}{t}$$

and integrating with respect to t on both sides shows

$$\ln|y| = 2\ln t + c.$$

Exponentiating both sides shows $y = Ct^2$ for some $C \in \mathbb{R}$. In this expression, $y(0) = 0$, contradicting the initial conditions. Thus, this ODE has no solution with the given initial conditions.

Example 15.8 (Nonunique solutions). Now, consider the same ODE with $y(0) = 0$. Consider $y(t)$ given by $y(t) = Ct^2$ for *any* $C \in \mathbb{R}$. Then, $y'(t) = 2Ct$ and

$$\frac{2y}{t} = \frac{2Ct^2}{t} = 2Ct = y'(t),$$

showing that the ODE is solved by this function regardless of C. Thus, solutions of this equation with the new initial conditions are nonunique.

There is a rich theory characterizing behavior and stability of solutions to ordinary differential equations. Under weak conditions on F, it is possible to show that an ODE $f'(t) = F[f(t)]$ has a solution; in the next chapter, we will see that showing existence and/or uniqueness for PDEs rather than ODEs does not benefit from this structure. One such theorem guarantees existence of a solution when F is not sharply sloped:

Theorem 15.1 (ODE existence and uniqueness). Suppose F is continuous and Lipschitz, that is, $\|F[\vec{y}] - F[\vec{x}]\|_2 \leq L\|\vec{y} - \vec{x}\|_2$ for some fixed $L \geq 0$. Then, the ODE $f'(t) = F[f(t)]$ admits exactly one solution for all $t \geq 0$ regardless of initial conditions.

In our subsequent development, we will assume that the ODE we are attempting to solve satisfies the conditions of such a theorem. This assumption is realistic since the conditions guaranteeing existence and uniqueness are relatively weak.

15.2.3 Model Equations

One way to understand computational methods for integrating ODEs is to examine their behavior on well-understood *model equations*. Many ODEs locally can be approximated by these model equations, motivating our detailed examination of these simplistic test cases.

We start by introducing a model equation for ODEs with a single dependent variable. Given our simplifications in §15.2.1, we consider equations of the form $y' = F[y]$, where $y(t) : [0, \infty) \to \mathbb{R}$. Taking a linear approximation of F, we might define $y' = ay + b$ to be

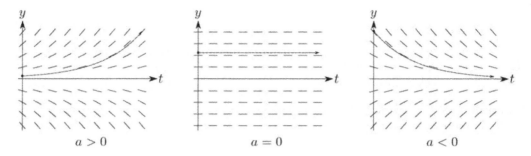

Figure 15.4 Three cases of the linear model equation $y' = ay$.

the model ODE, but we actually can fix $b = 0$. To justify using just one degree of freedom, define $\bar{y} \equiv y + b/a$. Then,

$$\bar{y}' = \left(y + \frac{b}{a}\right)' \text{ by definition of } \bar{y}$$

$$= y' \text{ since the second term is constant with respect to } t$$

$$= ay + b \text{ from the linearization}$$

$$= a(\bar{y} - b/a) + b \text{ by inverting the definition of } \bar{y}$$

$$= a\bar{y}.$$

This substitution satisfies $\bar{y}' = a\bar{y}$, showing that the constant b does not affect the qualitative behavior of the ODE. Hence, in the phenomenological study of model equations we safely take $b = 0$.

By the argument above, we locally can understand behavior of $y' = F[y]$ by studying the linear equation $y' = ay$. While the original ODE may not be solvable in closed form, applying standard arguments from calculus shows that the model equation is solved by the formula

$$y(t) = Ce^{at}.$$

Qualitatively, this formula splits into three cases, illustrated in Figure 15.4:

1. $a > 0$: Solutions get larger and larger; if $y(t)$ and $\hat{y}(t)$ both satisfy the ODE with slightly different starting conditions, as $t \to \infty$ they diverge.

2. $a = 0$: This system is solved by constant functions; solutions with different starting points stay the same distance apart.

3. $a < 0$: All solutions approach 0 as $t \to \infty$.

We say cases 2 and 3 are *stable*, in the sense that perturbing $y(0)$ yields solutions that do not diverge from each other over time; case 1 is *unstable*, since a small mistake in specifying the initial condition $y(0)$ will be amplified as time t advances.

Unstable ODEs generate ill-posed computational problems. Without careful consideration, we cannot expect numerical methods to generate usable solutions in this case, since theoretical solutions are already sensitive to perturbations of the input. On the other hand, stable problems are well-posed since small mistakes in $y(0)$ get diminished over time. Both cases are shown in Figure 15.5.

Extending to multiple dimensions, we study the linearized equation $\vec{y}' = A\vec{y}$; for simplicity, we will assume A is symmetric. As explained in §6.1.2, if $\vec{y}_1, \cdots, \vec{y}_k$ are eigenvectors of A

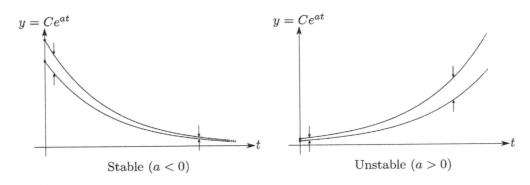

$y = Ce^{at}$ $y = Ce^{at}$

Stable $(a < 0)$ Unstable $(a > 0)$

Figure 15.5 A stable ODE diminishes the difference between solutions over time t if $y(0)$ is perturbed, while an unstable ODE amplifies this difference.

with eigenvalues $\lambda_1, \ldots, \lambda_k$ and $\vec{y}(0) = c_1\vec{y}_1 + \cdots + c_k\vec{y}_k$, then $\vec{y}(t) = c_1 e^{\lambda_1 t}\vec{y}_1 + \cdots + c_k e^{\lambda_k t}\vec{y}_k$. Based on this formula, the eigenvalues of A take the place of a in the one-dimensional model equation. From this result, it is not hard to intuit that a multivariable solution to $\vec{y}' = A\vec{y}$ is stable exactly when the eigenvalues of A are bounded above by zero.

As in the single-variable case, in reality we need to solve $\vec{y}' = F[\vec{y}]$ for general functions F. Assuming F is differentiable, we can approximate $F[\vec{y}] \approx F[\vec{y}_0] + J_F(\vec{y}_0)(\vec{y} - \vec{y}_0)$, yielding the model equation above after a shift. This argument shows that for short periods of time we expect behavior similar to the model equation with $A = J_F(\vec{y}_0)$, the Jacobian at $\vec{y}_0$.

15.3 TIME-STEPPING SCHEMES

We now describe several methods for solving the nonlinear ODE $\vec{y}' = F[\vec{y}]$ given potentially nonlinear functions F. Given a "time step" h, our methods will generate estimates of $\vec{y}(t+h)$ given $\vec{y}(t)$ and F. Applying these methods iteratively generates estimates $\vec{y}_0 \equiv \vec{y}(t)$, $\vec{y}_1 \approx \vec{y}(t + h)$, $\vec{y}_2 \approx \vec{y}(t + 2h)$, $\vec{y}_3 \approx \vec{y}(t + 3h)$, and so on. We call algorithms for generating approximations of $\vec{y}(t)$ *time-stepping schemes* or *integrators*, reflecting the fact that they are integrating out the derivatives in the input equation.

Of key importance to our consideration is the idea of *stability*. Even if an ODE theoretically is stable using the definition from §15.2.3, the integrator may produce approximations that diverge at an exponential rate. Stability usually depends on the time step h; when h is too large, differential estimates of the quality of an integrator fail to hold, yielding unpredictable output. Stability, however, can compete with *accuracy*. Stable schemes may generate bad approximations of $\vec{y}(t)$, even if they are guaranteed not to have wild behavior. ODE integrators that are both stable and accurate tend to require excessive computation time, indicating that we must compromise between these two properties.

15.3.1 Forward Euler

Our first ODE integrator comes from our construction of the forward differencing scheme in §14.3.2:

$$F[\vec{y}_k] = \vec{y}'(t) = \frac{\vec{y}_{k+1} - \vec{y}_k}{h} + O(h).$$

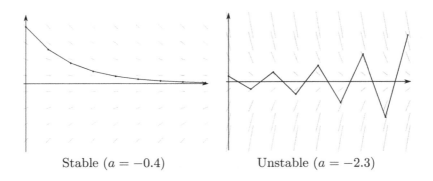

Stable $(a = -0.4)$ Unstable $(a = -2.3)$

Figure 15.6 Unstable and stable cases of forward Euler integration for the model equation $y' = ay$ with $h = 1$.

Solving this relationship for $\vec{y}_{k+1}$ shows

$$\vec{y}_{k+1} = \vec{y}_k + hF[\vec{y}_k] + O(h^2) \approx \vec{y}_k + hF[\vec{y}_k].$$

This *forward Euler* scheme applies the approximation on the right to estimate $\vec{y}_{k+1}$ from $\vec{y}_k$. It is one of the most computationally efficient strategies for time-stepping. Forward Euler is an *explicit* integrator, since there is an explicit formula for $\vec{y}_{k+1}$ in terms of $\vec{y}_k$ and F.

The forward Euler approximation of $\vec{y}_{k+1}$ holds to $O(h^2)$, so each step induces quadratic error. We call this the *localized truncation error* because it is the error induced by a single time step. The word "truncation" refers to the fact that we truncated a Taylor series to obtain the integrator. The iterate $\vec{y}_k$, however, already may be inaccurate thanks to accumulated truncation errors from previous iterations. If we integrate from t_0 to t with $k = O(1/h)$ steps, then the total error looks like $O(h)$. This estimate quantifies *global truncation error*, and thus we usually say that the forward Euler scheme is "first-order accurate."

The stability of forward Euler can be motivated by studying the model equation. We will work out the stability of methods in the one-variable case $y' = ay$, with the intuition that similar statements carry over to multidimensional equations by replacing a with a spectral radius. Substituting the one-variable model equation into the forward Euler scheme gives

$$y_{k+1} = y_k + ahy_k = (1 + ah)y_k.$$

Expanding recursively shows $y_k = (1+ah)^k y_0$. By this explicit formula for y_k in terms of y_0, the integrator is stable when $|1+ah| \leq 1$, since otherwise $|y_k| \to \infty$ exponentially. Assuming $a < 0$ (otherwise the theoretical problem is ill-posed), this condition takes a simpler form:

$$|1 + ah| \leq 1 \iff -1 \leq 1 + ah \leq 1 \text{ by expanding the absolute value}$$

$$\iff 0 \leq h \leq \frac{2}{|a|}, \text{ since } a < 0.$$

This derivation shows that forward Euler admits a *time step restriction*. That is, the output of forward Euler integration can explode even if $y' = ay$ is stable, when h is too large.

Figure 15.6 illustrates what happens when the stability condition is obeyed or violated. When time steps are too large—or equivalently when $|a|$ is too large—the forward Euler method is not only inaccurate but also has very different qualitative behavior. For nonlinear ODEs this formula gives a guide for stability at least locally in time; globally h may have to be adjusted if the Jacobian of F becomes worse conditioned.

Certain well-posed ODEs require tiny time steps h for forward Euler to be stable. In this case, even though the forward Euler formula is computationally inexpensive for a single step, integrating to some fixed time t may be infeasible because so many steps are needed. Such ODEs are called *stiff*, inspired by stiff springs requiring tiny time steps to capture their rapid oscillations. One text defines stiff problems slightly differently (via [60]): "Stiff equations are problems for which explicit methods don't work" [57]. With this definition in mind, in the next section we consider an *implicit* method with no stability time step restriction, making it more suitable for stiff problems.

15.3.2 Backward Euler

We could have applied backward differencing at $\vec{y}_{k+1}$ to design an ODE integrator:

$$F[\vec{y}_{k+1}] = \vec{y}'(t+h) = \frac{\vec{y}_{k+1} - \vec{y}_k}{h} + O(h).$$

Isolating $\vec{y}_k$ shows that this integrator requires solving the following potentially nonlinear system of equations for $\vec{y}_{k+1}$:

$$\boxed{\vec{y}_{k+1} = \vec{y}_k + hF[\vec{y}_{k+1}].}$$

This equation differs from forward Euler integration by the evaluation of F at $\vec{y}_{k+1}$ rather than at $\vec{y}_k$. Because we have to solve this equation for $\vec{y}_{k+1}$, this technique, known as *backward Euler* integration, is an *implicit* integrator.

Example 15.9 (Backward Euler). Suppose we wish to generate time steps for the ODE $\vec{y}' = A\vec{y}$, with fixed $A \in \mathbb{R}^{n \times n}$. To find $\vec{y}_{k+1}$ we solve the following system:

$$\vec{y}_k = \vec{y}_{k+1} - hA\vec{y}_{k+1} \implies \vec{y}_{k+1} = (I_{n \times n} - hA)^{-1}\vec{y}_k.$$

Backward Euler is first-order accurate like forward Euler by an identical argument. Its stability, however, contrasts considerably with that of forward Euler. Once again considering the model equation $y' = ay$, we write:

$$y_k = y_{k+1} - hay_{k+1} \implies y_{k+1} = \frac{y_k}{1 - ha}.$$

To prevent exponential blowup, we enforce the following condition:

$$\frac{1}{|1 - ha|} \leq 1 \iff h \leq \frac{2}{a} \text{ or } h \geq 0, \text{ for } a < 0.$$

We always choose $h \geq 0$, so backward Euler is *unconditionally* stable, as in Figure 15.7.

Even if backward Euler is stable, however, it may not be accurate. If h is too large, $\vec{y}_k$ will approach zero at the wrong rate. When simulating cloth and other physical materials that require lots of high-frequency detail to be realistic, backward Euler may exhibit undesirable dampening. Furthermore, we have to invert $F[\cdot]$ to solve for $\vec{y}_{k+1}$.

Figure 15.7 Backward Euler integration is unconditionally stable, so no matter how large a time step h with the same initial condition, the resulting approximate solution of $y' = ay$ does not diverge. While the output is stable, when h is large the result does not approximate the continuous solution $y = Ce^{at}$ effectively.

15.3.3 Trapezoidal Method

Suppose that in addition to having $\vec{y}_k$ at time t and $\vec{y}_{k+1}$ at time $t + h$, we also know $\vec{y}_{k+1/2}$ at the halfway point in time $t + {}^h\!/_2$. Then, by our derivation of centered differencing

$$\vec{y}_{k+1} = \vec{y}_k + hF[\vec{y}_{k+1/2}] + O(h^3).$$

In our derivation of error bounds for the trapezoidal rule in §14.2.3, we derived the following relationship via Taylor's theorem:

$$\frac{F[\vec{y}_{k+1}] + F[\vec{y}_k]}{2} = F[\vec{y}_{k+1/2}] + O(h^2).$$

Substituting this equality into the expression for $\vec{y}_{k+1}$ yields a second-order ODE integrator, the *trapezoid method*:

$$\boxed{\vec{y}_{k+1} = \vec{y}_k + h\frac{F[\vec{y}_{k+1}] + F[\vec{y}_k]}{2}}$$

Like backward Euler, this method is implicit since we must solve this equation for $\vec{y}_{k+1}$.

Example 15.10 (Trapezoidal integrator). Returning to the ODE $\vec{y}' = A\vec{y}$ from Example 15.9, trapezoidal integration solves the system

$$\vec{y}_{k+1} = \vec{y}_k + h\frac{A\vec{y}_{k+1} + A\vec{y}_k}{2} \implies \vec{y}_{k+1} = \left(I_{n\times n} - \frac{hA}{2}\right)^{-1}\left(I_{n\times n} + \frac{hA}{2}\right)\vec{y}_k.$$

To carry out stability analysis on $y' = ay$, the example above shows time steps of the trapezoidal method satisfy

$$y_k = \left(\frac{1 + \frac{1}{2}ha}{1 - \frac{1}{2}ha}\right)^k y_0.$$

Consequently, the method is stable when

$$\left|\frac{1 + \frac{1}{2}ha}{1 - \frac{1}{2}ha}\right| < 1.$$

This inequality holds whenever $a < 0$ and $h > 0$, showing that the trapezoid method is unconditionally stable.

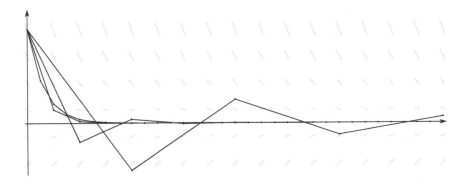

Figure 15.8 The trapezoidal method is unconditionally stable, so regardless of the step size h the solution curves always approach $y = 0$; when h is large, however, the output oscillates about zero as it decays.

Despite its higher order of accuracy with maintained stability, the trapezoid method has some drawbacks that make it less popular than backward Euler for large time steps. In particular, consider the ratio

$$R \equiv \frac{y_{k+1}}{y_k} = \frac{1 + \frac{1}{2}ha}{1 - \frac{1}{2}ha}.$$

When $a < 0$, for large enough h this ratio eventually becomes negative; as $h \to \infty$, we have $R \to -1$. As illustrated in Figure 15.8, this observation shows that if time steps h are too large, the trapezoidal method of integration tends to introduce undesirable oscillatory behavior not present in theoretical solutions Ce^{at} of $y' = ay$.

15.3.4 Runge-Kutta Methods

A class of integrators can be derived by making the following observation:

$$\vec{y}_{k+1} = \vec{y}_k + \int_{t_k}^{t_k+h} \vec{y}'(t)\,dt \text{ by the Fundamental Theorem of Calculus}$$

$$= \vec{y}_k + \int_{t_k}^{t_k+h} F[\vec{y}(t)]\,dt \text{ since } \vec{y} \text{ satisfies } \vec{y}'(t) = F[\vec{y}(t)].$$

Using this formula outright does not help design a method for time-stepping, since we do not know $\vec{y}(t)$ *a priori*. Approximating the integral using quadrature rules from the previous chapter, however, produces a class of well-known strategies for ODE integration.

Suppose we apply the trapezoidal quadrature rule to the integral for $\vec{y}_{k+1}$. Then,

$$\vec{y}_{k+1} = \vec{y}_k + \frac{h}{2}(F[\vec{y}_k] + F[\vec{y}_{k+1}]) + O(h^3).$$

This is the formula we wrote for the trapezoidal method in §15.3.3. If we wish to find an explicit rather than implicit method with the accuracy of the trapezoidal time-stepping, however, we must replace $F[\vec{y}_{k+1}]$ with a high-accuracy approximation that is easier to evaluate:

$$F[\vec{y}_{k+1}] = F[\vec{y}_k + hF[\vec{y}_k] + O(h^2)] \text{ by the forward Euler order of accuracy}$$

$$= F[\vec{y}_k + hF[\vec{y}_k]] + O(h^2) \text{ by Taylor's theorem.}$$

Since it gets scaled by h, making this substitution for $\vec{y}_{k+1}$ does not affect the order of approximation of the trapezoidal time step. This change results in a new approximation:

$$\vec{y}_{k+1} = \vec{y}_k + \frac{h}{2}(F[\vec{y}_k] + F[\vec{y}_k + hF[\vec{y}_k]]) + O(h^3).$$

Ignoring the $O(h^3)$ terms yields a new integrator known as *Heun's method*, which is second-order accurate and explicit.

To evaluate the stability of Heun's method for $y' = ay$ with $a < 0$, we expand

$$y_{k+1} = y_k + \frac{h}{2}(ay_k + a(y_k + hay_k)) = \left(\frac{1}{2}h^2 a^2 + ha + 1\right) y_k.$$

From this substitution, the method is stable when

$$-1 \leq 1 + ha + \frac{1}{2}h^2 a^2 \leq 1 \iff -4 \leq 2ha + h^2 a^2 \leq 0.$$

The inequality on the right is equivalent to writing $h \leq \frac{2}{|a|}$, and the inequality on the left is always true for $h > 0$ and $a < 0$. Hence, the stability condition for Heun's method can be written $h \leq \frac{2}{|a|}$, the same as the stability condition for forward Euler.

Heun's method is an example of a *Runge-Kutta* integrator derived by starting from a quadrature rule and substituting Euler steps to approximate $F[\vec{y}_{k+\ell}]$, for $\ell > 0$. Forward Euler is a first-order accurate Runge-Kutta method, and Heun's method is second-order. A popular fourth-order Runge-Kutta method (abbreviated "RK4") is given by:

$$\vec{y}_{k+1} = \vec{y}_k + \frac{h}{6}(\vec{k}_1 + 2\vec{k}_2 + 2\vec{k}_3 + \vec{k}_4)$$
$$\text{where } \vec{k}_1 = F[\vec{y}_k]$$
$$\vec{k}_2 = F\left[\vec{y}_k + \frac{1}{2}h\vec{k}_1\right]$$
$$\vec{k}_3 = F\left[\vec{y}_k + \frac{1}{2}h\vec{k}_2\right]$$
$$\vec{k}_4 = F\left[\vec{y}_k + h\vec{k}_3\right]$$

This formula is constructed from Simpson's quadrature rule.

Runge-Kutta methods are popular because they are explicit but provide high degrees of accuracy. The cost of this accuracy, however, is that $F[\cdot]$ must be evaluated more times to carry out a single time step. Implicit Runge-Kutta integrators also have been constructed, for poorly conditioned ODEs.

15.3.5 Exponential Integrators

We have focused our stability and accuracy analyses on the model equation $y' = ay$. If this ODE is truly an influential test case, however, we have neglected a key piece of information: We know the solution of $y' = ay$ in closed form as $y = Ce^{at}$! We might as well incorporate this formula into an integration scheme to achieve 100% accuracy on the model equation. That is, we can design a class of integrators that achieves strong accuracy when $F[\cdot]$ is nearly linear, potentially at the cost of computational efficiency.

Assuming A is symmetric, using the eigenvector method from §15.2.3 we can write the solution of the ODE $\vec{y}' = A\vec{y}$ as $\vec{y}(t) = e^{At}\vec{y}(0)$, where e^{At} is a matrix encoding the transformation from $\vec{y}(0)$ to $\vec{y}(t)$ (see Exercise 6.10). Starting from this formula, integrating in time by writing $\vec{y}_{k+1} = e^{Ah}\vec{y}_k$ achieves perfect accuracy on the linear model equation; our strategy is to use this formula to construct integrators for the nonlinear case.

When F is smooth, we can attempt to factor the ODE $\vec{y}' = F[\vec{y}]$ as

$$\vec{y}' = A\vec{y} + G[\vec{y}],$$

where G is a nonlinear but small function and $A \in \mathbb{R}^{n \times n}$. Taking A to be the Jacobian of F makes this factorization agree with its first-order Taylor expansion. *Exponential integrators* integrate the $A\vec{y}$ part using the exponential formula and approximate the effect of the nonlinear G part separately.

We start by deriving a "variation of parameters" formula from the classical theory of ODEs. Rewriting the original ODE as $\vec{y}' - A\vec{y} = G[\vec{y}]$, suppose we multiply both sides by e^{-At} to obtain $e^{-At}(\vec{y}' - A\vec{y}) = e^{-At}G[\vec{y}]$. The left-hand side satisfies

$$e^{-At}(\vec{y}' - A\vec{y}) = \frac{d}{dt}\left(e^{-At}\vec{y}(t)\right),$$

after applying the identity $Ae^{At} = e^{At}A$ (see Exercise 15.2), implying $d/dt(e^{-At}\vec{y}(t)) = e^{-At}G[\vec{y}]$. Integrating this expression from 0 to t shows

$$e^{-At}\vec{y}(t) - \vec{y}(0) = \int_0^t e^{-A\tau}G[\vec{y}(\tau)]\, d\tau,$$

or equivalently,

$$\vec{y}(t) = e^{At}\vec{y}(0) + e^{At}\int_0^t e^{-A\tau}G[\vec{y}(\tau)]\, d\tau$$

$$= e^{At}\vec{y}(0) + \int_0^t e^{A(t-\tau)}G[\vec{y}(\tau)]\, d\tau.$$

Slightly generalizing this formula shows

$$\vec{y}_{k+1} = e^{Ah}\vec{y}_k + \int_{t_k}^{t_k+h} e^{A(t_k+h-t)}G[\vec{y}(t)]\, dt.$$

Similar to the Runge-Kutta methods, exponential integrators apply quadrature to the integral on the right-hand side to approximate the time step to $\vec{y}_{k+1}$.

For example, the *first-order exponential integrator* applies forward Euler to the nonlinear G term by making a constant approximation $G[\vec{y}(t)] \approx G[\vec{y}_k]$, yielding

$$\vec{y}_{k+1} \approx e^{Ah}\vec{y}_k + \left[\int_0^h e^{A(h-t)}\, dt\right]G[\vec{y}_k].$$

As shown in Exercise 15.5, the integral can be taken in closed form, leading to the expression

$$\boxed{\vec{y}_{k+1} = e^{Ah}\vec{y}_k + A^{-1}(e^{Ah} - I_{n \times n})G[\vec{y}_k].}$$

Analyzing exponential integrators like this one requires techniques beyond using the linear model equation, since they are designed to integrate linear ODEs exactly. Intuitively, exponential integrators behave best when $G \approx 0$, but the cost of this high numerical performance is the use of a matrix exponential, which is difficult to compute or apply efficiently.

15.4 MULTIVALUE METHODS

The transformations in §15.2.1 reduced all explicit ODEs to the form $\vec{y}' = F[\vec{y}]$, which can be integrated using the methods introduced in the previous section. While all explicit ODEs *can* be written this way, however, it is not clear that they always *should* be when designing a high-accuracy integrator.

When we reduced k-th order ODEs to first order, we introduced new variables representing the first through $(k-1)$-st derivatives of the desired output function $\vec{y}(t)$. The integrators in the previous section then approximate $\vec{y}(t)$ and these $k-1$ derivatives with equal accuracy, since in some sense they are treated "democratically" in first-order form. A natural question is whether we can relax the accuracy of the approximated derivatives of $\vec{y}(t)$ without affecting the quality of the $\vec{y}(t)$ estimate itself.

To support this perspective, consider the Taylor series

$$\vec{y}(t_k + h) = \vec{y}(t_k) + h\vec{y}'(t_k) + \frac{h^2}{2}\vec{y}''(t_k) + O(h^3).$$

If we perturb $\vec{y}'(t_k)$ by some value on the order $O(h^2)$, the quality of this Taylor series approximation does not change, since

$$h \cdot [\vec{y}'(t_k) + O(h^2)] = h\vec{y}'(t_k) + O(h^3).$$

Perturbing $\vec{y}''(t_k)$ by a value on the order $O(h)$ has a similar effect, since

$$\frac{h^2}{2} \cdot [\vec{y}''(t_k) + O(h)] = \frac{h^2}{2}\vec{y}''(t_k) + O(h^3).$$

Based on this argument, *multivalue methods* integrate $\vec{y}^{(k)}(t) = F[t, \vec{y}'(t), \vec{y}''(t), \ldots, \vec{y}^{(k-1)}(t)]$ using less accurate estimates of the higher-order derivatives of $\vec{y}(t)$.

We will restrict our discussion to the second-order case $\vec{y}''(t) = F[t, \vec{y}, \vec{y}']$, the most common case for ODE integration thanks to Newton's second law $F = ma$. Extending the methods we consider to higher order, however, follows similar if notationally more complex arguments. For the remainder of this section, we will define a "velocity" vector $\vec{v}(t) \equiv \vec{y}'(t)$ and an "acceleration" vector $\vec{a} \equiv \vec{y}''(t)$. By the reduction to first order, we wish to solve the following order system:

$$\vec{y}'(t) = \vec{v}(t)$$
$$\vec{v}'(t) = \vec{a}(t)$$
$$\vec{a}(t) = F[t, \vec{y}(t), \vec{v}(t)].$$

Our goal is to derive integrators tailored to this system, evaluated based on the accuracy of estimating $\vec{y}(t)$ rather than $\vec{v}(t)$ or $\vec{a}(t)$.

15.4.1 Newmark Integrators

We begin by deriving the class of *Newmark* integrators following the development in [46]. Denote $\vec{y}_k$, $\vec{v}_k$, and $\vec{a}_k$ as position, velocity, and acceleration vectors at time t_k; our goal is to advance to time $t_{k+1} \equiv t_k + h$.

By the Fundamental Theorem of Calculus,

$$\vec{v}_{k+1} = \vec{v}_k + \int_{t_k}^{t_{k+1}} \vec{a}(t) \, dt.$$

We also can write $\vec{y}_{k+1}$ as an integral involving $\vec{a}(t)$ by deriving an error estimate developed in some proofs of Taylor's theorem:

$$\vec{y}_{k+1} = \vec{y}_k + \int_{t_k}^{t_{k+1}} \vec{v}(t)\, dt \text{ by the Fundamental Theorem of Calculus}$$

$$= \vec{y}_k + [t\vec{v}(t)]_{t_k}^{t_{k+1}} - \int_{t_k}^{t_{k+1}} t\vec{a}(t)\, dt \text{ after integration by parts}$$

$$= \vec{y}_k + t_{k+1}\vec{v}_{k+1} - t_k\vec{v}_k - \int_{t_k}^{t_{k+1}} t\vec{a}(t)\, dt \text{ by expanding the difference term}$$

$$= \vec{y}_k + h\vec{v}_k + t_{k+1}\vec{v}_{k+1} - t_{k+1}\vec{v}_k - \int_{t_k}^{t_{k+1}} t\vec{a}(t)\, dt \text{ by adding and subtracting } h\vec{v}_k$$

$$= \vec{y}_k + h\vec{v}_k + t_{k+1}(\vec{v}_{k+1} - \vec{v}_k) - \int_{t_k}^{t_{k+1}} t\vec{a}(t)\, dt \text{ after factoring out } t_{k+1}$$

$$= \vec{y}_k + h\vec{v}_k + t_{k+1}\int_{t_k}^{t_{k+1}} \vec{a}(t)\, dt - \int_{t_k}^{t_{k+1}} t\vec{a}(t)\, dt \text{ since } \vec{v}'(t) = \vec{a}(t)$$

$$= \vec{y}_k + h\vec{v}_k + \int_{t_k}^{t_{k+1}} (t_{k+1} - t)\vec{a}(t)\, dt.$$

Fix a constant $\tau \in [t_k, t_{k+1}]$. Then, we can write expressions for $\vec{a}_k$ and $\vec{a}_{k+1}$ using the Taylor series about τ:

$$\vec{a}_k = \vec{a}(\tau) + \vec{a}'(\tau)(t_k - \tau) + O(h^2)$$

$$\vec{a}_{k+1} = \vec{a}(\tau) + \vec{a}'(\tau)(t_{k+1} - \tau) + O(h^2).$$

For any constant $\gamma \in \mathbb{R}$, scaling the expression for $\vec{a}_k$ by $1 - \gamma$, scaling the expression for $\vec{a}_{k+1}$ by γ, and summing shows

$$\vec{a}(\tau) = (1 - \gamma)\vec{a}_k + \gamma\vec{a}_{k+1} + \vec{a}'(\tau)((\gamma - 1)(t_k - \tau) - \gamma(t_{k+1} - \tau)) + O(h^2)$$

$$= (1 - \gamma)\vec{a}_k + \gamma\vec{a}_{k+1} + \vec{a}'(\tau)(\tau - h\gamma - t_k) + O(h^2) \text{ after substituting } t_{k+1} = t_k + h.$$

Integrating $\vec{a}(t)$ from t_k to t_{k+1} yields the change in velocity. Substituting the approximation above shows:

$$\vec{v}_{k+1} - \vec{v}_k = \int_{t_k}^{t_{k+1}} \vec{a}(\tau)\, d\tau = (1 - \gamma)h\vec{a}_k + \gamma h\vec{a}_{k+1} + \int_{t_k}^{t_{k+1}} \vec{a}'(\tau)(\tau - h\gamma - t_k)\, d\tau + O(h^3)$$

$$= (1 - \gamma)h\vec{a}_k + \gamma h\vec{a}_{k+1} + O(h^2),$$

where the second step holds because $(\tau - t_k) - h\gamma = O(h)$ for $\tau \in [t_k, t_{k+1}]$ and the interval of integration is of width h. Rearranging shows

$$\vec{v}_{k+1} = \vec{v}_k + (1 - \gamma)h\vec{a}_k + \gamma h\vec{a}_{k+1} + O(h^2).$$

Starting again from the approximation we wrote for $\vec{a}(\tau)$—this time using a new constant β rather than γ—we can also develop an approximation for $\vec{y}_{k+1}$. To do so, we will work with the integrand in the Taylor estimate for $\vec{y}_{k+1}$:

$$\int_{t_k}^{t_{k+1}} (t_{k+1} - t)\vec{a}(t)\, dt = \int_{t_k}^{t_{k+1}} (t_{k+1} - \tau)((1 - \beta)\vec{a}_k + \beta\vec{a}_{k+1} + \vec{a}'(\tau)(\tau - h\beta - t_k))\, d\tau$$

$$+ O(h^3)$$

$$= \frac{1}{2}(1 - \beta)h^2\vec{a}_k + \frac{1}{2}\beta h^2\vec{a}_{k+1} + O(h^2) \text{ by a similar simplification.}$$

We can use this observation to write the Taylor series error estimate for $\vec{y}_{k+1}$ in a different form:

$$\vec{y}_{k+1} = \vec{y}_k + h\vec{v}_k + \int_{t_k}^{t_{k+1}} (t_{k+1} - t)\vec{a}(t)\,dt \text{ from before}$$

$$= \vec{y}_k + h\vec{v}_k + \left(\frac{1}{2} - \beta\right) h^2 \vec{a}_k + \beta h^2 \vec{a}_{k+1} + O(h^2).$$

Summarizing this technical argument, we have derived the class of Newmark schemes, each characterized by the two fixed parameters γ and β:

$$\boxed{\begin{aligned} \vec{y}_{k+1} &= \vec{y}_k + h\vec{v}_k + \left(\frac{1}{2} - \beta\right) h^2 \vec{a}_k + \beta h^2 \vec{a}_{k+1} \\ \vec{v}_{k+1} &= \vec{v}_k + (1 - \gamma)h\vec{a}_k + \gamma h\vec{a}_{k+1} \\ \vec{a}_k &= F[t_k, \vec{y}_k, \vec{v}_k] \end{aligned}}$$

This integrator is accurate up to $O(h^2)$ in each time step, making it globally first-order accurate. Depending on γ and β, the integrator can be implicit, since $\vec{a}_{k+1}$ appears in the expressions for $\vec{y}_{k+1}$ and $\vec{v}_{k+1}$.

Specific choices of β and γ yield integrators with additional properties:

- $\beta = \gamma = 0$ gives the *constant acceleration* integrator:

$$\vec{y}_{k+1} = \vec{y}_k + h\vec{v}_k + \frac{1}{2}h^2 \vec{a}_k$$
$$\vec{v}_{k+1} = \vec{v}_k + h\vec{a}_k.$$

This integrator is explicit and holds exactly when the acceleration is a constant function of time.

- $\beta = 1/2, \gamma = 1$ gives the *constant implicit acceleration* integrator:

$$\vec{y}_{k+1} = \vec{y}_k + h\vec{v}_k + \frac{1}{2}h^2 \vec{a}_{k+1}$$
$$\vec{v}_{k+1} = \vec{v}_k + h\vec{a}_{k+1}.$$

The velocity is stepped implicitly using backward Euler, giving first-order accuracy. The $\vec{y}$ update, however, can be written

$$\vec{y}_{k+1} = \vec{y}_k + \frac{1}{2}h(\vec{v}_k + \vec{v}_{k+1}),$$

which coincides with the trapezoidal rule. Hence, this is our first example of a scheme where the velocity and position updates have different orders of accuracy. This technique, however, is still only globally first-order accurate in $\vec{y}$.

- $\beta = 1/4, \gamma = 1/2$ gives the following second-order trapezoidal scheme after some algebra:

$$\vec{y}_{k+1} = \vec{y}_k + \frac{1}{2}h(\vec{v}_k + \vec{v}_{k+1})$$
$$\vec{v}_{k+1} = \vec{v}_k + \frac{1}{2}h(\vec{a}_k + \vec{a}_{k+1}).$$

- $\beta = 0, \gamma = 1/2$ gives a second-order accurate *central differencing* scheme. In the canonical form, it is written

$$\vec{y}_{k+1} = \vec{y}_k + h\vec{v}_k + \frac{1}{2}h^2\vec{a}_k$$

$$\vec{v}_{k+1} = \vec{v}_k + \frac{1}{2}h(\vec{a}_k + \vec{a}_{k+1}).$$

The method earns its name because simplifying the equations above leads to the alternative form:

$$\vec{v}_{k+1} = \frac{\vec{y}_{k+2} - \vec{y}_k}{2h}$$

$$\vec{a}_{k+1} = \frac{\vec{y}_{k+2} - 2\vec{y}_{k+1} + \vec{y}_k}{h^2}.$$

Newmark integrators are unconditionally stable when $4\beta > 2\gamma > 1$, with second-order accuracy exactly when $\gamma = 1/2$.

15.4.2   Staggered Grid and Leapfrog

A different way to achieve second-order accuracy in stepping $\vec{y}$ is to use centered differences about $t_{k+1/2} \equiv t_k + h/2$:

$$\vec{y}_{k+1} = \vec{y}_k + h\vec{v}_{k+1/2}.$$

Rather than attempting to approximate $\vec{v}_{k+1/2}$ from $\vec{v}_k$ and/or $\vec{v}_{k+1}$, we can process velocities $\vec{v}$ directly at *half* points on the grid of time steps.

A similar update steps forward the velocities with the same accuracy:

$$\vec{v}_{k+3/2} = \vec{v}_{k+1/2} + h\vec{a}_{k+1}.$$

A lower-order approximation suffices for the acceleration term since it is a higher-order derivative:

$$\vec{a}_{k+1} = F\left[t_{k+1}, \vec{x}_{k+1}, \frac{1}{2}(\vec{v}_{k+1/2} + \vec{v}_{k+3/2})\right].$$

This expression can be substituted into the equation for $\vec{v}_{k+3/2}$.

When $F[\cdot]$ has no dependence on $\vec{v}$, e.g., when simulating particles without wind resistance, the method is fully explicit:

$$\boxed{\begin{aligned} \vec{y}_{k+1} &= \vec{y}_k + h\vec{v}_{k+1/2} \\ \vec{a}_{k+1} &= F[t_{k+1}, \vec{y}_{k+1}] \\ \vec{v}_{k+3/2} &= \vec{v}_{k+1/2} + h\vec{a}_{k+1} \end{aligned}}$$

This is known as the *leapfrog* integrator, thanks to the staggered grid of times and the fact that each midpoint is used to update the next velocity or position.

A distinguishing property of the leapfrog scheme is its *time reversibility*.[*] Assume we have used the leapfrog integrator to generate $(\vec{y}_{k+1}, \vec{v}_{k+3/2}, \vec{a}_{k+1})$. Starting at t_{k+1}, we might reverse the direction of time to step backward. The leapfrog equations give

$$\vec{v}_{k+1/2} = \vec{v}_{k+3/2} + (-h)\vec{a}_{k+1}$$

$$\vec{y}_k = \vec{y}_{k+1} - h\vec{v}_{k+1/2}.$$

These formulas invert the forward time step exactly. That is, if we run the leapfrog in reverse, we trace the solution back to where it started *exactly*, up to rounding error.

---

[*]Discussion of time reversibility contributed by Julian Kates-Harbeck.

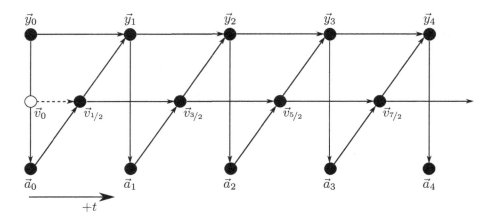

Figure 15.9 Leapfrog integration computes velocities at half time steps; here arrows denote dependencies between computed values. If the initial conditions specify $\vec{v}$ at $t = 0$, an initial half time step must be carried out to approximate $\vec{v}_{1/2}$.

A consequence of reversibility is that errors in position, energy, and angular momentum tend to cancel out over time as opposed to accumulating. For instance, for problems where the acceleration only depends on position, angular momentum is conserved exactly by leapfrog integration, and energy remains stable over time, whereas other even higher-order schemes can induce significant "drift" of these quantities. Symmetry, second-order accuracy for "first-order work" (i.e., the same amount of computation as forward Euler integration), and conservation properties make leapfrog integration a popular method for physical simulation. These properties classify the leapfrog method as a *symplectic* integrator, constructed to conserve the continuous structure of ODEs coming from Hamiltonian dynamics and related physical systems.

If $F[\cdot]$ has dependence on $\vec{v}$, then this "staggered grid" method becomes implicit. Such dependence on velocity often is symmetric. For instance, wind resistance changes sign if you reverse the direction in which you are moving. This property makes the matrices symmetric in the implicit step for updating velocities, enabling the application of conjugate gradients and related iterative methods.

15.5   COMPARISON OF INTEGRATORS

This chapter has introduced a sampling from the remarkably large pantheon of ODE integrators. Choosing the right ODE integrator for a given problem is a challenging task representing a careful balancing act between accuracy, stability, computational efficiency, and assorted special properties like reversibility. The table in Figure 15.10 compares the basic properties of the methods we considered.

In practice, it may require some experimentation to determine the proper integrator given an ODE problem; thankfully, most of the integrators we have introduced are relatively easy to implement. In addition to the generic considerations we have discussed in this chapter, additional "domain-specific" concerns also influence the choice of ODE integrators, including the following:

- In computer graphics and other fields prioritizing visual effect over reproducibility in the real world, it may be more important that a time-stepping method *looks* right

Integrator	Section	Accuracy	Implicit or explicit?	Stability	Notes
Forward Euler	§15.3.1	First	Explicit	Conditional	
Backward Euler	§15.3.2	First	Implicit	Unconditional	
Trapezoidal	§15.3.3	Second	Implicit	Unconditional	Large steps oscillate
Heun	§15.3.4	Second	Explicit	Conditional	
RK4	§15.3.4	Fourth	Explicit	Conditional	
1st-order exponential	§15.3.5	First	Explicit	Conditional	Needs matrix exponential
Newmark	§15.4.1	First	Implicit	Conditional	For 2nd-order ODE; 2nd-order accurate when $\gamma = 1/2$; explicit when $\beta = \gamma = 0$
Staggered	§15.4.2	Second	Implicit	Conditional	For 2nd-order ODE
Leapfrog	§15.4.2	Second	Explicit	Conditional	For 2nd-order ODE; reversible; $F[\cdot]$ must not depend on $\vec{v}$

Figure 15.10 Comparison of ODE integrators.

than whether the numerical output is perfect. For instance, simulation tools for visual effects need to produce fluids, gases, and cloth that exhibit high-frequency swirls, vortices, and folds. These features may be dampened by a backward Euler integrator, even if it is more likely to be stable than other alternatives.

- Most of our analysis used Taylor series and other localized arguments, but *long-term behavior* of certain integrators can be favorable even if individual time steps are suboptimal. For instance, forward Euler integration tends to add energy to oscillatory ODEs, while backward Euler removes it. If we wish to simulate a pendulum swinging in perpetuity, neither of these techniques will suffice.

- Some ODEs operate in the presence of constraints. For instance, if we simulate a ball attached to a string, we may not wish for the string to stretch beyond its natural length. Methods like forward Euler and leapfrog integration can overshoot such constraints, so an additional projection step may be needed to enforce the constraints more exactly.

- A degree of adaptivity is needed for applications in which discrete events can happen during the course of solving an ODE. For instance, when simulating the dynamics of a piece of cloth, typically parts of the cloth can run into each other or into objects in their surroundings. These collision events can occur at fractional time steps and must be handled separately to avoid interpenetration of objects in a scene [5].

- For higher-quality animation and physical predictions, some ODE integrators can output not only the configuration at discrete time steps but also some indicator (e.g., an interpolatory formula) approximating continuous behavior between the time steps.

- If the function F in $\vec{y}' = F[\vec{y}]$ is smooth and differentiable, the derivatives of F can be used to improve the quality of time-stepping methods.

Many of these problems are difficult to handle efficiently in large-scale simulations and in cases where computational power is relatively limited.

15.6 EXERCISES

15.1 Some practice discretizing an ODE:

   (a) Suppose we wish to solve the ODE $dy/dt = -\sin y$ numerically. For time step $h > 0$, write the implicit backward Euler equation for approximating y_{k+1} at $t = (k+1)h$ given y_k at $t = kh$.

   (b) Write the Newton iteration for solving the equation from Exercise 15.1a for y_{k+1}.

15.2 We continue our discussion of the matrix exponential introduced in Exercise 6.10 and used in our discussion of exponential integrators. For this problem, assume $A \in \mathbb{R}^{n \times n}$ is a symmetric matrix.

   (a) Show that A commutes with e^{At} for any $t \geq 0$. That is, justify the formula $Ae^{At} = e^{At}A$.

   (b) Recall that we can write

$$e^{At} = I_{n \times n} + At + \frac{(At)^2}{2!} + \frac{(At)^3}{3!} + \cdots.$$

   For sufficiently small $h \geq 0$, prove a similar formula for matrix inverses:

$$(I_{n \times n} - hA)^{-1} = I_{n \times n} + hA + (hA)^2 + (hA)^3 + \cdots$$

   (c) Which of the two series from Exercise 15.2b should converge faster? Based on this observation, compare the computational cost of a single backward Euler iteration (see Example 15.9) versus that of an iteration of the exponential integrator from §15.3.5 using these formulas.

15.3 Suppose we are solving a second-order ODE using the leapfrog integrator. We are given initial conditions $\vec{y}(0)$ and $\vec{v}(0)$, the position and velocity vectors at time $t = 0$. But, the leapfrog scheme maintains velocities at the half time steps. Propose a way to initialize $\vec{v}_{1/2}$ at time $t = h/2$, and argue that your initialization does not affect the order of accuracy of the leapfrog integrator if it is run for sufficiently many time steps.

15.4 Suppose we wish to approximate solutions to $\vec{y}'' = F[\vec{y}]$. Add together Taylor expansions for $\vec{y}(t+h)$ and $\vec{y}(t-h)$ to derive the *Verlet algorithm* for predicting $\vec{y}_{k+1}$ from $\vec{y}_k$ and $\vec{y}_{k-1}$, which induces $O(h^4)$ integration error in a single time step.

15.5 Verify the following formula used in §15.3.5 for symmetric $A \in \mathbb{R}^{n \times n}$:

$$\int_0^h e^{A(h-t)} \, dt = A^{-1}(e^{Ah} - I_{n \times n}).$$

   Also, derive a global order of accuracy in the form $O(h^k)$ for some $k \in \mathbb{N}$ for the first-order exponential integrator.

15.6 In this problem, we will motivate an ODE used in computer graphics applications that does not come from Newton's laws. Throughout this problem, assume $f, g : [0, 1] \to \mathbb{R}$ are differentiable functions with $g(0) = g(1) = 0$. We will derive continuous and discrete versions of the *screened Poisson equation*, used for smoothing (see, e.g., [24]).

(a) So far our optimization problems have been to find points $\vec{x}^* \in \mathbb{R}^n$ minimizing some function $h(\vec{x})$, but sometimes our unknown is an entire function. Thankfully, the "variational" approach still is valid in this case. Explain in words what the following energies, which take a function f as input, measure about f:

(i) $E_1[f] \equiv \int_0^1 (f(t) - f_0(t))^2 \, dt$ for some fixed function $f_0 : [0,1] \to \mathbb{R}$.

(ii) $E_2[f] \equiv \int_0^1 (f'(t))^2 \, dt$.

(b) For an energy functional $E[\cdot]$ like the two above, explain how the following expression for $dE(f; g)$ (the Gâteaux derivative of E) can be thought of as the "directional derivative of E at f in the g direction":

$$dE(f; g) = \frac{d}{d\varepsilon} E[f + \varepsilon g]\Big|_{\varepsilon=0}.$$

(c) Again assuming $g(0) = g(1) = 0$, derive the following formulae:

(i) $dE_1(f, g) = \int_0^1 2(f(t) - f_0(t))g(t) \, dt$.

(ii) $dE_2(f, g) = \int_0^1 -2f''(t)g(t) \, dt$.
   Hint: Apply integration by parts to get rid of $g'(t)$; recall our assumption $g(0) = g(1) = 0$.

(d) Suppose we wish to approximate f_0 with a smoother function f. One reasonable model for doing so is to minimize $E[f] \equiv E_1[f] + \alpha E_2[f]$ for some $\alpha > 0$ controlling the trade-off between similarity to f_0 and smoothness. Using the result of 15.6c, argue informally that an f minimizing this energy should satisfy the differential equation $f(t) - f_0(t) = \alpha f''(t)$ for $t \in (0, 1)$.

(e) Now, suppose we discretize f on $[0, 1]$ using n evenly spaced samples $f^1, f^2, \ldots, f^n \in \mathbb{R}$ and f_0 using samples $f_0^1, f_0^2, \ldots, f_0^n$. Devise a discrete analog of $E[f]$ as a quadratic energy in the f^k's. For $k \notin \{1, n\}$, does differentiating E with respect to f_k yield a result analogous to Exercise 15.6d?

15.7 (Adapted from [21]) The swing angle θ of a pendulum under gravity satisfies the following ODE:

$$\theta'' = -\sin\theta,$$

where $|\theta(0)| < \pi$ and $\theta'(0) = 0$.

(a) Suppose $\theta(t)$ solves the ODE. Show that the following value (representing the energy of the system) is constant as a function of t:

$$E(t) \equiv \frac{1}{2}(\theta')^2 - \cos\theta.$$

(b) Many ODE integrators drift away from the desired output as time progresses over larger periods. For instance, forward Euler can add energy to a system by overshooting, while backward Euler tends to damp out motion and remove energy. In many computer graphics applications, quality long-term behavior can be prioritized, since large-scale issues cause visual artifacts. The class of *symplectic* integrators is designed to avoid this issue.

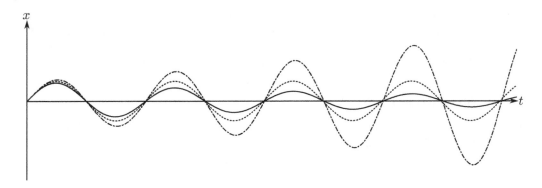

Figure 15.11 Three simulations of an undamped oscillator.

Denote $\omega \equiv \theta'$. The *symplectic Euler* scheme makes a series of estimates $\theta_0, \theta_1, \theta_2, \theta_3, \ldots$ and $\omega_0, \omega_1, \omega_2, \omega_3, \ldots$ at time $t = 0, h, 2h, 3h, \ldots$ using the following iteration:

$$\theta_{k+1} = \theta_k + h\omega_k$$
$$\omega_{k+1} = \omega_k - h\sin\theta_{k+1}.$$

Define

$$E_k \equiv \frac{1}{2}\omega_k^2 - \cos\theta_k.$$

Show that $E_{k+1} = E_k + O(h^2)$.

(c) Suppose we make the small-angle approximation $\sin\theta \approx \theta$ and decide to solve the linear ODE $\theta'' = -\theta$ instead. Now, symplectic Euler takes the following form:

$$\theta_{k+1} = \theta_k + h\omega_k$$
$$\omega_{k+1} = \omega_k - h\theta_{k+1}.$$

Write a 2×2 matrix A such that

$$\begin{pmatrix} \theta_{k+1} \\ \omega_{k+1} \end{pmatrix} = A \begin{pmatrix} \theta_k \\ \omega_k \end{pmatrix}.$$

(d) If we define $E_k \equiv \omega_k^2 + h\omega_k\theta_k + \theta_k^2$, show that $E_{k+1} = E_k$ in the iteration from 15.7c. In other words, E_k is constant from time step to time step.

15.8 Suppose we simulate a spring by solving the ODE $y'' = -y$ with $y(0) = 0$ and $y'(0) = 1$. We obtain the three plots of $y(t)$ in Figure 15.11 by using forward Euler, backward Euler, and symplectic Euler time integration. Determine which plot is which, and justify your answers using properties of the three integrators.

15.9 Suppose we discretize Schrödinger's equation for a particular quantum simulation yielding an ODE $\vec{x}' = A\vec{x}$, for $\vec{x}(t) \in \mathbb{C}^n$ and $A \in \mathbb{C}^{n \times n}$. Furthermore, suppose that A is *self-adjoint* and *negative definite*, that is, A satisfies the following properties:

- Self-adjoint: $a_{ij} = \bar{a}_{ji}$, where $\overline{a + bi} = a - bi$.

- Negative definite: $\vec{x}^\top A\vec{x} \leq 0$ (and is real) for all $\vec{x} \in \mathbb{C}^n\backslash\{\vec{0}\}$. Here we define $(\bar{\vec{x}})_i \equiv \bar{x}_i$.

Derive a backward Euler formula for solving this ODE and show that each step can be carried out using conjugate gradients.

Hint: Before discretizing, convert the ODE to a real-valued system by separating imaginary and real parts of the variables and constants.

15.10 ("Phi functions," [89]) Exponential integrators made use of ODEs with known solutions to boost numerical quality of time integration. This strategy can be extended using additional closed-form solutions.

(a) Define $\varphi_k(x)$ recursively by defining $\varphi_0(x) \equiv e^x$ and recursively writing

$$\varphi_{k+1}(x) \equiv \frac{1}{x}\left(\varphi_k(x) - \frac{1}{k!}\right).$$

Write the Taylor expansions of $\varphi_0(x)$, $\varphi_1(x)$, $\varphi_2(x)$, and $\varphi_3(x)$ about $x = 0$.

(b) Show that for $k \geq 1$,

$$\varphi_k(x) = \frac{1}{(k-1)!}\int_0^1 e^{(1-\theta)x}\theta^{k-1}\,d\theta.$$

Hint: Use integration by parts to show that the recursive relationship from Exercise 15.10a holds.

(c) Check the following formula for $\varphi_k'(x)$ when $k \geq 1$:

$$\varphi_k'(x) = \frac{1}{x}\left[\varphi_k(x)(x-k) + \frac{1}{(k-1)!}\right].$$

(d) Show that the ODE

$$\vec{u}'(t) = L\vec{u}(t) + \vec{v}_0 + \frac{1}{1!}t\vec{v}_1 + \frac{1}{2!}t^2\vec{v}_2 + \frac{1}{3!}t^3\vec{v}_3 + \cdots$$

subject to $\vec{u}(0) = \vec{u}_0$ is solved by

$$\vec{u}(t) = \varphi_0(tL)\vec{u}_0 + t\varphi_1(tL)\vec{v}_0 + t^2\varphi_2(tL)\vec{v}_1 + t^3\varphi_3(tL)\vec{v}_2 + \cdots.$$

When L is a matrix, assume $\varphi_k(tL)$ is evaluated using the formula from Exercise 15.10b.

(e) Use the closed-form solution from Exercise 15.10d to propose an integrator for the ODE $\vec{y}' = A\vec{y} + \sum_{k=1}^\ell \frac{t^k}{k!}\vec{v}_k + G[\vec{y}]$ that provides exact solutions when $G[\vec{y}] \equiv \vec{0}$.

15.11 ("Fehlberg's method," [39] via notes by J. Feldman) We can approximate the error of an ODE integrator to help choose appropriate step sizes given a desired level of accuracy.

(a) Suppose we carry out a single time step of $\vec{y}' = F[\vec{y}]$ with size h starting from $\vec{y}(0) = \vec{y}_0$. Make the following definitions:

$$\vec{v}_1 \equiv F[\vec{y}_0]$$
$$\vec{v}_2 \equiv F[\vec{y}_0 + h\vec{v}_1]$$
$$\vec{v}_3 \equiv F\left[\vec{y}_0 + \frac{h}{4}(\vec{v}_1 + \vec{v}_2)\right].$$

We can write two estimates of $\vec{y}(h)$:

$$\vec{y}^{(1)} \equiv \vec{y}_0 + \frac{h}{2}(\vec{v}_1 + \vec{v}_2)$$
$$\vec{y}^{(2)} \equiv \vec{y}_0 + \frac{h}{6}(\vec{v}_1 + \vec{v}_2 + 4\vec{v}_3).$$

Show that there is some $K \in \mathbb{R}$ such that $\vec{y}^{(1)} = \vec{y}(h) + Kh^3 + O(h^4)$ and $\vec{y}^{(2)} = \vec{y}(h) + O(h^4)$.

(b) Use this relationship to derive an approximation of the amount of error introduced per unit increase of time t if we use $\vec{y}^{(1)}$ as an integrator. If this value is too large, adaptive integrators reject the step and try again with a smaller h.

CHAPTER 16

Partial Differential Equations

CONTENTS

16.1	Motivation	330
16.2	Statement and Structure of PDEs	335
	16.2.1 Properties of PDEs	335
	16.2.2 Boundary Conditions	336
16.3	Model Equations	338
	16.3.1 Elliptic PDEs	338
	16.3.2 Parabolic PDEs	339
	16.3.3 Hyperbolic PDEs	340
16.4	Representing Derivative Operators	341
	16.4.1 Finite Differences	342
	16.4.2 Collocation	346
	16.4.3 Finite Elements	347
	16.4.4 Finite Volumes	350
	16.4.5 Other Methods	351
16.5	Solving Parabolic and Hyperbolic Equations	352
	16.5.1 Semidiscrete Methods	352
	16.5.2 Fully Discrete Methods	353
16.6	Numerical Considerations	354
	16.6.1 Consistency, Convergence, and Stability	354
	16.6.2 Linear Solvers for PDE	354

INTUITION for ordinary differential equations largely stems from the time evolution of physical systems. Equations like Newton's second law, determining the motion of physical objects over time, dominate the literature on ODE problems; additional examples come from chemical concentrations reacting over time, populations of predators and prey interacting from season to season, and so on. In each case, the initial configuration—e.g., the positions and velocities of particles in a system at time zero—is known, and the task is to predict behavior as time progresses. Derivatives only appear in a single time variable.

In this chapter, we entertain the possibility of *coupling* relationships between different derivatives of a function. It is not difficult to find examples where this coupling is necessary. When simulating gases or fluids, quantities like "pressure gradients," which encode the derivatives of pressure in *space*, figure into how material moves over *time*. These gradients appear since gases and fluids naturally move from high-pressure regions to low-pressure regions. In image processing, coupling the horizontal and vertical partial derivatives of an image can be used to describe its edges, characterize its texture, and so on.

Equations coupling together derivatives of functions in more than one variable are known as *partial differential equations*. They are the subject of a rich, nuanced theory worthy of

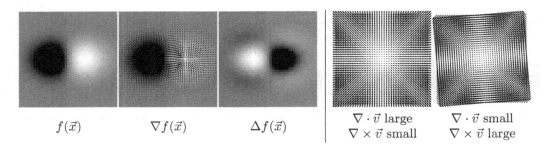

$$f(\vec{x}) \qquad \nabla f(\vec{x}) \qquad \Delta f(\vec{x})$$

$$\nabla \cdot \vec{v} \text{ large} \qquad \nabla \cdot \vec{v} \text{ small}$$
$$\nabla \times \vec{v} \text{ small} \qquad \nabla \times \vec{v} \text{ large}$$

Figure 16.1 Vector calculus notation. On the left, we show a function $f(\vec{x})$ for $\vec{x} \in \mathbb{R}^2$ colored from black to white, its gradient ∇f, and its Laplacian $\nabla^2 f$; on the right are vector fields $\vec{v}(\vec{x})$ with different balances between divergence and curl.

larger-scale treatment, so we simply will summarize key ideas and provide sufficient material to approach problems commonly appearing in practice.

16.1 MOTIVATION

Partial differential equations (PDEs) provide one or more relationships between the partial derivatives of a function $f : \mathbb{R}^n \to \mathbb{R}^m$; the goal is to find an f satisfying the criteria. PDEs appear in nearly any branch of applied mathematics, and we list just a few below. Unlike in previous chapters, the algorithms in this chapter will be far from optimal with respect to accuracy or speed when applied to many of the examples. Our goals are to explore the vast space of problems that can be expressed as PDEs, to introduce the language needed to determine necessary numerical machinery, and to highlight key challenges and techniques for different classes of PDEs.

There are a few combinations of partial derivatives that appear often in the world of PDEs. If $f : \mathbb{R}^3 \to \mathbb{R}$ is a function and $\vec{v} : \mathbb{R}^3 \to \mathbb{R}^3$ is a vector field, then the following operators from vector calculus, illustrated in Figure 16.1, are worth remembering:

Name	Notation	Definition
Gradient	∇f	$\left(\frac{\partial f}{\partial x_1}, \frac{\partial f}{\partial x_2}, \frac{\partial f}{\partial x_3} \right)$
Divergence	$\nabla \cdot \vec{v}$	$\frac{\partial v_1}{\partial x_1} + \frac{\partial v_2}{\partial x_2} + \frac{\partial v_3}{\partial x_3}$
Curl	$\nabla \times \vec{v}$	$\left(\frac{\partial v_3}{\partial x_2} - \frac{\partial v_2}{\partial x_3}, \frac{\partial v_1}{\partial x_3} - \frac{\partial v_3}{\partial x_1}, \frac{\partial v_2}{\partial x_1} - \frac{\partial v_1}{\partial x_2} \right)$
Laplacian	$\nabla^2 f$	$\frac{\partial^2 f}{\partial x_1^2} + \frac{\partial^2 f}{\partial x_2^2} + \frac{\partial^2 f}{\partial x_3^2}$

For PDEs involving fluids, electrodynamics, and other physical quantities, by convention we think of the derivatives above as acting on the *spatial* variables (x, y, z) rather than the time variable t. For instance, the gradient of a function $f : (x, y, z; t) \to \mathbb{R}$ will be written $\nabla f \equiv (\partial f / \partial x, \partial f / \partial y, \partial f / \partial z)$; the partial derivative in time $\partial f / \partial t$ is treated separately.

Example 16.1 (Fluid simulation). The flow of fluids and smoke is governed by the *Navier-Stokes equations*, a system of PDEs in many variables. Suppose a fluid is moving in a region $\Omega \subseteq \mathbb{R}^3$. We define the following quantities:

$t \in [0, \infty)$	Time
$\vec{v}(t) : \Omega \to \mathbb{R}^3$	Velocity
$p(t) : \Omega \to \mathbb{R}$	Pressure
$\vec{f}(t) : \Omega \to \mathbb{R}^3$	External forces (e.g., gravity)

Boundary conditions (on $\partial\Omega$) Laplace solution (on Ω)

Figure 16.2 Laplace's equation takes a function on the boundary $\partial\Omega$ of a domain $\Omega \subseteq \mathbb{R}^2$ (left) and interpolates it to the interior of Ω as smoothly as possible (right).

If the fluid has fixed viscosity μ and density ρ, then the (incompressible) Navier-Stokes equations state

$$\rho \cdot \left(\frac{\partial \vec{v}}{\partial t} + \vec{v} \cdot \nabla \vec{v}\right) = -\nabla p + \mu \nabla^2 \vec{v} + \vec{f} \quad \text{with} \quad \nabla \cdot \vec{v} = 0.$$

This system of equations determines the time dynamics of fluid motion and can be constructed by applying Newton's second law to tracking "particles" of fluid. Its statement involves derivatives in time $\partial/\partial t$ and derivatives in space ∇, making it a PDE.

Example 16.2 (Maxwell's equations). Maxwell's equations determine the interaction between electric fields $\vec{E}$ and magnetic fields $\vec{B}$ over time. As with the Navier-Stokes equations, we think of the gradient, divergence, and curl operators as taking partial derivatives in space (x, y, z) and not time t. In a vacuum, Maxwell's system (in "strong" form) can be written:

$$\text{Gauss's law for electric fields: } \nabla \cdot \vec{E} = \frac{\rho}{\varepsilon_0}$$

$$\text{Gauss's law for magnetism: } \nabla \cdot \vec{B} = 0$$

$$\text{Faraday's law: } \nabla \times \vec{E} = -\frac{\partial \vec{B}}{\partial t}$$

$$\text{Ampère's law: } \nabla \times \vec{B} = \mu_0 \left(\vec{J} + \varepsilon_0 \frac{\partial \vec{E}}{\partial t}\right)$$

Here, ε_0 and μ_0 are physical constants and $\vec{J}$ encodes the density of electrical current. Just like the Navier-Stokes equations, Maxwell's equations relate derivatives of physical quantities in time t to their derivatives in space (given by curl and divergence terms).

Example 16.3 (Laplace's equation). Suppose Ω is a domain in $\mathbb{R}^2$ with boundary $\partial\Omega$ and that we are given a function $g : \partial\Omega \to \mathbb{R}$, illustrated in Figure 16.2. We may wish to interpolate g to the interior of Ω as smoothly as possible. When Ω is an irregular shape, however, our strategies for interpolation from Chapter 13 can break down.

Take $f(\vec{x}) : \Omega \to \mathbb{R}$ to be an interpolating function satisfying $f(\vec{x}) = g(\vec{x})$ for all $\vec{x} \in \partial\Omega$. One metric for evaluating the quality of f as a smooth interpolant is to define an energy functional:

$$E[f] = \int_{\Omega} \|\nabla f(\vec{x})\|_2^2 \, d\vec{x}.$$

Here, the notation $E[\cdot]$ does not stand for "expectation" as it might in probability theory, but rather is an "energy" functional; it is standard notation in variational analysis. $E[f]$ measures the "total derivative" of f measured by taking the norm of its gradient and integrating this quantity over all of Ω. Wildly fluctuating functions f will have high values of $E[f]$ since the slope ∇f will be large in many places; smooth functions f, on the other hand, will have small $E[f]$ since their slope will be small everywhere.

We could ask that f interpolates g while being as smooth as possible in the interior of Ω using the following optimization:

$$\text{minimize}_f \; E[f]$$
$$\text{subject to } f(\vec{x}) = g(\vec{x}) \, \forall x \in \partial\Omega.$$

This setup *looks* like optimizations we have solved elsewhere, but now our unknown is a function f rather than a point in $\mathbb{R}^n$.

If f minimizes E subject to the boundary conditions, then $E[f + h] \geq E[f]$ for all functions $h(\vec{x})$ with $h(\vec{x}) = 0$ for all $\vec{x} \in \partial\Omega$. This statement is true even for small perturbations $E[f + \varepsilon h]$ as $\varepsilon \to 0$. Subtracting $E[f]$, dividing by ε, and taking the limit as $\varepsilon \to 0$, we must have $\frac{d}{d\varepsilon} E[f + \varepsilon h]|_{\varepsilon=0} = 0$; this expression is akin to setting directional derivatives of a function equal to zero to find its minima. We can simplify:

$$E[f + \varepsilon h] = \int_{\Omega} \|\nabla f(\vec{x}) + \varepsilon \nabla h(\vec{x})\|_2^2 \, d\vec{x}$$
$$= \int_{\Omega} (\|\nabla f(\vec{x})\|_2^2 + 2\varepsilon \nabla f(\vec{x}) \cdot \nabla h(\vec{x}) + \varepsilon^2 \|\nabla h(\vec{x})\|_2^2) \, d\vec{x}.$$

Differentiating with respect to ε shows

$$\frac{d}{d\varepsilon} E[f + \varepsilon h] = \int_{\Omega} (2\nabla f(\vec{x}) \cdot \nabla h(\vec{x}) + 2\varepsilon \|\nabla h(\vec{x})\|_2^2) \, d\vec{x}$$
$$\implies \frac{d}{d\varepsilon} E[f + \varepsilon h]|_{\varepsilon=0} = 2 \int_{\Omega} [\nabla f(\vec{x}) \cdot \nabla h(\vec{x})] \, d\vec{x}.$$

Applying integration by parts and recalling that h is zero on $\partial\Omega$,

$$\frac{d}{d\varepsilon} E[f + \varepsilon h]|_{\varepsilon=0} = -2 \int_{\Omega} h(\vec{x}) \nabla^2 f(\vec{x}) \, d\vec{x}.$$

This expression must equal zero for *all* perturbations h that are zero on $\partial\Omega$. Hence, $\nabla^2 f(\vec{x}) = 0$ for all $\vec{x} \in \Omega \backslash \partial\Omega$ (a formal proof is outside of the scope of our discussion).

We have shown that the boundary interpolation problem above amounts to solving the following PDE:

$$\nabla^2 f(\vec{x}) = 0 \; \forall \vec{x} \in \Omega \backslash \partial\Omega$$
$$f(\vec{x}) = g(\vec{x}) \; \forall \vec{x} \in \partial\Omega.$$

This PDE is known as *Laplace's equation*.

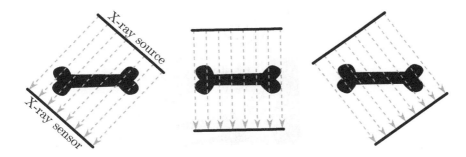

Figure 16.3 A CT scanner passes x-rays through an object; sensors on the other side collect the energy that made it through, giving the integrated density of the object along the x-ray path. Placing the source and sensor in different rotated poses allows for reconstruction of the pointwise density function.

Example 16.4 (X-ray computerized tomography). Computerized tomography (CT) technology uses x-rays to see inside an object without cutting through it. The basic model is shown in Figure 16.3. Essentially, by passing x-rays through an object, the density of the object integrated along the x-ray path can be sensed by collecting the proportion that makes it through to the other side.

Suppose the density of an object is given by a function $\rho : \mathbb{R}^3 \to \mathbb{R}^+$. For any two points $\vec{x}, \vec{y} \in \mathbb{R}^3$, we can think of a CT scanner abstractly as a device that can sense the integral u of ρ along the line connecting $\vec{x}$ and $\vec{y}$:

$$u(\vec{x}, \vec{y}) \equiv \int_{-\infty}^{\infty} \rho(t\vec{x} + (1-t)\vec{y}) \, dt.$$

The function $u : \mathbb{R}^3 \times \mathbb{R}^3 \to \mathbb{R}^+$ is known as the *Radon transform* of ρ.

Suppose we take a second derivative of u in an $\vec{x}$ and then a $\vec{y}$ coordinate:

$$\frac{\partial}{\partial x_i} u(\vec{x}, \vec{y}) = \int_{-\infty}^{\infty} \frac{\partial}{\partial x_i} \rho(t\vec{x} + (1-t)\vec{y}) \, dt \text{ by definition of } u$$

$$= \int_{-\infty}^{\infty} t\vec{e}_i \cdot \nabla\rho(t\vec{x} + (1-t)\vec{y}) \, dt$$

$$\implies \frac{\partial^2}{\partial y_j \partial x_i} u(\vec{x}, \vec{y}) = \int_{-\infty}^{\infty} \frac{\partial}{\partial y_j} t\vec{e}_i \cdot \nabla\rho(t\vec{x} + (1-t)\vec{y}) \, dt$$

$$= \int_{-\infty}^{\infty} t(1-t)\vec{e}_i^{\top} H_\rho(t\vec{x} + (1-t)\vec{y})\vec{e}_j \, dt \text{ for Hessian } H_\rho \text{ of } \rho.$$

An identical set of steps shows that the derivative $\frac{\partial^2 u}{\partial x_j \partial y_i}$ equals the same expression after applying symmetry of H_ρ. That is, u satisfies the following relationship:

$$\frac{\partial^2 u}{\partial y_j \partial x_i} = \frac{\partial^2 u}{\partial x_j \partial y_i}.$$

This equality, known as the Fritz John equation [68], gives information about u without involving the unknown density function ρ. In a computational context, it can be used to fill in data missing from incomplete x-ray scans or to smooth data from a potentially noisy x-ray sensor before reconstructing ρ.

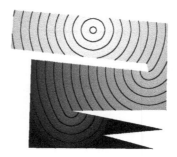

Figure 16.4 Shortest-path distances constrained to move within the interior of a non-convex shape have to wrap around corners; level sets of the distance function (shown as black lines) are no longer circles beyond these corner points.

Example 16.5 (Eikonal equation). Suppose Ω is a closed region in $\mathbb{R}^n$. For a fixed point $\vec{x}_0 \in \Omega$, we might wish to find a function $d(\vec{x}) : \Omega \to \mathbb{R}^+$ measuring the length of the shortest path from $\vec{x}_0$ to $\vec{x}$ restricted to move only within Ω. When Ω is convex, we can write d in closed form as

$$d(\vec{x}) = \|\vec{x} - \vec{x}_0\|_2.$$

As illustrated in Figure 16.4, however, if Ω is non-convex or is a complicated domain like a surface, these distance functions become more challenging to compute. Solving for d, however, is a critical step for tasks like planning paths of robots by minimizing the distance they travel while avoiding obstacles marked on a map.

If Ω is non-convex, away from singularities, the function $d(\vec{x})$ still satisfies a derivative condition known as the *eikonal equation*:

$$\|\nabla d\|_2 = 1.$$

Intuitively, this PDE states that a distance function should have unit rate of change everywhere. As a sanity check, this relationship is certainly true for the absolute value function $|x - x_0|$ in one dimension, which measures the distance along the real line between x_0 and x. This equation is nonlinear in the derivative ∇d, making it a particularly challenging problem to solve for $d(\vec{x})$.

Specialized algorithms known as *fast marching methods* and *fast sweeping methods* estimate $d(\vec{x})$ over all of Ω by integrating the eikonal equation. Many algorithms for approximating solutions to the eikonal equation have structure similar to Dijkstra's algorithm for computing shortest paths along graphs; see Exercise 16.8 for one example.

Example 16.6 (Harmonic analysis). Different objects respond differently to vibrations, and in large part these responses are functions of the *geometry* of the objects. For example, cellos and pianos can play the same note, but even an inexperienced listener can distinguish between the sounds they make.

From a mathematical standpoint, we can take $\Omega \subseteq \mathbb{R}^3$ to be a shape represented either as a surface or a volume. If we clamp the edges of the shape, then its *frequency spectrum* is given by eigenvalues coming from the following problem:

$$\nabla^2 \phi = \lambda \phi$$
$$\phi(\vec{x}) = 0 \; \forall \vec{x} \in \partial\Omega,$$

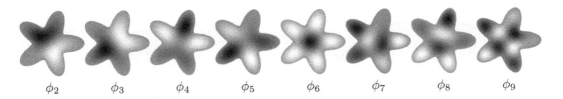

Figure 16.5 The first eight eigenfunctions ϕ_i of the Laplacian operator of the domain Ω from Figure 16.2, which satisfy $\nabla^2 \phi_i = \lambda_i \phi_i$ in order of increasing frequency; we omit ϕ_1, which is the constant function with $\lambda = 0$.

where ∇^2 is the Laplacian of Ω and $\partial\Omega$ is the boundary of Ω. Figure 16.5 shows examples of these functions on a two-dimensional domain Ω.

Relating to the one-dimensional theory of waves, $\sin kx$ solves this problem when Ω is the interval $[0, 2\pi]$ and $k \in \mathbb{Z}$. To check, the Laplacian in one dimension is $\partial^2/\partial x^2$, and thus

$$\frac{\partial^2}{\partial x^2} \sin kx = \frac{\partial}{\partial x} k \cos kx$$
$$= -k^2 \sin kx$$
$$\sin(k \cdot 0) = 0$$
$$\sin(k \cdot 2\pi) = 0.$$

That is, the eigenfunctions are $\sin kx$ with eigenvalues $-k^2$.

16.2 STATEMENT AND STRUCTURE OF PDES

Vocabulary used to describe PDEs is extensive, and each class of PDEs has substantially different properties from the others in terms of solvability, theoretical understanding of solutions, and discretization challenges. Our main focus eventually will be on developing algorithms for a few common tasks rather than introducing the general theory of continuous or discretized PDE, but it is worth acknowledging the rich expressive possibilities—and accompanying theoretical challenges—that come with using PDE language to describe numerical problems.

Following standard notation, in our subsequent development we will assume that our unknown is some function $u(\vec{x})$. For ease of notation, we will use subscript notation to denote partial derivatives:

$$u_x \equiv \frac{\partial u}{\partial x}, \qquad u_y \equiv \frac{\partial u}{\partial y}, \qquad u_{xy} \equiv \frac{\partial^2 u}{\partial x \partial y},$$

and so on.

16.2.1 Properties of PDEs

Just as ODEs couple the time derivatives of a function, PDEs typically are stated as relationships between two or more partial derivatives of u. By examining the algebraic form of a PDE, we can check if it has any of a number of properties, including the following:

- *Homogeneous* (e.g., $x^2 u_{xx} + u_{xy} - u_y + u = 0$): The PDE can be written using linear combinations of u and its derivatives; the coefficients can be scalar values or func-

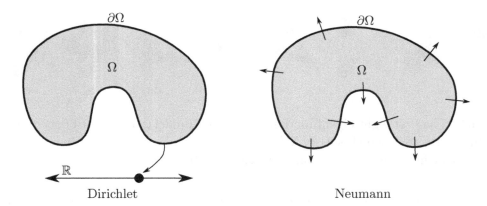

Figure 16.6 Dirichlet boundary conditions prescribe the values of the unknown function u on the boundary $\partial\Omega$ of the domain Ω, while Neumann conditions prescribe the derivative of u orthogonal to $\partial\Omega$.

tions of the independent variables. The equation can be nonlinear in the independent variables (x and y in our example).

- *Linear* (e.g., $u_{xx} - yu_{yy} + u = xy^2$): Similar to homogeneous PDE, but potentially with a nonzero (inhomogeneous) right-hand side built from scalars or the dependent variables. PDEs like the eikonal equation (or $u_{xx}^2 = u_{xy}$) are considered *nonlinear* because they are nonlinear in u.

- *Quasi-linear* (e.g., $u_{xy} + 2u_{xx} + u_y^2 + u_x^2 = y$): The statement is linear in the highest-order derivatives of u.

- *Constant-coefficient* (e.g., $u_{xx} + 3u_y = u_z$): The coefficients of u and its derivatives are not functions of the independent variables.

One potentially surprising observation about the properties above is that they are more concerned with the role of u than those of the independent variables like x, y, and z. For instance, the definition of a "linear" PDE allows u to have coefficients that are nonlinear functions of these variables. While this may make the PDE appear nonlinear, it is still linear in the unknowns, which is the distinguishing factor.

The *order* of a PDE is the order of its highest derivative. Most of the PDEs we consider in this chapter are second-order and already present considerable numerical challenges. Methods analogous to reduction of ODEs to first order (§15.2.1) can be carried out but do not provide as much benefit for solving PDEs.

16.2.2 Boundary Conditions

ODEs typically are considered *initial-value problems*, because given a configuration that is known at the initial time $t = 0$, they evolve the state forward indefinitely. With few exceptions, the user does not have to provide information about the state for $t > 0$.

PDE problems also can be *boundary-value problems* rather than or in addition to being initial value problems. Most PDEs require information about behavior at the boundary of the domain of all the variables. For instance, Laplace's equation, introduced in Example 16.3, requires fixed values on the boundary $\partial\Omega$ of Ω. Similarly, the heat equation used to

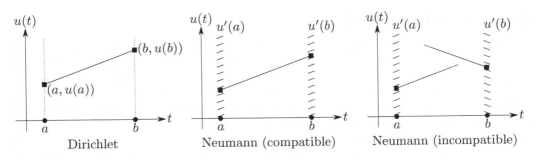

Figure 16.7 Boundary conditions for the PDE $u_{tt} = 0$ from Example 16.7.

simulate conductive material like metals admits a number of possible boundary conditions, corresponding to whether the material is attached to a heat source or dispersing heat energy into the surrounding space.

If the unknown of a PDE is a function $u : \Omega \to \mathbb{R}$ for some domain $\Omega \subseteq \mathbb{R}^n$, typical boundary conditions include the following:

- *Dirichlet conditions* directly specify the values of $u(\vec{x})$ for all $\vec{x} \in \partial\Omega$.

- *Neumann conditions* specify the derivative of $u(\vec{x})$ in the direction orthogonal to $\partial\Omega$.

- *Mixed* or *Robin conditions* specify a relationship between the value and normal derivatives of $u(\vec{x})$ on $\partial\Omega$.

The first two choices are illustrated in Figure 16.6.

Improperly encoding boundary conditions is a subtle oversight that creeps into countless discretizations of PDEs. There are many sources of confusion that explain this common issue. Different discretizations of the same boundary conditions can yield qualitatively different outputs from a PDE solver if they are expressed improperly. Indeed, some boundary conditions are not realizable even in theory, as illustrated in the example below.

Example 16.7 (Boundary conditions in one dimension). Suppose we are solving the following PDE (more precisely an ODE, although the distinction here is not relevant) in one variable t over the interval $\Omega = [a, b]$:

$$u_{tt} = 0.$$

From one-variable calculus, that solutions must take the form $u(t) = \alpha t + \beta$.

Consider the effects of assorted choices of boundary conditions on $\partial\Omega = \{a, b\}$, illustrated in Figure 16.7:

- Dirichlet conditions specify the values $u(a)$ and $u(b)$ directly. There is a unique line that goes through any pair of points $(a, u(a))$ and $(b, u(b))$, so a solution to the PDE always exists and is unique in this case.

- Neumann conditions specify $u'(a)$ and $u'(b)$. From the general form of $u(t)$, $u'(t) = \alpha$, reflecting the fact that lines have constant slope. Neumann conditions specifying different values for $u'(a)$ and $u'(b)$ are *incompatible* with the PDE itself. Compatible Neumann conditions, on the other hand, specify $u'(a) = u'(b) = \alpha$ but are satisfied for any choice of β.

16.3   MODEL EQUATIONS

In §15.2.3, we studied properties of ODEs and their integrators by examining the model equation $y' = ay$. We can pursue a similar analytical technique for PDEs, although we will have to separate into multiple special cases to cover the qualitative phenomena of interest.

We will focus on the linear, constant-coefficient, homogeneous case. As mentioned in §16.2.1, the non-constant coefficient and inhomogeneous cases often have similar qualitative behavior, and nonlinear PDEs require special consideration beyond the scope of our discussion. We furthermore will study *second-order* systems, that is, systems containing at most the second derivative of u. While the model ODE $y' = ay$ is first-order, a reasonable model PDE needs at least two derivatives to show how derivatives in different directions interact.

Linear, constant-coefficient, homogeneous second-order PDEs have the following general form, for unknown function $u : \mathbb{R}^n \to \mathbb{R}$:

$$\sum_{ij} a_{ij} \frac{\partial u}{\partial x_i \partial x_j} + \sum_i b_i \frac{\partial u}{\partial x_i} + cu = 0.$$

To simplify notation, we can define a formal "gradient operator" as the vector of derivatives

$$\nabla \equiv \left(\frac{\partial}{\partial x_1}, \frac{\partial}{\partial x_2}, \dots, \frac{\partial}{\partial x_n} \right).$$

Expressions like ∇f, $\nabla \cdot \vec{v}$, and $\nabla \times \vec{v}$ agree with the definitions of gradients, divergence, and curl on $\mathbb{R}^3$ using this formal definition of ∇. In this notation, the model PDE takes a matrix-like form:

$$(\nabla^\top A \nabla + \nabla \cdot \vec{b} + c)u = 0.$$

The operator $\nabla^\top A \nabla + \nabla \cdot \vec{b} + c$ acting on u abstractly looks like a quadratic form in ∇ as a vector; since partial derivatives commute, we can assume A is symmetric.

The definiteness of A determines the *class* of the model PDE, just as the definiteness of a matrix determines the convexity of its associated quadratic form. Four cases bring about qualitatively different behavior for u:

- If A is *positive or negative definite*, the system is *elliptic*.

- If A is *positive or negative semidefinite*, the system is *parabolic*.

- If A has only one eigenvalue of different sign from the rest, the system is *hyperbolic*.

- If A satisfies none of these criteria, the system is *ultrahyperbolic*.

These criteria are listed approximately in order of the difficulty level of solving each type of equation. We consider the first three cases below and provide examples of corresponding behavior by specifying different matrices A; ultrahyperbolic equations do not appear as often in practice and require highly specialized solution techniques.

16.3.1   Elliptic PDEs

Positive definite linear systems can be solved using efficient algorithms like Cholesky decomposition and conjugate gradients that do not necessarily work for indefinite matrices. Similarly, elliptic PDEs, for which A is positive definite, have strong structure that makes them the most straightforward equations to characterize and solve, both theoretically and computationally.

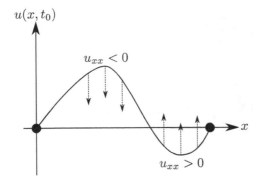

Figure 16.8 The heat equation in one variable $u_t = \alpha u_{xx}$ decreases u over time where it is curved down and increases u over time where u is curved up, as measured using the second derivative in space u_{xx}. Here, we show a solution of the heat equation $u(x,t)$ at a fixed time t_0; the arrows indicate how values of u will change as t advances.

The model elliptic PDE is the *Laplace equation*, given by $\nabla^2 u = 0$, as in Example 16.3. In two variables, the Laplace equation is written

$$u_{xx} + u_{yy} = 0.$$

Figure 16.2 illustrated a solution of the Laplace equation, which essentially interpolates information from the boundary of the domain of u to its interior.

Elliptic equations are well-understood theoretically and come with strong properties characterizing their behavior. Of particular importance is *elliptic regularity*, which states that solutions of elliptic PDEs automatically are differentiable to higher order than their building blocks. Physically, elliptic equations characterize stable equilbria like the rest pose of a stretched rubber sheet, which naturally resists kinks and other irregularities.

16.3.2 Parabolic PDEs

Positive *semi*definite linear systems are only marginally more difficult to deal with than positive definite ones, at least if their null spaces are known and relatively small. Positive semidefinite matrices have null spaces that prevent them from being invertible, but orthogonally to the null space they behave identically to definite matrices. In PDE, these systems correspond to *parabolic* equations, for which A is positive semidefinite.

The heat equation is the model parabolic PDE. Suppose $u_0(x,y)$ is a fixed distribution of temperature in some region $\Omega \subseteq \mathbb{R}^2$ at time $t = 0$. Then, the heat equation determines how heat diffuses over time $t > 0$ as a function $u(t; x, y)$:

$$u_t = \alpha(u_{xx} + u_{yy}),$$

where $\alpha > 0$. If $\nabla = (\partial/\partial x, \partial/\partial y)$, the heat equation can be written $u_t = \alpha \nabla^2 u$. There is no second derivative in time t, making the equation parabolic rather than elliptic.

Figure 16.8 provides a phenomenological interpretation of the heat equation in one variable $u_t = \alpha u_{xx}$. The second derivative $\nabla^2 u$ measures the convexity of u. The heat equation increases u with time when its value is "cupped" upward, and decreases u otherwise. This

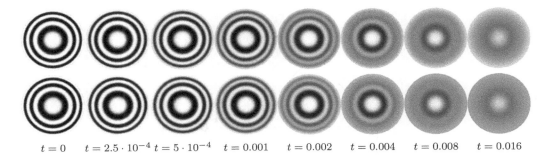

$t = 0 \qquad t = 2.5 \cdot 10^{-4}\, t = 5 \cdot 10^{-4} \qquad t = 0.001 \qquad t = 0.002 \qquad t = 0.004 \qquad t = 0.008 \qquad t = 0.016$

Figure 16.9 Solution to the heat equation $u_t = u_{xx} + u_{yy}$ on the unit circle with Dirichlet (top) and Neumann (bottom) boundary conditions. Solutions are colored from -1 (black) to 1 (white).

negative feedback is stable and leads to equilibrium as $t \to \infty$. Example solutions to the heat equation with different boundary conditions are shown in Figure 16.9.

The corresponding second-order term matrix A for the heat equation is:

$$A = \begin{array}{c} \\ t \\ x \\ y \end{array} \begin{array}{ccc} t & x & y \\ \begin{pmatrix} 0 & 0 & 0 \\ 0 & 1 & 0 \\ 0 & 0 & 1 \end{pmatrix} \end{array}.$$

The heat equation is parabolic since this matrix has eigenvalues 0, 1, and 1.

There are two boundary conditions needed for the heat equation, both of which have physical interpretations:

- The distribution of heat $u(0; x, y) \equiv u_0(x, y)$ at time $t = 0$ at all points $(x, y) \in \Omega$.

- Behavior of u when $t > 0$ at boundary points $(x, y) \in \partial\Omega$. Dirichlet conditions fix $u(t; x, y)$ for all $t \geq 0$ and $(x, y) \in \partial\Omega$, e.g., if Ω is a piece of foil sitting next to a heat source like an oven whose temperature is controlled externally. Neumann conditions specify the derivative of f in the direction normal to the boundary $\partial\Omega$; they correspond to fixing the *flux* of heat out of Ω caused by different types of insulation.

16.3.3 Hyperbolic PDEs

The final model equation is the wave equation, corresponding to the indefinite matrix case:

$$u_{tt} = c^2(u_{xx} + u_{yy}).$$

The wave equation is hyperbolic because the second derivative in time t has opposite sign from the two spatial derivatives when all terms involving u are isolated on the same side. This equation determines the motion of waves across an elastic medium like a rubber sheet. It can be derived by applying Newton's second law to points on a piece of elastic, where x and y are positions on the sheet and $u(t; x, y)$ is the height of the piece of elastic at time t.

Figure 16.10 illustrates a solution of the wave equation with Dirichlet boundary conditions; these boundary conditions correspond to the vibrations of a drum whose outer boundary is fixed. As illustrated in the example, wave behavior contrasts considerably with

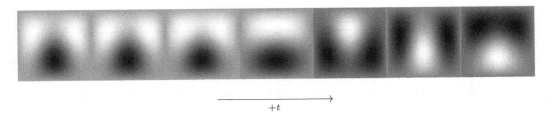

$$\xrightarrow{}$$
$$+t$$

Figure 16.10 The wave equation on a square with Dirichlet boundary conditions; time is sampled evenly and progresses left to right. Color is proportional to the height of the wave, from -1 (black) to 1 (white).

heat diffusion in that as $t \to \infty$ the energy of the system does not disperse; waves can bounce back and forth across a domain indefinitely. For this reason, implicit integration strategies may not be appropriate for integrating hyperbolic PDEs because they tend to damp out motion.

Boundary conditions for the wave equation are similar to those of the heat equation, but now we must specify both $u(0; x, y)$ and $u_t(0; x, y)$ at time zero:

- The conditions at $t = 0$ specify the position and velocity of the wave at the start time.

- Boundary conditions on $\partial\Omega$ determine what happens at the ends of the material. Dirichlet conditions correspond to fixing the sides of the wave, e.g., plucking a cello string that is held flat at its two ends on the instrument. Neumann conditions correspond to leaving the ends of the wave untouched, like the end of a whip.

16.4   REPRESENTING DERIVATIVE OPERATORS

A key intuition that underlies many numerical techniques for PDEs is the following:

> **Derivatives act on functions in the same way that sparse matrices act on vectors.**

Our choice of notation reflects this parallel: The derivative $d/dx[f(x)]$ looks like the product of an operator d/dx and a function f.

Formally, differentiation is a *linear operator* like matrix multiplication, since for all smooth functions $f, g : \mathbb{R} \to \mathbb{R}$ and scalars $a, b \in \mathbb{R}$,

$$\frac{d}{dx}(af(x) + bg(x)) = a\frac{d}{dx}f(x) + b\frac{d}{dx}g(x).$$

The derivatives act on functions, which can be thought of as points in an infinite-dimensional vector space. Many arguments from Chapter 1 and elsewhere regarding the linear algebra of matrices extend to this case, providing conditions for invertibility, symmetry, and so on of these abstract operators.

Nearly all techniques for solving linear PDEs make this analogy concrete. For example, recall the model equation $(\nabla^\top A \nabla + \nabla \cdot \vec{b} + c)u = 0$ subject to Dirichlet boundary conditions $u|_{\partial\Omega} = u_0$ for some fixed function u_0. We can define an operator $R_{\partial\Omega} : C^\infty(\Omega) \to C^\infty(\partial\Omega)$, that is, an operator taking functions on Ω and returning functions on its boundary $\partial\Omega$,

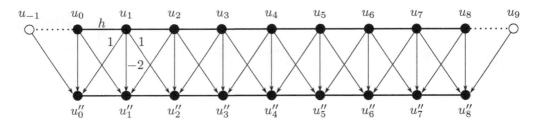

Figure 16.11 The one-dimensional finite difference Laplacian operator L takes samples u_i of a function $u(x)$ and returns an approximation of u'' at the same grid points by combining neighboring values using weights (1)—(−2)—(1); here $u(x)$ is approximated using nine samples $u_0, \ldots, u_8$. Boundary conditions are needed to deal with the unrepresented quantities at the white endpoints.

by restriction: $[R_{\partial\Omega} u](\vec{x}) \equiv u(\vec{x})$ for all $\vec{x} \in \partial\Omega$. Then, the model PDE and its boundary conditions can be combined in matrix-like notation:

$$\begin{pmatrix} (\nabla^\top A \nabla + \nabla \cdot \vec{b} + c) \\ R_{\partial\Omega} \end{pmatrix} u = \begin{pmatrix} 0 \\ u_0 \end{pmatrix}.$$

In this sense, we wish to solve $Mu = w$ where M is a linear operator. If we discretize M as a matrix, then recovering the solution u of the original equation is as easy as writing

$$\text{``} u = M^{-1} w.\text{''}$$

Many discretizations exist for M and u, often derived from the discretizations of derivatives introduced in §14.3. While each has subtle advantages, disadvantages, and conditions for effectiveness or convergence, in this section we provide constructions and high-level themes from a few popular techniques. Realistically, a legitimate and often-applied technique for finding the best discretization for a given application is to try a few and check empirically which is the most effective.

16.4.1 Finite Differences

Consider a function $u(x)$ on $[0,1]$. Using the methods from Chapter 14, we can approximate the second derivative $u''(x)$ as

$$u''(x) = \frac{u(x+h) - 2u(x) + u(x-h)}{h^2} + O(h^2).$$

In the course of solving a PDE in u, assume $u(x)$ is discretized using $n+1$ evenly spaced samples $u_0, u_1, \ldots, u_n$, as in Figure 16.11, and take h to be the spacing between samples, satisfying $h = 1/n$. Applying the formula above provides an approximation of u'' at each grid point:

$$u_k'' \approx \frac{u_{k+1} - 2u_k + u_{k-1}}{h^2}.$$

That is, the second derivative of a function on a grid of points can be estimated using the (1)—(−2)—(1) stencil illustrated in Figure 16.12.

Boundary conditions are needed to compute u_0'' and u_n'' since we have not included u_{-1} or u_{n+1} in our discretization. Keeping in mind that $u_0 = u(0)$ and $u_n = u(1)$, we can incorporate them as follows:

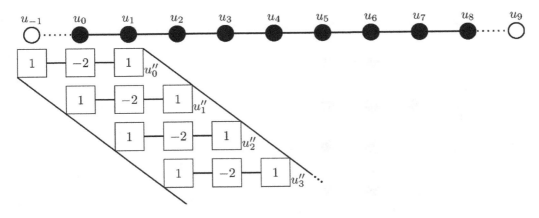

Figure 16.12 The one-dimensional finite difference Laplacian can be thought of as dragging a (1)—(−2)—(1) stencil across the domain.

- *Dirichlet:* $u_{-1} \equiv u_{n+1} = 0$, that is, fix the value of u beyond the endpoints to be zero.

- *Neumann:* $u_{-1} = u_0$ and $u_{n+1} = u_n$, encoding the condition $u'(0) = u'(1) = 0$.

- *Periodic:* $u_{-1} = u_n$ and $u_{n+1} = u_0$, making the identification $u(0) = u(1)$.

Suppose we stack the samples u_k into a vector $\vec{u} \in \mathbb{R}^{n+1}$ and the samples u_k'' into a second vector $\vec{w} \in \mathbb{R}^{n+1}$. The construction above shows that $h^2 \vec{w} = L\vec{u}$, where L is one of the choices below:

$$
\begin{array}{ccc}
\textbf{Dirichlet} & \textbf{Neumann} & \textbf{Periodic} \\[4pt]
\begin{pmatrix}
-2 & 1 & & & \\
1 & -2 & 1 & & \\
& \ddots & \ddots & \ddots & \\
& & 1 & -2 & 1 \\
& & & 1 & -2
\end{pmatrix}
&
\begin{pmatrix}
-1 & 1 & & & \\
1 & -2 & 1 & & \\
& \ddots & \ddots & \ddots & \\
& & 1 & -2 & 1 \\
& & & 1 & -1
\end{pmatrix}
&
\begin{pmatrix}
-2 & 1 & & & 1 \\
1 & -2 & 1 & & \\
& \ddots & \ddots & \ddots & \\
& & 1 & -2 & 1 \\
1 & & & 1 & -2
\end{pmatrix}
\end{array}
$$

The matrix L can be thought of as a discretized version of the operator $\frac{d^2}{dx^2}$ acting on $\vec{u} \in \mathbb{R}^{n+1}$ rather than functions $u : [0,1] \to \mathbb{R}$.

In two dimensions, we can use a similar approximation of the Laplacian $\nabla^2 u$ of $u :$ $[0,1] \times [0,1] \to \mathbb{R}$. Now, we sample using a grid of values shown in Figure 16.13. In this case, $\nabla^2 u = u_{xx} + u_{yy}$, so we sum up x and y second derivatives constructed in the one-dimensional example above. If we number our samples as $u_{k,\ell} \equiv u(kh, \ell h)$, then the formula for the Laplacian of u becomes

$$(\nabla^2 u)_{k,\ell} \approx \frac{u_{(k-1),\ell} + u_{k,(\ell-1)} + u_{(k+1),\ell} + u_{k,(\ell+1)} - 4u_{k,\ell}}{h^2}.$$

This approximation implies a (1)—(−4)—(1) stencil over a 3×3 box. If we once again combine our samples of u and ∇u into $\vec{u}$ and $\vec{w}$, respectively, then $h^2 \vec{w} = L_2 \vec{y}$ where L_2 comes from the stencil we derived. This two-dimensional grid Laplacian L_2 appears in many image processing applications, where (k, ℓ) is used to index pixels on an image.

Regardless of dimension, given a discretization of the domain and a Laplacian matrix L, we can approximate solutions of elliptic PDEs using linear systems of equations. Consider the Poisson equation $\nabla^2 u = w$. After discretization, given a sampling $\vec{w}$ of $w(\vec{x})$, we can obtain an approximation $\vec{u}$ of the solution by solving $L\vec{u} = h^2 \vec{w}$.

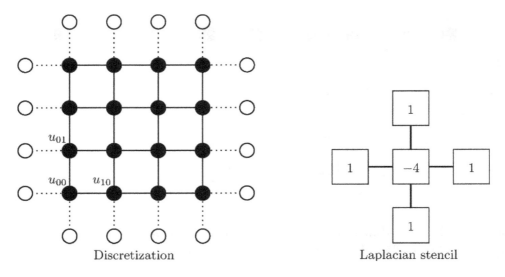

Discretization   Laplacian stencil

Figure 16.13 For functions $u(x, y)$ discretized on a two-dimensional grid (left), the Laplacian L_2 has a (1)—(-4)—(1) stencil.

This approach can be extended to inhomogeneous boundary conditions. For example, if we wish to solve $\nabla^2 u = w$ on a two-dimensional grid subject to Dirichlet conditions prescribed by a function u_0, we can solve the following linear system of equations for $\vec{u}$:

$$u_{k,\ell} = u_0(kh, lh) \text{ when } k \in \{0, n\} \text{ or } \ell \in \{0, n\}$$
$$u_{(k-1),\ell} + u_{k,(\ell-1)} + u_{(k+1),\ell} + u_{k,(\ell+1)} - 4u_{k,\ell} = 0 \text{ otherwise.}$$

This system of equations uses the 3×3 Laplacian stencil for vertices in the interior of $[0, 1]^2$ while explicitly fixing the values of u on the boundary.

These discretizations exemplify the *finite differences* method of discretizing PDEs, usually applied when the domain can be approximated using a grid. The finite difference method essentially treats the divided difference approximations from Chapter 14 as linear operators on grids of function values and then solves the resulting discrete system of equations.

Quoting results from Chapter 14 directly, however, comprises a serious breach of notation. When we write that an approximation of $u'(x)$ or $u''(x)$ holds to $O(h^k)$, we implicitly assume that $u(x)$ is sufficiently differentiable. Hence, what we need to show is that the result of solving systems like $L\vec{u} = h^2 \vec{w}$ produces a $\vec{u}$ that actually approximates samples from a smooth function $u(x)$ rather than oscillating crazily. The following example shows that this issue is practical rather than theoretical, and that reasonable but non-convergent discretizations can fail catastrophically.

Example 16.8 (Lack of convergence). Suppose we again sample a function $u(x)$ of one variable and wish to solve an equation that involves a first-order u' term. Interestingly, this task can be more challenging than solving second-order equations.

First, if we define u'_k as the forward difference $\frac{1}{h}(u_{k+1} - u_k)$, then we will be in the unnaturally asymmetric position of needing a boundary condition at u_n but not at u_0 as shown in Figure 16.14. Backward differences suffer from the reverse problem.

We might attempt to solve this problem and simultaneously gain an order of accuracy by using the symmetric difference $u'_k \approx \frac{1}{2h}(u_{k+1} - u_{k-1})$, but this discretization suffers

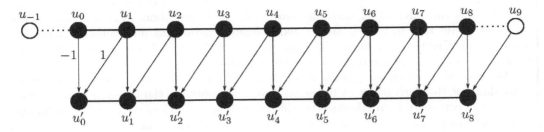

Figure 16.14 Forward differencing to approximate $u'(x)$ asymmetrically requires boundary conditions on the right but not the left.

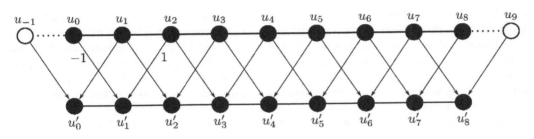

Figure 16.15 Centered differencing yields a symmetric approximation of $u'(x)$, but u'_k is not affected by the value of u_k using this formula.

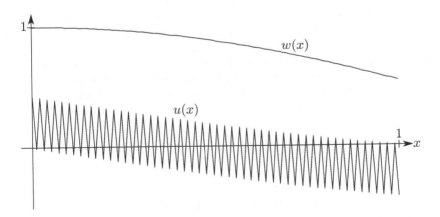

Figure 16.16 Solving $u'(x) = w(x)$ for $u(x)$ using a centered difference discretization suffers from the fencepost problem; odd- and even-indexed values of u have completely separate behavior. As more gridpoints are added in x, the resulting $u(x)$ does not converge to a smooth function, so $O(h^k)$ estimates of derivative quality do *not* apply.

from a more subtle *fencepost problem* illustrated in Figure 16.15. In particular, this version of u'_k ignores the value of u_k itself and only looks at its neighbors u_{k-1} and u_{k+1}. This oversight means that u_k and u_ℓ are treated differently depending on whether k and ℓ are even or odd. Figure 16.16 shows the result of attempting to solve a numerical problem with this discretization; the result is not differentiable.

As with the leapfrog integration algorithm in §15.4.2, one way to avoid these issues is to think of the derivatives as living on *half* gridpoints. In the one-dimensional case, this change corresponds to labeling the difference $\frac{1}{h}(y_{k+1} - y_k)$ as $y'_{k+1/2}$. This technique of placing different derivatives on vertices, edges, and centers of grid cells is particularly common in fluid simulation, which often maintains pressures, fluid velocities, and other physical quantities at locations suggested by the discretization.

16.4.2 Collocation

A challenge when working with finite differences is that we must justify that the end result "looks like" the theoretical solution we are seeking to approximate. That is, we have replaced a continuous unknown $u(\vec{x})$ with a sampled proxy on a grid but may inadvertently lose the connection to continuous mathematics in the process; Example 16.8 showed one example where a discretization is not convergent and hence yields unusable output. To avoid these issues, many numerical PDE methods attempt to make the connection between continuous and discrete less subtle.

One way to link continuous and discrete models is to write $u(\vec{x})$ in a basis $\phi_1, \ldots, \phi_k$:

$$u(\vec{x}) \approx \sum_{i=1}^{k} a_i \phi_i(\vec{x}).$$

This strategy should be familiar, as it underlies machinery for interpolation, quadrature, and differentiation. The philosophy here is to find coefficients $a_1, \ldots, a_k$ providing the *best possible approximation* of the solution to the continuous problem in the ϕ_i basis. As we add more functions ϕ_i to the basis, in many cases the approximation will converge to the theoretical solution, so long as the ϕ_i's eventually cover the relevant part of function space.

Perhaps the simplest method making use of this new construction is the *collocation* method. In the presence of k basis functions, this method samples k points $\vec{x}_1, \ldots, \vec{x}_k \in \Omega$ and requires that the PDE holds exactly at these locations. For example, if we wish to solve the Poisson equation $\nabla^2 u = w$, then for each $i \in \{1, \ldots, k\}$ we write

$$w(\vec{x}_i) = \nabla^2 u(\vec{x}_i) = \sum_{j=1}^{k} a_j \nabla^2 \phi_j(\vec{x}_i).$$

The only unknown quantities in this expression are the a_j's, so it can be used to write a square linear system for the vector $\vec{a} \in \mathbb{R}^k$ of coefficients. It can be replaced with a least-squares problem if more than k points are sampled in Ω.

Collocation requires a choice of basis functions $\phi_1, \ldots, \phi_k$ and a choice of *collocation points* $\vec{x}_1, \ldots, \vec{x}_k$. Typical basis functions include full or piecewise polynomial functions and trigonometric functions. When the ϕ_i's are compactly supported, that is, when $\phi_i(\vec{x}) = 0$ for most $\vec{x} \in \Omega$, the resulting system of equations is sparse. Collocation outputs a set of coefficients rather than a set of function values as in finite differences. Since the basis functions do not have to have any sort of grid structure, it is well-suited to non-rectangular domains, which can provide some challenge for finite differencing.

A drawback of collocation is that it does not regularize the behavior of the approximation $u(\vec{x})$ between the collocation points. Just as interpolating a polynomial through a set of sample points can lead to degenerate and in some cases highly oscillatory behavior between the samples, the collocation method must be used with caution to avoid degeneracies, for instance by optimizing the choice of basis functions and collocation points. Another option is to use a method like finite elements, considered below, which integrates behavior of an approximation over more than one sample point at a time.

16.4.3 Finite Elements

Finite element discretizations also make use of basis functions but do so by examining integrated quantities rather than pointwise values of the unknown function $u(\vec{x})$. This type of discretization is relevant to simulating a wide variety of phenomena and remains a popular choice in a diverse set of fields including mechanical engineering, digital geometry processing, and cloth simulation.

As an example, suppose that $\Omega \subseteq \mathbb{R}^2$ is a region on the plane and that we wish to solve the Dirichlet equation $\nabla^2 u = 0$ in its interior. Take any other function $v(\vec{x})$ satisfying $v(\vec{y}) = 0$ for all $\vec{y} \in \partial\Omega$. If we solve the PDE for u successfully, then the function $u(\vec{x})$ will satisfy the relationship

$$\int_\Omega v(\vec{x})\nabla^2 u(\vec{x})\, d\vec{x} = \int_\Omega v(\vec{x}) \cdot 0\, d\vec{x} = 0,$$

regardless of the choice of $v(\vec{x})$.

We can define a bilinear operator $\langle u, v \rangle_{\nabla^2}$ as the integral

$$\langle u, v \rangle_{\nabla^2} \equiv \int_\Omega v(\vec{x})\nabla^2 u(\vec{x})\, d\vec{x}.$$

Any function $u(\vec{x})$ for which $\langle u, v \rangle_{\nabla^2} = 0$ for all reasonable $v : \Omega \to \mathbb{R}$ defined above is called a *weak solution* to the Dirichlet equation. The functions v are known as *test functions*.

A remarkable observation suggests that weak solutions to PDEs may exist even when a strong solution does not. When $v(\vec{x})$ vanishes on $\partial\Omega$, the *divergence theorem* from multivariable calculus implies the following alternative form for $\langle u, v \rangle_{\nabla^2}$:

$$\langle u, v \rangle_{\nabla^2} = -\int_\Omega \nabla u(\vec{x}) \cdot \nabla v(\vec{x})\, d\vec{x}.$$

We used a similar step in Example 16.3 to derive Laplace's equation. Whereas the Laplacian ∇^2 in the Dirichlet equation requires the second derivative of u, this expression only requires u to be *once* differentiable. In other words, we have expressed a second-order PDE in first-order language. Furthermore, this form of $\langle \cdot, \cdot \rangle_{\nabla^2}$ is symmetric and negative semidefinite, in the sense that

$$\langle u, u \rangle_{\nabla^2} = -\int_\Omega \|\nabla u(\vec{x})\|_2^2\, d\vec{x} \leq 0.$$

Our definition of weak PDE solutions above is far from formal, since we were somewhat cavalier about the *space* of functions we should consider for u and v. Asking that $\langle u, v \rangle_{\nabla^2} = 0$ for all possible functions $v(\vec{x})$ is an unreasonable condition, since the space of all functions includes many degenerate functions that may not even be integrable. For the theoretical study of PDEs, it is usually sufficient to assume v is sufficiently smooth and has small support. Even with this restriction, however, the space of functions is far too large to be discretized in any reasonable way.

The *finite elements method* (FEM), however, makes the construction above tractable by restricting functions to a finite basis. Suppose we approximate u in a basis $\phi_1(\vec{x}), \ldots, \phi_k(\vec{x})$ by writing $u(\vec{x}) \approx \sum_{i=1}^{k} a_i \phi_i(\vec{x})$ for unknown coefficients $a_1, \ldots, a_k$. Since the actual solution $u(\vec{x})$ of the PDE is unlikely to be expressible in this form, we cannot expect $\langle \sum_i a_i \phi_i, v \rangle_{\nabla^2} = 0$ for all test functions $v(\vec{x})$. Hence, we not only approximate $u(\vec{x})$ but also restrict the class of test functions $v(\vec{x})$ to one in which we are more likely to be successful.

The best-known finite element approximation is the *Galerkin method*. In this method, we require that $\langle u, v \rangle_{\nabla^2} = 0$ for all test functions v that also can be written in the ϕ_i basis. By linearity of $\langle \cdot, \cdot \rangle_{\nabla^2}$, this method amounts to requiring that $\langle u, \phi_i \rangle_{\nabla^2} = 0$ for all $i \in \{1, \ldots, k\}$. Expanding this relationship shows

$$\langle u, \phi_i \rangle_{\nabla^2} = \left\langle \sum_j a_j \phi_j, \phi_i \right\rangle_{\nabla^2} \quad \text{by our approximation of } u$$

$$= \sum_j a_j \langle \phi_i, \phi_j \rangle_{\nabla^2} \text{ by linearity and symmetry of } \langle \cdot, \cdot \rangle_{\nabla^2}.$$

Using this final expression, we can recover the vector $\vec{a} \in \mathbb{R}^k$ of coefficients by solving the following linear system of equations:

$$\begin{pmatrix} \langle \phi_1, \phi_1 \rangle_{\nabla^2} & \langle \phi_1, \phi_2 \rangle_{\nabla^2} & \cdots & \langle \phi_1, \phi_k \rangle_{\nabla^2} \\ \langle \phi_2, \phi_1 \rangle_{\nabla^2} & \langle \phi_2, \phi_2 \rangle_{\nabla^2} & \cdots & \langle \phi_2, \phi_k \rangle_{\nabla^2} \\ \vdots & \vdots & \ddots & \vdots \\ \langle \phi_k, \phi_1 \rangle_{\nabla^2} & \langle \phi_k, \phi_2 \rangle_{\nabla^2} & \cdots & \langle \phi_k, \phi_k \rangle_{\nabla^2} \end{pmatrix} \vec{a} = \vec{0},$$

subject to the proper boundary conditions. For example, to impose nonzero Dirichlet boundary conditions, we can fix those values a_i corresponding to elements on the boundary $\partial \Omega$.

Approximating solutions to the Poisson equation $\nabla^2 u = w$ can be carried out in a similar fashion. If we write $w = \sum_i b_i \phi_i$, then Galerkin's method amounts to writing a slightly modified linear system of equations. The weak form of the Poisson equation has the same left-hand side but now has a nonzero right-hand side:

$$\int_\Omega v(\vec{x}) \nabla^2 u(\vec{x}) \, d\vec{x} = \int_\Omega v(\vec{x}) w(\vec{x}) \, d\vec{x},$$

for all test functions $v(\vec{x})$. To apply Galerkin's method in this case, we not only approximate $u(\vec{x}) = \sum_i a_i \phi_i(\vec{x})$ but also assume the right-hand side $w(\vec{x})$ can be written $w(\vec{x}) = \sum_i b_i \phi_i(\vec{x})$. Then, solving the weak Poisson equation in the ϕ_i basis amounts to solving:

$$\begin{pmatrix} \langle \phi_1, \phi_1 \rangle_{\nabla^2} & \langle \phi_1, \phi_2 \rangle_{\nabla^2} & \cdots & \langle \phi_1, \phi_k \rangle_{\nabla^2} \\ \langle \phi_2, \phi_1 \rangle_{\nabla^2} & \langle \phi_2, \phi_2 \rangle_{\nabla^2} & \cdots & \langle \phi_2, \phi_k \rangle_{\nabla^2} \\ \vdots & \vdots & \ddots & \vdots \\ \langle \phi_k, \phi_1 \rangle_{\nabla^2} & \langle \phi_k, \phi_2 \rangle_{\nabla^2} & \cdots & \langle \phi_k, \phi_k \rangle_{\nabla^2} \end{pmatrix} \vec{a} = \begin{pmatrix} \langle \phi_1, \phi_1 \rangle & \langle \phi_1, \phi_2 \rangle & \cdots & \langle \phi_1, \phi_k \rangle \\ \langle \phi_2, \phi_1 \rangle & \langle \phi_2, \phi_2 \rangle & \cdots & \langle \phi_2, \phi_k \rangle \\ \vdots & \vdots & \ddots & \vdots \\ \langle \phi_k, \phi_1 \rangle & \langle \phi_k, \phi_2 \rangle & \cdots & \langle \phi_k, \phi_k \rangle \end{pmatrix} \vec{b},$$

where $\langle f, g \rangle \equiv \int_\Omega f(\vec{x}) g(\vec{x}) \, d\vec{x}$, the usual inner product of functions. The matrix next to $\vec{a}$ is known as the *stiffness matrix*, and the matrix next to $\vec{b}$ is known as the *mass matrix*. This is still a linear system of equations, since $\vec{b}$ is a fixed input to the Poisson equation.

Finite element discretizations like Galerkin's method boil down to choosing appropriate spaces for approximation solutions u and test functions v. Once these spaces are chosen, the mass and stiffness matrices can be worked out offline, either in closed form or by using a quadrature method as explained in Chapter 14. These matrices are computable from the choice of basis functions. A few common choices are documented below:

- In two dimensions, the most typical use case for FEM makes use of a triangulation of the domain $\Omega \subset \mathbb{R}^2$ and takes the ϕ_i basis to be localized small neighborhoods of triangles. For example, for the Poisson equation it is sufficient to use piecewise-linear "hat" basis functions as discussed in §13.2.2 and illustrated in Figure 13.9. In this case, the mass and stiffness matrices are very sparse, because most of the basis functions ϕ_i have no overlap. Exercise 16.2 works out the details of one such approach on the plane. Volumes in $\mathbb{R}^3$ admit similar formulations with triangles replaced by tetrahedra.

- Spectral methods use bases constructed out of cosine and sine, which have the advantage of being orthogonal with respect to $\langle \cdot, \cdot \rangle$; in particularly favorable situations, this orthogonality can make the mass or stiffness matrices diagonal. Furthermore, the fast Fourier transform and related algorithms accelerate computations in this case.

- Adaptive finite element methods analyze the output of a FEM solver to identify regions of Ω in which the solution has poor quality. Additional basis functions ϕ_i are added to refine the output in those regions.

Example 16.9 (Piecewise-linear FEM). Suppose we wish to solve the Poisson equation $u''(x) = w(x)$ for $u(x)$ on the unit interval $x \in [0, 1]$ subject to Dirichlet boundary conditions $u(0) = c$ and $u(1) = d$. We will use the piecewise linear basis functions introduced in §13.1.3. Define

$$\phi(x) \equiv \begin{cases} 1 + x & \text{when } x \in [-1, 0] \\ 1 - x & \text{when } x \in [0, 1] \\ 0 & \text{otherwise.} \end{cases}$$

We define $k + 1$ basis elements using the formula $\phi_i(x) \equiv \phi(kx - i)$ for $i \in \{0, \dots, k\}$.

For convenience, we begin by computing the following integrals:

$$\int_{-1}^{1} \phi(x)^2 \, dx = \int_{-1}^{0} (1 + x)^2 \, dx + \int_{0}^{1} (1 - x)^2 \, dx = \frac{2}{3}$$

$$\int_{-1}^{1} \phi(x)\phi(x - 1) \, dx = \int_{0}^{1} x(1 - x) \, dx = \frac{1}{6}.$$

After applying change of coordinates, these integrals show

$$\langle \phi_i, \phi_j \rangle = \frac{1}{6k} \cdot \begin{cases} 4 & \text{when } i = j \\ 1 & \text{when } |i - j| = 1 \\ 0 & \text{otherwise.} \end{cases}$$

Furthermore, the derivative $\phi'(x)$ satisfies

$$\phi'(x) \equiv \begin{cases} 1 & \text{when } x \in [-1, 0] \\ -1 & \text{when } x \in [0, 1] \\ 0 & \text{otherwise.} \end{cases}$$

Hence, after change-of-variables we have

$$\langle \phi_i, \phi_j \rangle_{d^2/dx^2} = -\langle \phi_i', \phi_j' \rangle_2 = k \cdot \begin{cases} -2 & \text{when } i = j \\ 1 & \text{when } |i - j| = 1 \\ 0 & \text{otherwise.} \end{cases}$$

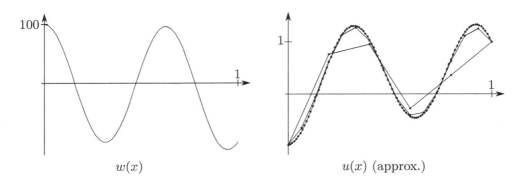

$w(x)$ $\qquad\qquad$ $u(x)$ (approx.)

Figure 16.17 Approximated piecewise linear solutions of $u''(x) = w(x)$ computed using finite elements as derived in Example 16.9; in these examples, we take $c = -1$, $d = 1$, and $k \in \{5, 15, 100\}$.

Up to the constant k, these values coincide with the divided difference second-derivative from §16.4.1.

We will apply the Galerkin method to discretize $u(x) \approx \sum_i a_i \phi_i(x)$. Assume we sample $b_i = w(i/k)$. Then, based on the integrals above, we should solve:

$$
k \begin{pmatrix}
1/k & & & & \\
1 & -2 & 1 & & \\
& 1 & -2 & 1 & \\
& & \ddots & \ddots & \ddots & \\
& & & 1 & -2 & 1 \\
& & & & & 1/k
\end{pmatrix} \vec{a} = \frac{1}{6k} \begin{pmatrix}
6k & & & & \\
1 & 4 & 1 & & \\
& 1 & 4 & 1 & \\
& & \ddots & \ddots & \ddots & \\
& & & 1 & 4 & 1 \\
& & & & & 6k
\end{pmatrix} \begin{pmatrix}
c \\
b_1 \\
\vdots \\
b_{k-1} \\
d
\end{pmatrix}.
$$

The first and last rows of this equation encode the boundary conditions, and the remaining rows come from the finite elements discretization. Figure 16.17 shows an example of this discretization in practice.

16.4.4 Finite Volumes

The *finite volume* method might be considered somewhere on the spectrum between finite elements and collocation. Like collocation, this method starts from the pointwise formulation of a PDE. Rather than asking that the PDE holds at a particular set of points in the domain Ω, however, finite volumes requires that the PDE is satisfied *on average* by integrating within the cells of a partition of Ω.

Suppose $\Gamma \subseteq \Omega$ is a region contained within the domain Ω and that we once again wish to solve the Laplace equation $\nabla^2 u = 0$. A key tool for the finite volume method is the divergence theorem, which states that the divergence of a smooth vector field $\vec{v}(x)$ can be integrated over Γ two different ways:

$$
\int_\Gamma \nabla \cdot \vec{v}(\vec{x}) \, d\vec{x} = \int_{\partial\Gamma} \vec{v}(\vec{x}) \cdot \vec{n}(\vec{x}) \, d\vec{x}.
$$

Here, $\vec{n}$ is the normal to the boundary $\partial\Gamma$. In words, the divergence theorem states that the total divergence of a vector field $\vec{v}(x)$ in the interior of Γ is the same as summing the amount of $\vec{v}$ "leaving" the boundary $\partial\Gamma$.

Suppose we solve the Poisson equation $\nabla^2 u = w$ in Ω. Integrating over Γ shows

$$\int_\Gamma w(\vec{x}) \, d\vec{x} = \int_\Gamma \nabla^2 u(\vec{x}) \, d\vec{x} \text{ since we solved the Poisson equation}$$

$$= \int_\Gamma \nabla \cdot (\nabla u(\vec{x})) \, d\vec{x} \text{ since the Laplacian is the divergence of the gradient}$$

$$= \int_{\partial\Gamma} \nabla u(\vec{x}) \cdot \vec{n}(\vec{x}) \, d\vec{x} \text{ by the divergence theorem.}$$

This final expression characterizes solutions to the Poisson equation when they are averaged over Γ.

To derive a finite-volume approximation, again write $u(\vec{x}) \approx \sum_{i=1}^{k} a_i \phi_i(\vec{x})$ and now divide Ω into k regions $\Omega = \cup_{i=1}^{k} \Omega_i$. For each Ω_i,

$$\int_{\Omega_i} w(\vec{x}) \, d\vec{x} = \int_{\partial\Omega_i} \nabla \left(\sum_{j=1}^{k} a_j \phi_j(\vec{x}) \right) \cdot \vec{n}(\vec{x}) \, d\vec{x} = \sum_{j=1}^{k} a_j \left[\int_{\partial\Omega_i} \nabla \phi_j(\vec{x}) \cdot \vec{n}(\vec{x}) \, d\vec{x} \right].$$

This is a linear system of equations for the a_i's. A typical discretization in this case might take the ϕ_i's to be piecewise-linear hat functions and the Ω_i's to be the Voronoi cells associated with the triangle centers (see §13.2.1).

16.4.5 Other Methods

Countless techniques exist for discretizing PDEs, and we have only scraped the surface of a few common methods in our discussion. Texts such as [78] are dedicated to developing the theoretical and practical aspects of these tools. Briefly, a few other notable methods for discretization include the following:

- *Domain decomposition* methods solve small versions of a PDE in different subregions of the domain Ω, iterating from one to the next until a solution to the global problem is reached. The subproblems can be made independent, in which case they are solvable via parallel processors. A single iteration of these methods can be used to approximate the global solution of a PDE to precondition iterative solvers like conjugate gradients.

- The *boundary element* and *analytic element* methods solve certain PDEs using basis functions associated with points on the boundary $\partial\Omega$, reducing dependence on a triangulation or other discretization of the interior of Ω.

- *Mesh-free methods* simulate dynamical phenomena by tracking particles rather than meshing the domain. For example, the *smoothed-particle hydrodynamics* (SPH) technique in fluid simulation approximates a fluid as a collection of particles moving in space; particles can be added where additional detail is needed, and relatively few particles can be used to get realistic effects with limited computational capacity.

- *Level set methods*, used in image processing and fluid simulation, discretize PDEs governing the evolution and construction of curves and surfaces by representing those objects as level sets $\{\vec{x} \in \mathbb{R}^n : \psi(\vec{x}) = 0\}$. Geometric changes are represented by evolution of the level set function ψ.

16.5   SOLVING PARABOLIC AND HYPERBOLIC EQUATIONS

In the previous section, we mostly dealt with the Poisson equation, which is an elliptic PDE. Parabolic and hyperbolic equations generally introduce a *time* variable into the formulation, which also is differentiated but potentially to lower order or with a different sign. Discretizing time in the same fashion as space may not make sense for a given problem, since the two play fundamentally different roles in most physical phenomena. In this section, we consider options for discretizing this variable independently of the others.

16.5.1   Semidiscrete Methods

Semidiscrete methods apply the discretizations from §16.4 to the spatial domain but not to time, leading to an ODE with a continuous time variable that can be solved using the methods of Chapter 15. This strategy is also known as the *method of lines*.

> **Example 16.10** (Semidiscrete heat equation). Consider the heat equation in one variable, given by $u_t = u_{xx}$, where $u(t; x)$ represents the heat of a wire at position $x \in [0, 1]$ and time t. As boundary data, the user provides a function $u_0(x)$ such that $u(0; x) \equiv u_0(x)$; we also attach the boundary $x \in \{0, 1\}$ to a refrigerator and enforce Dirichlet conditions $u(t; 0) = u(t; 1) = 0$.
>
> Suppose we discretize x using evenly spaced samples but leave t as a continuous variable. If we use the finite differences technique from §16.4.1, this discretization results in functions $u_0(t), u_1(t), \ldots, u_n(t)$, where $u_i(t)$ represents the heat at position i as a function of time. Take L to be the corresponding second derivative matrix in the x samples with Dirichlet conditions. Then, the semidiscrete heat equation can be written $h^2 \vec{u}'(t) = L\vec{u}(t)$, where $h = 1/n$ is the spacing between samples. This is an ODE for $\vec{u}(t)$ that could be time-stepped using backward Euler integration:
>
> $$\vec{u}(t_{k+1}) \approx \left(I_{(n+1) \times (n+1)} - \frac{1}{h}L \right)^{-1} \vec{u}(t_k).$$

The previous example is an instance of a general pattern for parabolic equations. PDEs for *diffusive* phenomena like heat moving across a domain or chemicals moving through a membrane usually have one lower-order time variable and several spatial variables that are differentiated in an elliptic way. When we discretize the spatial variables using finite differences, finite elements, or another technique, the resulting semidiscrete formulation $\vec{u}' = A\vec{u}$ usually contains a negative definite matrix A. This makes the resulting ODE unconditionally stable.

As outlined in the previous chapter, there are many choices for solving the ODE after spatial discretization. If time steps are small, explicit methods may be acceptable. Implicit solvers, however, often are applied to solving parabolic PDEs; diffusive behavior of implicit Euler agrees behaviorally with diffusion from the heat equation and may be acceptable even with fairly large time steps. Hyperbolic PDEs, on the other hand, may require implicit steps for stability, but advanced integrators can combine implicit and explicit terms to prevent oversmoothing of non-diffusive phenomena.

When A does not change with time, one contrasting approach is to write solutions of semidiscrete systems $\vec{u}' = A\vec{u}$ in terms of eigenvectors of A. Suppose $\vec{v}_1, \ldots, \vec{v}_n$ are eigenvectors of A with eigenvalues $\lambda_1, \ldots, \lambda_n$ and that $\vec{u}(0) = c_1 \vec{v}_1 + \cdots + c_n \vec{v}_n$. As we showed in §6.1.2, the solution of $\vec{u}' = A\vec{u}$ is

$$\vec{u}(t) = \sum_i c_i e^{\lambda_i t} \vec{v}_i.$$

The eigenvectors and eigenvalues of A may have physical interpretations in the case of a semidiscrete PDE. Most commonly, the eigenvalues of the Laplacian ∇^2 on a domain Ω correspond to resonant frequencies of a domain, that is, the frequencies that sound when hitting the domain with a hammer. The eigenvectors provide closed-form "low-frequency approximations" of solutions to common PDEs after truncating the sum above.

16.5.2 Fully Discrete Methods

Rather than discretizing time and then space, we might treat the space and time variables more democratically and discretize them both simultaneously. This one-shot discretization is in some sense a more direct application of the methods we considered in §16.4, just by including t as a dimension in the domain Ω under consideration. Because we now multiply the number of variables needed to represent Ω by the number of time steps, the resulting linear systems of equations can be large if dependence between time steps has global reach.

Example 16.11 (Fully discrete heat diffusion, [58]). Consider the heat equation $u_t = u_{xx}$. Discretizing x and t simultaneously via finite differences yields a matrix of u values, which we can index as u_i^j, representing the heat at position i and time j. Take Δx and Δt to be the spacing of x and t in the grid, respectively. Choosing where to evaluate the different derivatives leads to different discretization schemes stepping from time j to time $j + 1$.

For example, evaluating the x derivative at time j produces an *explicit* formula:

$$\frac{u_i^{j+1} - u_i^j}{\Delta t} = \frac{u_{i+1}^j - 2u_i^j + u_{i-1}^j}{(\Delta x)^2}.$$

Isolating u_i^{j+1} gives a formula for obtaining u at time $j + 1$ without a linear solve.

Alternatively, we can evaluate the x derivative at time $j + 1$ for an *implicit* integrator:

$$\frac{u_i^{j+1} - u_i^j}{\Delta t} = \frac{u_{i+1}^{j+1} - 2u_i^{j+1} + u_{i-1}^{j+1}}{(\Delta x)^2}.$$

This integrator is unconditionally stable but requires a linear solve to obtain the u values at time $j + 1$ from those at time j.

These implicit and explicit integrators inherit their accuracy from the quality of the finite difference formulas, and hence—stability aside—both are first-order accurate in time and second-order accurate in space. To improve the accuracy of the time discretization, we can use the *Crank-Nicolson* method, which applies a trapezoidal time integrator:

$$\frac{u_i^{j+1} - u_i^j}{\Delta t} = \frac{1}{2}\left[\frac{u_{i+1}^j - 2u_i^j + u_{i-1}^j}{(\Delta x)^2} + \frac{u_{i+1}^{j+1} - 2u_i^{j+1} + u_{i-1}^{j+1}}{(\Delta x)^2}\right].$$

This method inherits the unconditional stability of trapezoidal integration and is second-order accurate in time and space. Despite this stability, however, as explained in §15.3.3, taking time steps that are too large can produce unrealistic oscillatory behavior.

In the end, even semidiscrete methods can be considered fully discrete in that the time-stepping ODE method still discretizes the t variable; the difference between semidiscrete and fully discrete is mostly for classification of how methods were derived. One advantage of semidiscrete techniques, however, is that they can adjust the time step for t depending on the current iterate, e.g., if objects are moving quickly in a physical simulation, it might make sense to take more dense time steps and resolve this motion. Some methods also adjust the discretization of the domain of x values in case more resolution is needed near local discontinuities such as shock waves.

16.6 NUMERICAL CONSIDERATIONS

We have considered several options for discretizing PDEs. As with choosing time integrators for ODEs, the trade-offs between these options are intricate, representing different compromises between computational efficiency, numerical quality, stability, and so on. We conclude our treatment of numerical methods for PDE by outlining a few considerations when choosing a PDE discretization.

16.6.1 Consistency, Convergence, and Stability

A key consideration when choosing ODE integrators was *stability*, which guaranteed that errors in specifying initial conditions would not be amplified over time. Stability remains a consideration in PDE integration, but it also can interact with other key properties:

- A method is *convergent* if solutions to the discretized problem converge to the theoretical solution of the PDE as spacing between discrete samples approaches zero.

- A method is *consistent* if the accompanying discretization of the differential operators better approximates the derivatives taken in the PDE as spacing approaches zero.

For finite differencing schemes, the Lax-Richtmyer Equivalence Theorem states that if a linear problem is well-posed, *consistency* and *stability* together are necessary and sufficient for *convergence* [79]. Consistency and stability tend to be easier to check than convergence. Consistency arguments usually come from Taylor series. A number of well-established methods establish stability or lack thereof; for example, the well-known *CFL condition* states that the ratio of time spacing to spatial spacing of samples should exceed the speed at which waves propagate in the case of hyperbolic PDE [29]. Even more caution must be taken when simulating advective phenomena and PDEs that can develop fronts and shocks; specialized *upwinding* schemes attempt to detect the formation of these features to ensure that they move in the right direction and at the proper speed.

Even when a time variable is not involved, some care must be taken to ensure that a PDE approximation scheme reduces error as sampling becomes more dense. For example, in elliptic PDE, convergence of finite elements methods depends on the choice of basis functions, which must be sufficiently smooth to represent the theoretical solution and must span the function space in the limit [16].

The subtleties of consistency, convergence, and stability underlie the theory of numerical PDE, and the importance of these concepts cannot be overstated. Without convergence guarantees, the output of a numerical PDE solver cannot be trusted. Standard PDE integration packages often incorporate checks for assorted stability conditions or degenerate behavior to guide clients whose expertise is in modeling rather than numerics.

16.6.2 Linear Solvers for PDE

The matrices resulting from PDE discretizations have many favorable properties that make them ideal inputs for the methods we have considered in previous chapters. For instance, as motivated in §16.3.1, elliptic PDEs are closely related to positive definite matrices, and typical discretizations require solution of a positive definite linear system. The same derivative operators appear in parabolic PDEs, which hence have well-posed semidiscretizations. For this reason, methods like Cholesky decomposition and conjugate gradients can be applied to these problems. Furthermore, derivative matrices tend to be sparse, inducing additional memory and time savings. Any reasonable implementation of a PDE solver should include these sorts of optimizations, which make them scalable to large problems.

Example 16.12 (Elliptic operators as matrices). Consider the one-dimensional second derivative matrix L with Dirichlet boundary conditions from §16.4.1. L is sparse and negative definite. To show the latter property, we can write $L = -D^\top D$ for the matrix $D \in \mathbb{R}^{(n+1) \times n}$ given by

$$
D = \begin{pmatrix}
1 & & & & \\
-1 & 1 & & & \\
& -1 & 1 & & \\
& & \ddots & \ddots & \\
& & & -1 & 1 \\
& & & & -1
\end{pmatrix}.
$$

This matrix is a finite-differenced *first* derivative, so this observation parallels the fact that $d^2 y/dx^2 = d/dx(dy/dx)$. For any $\vec{x} \in \mathbb{R}^n$, $\vec{x}^\top L \vec{x} = -\vec{x}^\top D^\top D \vec{x} = -\|D\vec{x}\|_2^2 \le 0$, showing L is negative semidefinite. Furthermore, $D\vec{x} = 0$ only when $\vec{x} = 0$, completing the proof that L is negative definite.

Example 16.13 (Stiffness matrix is positive semidefinite). Regardless of the basis $\phi_1, \ldots, \phi_k$, the stiffness matrix from discretizing the Poisson equation via finite elements (see §16.4.3) is negative semidefinite. Taking M_{∇^2} to be the stiffness matrix and $\vec{a} \in \mathbb{R}^k$,

$$
\vec{a}^\top M_{\nabla^2} \vec{a} = \sum_{ij} a_i a_j \langle \phi_i, \phi_j \rangle_{\nabla^2} \text{ by definition of } M_{\nabla^2}
$$

$$
= \left\langle \sum_i a_i \phi_i, \sum_j a_j \phi_j \right\rangle_{\nabla^2} \text{ by bilinearity of } \langle \cdot, \cdot \rangle_{\nabla^2}
$$

$$
= \langle \psi, \psi \rangle_{\nabla^2} \text{ if we define } \psi \equiv \sum_i a_i \phi_i
$$

$$
= -\int_\Omega \|\nabla \psi(\vec{x})\|_2^2 \, d\vec{x} \text{ by definition of } \langle \cdot, \cdot \rangle_{\nabla^2}
$$

$$
\le 0 \text{ since the integrand is nonnegative.}
$$

16.7 EXERCISES

16.1 ("Shooting method," [58]) The *two-point boundary value problem* inherits some structure from ODE and PDE problems alike. In this problem, we wish to solve the ODE $\vec{y}' = F[\vec{y}]$ for a function $\vec{y}(t) : [0, 1] \to \mathbb{R}^n$. Rather than specifying initial conditions, however, we specify some relationship $g(\vec{y}(0), \vec{y}(1)) = \vec{0}$.

(a) Give an example of a two-point boundary value problem that does not admit a solution.

(b) Assume we have checked the conditions of an existence/uniqueness theorem, so given $\vec{y}_0 = \vec{y}(0)$ we can generate $\vec{y}(t)$ for all $t > 0$ satisfying $\vec{y}'(t) = F[\vec{y}(t)]$.

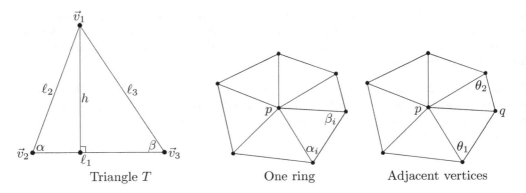

Figure 16.18 Notation for Exercise 16.2.

Denote $\vec{y}(t; \vec{y}_0) : \mathbb{R}^+ \times \mathbb{R}^n \to \mathbb{R}$ as the function returning $\vec{y}$ at time t given $\vec{y}(0) = \vec{y}_0$. In this notation, pose the two-point boundary value problem as a root-finding problem.

(c) Use the ODE integration methods from Chapter 15 to propose a computationally feasible root-finding problem for approximating a solution $\vec{y}(t)$ of the two-point boundary value problem.

(d) As discussed in Chapter 8, most root-finding algorithms require the Jacobian of the objective function. Suggest a technique for finding the Jacobian of your objective from Exercise 16.1c.

16.2 In this problem, we use first-order finite elements to derive the famous *cotangent Laplacian* formula used in geometry processing. Refer to Figure 16.18 for notation.

(a) Suppose we construct a planar triangle T with vertices $\vec{v}_1, \vec{v}_2, \vec{v}_3 \in \mathbb{R}^2$ in counterclockwise order. Take $f_1(\vec{x})$ to be the affine *hat function* $f_1(\vec{x}) \equiv c + \vec{d} \cdot \vec{x}$ satisfying $f_1(\vec{v}_1) = 1$, $f_1(\vec{v}_2) = 0$, and $f_1(\vec{v}_3) = 0$. Show that ∇f_1 is a constant vector satisfying:

$$\nabla f_1 \cdot (\vec{v}_1 - \vec{v}_2) = 1$$
$$\nabla f_1 \cdot (\vec{v}_1 - \vec{v}_3) = 1$$
$$\nabla f_1 \cdot (\vec{v}_2 - \vec{v}_3) = 0.$$

The third relationship shows that ∇f_1 is perpendicular to the edge from $\vec{v}_2$ to $\vec{v}_3$.

(b) Show that $\|\nabla f_1\|_2 = \frac{1}{h}$, where h is the height of the triangle as marked in Figure 16.18 (left).
Hint: Start by showing $\nabla f_1 \cdot (\vec{v}_1 - \vec{v}_3) = \|\nabla f_1\|_2 \ell_3 \cos\left(\frac{\pi}{2} - \beta\right)$.

(c) Integrate over the triangle T to show

$$\int_T \|\nabla f_1\|_2^2 \, dA = \frac{1}{2}(\cot \alpha + \cot \beta).$$

Hint: Since ∇f_1 is a constant vector, the integral equals $\|\nabla f_1\|_2^2 A$, where A is the area of T. From basic geometry, $A = \frac{1}{2}\ell_1 h$.

(d) Define $\theta \equiv \pi - \alpha - \beta$, and take f_2 and f_3 to be the hat functions associated with $\vec{v}_2$ and $\vec{v}_3$, respectively. Show that

$$\int_T \nabla f_2 \cdot \nabla f_3 \, dA = -\frac{1}{2} \cot \theta.$$

(e) Now, consider a vertex p of a triangle mesh (Figure 16.18, middle), and define $f_p : \mathbb{R}^2 \to [0, 1]$ to be the *piecewise linear hat function* associated with p (see §13.2.2 and Figure 13.9). That is, restricted to any triangle adjacent to p, the function f_p behaves as constructed in Exercise 16.2a; $f_p \equiv 0$ outside the triangles adjacent to p. Based on the results you already have constructed, show:

$$\int_{\mathbb{R}^2} \|\nabla f_p\|_2^2 \, dA = \frac{1}{2} \sum_i (\cot \alpha_i + \cot \beta_i),$$

where $\{\alpha_i\}$ and $\{\beta_i\}$ are the angles opposite p in its neighboring triangles.

(f) Suppose p and q are adjacent vertices on the same mesh, and define θ_1 and θ_2 as shown in Figure 16.18 (right). Show

$$\int_{\mathbb{R}^2} \nabla f_p \cdot \nabla f_q \, dA = -\frac{1}{2} (\cot \theta_1 + \cot \theta_2).$$

(g) Conclude that in the basis of hat functions on a triangle mesh, the stiffness matrix for the Poisson equation has the following form:

$$L_{ij} \equiv -\frac{1}{2} \begin{cases} \sum_{i \sim j} (\cot \alpha_j + \cot \beta_j) & \text{if } i = j \\ -(\cot \alpha_j + \cot \beta_j) & \text{if } i \sim j \\ 0 & \text{otherwise.} \end{cases}$$

Here, $i \sim j$ denotes that vertices i and j are adjacent.

(h) Write a formula for the entries of the corresponding mass matrix, whose entries are

$$\int_{\mathbb{R}^2} f_p f_q \, dA.$$

Hint: This matrix can be written completely in terms of triangle areas. Divide into cases: (1) $p = q$, (2) p and q are adjacent vertices, and (3) p and q are not adjacent.

16.3 Suppose we wish to approximate Laplacian eigenfunctions $f(\vec{x})$, satisfying $\nabla^2 f = \lambda f$. Show that discretizing such a problem using FEM results in a generalized eigenvalue problem $A\vec{x} = \lambda B\vec{x}$.

16.4 Propose a semidiscrete form for the one-dimensional wave equation $u_{tt} = u_{xx}$, similar to the construction in Example 16.10. Is the resulting ODE well-posed (§15.2.3)?

16.5 *Graph-based semi-supervised learning* algorithms attempt to predict a quantity or label associated with the nodes of a graph given labels on a few of its vertices. For instance, under the (dubious) assumption that friends are likely to have similar incomes, it could be used to predict the annual incomes of all members of a social network given the incomes of a few of its members. We will focus on a variation of the method proposed in [132].

(a) Take $G = (V, E)$ to be a connected graph, and define $f_0 : V_0 \to \mathbb{R}$ to be a set of scalar-valued labels associated with the nodes of a subset $V_0 \subseteq V$. The *Dirichlet energy* of a full assignment of labels $f : V \to \mathbb{R}$ is given by

$$E[f] \equiv \sum_{(v_1, v_2) \in E} (f(v_2) - f(v_1))^2.$$

Explain why $E[f]$ can be minimized over f satisfying $f(v_0) = f_0(v_0)$ for all $v_0 \in V_0$ using a linear solve.

(b) Explain the connection between the linear system from Exercise 16.5a and the 3×3 Laplacian stencil from §16.4.1.

(c) Suppose f is the result of the optimization from Exercise 16.5a. Prove the *discrete maximum principle*:

$$\max_{v \in V} f(v) = \max_{v_0 \in V_0} f_0(v_0).$$

Relate this result to a physical interpretation of Laplace's equation.

16.6 Give an example where discretization of the Poisson equation via finite differences and via collocation lead to the same system of equations.

16.7 ("Von Neumann stability analysis," based on notes by D. Levy) Suppose we wish to approximate solutions to the PDE $u_t = au_x$ for some fixed $a \in \mathbb{R}$. We will use initial conditions $u(x, 0) = f(x)$ for some $f \in C^\infty([0, 2\pi])$ and periodic boundary conditions $u(0, t) = u(2\pi, t)$.

(a) What is the order of this PDE? Give conditions on a for it to be elliptic, hyperbolic, or parabolic.

(b) Show that the PDE is solved by $u(x, t) = f(x + at)$.

(c) The Fourier transform of $u(x, t)$ in x is

$$[\mathcal{F}_x u](\omega, t) \equiv \frac{1}{\sqrt{2\pi}} \int_0^{2\pi} u(x, t) e^{-i\omega x} \, dx,$$

where $i = \sqrt{-1}$ (see Exercise 4.15). It measures the frequency content of $u(\cdot, t)$. Define $v(x, t) \equiv u(x + \Delta x, t)$. If u satisfies the stated boundary conditions, show that $[\mathcal{F}_x v](\omega, t) = e^{i\omega \Delta x} [\mathcal{F}_x u](\omega, t)$.

(d) Suppose we use a forward Euler discretization:

$$\frac{u(x, t + \Delta t) - u(x, t)}{\Delta t} = a \frac{u(x + \Delta x, t) - u(x - \Delta x, t)}{2\Delta x}.$$

Show that this discretization satisfies

$$[\mathcal{F}_x u](\omega, t + \Delta t) = \left(1 + \frac{ai\Delta t}{\Delta x} \sin(\omega \Delta x)\right) [\mathcal{F}_x u](\omega, t).$$

(e) Define the *amplification factor*

$$\hat{Q} \equiv 1 + \frac{ai\Delta t}{\Delta x} \sin(\omega \Delta x).$$

Show that $|\hat{Q}| > 1$ for almost any choice of ω. This shows that the discretization amplifies frequency content over time and is *unconditionally unstable*.

(f) Carry out a similar analysis for the alternative discretization

$$u(x, t+\Delta t) = \frac{1}{2} \left(u(x - \Delta x, t) + u(x + \Delta x, t) \right) + \frac{a\Delta t}{2\Delta x} \left[u(x + \Delta x, t) - u(x - \Delta x, t) \right].$$

Derive an upper bound on the ratio $\Delta t / \Delta x$ for this discretization to be stable.

16.8 ("Fast marching," [19]) Nonlinear PDEs require specialized treatment. One nonlinear PDE relevant to computer graphics and medical imaging is the eikonal equation $\|\nabla d\|_2 = 1$ considered in §16.5. Here, we outline some aspects of the *fast marching* method for solving this equation on a triangulated domain $\Omega \subset \mathbb{R}^2$ (see Figure 13.9).

   (a) We might approximate solutions of the eikonal equation as shortest-path distances along the edges of the triangulation. Provide a way to triangulate the unit square $[0, 1] \times [0, 1]$ with arbitrarily small triangle edge lengths and areas for which this approximation gives distance 2 rather than $\sqrt{2}$ from $(0, 0)$ to $(1, 1)$. Hence, can the edge-based approximation be considered convergent?

   (b) Suppose we approximate $d(\vec{x})$ with a linear function $d(\vec{x}) \approx \vec{n}^\top \vec{x} + p$, where $\|\vec{n}\|_2 = 1$ by the eikonal equation. Given $d_1 = d(\vec{x}_1)$ and $d_2 = d(\vec{x}_2)$, show that p can be recovered by solving a quadratic equation and provide a geometric interpretation of the two roots. You can assume that $\vec{x}_1$ and $\vec{x}_2$ are linearly independent.

   (c) What geometric assumption does the approximation in Exercise 16.8b make about the shape of the level sets $\{\vec{x} \in \mathbb{R}^2 : d(\vec{x}) = c\}$? Does this approximation make sense when d is large or small? See [91] for a contrasting circular approximation.

   (d) Extend Dijkstra's algorithm for graph-based shortest paths to triangulated shapes using the approximation in Exercise 16.8b. What can go wrong with this approach?
   Hint: Dijkstra's algorithm starts at the center vertex and builds the shortest path in breadth-first fashion. Change the update to use Exercise 16.8b, and consider when the approximation will make distances decrease unnaturally.

16.9 Constructing *higher-order elements* can be necessary for solving certain differential equations.

   (a) Show that the parameters $a_0, \ldots, a_5$ of a function $f(x, y) = a_0 + a_1 x + a_2 y + a_3 x^2 + a_4 y^2 + a_5 xy$ are uniquely determined by its values on the three vertices and three edge midpoints of a triangle.

   (b) Show that if (x, y) is on an edge of the triangle, then $f(x, y)$ can be computed knowing only the values of f at the endpoints and midpoint of that edge.

   (c) Use these facts to construct a basis of continuous, piecewise-quadratic functions on a triangle mesh, and explain why it may be useful for solving higher-order PDEs.

16.10 For matrices $A, B \in \mathbb{R}^{n \times n}$, the Lie-Trotter-Kato formula states

$$e^{A+B} = \lim_{n \to \infty} (e^{A/n} e^{B/n})^n,$$

where e^M denotes the matrix exponential of $M \in \mathbb{R}^{n \times n}$ (see §15.3.5).

Suppose we wish to solve a PDE $u_t = \mathcal{L}u$, where $\mathcal{L}$ is some differential operator that admits a *splitting* $\mathcal{L} = \mathcal{L}_1 + \mathcal{L}_2$. How can the Lie-Trotter-Kato formula be applied to designing PDE time-stepping machinery in this case?

Note: Such splittings are useful for breaking up integrators for complex PDEs like the Navier-Stokes equations into simpler steps.

Bibliography

[1] S. Ahn, U. J. Choi, and A. G. Ramm. A scheme for stable numerical differentiation. *Journal of Computational and Applied Mathematics*, 186(2):325–334, 2006.

[2] E. Anderson, Z. Bai, and J. Dongarra. Generalized QR factorization and its applications. *Linear Algebra and Its Applications*, 162–164(0):243–271, 1992.

[3] D. Arthur and S. Vassilvitskii. K-means++: The advantages of careful seeding. In *Proceedings of the Symposium on Discrete Algorithms*, pages 1027–1035. Society for Industrial and Applied Mathematics, 2007.

[4] S. Axler. Down with determinants! *American Mathematical Monthly*, 102:139–154, 1995.

[5] D. Baraff, A. Witkin, and M. Kass. Untangling cloth. *ACM Transactions on Graphics*, 22(3):862–870, July 2003.

[6] J. Barbič and Y. Zhao. Real-time large-deformation substructuring. *ACM Transactions on Graphics*, 30(4):91:1–91:8, July 2011.

[7] R. Barrett, M. Berry, T. Chan, J. Demmel, J. Donato, J. Dongarra, V. Eijkhout, R. Pozo, C. Romine, and H. van der Vorst. *Templates for the Solution of Linear Systems: Building Blocks for Iterative Methods*. Society for Industrial and Applied Mathematics, 1994.

[8] M. Bartholomew-Biggs, S. Brown, B. Christianson, and L. Dixon. Automatic differentiation of algorithms. *Journal of Computational and Applied Mathematics*, 124(12):171–190, 2000.

[9] H. Bauschke and J. Borwein. On projection algorithms for solving convex feasibility problems. *SIAM Review*, 38(3):367–426, 1996.

[10] H. H. Bauschke and Y. Lucet. What is a Fenchel conjugate? *Notices of the American Mathematical Society*, 59(1), 2012.

[11] A. Beck and M. Teboulle. A fast iterative shrinkage-thresholding algorithm for linear inverse problems. *SIAM Journal on Imaging Sciences*, 2(1):183–202, Mar. 2009.

[12] J.-P. Berrut and L. Trefethen. Barycentric Lagrange interpolation. *SIAM Review*, 46(3):501–517, 2004.

[13] C. Bishop. *Pattern Recognition and Machine Learning*. Information Science and Statistics. Springer, 2006.

[14] S. Boyd, N. Parikh, E. Chu, B. Peleato, and J. Eckstein. Distributed optimization and statistical learning via the alternating direction method of multipliers. *Foundations and Trends in Machine Learning*, 3(1):1–122, Jan. 2011.

[15] S. Boyd and L. Vandenberghe. *Convex Optimization*. Cambridge University Press, 2004.

[16] S. Brenner and R. Scott. *The Mathematical Theory of Finite Element Methods*. Texts in Applied Mathematics. Springer, 2008.

[17] R. Brent. *Algorithms for Minimization without Derivatives*. Dover Books on Mathematics. Dover, 2013.

[18] J. E. Bresenham. Algorithm for computer control of a digital plotter. *IBM Systems Journal*, 4(1):25–30, 1965.

[19] A. Bronstein, M. Bronstein, and R. Kimmel. *Numerical Geometry of Non-Rigid Shapes*. Monographs in Computer Science. Springer, 2008.

[20] S. Bubeck. Theory of convex optimization for machine learning. *arXiv preprint arXiv:1405.4980*, 2014.

[21] C. Budd. Advanced numerical methods (MA50174): Assignment 3, initial value ordinary differential equations. University Lecture, 2006.

[22] R. Burden and J. Faires. *Numerical Analysis*. Cengage Learning, 2010.

[23] W. Cheney and A. A. Goldstein. Proximity maps for convex sets. *Proceedings of the American Mathematical Society*, 10(3):448–450, 1959.

[24] M. Chuang and M. Kazhdan. Interactive and anisotropic geometry processing using the screened Poisson equation. *ACM Transactions on Graphics*, 30(4):57:1–57:10, July 2011.

[25] C. Clenshaw and A. Curtis. A method for numerical integration on an automatic computer. *Numerische Mathematik*, 2(1):197–205, 1960.

[26] A. Colorni, M. Dorigo, and V. Maniezzo. Distributed optimization by ant colonies. In *Proceedings of the European Conference on Artificial Life*, pages 134–142, 1991.

[27] D. Comaniciu and P. Meer. Mean shift: A robust approach toward feature space analysis. *Transactions on Pattern Analysis and Machine Intelligence*, 24(5):603–619, May 2002.

[28] P. G. Constantine and D. F. Gleich. Tall and skinny QR factorizations in MapReduce architectures. In *Proceedings of the Second International Workshop on MapReduce and Its Applications*, pages 43–50. ACM, 2011.

[29] R. Courant, K. Friedrichs, and H. Lewy. Über die partiellen differenzengleichungen der mathematischen physik. *Mathematische Annalen*, 100(1):32–74, 1928.

[30] Y. H. Dai and Y. Yuan. A nonlinear conjugate gradient method with a strong global convergence property. *SIAM Journal on Optimization*, 10(1):177–182, May 1999.

[31] I. Daubechies, R. DeVore, M. Fornasier, and C. S. Güntürk. Iteratively reweighted least squares minimization for sparse recovery. *Communications on Pure and Applied Mathematics*, 63(1):1–38, 2010.

[32] T. Davis. *Direct Methods for Sparse Linear Systems*. Fundamentals of Algorithms. Society for Industrial and Applied Mathematics, 2006.

[33] M. de Berg. *Computational Geometry: Algorithms and Applications*. Springer, 2000.

[34] J. Duchi, E. Hazan, and Y. Singer. Adaptive subgradient methods for online learning and stochastic optimization. *Journal of Machine Learning Research*, 12:2121–2159, July 2011.

[35] S. T. Dumais. Latent semantic analysis. *Annual Review of Information Science and Technology*, 38(1):188–230, 2004.

[36] R. Eberhart and J. Kennedy. A new optimizer using particle swarm theory. In *Micro Machine and Human Science*, pages 39–43, Oct 1995.

[37] M. Elad. *Sparse and Redundant Representations: From Theory to Applications in Signal and Image Processing*. Springer, 2010.

[38] M. A. Epelman. Continuous optimization methods (IOE 511): Rate of convergence of the steepest descent algorithm. University Lecture, 2007.

[39] E. Fehlberg. *Low-order classical Runge-Kutta formulas with stepsize control and their application to some heat transfer problems*. NASA technical report. National Aeronautics and Space Administration, 1969.

[40] R. Fletcher. Conjugate gradient methods for indefinite systems. In G. A. Watson, editor, *Numerical Analysis*, volume 506 of *Lecture Notes in Mathematics*, pages 73–89. Springer, 1976.

[41] R. Fletcher and C. M. Reeves. Function minimization by conjugate gradients. *The Computer Journal*, 7(2):149–154, 1964.

[42] D. C.-L. Fong and M. Saunders. LSMR: An iterative algorithm for sparse least-squares problems. *SIAM Journal on Scientific Computing*, 33(5):2950–2971, Oct. 2011.

[43] M. Frank and P. Wolfe. An algorithm for quadratic programming. *Naval Research Logistics Quarterly*, 3(1–2):95–110, 1956.

[44] R. W. Freund and N. M. Nachtigal. QMR: A quasi-minimal residual method for non-Hermitian linear systems. *Numerische Mathematik*, 60(1):315–339, 1991.

[45] C. Führer. Numerical methods in mechanics (FMN 081): Homotopy method. University Lecture, 2006.

[46] M. Géradin and D. Rixen. *Mechanical Vibrations: Theory and Application to Structural Dynamics*. Wiley, 1997.

[47] T. Gerstner and M. Griebel. Numerical integration using sparse grids. *Numerical Algorithms*, 18(3–4):209–232, 1998.

[48] W. Givens. Computation of plane unitary rotations transforming a general matrix to triangular form. *Journal of the Society for Industrial and Applied Mathematics*, 6(1):26–50, 1958.

[49] D. Goldberg. What every computer scientist should know about floating-point arithmetic. *ACM Computing Surveys*, 23(1):5–48, Mar. 1991.

[50] G. Golub and C. Van Loan. *Matrix Computations*. Johns Hopkins Studies in the Mathematical Sciences. Johns Hopkins University Press, 2012.

[51] M. Grant and S. Boyd. CVX: MATLAB software for disciplined convex programming, version 2.1.

[52] M. Grant and S. Boyd. Graph implementations for nonsmooth convex programs. In V. Blondel, S. Boyd, and H. Kimura, editors, *Recent Advances in Learning and Control*, Lecture Notes in Control and Information Sciences, pages 95–110. Springer, 2008.

[53] E. Grinspun and M. Wardetzky. Discrete differential geometry: An applied introduction. In *SIGGRAPH Asia Courses*, 2008.

[54] C. W. Groetsch. Lanczos' generalized derivative. *American Mathematical Monthly*, 105(4):320–326, 1998.

[55] L. Guibas, D. Salesin, and J. Stolfi. Epsilon geometry: Building robust algorithms from imprecise computations. In *Proceedings of the Fifth Annual Symposium on Computational Geometry*, pages 208–217. ACM, 1989.

[56] W. Hackbusch. *Iterative Solution of Large Sparse Systems of Equations*. Applied Mathematical Sciences. Springer, 1993.

[57] G. Hairer. *Solving Ordinary Differential Equations II: Stiff and Differential-Algebraic Problems*. Springer, 2010.

[58] M. Heath. *Scientific Computing: An Introductory Survey*. McGraw-Hill, 2005.

[59] M. R. Hestenes and E. Stiefel. Methods of conjugate gradients for solving linear systems. *Journal of Research of the National Bureau of Standards*, 49(6):409–436, Dec. 1952.

[60] D. J. Higham and L. N. Trefethen. Stiffness of ODEs. *BIT Numerical Mathematics*, 33(2):285–303, 1993.

[61] N. Higham. Computing the polar decomposition with applications. *SIAM Journal on Scientific and Statistical Computing*, 7(4):1160–1174, Oct. 1986.

[62] N. Higham. *Accuracy and Stability of Numerical Algorithms*. Society for Industrial and Applied Mathematics, 2 edition, 2002.

[63] G. E. Hinton. Training products of experts by minimizing contrastive divergence. *Neural Computation*, 14(8):1771–1800, Aug. 2002.

[64] M. Hirsch, S. Smale, and R. Devaney. *Differential Equations, Dynamical Systems, and an Introduction to Chaos*. Academic Press, 3rd edition, 2012.

[65] A. S. Householder. Unitary triangularization of a nonsymmetric matrix. *Journal of the ACM*, 5(4):339–342, Oct. 1958.

[66] M. Jaggi. Revisiting Frank-Wolfe: Projection-free sparse convex optimization. *Journal of Machine Learning Research: Proceedings of the International Conference on Machine Learning*, 28(1):427–435, 2013.

[67] D. L. James and C. D. Twigg. Skinning mesh animations. *ACM Transactions on Graphics*, 24(3):399–407, July 2005.

[68] F. John. The ultrahyperbolic differential equation with four independent variables. *Duke Mathematical Journal*, 4(2):300–322, 6 1938.

[69] W. Kahan. Pracniques: Further remarks on reducing truncation errors. *Communications of the ACM*, 8(1):47–48, Jan. 1965.

[70] J. T. Kajiya. The rendering equation. In *Proceedings of SIGGRAPH*, volume 20, pages 143–150, 1986.

[71] Q. Ke and T. Kanade. Robust L_1 norm factorization in the presence of outliers and missing data by alternative convex programming. In *Proceedings of the 2005 IEEE Computer Society Conference on Computer Vision and Pattern Recognition*, pages 739–746. IEEE, 2005.

[72] J. Kennedy and R. Eberhart. Particle swarm optimization. In *Proceedings of the International Conference on Neural Networks*, volume 4, pages 1942–1948. IEEE, 1995.

[73] S. Kirkpatrick, C. D. Gelatt, and M. P. Vecchi. Optimization by simulated annealing. *Science*, 220(4598):671–680, 1983.

[74] K. Kiwiel. *Methods of Descent for Nondifferentiable Optimization*. Lecture Notes in Mathematics. Springer, 1985.

[75] A. Knyazev. A preconditioned conjugate gradient method for eigenvalue problems and its implementation in a subspace. In *Numerical Treatment of Eigenvalue Problems*, volume 5, pages 143–154. Springer, 1991.

[76] A. Knyazev. Toward the optimal preconditioned eigensolver: Locally optimal block preconditioned conjugate gradient method. *SIAM Journal on Scientific Computing*, 23(2):517–541, 2001.

[77] C. Lanczos. *Applied Analysis*. Dover Books on Mathematics. Dover Publications, 1988.

[78] S. Larsson and V. Thomée. *Partial Differential Equations with Numerical Methods*. Texts in Applied Mathematics. Springer, 2008.

[79] P. D. Lax and R. D. Richtmyer. Survey of the stability of linear finite difference equations. *Communications on Pure and Applied Mathematics*, 9(2):267–293, 1956.

[80] R. B. Lehoucq and D. C. Sorensen. Deflation techniques for an implicitly restarted Arnoldi iteration. *SIAM Journal on Matrix Analysis and Applications*, 17(4):789–821, Oct. 1996.

[81] M. Leordeanu and M. Hebert. Smoothing-based optimization. In *Proceedings of the Conference on Computer Vision and Pattern Recognition*. IEEE, June 2008.

[82] K. Levenberg. A method for the solution of certain non-linear problems in least-squares. *Quarterly of Applied Mathematics*, 2(2):164–168, July 1944.

[83] M. S. Lobo, L. Vandenberghe, S. Boyd, and H. Lebret. Applications of second-order cone programming. *Linear Algebra and Its Applications*, 284(13):193–228, 1998.

[84] D. Luenberger and Y. Ye. *Linear and Nonlinear Programming*. International Series in Operations Research & Management Science. Springer, 2008.

[85] D. W. Marquardt. An algorithm for least-squares estimation of nonlinear parameters. *Journal of the Society for Industrial and Applied Mathematics*, 11(2):431–441, 1963.

[86] J. McCann and N. S. Pollard. Real-time gradient-domain painting. *ACM Transactions on Graphics*, 27(3):93:1–93:7, Aug. 2008.

[87] M. Mitchell. *An Introduction to Genetic Algorithms*. MIT Press, 1998.

[88] Y. Nesterov and I. Nesterov. *Introductory Lectures on Convex Optimization: A Basic Course*. Applied Optimization. Springer, 2004.

[89] J. Niesen and W. M. Wright. Algorithm 919: A Krylov subspace algorithm for evaluating the φ-functions appearing in exponential integrators. *ACM Transactions on Mathematical Software*, 38(3):22:1–22:19, Apr. 2012.

[90] J. Nocedal and S. Wright. *Numerical Optimization*. Series in Operations Research and Financial Engineering. Springer, 2006.

[91] M. Novotni and R. Klein. Computing geodesic distances on triangular meshes. *Journal of the Winter School of Computer Graphics (WSCG)*, 11(1–3):341–347, Feb. 2002.

[92] J. M. Ortega and H. F. Kaiser. The LLT and QR methods for symmetric tridiagonal matrices. *The Computer Journal*, 6(1):99–101, 1963.

[93] C. Paige and M. Saunders. Solution of sparse indefinite systems of linear equations. *SIAM Journal on Numerical Analysis*, 12(4):617–629, 1975.

[94] C. C. Paige and M. A. Saunders. LSQR: An algorithm for sparse linear equations and sparse least squares. *ACM Transactions on Mathematical Software*, 8(1):43–71, Mar. 1982.

[95] T. Papadopoulo and M. I. A. Lourakis. Estimating the Jacobian of the singular value decomposition: Theory and applications. In *Proceedings of the European Conference on Computer Vision*, pages 554–570. Springer, 2000.

[96] S. Paris, P. Kornprobst, and J. Tumblin. *Bilateral Filtering: Theory and Applications*. Foundations and Trends in Computer Graphics and Vision. Now Publishers, 2009.

[97] S. Paris, P. Kornprobst, J. Tumblin, and F. Durand. A gentle introduction to bilateral filtering and its applications. In *ACM SIGGRAPH 2007 Courses*, 2007.

[98] B. N. Parlett and J. Poole, W. G. A geometric theory for the QR, LU and power iterations. *SIAM Journal on Numerical Analysis*, 10(2):389–412, 1973.

[99] K. Petersen and M. Pedersen. *The Matrix Cookbook*. Technical University of Denmark, November 2012.

[100] E. Polak and G. Ribière. Note sur la convergence de méthodes de directions conjuguées. *Modélisation Mathématique et Analyse Numérique*, 3(R1):35–43, 1969.

[101] W. Press. *Numerical Recipes in C++: The Art of Scientific Computing*. Cambridge University Press, 2002.

[102] L. Ramshaw. *Blossoming: A Connect-the-Dots Approach to Splines*. Number 19 in SRC Reports. Digital Equipment Corporation, 1987.

[103] C. P. Robert and G. Casella. *Monte Carlo Statistical Methods*. Springer Texts in Statistics. Springer, 2005.

[104] R. Rockafellar. Monotone operators and the proximal point algorithm. *SIAM Journal on Control and Optimization*, 14(5):877–898, 1976.

[105] Y. Saad. *Iterative Methods for Sparse Linear Systems.* Society for Industrial and Applied Mathematics, 2nd edition, 2003.

[106] Y. Saad and M. H. Schultz. GMRES: A generalized minimal residual algorithm for solving nonsymmetric linear systems. *SIAM Journal on Scientific and Statistical Computing*, 7(3):856–869, July 1986.

[107] S. Shalev-Shwartz. Online learning and online convex optimization. *Foundations and Trends in Machine Learning*, 4(2):107–194, 2012.

[108] D. Shepard. A two-dimensional interpolation function for irregularly-spaced data. In *Proceedings of the 1968 23rd ACM National Conference*, pages 517–524. ACM, 1968.

[109] J. R. Shewchuk. An introduction to the conjugate gradient method without the agonizing pain. Technical report, Carnegie Mellon University, 1994.

[110] J. Shi and J. Malik. Normalized cuts and image segmentation. *Transactions on Pattern Analysis and Machine Intelligence*, 22(8):888–905, Aug 2000.

[111] K. Shoemake and T. Duff. Matrix animation and polar decomposition. In *Proceedings of the Conference on Graphics Interface*, pages 258–264. Morgan Kaufmann, 1992.

[112] N. Z. Shor, K. C. Kiwiel, and A. Ruszcayñski. *Minimization Methods for Non-differentiable Functions.* Springer, 1985.

[113] M. Slawski and M. Hein. Sparse recovery by thresholded non-negative least squares. In *Advances in Neural Information Processing Systems*, pages 1926–1934, 2011.

[114] S. Smolyak. Quadrature and interpolation formulas for tensor products of certain classes of functions. *Soviet Mathematics, Doklady*, 4:240–243, 1963.

[115] P. Sonneveld. CGS: A fast Lanczos-type solver for nonsymmetric linear systems. *SIAM Journal on Scientific and Statistical Computing*, 10(1):36–52, 1989.

[116] O. Sorkine and M. Alexa. As-rigid-as-possible surface modeling. In *Proceedings of the Symposium on Geometry Processing*, pages 109–116. Eurographics Association, 2007.

[117] J. Stoer and R. Bulirsch. *Introduction to Numerical Analysis.* Texts in Applied Mathematics. Springer, 2002.

[118] L. H. Thomas. Elliptic problems in linear differential equations over a network. Technical report, Columbia University, 1949.

[119] R. Tibshirani. Regression shrinkage and selection via the lasso. *Journal of the Royal Statistical Society, Series B*, 58:267–288, 1994.

[120] C. Tomasi and R. Manduchi. Bilateral filtering for gray and color images. In *Proceedings of the Sixth International Conference on Computer Vision*, pages 839–846. IEEE, 1998.

[121] J. A. Tropp. Column subset selection, matrix factorization, and eigenvalue optimization. In *Proceedings of the Symposium on Discrete Algorithms*, pages 978–986. Society for Industrial and Applied Mathematics, 2009.

[122] M. Turk and A. Pentland. Eigenfaces for recognition. *Journal of Cognitive Neuroscience*, 3(1):71–86, Jan. 1991.

[123] W. T. Tutte. How to draw a graph. *Proceedings of the London Mathematical Society*, 13(1):743–767, 1963.

[124] H. Uzawa and K. Arrow. *Iterative Methods for Concave Programming*. Cambridge University Press, 1989.

[125] J. van de Weijer and R. van den Boomgaard. Local mode filtering. In *Proceedings of the 2001 IEEE Computer Society Conference on Computer Vision and Pattern Recognition*, pages 428–433. IEEE, 2001.

[126] H. A. van der Vorst. Bi-CGSTAB: A fast and smoothly converging variant of BI-CG for the solution of nonsymmetric linear systems. *SIAM Journal on Scientific and Statistical Computing*, 13(2):631–644, Mar. 1992.

[127] S. Wang and L. Liao. Decomposition method with a variable parameter for a class of monotone variational inequality problems. *Journal of Optimization Theory and Applications*, 109(2):415–429, 2001.

[128] M. Wardetzky, S. Mathur, F. Kälberer, and E. Grinspun. Discrete Laplace operators: No free lunch. In *Proceedings of the Fifth Eurographics Symposium on Geometry Processing*, pages 33–37. Eurographics Association, 2007.

[129] O. Weber, M. Ben-Chen, and C. Gotsman. Complex barycentric coordinates with applications to planar shape deformation. *Computer Graphics Forum*, 28(2), 2009.

[130] K. Q. Weinberger and L. K. Saul. Unsupervised learning of image manifolds by semidefinite programming. *International Journal of Computer Vision*, 70(1):77–90, Oct. 2006.

[131] J. H. Wilkinson. *The perfidious polynomial*. Mathematical Association of America, 1984.

[132] X. Zhu, Z. Ghahramani, J. Lafferty, et al. Semi-supervised learning using Gaussian fields and harmonic functions. In *Proceedings of the International Conference on Machine Learning*, volume 3, pages 912–919. MIT Press, 2003.

Index

== operator, 36–37

∞-norm, 82, 83

1-norm, 82, 83

Absolute error, 33

Accuracy, 36

A-conjugate vectors, 213, 215

Active constraints, 190

Adaptive quadrature, 287–289

Additive associativity, 4–5

Additive commutativity, 4–5

Additive identity, 4–5

Additive inverse, 4–5

Affine, 266

Algebraic multiplicity, 116

Alternating direction method of multipliers (ADMM) algorithm, 237–240

Alternating least-squares (ALS) algorithm, 232, 248

Alternating projection method, 250

Alternation, 231–235

Analytic element method, 351

Annealing, 250–251

Approximations

    centered differences, 292, 345

    forward difference, 292, 345

    Laplace, 25

    low-rank, 135–136

    Taylor, 17

    via piecewise polynomials, 272

Arbitrary-precision arithmetic, 31–32

Arithmetic logic unit (ALU), 29

As-rigid-as-possible (ARAP) optimization, 188–189, 232–233

Augmented Lagrangian optimization, 235–240

Automatic differentiation, 295–296

Back-substitution, 56, 57, 59

Backward error, 34–37

Backward Euler, 313–314

Banded matrix, 81

Barrier methods, 194

Barycentric interpolation, 266–268

Barycentric Lagrange interpolation, 273–274

Basis, 7, 258

Bayes' rule, 279

BFGS (Broyden-Fletcher-Goldfarb-Shanno) algorithm, 175–178, 180, 182–183

Bicubic interpolation, 269

Big-O notation, 17

Bilateral filter, 252

Bilinear interpolation, 268–269

Binary encoding, 27–28

Bisection, 148–149, 155

Block matrix notation, 76

Boolean algebra, 201

Boundary conditions, 336–337, 341–343

Boundary element method, 351

Boundary-value problems, 336–337

Brent's method, 155

Broyden's method, 157–158, 160

Bundle adjustment, 187–188

Canonical ODE form, 305–306

Cardinality function, 204–205

Catastrophic cancellation, 33–34, 37

Cauchy-Schwarz inequality, 8

Centered differences approximation, 292, 345

Central differencing integrator, 321

CFL condition, 354

Characteristic polynomial, 116

Chebyshev points, 271, 276

Chebyshev polynomials, 271, 276

Cholesky factorization, 75–79, 80, 88, 91, 200

Circulant matrix, 81

C^k function, 148

Closed Newton-Cotes quadrature, 282–283

Collocation, 346–347

Collocation points, 346

Column-major ordering, 14

Column space, 15, 91–106

Compact support, 263–265

Compensated summation, 38–39

Complex conjugate, 90, 114

Complex numbers, 3, 62

Complex vector space, 4–5

Composite Simpson's rule, 284, 285

Composite trapezoidal rule, 284

Compressed sensing, 197

Computational geometry, 31, 43, 79

Computational physics, 32–33, 62, 109, 304, 330–331

Computerized tomography (CT), 333

Conditioning, 158, 159, 290

Condition numbers, 35–36, 40, 84–86, 91

Conjugate gradient normal equation error (CGNE), 222

Conjugate gradient normal equation residual (CGNR), 222

Conjugate gradients algorithm, 211–221
    convergence and stopping conditions, 219
    formulating, 217–219
    generating A-conjugate directions, 215–216
    motivation for, 212–213
    with preconditioning, 220–221

Conjugate transpose, 114

Consistency, 354

Constant implicit acceleration integrator, 320

Constrained optimization, 21–22, 185–206
    applications of, 185–189
    barrier methods, 194
    convex programming, 194–201
    critical point of, 189
    equality-constrained, 189, 190, 235–240
    general form of, 185
    integer programs, 200–201
    Karush-Kuhn-Tucker (KKT) conditions, 189–192
    linear programming, 196–197, 202
    optimization algorithms, 192–194
    relaxations, 200–201
    second-order cone programming, 197–200
    semidefinite programming, 199–200
    sequential quadratic programming, 193–194
    theory of, 189–192

Continuity, 148–149, 170

Contractions, 149

Convergence, 149, 151, 155, 170, 209–211, 219, 240, 354

Convergence rate, 149

Convex functions, 168–169, 178, 179, 194–195, 247

Convex programming, 194–201

Convex sets, 194–195

Convex shapes, 194

Coordinate descent, 231, 233–234

Cotangent Laplacian formula, 356

Critical points, 20, 21, 167, 189

Crowd simulation, 305

Cubic blossom function, 274–275

Cubic convergence, 155

Cubic Hermite interpolation, 274

Cubic polynomials, 6

Cumulative distribution function (CDF), 278

Cumulative loss, 246

Curvature, 297
    discrete, 298
    integrated, 297

Dai-Yuan algorithm, 223

Damping, 229

Davidon-Fletcher-Powell (DFP) algorithm, 176, 180

Deconvolution, 73–74

Deflation, 120–121

Dekker's method, 155

Delaunay triangulation, 266

De Moivre's formula, 90

Derivative operators, 341–351

Determinants, 116

Diagonally dominant, 63, 88, 224

Diagonal preconditioner, 221

Differentiability, 148

Differential calculus, 15–23
    differentiation in multiple variables, 17–20
    differentiation in one variable, 16–17
    optimization, 20–23

Differential equations, 109–110
    ordinary, 303–328
    partial, 303–328, 329–360

Differential optimality, 166–168

Differentiation, 277–278, 290–298, 300, 301
    applications of, 278–279
    automatic, 295–296
    basis functions, 291
    choosing step size, 294–295
    finite differences, 291–293, 295
    integrated quantities, 296–298
    by integration, 299

numerical, 300, 301
    Richardson extrapolation, 293–294
    structure preservation, 296–298
Digits of precision, 29
Dijkstra's algorithm, 359
Dirichlet boundary conditions, 336–337, 343
Dirichlet energy, 88
Disciplined convex programming, 195
Discrete curvature, 298
Discrete Fourier transform, 90
Discretization error, 32
Distributivity, 4–5
Divided differences, 32
Domain decomposition, 222, 351
Dot product, 7–8, 12
Duality gap, 254

ε-geometry, 43
Eigenfaces, 140–141
Eigenvalues, 107–108, 111, 112–117, *see also*
        Eigenvectors
    algebraic multiplicity of, 116
    computation of single, 117–120
    defective, 116
    finding multiple, 120–126
    of positive definite matrices, 116
    specialized properties of, 116–117
Eigenvectors, 107–130
    applications of, 107–111
    approximations, 200
    computation using, 115
    defined, 112
    deflation, 120–121
    differential equations, 109–110
    inverse iteration, 118–119
    Krylov subspace methods, 126
    power iteration, 117–118, 119–120
    properties of, 112–117
    QR iteration, 121–125
    Rayleigh quotient iteration, 119, 120
    sensitivity and conditioning, 126–127
    shifting, 119–120
    spectral embedding, 110–111
    statistics, 108–109
Eikonal equation, 334
Elimination matrix, 52–53
Elliptic operators, 355
Elliptic PDEs, 338–339
Epidemiology, 129
Equality-constrained optimization, 21–22,
        189, 190, 193, 235–240

Equations
    differential, 16–20, 109–110
    eikonal, 334
    Fritz John, 333
    hyperbolic, 352–354
    integral, 278
    Laplace's, 331–332, 336–337, 339
    linear systems of, 14–15, 35. *see* Linear
        systems
    Lorenz, 308
    Maxwell's, 331
    model, 309–311, 338–341
    Navier-Stokes, 329–330
    nonlinear systems of. *see* Nonlinear
        systems
    normal, 69, 91–92
    ordinary differential, 303–328
    parabolic, 352–354
    partial differential, 329–360
    rendering, 278–279
Equivalent norms, 82–83
Error
    absolute, 33
    backward, 34–37
    catastrophic cancellation, 33–34, 37
    classifying, 33–35
    discretization, 32
    forward, 34, 35–36
    input, 32, 33
    modeling, 32
    relative, 33, 34, 37, 40
    rounding, 31, 32
    truncation, 32
Euclidean TSP, 251
Euler's formula, 90
Explicit integrator, 312
Exponential integrators, 316–317

Factorization
    Cholesky, 75–79, 80, 88, 91, 200
    constructing, 59–60
    LDLT, 88
    LU, 58–61, 63
    QR, 94–103, 122
    SVD, 131–133
Fast marching methods, 334, 359
Fast sweeping methods, 334
Feasible point, 189
Feasible set, 189
Fehlberg's method, 327–328
Fencepost problem, 346

Fenchel duality, 203
Finite differences, 291–293, 295, 342–346
Finite element method (FEM), 347–350
Finite-precision arithmetic, 37–39
Finite volume method, 350–351
Fixed point iteration, 149–151
Fixed-point representations, 28–29
Fletcher-Reeves algorithm, 223
Floating-point representations, 29–31
Fluid simulation, 329–330
Follow the leader (FTL) optimization,
    246–247
Follow the regularized leader (FTRL)
    optimization, 247–248, 254
Forward difference approximation, 292, 345
Forward error, 34, 35–36
Forward Euler, 311–313
Forward-substitution, 55–56, 58–59, 77
Fourier series/transform, 90, 258, 299
Fractional numbers, storing, 27–32
Frank-Wolfe algorithm, 253–254
Fritz John equations, 333
Frobenius norm, 83, 136–137
Full pivoting, 58
Fully discrete PDE integration, 353–354
Functional analysis, 269
Functions
    bisection, 148–149
    C^k, 148
    classifying, 148
    convex, 168–169, 178, 179, 194–195,
        247
    hat, 356–357
    inner products of, 269–270
    linear, 9–10, 19
    linear algebra of, 269–271
    Lipschitz continuous, 148
    overfitting, 68, 69
    phi, 327
    piecewise affine, 267
    quadratic, 20–21
    quasiconvex, 169
    rational, 262–263
    unimodular, 170–173
Fundamental Theorem of Algebra, 112
Fundamental Theorem of Calculus, 253,
    297, 300, 319

Galerkin method, 348–350
Gaussian elimination, 54–58, 59, 77, 94,
    207, 211

analysis of, 56–58
back-substitution, 56, 57, 59
forward-substitution, 55–56, 58–59
implementation of, 61
Gaussian quadrature, 286–287
Gauss-Newton algorithm, 228, 248
Generalized barycentric coordinates,
    266–267
Generalized PCA, 232
Generalized Rayleigh quotient, 226
Geometric median problem, 165, 239–240
Geometric multiplicity, 113
Geometric programs, 204
Geometric projection, 186
Geometry
    computational, 31, 43, 79
    ε-geometry, 43
Givens rotations, 105
Global minimum, 166, 169, 195
Global optimization, 240–244
    graduated, 241–242
    homotopy methods, 242
    particle swarm, 243–244
    randomized, 243–244
    scale space methods, 241
    simulated annealing, 250–251
Global truncation error, 312
Golden ratio, 154, 172
Golden section search, 170–173, 178–179
Gradient descent algorithm, 173–174, 181,
    205–206, 208–211, 304–305
    convergence, 209–211
    for linear systems, 208–209
    suboptimality for linear systems,
        214–215
Gradient domain painting, 225
Graduated optimization, 241–243
Gram matrix, 69, 114
Gram-Schmidt orthogonalization, 94–99,
    215, 276
    algorithm, 96–99
    projections, 94–96
Graph-based semi-supervised learning,
    357–358
Graphical models, 80
Graph layout, 224
Grasping force optimization, 205
Grid-based interpolation, 268–269

Halley's method, 152
Harmonic analysis, 334–335

Harmonic condition, 74
Harmonic parameterization, 74–75, 88
Hat function, 356–357
Hermitian matrices, 114–115
Hessian matrix, 168, 174–175, 178, 180
Hestenes-Stiefel algorithm, 223
Higher-order elements, 359
Homotopic functions, 242
Homotopy methods, 242–243, 249
Hooke's Law, 109
Horner's rule, 275–276
Householder transformations, 99–103
Huber loss function, 249
Hyperbolic PDE, 340–341, 352–354

Identity
    additive, 4–5
    multiplicative, 4–5
Identity matrix, 11
Image alignment, 71–73, 241–242
Image processing, 58, 79, 268, 279
Inactive constraints, 190
Incomplete Cholesky preconditioner, 222
Indefinite matrices, 168
Independent variables, 66–67
Induced norm, 83–84
Inequality constraints, 191, 193–194
Infinite-precision arithmetic, 223
Infinitesimal analysis, 16–17
Initial-value problems, 336–337
Inner products, 114, 128
    A-inner product, 213
    of functions, 269–270, 348
Input error, 32, 33
Integer programs, 200–201
Integers, 3
Integral equations, 278
Integrated curvature, 297
Integrated quantities, 296–298
Integration, 277–290
Interior point linear programming
        algorithms, 196
Intermediate Value Theorem, 148–149, 170
Interpolants, 258
Interpolation, 68–69, 257–276
    alternative bases, 262–263
    barycentric, 266–268
    barycentric Lagrange, 273–274
    bicubic, 269
    bilinear, 268–269
    cubic Hermite, 274

grid-based, 268–269
    Lagrange basis, 259–260
    Lanczos, 269
    multivariable, 265–269
    nearest-neighbor, 265–266
    Newton basis, 260–262
    piecewise, 263–265
    piecewise constant, 272
    polynomial, 258–262
    in single variable, 258–265
    theory of, 269–272
Interpolatory quadrature, 280
Interval arithmetic, 43
Inverse distance weighting, 273
Inverse iteration, 118–119
Isometries, 93, 133
Iterated integral, 289
Iterative linear solvers, 207–226
    conjugate gradients, 211–219
    gradient descent, 208–211
    need for, 207–208
    preconditioning, 219–222
Iteratively reweighted least-squares (IRLS)
        algorithm, 230–231
Iterative shrinkage-thresholding algorithm
        (ISTA), 252–253

Jacobian, 19–20, 156
    Broyden approximation, 156–158
Jordan normal form, 116–117

Kahan summation algorithm, 38–39
Karush-Kuhn-Tucker (KKT) conditions,
        189–192
Kernel density estimator, 251–252
Kernel trick, 89–90
k-means clustering, 234–235
Kronrod quadrature, 287
Krylov subspace methods, 126

Lagrange interpolation basis, 259–260
Lagrange multipliers, 22–23, 111, 177, 189,
        191, 236–240
Lanczos differentiator, 299
Lanczos interpolation, 269
Laplace approximation, 25
Laplace's equation, 331–332, 336–337, 339
Laplacian operator, 342, 356
Latent semantic analysis, 143
Lax-Richtmyer Equivalence Theorem, 354
LDLT decomposition, 88

Leapfrog integration, 321–322
Least absolute deviations, 250
Least-squares, 68–69, 89–92, 160, 197–198, 270
    alternating, 232, 248
    iteratively reweighted, 230–231
    linear, 68–69
    nonlinear, 164, 227–229
    nonnegative, 187, 238–239, 249
    normal equations, 69
Legendre polynomials, 270
Level set methods, 351
Levenberg-Marquardt algorithm, 229, 248
Lie-Trotter-Kato formula, 359–360
Linear algebra, of functions, 269–271
Linear combination, 5
Linear convergence, 149, 155
Linear dependence, 6–7
Linear fractional transformation, 276
Linearity, 9–15, 19
    matrices, 10–14
    scalars, 12–13
    vectors, 12–13
Linear operators, 9–10, 341
Linear programming, 196–197, 202
Linear regression, 66–68
Linear systems, 35
    ad-hoc solution strategies, 49–50
    condition numbers of, 84–86
    designing and analyzing, 65–90
    encoding row operations, 51–54
    Gaussian elimination, 54–58
    gradient descent for, 208–209
    iterative linear solvers, 207–226
    LU factorization, 58–61
    sensitivity analysis, 81–86
    solvability of, 47–49
    solving via SVD, 134–135
    special properties of, 75–81
    square systems, 65–75
    Tikhonov regularization, 70–71
    underdetermined, 48
Lipschitz continuous functions, 148
Localized truncation error, 312
Locally optimal block preconditioned conjugate gradient (LOBPCG) algorithm, 225
Local maximum, 167
Local minimum, 166, 167, 169, 207
Log likelihood, 165
Log-sum-exp, 40

Lorenz equations, 308
Low-order functions, 265
Low-rank approximations, 135–136
LSMR algorithm, 222
LSQR algorithm, 222
LU factorization, 58–61, 63

Machine learning, 80, 89, 128, 164, 174, 181, 244, 251, 279, 296, 357
Machine precision, 30
Magenetic resonance imaging (MRI), 268
Mahalanobis metric, 128
Manhattan norm, 82
Manufacturing problems, 186–187
Mass matrix, 109
Matrices, 7, 10–13
    circulant, 81
    column space, 15, 91–106
    condition numbers, 84–86
    determinants of, 116
    elliptic operators as, 355
    Gaussian elimination, 54–58
    Givens rotation, 105
    Gram, 69, 114
    Hermitian, 114–115
    Hessian, 168, 174–175, 178, 180
    identity, 11
    indefinite, 168
    Jordan normal form, 116–117
    Krylov, 126
    mass, 109
    matrix-vector multiplication, 11–14
    multiplication, 11, 20
    negative definite, 168
    nondefective, 113
    non-orthogonal, 93–94
    occurrence, 143
    orthogonal, 92–93, 122, 188
    positive definite, 75–79, 114–116, 168
    positive semidefinite, 75–76
    row operations, 51–54
    semidefinite, 168, 199–200
    sensitivity analysis, 81–86
    similar, 113–114
    simplification, 51
    sparsity, 79–80
    special structures, 80–81
    storage, 13–14
    symmetric, 114–116, 127
    transpose, 12
    Vandermonde, 258–259, 262
    vector norms and, 81–84

Matrix calculus, 87, 142
Matrix norms, 136–137
Matrix-vector products, 11, 12
Maximum likelihood estimation, 164–165
Maxwell's equations, 331
Mean shift algorithm, 251–252
Medical imaging, 268
Mesh-free methods, 351
Method of lines, 352–353
Method of undetermined coefficients, 281–282
Metric, 8
Metric learning, 128
Midpoint rule, 283, 288, 298
Minimax problem, 198
MINRES algorithm, 222
Mixed conditions, 337
Mixed-integer programming, 200–201
Model equations, 309–311, 338–341
Modeling error, 32
Modified Gram-Schmidt (MGS) algorithm, 98–99
Monte Carlo integration, 289–290
Monomials, 204
Multiplication, matrix-vector, 11–14, 20
Multiplicative compatibility, 4–5
Multiplicative identity, 4–5
Multivariable interpolation, 265–269

Natural numbers, 3
Navier-Stokes equations, 329–330
n-dimensional Euclidean space, 7–8
Nearest-neighbor interpolation, 265–266
Negative definite matrices, 168
Negative log likelihood function, 25
Neumann conditions, 337, 343
Newmark integrators, 318–321
Newton basis, 260–262
Newton-Cotes quadrature, 282–286, 301
Newton's method, 156, 170, 208, 240, 241
    in multiple variables, 174–175
    of root-finding, 151–153
Newton's second law, 32, 109, 304
Nonconvex shapes, 194
Nondefective matrix, 113
Nonlinearity, 15–23
Nonlinear least-squares, 164, 227–229
Nonlinear systems, 147–161
    conditioning, 158, 159
    multivariable problems, 156–158
    root-finding in single variable, 147–155

Nonlinear techniques
    constrained optimization, 185–206
    specialized optimization methods, 227–254
    unconstrained optimization, 163–183
Nonnegative least-squares, 187, 238–239, 249
Nonparametic regression, 89–90
Normal distribution, 164
Normal equations, 69, 91–92
Normalized cuts, 130
Normalized power iteration algorithm, 118
Norms
    equivalence of, 82
    Frobenius, 83, 136–137
    induced, 83
    matrix, 136–137
    nuclear, 141
    vector, 8, 37, 81–84
    weighted Frobenius, 177
Nuclear norm, 141
Numbers, 3–4
    complex, 3, 62
    condition, 35–36, 40, 84–86, 91
    with fractional parts, storing, 27–32
    integers, 3
    natural, 3
    rational, 3
    real, 4
Numerical algorithms
    column spaces, 91–106
    constrained optimization, 185–206
    differentiation, 277–279, 290–298
    eigenvectors, 107–130
    Gram-Schmidt algorithm, 96–99
    integration, 277–290
    interpolation, 257–276
    iterative linear solvers, 207–226
    linear systems, 47–64, 65–90
    nonlinear, 147–162
    numerics and number analysis, 27–43
    ordinary differential equations, 303–328
    orthogonality, 92–93
    partial differential equations, 329–360
    practical aspects of, 36–39
    QR factorization, 94–103
    singular value decomposition, 131–144
    specialized optimization methods, 227–254
    stability, 36
    unconstrained optimization, 163–183

Numerical differentiation, *see* Differentiation
Numerical integration, *see* Integration

Objective function, 20, 163
Occurrence matrix, 143
Online optimization, 244–248
Open Newton-Cotes quadrature, 282, 283
Optimality conditions, 21–22, 165–166, 168–169, 191
Optimization, 20–23, 163–165, 186–189
   alternating direction method of multipliers (ADMM), 237–240
   alternation, 231–235
   as-rigid-as-possible (ARAP), 188–189, 232–233
   augmented Lagrangian, 235–240
   constrained, 185–206
   coordinate descent, 231, 233–234
   global, 240–244, 250–251
   graduated, 241–243
   iteratively reweighted least-squares, 230–231
   nonlinear least-squares, 227–229
   online, 244–248
   particle swarm, 243–244, 245
   specialized methods, 227–254
   unconstrained, 163–183
Ordinary differential equations (ODEs), 303–328
   applications of, 304–305
   backward Euler, 313–314
   canonical form, 305–306
   comparison of integrators, 322–323
   existence and uniqueness, 307–309
   expansion, 307
   explicit, 306
   exponential integrators, 316–317
   first-order, 306–307
   forward Euler, 311–313
   implicit, 306
   leapfrog, 321–322
   model equations, 309–311
   multivalue methods, 318–322
   Newmark integrators, 318–321
   Runge-Kutta methods, 315–316
   second-order, 306–307
   solvability of, 309
   staggered grid, 321–322
   theory of, 305–311
   time-stepping schemes, 311–317

   trapezoidal method, 314–315
Orthogonality, 8, 92–93, 122
   Gram-Schmidt orthogonalization, 94–99
Orthogonal matrices, 188
Orthogonal Procrustes problem, 137–139
Orthonormal basis, 93
Oscillation, 68
Outer products, 135–136
Overfitting, 68, 69

Parabolas, 178
Parabolic PDEs, 339–340
Parameter estimation, 164
Parameterization, 74–75, 88
   by arc length, 297
Parametric regression, 66–67
Parabolic equations, 352–354
Pareto dominate, 181
Pareto optimality, 181–182
Partial derivative, 17–18
Partial differential equations (PDEs), 303–304, 329–360
   applications of, 330–335
   boundary conditions, 336–337, 341–343
   collocation, 346–347
   derivative operators, 341–351
   elliptic, 338–339
   finite differences, 342–346
   finite elements, 347–350
   finite volumes, 350–351
   hyperbolic, 340–341, 352–354
   linear solvers for, 354–355
   model equations, 338–341
   numerical considerations, 354–355
   parabolic, 339–340, 352–354
   properties of, 335–336
   second-order, 338
   statement and structure of, 335–337
Partial pivoting, 57–58
Particle swarm method, 243–244, 245
Periodic boundary conditions, 343
Permutation, 51–52
Perturbation of linear systems, 81
Per-vertex shading, 267–268
Phase space diagram, 308
Phi functions, 327
Physical equilibria, 165
Piecewise affine functions, 267
Piecewise constant interpolation, 272
Piecewise interpolation, 263–265

Piecewise-linear FEM, 349–350
Piecewise linear hat function, 357
Piecewise polynomials, 264–265, 272
Pivoting strategies, 57–58
p-norm, 82
Point cloud alignment, 137–139
Polak-Ribière algorithm, 223
Polar decomposition, 142–143
Polynomial interpolation, 258–262
Polynomial regression, 67
Polynomials, 5
    characteristics, 116
    Chebyshev, 271, 276
    cubic, 6
    Legendre, 270
    piecewise, 264–265, 272
Positive definite matrices, 70, 75–79,
    114–116, 168, 208
Positive semidefinite matrices, 75–76, 199
Posynomials, 204
Power iteration, 117–120
Powers, of sets, 4
Preconditioning, 219–222
Pressure gradients, 329
Primitive n-th root of unity, 90
Principal component analysis (PCA),
    139–141
Procrustes problem, 137–139
Projection, 94–96, 100, 120, 186, 250
Protein folding, 304
Pseudoinverse, 134–135
Pseudometrics, 128

QR factorization, 122
    Givens rotation, 105
    Gram-Schmidt orthogonalization,
      94–99
    Householder transformations, 99–103
    reduced, 103
QR iteration, 121–125
Quadratic convergence, 151, 155
Quadratic functions, 20–21
Quadrature, 279–290
    adaptive, 287–289
    conditioning, 290
    Gaussian, 286–287
    interpolatory, 280
    Kronrod, 287
    multiple variables, 289–290
    Newton-Cotes, 282–286, 301
    recursive-quadrature, 288

Romberg, 300
    rules, 281–282, 298
Quasiconvex functions, 169, 178
Quasi-Newton algorithms, 156–157, 175

Randomized global optimization, 243–244
Rational functions, 262–263
Rational numbers, 3
Rayleigh quotient iteration, 119, 120, 128
Real numbers, 4, 28
Recursive quadrature, 288
Reduced QR factorization, 103
Regression, 66–68
    nonparametic, 89–90
Regret, 246
Relative error, 33, 34, 37, 40
Relativity, 18
Relaxations, 200–201
Rendering equation, 278–279
Representations
    fixed-point, 28–29
    floating-point, 29–31
    for real numbers, 28–32
Residual norm, 12–13
Richardson extrapolation, 293–294, 300
Riemann integral, 281
Right singular vectors, 133
Robin conditions, 337
Robust PCA, 232
Romberg quadrature, 300
Root-finding, 36
    bisection, 148–149, 155
    Broyden's method, 157–158, 160
    continuity, 148–149
    fixed point iteration, 149–151
    hybrid techniques, 155
    multivariable problems, 156–158
    Newton's method, 151–153, 156
    problem characterization, 147–148
    quasi-Newton algorithms, 156–157
    secant method, 153–154, 155
    in single variable, 147–155
Rounding errors, 31, 32
Row-major ordering, 14
Row operations, 51–54
    elimination, 52–53
    permutation, 51–52
Row scaling, 52
Runge-Kutta methods, 315–316

Saddle point, 167

Sampling, 278
Scalarizations, 182
Scalar product preservation, 9
Scalars, 12–13
Scientific notation, 29–30
Screened Poisson smoothing, 89
Secant method, 153–154, 155
Second dividend difference, 275
Second-order cone programming (SOCP), 197–200, 202
Second-order PDEs, 338
Semidefinite embedding, 199
Semidefinite matrices, 168
Semidefinite programming, 199–200
Semidiscrete PDE integration, 352–353
Sensitivity analysis, 81–86
Sequence acceleration, 293–294, 300
Sequential quadratic programming (SQP), 193–194
Sets, 3–4, 6
    convex, 194–195
    feasible, 189
Shading, 267–268
Shifted QR iteration, 129
Shifting, 119–120
Shortest-path distances, 334
Significand, 30
Similarity transformation, 113–114
Similar matrices, 113–114
Simplex algorithm, 196
Simpson's rule, 283, 284, 285
Simulated annealing, 250–251
Singular value decomposition (SVD), 70, 131–144
    applications of, 134–141
    computing, 133
    derivative of, 141–142
    deriving, 131–133
    geometric interpretation for, 133
Slope, 16
Smolyak grid, 290
Smoothed-particle hydrodynamics (SPH), 351
Solution path, 243
Span, 5–6
Sparse approximate inverse preconditioner, 221
Sparse grid, 290
Sparse vectors, 197
Sparsity, 79–80
Specialized optimization methods, 227–254

alternating direction method of multipliers (ADMM), 237–240
    alternation, 231–235
    augmented Lagrangian optimization, 235–240
    coordinate descent, 231, 233–234
    global optimization, 240–244, 250–251
    iteratively reweighted least-squares, 230–231
    nonlinear least-squares, 227–229
    online optimization, 244–248
Special structures, 80–81
Spectral embedding, 110–111
Spectral norm, 84
Spectral radius, 112
Spectral theorem, 115
Spectrum, 112
Splitting methods, 222, 223–224
Square systems, solution of, 65–75
Stability, 36, 311, 354
Stable rank, 143–144
Staggered grid, 321–322
Standard basis, 7
Stationary point, 167–168
Stochastic gradient descent algorithm, 181
Storage, of numbers with fractional parts, 27–32
Strongly convex, 247
Structure preservation, 296–298
Subdifferentials, 179
Subgradient method, 179–180
Subnormal values, 31
Subspace, 5
Substitution
    back-substitution, 56, 57, 59
    forward-substitution, 55–56, 58–59, 77
Successive over-relaxation (SOR) method, 224–225
Successive parabolic interpolation, 170
Summation, 38–39
Superdiagonal, 116
Superlinear convergence, 155
Swarm optimization, 243–244
Symmetric matrices, 114–116, 127
Symmetric positive definite (SPD) system, 76, 208
SYMMLQ method, 222
Symplectic integrator, 322

Taxicab norm, 82
Taylor approximation, 17, 36, 240, 258, 272, 292, 323

Tikhonov regularization, 70–71, 198
Time reversibility, 321–322
Time-stepping schemes, 311–317, 322–323
Time step restriction, 312
Tolerance, 36
Transformations
    linear fractional, 276
    similarity, 113–114
Transpose, 12
Trapezoidal method, 314–315
Trapezoidal rule, 283, 284, 288
Traveling salesman problem (TSP), 251
Triangle mesh, 74, 188, 267, 357
Triangular systems, 58–60
Tridiagonal systems, 80–81, 88
Truncation error, 32
Turning number theorem, 297
Two-point boundary value problem,
    355–356

Unconstrained optimization, 163–183
    applications of, 163–165
    golden section search, 170–173
    gradient descent algorithm, 173–174
    multivariable strategies, 173–178
    Newton's method, 170, 174–175
    one-dimensional strategies, 169–173
    optimality, 165–169
    without Hessians, 175–178
Underdetermined, 266
Unimodular functions, 170–173
Upper-triangular system, 58–60
Upwinding schemes, 354
Uzawa iteration, 237

Vandermonde matrix, 67, 258–259, 262
Variational problems, xv, 20–23
Vector, 4–5
Vector calculus, 330
Vector norms, 8, 81–84
    computation of, 37–38
Vectors
    A-conjugate, 213, 215
    eigenvectors, 23, 107–130
    matrices and, 12–13
    matrix-vector multiplication, 11–14
    outer products of, 135–136
    singular, 133
Vector spaces
    basis, 7
    complex, 4–5
    defined, 4–5
    dimension of, 7
    linear dependence, 6–7
    n-dimensional Euclidean space, 7–8
    orthogonal, 8
    span, 5–6
Von Neumann stability analysis, 358–359
Voronoi cells, 265–266

Weighted Frobenius norm, 177
Weiszfeld algorithm, 231
Well-conditioned problems, 35–36
Wilkinson's polynomial, 42

X-ray computerized tomography, 333

Zero-one programming, 200–201
z-fighting, 40